BINDING
Vol. XVI

The binding of this volume is a facsimile of the original belonging to the present Emperor of Germany. It was exhibited at the St. Louis Exposition as a choice example of Art Nouveau binding.

The binding was executed by P. Claessens, of Brussels, after a design by H. Van de Velde.

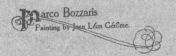

Marco Bozzaris
Painting by Jean Léon Gérôme.

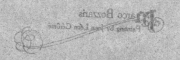

THE GREAT EVENTS

BY

FAMOUS HISTORIANS

A COMPREHENSIVE AND READABLE ACCOUNT OF THE WORLD'S HISTORY, EMPHASIZING THE MORE IMPORTANT EVENTS, AND PRESENTING THESE AS COMPLETE NARRATIVES IN THE MASTER-WORDS OF THE MOST EMINENT HISTORIANS

NON-SECTARIAN   NON-PARTISAN   NON-SECTIONAL

ON THE PLAN EVOLVED FROM A CONSENSUS OF OPINIONS GATH-
ERED FROM THE MOST DISTINGUISHED SCHOLARS OF AMERICA
AND EUROPE, INCLUDING BRIEF INTRODUCTIONS BY SPECIALISTS
TO CONNECT AND EXPLAIN THE CELEBRATED NARRATIVES, AR-
RANGED CHRONOLOGICALLY, WITH THOROUGH INDICES, BIBLIOG-
RAPHIES, CHRONOLOGIES, AND COURSES OF READING

EDITOR-IN-CHIEF

ROSSITER JOHNSON, LL.D.

ASSOCIATE EDITORS

CHARLES F. HORNE, Ph.D.
JOHN RUDD, LL.D.

With a staff of specialists

VOLUME XVI

The National Alumni

CONTENTS

VOLUME XVI

CONTENTS

CONTENTS

ILLUSTRATIONS

VOLUME XVI

AN OUTLINE NARRATIVE

TRACING BRIEFLY THE CAUSES, CON-
NECTIONS, AND CONSEQUENCES OF

THE GREAT EVENTS

(PROGRESS AND REPRESSION)

CHARLES F. HORNE

EEKING the most important, the most prominent characteristic of the quarter century
that followed Napoleon's downfall, we find
it in the struggles of awakened democracy,
or perhaps in the vastly increased material
prosperity of the age, the marvellous progress of the common man in knowledge, in
comfort, and in power. This was a period of peace, in which
man, relieved from the dread incubus of universal war, became
once more a toiler and a thinker. Honest labor did for the world
what strife has never done; and genius, instead of planning new
ways of inflicting death, sought to add to the happiness of life.

Many of the industrial changes that make our own times
seem so widely at variance with the past had their origin in this
era. Fulton had but recently given America the steamboat.
Stephenson now gave to all the world its system of steam railroads.[1] The plan of the electric telegraph arose from the brain
of Morse. Photography became of practical value through the
experiments of Daguerre.[2] More noteworthy still in its bearing
on the future was the rapid spread of education among the lower
classes. Something of the value of what we now call "common"
schools had long been recognized in America; Napoleon had insisted on their maintenance in France; Pestalozzi showed their

[1] See *Beginning of Railway Locomotion*, page 157.
[2] See *The Invention of Photography*, page 338.

xiii

worth to Germany, and Froebel carried on his work. The schoolmaster became the regenerator of the world.

Our own age has grown so accustomed to the rule of the people, the *demos*, "democracy," that we hardly realize how differently society was managed less than a century ago. In 1815 it was only in America that the people had established their control. There, Jefferson had taught the leaders of the State to hold their power by following the voice of the people—not drowning it as Napoleon had drowned it with the roar of his cannon; not hushing it as Washington had hushed it by the weight of noble character and highest argument, but listening for it, courting it, obeying.

In other lands, however, the struggle of democracy had only just begun. England was ruled by a narrow aristocracy. The great mass of the people had no vote whatever in the elections to Parliament; they could only parade the streets and shout; and they were too ignorant to realize what they lacked. On the Continent of Europe matters were even worse. In 1814, when the widespread patriotic uprising of the masses had overthrown Napoleon, many of the monarchs of Europe in a first not unnatural burst of gratitude assured their subjects of a share in the governments they had rescued, promised them "constitutions." What these precious documents were to say or by what magic they would revolutionize the world most of their worshippers had only the vaguest idea, except that a constitution meant electing somebody to govern for the popular good, as opposed to the old system of absolutism and tyranny.

THE HOLY ALLIANCE

After cooler second thought, however, most of the rulers "by divine right" concluded not to lay aside any portion of their supreme authority. Some of them may have been actuated by selfishness, others by an honest horror of the excesses of the French democracy. The practical result was, that the great Congress of the Diplomats at Vienna, from which Liberty had hoped so much, ended in an alliance among all the larger governments to suppress the people.

This union and the fear that underlay it account for the long peace that now spread its beneficent effects over Europe. Mon-

archs dared not fight one another, lest their weakness give their subjects the eagerly awaited opportunity to escape from bondage. Thus from evil came good, and thus the issue between kings and commons was sharply outlined as never before. The people had grown so strong in the knowledge of what they wished, that they could no longer be armed and used as brainless weapons in the strife for empire.

The real ruler of Europe during this period was Prince Metternich, the chief minister of Austria. It was he who had dominated the Vienna Congress and impressed upon the various governments this widespread policy of alliance and repression. Among the most hesitant to follow him at first was the Russian Emperor, Alexander I, who by his resolute struggle against Napoleon had become the chief sovereign of the world. Alexander was an enthusiast; he believed in progress; and he persuaded the other sovereigns to join him in a personal compact, the "Holy Alliance," which pledged them to accept as their principles of government a string of high-sounding phrases of pure but somewhat vague nobility. Yet even Alexander thought certain repressive measures necessary. These led to murmurings and protest, and at length to the murder of one of the Czar's counsellors, whereupon the unhappy ruler became angrily convinced that Metternich was right, that "nobility" bade him suppress with iron hand the madness of the people.[1]

Such constitutions as had been granted by lesser monarchs, in the first moments of enthusiasm or necessity, were withdrawn under Metternich's protection. Bavaria, it is true, and a few lesser German States still retained some shadow of representative government. So also did France, but all real power there was in the hands of the reactionaries; and thus the year 1820 saw Europe once more in the grasp of an absolutism as complete in its authority as before 1789, and grown far more watchful and wise and cautious.

Was it to prove as strong as previously? Naturally there were upflarings of revolt from the deluded people. Their dream of self-government was not lightly to be abandoned. Spain, which had the cruellest tyrant, rose first in rebellion. Some troops, that were being despatched to America to aid in the suppression of the

[1] See *The Holy Alliance*, page 1.

revolted Spanish colonies, turned upon the oppressive Government instead, and clamored for a constitution. The helpless King gave them all they asked. When the people of southern Italy heard the news they rose also, demanding—pitiful picture of an ignorance that hardly knew how to frame its longing in words!—demanding "the Spanish constitution." The frightened King of Naples yielded as promptly as had the equally worthless lord of Spain, and with all his ministers solemnly swore to obey this constitution, of whose actual terms he knew no more than his subjects. Greece rose in revolt against the Turks. Portugal sprang to arms. The flame seemed to leap as by magic through all the southern peninsulas of Europe (1820–1821).[1]

Metternich and his "good friends" of the Holy Alliance were horrified. This would never do. Much of northern Italy belonged to Austria, and the evil example of the southern part was spreading fast. Large bodies of Austrian troops were employed to trample out the dangerous symptoms shown not only in Naples but in Sicily, Piedmont, and other States. A French army was despatched to crush the spirit of revolt in Spain; and the vindictive southern kings to whose hands power was thus restored, took murderous vengeance on their now helpless subjects.

So extreme was the fear in which the allied forces held "revolt" that they refused even to aid unhappy Greece, refused to aid Christians striving to save themselves from the brutal dominance of the Turks. The religious feeling of Europe had thus swung far indeed from the enthusiasm that thrilled it in the time of the Crusades, from the passion that swayed the Reformation. There could be no clearer mark of the changing times, no more striking evidence of the desperation to which monarchy had been driven in its terror of the people.

At least, however, Christian troops were not actually despatched to Greece as they had been to Italy and Spain; the insurgents were not crushed and handed over helpless to the mercy of their savage masters. Left to their own resources, the Greeks made resolute resistance; and gradually all that was most romantic in Europe rallied to their aid.[2] "Philhellenes," lovers of the ancient glory of classic Greece, sent money or marched in bodies

[1] See *The Spanish Demand for a Constitution*, page 41.
[2] See *The Greek War for Independence*, page 65.

to join the fight. Lord Byron, the famous poet, threw in his lot with theirs. They talked of making him their king. The two heroic sieges of Missolonghi proclaimed abroad the desperate nature of the strife.[1] The enfeebled Turks were fought to a standstill until at length the Sultan secured the aid of Mehemet Ali, who in Napoleon's time had made Egypt almost wholly independent of the sultans, her former rulers. The exhausted Greeks proved no match for Ali's trained Egyptians; but Greece was saved by a new turn in the wheel of European politics.

Alexander I of Russia died in 1825, and was succeeded by his brother Nicholas I. Nicholas believed in the established policy of repression, but he believed still more in the strength and destiny of Russia. He thought there could be no possibility of rebellion among his own ignorant, superstitious, and patriotic people; and he wished to enlarge Russia at the expense of Turkey. Therefore he began to extend a helping hand to Greece.

At the same time the Sultan, having caught the spirit of the times, was engaged in some rather vigorous repression on his own account. The flower of the Turkish armies had long been the warlike but turbulent body known as the Janizaries. These troops were almost as much masters of Turkey as the Sultan himself, and, in imitation of Mehemet Ali's course with the Egyptian Mamelukes, the Sultan now planned and dexterously executed the massacre of the entire corps of Janizaries. His success left him master indeed, but master of a ruined cause. The last vestige of the ancient military power of Mahometanism perished with the Janizaries and left Turkey and the East helpless before advancing Russia.[2]

In the changed condition of affairs both England and France hurried warships to the East to preserve the European peace and balance of power, if necessary, by force of arms. These vessels, accompanied by those of Russia, met the Turkish fleet in Navarino Bay. The haughty Mahometan commander, not at all awake to the true proportions of his country and the others, took occasion of some disagreement to open fire on the allies' men-of-war. In less than an hour no Turkish fleet was left. The

[1] See *Siege of Missolonghi*, page 112.
[2] See *Massacre of the Janizaries*, page 128.

naval strength of the East had disappeared in the wake of its military power.[1]

This "untoward event," as it was called in the English politics of the time, left Greek freedom inevitable. Russia, in her new rôle of Greece's champion and ally, even permitted the little land to become a republic. Then this suddenly self-constituted champion of freedom engaged in a territorial war with Turkey on her own account, and won a series of easy victories. She seemed on the point of swallowing the entire Ottoman domain, when the other Powers, jealous of her progress, threatened to form a Turkish alliance against her. This menace stopped the war, saved the "sick man of the East," and restored the much disordered European peace. The little Greek republic, having proved quite as turbulent as the former French one, was compelled by the Powers to assume a monarchical government, and had to go begging through the various royal families of Europe to find a younger son to act as its king.

UPRISINGS OF 1830

Soon afterward the cause of absolutism, so rudely jarred in eastern Europe, received an even sharper setback in the west. In France, the restored Bourbon monarch, Louis XVIII, had died (1824) and been succeeded by his brother, Charles X. Louis, fearing the temper of his people, had governed them with moderation; but Charles was among the most intense of the reactionaries. Slight as was the semblance of popular government in France, the new king hated it and was forever planning its downfall. In 1830 French troops took advantage of the general disintegration of Mahometan power to seize upon Algiers and attempt to make a colony of it.[2] The first slight successes of the invaders pleased the French lovers of "glory," and Charles used his momentary popularity to follow the illustrious example of the kings of Spain and Naples. The constitution which he had sworn to defend, he deliberately declared abolished, offering in its stead another even more attenuated.

Unfortunately for himself, Charles had not waited, like the other monarchs, until he had a foreign army at his back. There

[1] See *Battle of Navarino*, page 135.
[2] See *Algiers Taken by the French*, page 199.

was a sudden spontaneous revolution. The few troops that
clung to the King were attacked; about six thousand persons perished; and the last of the Bourbon kings fled from France forever.[1]

For a moment the French hardly knew what use to make of
their unanticipated freedom. To declare their land again a republic would be to challenge the interference of all the other
Powers. So they established another monarchy, a really constitutional one this time, and placed upon the throne Louis Philippe, a relative of the former royal house. Despite this moderation France might have found herself facing another alliance
such as that of 1815, had not the sudden success of her revolution
stimulated democracy all over Europe into hope, and into action
too swift for entire control.

There were uprisings in several little German States, where
constitutional concessions were wrung from unwilling rulers.
There was civil war in Switzerland between the aristocratic and
democratic cantons, resulting in victory for the latter. There
was armed and successful rebellion in Italy, so that Policeman
Metternich had again to march his Austrians through the land
and replace his puppets on their toppling thrones. Poland
flared out in a last desperate revolt. Of this ancient and much
conquered land, the Congress of Vienna had left some fragment
as a semi-independent kingdom under a Russian viceroy. The
viceroy had naturally proved a tyrant and an absolutist. Now
he was expelled, and the Poles cried to Europe, and especially
to France their old ally, for aid against Russia. But Louis
Philippe, the "tradesman king" as his own people learned bitterly to call him, made use of the strife in other lands only to
exact from Austria and Russia an acceptance of his own newly
established government. That being granted, he left Poland to
her fate; and the last spark of her independence was trampled
out by the brute force of Russia.[2]

In Belgium the revolutionary movement was more successful.
The Congress of Vienna, much against the will of the Belgians,
had united them with Holland as a single State, known as the
Kingdom of the United Netherlands. The Dutch dominated

---

[1] See *End of Absolutism in France*, page 207.
[2] See *Insurrection in Russian Poland*, page 245.

this union; its king was Dutch; and the Belgians, a people more than half French in language and in feeling, became mere tributaries, dependent and despised. Immediately on the success of the French uprising, the Belgians threw off their yoke, and drove the Dutch soldiers from the land. They would have joined themselves to France; but Louis Philippe cautiously refused any addition to French territory which should seem to proclaim a return to the aggrandizing spirit of the democracy of 1789. The Belgians, ready for any course that would win the support of the great Powers, then declared their land an independent constitutional kingdom, and offered the throne to a French prince. This also the cautious Louis forbade. So the crown was given to a German prince with English family alliances; and the Powers, accepting this as the best way out of the difficulty, admitted the new State upon their map.[1]

Holland, however, refused angrily to assent to this diminution of her authority, and there was much fierce fighting between the two little States, until France and England stepped in and by force compelled the Dutch to acquiesce in the arrangement that Europe had approved.

By this time Spain also had joined the ranks of constitutional kingdoms. Her tyrant monarch, Ferdinand, had died in 1833, his final folly casting one more cause of disruption and destruction into the land he had ruined. He changed the ancient laws of succession to the throne, and arranged that instead of passing to his brother, Don Carlos, it should go to his young daughter, Isabella. This led to a civil war, which has flared out again and again, the Carlists ever seeking to regain the crown. Temporarily Isabella, or rather her mother, got the upper hand by conferring a constitution on her subjects, so that they fought the Carlists to defend this unexpected prize.[2]

REFORM IN ENGLAND

In England also the cause of democracy had been rapidly advancing, though by less spectacular means. After a long parliamentary struggle, Protestants of other denominations than the Anglican or State Church were admitted to a share in the

[1] See *The Revolution in Belgium*, page 220.
[2] See *Carlist Revolt in Spain*, page 287.

government. This concession was followed by a determined
effort, headed by the great Irish statesman Daniel O'Connell, to
secure the same right for Roman Catholics. The struggle culminated in the "Emancipation Act" of 1829.[1]

More widespread still was the agitation for the reform of
Parliament itself, which had begun generations before. Gradually the lower classes became so angered at their exclusion from
voting, and so determined to have a voice in the government, that
the aristocracy felt itself approaching such a revolution as had
exterminated the French *noblesse*. Even the Duke of Wellington, conqueror of Napoleon, was mobbed by infuriated London-
ers. The democratic movements of 1830 added such intensity
to the excitement that at length the aristocracy yielded. In
1832 was passed the famous first Reform Bill.[2] It did not make
Parliament what we to-day should call a really representative
body. But it was a step in that direction, and the first step soon
involved others, until the English Government to-day is quite as
representative as that of the United States.

The reform brought others in its train. The spirit of democracy, of man's universal equality, had already raised widespread protest against negro slavery, and the first English Parliament elected under the Act of 1832 passed laws abolishing
slavery through all England's broad domains. The other countries of Western Europe soon followed her example, until America was left the only prison of the negro slave.[3]

The demand for equality, and for a share in the government,
spread from England to her colonies and caused a serious Canadian revolt in 1837.[4] This led to investigations and reforms, and
finally, in 1841, to the union of the separate Provinces of Ontario and Quebec into the single State known as Canada.[5] This
was the beginning of the extensive movement toward union and
self-government which has since been so wisely followed by England in her colonial affairs.

This period of history saw also the intrusion of European

[1] See *Catholic Emancipation*, page 175.
[2] See *The Passage of the English Reform Bill*, page 252.
[3] See *Abolition of the Slave-trade*, page 296.
[4] See *The Canadian Rebellion*, page 325.
[5] See *Union of Upper and Lower Canada*, page 372.

governments into the affairs of the Farthest East. Hitherto the relations of Europe to China and the surrounding nations had been confined merely to trade, but now, this trade had grown so valuable, and the military weakness of the Asiatics so obvious, that England prepared to assert her trading claims by force, and engaged in the "Opium War" with China.[1]

THE ADVANCE OF DEMOCRACY IN AMERICA

Through all this period of democratic struggle and repression in Europe, America was enjoying the benefits of popular government. The United States was thus, if not the most important country in the world, at least the most advanced, looked upon by other governments with curiosity as an experiment, or rather as a volcano which might destroy itself at any moment, an impossible extravagance expected to disappear with each decade.

Instead, the land grew ever greater and stronger. The difficulties of Europe became the opportunities of the freer government. Just as Napoleon had sold Louisiana when he could no longer defend it, so in 1821 Spain sold Florida when rebellion at home had made the re-conquest of her South American colonies manifestly impossible, and money had become a necessity to her bankrupt king.[2] The United States had begun to see the possibility of settling the vast waste lands which extended all around her. The Mississippi River gave her access to the Central West. New York State, at an expense unparalleled in those days, built the Erie Canal, which opened traffic with the Great Lakes and made New York the metropolis of America.[3]

The giant possibilities of the future dawned upon the nation, and the period of "earth-hunger," the passion for expanding territory, seized upon the United States as it had already seized on England, France, and Russia. To check the encroachments of European nations, our Government proclaimed the much-discussed "Monroe Doctrine," which declared that no more of the American continent was to be appropriated by foreign States, that America was "no longer a subject for colonization."[4]

[1] See *The Opium War*, page 352.
[2] See *Florida Acquired by the United States*, page 57.
[3] See *Opening of the Erie Canal*, page 94.
[4] See *The Monroe Doctrine*, page 80.

Yet the very vastness of the United States was already threatening to rend its Government apart. It was impossible that regions so widely separated, so diverse in climate and in occupations, should have always a common interest. What was advantageous to one section must often prove harmful to another. Thus the prosperity of the Mississippi valley had been impossible while a foreign power held the mouth of the great river; yet the East cared nothing for New Orleans. The War of 1812, upheld by the South, had ruined the shipping interests of the North. And, again, the employment of slave labor, then considered essential by the South for the cultivation of its cotton and its rice, grew ever more offensive to the moral sense of the North.

Threats of disunion were not uncommon to the heat of controversy, and, as it became increasingly apparent that the material interests of North and South were specially divergent, clearly marked parties, sectional factions, struggled for control of the central government. At length, over the admission of Missouri to the Union as a new slave State, flashed up a controversy so sharp, so bitter, that statesmen drew back in horror. Jefferson, speaking from the honored retirement of his age, declared he felt the tumult "like a fire-bell in the night"; he feared it as "the knell of the Union." Men asked themselves despondently, whether Europe could be right, whether the government of which they had been so proud could indeed be doomed to dissolution. A geographical compromise was hastily arranged, which, it was hoped, might settle the slavery dispute forever.[1]

Soon there were other causes of disagreement. The South had at first approved a high protective tariff, but by degrees found that this policy, while aiding Northern manufactures, was hampering Southern agricultural prosperity. Tariff compromises became necessary. The common people, seeing their college-bred leaders at variance, thought to place common-sense above learning and subtle acuteness; and in 1828 a further democratic revolution occurred in the election to the presidency of General Jackson, the popular soldier. One of the rallying cries of his campaign was that he was *not* a college graduate.[2]

Another change, even more noteworthy in its influence on

[1] See *Passage of the Missouri Compromise*, page 14.
[2] See *Jackson Elected President of the United States*, page 143.

the future, found expression during Jackson's administration. This was the pride of the people in the nation as a whole, patriotism for the country, not for a single ancient colony.   Jackson represented the West, the States that had come into existence since the forming of the Union, States which had never known a separate existence, and which looked on all talk of disunion as treason to the central government.   To the West, as opposed to the East, we owe that we are still a united nation.   When, in 1832, the tariff laws seemed to press especially hard on South Carolina, that State declared them "null and void," and took measures obviously meant to lead to separation from the Union. Jackson, the plain man, undeterred by subtleties of law, the man of the West, horrified at the suggestion of disloyalty, the soldier accustomed to prompt action, gathered troops to crush the incipient rebellion.   A compromise was hastily arranged in Congress, and Carolina receded from her dangerous position.[1]

Yet, despite these internal difficulties sprung from the country's already unwieldy size, the earth-hunger of the nation did not abate.   An opportunity was offered for its satisfaction by the rebellion of the Texans against Mexico.   The inhabitants of Texas, mostly belonging to the Teutonic races, naturally appealed to the United States for help against the Spanish blood of their opponents.   That help being refused, they achieved a glorious independence by their own unaided prowess.[2]

Texas then applied as an independent State for admission to the Union.   But the North, dreading this enormous expansion of slave territory, hesitated to receive her.   Moreover, Mexico, not yet content to acknowledge the loss of her rebellious province, declared positively that she would regard its admission as an act of war.   For some years the subject was in dispute, but Texas was finally admitted, and the Mexican War followed.   The democracy of America entered 'on a new era—an era of expansion by force of arms.   For all the world the period of external peace ended, and alliance against internal democratic revolution, and a period of widespread war and democratic triumph began.

[1] See *Nullification in South Carolina*, page 267.
[2] See *The Texan Revolution*, page 305.

[FOR THE NEXT SECTION OF THIS GENERAL SURVEY SEE VOLUME XVII]

THE HOLY ALLIANCE

EUROPEAN REACTION UNDER METTERNICH

A.D. 1816

C. EDMUND MAURICE

Before the allies had withdrawn from Paris after the fall of Napoleon in 1815, three Continental powers of Europe entered into a new alliance, from which England held aloof. It was formed by Alexander I of Russia, Francis I of Austria, and Frederick William III of Prussia, each of whom personally signed the agreement at Paris, September 26, 1815, when France also joined the alliance.

This event marked the beginning of a concerted reactionary policy on the part of the contracting powers, and led to the long ascendency of Prince Metternich, the Austrian minister, in European affairs. From this time he was leader of the repressive movement against popular aspirations for constitutional government and liberal institutions. The declared purpose of the alliance was to follow the teachings of the New Testament in political conduct. The sovereigns promised to rule "strictly in accordance with the precepts of justice and Christian love and peace." The relation of sovereign and subject was to be that of father and son. However sincerely founded, the alliance was soon perverted into an instrument of tyranny, sure to provoke fresh revolts, and after the French revolution of 1830 the league came to an end.

The part played by Metternich, the principal actor in those affairs with which the Holy Alliance concerned itself, is skilfully portrayed by Maurice, the historian of the later revolutionary period in Europe, who speaks with the highest authority of the reactionary influences against which, in due time, the progressive forces themselves reacted.

IN the year 1814 Napoleon Bonaparte ceased to reign over Europe, and, after a very short interregnum, Clemens Metternich reigned in his stead. Ever since the fall of Stadion, and the collapse of Austria in 1809, this statesman had exercised the chief influence in Austrian affairs; and, by his skilful diplomacy, the Emperor had been enabled to play a part in Europe which, though neither honorable nor dignified, was eminently calculated to enable that prince to take a leading position in politics, when the other powers were exhausted by war, and uncertain of what was to follow. But Francis of Austria, though in agreement with Metternich, was really his hand rather than his head; and thus the crafty minister easily assumed the real headship of Europe, while professing to be the humble servant of the Emperor of Austria.

The system of the new ruler resembled that of Napoleon in its contempt for the rights of men and of nations; but it was to be varnished over with an appearance of legality, a seeming respect for the rights of kings, and a determination to preserve peace and avoid dramatic sensations, which made it welcome to Europe, after eighteen years of almost incessant wars or rumors of wars. As he looked round upon the countries that had fallen under his rule, the contemplation of the existing state of Europe seemed to promise the new monarch a fairly successful reign. France had been satisfied by the preservation of Alsace and Lorraine, and by the sense that, from having been the focus of revolution, she had now become the corner-stone of legitimacy. England had at first seemed to give pledges to the cause of liberty by her promise of independence to Genoa, and her guarantee of the Sicilian Constitution; but with the help of Castlereagh, whom Metternich described as "that upright and enlightened statesman," the Austrian Government had succeeded in persuading the English to consent to look on quietly while Genoa was absorbed in the kingdom of Sardinia, and while the Anglo-Sicilian Constitution was destroyed by Ferdinand of Naples; and the English zeal for independence had been happily diverted from the support of constitutions and civic liberties to the championship of the most contemptible of Napoleon's puppets, the King of Saxony.

The King of Prussia, who in 1813 had seemed in danger of becoming the champion of popular rights and German freedom, was now, with his usual feebleness, swaying toward the side of despotism; and any irritation which he may have felt at the opposition to his claim upon Saxony had been removed by the concession of the Rhine province.

Among the smaller sovereigns of Europe, the King of Sardinia and Pope Pius VII alone showed any signs of rebellion against the new ruler of Europe. The former had objected to the continued occupation of Alessandria by Austrian forces; while the representatives of the Pope had even entered a protest against that vague and dangerous clause in the Treaty of Vienna which gave Austria a right to occupy Ferrara.

But, on the other hand, the King of Sardinia had shown more zeal than any other ruler of Italy in restoring the old feudal and absolutist *régime* which the French had overthrown. And though Cardinal Consalvi, the chief adviser of the Pope, was following for the present a semi-liberal policy, he might as yet be considered as only having established a workable government in Rome. And the Pope, who had been kidnapped by Napoleon, was hardly likely to offer much opposition to the man who, in his own opinion, was the overthrower of Napoleon.

Yet there were two difficulties which seemed likely to hinder the prosperity of Metternich's reign. These were the character of Alexander I of Russia and the aspirations of the German nation.

Alexander, indeed, if occasionally irritating Metternich, evidently afforded him considerable amusement, and the sort of pleasure which every man finds in a suitable subject for the exercise of his peculiar talents. For Alexander was eminently a man to be managed. Enthusiastic, dreamy, and vain; now bent on schemes of conquest, now on the development of some ideal of liberty, now filled with some confused religious mysticism; at one time eager to divide the world with Napoleon, then anxious to restore Poland to its independence; now listening to the appeals of Metternich to his fears, at another time to the nobler and more liberal suggestions of Stein and Pozzo di Borgo; he was only consistent in the one desire to play an impressive and melodramatic part in European affairs.

But, amusing as Alexander was to Metternich, there were circumstances connected with the condition of Europe which might make his weak love of display as dangerous to Metternich's policy as a more determined opponent could be. There were still scattered over Europe traces of the old aspirations after liberty which had been first kindled by the French Revolution, and again awakened by the rising against Napoleon. Setting aside, for the moment, the leaders of German thought, there were men who had hoped that even Napoleon might give liberty to

Poland; there were Spanish popular leaders who had arisen for the independence of their country; Lombards who had sat in the Assembly of the Cisalpine Republic; Carbonari in Naples, who had fought under Murat, and who had at one time received some little encouragement, even from their present king. If the Emperor of Russia should put himself at the head of such a combination as this, the consequences to Europe might indeed be serious. But the stars in their courses fought for Metternich; and a force that he had considered almost as dangerous as the character of Alexander proved the means of securing the Czar to the side of despotism.

Nothing is more characteristic of Metternich and his system than his attitude toward any kind of religious feeling. It might have been supposed that the anti-religious spirit which had shown itself in the fiercest period of the French Revolution, and to a large extent also in the career of Napoleon, would have induced the restorers of the old system to appeal both to clerical feeling and to religious sentiment as the most hopeful bulwark of legitimate despotism. Metternich was far wiser. He knew, in spite of the accidental circumstances which had connected atheism with the fiercer forms of Jacobinism, that, from the time of Moses to the time of George Washington, religious feeling had constantly been a tremendous force on the side of liberty; and although he might try to believe that to himself alone was due the fall of Napoleon, yet he could not but be aware that there were many who still fancied that the popular risings in Spain and Germany had contributed to that end, and that in both these cases the element of religious feeling had helped to strengthen the popular enthusiasm. He felt, too, that however much the clergy might at times have been made the tools of despotism, they did represent a spiritual force which might become dangerous to those who relied on the power of armies, the traditions of earthly kings, or the tricks of diplomatists. Much, therefore, as he may have disliked the levelling and liberating part of the policy of Joseph II, Metternich shared the hostility of that prince to the power of the clergy.

Nor was it purely from calculations of policy that Metternich was disposed to check religious enthusiasm. Like many of the nobles of his time he had come under the influence of the French philosophers of the eighteenth century; his hard and cynical spirit had easily caught the impress of their teaching; and he found it no difficult matter to flavor Voltairism with a slight tincture of respectable orthodox Toryism.

The method by which he achieved this end should be given in his own words: "I read every day one or two chapters of the Bible. I discover new beauties daily, and prostrate myself before this admirable book; while at the age of twenty I found it difficult not to think the family of Lot unworthy to be saved, Noah unworthy to have lived, Saul a great criminal, and David a terrible man. At twenty I tried to understand the Apocalypse; now I am sure that I never shall understand it. At the age of twenty a deep and long-continued search in the Holy Books made me an atheist after the fashion of Alembert and Lalande; or a Christian after that of Châteaubriand. Now I believe, and do not criticise. Accustomed to occupy myself with great moral questions, what have I not accomplished or allowed to be wrought out, before arriving at the point where the Pope and my *curé* begged me to accept from them the most portable edition of the Bible? Is it bold in me to take for certain that among a thousand individuals chosen from the men of whom the people are composed, there will be found, owing to their intellectual faculties, their education, or their age, very few who have arrived at the point where I find myself?"

This statement of his attitude of mind is taken from a letter written to remonstrate with the Russian ambassador on the patronage afforded by the Emperor Alexander to the Bible societies. But how much more would such an attitude of mind lead him to look with repugnance on the religious excitement that was displaying itself even in the archduchy of Austria! And to say the truth, men of far deeper religious feeling than Metternich might well be satisfied with the influence of the person who was the chief mover in this excitement.

The Baroness de Kruedener, formerly one of the gayest of Parisian ladies of fashion, and at least suspected of not having been too scrupulous in her conduct, had gone through the process which Carlyle so forcibly describes in his sketch of Ignatius Loyola. She had changed the excitements of religion, and was now preaching and prophesying a millennium of good things to

come, in another world, to those who would abandon some of the
more commonplace amusements of the present.   The disturbance that she was producing in men's minds especially alarmed
Metternich; and, under what influence it may be difficult to
prove, she was induced to retire to Russia, and there came in
contact with the excitable Czar.

Under her influence Alexander drew up a manifesto, from
which it appeared that, while all men were brothers, kings were
the fathers of their peoples; Russia, Austria, and Prussia were
different branches of one Christian people, who recognized no
ruler save the Highest; and they were to combine to enforce
Christian principles on the peoples of Europe.   When the draft
of this proclamation was first placed before Metternich it was so
alien from his manner of thinking that he could only treat it with
scorn; and Frederick William of Prussia was the only ruler who
regarded it with even modified approval.   But with all his scorn
Metternich had the wit to see that the piety of Alexander of Russia
had now been turned into a direction which might be made use of
for the enforcement of Metternich's own system of government;
and thus, having induced Alexander, much against his will, to
modify and alter the original draft, Metternich laid the foundation of the Holy Alliance.

But there still remained the troublesome question of the aspirations of the German nation; and these seemed likely at first to
centre in a man of far higher type and far more steady resolution
than Alexander.   This was Baron von Stein,[1] who, driven from
office by Napoleon, had been in exile the point of attraction to all
those who labored for the liberty of Germany.   He had declared,
at an early period, in favor of a German parliament.   But Metternich had ingeniously succeeded in pitting against him the
local feeling of the smaller German states; and instead of the
real parliament which Stein desired, there arose that curious
device for hindering national development called the "German
Bund."

This was composed of thirty-nine members, representatives
of all the different German governments.   Its object was said to
be to preserve the outward and inward safety of Germany, and

[1] This Prussian statesman had become the intimate counsellor of Al
exander.—ED.

the independence and inviolability of her separate states. If any change were to be made in fundamental laws, it could only be done by a unanimous vote. Some form of constitution was to be introduced in each state of the bund; arrangements were to be made with regard to the freedom of the press, and the bund was also to take into consideration the question of trade and intercourse between the different states. All the members of the *bundestag* were to protect Germany, and each individual state, against every attack. The vagueness and looseness of these provisions enabled Metternich so to manage the bundestag as to defeat the object of Stein and his friends, and gradually to use this weakly constituted assembly as an effective engine of despotism.

But in fact Stein was ill fitted to represent the popular feeling in any efficient manner. His position is not altogether easy to explain. He believed, to some extent, in the people, especially the German people. That is to say, he believed in the power of that people to feel justly and honorably; and, as long as that feeling was expressed in the form of a cry to their rulers to guide and lead justly, he was as anxious as anyone that that cry be heard. He liked, too, the sense of the compact embodiment of this feeling in some institution representing the unity of the nation. But with the ideas connected with popular representation in the English sense he had little sympathy. That the people or their representatives should reason or act, independently of their sovereigns, was a political conception which was abhorrent to him.

In short, Stein's antagonism to Metternich was as intense as that of the most advanced democrat; but it was not so much the opposition of a champion of freedom to a champion of despotism as the opposition of an honest man to a rogue. Metternich wrote in his *Memoirs*, when he was taking office for the first time in 1809: "From the day when peace is signed we must confine our system to tacking and turning and flattering. Thus alone may we possibly preserve our existence till the day of general deliverance." This policy had been consistently followed. The abandonment of Andrew Hofer after the Tyrolese rising of 1809, the marriage of Maria Louisa, the alliance with Napoleon, the discouragement of all popular effort to throw off the French yoke, the timely desertion of Napoleon's cause, just soon enough to give importance to the alliance of Austria with Prussia and Russia and England, just late enough to prevent any danger of defeat and misfortune—these acts marked the character of Metternich's policy and excited the loathing of Stein.

As he had been repelled from Metternich by arts like these, so Stein had been drawn to Arndt, Schleiermacher, and Steffens by a common love of honesty and by a common power of self-sacrifice; but he looked upon them none the less as to a large extent dreamers and theorists; and this want of sympathy with them grew, as the popular movement took a more independent form, until at last the champion of parliamentary government, the liberator of the Prussian peasant, the leader of the German people in the struggle against Napoleon, drifted entirely out of political life from want of sympathy with all parties.

But it was not to Stein alone that the Germans of 1813 had looked for help and encouragement in their struggle against Napoleon. The people had found other noble leaders at that period and it remembered them. The King of Prussia remembered them too, to his shame. He was perfectly aware that he had played a very sorry part in the beginning of the struggle, and that, instead of leading his people, he had been forced by them most unwillingly into the position of a champion of liberty. It was not, therefore, merely from a fear of the political effects of the constitutional movement, but from a more personal feeling, that Frederick William III was eager to forget the events of 1813.

But if the King wished to put aside uncomfortable facts, his flatterers were disposed to go much further, and to deny them. A man named Schmalz, who had been accused, rightly or wrongly, of having acted in 1808 with Scharnhorst in promoting the "*Tugendbund*," and of writing in a democratic sense about popular assemblies, now wrote a pamphlet to vindicate himself against these charges. Starting from this personal standpoint, he went on to maintain that all which was useful in the movement of 1813 came directly from the King; that enterprises like that by which Schill endeavored to rouse the Prussians to a really popular struggle against the French were an entire mistake; that the political unions did nothing to stir up the people; that the alliance between Prussia and France in 1812 had saved Europe; and that it was not till the King gave the word in February, 1813, that the German people had shown any wish to throw off the yoke of Napoleon.

This pamphlet at once called forth a storm of indignation. Niebuhr and Schleiermacher both wrote answers to it, and the remaining popularity of the King received a heavy blow when it was found that he was checking the opposition, and had even singled out Schmalz for special honor. The great centre of discontent was in the newly acquired Rhine province. The King of Prussia, indeed, had hoped that by founding a university at Bonn, by appointing Arndt professor of history, and Goerres, the former editor of the *Rhenish Mercury (Rheinischer Merkur)*, director of public instruction, he might have secured the popular feeling in the province to his side.

But Arndt and Goerres were not men to be silenced by favor, any more than by fear. Goerres remonstrated with the King for giving a decoration to Schmalz, and organized petitions for enforcing the clause in the Treaty of Vienna which enabled the bund to summon the *staende* of the different provinces. Arndt renewed his demand for the abolition of serfdom in his own province of Ruegen, advocated peasant proprietorship, and, above all, parliamentary government for Germany. The feeling of discontent, which these pamphlets helped to keep alive, was further strengthened in the Rhine province by a growing feeling that Frederick William was trying to crush out local traditions and local independence by the help of Prussian officials.

So bitter was the anti-Prussian feeling produced by this conduct, that a temporary liking was excited for the Emperor of Austria, as an opponent of the Prussianizing of Germany; and Metternich, travelling in 1817 through this province, remarked that it is "no doubt the part of Europe where the Emperor is most loved, more even than in our own country." But it was but a passing satisfaction that the ruler of Europe could derive from this accidental result of German discontent. He had already begun to perceive that his opposition to the unity of Germany, and his consequent attempt to pose as the champion of the separate states, had not tended to secure the despotic system which his soul loved.

Stein had opposed the admission of the smaller German states to the Vienna Congress, no doubt holding that unity of

Germany would be better accomplished in this manner, and very likely distrusting Bavaria and Wurtemberg as former allies of Napoleon. Metternich, by the help of Talleyrand, had defeated this attempt at exclusion, and had secured the admission of Bavaria and Wurtemberg to the Congress. But he now found that these very states were thorns in his side.

They resented the attempts of Metternich to dictate to them in their internal affairs; and, though the King of Bavaria might confine himself to vague phrases about liberty, the King of Wurtemberg actually went the length of granting a constitution. Had the King lived much longer, Metternich might have been able to revive against him the remembrance of his former alliance with Napoleon. But when, after his death in 1816, the new King of Wurtemberg, a genuine German patriot, continued, in defiance of his nobles, to uphold his father's constitution, this hope was taken away, and the South German states remained to the last, with more or less consistency, a hinderance to the completeness of Metternich's system.

But the summary of Metternich's difficulties in Germany is not yet complete. The ruler of another small principality, the Duke of Weimar, like the King of Wurtemberg, had taken advantage of the permission to grant a constitution to his people; and had been more prominent than even the King of Wurtemberg in encouraging freedom of discussion in his dominions. This love of freedom, in Weimar as in most countries of Europe, connected itself with university life, and thus found its centre in the celebrated University of Jena; and on June 18, 1816, the students of the university met to celebrate the anniversary of the battle of Leipsic. There, to the great alarm of the authorities, they publicly burned the pamphlet of Schmalz, and another written by the playwriter Kotzebue, who was believed to have turned away Alexander of Russia from the cause of liberty, and now to be acting as his tool and spy.

The head of the Rhine police, conscious, no doubt, of the ferment in his own province, remonstrated with the Duke of Weimar on permitting such disturbances. The opposition increased the movement which it was designed to check. Jahn, who had founded the gymnastic schools which had speedily become places of military exercise for patriotic Germans during the war, now came forward to organize a *"Burschenschaft,"* a society that was to include all the patriotic students of Germany. Metternich and his friend had become thoroughly alarmed at the progress of the opposition, but again events seemed to work for him; and the enthusiasm of the students, ill-regulated and ill-guided, was soon to give an excuse for the blow that would secure the victory for a time to the champions of absolutism. The desire for liberty seems always to connect itself with love of symbolism; and the movement for reform naturally led to the revival of sympathy with earlier reformers. Actuated by these feelings, the students of Leipsic and other German universities gathered at the Wartburg, in 1817, to revive the memory of Luther's testimony for liberty of thought; and they seized the opportunity for protesting against the tyranny of their own time.

Apparently the enthusiasm for the Emperor of Austria had not extended to Saxony; for an Austrian corporal's staff was one of the first objects cast into the bonfire that was lighted by the students; while the dislike to Prussia was symbolized by the burning of a pair of Prussian military stays, and the hatred of the tyranny which prevailed in the smaller states found vent in the burning of a Hessian pigtail. The demonstration excited much disapproval among the stricter followers of Metternich; but Stein and others protested against any attempt to hinder the students in their meeting.

In the following year the Burschenschaft, which Jahn desired to form, began to take shape and to increase the alarm of the lovers of peace at all costs. Metternich rose to the occasion, and boasted that he had become a moral power in Europe, which would leave a void when it disappeared. In March, 1819, the event took place which at last gave this "moral power" a success that seemed for the moment likely to be lasting. Ludwig Sand, a young man who had studied first at Erlangen and afterward at Jena, went, on March 23, 1819, to the house of Kotzebue at Mannheim, and stabbed him to the heart. It was said, truly or falsely, that a paper was found with Sand, declaring that he acted with the authority of one of the universities. It was said also that Sand had played a prominent part in the Wartburg celebration. With the logic usual with panicmongers, Metternich was easily able to deduce from these facts that the universities must, if left to themselves, become schools of sedition and murder.

The Duke of Weimar, with more courage, perhaps, than tact, had anticipated the designs of Metternich by a proclamation in favor of freedom of thought and teaching at the universities, as the best security for attaining truth. This proclamation strengthened still further the hands of Metternich. Abandoning the position which he had assumed at the Congress of Vienna, of champion of the smaller states of Germany, he appealed to the King of Prussia for help to coerce the Duke of Weimar and the German universities.

Frederick William, in spite of his support of Schmalz, was still troubled by some scruples of conscience. In May, 1815, he had made a public promise of a constitution to Prussia; Stein and Humboldt were eager that he should fulfil this promise, and even the less scrupulous Hardenberg held that it ought to be fulfilled sooner or later. But Metternich urged upon the King that he had allowed dangerous principles to grow in Prussia; that his kingdom was the centre of conspiracy against the peace and order of Germany; and that, if he once conceded representative government, the other powers would be obliged to leave him to his fate. The King, already alarmed by the course which events were taking, was easily persuaded by Metternich to abandon a proposal that seemed to have nothing in its favor except the duty of keeping his word. Arndt was deprived of his professorship, and tried by commission on the charge of taking part in a republican conspiracy; Jahn was arrested, and Goerres fled from the country, to reappear in Bavaria as a champion of ultramontanism against the hateful influence of Prussia.

Then Metternich proceeded to his master-stroke. He called a conference at Carlsbad to crush the revolutionary spirit of the universities. A commission of five members was appointed, under whose superintendence an official was to be placed over every university, to direct the minds and studies of students to sound political conclusions. Each government of Germany was to pledge itself to remove any teacher pronounced dangerous by this commission, and if any government resisted, the commission would compel it. No government was ever to accept a teacher so expelled from any other university. No newspaper of fewer than twenty pages was to appear without leave of a board, appointed for the purpose, and every state of Germany was to be answerable to the bund for the contents of its newspapers. The editor of a suppressed paper was to be, *ipso facto*, prohibited from establishing another paper for five years in any state of the bund; and a central board was to be founded for inquiry into demagogic plots.

These decrees seem a sufficiently crushing engine of despotism; but there still remained a slight obstacle to be removed from Metternich's path. The Thirteenth Article of the Treaty of Vienna had suggested the granting of constitutions by different rulers of Germany; and, vaguely as it had been drawn, both Metternich and Francis felt this clause an obstacle in their path. As soon, therefore, as the Carlsbad Decrees had been passed, Metternich summoned anew the different states of Germany, to discuss the improvement of this clause. The representatives of Bavaria and Wurtemberg protested against this interference with the independence of the separate states; and, although the representative of Prussia steadily supported Metternich, it was necessary to make some concession in form to the opponents of his policy.

It was, therefore, decided that the princes of Germany should not be hindered in the exercise of their power, nor in their duty as members of the bund, by any constitutions. By this easy device Metternich was able to assume, without resistance, the imperial tone that suited his position. The entry in his *Memoirs* naturally marks this supreme moment of triumph. "I told my five-and-twenty friends," he says, "what we want, and what we do not want; on this avowal there was a general declaration of approval, and each one asserted he had never wanted more or less, nor indeed anything different."

Thus was Metternich recognized as the undisputed ruler of Germany, and, for the moment, of Europe.

PASSAGE OF THE MISSOURI COMPROMISE

A.D. 1820

JAMES ALBERT WOODBURN

A climax in the political endeavor to adjust questions concerning slavery in the United States was reached in 1820, and was temporarily met by the passage in Congress of the Missouri Compromise. This was an agreement between the proslavery and the antislavery members of Congress for admitting Missouri into the Union as a slave State, and prohibiting slavery forever north of the line of 36° 30', the southern boundary of Missouri. The compromise continued in force until 1854, when it was repealed.

As early as 1790 the Quaker Yearly Meeting in Pennsylvania presented a memorial asking Congress to remove the reproach of slavery from the land. The memorial was referred to a committee, upon whose report Congress resolved that the Federal Government was prohibited from interfering with the slave trade for domestic supply until 1808, although Congress could prevent such trade for foreign supply; that Congress could neither emancipate the slaves nor regulate their treatment in the States, since it remained with the States to regulate their own institutions. This constitutional limitation of the power of Congress in the premises was ever after generally admitted. In 1793 a fugitive-slave law was enacted by Congress, and its enforcement met with little opposition. By the Ordinance of 1787 slavery was prohibited in the Northwest Territory. Unsuccessful efforts were made in 1802 and afterward to secure the repeal of this restriction. By the terms of the Louisiana treaty, in 1803, the people living in Louisiana under French law were guaranteed all the rights of person and property which they enjoyed at the time of the transfer of the territory to the United States. The right to their property included the right to their slaves. In 1812 the State of Louisiana was admitted to the Union on terms conformed to this treaty, although without specific mention of slavery.

The slave trade was prohibited by Congress to foreign carriers in 1794. By act of 1807 it was wholly outlawed after 1808; in 1815 the United States joined England (Treaty of Ghent) in an agreement to suppress it, and in 1820 declared it piracy. Meanwhile, on the subject of slavery itself, the attention of political leaders was mainly given to maintaining a certain balance between slave States and free States, by alternate admission. This was the rule from the early days of the Union, and it was carefully observed as long as slavery remained. At the assembling of Congress in 1817 the distribution of political power between the free and the slave sections was a question of paramount importance, the balance, in number of States, being then in favor of the free-State section by one, with the admission of Alabama as a slave State admitted. Out of this situation arose the struggle over Missouri, the progress and issue of which are traced by Professor Woodburn, whose exhaustive yet concise account has taken rank among the authoritative publications of the American Historical Association.

THE struggle for the restriction of African slavery in the United States is the central theme in American political history during a large part of the nineteenth century.   That struggle suggests to the student of American politics a long series of contests culminating at last in one of the greatest civil wars in human history. The struggle over the admission of Missouri into the Union (1818–1821) involves the merits of the whole controversy.   In attempting to interpret the significance of that struggle and to estimate the principles which it involved, it is first essential to have, if possible, a candid recital of the facts.

The Fifteenth Congress assembled at Washington, December 1, 1817.   Henry Clay was chosen Speaker of the House.   John Scott appeared as the delegate from the Missouri Territory.   On March 16, 1818, Mr. Scott presented a petition from Missouri praying for Statehood, which together with former similar petitions was referred to a select committee.   At the same time Scott presented a petition from the inhabitants of the southern part of Missouri praying for a division of the Territory.   On April 18, 1818, Mr. Scott, chairman of this committee, reported to the House an enabling act to authorize Missouri Territory to form a constitution and State government and for the admission of the State into the Union on an equal footing with the other States. The bill was read twice and referred to the committee of the whole, where it slept for the remainder of the session.

The same Congress met in second session, November 16, 1818.   On December 18, 1818, the Speaker presented a memorial from the Territorial Legislature of Missouri again praying to be permitted to form a constitution and State government preparatory for admission.   The memorial was referred.   On Saturday, February 13, 1819, the House, on motion of Mr. Scott of Missouri, went into committee of the whole on the enabling acts for Missouri and Alabama.   The Missouri bill was taken up first, and James Tallmadge Jr., a representative from New York, offered the following amendment:

"*Provided*, That the further introduction of slavery or involuntary servitude be prohibited, except for the punishment of crimes whereof the party shall have been duly convicted; and that all children born within the said State after the admission thereof into the Union shall be free, but may be held to service until the age of twenty-five years."[1]

It is to be noticed that there were two distinct parts to this amendment: (1) Provision against the further introduction of slaves; (2) provision for gradual emancipation of the slaves already there.

Neither of these was a radical proposition. Neither proposed to interfere with the rights of property in that Territory. "The motion of Tallmadge," says the *Annals*, "gave rise to an interesting and pretty wide debate." On February 17th the House passed the bill with the Tallmadge amendment. The vote stood 87 to 76, one from the slave States favoring restriction, and ten from the free States opposing restriction. It was clearly a sectional vote.

The House bill for Missouri reached the Senate February 17, 1819, and was read twice and referred to the committee on the memorial from Alabama. On February 21st, Senator Tait, of Georgia, chairman of this committee, reported the bill back to the Senate with an amendment striking out restriction. On February 27th the bill "was again resumed," and various motions gave rise to a long and animated debate. The Senate struck out the Tallmadge amendment—the latter clause, which provided for gradual emancipation, by a vote of 31 to 7; the first clause, which prohibited further introduction of slavery, by a vote of 22 to 16—and on March 2, 1819, the amended bill passed the Senate.

On the return of the bill to the House, March 2d, Tallmadge moved the indefinite postponement of the bill, a motion which was barely lost. The House then refused to concur in the Senate amendments, and the bill was returned to the Senate. A message came back immediately that the Senate still adhered to its

[1] In Seaton's *Annals of Congress* the last clause of this amendment reads: "That all children born within the said State, after the admission thereof into the Union, shall be free at the age of twenty-five years."

amendment, and thereupon, by motion of Mr. Taylor, of New York, the House voted to adhere to its disagreement, and the bill was lost with the Fifteenth Congress in deadlock. This was the end of the first struggle.

The struggle for restriction in the Fifteenth Congress was not confined, in the minds of the restrictionists, to the question of the admission of the new State of Missouri. The southern portion of that Territory was cut off from the proposed new State and organized as the Territory of Arkansas. During the consideration of the bill to provide a Territorial government for the Arkansas country, Mr. Taylor, of New York, moved an amendment containing the substance of the Tallmadge amendment to the Missouri bill—to prohibit the existence of slavery in the new Territory. "This motion," says the *Annals*, "gave rise to a wide and long-continued debate, covering part of the ground previously occupied on this subject, but differing in part, as the proposition for Arkansas was to impose a condition on a Territorial government instead of, as in the former case, to enjoin the adoption of the (prohibitive) principle in the constitution of a State."

This distinction is important, in view of the fact that the chief argument against restriction on Missouri was based on the assumed sovereignty and equality of the States. The fact of the discussion over Arkansas is important as indicating the temper of the lower House, and that the prime motive, the uppermost desire, of those who wished to impose conditions upon Missouri, was to limit the area of human slavery. The House first adopted one clause of the Taylor amendment, that providing for gradual emancipation in Arkansas, but by the casting vote of the Speaker, Mr. Clay, the bill was recommitted; and in the final decision, the House determined by a majority of two votes to strike out all the antislavery restriction on the Territory of Arkansas. Territorial restriction failed only because of complication with the Missouri question. Thus, we see, the Fifteenth Congress expired with the House refusing to admit Missouri without restriction, the Senate refusing to admit her with restriction.

The fact that the Fifteenth Congress left Missouri without authority to organize as a State was the occasion of great excitement among the people of that Territory, and from the adjournment of the Fifteenth Congress to the assembling of the Sixteenth the whole Union was agitated.   The legislatures of the States passed resolutions in favor of and against restriction, according to their respective sections, sending copies of these to one another and to the General Government; popular assemblies in all parts of the country debated the question, adopted resolutions, petitioned Congress, and appealed to the public sentiment of the country in whatever demonstration they could use for their cause; the press kept up a continual agitation, and a multitude of pamphleteers entered the field, adding to the momentum and excitement of the great national argument.

Such was the state of the public mind when the Sixteenth Congress assembled, December 6, 1819.   Mr. Clay was again elected Speaker.   On December 8, 1819, by motion of Scott, of Missouri, the memorial from that State praying for admission was referred to a select committee.   On the same day Mr. Strong, of New York, gave notice of his intention to introduce a bill to prohibit the further extension of slavery in the Territories of the United States.   On the following day Mr. Scott, chairman of the special committee, all but one of whom were from the slave States, reported an enabling act for Missouri which was read twice and referred to the committee of the whole.   At the same time Strong waived his notice of the previous day in view of the fact that the same issue would be presented in the proposed Missouri bill.

The Missouri bill did not again come up in the House till January 24, 1820.   On the 26th Mr. Taylor, of New York, offered an amendment requiring that Missouri should "ordain and establish that there shall be neither slavery nor involuntary servitude, otherwise than in punishment of crimes whereof the party shall have been duly convicted," followed by the usual provision for the rendition of fugitive slaves.

This restrictive amendment was debated, almost daily for nearly a month, until February 19th, when a bill came from the Senate "to admit the State of Maine into the Union," carrying the whole Missouri bill, without restriction, as a "rider."

A word of retrospect as to Maine: By an act of the State of Massachusetts of June 19, 1819, the people of that part of Massachusetts known as Maine were permitted to form themselves into an independent State.   In this instance Massachusetts freely consented to her own division, but these proceedings were to be void unless Maine were admitted to the Union by March 4, 1820, Accordingly, the people of Maine formed a constitution, organized a State government, and petitioned Congress for admission to the Union. Her case was exactly parallel with that of Kentucky, and, as in Kentucky's case, it was only necessary that the bill admitting Maine should be a brief enactment, "that from and after March 3, 1820, the State of Maine is hereby declared to be one of the United States of America," and should extend the United States laws over her territory and assign her a fair proportion of representatives. Ordinarily this simple process of admission would be an easy matter, and but for the issue over Missouri, Maine's admission would have passed unquestioned. The House had passed an ordinary Maine bill, January 3, 1820. The Senate had already passed a similar bill to a second reading, merely declaring the consent of Congress to Maine's admission as early as December 22, 1819, the first month of the session. It was not until January 6, 1820, three days after the House Maine bill had come to the Senate, that the scheme of carrying Missouri through on the back of Maine was put into formal shape. On that day the Senate committee having the Maine bill in charge reported it with the Missouri "rider," but on the 13th the House Maine bill was substituted with the Missouri attachment.

It is not known what politician first suggested the party stroke of forcing this combination of the two bills in one—that the admission of Maine should be made dependent upon unconditional admission of Missouri. It is known, however, that Henry Clay gave public approval to the idea two weeks before in the House discussion on the Maine bill.

Holmes expressed the hope, in discussing the bill for Maine, that the question had not gone to the extent of making one distinct measure depend upon another, and that the admission of Maine did not depend upon giving up restriction on Missouri. Clay, in an undertone, said that it did, and then answering Holmes he asserted publicly that he did not intend to give his consent to the admission of Maine until the doctrine of imposing conditions were given up. This was in December, 1819. Clay gave, perhaps, the most plausible statement in defence of a position which is usually regarded only as a politician's resort of forcing a compensation for doing his duty. "A State in the quarter of the country from which I come," says Clay, "asks to be admitted to the Union. What say the gentlemen who ask the admission of Maine? Why, they will not admit Missouri without a condition which strips her of an essential attribute of sovereignty. What, then, do I say to them? That justice is due to all parts of the Union; your State shall be admitted free of condition, but if you refuse to admit Missouri also free of condition we see no reason why you shall take to yourselves privileges which you deny to her, and until you grant them also to her we will not admit you. This notion of an equivalent is not a new one; it is one upon which commonwealths and states have acted from time immemorial."

Holmes then pertinently remarked that in this Clay had taken the position that "unless others do what they think is wrong you will not do what you acknowledge to be right." And Livermore, of New Hampshire, pointedly inquired of Clay why he had not "called a pause" on the usual admission of States before the admission of Alabama in that very year. The situation clearly shows us that the real issue, that which divided men into party contestants and was decisive of their votes and conduct, was the question of slavery and its interests. The doctrine of the sovereignty and equality of States was put forward to defend the interests of slavery.

When the Maine bill was reported to the Senate by the committee, with the Missouri "rider," January 13, 1820, Senator Roberts, of Pennsylvania, endeavored to secure a recommitment of the bill with a view to their separation. Failing in this, he moved, on January 17th, an absolute antislavery restriction. After this was voted down the restrictionists in the Senate came again to the conflict by a motion from Senator Burrill, of Rhode Island, to apply to Missouri "the first three articles of compact in the Ordinance of 1787." The great debate then continued in the Senate for a month, and on February 16, 1820, the Senate agreed to the amendment of its committee combining the Maine and Missouri bills in one. Then Mr. Thomas, of Illinois, amid the highest excitement of the debate, offered the following important amendment to the Missouri section of the bill:

"*And be it further enacted*, That in all that territory ceded by

France to the United States under the name of Louisiana, which lies north of 36° and 30′ north latitude, excepting only such part thereof as is included within the limits of the State contemplated by this act, slavery and involuntary servitude, otherwise than in punishment of crime whereof the party shall have been duly convicted, shall be and is hereby forever prohibited."

This amendment contains the substance of the final settlement. Barbour, of Virginia, attempted to have the line fixed at 40° and 30′; only three Senators voted for his proposition. Eaton, of Tennessee, offered as a substitute for the Thomas amendment a section prescribing the same limits as the Thomas amendment, but providing that the restriction apply only while said portion of country remains a Territory. Eaton found it useless to press the substitute, which was merely an abstract declaration against the right of Congress to impose conditions upon a State, and he withdrew it. Trimble, of Ohio, proposed to make the restriction apply to all territory west of the Mississippi except Missouri. After these three suggestions had been made in vain the Thomas amendment was adopted the next day in the Senate by a vote of 34 to 10, without change and without debate, and on the 18th the Maine and Missouri bills in one, with the compromise amendment, were formally passed.

On February 19, 1820, the House took up these Senate amendments to the Maine bill. Taylor moved that the House disagree, whereupon Scott moved that the amendments be sent to the committee of the whole, which was then, and had been for days, considering the House Missouri bill. This motion took precedence and a spirited debate followed, but commitment was defeated by a vote of 107 to 70. The question then came up on the motion to disagree, which was debated for three days, when, on February 23d, the House disagreed to the Missouri attachment by a vote of 93 to 73, and then to the restrictive amendment by 159 to 18. So the Senate Maine-Missouri bill with the Thomas amendment was defeated in the House. The House then went into the committee of the whole on its own bill with the Taylor restriction, which was still pending. The House continued the debate on this restrictive clause February 24th and 25th.

On the 26th Mr. Storrs, of New York, moved the substance of the Thomas amendment, and supported it in a speech "embracing incidentally an examination of the right of imposing the slavery restriction on Missouri." On February 28th the Senate sent a message to the House saying that it insisted on its amendments. Taylor moved that the House insist upon its disagreement. By a vote of 97 to 76 the House again refused to agree to the rolling of Maine and Missouri into one bill. Then disagreement to the restrictive compromise amendment was voted by 160 to 14, Lowndes, of South Carolina, explaining for the friends of Missouri that though he favored such a proposition, yet, since the free admission of Missouri had been defeated, the restrictive amendment was useless, and there was no motive to vote for it with the Maine bill alone. The chief desire of the men for whom Lowndes spoke was to secure the immediate admission of Missouri without restriction; to that end they were ready to consent to restriction on the Territories. The House had again disagreed to both amendments of the Senate.

Mr. Thomas, of Illinois, moved that a committee of conference be appointed, which was the occasion of a debate of "vehemence and warm feeling." The Senate voted to request a conference, and Senators Thomas of Illinois, Pinkney of Maryland, and Barbour of Virginia were appointed the Senate conferrees. On the following day, February 29th, the House agreed to confer, and Messrs. Holmes of Massachusetts, Taylor of New York, Lowndes of South Carolina, Parker of Massachusetts, and Kinsey of New Jersey were appointed to manage the conference on the part of the House.

On March 1st the House passed its Missouri bill with restriction. It was immediately taken up in the Senate and on March 2d it was passed, after striking out restriction and substituting the Thomas compromise amendment. This agreed with what, it seemed to be understood, would be the report of the conference committee. This report, made in the House by Mr. Holmes on March 2d, contained three distinct recommendations: (1) The Senate should give up a combination of Missouri in the same bill with Maine, and Maine should be admitted; (2) the House should abandon the attempt to restrict slavery in Missouri; (3) both houses should agree to pass the Senate's Missouri bill with the Thomas restriction excluding slavery north and west of that State.

After the reading of the report the first and vital question was then put to the House: Will the House concur with the Senate in admitting Missouri without restriction as to slavery? On this, a last, short, fervent debate occurred. Lowndes of South Carolina, Holmes of Massachusetts, and Mercer of Virginia spoke vigorously. Kinsey, of New Jersey, as one of those holding the balance of power between the contending forces, voiced the opinion of the moderate restrictionists who were now ready to compromise. The cause upon which he relied was the cause of the Union, and to the desire and love of Union he appealed. This had been the cause of compromise before, as it was destined to be many a time later.

The House decided to give up restriction, by a vote of 90 to 87. Fourteen of those who voted to forego restriction on Missouri were from the free States. Taylor, the persistent and valiant leader of the early free-soilers, who, as a member of the conference committee from the House, was the only one of all the committee that refused to concur in the report, made a last effort for his cause by endeavoring to secure the insertion of a line excluding slavery from all the territory west of the Mississippi except Missouri, Arkansas, and Louisiana, but the phalanx of restriction had been broken and his worthy effort failed. The Missouri bill, enabling Missouri to form her constitution, passed both houses March 2, 1820. The following day the Maine bill passed the Senate. Maine was admitted, and the people of Missouri were authorized to form a State government and constitution. And this was the end of the second struggle.

In reviewing the struggle in his mind the careful student will distinguish here between the two totally distinct propositions in reference to restriction: (1) The original restriction of Tallmadge, which Clay vehemently opposed, proposed the exclusion of slavery from Missouri: this was restriction on a State, and was opposed on that ground; (2) the final restriction of Thomas proposed the exclusion of slavery from the Territories of the United States north and west of Missouri. This proposition was adopted; but it did not emanate from the original Missouri restrictionists, nor did it by any means satisfy them. The final compromise measure was proposed by a steadfast opponent of the original Tallmadge amendment. "The current assumption," says Greeley, "that this restriction was proposed by Rufus King, of New York, and mainly sustained by the antagonists of slavery, is wholly mistaken. The truth, doubtless, is that it was suggested by the more moderate opponents of restriction on Missouri as a means of overcoming the resistance of the House to slavery in Missouri. It was, in effect, an offer from the milder opponents of slavery restriction to the more moderate and flexible advocates of that restriction. 'Let us have slavery in Missouri, and we will unite with you in excluding it from all the uninhabited territories north and west of that State.' It was in substance an agreement between the North and the South to that effect, though the more determined champions, whether of slavery extension or slavery restriction, did not unite in it."

This statement of Greeley's is borne out by the record and the final vote. After the prolonged and bitter contest; after a debate then without a parallel in the history of Congress, a debate equalled only in the Constitutional Convention of 1787, which itself had settled the slavery question by compromises; facing bitter prophecies of disunion as an alternative; with earnest and impassioned appeals for compromise still resounding in their ears, eighty-seven original restrictionists held out for restriction on Missouri. They would not consent to a single other slave State in the American Union, and restriction was finally abandoned only by a majority of three votes. Slavery was allowed in Missouri, and restriction was beaten only by the plan of proffering instead an exclusion of slavery from all the then Federal territory west and north of that State. Without this compromise, or its equivalent, the Northern votes needed to pass the bill could not have been obtained.

Maine was now admitted, and nothing remained but that Missouri should form her constitution, that it be formally accepted by Congress, and that the new State take her place with the rest.

A Missouri convention assembled at St. Louis and adopted a constitution for the new State, July 19, 1820. The people of Missouri were displeased with the long delay which had been imposed upon them by the introduction of a subject which they felt was a concern of themselves alone. It was their right, in their opinion, to settle the slavery question for themselves. In this feeling of resentment, and led by extremists in the convention, they inserted a provision in their constitution declaring that "It shall be the duty of the General Assembly, as soon as may be, to pass such laws as may be necessary to prevent free negroes or mulattoes from coming to or settling in this State under any pretext whatever."[1]

This constitution was laid before Congress by Mr. Scott, the delegate from Missouri, on November 20, 1820. The objectionable clause in her constitution gave rise to a stouter and more serious contest than any that had preceded. There arose once more a bitter parliamentary struggle, which provoked dire threats of the dissolution of the Union. The lines of the old contest formed again. The antislavery men and restrictionists who had so hotly contested Missouri's admission as a slave State determined to continue that opposition. They were joined by some who had formerly voted against restriction, but who were now ready to vote against admission. They based their opposition on the ground that the obnoxious clause in Missouri's Constitution was an insulting reflection upon every State in which colored men were citizens, and that it was in direct contravention of that clause in the United States Constitution which declares that "the citizens of each State shall be entitled to all the privileges and immunities of citizens of the several States."

Missouri's Constitution, upon its presentation, was referred to a committee of which Mr. Lowndes, of South Carolina, was chairman. Within a week the committee reported in favor of admission, proposing to effect this by a simple resolution, "That the State of Missouri shall be, and is hereby declared to be, one of the United States of America, and is admitted to the Union on an equal footing with the original States." The report considered the objection which had been urged to Missouri's ready admission, although this objection had not yet come under the cognizance of Congress.

Mr. Lowndes, in a notable speech advocating the immediate

---

[1] The constitution also forbade the legislative emancipation of slaves without the consent of the masters. These two new subjects were to be presented for the consideration of Congress, and it was evident that the whole subject would again be reopened. It seemed as if Missouri wished to meet Congress in a spirit of defiance.

recognition of Missouri as a State, held that the enabling act of the former session was a complete act of admission, that the time and circumstances which made a people a State were the time at which its people formed a constitution, and the act of forming it. This view, Mr. Lowndes contended, was according to precedent. In the case of Indiana, December 11, 1816, the practice of a subsequent declaration of admission first occurred, and this declaration was but a formal notification to the other States that a new member had been admitted. The act of the last session which had been agreed to by the compromise after so long a struggle did not merely give to the people of Missouri the right to propose a constitution, but it conferred on that people all the rights of the proudest and oldest States. This is clearly seen, urged Mr. Lowndes, from the fact that while the act was under discussion Mr. Taylor, of New York, the leader of the restrictionists, had moved to insert an amendment providing that if the constitution of the new State "shall be approved by Congress, the said Territory shall be admitted as a State upon the same footing as the original States." This amendment was voted down, implying that Missouri would be admitted without such condition. We had given Missouri the right of self-government, and we cannot now take it from her.

Mr. Lowndes would not undertake to decide whether or not the objectionable clause was constitutional. He would leave that for the Supreme Court to determine. He was aware that a very large majority of the free blacks of the United States were not considered citizens in their respective States, and this provision of Missouri might be construed as intending to exempt from its provision such of the blacks as were citizens in other States. A similar provision discriminating against free colored persons was in the Constitution of Delaware. No one contended that Congress could sit in judgment on the various constitutional provisions of the old States. The States, old and new, must be equal, and why should Missouri be singled out for invidious distinction? The question should be left to the judiciary as the proper tribunal to interpret the law. When Tennessee presented herself for admission, having formed a constitution without an enabling act of Congress, Mr. Smith, of South Carolina, objected, on the ground that the Constitution of Tennessee was incompatible with that of the United States; Mr. Baldwin replied that "if there should be things in the Constitution of Tennessee not compatible with the Constitution of the United States it was well known that the Constitution of the United States would be paramount; they can therefore be of no effect." In that case the question of constitutional law was left to the supreme judicial tribunal.

Mr. Sergeant, of Pennsylvania, replied to Mr. Lowndes. He did not consider that a Territory became an independent and sovereign State at the time it formed a constitution. Congress could not admit a State by anticipation. Congress could not bind itself to the admission of a State so as to have no choice but to accept such a constitution as that State chose to offer. Giving authority to the people of a Territory to form a State constitution did not admit them into the Union, unless their constitution should be such as the people of the United States, through their representatives, thought fit to accept as a fundamental rule of government. If it be true that Missouri has already the "rights of the oldest and proudest States," why are we deliberating? Why is this resolution now under consideration? Why are the Senators and the Representative from Missouri kept waiting at our doors until they learn the fate of this resolution? Why was Missouri's Constitution submitted to a committee? Why has that committee made a report which we are now discussing? And why did the committee consider it necessary to go into an examination of a particular clause of that constitution, pointing out a mode by which Congress might relieve itself from the task of deciding on its constitutionality by leaving it to the judiciary? The reason assigned by the committee in the "whereas" of the resolution is that Missouri has formed a constitution in conformity with our act of the last session. How could the committee know this?

In the act authorizing the formation of this constitution were found two limitations—that the constitution should be republican, and that it should not be repugnant to the Constitution of the United States. Is it not indispensable before passing a resolution like this that the members of this House should be satisfied that these requisitions have been complied with? Can it be said that Congress has parted with the power of looking into the Constitution of Missouri when it had expressly prescribed conditions which should be indispensable to its acceptance? If Missouri is now involved in difficulty it is the fault of the people of Missouri. This is a difficulty which they themselves have created; the failure to fulfil the compact is on the part of the people of that Territory. Would the people of Missouri think more highly of Congress were we to yield to them on this occasion? How much better it would be for Congress at once to take its ground and refuse to sanction the constitution of any State which is in any respect repugnant to that of the United States. Would anyone pretend, if this constitution instead of being faulty in one particular were faulty from beginning to end, that Missouri would be entitled to admission? Yet the surrender of our right to decide in one particular involves the whole. With respect to the proposition to turn the question over to the judiciary, Mr. Sergeant said that he must declare, with the greatest respect for that judicial body, that he could not consent, on a question which was properly presented for his own decision, to say, "Let the question sleep till some humble individual, some poor citizen, shall come forward and claim a decision of it." He would not leave to some individual to do what it was the duty of Congress to do.

These speeches opened a long and animated debate. The principal theme of discussion was the citizenship of free persons of color, and the subject was examined from every point of view. Mr. Barbour, of Virginia, attempted a definition of the term citizen. There was not a State in the Union, in his opinion, in which colored men were citizens in the sense in which the Constitution uses the term—no State in which they have all the civil rights of other citizens; and therefore the Constitution of Missouri did not infringe the Constitution of the United States.

Mr. Archer, of Virginia, remarked that if there were colored persons who were citizens in some of the States, there was notoriously a much larger class who did not belong to this description, and the clause in Missouri's Constitution might be considered as operating only on this latter class. To reject her constitution in the present state of the public mind would lead to suspicion that the policy of restriction was to be reopened; in that case the wound inflicted on the harmony of the country would be incurable; every man must perceive that the Union would be gone.

Mr. McLane, of Delaware, asserted that free negroes and mulattoes are not that description of citizens contemplated by the Constitution of the United States as entitled to Federal rights. What rights they have are of a local nature, dependent upon the gratuitous favor of the municipal authorities of the States; these rights are limited to the States granting them and confer no Federal privileges and immunities. The free negro must be shown to be of "that description of citizen" to whom the Constitution meant to guarantee equal rights in every State.

Mr. McLane was answered by Mr. Eustis, of Massachusetts, who showed that the rights of citizenship in the States were left to the States themselves, and that in Massachusetts the free negro was in the enjoyment of equal citizenship under the laws; there the free negro was in the enjoyment of civil rights, which were guaranteed to him by the Constitution of the United States, and of which he should not be deprived.

On December 13, 1820, the House rejected the resolution for the admission of Missouri by a vote of 93 to 79. Mr. Lowndes then said that while he did not wish to be disrespectful to the majority of the House, he now called upon that majority "to devise and propose means necessary to protect the Territory, property, and rights of the United States in the Missouri country." The Missouri question now disappears from the Congressional debates for two weeks. On January 5, 1821, Mr. Archer, of Virginia, offered in the House a resolution instructing the committee on the judiciary to inquire into the legal relation of Missouri to the United States—to ascertain whether there were United States tribunals there "competent to exercise jurisdiction and to determine controversies, and, if there be no such tribunals, to report such measures as will cause the laws of the United States to be respected there."

Mr. Archer asserted that in his opinion Missouri stood entirely disconnected from any legal or political relation with the United States Government. "With our own hands we have cut all the moorings, and she floats entirely liberated and at large. She stood formerly in the relation of a Territory; she had proposed to assume the relation of a State. This House had refused her permission to do so, and Missouri stands discharged from all relation to the Union." This resolution was the next phase of the

Missouri question, which gave rise to a spirited debate. The friends of Missouri held that their position was anomalous. She was not a Territory, she was not a State; the authority of the Union hung over her, but there was no legal mode by which it could be exercised—the channels through which the authority of the United States Government could be exercised had been cut off. On the other hand, the opponents of Missouri's admission held that her relations to the Union were as they had been, and they succeeded in laying the Archer resolution of inquiry on the table. This prevented the House judiciary committee from giving a public legal declaration of Missouri's relations and rights, and by this action the House assumed the existence of the Territorial relation, without, however, any express settlement of the question.

Missouri next came up in the House debates on a question of amending the Journal. On January 11th Mr. Lowndes presented three memorials from the Senate and House of Representatives of Missouri. On the 12th Mr. Cobb, of Georgia, moved to amend the Journal by inserting the words "the State of" before the word "Missouri." After some rapid sparring in debate the parties ranged themselves for another vote, and the motion of Mr. Cobb was lost by the casting vote of the Speaker, and the House thus again refused to recognize Missouri as a State. Mr. Parker, of Virginia, then moved to amend the Journal by inserting before "Missouri" the words "the Territory of." The House had denied what Missouri is not, they must now say what she is. The Speaker then explained from the chair that the Journal should be prepared by the clerk. The rules of the House made it the duty of the Speaker "to examine and correct the Journal before it is read."

In this case the memorials had been purposely made to read so as neither to affirm nor deny that Missouri was a State, since the House was divided upon that question. The motion of Mr. Parker was voted down, and the House proceeded to discuss the right of the Speaker to make the alterations in the Journal which he had made in these memorials. Thus, while refusing to acknowledge Missouri as a State, the House refused to declare that she was a Territory.

On January 24, 1820, Mr. Eustis, of Massachusetts, offered

a resolution declaring the admission of Missouri on condition that the objectionable clause in her constitution be expunged. His object was to remove the only objection to the admission of Missouri. This resolution was negatived by a large majority.

On January 29, 1820, a resolution from the Senate came to the House and was taken up there in committee of the whole. This Senate resolution admitted Missouri, and provided:

"That nothing herein contained shall be so construed as to give the assent of Congress to any provision in the Constitution of Missouri (if any such there be) which contravenes that clause of the Constitution of the United States which declares that the citizens of each State shall be entitled to all the privileges and immunities of citizens of the several States."

One objection which had been urged to admitting Missouri with her objectionable constitution was that to do so would be to consent to the unconstitutional provision of her fundamental law. The Senate resolution was intended to meet this objection. It admitted the probability that Missouri's objectionable clause contravened the Constitution of the United States and merely asserted the Senate's unwillingness to have its admission of Missouri interpreted as making Congress a party to such violation. This was not satisfactory to the opponents of Missouri, who held that the responsibility was on Congress; it was the duty of Congress to prevent a violation of the Constitution, and this resolution merely shirked the responsibility. It was seen that the resolution would be rejected by the House.

Between January 29th and February 2d six amendments were proposed in the nature of binding Missouri either to expunge the offensive clause of her constitution or never to enact a law in obedience to that clause. The debates of these days covered the evils of slavery, the rights of the South, the balance of power, and the nature, obligations, and benefits of the Union. On February 2d Mr. Clay, seeing that all efforts at amendment had failed, and anxious to make a last effort to settle this distracting question, moved to refer the Senate's resolution to a special committee of thirteen members.

On February 10th Mr. Clay, in behalf of the committee of thirteen, reported. The committee had desired to arrive at a conclusion which would give general satisfaction; they had sought a full and frank comparison of opinion among themselves; the committee was of the unanimous opinion that no condition ought to be imposed on Missouri except those suggested at the last session of Congress, *i.e.*, that her constitution should be republican and in conformity with the Constitution of the United States; that the question of restriction should not be raised. This limited the consideration of the committee to the question whether Missouri's Constitution was in conformity with these conditions, and it was found that the only objection to her constitution was the clause to which exception had been taken. On that clause the same diversity of opinion appeared in the committee which had been made manifest in the House—"With these conflicting opinions the committee thought it best that, without either side abandoning its opinion, an endeavor should be made to form an amendment to the Senate resolution which should contain an adequate security against the violation of the privileges and immunities of citizens of other States in Missouri."

Accordingly, Missouri is to be admitted into the Union "upon the fundamental condition that she shall never pass any laws preventing any description of persons from going to or settling in the said State who now are, or hereafter may become, citizens of any of the States of this Union; and upon the Legislature of the said State signifying its assent to that condition, by a solemn public act, which is to be communicated to the President of the United States, he is to proclaim the fact, and thereupon the admission of the said State is to be complete. To prevent, however, this amendment from being considered as impairing any right which may appertain to Missouri, in common with other States, to exclude from her jurisdiction persons under peculiar circumstances (as paupers and vagabonds), a further proviso is added declaring Missouri's right to exercise any power which the original States may constitutionally exercise."

This report from the special committee of thirteen was laid on the table until February 12th. The debate was then again renewed, involving charges and countercharges on the balance of power between the sections and on the matter of slave representation. The majority in opposition to Missouri was still obdurate, and the Senate resolution, amendment and all, was rejected by the close vote of 83 to 80.   Members in ill-health, who had not been in the hall when their names were called, appeared and asked to have their votes recorded   This could not be done on cept by unanimous consent.   This was not given, and the work of the committee of thirteen seemed to have come to nothing. Mr. Livermore, however, an opponent of Missouri, who had objected to the contested votes, gave notice of a motion to reconsider in order that the question might be fairly tested in a full vote of the House.   On the next day, February 13, 1821, Mr. Livermore made his motion for reconsideration.   Some of the friends of Missouri opposed the motion for reconsideration, partly because they would not have Missouri burdened with any conditions whatever, holding that she was only kept out of the Union by violence and injustice; partly because, as in the case of Mr. Randolph, of Virginia, they held that the battle had been fairly fought and won by the other side, and that another way must be found to settle this question.   Mr. Clay made a successful plea for reconsideration, and again the House plunged into a heated debate.

At this stage of the controversy Mr. Pinckney, of South Carolina, made a notable speech.   He considered that the country "had now arrived at the most awful period which had hitherto occurred on this delicate and distressing subject."   He quoted from a letter of Jefferson, lately published, indicating the portentous character of the Missouri question.[1]   "I agree perfectly with him," said Mr. Pinckney, "and I consider this, beyond all comparison, the second question in importance which has been agitated among us since our revolt from the parent State.   The first was the memorable declaration which confirmed the Union and gave birth to the independence of our country.   This is the only one which may, in its consequences, lead to the dissolution of that very Union, and prove the death-blow to all our political happiness and national importance.   I express this fear from the fact that gentlemen of the opposition have seen fit to throw off the veil and expressly declare their intention to leave this question to the next Congress; to leave to them unfettered by any act of ours the power to decide how far the true interests of the Union

[1] "The Missouri question is the most portentous one that ever threatened our Union.   In the gloomiest moments of the Revolutionary War I never had any apprehension equal to that I feel now from this source."

make it necessary to renew the struggle for restriction of slavery in Missouri—a struggle which has during the last three sessions shaken the Union to its very foundations.   They openly avow that they do not consider themselves bound by the compact of last year, but aver, if they have the strength to do so, to leave the next Congress free to decide this question as they please."

Mr. Pinckney then went into an examination of the Constitution of Missouri, claiming for it an excellence and superiority over the constitutions of other States.   "Can it be possible," he asked, "that so excellent a system can be rejected for the trifling reason that it inadvertently contains a provision prohibiting the settlement of free negroes and mulattoes among them?   Or is it not infinitely more probable that other reasons of a much more serious nature, and pregnant with the most disastrous events to the future union and peace of these States, are at the bottom of this unexpected and inexcusable opposition?   The article of the Constitution on which now so much stress is laid—'the citizens in each State shall be entitled to all the privileges and immunities in every State,'—having been made by me, it is supposed that I must know, or perfectly recollect, what I meant by it.   In answer, I say that, at the time I drew that article, I perfectly knew that there did not then exist such a thing in the Union as a black or colored citizen, nor could I have conceived it possible such a thing could ever have existed in it.[1]

"Missouri having no idea of the existence of such a thing as a black or colored citizen of the United States, and knowing that all the Southern and Western States had for many years passed laws to the same effect, which laws are well known to Congress, being at this moment in their library, and within the walls of the capitol, and which were never before objected to by them or their courts, they (the people of Missouri) were no doubt warranted in supposing they had the same right.   The silence of Congress on the antecedent laws of Southern and Western States might fairly be considered a sanction to Missouri's proceeding."

This speech of Mr. Pinckney gave indirect public expression to the charge, which had been frequently bandied in political circles, that the antislavery restrictionists, having secured the ad-

---

[1] Gen. Charles Pinckney was a member of the Constitutional Convention of 1787.

mission of Maine, were now not willing to fulfil the terms of the compromise; that they were guilty of a breach of faith. The in justice of this view is indicated by the fact that some members who had voted against restriction on Missouri in the previous session, were now opposing her admission under her objectionable constitution. Mr. Foot, of Connecticut, was of this number, and he asserted at this stage of the controversy that he would never vote for Missouri's admission unless the offensive clause were expunged. But, no doubt, the original restrictionists were ready to seize this opportunity to put an obstacle in the way of the admission of another slave State. Mr. Clay, struggling for conciliation, closed the debate. He alternately reasoned, remonstrated, and entreated the House, but his effort was in vain, and his compromise resolution was rejected by a vote of 88 to 82.

It was the day after this seemingly final rejection of Missouri that the two Houses were appointed to meet to count the electoral vote for President and Vice-President. It had been seen, of course, that the question would arise whether the vote of Missouri should be counted, or whether it was entitled to be cast. It had not yet been decided whether Missouri was a State. In order to come to some arrangement by which the Houses could avoid this question when they should come into joint session, Mr. Clay had, ten days before, on February 4th, offered in the House a resolution providing that if any objection be made to the vote of Missouri the President of the Senate, who was to preside on this occasion, should be directed to announce what the result would be if the votes of Missouri were counted and what it would be if the votes of Missouri were not counted; "but in either case A. B. is elected President of the United States."

This resolution was adopted only after considerable debate as to the status of Missouri. The Senate also agreed to this plan, but there was still much fear that it would not be successful in keeping the peace, and the fear was realized. The joint meeting of the two Houses on February 14th was one of turbulent excitement. It was frequently interrupted by simultaneous challenges of Missouri's vote. When the vote of Missouri was announced Mr. Livermore, of New Hampshire, arose and said: "Mr. President and Mr. Speaker, I object to receiving any votes for President and Vice-President from Missouri, as Missouri is not a State of this Union." This objection was numerously and clamor-ously seconded. Confusion and tumult followed, till "at last a Senator, with a voice above the wildness of the scene, moved that the Senate withdraw, which was immediately obeyed, and the House was left in sole possession of the field." Disorder con-tinued in the House after the Senate's withdrawal, one member crying, "Missouri is not a State," another shouting, "Missouri is a State." An hour of wrangling followed. When order was re-stored, Mr. Floyd, of Virginia, arose and offered the following:

"*Resolved*, That Missouri is one of the States of this Union, and her votes for President and Vice-President of the United States ought to be received and counted."

Mr. Floyd said that he now considered the House brought to the brink of the precipice. "The votes of other States had been received and counted before their admission had been formally declared. The question of Missouri was now brought fairly to issue. Let us know whether Missouri be a State in the Union or not. If not, let us send her an ambassador, and treat for her admission. Sir, we cannot take another step without hurling this Government into the gulf of destruction. For one, I say I have gone as far as I can go in the way of compromise, and if there is to be a compromise beyond that point it must be at the edge of the sword."

Mr. Archer, of Maryland, moved the indefinite postponement of Mr. Floyd's resolution. He was a friend of Missouri, but he could not assert by his vote that she was a member of the Union without the acceptance of her constitution by Congress, as much as he "reprobated the foul combination for her rejection."

John Randolph, of Virginia, considered that in this resolu-tion Missouri had for the first time presented herself in visible and tangible shape. "Now comes the question whether we will not merely repel her, but repel her with scorn and contumely." He would have had this question of Missouri at an earlier stage of the proceedings in this concrete shape, as, for instance, the right of her representatives to a seat on the floor. Missouri's vote was now presented in her own person and Congress had no power to reject. Randolph here laid down the strange doctrine that the electoral college was as independent of Congress as Congress was of the college. The duty of the Houses in counting the vote was purely ministerial; it is to count the votes, not to reject; there was power to receive the return, but no power to pass judgment on the validity of the return. It must count the vote; but it had no power to determine what were votes. "This was the first instance in which Missouri had knocked at the door and demanded her rights. It is now for us to determine whether she shall now be one of our commonwealths. No doubt Congress may drive Missouri into the wilderness, like another son of Hagar, but if we do we drive her at our own peril."

After this spirited and heated debate, in which Mr. Clay took a prominent part, the resolution of Mr. Floyd was laid on the table, and a message was sent to the Senate that the House was again ready to receive it for the purpose of counting the electoral vote. I quote from the *Annals of Congress:*

"The Senate again appeared and took seats in the House as before. The President of the Senate, in the presence of both Houses, proceeded to open the certificates of the electors of the State of Missouri, which he delivered to the tellers, by whom they were read and who registered the same. And the votes of all the States having been thus counted, registered, and the list thereof compared, they were delivered to the president of the Senate, by whom they were read as already printed. The president of the Senate then, in pursuance of the resolution adopted by the two Houses, proceeded to announce the vote as follows:

"'Were the vote of Missouri to be counted, the result would be for James Monroe, of Virginia, for President of the United States, 231 votes; if not counted, for James Monroe, of Virginia, 228 votes. For Daniel D. Tompkins, of New York, for Vice-President of the United States, 218 votes; if not counted, for Daniel D. Tompkins, of New York, for Vice-President, 215. But in either event, James Monroe, of Virginia, has a majority of the votes of the whole number of electors for President, and Daniel D. Tompkins, of New York, a majority of the whole number of electors for Vice-President of the United States.'

"The President of the Senate had proceeded thus far, or nearly thus far, in the proclamation when Mr. Floyd, of Virginia, addressed the Chair and inquired whether the votes of Missouri were or were not counted. Cries of 'Order! Order!' were so loud as to drown Mr. Floyd's voice. The president of the

Senate had hesitated in the proclamation on Mr. Floyd's addressing the Chair.

"Mr. Randolph rose and was addressing the Chair, when loud cries of 'Order! Order!' resounded from many voices.

"The Speaker pronounced Mr. Randolph to be out of order and invited him to take his seat.

"Mr. Brush demanded that Mr. Randolph should be allowed to proceed, and declared his determination to sustain his right to do so.

"Mr. Floyd was also declared out of order, and though there was considerable murmuring at the decision, order was restored and the President of the Senate completed the announcement of the election of Monroe and Tompkins.

"Mr. Randolph addressed the Chair, but was required to take his seat. On motion, the Senate retired from the hall. After they retired, the House being called to order, Mr. Randolph, who had still retained the floor, was heard addressing the Chair. 'He had,' he said, 'seen every election of President of the United States except that of the present chief magistrate, and he had never before heard any other form of proclamation than that such was the whole number of votes given in. Sir, your election is vitiated; you have flinched from the question; you have attempted to evade the decision of that which was essential to the determination of who is or who is not elected chief magistrate of the United States.' And Mr. Randolph concluded his remarks with resolutions declaring the election illegal. When he suspended his remarks to reduce his resolutions to writing, a motion was made and carried to adjourn the House."

The next day, February 15th, the formal resolution was again repeated by Mr. Clark, of New York, to admit Missouri on condition that she expunge the objectionable clause, but the resolution was laid over without discussion. The House was tired of all the old aspects of the question. The next aspect of the question which excited discussion arose on the proposition of Mr. Brown, of Kentucky, made February 21st, to repeal the enabling act for Missouri. Missouri had not been admitted according to the terms of the compact, and Mr. Brown now demanded, "on the principle of justice which governs contracts, that the antislavery restriction should be raised from the rest of the Territory. The consideration promised for this restriction has not been paid; the plighted faith of Congress for the admission of Missouri has been violated then made off the restriction. Sir, the course of the majority can be justified by no principle of reason or sound policy, but must rest for its support on pious fraud."

On the day following Mr. Clay moved the appointment of a joint committee, to consist of twenty-three members on the part of the House, to take into consideration the admission of Missouri. The committee appointed by ballot reported on February 24th, the report embodying substantially the conclusions of the former committee of thirteen. It was agreed that "Missouri shall be admitted into this Union on an equal footing with the original States, upon the fundamental condition" that the objectionable clause of her constitution should "never be construed to authorize the passage of any laws, and that no law should ever be passed, by which any citizen of either of the States of the Union shall be excluded from the enjoyment of any of the privileges and immunities to which such citizen is entitled under the Constitution of the United States; that the Legislature of said State, by a solemn public act, shall declare the assent of said State to the said fundamental condition." Upon the transmission of this act to the Chief Executive, the President was to proclaim the admission of Missouri.

This report came back to the two Houses with the unanimous approval of the committee from the Senate and with almost the unanimous vote of the committee of the House. But it did not pass the House without another animated debate; and it then passed only by the close vote of 86 to 82. And the Missouri struggle was ended. Missouri agreed to the "fundamental condition of her admission," June 26, 1821, and the President's proclamation announcing her admission was dated August 10, 1821.

It was this last phase of the struggle—which seems only like an appendix to the real issue itself—in which Mr. Clay took such an active and prominent part, a part which helped to gain for him the title of "Pacificator." It was in this final compromise, not in the former and more important one, that Mr. Clay was the leading spirit. The final phase of the Missouri struggle has almost disappeared from general knowledge. The first struggle and compromise involved the chief merits of the controversy and dealt with the subjects of permanent interest.   But it was in the last phase that the greatest excitement, antagonism, and bitterness were aroused, and it was in this stage that the struggle appeared the most dangerous.   But the excitement and danger which this involved were merely temporary.   The enduring nature of the Missouri question was involved, not in the final heated struggle, but in the original contest over restriction and the compromise by which this was settled.

THE SPANISH DEMAND FOR A CONSTITUTION

A.D. 1820

CHARLES A. FYFFE

In Spain, as in the rest of Europe, the overthrow of Napoleon was followed by a restoration of the ancient forms of authority. King Ferdinand VII had received from the Spanish people evidences of the most devoted loyalty. In his name they had maintained their long struggle against Bonaparte, Ferdinand himself meanwhile being a prisoner-guest in France, receiving from Napoleon an enormous income, and writing to him letters overflowing with professions of warm attachment.

In 1812 the Spanish people, with English help, had driven back the French invaders and established a constitutional government. In 1814 King Ferdinand returned from France to resume the rule of a country that was half tempted to disown him in scorn at the contemptible figure he had so far made in every epoch of his life. He evaded the swearing of allegiance to the newly established constitution, which he presently rejected altogether, imprisoning the men who had established it. Having thus punished those who had made his restoration possible, he began a career of the most unbridled and savage despotism.

Fyffe, the English historian of modern Europe, has given one of the latest and certainly most dramatic accounts of the causes, progress, and significance of the rebellion that ensued.

WHEN the guardians of Europe, at the end of the first three years of peace, scanned from their council-chamber at Aix-la-Chapelle[1] that goodly heritage which, under Providence, their own parental care was henceforth to guard against the assaults of malice and revolution, they had fixed their gaze chiefly on France, Germany, and the Netherlands as the regions most threatened by the spirit of change. The forecast was not accurate. In each of these countries government proved during the succeeding years to be much more than a match for

[1] The Congress of Aix-la-Chapelle (October, 1818), representatives of the powers, concerted measures for the settlement of European affairs. This was three years after the Second Peace of Paris, which ended the Napoleonic Wars.—ED.

41

its real or imaginary foes: it was in the Mediterranean states, which had excited comparatively little anxiety, that the first successful attack was made upon established power. Three movements arose successively in the three southern peninsulas, at the time when Metternich was enjoying the silence which he had imposed upon Germany, and the Ultraroyalists of France were making good the advantage which the crime of an individual and the imprudence of a party had thrown into their hands. In Spain and in Italy a body of soldiers rose in behalf of constitutional government: in Greece a nation rose against the rule of the foreigner.

In all three countries the issue of these movements was determined by the Northern powers. All three movements were at first treated as identical, and all alike condemned as the work of Jacobinism. But the course of events, and a change of persons in the government of one great state, brought about a truer view of the nature of the struggle in Greece. The ultimate action of Europe in the affairs of that country was different from its action in the affairs of Italy and Spain. It is now only remembered as an instance of political recklessness or stupidity that a conflict of race against race and of religion against religion should for a while have been confused by some of the leading ministers of Europe with the attempt of a party to make the form of domestic government more liberal. The Hellenic rising had indeed no feature in common with the revolutions of Naples and Cadiz; and, although in order of time the opening of the Greek movement long preceded the close of the Spanish movement, the historian, who has neither the politician's motive for making a confusion, nor the protection of his excuse of ignorance, must in this case neglect the accidents of chronology, and treat the two as altogether apart.

King Ferdinand of Spain, after overthrowing the constitution which he found in existence on his return to his country, had conducted himself as if his object had been to show to what lengths a legitimate monarch might abuse the fidelity of his subjects and defy the public opinion of Europe. The leaders of the Cortes, whom he had arrested in 1814, after being declared innocent by one tribunal after another, were sentenced to long terms of imprisonment by an arbitrary decree of the King, without even the pretence of judicial forms. Men who had been conspicuous in the struggle of the nation against Napoleon were neglected or disgraced; many of the highest posts were filled by politicians who had played a double part, or had even served under the invader. Priests and courtiers intrigued for influence over the King; even when a capable minister was placed in power through the pressure of the ambassadors, and the King's name was set to edicts of administrative reform, these edicts were made a dead letter by the powerful band who lived upon the corruption of the public service. The peasant, who knew that his house would not now be burned by the French, and who heard that true religion had at length triumphed over its enemies, understood, and cared to understand, nothing more. Rumors of kingly misgovernment and oppression scarcely reached his ears. Ferdinand was still the child of Spain and of the Church; his return had been the return of peace; his rule was the victory of the Catholic faith.

But the acquiescence of the mass of the people was not shared by the officers of the army and the educated classes in the towns. The overthrow of the constitution was from the first condemned by soldiers who had won distinction under the government of the Cortes; and a series of acts of military rebellion, though isolated and on the smallest scale, showed that the course on which Ferdinand had entered was not altogether free from danger. The attempts of General Mina in 1814, and of Porlier and Lacy in succeeding years, to raise the soldiery in behalf of the constitution, failed, through the indifference of the soldiery themselves.

Discontent made its way in the army by slow degrees; and the ultimate declaration of a military party against the existing Government was due at least as much to Ferdinand's absurd system of favoritism, and to the wretched condition into which the army had been thrown, as to an attachment to the memory or the principles of constitutional rule. Misgovernment made the treasury bankrupt; soldiers and sailors received no pay for years together; and the hatred with which the Spanish people had now come to regard military service is curiously shown by an order of the Government that all the beggars in Madrid and other great towns should be seized on a certain night (July 23,

1816) and enrolled in the army. But the very beggars were more than a match for Ferdinand's administration. They heard of the fate in store for them, and mysteriously disappeared, so frustrating a measure by which it had been calculated that Spain would gain sixty thousand warriors.

The military revolution which at length broke out in the year 1820 was closely connected with the struggle for independence now being made by the American colonies of Spain; and in its turn it affected the course of this struggle and its final result. The colonies had refused to accept the rule either of Joseph Bonaparte, or of the Cortes of Cadiz when their legitimate sovereign was dispossessed by Napoleon. While acting for the most part in Ferdinand's name, they had engaged in a struggle with the National Government of Spain. They had tasted independence; and although after the restoration of Ferdinand they would probably have recognized the rights of the Spanish crown if certain concessions had been made, they were not disposed to return to the condition of inferiority in which they had been held during the last century, or to submit to rulers who proved themselves as cruel and vindictive in moments of victory as they were incapable of understanding the needs of the time. The struggle accordingly continued. Regiment after regiment was sent from Spain, to perish of fever, of forced marches, or on the field. The Government of King Ferdinand, despairing of its own resources, looked around for help among the European powers.

England would have lent its mediation, and possibly even armed assistance, if the court of Madrid would have granted a reasonable amount of freedom to the colonies and have opened their ports to British commerce. This, however, was not in accordance with the views of Ferdinand's advisers. Strange as it may appear, the Spanish Government demanded that the alliance of sovereigns, which had been framed for the purpose of resisting the principle of rebellion and disorder in Europe, should intervene against its revolted subjects on the other side of the Atlantic, and it implied that England, if acting at all, should act as the instrument of the Alliance. Encouragement was given to the design by the courts of Paris and St. Petersburg. Whether a continent claimed its independence, or a German schoolboy wore a forbidden ribbon in his cap, the chiefs of the Holy Alliance now assumed the frown of offended Providence, and prepared to interpose their own superior power and wisdom to save a misguided world from the consequences of its own folly.

Alexander had indeed for a time hoped that the means of subduing the colonies might be supplied by himself; and in his zeal to supplant England in the good graces of Ferdinand he sold the King a fleet of war on very moderate terms. To the scandal of Europe the ships, when they reached Cadiz, turned out to be thoroughly rotten and unseaworthy. As it was certain that the Czar's fleet, and the Spanish soldiers, however holy their mission, would all go to the bottom together as soon as they encountered the waves of the Atlantic, the expedition was postponed, and the affairs of America were brought before the Congress of Aix-la-Chapelle. The envoys of Russia and France submitted a paper, in which, anticipating the storm-warnings of more recent times, they described the dangers to which monarchical Europe would be exposed from the growth of a federation of republics in America; and they suggested that Wellington, as "the man of Europe," should go to Madrid, to preside over a negotiation between the court of Spain and all the ambassadors with reference to the terms to be offered to the transatlantic states. England, however, in spite of Lord Castlereagh's dread of revolutionary contagion, adhered to the principles which it had already laid down; and as the counsellors of King Ferdinand declined to change their policy, Spain was left to subdue its colonies by itself.

It was in the army assembled at Cadiz for embarkation in the summer of 1819 that the conspiracy against Ferdinand's government found its leaders. Secret societies had now spread themselves over the principal Spanish towns, and looked to the soldiery on the coast for the signal of revolt. Abisbal, commander at Cadiz, intending to make himself safe against all contingencies, encouraged for a while the plots of the discontented officers: then, foreseeing the failure of the movement, he arrested the principal men by a stratagem, and went off to Madrid to reveal the conspiracy to the court and to take credit for saving the King's crown (July, 1819). If the army could have been immediately despatched to America, the danger would possibly

have passed away. This, however, was prevented by an outbreak of yellow fever, which made it necessary to send the troops
into cantonments for several months. The conspirators gained
time to renew their plans. The common soldiers, who had
hitherto been faithful to the Government, heard in their own
squalor and inaction the fearful stories of the few sick and
wounded who returned from beyond the seas, and learned to
regard the order of embarkation as a sentence of death. Several battalions were won over to the cause of constitutional liberty by their commanders. The leaders imprisoned a few months
before were again in communication with their followers.

After the treachery of Abisbal, it was agreed to carry out the
revolt without the assistance of generals or grandees. The leaders chosen were two colonels, Quiroga and Riego, of whom the
former was in nominal confinement in a monastery near Medina
Sidonia, twenty miles east of Cadiz, while Riego was stationed
at Cabeza, a few marches distant on the great road to Seville.
The first day of the year 1820 was fixed for the insurrection. It
was determined that Riego should descend upon the headquarters,
which were at Arcos, and arrest the generals before they could
hear anything of the movement, while Quiroga, moving from the
east, gathered up the battalions stationed on the road, and threw
himself into Cadiz, there to await his colleague's approach.

The first step in the enterprise proved successful. Riego,
proclaiming the Constitution of 1812, surprised the headquarters, seized the generals, and rallied several companies to his
standard. Quiroga, however, though he gained possession of
San Fernando, at the eastern end of the peninsula of Leon, on
which Cadiz is situated, failed to make his entrance into Cadiz.
The commandant, hearing of the capture of the headquarters,
had closed the city gates and arrested the principal inhabitants
whom he suspected of being concerned in the plot. The troops
within the town showed no sign of mutiny. Riego, when he arrived at the peninsula of Leon, found that only five thousand
men in all had joined the good cause, while Cadiz, with a considerable garrison and fortifications of great strength, stood hostile before him. He accordingly set off with a small force to visit
and win over the other regiments which were lying in the neighboring towns and villages. The commanders, however, while

not venturing to attack the mutineers, drew off their troops to a distance, and prevented them from entering into any communication with Riego.

The adventurous soldier, leaving Quiroga in the peninsula of Leon, then marched into the interior of Andalusia (January 27th), endeavoring to raise the inhabitants of the towns. But the small numbers of his band, and the knowledge that Cadiz and the greater part of the army still held by the Government, prevented the inhabitants from joining the insurrection, even where they received Riego with kindness and supplied the wants of his soldiers. During week after week the little column traversed the country, now cut off from retreat, exhausted by forced marches in drenching rain, and harassed by far stronger forces sent in pursuit. The last town that Riego entered was Cordova. The enemy was close behind him. No halt was possible. He led his band, now numbering only two hundred men, into the mountains, and there bade them disperse (March 11th).

With Quiroga lying inactive in the peninsula of Leon and Riego hunted from village to village, it seemed as if the insurrection which they had begun could only end in the ruin of its leaders. But the movement had in fact effected its object. While the courtiers around King Ferdinand, unwarned by the news from Cadiz, continued their intrigues against one another, the rumor of rebellion spread over the country. If no great success had been achieved by the rebels, it was also certain that no great blow had been struck by the Government. The example of bold action had been set; the shock given at one end of the peninsula was felt at the other; and a fortnight before Riego's band dispersed, the garrison and the citizens of Corunna together declared for the constitution (February 20th). From Corunna the revolutionary movement spread to Ferrol and to all the other coast towns of Galicia. The news reached Madrid, terrifying the Government and exciting the spirit of insurrection in the capital itself. The King summoned a council of the leading men around him. The wisest of them advised him to publish a moderate constitution, and, by convoking a parliament immediately, to stay the movement, which would otherwise result in the restoration of the Assembly and the Constitution of 1812.

They also urged the King to abolish the Inquisition forthwith. Ferdinand's brother, Don Carlos, the head of the clerical party, succeeded in preventing both measures. Though the generals in all quarters of Spain wrote that they could not answer for the troops, there were still hopes of keeping down the country by force of arms. Abisbal, who was at Madrid, was ordered to move with reënforcements toward the army in the South. He set out, protesting to the King that he knew the way to deal with rebels. When he reached Ocaña he proclaimed the constitution himself (March 4th).

It was now clear that the cause of absolute monarchy was lost. The ferment in Madrid increased. On the night of March 6th all the great bodies of state assembled for council in the King's palace, and early on the 7th Ferdinand published a proclamation stating that he had determined to summon the Cortes immediately. This declaration satisfied no one, for the Cortes designed by the King might be the mere revival of a medieval form, and the history of 1814 showed how little value was to be attached to Ferdinand's promises. Crowds gathered in the great squares of Madrid, crying for the Constitution of 1812. The statement of the Minister of War that the guard was on the point of joining the people now overcame even the resistance of Don Carlos and the confessors; and after a day wasted in dispute, Ferdinand announced to his people that he was ready to take the oath to the constitution which they desired. The next day was given up to public rejoicings; the book of the constitution was carried in procession through the city with the honors paid to the holy sacrament, and all political prisoners were set at liberty. The prison of the Inquisition was sacked, the instruments of torture broken in pieces.

On the 9th the leaders of the agitation took steps to make the King fulfil his promise. A mob invaded the court and threshold of the palace. At their demand the municipal council of 1814 was restored; its members were sent, in company with six deputies chosen by the populace, to receive the pledges of the King. Ferdinand, all smiles and bows, while he looked forward to the day when force or intrigue should make him again absolute master of Spain and enable him to take vengeance upon the men who were humiliating him, took the oath of fidelity to the Constitution of 1812. New ministers were immediately called to office, and a provisional Junta was placed by their side as the representative of the public until the new Cortes should be duly elected. Tidings of the Spanish revolution passed rapidly over Europe, disquieting the courts and everywhere reviving the hopes of the friends of popular right. Before four months had passed, the constitutional movement begun in Cadiz was taken up in Southern Italy.

It was the boast of the Spanish and Italian liberals that the revolutions effected in 1820 were undisgraced by the scenes of outrage which had followed the capture of the Bastille and the overthrow of French absolutism thirty years before. The gentler character of these southern movements proved, however, no extenuation in the eyes of the leading statesmen of Europe: on the contrary, the declaration of soldiers in favor of a constitution seemed in some quarters more ominous of evil than any excess of popular violence. The alarm was first sounded at St. Petersburg. As soon as the Czar heard of Riego's proceedings at Cadiz, he began to meditate intervention; and when it was known that Ferdinand had been forced to accept the Constitution of 1812, he ordered his ambassadors to propose that all the great powers, acting through their ministers at Paris, should address a remonstrance to the representative of Spain, requiring the Cortes to disavow the crime of March 8th, by which they had been called into being, and to offer a pledge of obedience to the King by enacting the most rigorous laws against sedition and revolt. In that case, and in that alone, the Czar desired to add, would the powers maintain their relations of confidence and amity with Spain.

This Russian proposal was viewed with some suspicion at Vienna; it was answered with a direct and energetic negative from London. Canning was still in the Ministry. The words with which in 1818 he had protested against a league between England and autocracy were still ringing in the ears of his colleagues. Lord Liverpool's government knew itself to be unpopular in the country; every consideration of policy as well as of self-interest bade it resist the beginnings of an intervention which, if confined to words, was certain to be useless, and, if supported by action, was likely to end in that alliance between France and

Russia which had been the nightmare of English statesmen ever since 1814, and in a second occupation of Spain by the very generals whom Wellington had spent so many years in dislodging. Castlereagh replied to the Czar's note in terms which made it clear that England would never give its sanction to a collective interference with Spain. Richelieu, the nominal head of the French Government, felt too little confidence in his position to act without the concurrence of Great Britain; and the crusade of absolutism against Spanish liberty was in consequence postponed until the victory of the Ultraroyalists at Paris was complete, and the overthrow of Richelieu had brought to the head of the French State a group of men who felt no scruple in entering upon an aggressive war.

The condition of Spain in the year 1822 gave ample encouragement to those who longed to employ the arms of France in the Royalist cause. The hopes of peaceful reform, which for the first few months after the revolution had been shared even by foreign politicians at Madrid, had long vanished. In the moment of popular victory Ferdinand had brought the leaders of the Cortes from their prisons and placed them in office. These men showed a dignified forgetfulness of the injuries which they had suffered. Misfortune had calmed their impetuosity and taught them more of the real condition of the Spanish people. They entered upon their task with seriousness and good faith, and would have proved the best friends of constitutional monarchy if Ferdinand had had the least intention of coöperating with them loyally. But they found themselves encountered from the first by a double enemy. The more violent of the liberals, with Riego at their head, abandoned themselves to extravagances like those of the club-orators of Paris in 1791, and did their best to make any peaceable administration impossible. After combating these anarchists, or *exaltados*, with some success, the Ministry was forced to call in their aid, when, at the suggestion of the papal nuncio, the King placed his veto upon a law dissolving most of the monasteries (October, 1820).

Ferdinand now openly combined with the enemies of the constitution, and attempted to transfer the command of the army to one of his own agents. The plot failed; the Ministry sent the alarm over the whole country, and Ferdinand stood convicted before his people as a conspirator against the constitution which he had sworn to defend. The agitation of the clubs, which the Ministry had hitherto suppressed, broke out anew. A storm of accusations assailed Ferdinand himself. He was compelled at the end of the year 1820 to banish from Madrid most of the persons who had been his confidants; and although his dethronement was not yet proposed, he had already become, far more than Louis XVI of France under similar conditions, the recognized enemy of the revolution and the suspected patron of every treason against the nation.

The attack of the despotic courts on Naples in the spring of 1821 heightened the fury of parties in Spain, encouraging the "Serviles," or "Absolutists," in their plots, and forcing the Ministry to yield to the cry for more violent measures against the enemies of the constitution. In the South of Spain the "Exaltados" gained possession of the principal military and civil commands, and openly refused obedience to the central Administration when it attempted to interfere with their action. Seville, Cartagena, and Cadiz acted as if they were independent republics, and even spoke of separation from Spain. Defied by its own subordinates in the provinces, and unable to look to the King for any sincere support, the moderate governing party lost all hold upon the nation. In the Cortes elected in 1822 the Exaltados formed the majority, and Riego was appointed president. Ferdinand now began to concert measures of action with the French Ultraroyalists.

The Serviles, supported by French money, broke into open rebellion in the North. When the session of the Cortes ended, the King attempted to overthrow his enemies by military force. Three battalions of the Royal Guard, which had been withdrawn from Madrid, received secret orders to march upon the capital (July 6, 1822), where Ferdinand was expected to place himself at their head. They were, however, met and defeated in the streets by other regiments, and Ferdinand, vainly attempting to dissociate himself from the action of his partisans, found his crown, if not his life, in peril. He wrote to Louis XVIII that he was a prisoner. Though the French King gave nothing more than good counsel, the Ultraroyalists in the French Cabinet and in the army now strained every nerve to accelerate a war between the two countries. The Spanish Absolutists seized the town of Seo d'Urgel, and there set up a provisional government. Civil war spread over the northern provinces.

The Ministry, which was now formed of Riego's friends, demanded and obtained from the Cortes dictatorial powers like those which the French Committee of Public Safety had wielded in 1793, but with far other result. Spain found no Danton, no Carnot, at this crisis, when the very highest powers of intellect and will would have been necessary to arouse and to arm a people far less disposed to fight for liberty than the French were in 1793. One man alone, General Mina, checked and overthrew the rebel leaders of the North with an activity superior to their own. The Government, boastful and violent in its measures, effected scarcely anything in the organization of a national force or in preparing the means of resistance against those foreign armies with whose attack the country was now plainly threatened.

The ambassadors of the three Eastern courts presented their notes at Madrid demanding a change in the constitution; and, after receiving a high-spirited answer from the Ministers, they quitted the country. Canning, while using every diplomatic effort to prevent an unjust war, had made it clear to the Spaniards that England could not render them armed assistance. The reasons against such an intervention were indeed overwhelming. Russia, Austria, and Prussia would have taken the field rather than have permitted the Spanish Constitution to triumph; and although, if leagued with Spain in a really national defence like that of 1808, Great Britain might perhaps have protected the Peninsula against all the powers of Europe combined, it was far otherwise when the cause at stake was one to which a majority of the Spanish nation had shown itself to be indifferent, and against which the northern provinces had actually taken up arms. The Government and the Cortes were therefore left to defend themselves as best they could against their enemies. They displayed their weakness by enacting laws of extreme severity against deserters, and by retiring, along with the recalcitrant King, from Madrid to Seville.

On April 7th the French troops, led by the Duke of Angoulême, crossed the frontier. The clergy and a great part of the peasantry welcomed them as deliverers; the forces opposed to them fell back without striking a blow. As the invader advanced toward the capital, gangs of Royalists spread such terror and devastation over the northern provinces that the presence of foreign troops became the only safeguard for the peaceable inhabitants. Madrid itself was threatened by the corps of a freebooter named Bessières. The commandant sent his surrender to the French while they were still at some distance, begging them to advance as quickly as possible in order to save the city from pillage. The message had scarcely been sent when Bessières and his bandits appeared in the suburbs. The Governor drove them back, and kept the Royalist mob within the city at bay for four days more. On May 23d the advance-guard of the French army entered the capital.

It had been the desire of King Louis XVIII and Angoulême to save Spain from the violence of Royalist misrule and fanaticism. On reaching Madrid, Angoulême intended to appoint a provisional government himself; he was, however, compelled by orders from Paris to leave the election in the hands of the Council of Castile, and a Regency came into power whose first acts showed in what spirit the victory of the French was to be used. Edicts were issued declaring all the acts of the Cortes affecting the monastic orders to be null and void, dismissing all officials appointed since March 7, 1820, and subjecting to examination those who, then being in office, had not resigned their posts.[1] The arrival of the ambassadors of the three Eastern powers encouraged the Regency in their antagonism to the French commander. It was believed that the Cabinet of Paris was unwilling to restore King Ferdinand as an absolute monarch, and intended to obtain from him the grant of institutions resembling those of the French "charta."

Any such limitation of absolute power was, however, an object of horror to the three despotic courts. Their ambassadors

[1] This process, which was afterward extended even to common soldiers, was called "*Purificacion*." Committees were appointed to whom all persons coming under the law had to send in detailed evidence of correct conduct in and since 1820, signed by well-known Royalists. But the committees also accepted any letters of denunciation that might be sent to them, and were bound by law to keep them secret, so that in practice the purificacion became a vast system of anonymous persecution.

formed themselves into a council with the express object of resisting the supposed policy of Angoulême. The Regency grew
bolder, and gave the signal for general retribution upon the Liberals by publishing an order depriving all persons who had served
in the voluntary militia since March, 1820, of their offices, pensions, and titles. The work inaugurated in the capital was carried much further in the provinces. The friends of the constitution, and even soldiers who were protected by their capitulation
with the French, were thrown into prison by the new local authorities. The violence of the reaction reached such a height that
Angoulême, now on the march to Cadiz, was compelled to publish an ordinance forbidding arrests to be made without the
consent of a French commanding officer, and ordering his generals to release the persons who had been arbitrarily imprisoned. The council of ambassadors, blind in their jealousy of
France to the danger of an uncontrolled restoration, drew up a
protest against his ordinance, and desired that the officers of the
Regency should be left to work their will.

After spending some weeks in idle debates at Seville, the
Cortes had been compelled by the appearance of the French on
the Sierra Morena to retire to Cadiz. As King Ferdinand refused
to accompany them, he was declared temporarily insane, and
forced to make the journey (June 12th). Angoulême, following
the French vanguard after a considerable interval, appeared before Cadiz in August, and sent a note to King Ferdinand, recommending him to publish an amnesty and to promise the restoration of the medieval Cortes. It was hoped that the terms
suggested in this note might be accepted by the Government in
Cadiz as a basis of peace, and so render an attack upon the city
unnecessary. The Ministry, however, returned a defiant answer in the King's name. The siege of Cadiz accordingly began in earnest. On August 30th the fort of the Trocadero was
stormed; three weeks later the city was bombarded. In reply to
all proposals for negotiation Angoulême stated that he could
only treat when King Ferdinand was within his own lines. There
was not the least hope of prolonging the defence of Cadiz with
success, for the combat was dying out even in those few districts of Spain where the constitutional troops had fought with
energy. Ferdinand himself pretended that he bore no grudge

Storming of the Trocadero at Cadiz, by the French forces under the Duke of Angoulême.

Painting by N. Megia.

Storming of the Trocadero at
Cadiz, by the French forces
under the Duke of
Angoulême.
Painting by N. Megin.

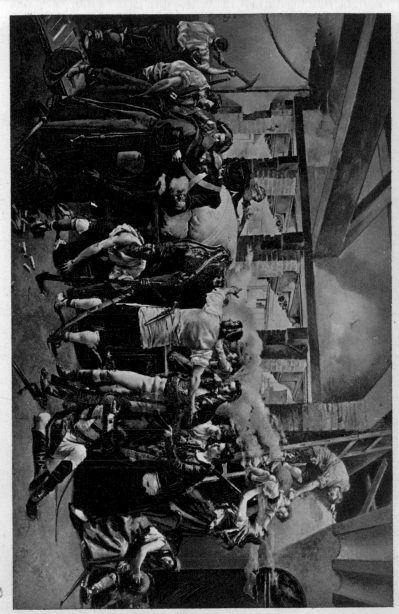

against his ministers, and that the Liberals had nothing to fear from his release. On September 30th he signed, as it with great satisfaction, an absolute and universal amnesty. On the following day he was conveyed with his family across the bay to Angoulême's headquarters.

The war was over: the real results of the French invasion now came into sight. Ferdinand had not been twelve hours in the French camp when, surrounded by Royalist desperadoes, he published a proclamation invalidating every act of the constitutional Government of the last three years, on the ground that his sanction had been given under constraint. The same proclamation ratified the acts of the Regency of Madrid. As the Regency of Madrid had declared all persons concerned in the removal of the King to Cadiz to be liable to the penalties of high treason, Ferdinand had in fact ratified a sentence of death against several of the men from whom he had just parted in friendship. Many of these victims of the King's perfidy were sent into safety by the French. But Angoulême was powerless to influence Ferdinand's policy and conduct. Don Saez, the King's confessor, was made First Secretary of State. On October 4th an edict was issued banishing forever from Madrid, and from the country fifty miles round it, every person who during the last three years had sat in the Cortes, or who had been a minister, counsellor of state, judge, commander, official in any public office, magistrate, or officer in the so-called voluntary militia.

Thus the war of revenge was openly declared against the defeated party. It was in vain that Angoulême indignantly reproached the King, and that the ambassadors of the three Eastern courts pressed him to draw up at least some kind of amnesty. Ferdinand travelled slowly toward Madrid, saying that he could take no such step until he reached the capital. On November 7th Riego was hanged. Thousands of persons were thrown into prison or compelled to fly from the country. Except where order was preserved by the French, life and property were at the mercy of Royalist mobs; and although the influence of the Russian statesman Pozzo di Borgo at length brought a respectable ministry into office, this only roused the fury of the clerical party, and led to a cry for the deposition of the King, and for the elevation of his more fanatical brother, Don Carlos, to the throne. Military commissions were instituted at the beginning of 1824 for the trial of accused persons, and a pretended amnesty, published six months later, included in its fifteen classes of exception the participators in almost every act of the revolution.

Ordinance followed upon ordinance, multiplying the acts punishable with death, and exterminating the literature which was believed to be the source of all religious and social heterodoxy. Every movement of life was watched by the police; every expression of political opinion was made high treason. Young men were shot for being freemasons; women were sent to prison for ten years for possessing a portrait of Riego. The relation of the restored Government to its subjects was in fact that which belonged to a state of civil war. Insurrections arose among the fanatics who were now taking the name of the Carlist or Apostolic party, as well as among a despairing remnant of the Constitutionalists. After a feeble outbreak of the latter at Tarifa, a hundred twelve persons were put to death by the military commissions within eighteen days. It was not until the summer of 1825 that the jurisdiction of these tribunals and Spain's "reign of terror" ended.

FLORIDA ACQUIRED BY THE UNITED STATES

A.D. 1821

RICHARD HILDRETH

Through the acquisition of Florida the United States territory was increased by about sixty-seven thousand square miles, and irritations of long standing, involving ill-feeling against Spain, were relieved. The Florida country, originally embracing a vastly larger area than that of the present State, was ceded by Spain, its discoverer, to Great Britain in 1763. In 1779–1781, while England was engaged in her disastrous American war, Spain reconquered the western part of Florida, and at the close of the Revolution the whole region known as " the Two Floridas " (Eastern and Western) was ceded by Great Britain to the Spanish Government.

The northern boundaries were not defined, and disputes quickly arose between the United States and Spain as to their respective limits. At last (1813) the United States took possession of Western Florida, and a few years later, in Monroe's administration, the First Seminole War broke out in the eastern part of the country. This led to events that culminated in the final acquisition of Florida by the United States.

GREAT complaints were made by the Georgia backwoodsmen of depredations by the Seminoles residing south of the Flint River, and principally within the Spanish territory. Gaines, who commanded at Fort Scott, on the north bank of the Flint, demanded of the Indians, on the opposite bank, the surrender of certain alleged murderers, but they refused to give them up, on the ground that the Georgians had been the first aggressors. Under authority from the War Department to expel these Indians from the lately ceded Creek district north of the Florida line, the Indian village of Fowltown, a few miles below Fort Scott, was attacked in the night, and three or four of the inhabitants killed or taken, the rest escaping into the woods. A second attempt, to bring off the Indian corn and cattle, brought on a fresh skirmish, in which two or three were killed on both sides.

The Indians revenged these attacks by waylaying a boat ascending the Apalachicola with supplies for Fort Scott. Of forty men and a number of women and children on board, all were killed except six men and one woman. Gaines thereupon called out a body of Georgia militia, having received, meanwhile, orders to carry the war into Florida if necessary; with directions, however, if the Indians took refuge under any Spanish fort, not to attack it, but to report the fact. When news arrived at Washington of the disaster on the Apalachicola, orders were sent to Jackson, who commanded in the Southern Department, to take the field in person, with authority to call additional militia from Tennessee.

Jackson on receiving these orders had issued a call for two thousand Tennessee volunteers. While they were preparing to march, he had hastened to Hartford, on the Ocmulgee, there to organize a body of Georgia militia, making, with those from Tennessee, and about a thousand regulars at Fort Scott, a force as numerous, perhaps, as the entire nation of the Seminoles, women and children included. Nor was this the whole of the force employed. The Creeks had just gratified the Georgians by the cession of two considerable additional tracts of territory, one on the Upper Ocmulgee, the other south of the Altamaha— for which the United States had undertaken to pay them twenty thousand dollars down, and an annuity of ten thousand dollars for ten years—and they hastened, also, on the call of Gaines, which, however, he had no authority to make, to take the field under their chief, M'Intosh.

There was great difficulty, in that wild and not very fertile region, in finding the means to feed an army. Jackson was obliged to march with his Georgians from Hartford with nothing to eat but lean cattle, and corn at the rate of a pint a day for each man, and that only obtained by his indefatigable personal exertions. He was joined on his march by a part of the Creeks, and at Fort Scott he found the regulars. The difficulty of subsistence had delayed the arrival of the Tennesseeans. Fort Scott being bare of supplies, Jackson hastened forward to meet the provision-boats expected up the Apalachicola from New Orleans; and, as a depot for those supplies, on the site of the late negro fort he built a new one, called Fort Gadsden. The expected provisions having at length arrived, Jackson marched eastward against the Seminole villages in the vicinity of the present town of Tallahassee, being joined on the way by a fresh body of Creeks and by a part of the Tennessee volunteers. The Indians made but a slight resistance; their villages were burned, and a considerable spoil was obtained in corn and cattle.

It is evident, from Jackson's despatches, that he had resolved from the first to find some pretence for taking possession of the fort at St. Mark's, the only Spanish post in this part of Florida. Under the allegation of some comfort or aid afforded to the Indians, he marched thither and demanded a surrender. The Spanish commandant hesitating a little, a detachment sent by Jackson entered the fort and took it by force, though without bloodshed.

One of the American armed vessels on the coast, having hoisted the British flag, enticed on board two refugee Red Stick Creek chiefs, one of whom, the prophet Francis, had lately visited England and had excited some sympathy there. Both these chiefs, by Jackson's orders, were forthwith hanged without ceremony. He next marched, with very small supplies, and through a country half covered with water, against another town on the Suwanee, not far from its mouth, inhabited principally by runaway negroes; but, having received timely warning, they had conveyed away their women and cattle, and after two considerable skirmishes, the only resistance which Jackson encountered, they abandoned the town, which was burned.

Notice of this intended attack had been sent to Suwanee by Arbuthnot, a Scotchman, last from the Bahamas, employed in trade with the Seminoles, whom Jackson had found at the fort at St. Mark's. Ambrister, a native of New Providence, who had served in Florida during the late war, and who had lately returned thither, apparently on some trading enterprises, in which he was connected with Arbuthnot, had headed the Indians and negroes in the defence of Suwanee and had been taken prisoner there. There seems to have been much rivalry for the Seminole trade between Arbuthnot and one Hambley, also a British subject, but who had espoused the American interest. On Jackson's return to St. Mark's—since neither the exhausted state of his men nor the failure of provisions would allow him to march against the more southern Indian towns—he put Arbuthnot and Ambrister on trial for their lives before a court-martial, of which Gaines was president. The court acquitted Arbuthnot of the charge of being a spy. Of the charge of stirring up the Indians to arrest the person and to seize the property of Hambley, they declined to take cognizance, as not within the range of a military court. Of the two charges of exciting and stirring up the Indians to war with the United States, and of furnishing the means of carrying it on, they found him guilty and sentenced him to death.

The proof consisted, first, in a letter of Arbuthnot's to one of the chiefs of the Lower Creeks, in which he insisted that, by the Treaty of Ghent, the Creeks were entitled to all the territories in their possession previous to the war; and, secondly, of copies of certain other letters found among Arbuthnot's papers, addressed to Bagot, the British ambassador at Washington, and to the Governor of New Providence, endeavoring to obtain some British aid and protection for these late British allies. To this was added the testimony of a discarded clerk of his, that Arbuthnot had supplied the Indians with powder. Ambrister was also found guilty of aiding, abetting, and comforting the enemy, supplying them with the means of war, and aiding them in it, and by two-thirds of the court was also sentenced to death; but, on reconsideration, the sentence was changed to fifty stripes on the bare back, and confinement at hard labor, with a ball and chain, for twelve months.

This last sentence was disapproved by Jackson, who reinstated the first one, and ordered the execution of both the unfortunate traders, on the extraordinary pretence that it was "an established principle of the law of nations, that an individual making war against the citizens of any other nation, the two nations being at peace, forfeits his allegiance, and becomes an outlaw and a pirate"—a principle which would have justified the British in hanging Lafayette and Kosciuszko, had they been taken prisoners in the war of the Revolution.

Jackson, meanwhile, on some rumor or pretended rumor, of encouragement from Pensacola to Indian inroads into Alabama, had marched for that place. He received, on the way, a protest from the Spanish Governor against the invasion of Florida, and a declaration of his intention to resist it; but this was construed by Jackson into an additional reason for seizing Pensacola, which he entered the next day, with only a show of opposition. The Governor fled to the fort at the Barancas, but, Jackson having erected batteries and begun a cannonade, he judged it best to capitulate.

Upon the arrival at Washington of the news of these proceedings, the Spanish minister protested against this violation of the Spanish territory pending a negotiation. In a cabinet council, Calhoun, Secretary of War, proposed bringing General Jackson to a trial; but this proposition met with no favor. John Quincy Adams, Secretary of State, replied to the Spanish minister by setting up the unfulfilled treaty obligation of Spain to restrain the Indians within her limits. The seizure of St. Mark's and Pensacola, though an act of the General's without orders, yet, considering the aid and encouragement afforded by these posts to the hostile Indians, was abundantly justified on the principle of self-defence. But as the war with the Seminoles was now ended, it was offered to restore Pensacola at once, and St. Mark's whenever Spain had a force ready to be stationed there competent to control the neighboring Indians.

A tardy ratification having arrived of the convention of indemnities of 1802, with additional instructions to Don Onis, the negotiation for the discharge of the American claims by the cession of Florida was presently renewed. Onis insisted upon a preliminary apology and indemnity for the seizure of St. Mark's and Pensacola; upon a confirmation of all the Spanish Floridian grants; and that the limits west of the Mississippi, between the United States and Spain, should be a due north line beginning on the Gulf east of the Sabine, between the Mermentau and Calcasiu, crossing the Red River at Natchitoches, and extending to the Missouri, that river thence to its source to be the boundary. Adams offered, as his ultimatum, to accept as a boundary the Sabine as far as 32° north latitude, a line thence due north to the Red River, that river to its source, the crest of the Rocky Mountains to 41° north latitude, and a line thence due west to the Pacific.

Onis offered to agree to the Sabine and a line due north to the Missouri, and the course of that river to its head. The

American claim to extend to the Pacific he pronounced a novelty, now heard of for the first time, and as to which he had no instructions. Adams rejoined by withdrawing his late offer as to boundary, proposing to let that question lie over for the present, and to settle the other points first. He took occasion, at the same time, to go into a long and very warm vindication of all Jackson's proceedings in Florida, which he defended on the ground taken by Jackson himself, that the war with the Seminoles had originated entirely in the instigations of Arbuthnot and Ambrister, who were described as only "pretended traders," and by implication as British emissaries, whom the Spanish commander was accused of having encouraged and abetted; a view of the case still more elaborately and zealously maintained in a despatch of the same date to Erving, the American minister in Spain.

Jackson's vigorous actions would seem not to have been without effect. Pending the discussion in Congress on his conduct, the Spanish minister, under new instructions from home, signed a treaty for the cession of Florida, in extinction of the various American claims, for the satisfaction of which the United States agreed to pay to the claimants five millions of dollars. The Louisiana boundary, as fixed by this treaty, was a compromise between the respective offers heretofore made, though leaning a good deal to the American side: the Sabine to 32° north latitude; thence a north meridian line to the Red River; the course of that river to 100° longitude east from Greenwich; thence north by that meridian to the Arkansas; up that river to its head and to 42° of north latitude, and along that degree to the Pacific. This treaty was immediately ratified by the Senate; and, in expectation of a like ratification by Spain, an act was passed to authorize the President to take possession of the ceded territory.

It was supposed that the British Government might make some stir about the execution of Arbuthnot and Ambrister. The subject was, indeed, mooted in Parliament; but the Ministers took the ground that British subjects mixing themselves up in the quarrels of other nations must abide the consequences, without expecting any interference of the British Government in their behalf.

The President's message of 1819 dwelt at length on the non-ratification of the Florida Treaty. The immediate cause appears to have been an announcement by Forsyth, who was sent as minister to Spain, and adopted a tone not flattering to Spanish pride, of an intention not to recognize certain large land grants, within the letter of the treaty, but not supposed by the President to be so when the treaty was signed. The Spanish court also complained of hostile expeditions in aid of her revolted colonies, set on foot within the United States, and especially of the attempts of certain adventurers to set up a republic of Texas. It was, perhaps, by way of menace, that the President intimated in his message a disposition to recognize the independence of the revolted South American colonies, so soon, at least, as the concurrence of Great Britain could be obtained. A new Spanish minister, who arrived shortly afterward, demanded, as preliminary to the ratification of the Florida Treaty, a stipulation not to make any such recognition. This the President indignantly refused; but on the arrival of news, pending the session of the overturn of Ferdinand's despotic power, and of the reëstablishment of the Cortes, the President recommended to Congress to give to this new Government an opportunity to act, before adopting any decisive measures. It was not until 1821 that the Spanish ratification of the treaty arrived and the cession of the territory was formally completed.

At length, on July 17, 1821, all the numberless preliminaries having been settled, the long-expected ceremony took place, and Florida became a Territory of the United States.

The great event was described, the day after, by an officer who took part in the proceedings: "Yesterday, after a series of delays and disappointments, of a piece with the whole tenor of our twenty years' negotiations with Spain, the American authorities were finally and formally put in possession of this city, of the fortress of the Barancas, and of the dominion of the Floridas. Out of tenderness to the feelings of the Spaniards, deeply excited by the painful separation about to take place between those who go and those who remain—and who are allied not only by ties of intimacy and friendship contracted during a long period of a common residence in this pleasant and salubrious region, and confirmed by a community of habits and religion, as well as of lineage and language, but knitted together by the most sacred and endearing bands of consanguinity and affiance, the ceremony was conducted with very little ostentation.

"The Spanish Governor's guard, consisting of a full company of dismounted dragoons of the regiment of Tarragona, elegantly clad and equipped, was paraded at an early hour of the morning in front of the Government House. About eight o'clock a battalion of the Fourth Regiment of United States infantry and a company of the Fourth Regiment of United States artillery, the whole under the command of Colonel Brooke, of the Fourth infantry, were drawn up on the public square, opposite to the Spanish guard, having marched into town from the encampment at Galvez's Spring. The usual military salute passed between them. Four companies of infantry from the American line, under the command of Major Dinkins, of the Fifth infantry, were then detached to take possession of the Barancas, which is nearly nine miles below this city.

"At ten o'clock, the hour previously appointed, General Jackson, attended by his aids, secretary, interpreters, etc., crossed the green, passed between the double line formed by the troops of both nations, who simultaneously saluted him by presenting arms, and entered the Government House, where the formality of the transfer was soon despatched, and the Spanish sergeant's guard at the gate was immediately relieved by an American guard. After a few minutes, Governor Jackson, accompanied by Colonel Callava, the late commandant, and their respective suites, left the Government House, and passed through the same double line of troops to the house which the American Governor has rented for the temporary accommodation of his family.

"The Spanish troops were then marched to the place of embarkation—the American flag was displayed upon the flagstaff, and grand salutes were fired by the artillery company and the United States ship Hornet, a gun being given to each State and Territory of the Federal Union, not forgetting Florida, and the regimental band, and that of the Hornet, playing the *Star Spangled Banner* all the while."

THE GREEK WAR FOR INDEPENDENCE

BYRON'S SERVICES TO GREECE

A.D. 1821

LEWIS SERGEANT   **JOHN NICHOL**

Europe, in the first quarter of the nineteenth century, saw several significant revolutions. Of these, the Greek movement (1821-1829), which resulted in the overthrow of Turkish rule, was the most important. Notwithstanding much gross mismanagement and many ignoble failures, in its more heroic aspects it marked a glorious period in the history of modern Greece, recalling memories of her ancient renown, and arousing the sympathy and admiration of lovers of freedom in every land. It was largely through the aid of these that her cause was ultimately won.

In 1820 occurred a revolution in Spain, which might have been permanently successful but for the intervention of France. This was soon followed by risings in Naples, Sicily, and Piedmont, and all Europe was stirred by these outbreaks. The Greeks, who had long suffered under Turkish oppression, from which they had vainly attempted to free themselves fifty years before, were now encouraged to begin anew the struggle for independence.

This war of liberty appealed to the adventurous spirit of Lord Byron, and " opened a new field for the exercise of his indomitable energy." The story of his joining the Greeks and dying in their cause, the eyes of the world upon him, forms a most dramatic conclusion of a striking and sometimes spectacular career. In presenting Byron's personality so prominently in connection with the Greek uprising, Nichol reproduces the figure which, to the general view, long dominated the history and typified the spirit of that movement. The best recent account of the opening events is that which immediately follows.

LEWIS SERGEANT

" IN the month of April, 1821," says Finlay, "a Mussulman population, generally of the Greek race, amounting to upward of twenty thousand souls, was living dispersed in Greece, employed in agriculture. Before two months had elapsed, the greater part were slain—men, women, and children were murdered on their own hearths, without mercy or remorse. Old men still point to heaps of stones and tell the traveller, ' There stood the *pyrgos* [tower] of Ali Aga, and there we slew him, his harem, and his slaves'; and the old man walks calmly on to plough the fields that once belonged to Ali Aga, without a thought that any vengeful fury can attend his path.   The crime was a nation's crime, and whatever perturbations it may produce must be in a nation's conscience, as the deed by which it can be expiated must be the act of a nation."

The judgment is not unfair, thought it may be questioned whether the whole responsibility for this slaughter, the whole perturbation of conscience, do not properly belong to the nation of the oppressors rather than to the nation of the oppressed. Revolutions, it has been said, are not made with rose-water; they are made, as a rule, with the same machinery as that of the tyrannies that call them forth.   In England people sign a monster petition, which requires two honorable members to carry it up the floor of the House; in France, a poet makes a speech, and the students raise a barricade.   In the Greece of 1821 there was a terrible accumulation of wrongs to be revenged—from the kidnapping of the tribute children to the cruelties of Veli and Khurshid and the extortions of the gypsy-haratcher.   The revenge springs from the injury, the responsibility rests with the oppressor.   We need not justify the extermination of the Turks in Greece, but we may fairly turn to the Ottoman Government for its expiation.

It would be useless to discuss the question where the Greek revolution first broke out.   The general uprising had been appointed for March 25th (April 6th), but many massacres and revolts took place during the preceding days.   The initial chapter in the history of New Greece was written simultaneously throughout the country.   In the mountains of Achaia, especially at Bersova and in the Crathis Valley, at Calavryta, at Patras and Vostitza (Aigion), in the Maina, and other parts of Messene, in short, throughout the peninsula, this vindictive passion burst all bounds.

"No more Turks, either in the Morea or in the whole world." It was sudden energy of instinct, a concentration of the passion of centuries.   Over and over again a militant Christianity has exhibited such a paroxysm of bloodthirsty rage, matching the murderous fury of the followers of the Prophet.

The Greek war, as was inevitable, was a war of *guerrilleros* ꜰꜰꜰꜰ Ｃꜰꜰꜰꜰꜰꜰꜰ, ꜰꜰꜰ ꜰꜰꜰꜰꜰ ꜰꜰꜰ ꜰꜰꜰꜰꜰꜰ ꜰꜰꜰ ꜰꜰ ꜰꜰꜰꜰꜰꜰꜰ ꜰꜰꜰ ꜰꜰ ꜰꜰꜰꜰꜰ military leader at their service, and those who began by shunning the Hetairists were in no better position.   One of the most promi- nent chiefs was Theodore Colokotronis, who, up to the time of the outbreak, had resided in one of the Ionian Islands, where he had attained the rank of major in the British army.   It was told of his father, who died at Castanitza in 1870, that he had killed with his own hands seven hundred Turks.   Major Colokotronis had done his best to persuade the British authorities that the cause of his countrymen deserved their active support; but, fail- ing in his endeavor, he had no hesitation about throwing in his lot with the Hetairists.   He had been in constant communication with both Capo d'Istria and Hupsilantes, and, when the latter embarked on his ill-fated expedition in the Danubian provinces, Major Colokotronis set out for the Maina, in company with an- other notable Hetairist, Anagnostaras, formerly a klephtic hero in the band of Zacharias.   Petros Mavromichaelis, bey of the Mainotes—the bold and independent inhabitants of the central promontory of the Morea—was generally expected to take the lead of his countrymen in their struggle for freedom.   Another prominent patriot at the outset of the insurrection was Germanos, Archbishop of Patras, who had been initiated in the Philike Hetairia, and who has left a narrative of many of the events which came under his observation.   The initial act of the revolu- tion is held to have been the raising of the cross by Archbishop Germanos at the monastery of Laura, whither he had fled on be- ing summoned to Tripolitza, March 25th (April 6th).   This day is still celebrated by the Greeks as the anniversary of their restora- tion to independence.

Greece had to wage with Europe a struggle more difficult and more protracted than its struggle with the Turks.   It had to per- suade the great powers—the great powers of the days of Laybach and Verona, of Metternich and Castlereagh—that it deserved its independence.   Not only so, but it had to overcome the indiffer- ence, the selfishness, in some instances the direct hostility, of these powers, and to enlist them actively on its side.   It was not enough to gain the ear of Britain, the favor of Russia, the consent of France.   Turkey must be smitten by Europe, as well as by her

Greek subjects, before she would be willing to resign herself to the loss of the peninsula. Who could be sanguine, in 1821, that all this would ever be accomplished? With Naples and Spain dragooned into submission, with the Wallachian patriots frowned down by Russia and snubbed by their own patriarch, who could have foreseen Navarino? The Greek outbreak was, in its first stages, a war of despair, and its most enthusiastic champions could scarcely tell how the sacrifice of their lives was likely to avail their cause. Men of discernment perceived that the freedom of Greece, though it depended in the first instance upon Greek patriotism, could never be definitely established without European aid; and it was for this aid that the best friends of Greece abroad were continually working and waiting.

Meanwhile the rising of the Greeks had already produced important results. Within three months a large part of the Peloponnese was liberated; the islands of Hydra, Spetzai, and Psara had proclaimed their union with the mainland; all the Cyclades and many of the Sporades were following suit; in Eubœa, in Crete, in Samos, in parts of Macedonia, the example of the Morea was bearing fruit. A large fleet of small vessels was at once devoted to the purposes of what was looked upon as a holy war, and the Greek sailors took a noble part in the struggle. Tricoupi gives an interesting account of the tactics pursued by the combined fleet of the Hydriotes, Spetziotes, and Psarians. It was under the command of Jakomiki Tombazis, who, having fallen in with a Turkish man-of-war (the Moving Mountain, 74 guns) off the north of Chios, pursued it to the roads of Erissos, and fired upon it without effect. He then determined to have recourse to a device which his countrymen had formerly found serviceable—the use of fire-ships. The plan was to take an old hulk, and fix upon its fore-deck and along one side three or four large cases of pitch and other combustible materials. A train of gunpowder connected these cases, and in addition the sails and rigging of the ship were soaked with turpentine. When the time came for action, the prepared vessel was driven upon the enemy, and fixed to her side by means of grappling-irons. The hardy crew would then fire the train, and escape by the port-holes into a small boat, taking their chance of surviving. In the case mentioned, one Pargios, of Psara, had the honor of making the first fire-ship in their war of independence; but his effort was unsuccessful. On the following day (June 18th) he constructed two more, one of which burned itself out without injuring the Turk, while the other set her on fire and utterly destroyed her, very few of her crew contriving to escape.

The remainder of the year 1821 brought both good and bad fortunes to the Greeks. A Turkish fleet under Cara Ali penetrated to the bottom of the Gulf of Corinth, and laid Galaxidhi in ashes; while the patriots, on their part, under Colokotronis, Anagnostaras, Giatracos, and Petrobey, captured Tripolitza after a long siege, and butchered the inhabitants with almost incredible ferocity. But perhaps the most significant events of the first year of the revolution were the assembling of the Greek notables at the Convent of Valtetzi, on June 7th, and the declaration of independence on the 27th of the following January.

JOHN NICHOL

This romantic struggle, begun in April, 1821, was carried on for two years with such remarkable success that at the close of 1822 Greece was beginning to be recognized as an independent state: but in the following months the tide seemed to turn; dissensions broke out among the leaders, the spirit of intrigue seemed to stifle patriotism, and the energies of the insurgents were hampered for want of the sinews of war. There was a danger of the movement being starved out, and the committee of London sympathizers—of which Byron's intimate friend and frequent correspondent, Douglas Kinnaird, and Captain Blaquière, were leading promoters—was impressed with the necessity of procuring funds in support of the cause. With a view to this it seemed of consequence to attach to it some shining name, and men's thoughts almost inevitably turned to Byron. No other Englishman seemed so fit to be associated with the enterprise as the warlike poet, who twelve years before had linked his fame to that of "gray Marathon" and "Athena's tower," and, more recently, immortalized the isles on which he cast so many a longing glance.

Hobhouse broke the subject to him early in the spring of 1823: the committee opened communications in April. After hesitating through May, in June Byron consented to meet Blaquière at

Zante, and, on hearing the results of the Captain's expedition to the Morea, to decide on future steps. His share in this enterprise has been assigned to purely personal and comparatively mean motives. It is said he was disgusted with his periodical, sick of his editor, tired of his mistress, and bent on any change, from China to Peru, that would give him a new theatre for display. One grows weary of the perpetual half-truths of inveterate detraction. It is granted that Byron was restless, vain, imperious, never did anything without a desire to shine in the doing of it, and was to a great degree the slave of circumstances.

Had the *Liberal* proved a lamp to the nations, instead of a mere "red flag flaunted in the face of John Bull," he might have cast anchor at Genoa; but the whole drift of his work and life demonstrates that he was capable on occasion of merging himself in what he conceived to be great causes, especially in their evil days.

Byron, indeed, left Italy in an unsettled state of mind: he spoke of returning in a few months, and, as the period for his departure approached, became more and more irresolute. A presentiment of his death seemed to brood over a mind always superstitious, though never fanatical. Shortly before his own departure, the Blessingtons were preparing to leave Genoa for England. On the evening of his farewell call he began to speak of his voyage with despondency, saying: "Here we are all now together; but when and where shall we meet again? I have a sort of boding that we see each other for the last time, as something tells me I shall never again return from Greece:" after which remark he leaned his head on the sofa, and burst into one of his hysterical fits of tears. The next week was given to preparations for an expedition, which, entered on with mingled motives—sentimental, personal, public—became more real and earnest to Byron at every step he took. He knew all the vices of the "hereditary bondsmen" among whom he was going, and went among them with still unquenched aspirations, but with the bridle of discipline in his hand, resolved to pave the way toward the nation becoming better, by devoting himself to making it free.

On the morning of July 14, 1823, he embarked in the brig Hercules, with Trelawney; Count Pietro Gamba, who remained with him to the last; Bruno, a brilliant young Italian doctor;

Scott, the captain of the vessel, and eight servants, including
Fletcher; besides the crew. They had on board two guns, with
other arms and ammunition, live horses, an ample supply of med-
icines, with fifty thousand Spanish dollars in coin and bills.   The
start was inauspicious.   A violent squall drove them back to port,
and in the course of a last ride with Gamba to Albaro, Byron
asked, "Where shall we be in a year?"   On the same day of the
same month of 1824 he was carried to the tomb of his ancestors.
They again set sail on the following evening, and in five days
reached Leghorn, where the poet received a salutation in verse
addressed to him by Goethe, and replied to it.   Here Hamilton
Brown, a Scotch gentleman with considerable knowledge of
Greek affairs, joined the party, and induced them to change their
course to Cephalonia, for the purpose of obtaining the advice and
assistance of the English resident, Colonel Napier.

This gentleman being absent from Cephalonia, Byron had
some pleasant social intercourse with his deputy, but, unable to
get from him any authoritative information, was left without advice, to be besieged by letters and messages from the factions.
Among these were brought to him hints that the Greeks wanted
a king, and he is reported to have said, "If they make me the
offer, I will perhaps not reject it."

The office would doubtless have been acceptable to a man
who never—amid his many self-deceptions—affected to deny that
he was ambitious; and who can say what might not have resulted
for Greece, had the poet lived to add lustre to her crown?   In the
mean time, while faring more frugally than a day-laborer, he yet
surrounded himself with a show of royal state, had his servants
armed with gilded helmets, and gathered around him a body-
guard of Suliotes.   These wild mercenaries becoming turbulent,
he was obliged to despatch them to Missolonghi, then threatened
with siege by the Turks and anxiously waiting relief.

Critics who have little history and less knowledge of war have
been accustomed to attribute Byron's lingering at Cephalonia to
indolence and indecision; they write as if he ought, on landing on
Greek soil, to have put himself at the head of an army and stormed
Constantinople.   Those who know more, confess that the delay
was deliberate and that it was judicious.   The Hellenic uprising
was animated by the spirit of a "lion after slumber," but it had

the heads of a Hydra hissing and tearing at one another.   The
chiefs who defended the country by their arms compromised her
by their arguments, and some of her best fighters were little better
than pirates and bandits.   Greece was a prey to factions—republican, monarchic, aristocratic—representing naval, military, and
territorial interests, and each beset by the adventurers who flock
round every movement, only representing their own.   During the
first two years of success they were held in embryo; during the
later years of disaster, terminated by the allies at Navarino, they
were buried; during the interlude of Byron's residence, when the
foes were like hounds in the leash, waiting for a renewal of the
struggle, they were rampant.   Had he joined any one of them, he
would have degraded himself to the level of a mere *condottiere*,
and helped to betray the common cause.

Beset by solicitations to go to Athens, to the Morea, to Acarnania, he resolutely held apart, biding his time, collecting information, making himself known as a man of affairs, endeavoring to
conciliate rival claimants for pension or place, and carefully
watching the tide of war.   Numerous anecdotes of the period
relate to acts of public or private benevolence, which endeared
him to the population of the island; but he was on the alert
against being fleeced or robbed.   "The bulk of the English,"
writes Colonel Napier, "came expecting to find the Peloponnesus
filled with Plutarch's men, and returned thinking the inhabitants
of Newgate more moral.   Lord Byron judged the Greeks fairly,
and knew that allowance must be made for emancipated slaves."
Among other incidents we hear of his passing a group, who were
"shrieking and howling as in Ireland" over some men buried in
the fall of a bank; he snatched a spade, began to dig, and threatened to horsewhip the peasants unless they followed his example.

On November 30th he despatched to the Central Government
a remarkable state paper, in which he dwells on the fatal calamity
of a civil war, and says that, unless union and order are established
all hopes of a loan—which, being every day more urgent, he was
in letters to England constantly pressing—are at an end.   "I desire," he concluded, "the wellbeing of Greece, and nothing else.
I will do all I can to secure it; but I will never consent that the
English public be deceived as to the real state of affairs.   You
have fought gloriously; act honorably toward your fellow-citizens

and the world, and it will then no more be said, as has been re-
iterated for two thousand years, with the Roman historians, that
Philopœmen was the last of the Grecians."

Prince Alexander Maurocordatos—the most prominent of the
practical patriotic leaders—having been deposed from the presidency, was sent to regulate the affairs of Western Greece, and was
now on his way with a fleet to relieve Missolonghi, in attempting
which the brave Marco Bozzaris had previously fallen.   In a letter, opening communication with a man for whom he always
entertained a high esteem, Byron writes: "Colonel Stanhope has
arrived from London, charged by our committee to act in concert
with me.   Greece is at present placed between three measures—
either to reconquer her liberty, to become a dependence of the
sovereigns of Europe, or to return to a Turkish province.   She
has the choice only of these three alternatives.   Civil war is but
a road that leads to the two latter."

At length the long-looked-for fleet arrived, and the Turkish
squadron, with the loss of a treasure-ship, retired up the Gulf of
Lepanto.   Maurocordatos, on entering Missolonghi, lost no time
in inviting the poet to join him, and placed a brig at his disposal,
adding: "I need not tell you to what a pitch your presence is desired by everybody, or what a prosperous direction it will give to
all our affairs.   Your councils will be listened to like oracles."

At the same date Stanhope writes, "The people in the streets
are looking forward to his lordship's arrival as they would to the
coming of the Messiah."   Byron was unable to sail in the ship
sent for him; but in spite of medical warnings, a few days later,
December 28th, he embarked in a small fast-sailing sloop called
a *mistico*, while the servants and baggage were stowed in a larger
vessel in charge of Count Gamba.   From Gamba's graphic account of the voyage we take the following:

"We sailed together till after ten at night; the wind favorable,
a clear sky, the air fresh, but not sharp.   Our sailors sang alternately patriotic songs, monotonous indeed, but to persons in our
situation extremely touching, and we took part in them.   We
were all, but Lord Byron particularly, in excellent spirits.   The
mistico sailed the fastest.   When the waves divided us, and our
voices could no longer reach other each, we made signals by firing
pistols and carbines.   To-morrow we meet at Missolonghi—to-

morrow. Thus, full of confidence and spirits, we sailed along.
At twelve we were out of sight of each other."

Byron's vessel, separated from her consort, came into the close
proximity of a Turkish frigate, and had to take refuge among the
Scrofes rocks. Emerging thence, he attained a small seaport of
Acarnania, called Dragomestri, whence sallying forth on January
2, 1824, under the convoy of some Greek gunboats, he was nearly
wrecked. On the 4th Byron made, when violently heated, an
imprudent plunge in the sea, and he never was afterward free
from a pain in his bones. On the 5th he arrived at Missolonghi,
and was received with salvos of musketry and music. Gamba
was waiting him. His vessel, the Bombarda, had been taken by
the Ottoman frigate, but the captain of the latter, recognizing the
Count as having formerly saved his life in the Black Sea, made
interest in his behalf with Yusuf Pacha at Patras, and obtained
his discharge. In recompense, the poet subsequently sent to the
Pacha some Turkish prisoners, with a letter requesting him to
endeavor to mitigate the inhumanities of the war.

Byron brought to the Greeks at Missolonghi the four thousand
pounds of his personal loan—applied in the first place to defraying the expenses of the fleet—with the spell of his name and presence. He was shortly afterward appointed to the command of
the intended expedition against Lepanto, and, with this view,
again took into his pay five hundred Suliotes. An approaching
general assembly to organize the forces of the West had brought
together a motley crew, destitute, discontented, and more likely
to wage war upon one another than on their enemies. Byron's
closest associates during the ensuing months were the engineer
Parry, an energetic artilleryman, "extremely active, and of strong
practical talents," who had travelled in America, and Colonel
Stanhope (afterward Lord Harrington), equally with himself devoted to the emancipation of Greece, but at variance about the
means of achieving it.

Stanhope, a moral enthusiast, beset by the fallacy of religious
missions, wished to cover the Morea with Wesleyan tracts, and
liberate the country by the agency of the press. He had imported
a converted blacksmith, with a cargo of Bibles, type, and paper,
who on twenty pounds a year undertook to accomplish the reform. Byron, backed by the good sense of Maurocordatos, pro-

posed to make cartridges of the tracts, and small shot of the type; he did not think that the turbulent tribes were ripe for freedom of the press, and had begun to regard republicanism itself as a matter of secondary moment.   The disputant allies in the common cause occupied each a flat of the same small house; the soldier by profession was bent on writing the Turks down, the poet on fighting them down, holding that "the work of the sword must precede that of the pen, and that camps must be the training-schools of freedom."   Their altercations were sometimes fierce. "Despot!" cried Stanhope, "after professing liberal principles from boyhood, you, when called to act, prove yourself a Turk." "Radical!" retorted Bryon, "if I had held up my finger I could have crushed your press"—but this did not prevent the recognition by each of them of the excellent qualities of the other.

Ultimately Stanhope went to Athens, and allied himself with Trelawney and Odysseus and the party of the Left.   Nothing can be more statesmanlike than some of Byron's papers of this and the immediately preceding period, nothing more admirable than the spirit which inspires them.   He had come into the heart of a revolution, exposed to the same perils as those which had wrecked the similar movement in Italy.   Neither trusting too much nor distrusting too much, with a clear head and a good will he set about enforcing a series of excellent measures.   From first to last he was engaged in denouncing dissension, in advocating unity, in doing everything that man could do to concentrate and utilize the disorderly elements with which he had to work.   He occupied himself in repairing fortifications, managing ships, restraining license, promoting courtesy between the foes, and regulating the disposal of the sinews of war.

On the morning of January 22d, his last birthday, he came from his room to Stanhope's, and said, smiling, "You were complaining that I never write any poetry now," and read the familiar stanzas beginning

> " 'Tis time this heart should be unmoved,"

and ending

> " Seek out—less often sought than found—
> A soldier's grave, for thee the best;
> Then look around, and choose thy ground,
> And take thy rest."

High thoughts, high resolves; but the brain that was overtasked, and the frame that was outworn, would be tasked and worn little longer. The lamp of a life that had burned too fiercely was flickering to its close. "If we are not taken off with the sword," he writes on February 5th, "we are like to march off with an ague in this mud-basket; and, to conclude with a very bad pun, better 'martially' than 'marsh-ally.' The dikes of Holland when broken down are the deserts of Arabia in comparison with Missolonghi." In April, when it was too late, Stanhope wrote from Salona, in Phocis, imploring him not to sacrifice health and perhaps life "in that bog."

Byron's house stood in the midst of the exhalations of a muddy creek, and his natural irritability was increased by a more than usually long ascetic regimen. In spite of his strength of purpose, his temper was not always proof against the rapacity and turbulence by which he was surrounded. About the middle of February, when the artillery had been got into readiness for the attack on Lepanto—the northern (as Patras was the southern) gate of the gulf, still in the hands of the Turks—the expedition was thrown back by an unexpected rising of the Suliotes.

These peculiarly forward Greeks, chronically seditious by nature, were on this occasion, as afterward appeared, stirred up by emissaries of Colocotronis, who, though assuming the position of the rival of Maurocordatos, was simply a brigand on a large scale in the Morea. Exasperation at this mutiny, and the vexation of having to abandon a cherished scheme, seem to have been the immediately provoking causes of a violent convulsive fit which, on the evening of the 15th, attacked the poet and endangered his life. Next day he was better, but complained of weight in the head, and, the doctors applying leeches too close to the temporal artery, he was bled till he fainted.

And now occurred the last of those striking incidents so frequent in his life, in reference to which we may quote the joint testimony of two witnesses. Colonel Stanhope writes: "Soon after his dreadful paroxysm, when he was lying on his sick-bed, with his whole nervous system completely shaken, the mutinous Suliotes, covered with dirt and splendid attires, broke into his apartments, brandishing their costly arms and loudly demanding their rights. Lord Byron, electrified by this unexpected act, seemed to recover from his sickness; and the more the Suliotes raged the ~~more his calm courage triumphed. The scene was truly sub~~ lime." "It is impossible," says Count Gamba, "to do justice to the coolness and magnanimity which he displayed upon every trying occasion. Upon trifling occasions he was certainly irritable; but the aspect of danger calmed him in an instant, and restored him the free exercise of all the powers of his noble nature. A more undaunted man in the hour of peril never breathed." A few days later, the riot being renewed, the disorderly crew were, on payment of their arrears, finally dismissed; but several of the English artificers under Parry left about the same time, in fear of their lives.

On the 4th, the last of the long list of Byron's letters to Moore resents, with some bitterness, the hasty acceptance of a rumor that he had been quietly writing *Don Juan* in some Ionian Island. At the same date he writes to Kennedy, "I am not unaware of the precarious state of my health. But it is proper I should remain in Greece, and it were better to die doing something than nothing."

Visions of enlisting Europe and America in behalf of the establishment of a new state, that might in course of time develop itself over the realm of Alexander, floated and gleamed in his fancy; but in his practical daily procedure the poet took as his text the motto *festina lente*, insisted on solid ground under his feet, and had no notion of sailing balloons over the sea. With this view he discouraged Stanhope's philanthropic and propagandist paper, the *Telegrapho*, and disparaged Doctor Mayer, its Swiss editor, saying, "Of all petty tyrants he is one of the pettiest, as are most demagogues."

Byron had none of the Slavonic leanings, and almost personal hatred of Ottoman rule, of some of our statesmen; but he saw on what side lay the forces and the hopes of the future. "I cannot calculate," he said to Gamba, during one of their latest rides together, "to what a height Greece may rise. Hitherto it has been a subject for the hymns and elegies of fanatics and enthusiasts; but now it will draw the attention of the politician. At present there is little difference, in many respects, between Greeks and Turks, nor could there be; but the latter must, in the common course of events, decline in power; and the former must as inevitably become better.   The English Government deceived itself at first in thinking it possible to maintain the Turkish empire in its integrity; but it cannot be done—that unwieldy mass is already putrefied, and must dissolve. If anything like an equilibrium is to be upheld, Greece must be supported."   These words have been well characterized as prophetic.   During this time Byron rallied in health and displayed much of his old spirit, vivacity, and humor, took part in such of his favorite amusements as circumstances admitted, fencing, shooting, riding, and playing with his pet dog, Lion.   The last of his recorded practical jokes is his rolling about cannon-balls and shaking the rafters, to frighten Parry in the room below with the dread of an earthquake.

On the 30th he was presented with the freedom of the city of Missolonghi.   On April 3d he intervened to prevent an Italian private, guilty of theft, from being flogged by order of some German officers.   On the 9th he took a long ride with Gamba and a few of the remaining Suliotes, and after being violently heated, and then drenched in a heavy shower, persisted in returning home in a boat, remarking with a laugh, in answer to a remonstrance, "I should make a pretty soldier if I were to care for such a trifle."

It soon became apparent that he had caught his death.   Almost immediately on his return he was seized with shiverings and violent pain.   The next day he rose as usual, and had his last ride in the olive woods.   On the 11th a rheumatic fever set in.   On the 14th, Bruno's skill being exhausted, it was proposed to call Doctor Thomas from Zante, but a hurricane prevented any ship being sent.   On the 15th another physician, Doctor Milligen, suggested bleeding to allay the fever, but Byron held out against it, quoting Doctor Reid to the effect that "less slaughter is effected by the lance than the lancet—that minute instrument of mighty mischief," and saying to Bruno, "If my hour is come I shall die, whether I lose my blood or keep it."   Next morning Milligen induced him to yield, by a suggestion of the possible loss of his reason.   Throwing out his arm he cried: "There! you are, I see, a d—d set of butchers.   Take away as much blood as you like, and have done with it."   The remedy, repeated on the following day, with blistering, was either too late or ill-advised.

On the 18th he saw more doctors, but was manifestly sinking, amid the tears and lamentations of attendants who could not understand one another's language. In his last hours his delirium bore him to the field of arms. He fancied he was leading the attack on Lepanto, and was heard exclaiming, "Forward! forward! follow me!" Who is not reminded of another death-bed, not remote in time from his, and the "*Tête d'armée*" of the great Emperor who with the great poet divided the wonder of Europe? The stormy vision passed, and his thoughts reverted home. "Go to my sister," he faltered out to Fletcher; "tell her—go to Lady Byron—you will see her, and say"—nothing more could be heard but broken ejaculations: "Augusta—Ada—my sister, my child. *Io lascio qualche cosa di caro nel mondo* ['There are things which make the world dear to me']. For the rest, I am content to die." At six on the evening of the 18th he uttered his last words, "Lord receive my spirit"; and on the 19th he passed away.

Never, perhaps, was there such a national lamentation. By order of Maurocordatos, thirty-seven guns—one for each year of the poet's life—were fired from the battery, and answered by the Turks from Patras with an exultant volley. All offices, tribunals, and shops were shut, and a general mourning for twenty-one days was proclaimed. Stanhope wrote, on hearing the news, "England has lost her brightest genius—Greece her noblest friend"; and Trelawney, on coming to Missolonghi, heard nothing in the streets but "Byron is dead!" like a bell tolling through the silence and the gloom. Intending contributors to the cause of Greece turned back when they heard the tidings, that seemed to them to mean she was headless. Her cities contended for the body, as of old for the birth of a poet. Athens wished him to rest in the Temple of Theseus. The funeral service was performed at Missolonghi. But on May 2d the embalmed remains left Zante and on the 29th arrived in the Downs. His relatives applied for permission to have them interred in Westminster Abbey, but it was refused; and on July 16th they were conveyed to the village church of Hucknall-Torkard.

THE MONROE DOCTRINE

A.D. 1823

ALFRED T. MAHAN[1]

President James Monroe, in his annual message to Congress in December, 1823, made certain statements that afterward became crystallized into a formula of American opinion and purpose, known as the Monroe Doctrine. The original utterance of this principle of policy by Monroe gave to his administration a "lasting mark of distinction," which to-day, perhaps more than at any former period, commands the interest of American statesmen and the attention of the world.

The statement of President Monroe simply expressed the demand of the people of the United States that there should be no intervention of European powers in affairs of the American continents. An earlier announcement of this political principle has been credited to John Quincy Adams, and also to the English statesman George Canning. And recent students of American political history have shown the gradual growth of the doctrine into a national tradition before the time of Monroe, who "merely formulated it, and made it a matter of distinct record."

Among contemporary writers none is better qualified to treat the subject in all its bearings than Captain Mahan, whose works are important contributions to American critical history in many departments.

THE formulation of the Monroe Doctrine, as distinguished from its origin, resulted, as is universally understood, from the political conditions caused by the revolt of the Spanish colonies in America. Up to that time, and for centuries previous, the name Spain had signified to Europe in general not merely the mother-country, but a huge colonial system, with its special economical and commercial regulation; the latter being determined through its colonial relations, upon the narrowest construction of colonial policy then known, which was saying a great deal. Spain stood for the Spanish empire, divisible primarily into two chief components, Spain and Greater Spain—the mother-country and the colonies. The passage of time had been gradually reversing the relative importance of the two in the apprehension of other European states.

[1] From the *National Review*, by permission of Captain Mahan.

In Sir Robert Walpole's day it was believed by many beside himself that Great Britain could not make head against France and Spain combined. The naval power of Spain, and consequently her political weight, still received awed consideration; a relic of former fears. This continued, though in a diminished degree, through the War of American Independence; but by the end of the century, while it may be too much to affirm that such apprehension had wholly disappeared—that no account was taken of the unwieldy numbers of ill-manned and often ill-officered ships that made up the Spanish navy—it is true that a Spanish war bore to British seamen an aspect rather commercial than military. It meant much more of prize-money than of danger; and that it did so was due principally to the wealth of the colonies.

This wealth was potential as well as actual, and in both aspects it appealed to Europe. To break in upon the monopoly enjoyed by Spain, and consecrated in international usage both by accepted ideas and long prescription, was an object of policy to the principal European maritime states. It was so conspicuously to Great Britain, on account of the preëminence which commercial considerations always had in her councils. In the days of William III the prospective failure of the Spanish royal house brought up the questions of what other family should succeed and to whom should be transferred the great inheritance won by Columbus, Cortés, and Pizarro. Thenceforth the thought of dividing this spoil of a decadent empire—the "sick man" of that day—remained in men's memory as a possible contingency of the future, even though momentarily out of the range of practical politics. The waning of Spain's political and military prestige was accompanied by an increasing understanding of the value of the commercial system appended to her in her colonies. The future disposition of these extensive regions, and the fruition of their wealth, developed and undeveloped, were conceived as questions of universal European policy. In the general apprehension of European rulers they were regarded as affecting the balance of power.

It was as the opponent of this conception, the perfectly natural outcome of previous circumstances and history, that the Monroe Doctrine entered the field; a newcomer in form, yet hav-

ing its own history and antecedent conditions as really as the conflicting European view. Far more than South America, which
had seen little contested occupation, the northern continent had
known what it was to be the scene of antagonistic European ambitions and exploitation. There had been within her territory a
balance of power, in idea, if not in achievement, quite as real as
any that had existed or been fought for in Europe. Canada in
the hands of France, and the mouth of the Mississippi in alien
control, were matters of personal memory to many, and of very
recent tradition to all Americans in active life in 1810. Florida
then was still Spanish, with unsettled boundary questions and
attendant evils. Not reason only, but feeling, based upon experience of actual inconvenience, suffering, and loss—loss of life and
loss of wealth, political anxiety and commercial disturbance—
conspired to intensify opposition to any avoidable renewal of
similar conditions. To quote the words of a distinguished American, Secretary of State, speaking twenty years ago: "This
sentiment is properly called a 'doctrine,' for it has no prescribed sanction, and its assertion is left to the exigency which
may invoke it." This accurate statement places it upon the
surest political foundation, much firmer than precise legal enactment or international convention, that of popular conviction.
The sentiment had existed beforehand; the first exigency which
invoked its formulated expression in 1823 was the announced intention of several great powers to perpetuate by force the European System, whether of colonial tenure or balance of power, of
monarchical forms in the Spanish colonies; they being then
actually in revolt against the mother-country and seeking, not
other political relations to Europe, but simply their own independence.

This political question of independence, however, involved
also necessarily that of commercial relations, and both were interesting to outside states. So far as then appeared, renewed
dependence meant the perpetuation of commercial exclusion
against foreign states. This characterized all colonial regulation
at that time, and continued in Spanish practice in Cuba and other
dependencies until the final downfall of her diminished empire in
1898. It must be recognized, therefore, that all outside parties
to the controversy, all parties other than Spain and her colonies,

which had special incitements of their own, were influenced by two classes of motives, political and commercial. These are logically separable, although in practice intertwined. That of the Continental powers—Austria, Prussia, and Russia, with the subsequent accession of France—was primarily political. Their object was to perpetuate in South America political conditions connected with the European System, by breaking down popular revolt against absolutist government, and maintaining the condition of dependence upon Spain. Whither this might lead in case of armed intervention, which was contemplated, was a question probably of the division of spoil; for in the end Spain could hardly pay the bill otherwise than by colonial cessions.

But whether the movement of the Holy Alliance, as it was self-styled, issued merely in the suppression of popular liberties or introduced further a European balance of power with its rivalries and conflicts, its wars and rumors of wars, both results were politically abhorrent to American feelings and disturbing to American peace. They gave rise to distinctly political objections by the people and statesmen of the United States. From these sentiments the exigency evoked the first reasoned official expression of the national conviction and purpose, which we now know as the Monroe Doctrine. Subsidiary to this political motive, but clearly recognized and avowed, was the legitimate inducement of commercial interest, benefited by the rejection of European rule, and to be injured by its restoration.

It will not be expected that a British Tory administration, before the Reform Bill of 1832 and with the protective system and Navigation Act in full force, should have shared the particular political prepossessions of the American States, geographically closely concerned, lately themselves colonies, and but very recently emerged from a prolonged conflict with British commercial regulations based upon the ancient conception of colonial administration. But Great Britain, in addition to commercial ambitions and interests greater then than those of the United States, and the outcome of a century of effort against Spanish monopoly, did have also a distinct political leaning in the matter. There ran through both political parties a real and deep sympathy with communities struggling for freedom. The iniquity of suppressing such efforts by external force of third parties, not immediately concerned, was strongly felt. There was accepted also among British statesmen a clearly defined rule of conduct, which had been conspicuously illustrated in the early days of the French Revolution, still a matter of recent memory in 1820, that interference in the intestine struggles of a foreign country, such as those then afflicting both the Spanish kingdom and colonies, was neither right in principle nor expedient in policy.

Basing its action firmly on these convictions, the British Ministry, under the influence of Canning, intimated clearly that, while neutral toward the intervention of the Holy Alliance in Spain itself, to restore there the old order of things, it would not permit the transport of armies to South America for a like purpose. The course of the Alliance in Spain was viewed with disapproval, but it did not immediately concern Great Britain to an extent demanding armed resistance. The case of the colonies was different. Intervention there would be prejudicial to British mercantile enterprise, already heavily engaged in their trade and economical development; while, politically, the occupation of the Peninsula by French armies would be offset by the detachment of the colonies from their previous dependence.

To the effect of this British attitude the position of the United States Government, defined by President Monroe in his message of December, 1823, constituted a powerful support, and the news of it evoked general satisfaction in England. However motived, without formal concert, still less in alliance, the two English-speaking countries occupied the same ground and announced the same purpose. Spain might conquer her colonies unaided, if she could; neither would interfere; but the attempt of other powers to give her armed assistance would be regarded by each as unfriendly to itself.

From this momentary community of position exaggerated inferences have been drawn as to the identity of impulses which had brought either state to it. It was a case of two paths converging; not thenceforth to unite, but to cross, and continue each in its former general direction, diverging rather than approximating. Though crumbling before the rising stream of progress, the ideas appropriate to the eighteenth century had not yet wholly disappeared from British conceptions; still less had the practice and policy of the state conformed themselves to the

changed point of view which, in the middle of the nineteenth century, began to characterise British statesmanship with reference
to colonies.   The battles of reformed political representation and
of free trade were yet to fight and win; old opinions continued
as to the commercial relationship of colonies to the mother-country, although modification in details was being introduced.   The
West Indies were still the most important group in the British
colonial system, and one of the latest acts of Canning, who died
in 1827, was to renew there commercial discrimination against
the United States; a measure which, however prompted, could
scarcely be said to reflect the image of the Monroe Doctrine.

For a generation then to come, British statesmen remained
under the domination of habits of thought which had governed
the course of the two Pitts; and they failed, as men usually fail,
to discern betimes changes of condition which modify, if not the
essentials, at least the application even of a policy sound in general
principle.   In 1823, not ten years had elapsed since the British
Government had contemplated exacting from the United States,
as the result of our prostration at the close of the War of 1812,
territorial cessions which might make an American of to-day, ignorant of the extremes to which his country was then reduced,
gasp with amazement.   How then could it be that Great Britain,
which for centuries had been acquiring territory, and to whom
the Americas were still the most immediate commercial interest,
should heartily accept the full scope of the Monroe Doctrine as
applicable to the extension of her own dominion by conquest or
otherwise, to any part of the American continents where she did
not at that moment have clear title?

As a matter of fact she did not in any wise accept this.   The
American declaration against "the extension of the system of
the allied powers to any portion of this hemisphere" was welcomed as supporting the attitude of Great Britain; for the phrase,
in itself ambiguous, was understood to apply not to the quintuple
alliance for the preservation of existing territorial arrangements
in Europe, to which Great Britain was a party, but to the Holy
Alliance, the avowed purpose of which was to suppress by external force revolutionary movements within any state—a course
into which she had refused to be drawn.   But the complementary
declaration in the President's message, that "the American con-

tinents are henceforth not to be considered as subjects for future colonization by any European power," was characterized in the *Annual Register* for 1823 as "scarcely less extravagant than that of the Russian ukase by which it was elicited" and which forbade any foreign vessel from approaching within a hundred miles of the Russian possession now known as Alaska. The British Government took the same view; and in the protocol to a conference held in 1827 expressly repudiated this American claim.

There was therefore between the two countries at this moment a clear opposition of principle, and agreement only as to a particular line of conduct in a special case. With regard to the interventions of the Holy Alliance in Europe, Great Britain, while reserving her independence of action, stood neutral for the time, but from motives of her own policy showed unmistakably that she would resist like action in Spanish America. The United States, impelled by an entirely different conception of national policy, now first offically enunciated, intimated in diplomatic phrase a similar disposition. The two supported each other in the particular contingency, and doubtless frustrated whatever intervention any members of the Holy Alliance may have entertained of projecting to the other side of the Atlantic their "union for the government of the world." In America, as in Europe, Great Britain deprecated the intrusion of external force to settle internal convulsions of foreign countries; but she did not commit herself, as the United States did, to the position that purchase or war should never entail a cession of territory by an American to a European state, a transaction which would be in so far colonization. In resisting any transfer of Spanish-American territory to a European power, Great Britain was not advancing a general principle, but maintaining an immediate interest. Her motive, in short, had nothing in common with the Monroe Doctrine. Such principles as were involved had been formulated long before, and had controlled her action in Europe as in America.

The United States dogma, on the contrary, planted itself squarely on the separate system and interests of America. This is distinctly shown by the comments of the Secretary of State, John Quincy Adams, in a despatch to the American minister in London, dated only two days before Monroe's message.

Alluding to Canning's most decisive phrase in a recent despatch, "Great Britain could not how hunt any part of the colonies transferred to any other power with indifference," he wrote. "We certainly do concur with her in this position; but the principles of that aversion, so far as they are common to both parties, resting only upon a casual coincidence of interests, in a national point of view selfish on both sides, would be liable to dissolution by every change of phase in the aspects of European politics. So that Great Britain, negotiating at once with the European alliance and with us concerning America, without being bound by any permanent community of principle, would still be free to accommodate her policy to any of those distributions of power and partitions of territory which for the last half-century have been the *ultima ratio* of all European political arrangements."

For this reason, Adams considered that recognition of the independence of the revolted colonies, already made by the United States, in March, 1822, must be given by Great Britain also, in order to place the two states on equal terms of coöperation. From motives of European policy, from which Great Britain could not dissociate herself, she delayed this recognition until 1825; and then Canning defined his general course toward the Spanish colonies in the famous words: "I called the New World into existence to redress the balance of the Old. I resolved that, if France had Spain, it should not be Spain with the Indies." His coincidence with the policy of the United States is thus seen to be based, and properly, upon British interests as involved in the European System, but that, so far from being the Monroe Doctrine, is almost the converse of it.

Nor was it only in direction that the impulses of the two states differed. They were unequal in inherent vital strength. The motive force of the one was bound to accumulate, and that of the other to relax, by the operation of purely natural conditions. An old order was beginning to yield to a new. After three centuries of tutelage America was slipping out of European control. She was reaching her majority and claiming her own. Within her sphere she felt the future to be hers. Of this sense the Monroe Doctrine was an utterance. It was a declaration of independence, not for a single nation only, but for a continent of nations, and it carried implicitly the assertion of all that logically follows

from such independence. Foremost among the conditions in-
suring its vitality was propinquity, with its close effect upon interest. Policy, as well as war, is a business of positions. This
maxim is perennial; a generation later it was emphasized in application, but not originated, by the peopling of the Pacific Coast,
the incidental discovery of gold in California, and the consequent
enhanced importance of the Isthmus of Panama to the political
strategy of nations. All this advanced the Monroe Doctrine on
the path of development, giving broader sweep to the corollaries
involved in the original proposition; but the transcendent posi-
tional interest of the United States no more needed demonstration in 1823 than in 1850, when the Clayton-Bulwer Treaty was
made, or than now, when, not the Pacific Coast only, but the
Pacific Ocean and the Farther East, lend increased consequence
to the isthmian communications.

The case of the United States is now stronger, but it is not
clearer. Correlatively, the admission of its force by others has
been progressive; gradual and practical, not at once or formal.
Its formulation in the Monroe Doctrine has not obtained the full
legislative sanction even of the country of its origin; and its
present development there rests upon successive utterances of
persons officially competent to define, but not of full authority to
commit the nation to their particular expressions. So, too, international acquiescence in the position now taken has been a work
of time, nor can there be asserted for it the final ratification of
international agreement. The Monroe Doctrine remains a policy, not a law, either municipal or international; but it has advanced in scope and in acceptance. The one progress, as the
other, has been the result of growing strength—strength of numbers and of resources. Taken with position, these factors constitute national power as they do military advantage, which in the
last analysis may always be resolved into two elements, force and
position.

In the conjunction of these two factors is to be found the birth
of the Monroe Doctrine and its development up to the present
time. It is a product of national interest, involved in position,
and of national power dependent upon population and resources.
These are the permanent factors of the Monroe Doctrine; and
it cannot be too strongly realized by Americans that the perma-

nence of the doctrine itself, as a matter of international consideration, depends upon the maintenance of both factors   To this
serious truth record is borne by history, the potent mother of
national warning and national encouragement.   That the doctrine at its first enunciation should not at once have obtained
either assent or influence, even in its most limited expression,
was entirely natural.   Although not without an antecedent history of conception and occasional utterance by American statesmen, its moment of birth was the announcement by Monroe;
and it had then all the weakness of the new-born, consequent upon
a national inadequacy to the display of organized strength which
had been pathetically manifested but ten years before.   After the
destruction of the rule of Spain in her colonies, except in Cuba
and Porto Rico, Great Britain remained the one great nation besides the United States possessed of extensive territory in America.   She also was the one state that had had experience of us as
an enemy, and known the weakness of our military system for
offensive action.   What more natural than that she should have
welcomed the first promulgation of the doctrine, in its original
scope directed apparently merely against a combination of Continental powers, the purposes of which were offensive to herself,
and yet failed to heed a root principle which in progress of time
should find its application to herself, contesting the expansion of
her own influence in the hemisphere, as being part of the European system and therefore falling under the same condemnation?
Yet even had she seen this, and fully appreciated the promise of
strength to come, it was to be expected that she should for the
mean time pursue her own policy, irrespective of the still distant
future.   It may be advantageous to retard that which must ultimately prevail; and at all events men who head the movements
of nations are not able at once to abandon the traditions of the
past, and conform their action to new ideas as yet unassimilated
by their people.

There is then this distinguishing feature of the Monroe Doctrine, which classifies it among principles of policy which are
essentially permanent.   From its correspondence to the nature
of things, to its environment, it possessed from the first a vitality
which insured growth and development.   Under such conditions
it could not remain in application at the end of a half-century

just what it had been in terms at the beginning. Apprehended
in leading features by American statesmen, and by them embraced with a conviction which the people shared—though probably not fully understanding—it received from time to time, as
successive exigencies arose to invoke assertion, definitions which
enlarged its scope; sometimes consistently with its true spirit,
sometimes apparently in excess of evident limitations, more
rarely in defect of them.

But from the fact of Great Britain's existing territorial possessions in America, and from her commercial preëminence and
ambitions, to which territorial acquisition is often desirable, it
was also in the nature of things that with her successive conten-
tions should arise. If not a balance of power, such as had distracted Europe, at least opposing scales existed from the first;
connected, not perhaps with the European system as a whole,
but certainly with a most important component of that system.
Moreover, the strength of Great Britain in America, relatively to
the United States, was not American strength, but European
strength. It was therefore unavoidably invidious to the sentiment breathed in the Monroe Doctrine, and much more so when
the United States was weak than when she became strong.

From these circumstances, it has been through discussion with
Great Britain chiefly that the doctrine, marking the advance of
the sentiment, has progressed from definition to definition, no
one of which is final in an authoritative sense, because in no case
clothed with full legislative sanction, but possessing, nevertheless, the weight which attaches to the utterances of those who
both by personal ability and official position are recognized as
competent interpreters. Such enunciations, *ex cathedra*, have
the force of judicial decisions, accepted as precedents to a degree
dependent upon the particular person or upon subsequent general acceptance. Not in every case have the positions of American administrations in this matter been indorsed by their successors or the public.

It is vain, therefore, to argue narrowly concerning what the
Monroe Doctrine is, from the precise application made of it to
any one particular emergency. Nor can there be finality of definition, antecedent to some national announcement, formally complete, which it is to be hoped will never be framed; but which, if

it were, would doubtless remain liable to contrary interpretations, ▓▓▓▓▓▓ ▓▓ ▓ ▓ ▓ ▓▓▓ ▓▓▓▓ ▓▓▓▓▓ ▓▓▓▓▓ ▓▓▓▓▓ ▓▓▓ ▓▓▓▓▓▓▓▓▓ of legis-latures nor the bull of a pope can claim exemption.   The virtue of the Monroe Doctrine, without which it would die deservedly, is that, through its correspondence with the national necessities of the United States, it possesses an inherent principle of life, which adapts itself with the flexibility of a growing plant to the successive conditions it encounters. One of these condi-tions of course is the growing strength of the nation itself. As Doctor Johnson ungraciously said of taxing Americans for the first time, "We do not put a calf to the plough: we wait till he is an ox." The Monroe Doctrine, without breach of its spirit, can now be made to bear a burden to which the nation a hundred years ago was unequal.

For these reasons it is more instructive, as to the present and future of the Monroe Doctrine, to consider its development by successive exhibitions in the past, than to strive to cage its free spirit within the bars of a definition attempted at any one mo-ment. Such an attempt the present writer certainly will not make. The international force of the proposition lies in its evolution, substantially consistent, broadening down from prece-dent to precedent; not in an alleged finality.

The aversion manifested by the Government of the War of Independence toward any attempted restoration of French do-minion in Canada, may be justly considered a premonition of the Monroe Doctrine, anticipatory of the ground taken by both Mon-roe and Canning against a transfer of Spanish colonies to any other European power. At the earlier period no remonstrance was raised against such transfers of West India Islands, which occurred frequently during both that war and those of the French Revolution and Napoleonic period. The cession of Louisiana by Spain to France, in 1801, excited the keenest susceptibilities. How far resistance might have been carried it is bootless to sur-mise; the inoperativeness of the transaction did not permit the full consequences to develop. Objection, however, appears to have turned upon the more immediate and special motive of the substitution of a strong power for a weak one, in control of an artery of trade essential to our people, than upon the formulated dogma that American territory was not matter for political exchange between European states. Moreover, it needed no broad maxim, wide-reaching in application, to arouse popular feeling, and guide national action, in a matter of such close and evident importance. Repulsion was a matter of instinct, of feeling, which did not need to give account of itself to reason. The Louisiana question laid its hand at once upon the heart of the nation. It concerned the country, not the hemisphere; and in essential principle did not lead out beyond itself, pointing the way to further action. It had finality.

The real stepping-stone by which national interest advanced to hemispheric considerations was Cuba. From every circumstance this island was eminently fitted to point the way of the future; to be the medium, and to mark the transition, from a strictly continental policy to one that embraced the hemisphere. It possessed in a very high degree the elements of power, from its position, size, and resources, which involved immense possibility for development of strength. Its intrinsic value was, therefore, very great; but further, while it had relations to our continental territory only less important than the lower course of the Mississippi, it nevertheless did not belong to the continent, to which the Jeffersonian school of thought, in power from 1801 to 1825, would strictly confine national expansion. The point where a powerful navy would be needed to maintain the integrity of the national possessions marked the limit of advance in the theory of Jefferson. Nevertheless, to him also, minimizing possibly the need of a fleet to insure access over so narrow a strip of sea, "the addition of Cuba to our confederacy is certainly exactly what is wanted to round our power as a nation to the point of its utmost interest." To prevent its falling as yet into the hands of any other European power, he expressed to Monroe in 1823 his approval of entering with Great Britain into a joint guarantee to preserve the island for Spain, for this, he argued, would bind the most dangerous and most suspected power. On subsequent information, however, that Great Britain had stated positively she would not acquire for herself any Spanish colony under the present distress of Spain, he retracted this opinion; for why, said he, by engaging in joint guarantee, concede to her an interest which she does not otherwise possess? Before this, however, Great Britain had offered to assure the island by her own sole action, on condition of Spain acknowledging the independence of her continental colonies; thus constituting for herself the interest from which Jefferson would have debarred the consent of the United States.

To such a point, anxiety for American ends and consciousness of American lack of organized strength would then carry a practical statesman of keen American instincts. To join with a European state in guaranteeing an American interest was not yet an anachronism. A like anxiety and a like consciousness were responsible for the Clayton-Bulwer Treaty, which proved so fertile a source of diplomatic contention and national ill-will in later days. Monroe's Secretary of State, John Quincy Adams, the contemporary and survivor of Jefferson, had clearer views and stronger purpose. Recognizing in Cuba an importance to the United States scarcely inferior to any part of the then existing Union, he held that there were still numerous and formidable objections to territorial dominion beyond sea. The aim of his policy, therefore, was that Spain should retain Cuba; but when he succeeded Monroe in the Presidency in 1825, having received the suggestion of a joint guarantee by Great Britain, France, and the United States upon condition of Spain acknowledging the independence of the Spanish-speaking continent, he replied merely that the matter would be held under advisement, and followed this in 1826 by an express refusal—"We can enter into no stipulations by treaty to guarantee the islands." At the same time it was clearly stated that "the United States would not consent to the occupation of Cuba and Porto Rico by any other European power than Spain, under any contingency whatever."

OPENING OF THE ERIE CANAL

A.D. 1825

WILLIAM H. SEWARD

Among internal improvements in the United States in the first half of the nineteenth century, the canal system, designed to furnish better communication for the Eastern States with the interior, was one of the most important. Of the canals then constructed, the Erie was the greatest in the world, and traversed the chief commercial route in the United States. It extends from the Hudson River at Albany to Lake Erie at Buffalo. Its present length is three hundred fifty and one-half miles; width at surface, seventy feet; at bottom, fifty-six feet; depth, seven feet. Its opening in 1825 was two years earlier than the building of the first railroad in America.

Although the building of railroads arrested canal navigation in the United States, interest in its revival has at times awakened, and at present (1905) the question of improving the canals of New York is one of the most important before the people and legislators of the State.

William H. Seward, the great Secretary of State under Lincoln, wrote valuable historical matter concerning New York, his native State, and his account of the Erie Canal enterprise and its successful accomplishment is the most complete and satisfactory that has ever appeared.

HISTORY will assign to Gouverneur Morris the merit of first suggesting a direct and continuous communication from Lake Erie to the Hudson. In 1800 he announced this idea from the shore of the Niagara River to a friend in Europe, in the following enthusiastic language: "Hundreds of large ships will, in no distant period, bound on the billows of these inland seas. Shall I lead your astonishment to the verge of incredulity? I will! Know then that one-tenth part of the expense borne by Britain in the last campaign would enable ships to sail from London through the Hudson into Lake Erie. As yet we only crawl along the outer shell of our country. The interior excels the part we inhabit in soil, in climate, in everything. The proudest empire of Europe is but a bauble compared with what America may be, must be."

The praise awarded to Gouverneur Morris must be qualified by the fact that the scheme he conceived was that of a canal with a uniform declination, and without locks, from Lake Erie to the Hudson. Morris communicated his project to Simeon De Witt in 1803, by whom it was made known to James Geddes in 1804. It afterward became the subject of conversation between Mr. Geddes and Jesse Hawley, and this communication is supposed to have given rise to the series of essays written by Mr. Hawley, under the signature of "Hercules," in the *Genesee Messenger*, continued from October, 1807, until March, 1808, which first brought the public mind into familiarity with the subject. These essays, written in a jail, were the grateful return, by a patriot, to a country which punished him with imprisonment for being unable to pay debts owed to another citizen. They bore evidences of deep research and displayed singular vigor and comprehensiveness of thought, and traced with prophetic accuracy a large portion of the outline of the Erie Canal.

In 1807 Albert Gallatin, then Secretary of the Treasury, in pursuance of a recommendation made by Thomas Jefferson, President of the United States, reported a plan for appropriating all the surplus revenues of the General Government to the construction of canals and turnpike roads; and it embraced in one grand and comprehensive view, nearly without exception, all the works which have since been executed or attempted by the several States in the Union.[1] This bold and statesmanlike, though premature, conception of that eminent citizen will remain the greatest among the many monuments of his forecast and wisdom.

In 1808 Joshua Forman, a representative in the New York Assembly from Onondaga County, submitted his memorable resolution:

"*Whereas*, The President of the United States did by his message to Congress, delivered at their meeting in October last, recommend that the surplus moneys in the treasury, over and above such sums as could be applied to the extinguishment of the national debt, be appropriated to the great national project of opening canals and making turnpike roads; and

"*Whereas*, The State of New York, holding the first commercial rank in the United States, possesses within herself the best

[1] This refers to a period ending about 1840.—ED.

mode of communication between the Atlantic and Western waters, by means of a canal between the tide-waters of the Hudson River and Lake Erie, through which the wealth and trade
of that large portion of the Union, bordering on the upper lakes,
would forever flow to our great commercial emporium; and

"*Whereas*, The legislatures of several of our sister-States have
made great exertions to secure to their own States the trade of
that widely extended country west of the Alleghanies, under natural advantages vastly inferior to those of this State; and

"*Whereas*, It is highly important that those advantages should
as speedily as possible be improved, both to preserve and increase the commercial and national importance of this State;
therefore be it

"*Resolved*, if the honorable the Senate concur herein, That a
joint committee be appointed to take into consideration the propriety of exploring and causing an accurate survey to be made of
the most eligible and direct route for a canal, to open a communication between the tide-waters of the Hudson River and
Lake Erie, to the end that Congress may be enabled to appropriate such sums as may be necessary to the accomplishment
of that great national object."

In pursuance of a recommendation by the committee, a resolution unanimously passed both houses, directing the surveyor-
general, Simeon De Witt, to cause an accurate survey to be made
of the various routes proposed for the contemplated communication. But how little the magnitude of that undertaking was
understood may be inferred from the fact that the appropriation
made by the resolution to defray the expenses of its execution
was limited to the sum of six hundred dollars.

There was then no civil engineer in the State. James Geddes,
a land surveyor, who afterward became one of our most distinguished engineers, by the force of native genius and application
in mature years, levelled and surveyed under instructions from
the surveyor-general, with a view to ascertain, first, whether a
canal could be made from the Oneida Lake to Lake Ontario, at
the mouth of Salmon Creek; secondly, whether navigation could
be opened from Oswego Falls to Lake Ontario, along the Oswego River; thirdly, what was the best route for a canal from
above the Falls of Niagara to Lewiston; and, fourthly, what was

the most direct route, and with the practicability of a canal from Lake Erie to the Genesee River, and thence to the waters run ning east to the Seneca River. The topography of the country between the Seneca River and the Hudson was at that time comparatively better known.

Mr. Geddes's report showed that a canal from Lake Erie to the Hudson was practicable, and could be made without serious difficulty. In 1810, on motion of Jonas Platt, of the Senate, who was distinguished throughout a pure and well-spent life by his zealous efforts to promote this great undertaking, Gouverneur Morris, De Witt Clinton, Stephen Van Rensselaer, Simeon De Witt, William North, Thomas Eddy, and Peter B. Porter were appointed commissioners "to explore the whole route for inland navigation from the Hudson River to Lake Ontario, and to Lake Erie." Cadwallader D. Colden, a contemporary historian, himself one of the earliest and ablest advocates of the canals, awards to Thomas Eddy the merit of having suggested this motion to Mr. Platt, and to both these gentlemen that of engaging De Witt Clinton's support, he being at that time a member of the Senate. Another writer commemorates the efficient and enlightened exertions, at this period, of Hugh Williamson, who wrote, with reference to the contemplated improvement, papers entitled *Observations on Navigable Canals* and also *Observations on the Means of Preserving the Commerce of New York*, which were published in magazines of that day.

The canal policy found, at the same time, earnest and vigorous supporters in the *American* and *Philosophical Register*, edited by Dr. David Hosack and Dr. John W. Francis.

The commissioners in March, 1811, submitted their report written by Gouverneur Morris, in which they showed the practicability and advantages of a continuous canal from Lake Erie to the Hudson, and stated their estimate of the cost at five million dollars, a sum which they ventured to predict would not exceed 5 per cent. of the value of the commodities which, within a century, would be annually transported on the proposed canal. We may pause here to remark that the annual value of the commodities carried on the canals, instead of requiring a century to attain the sum of one hundred millions, reached that limit in twenty-five years.

"By whom," added the commissioners, "shall the needful expense of the construction of the work be supported? We take the liberty of entering our feeble protest against a grant to private persons or companies. Too great a national interest is at stake. It must not become the subject of a job or of a fund for speculation. Among many other objections there is one insuperable, that it would defeat the contemplated cheapness of transportation. It remains to determine whether the canal shall be at the cost of the State or of the Union. If the State were not bound by the Federal band with her sister States, she might fairly ask compensation from those who own the soil along the Great Lakes, for giving permission to cut the canal at their expense; or her statesmen might deem it still more advisable to make the canal at her own expense, and take for the use of it a transit duty, raising or lowering the impost, as circumstances might direct, for her own advantage. This might be the better course if the State stood alone; but, fortunately for the peace and happiness of all, this is not the case. We are connected by a bond which, if the prayers of good men are favorably heard, will be indissoluble. It becomes proper, therefore, to resort, for the solution of the present question, to the principles of distributive justice. That which presents itself is the trite adage, that those who participate in the benefits should contribute to the expense. The commissioners presume not to go one step further. The wisdom, as well as the justice, of the National Legislature will no doubt lead to the exercise on their part of prudent munificence; but the proportion, the condition, the compact, in short, must be the subject of treaty."

From 1812 to 1815 the country suffered the calamities of war, and projects of internal improvement necessarily gave place to the patriotic efforts required to maintain the national security and honor. But those plans were not altogether forgotten, at least by those who distrusted their wisdom. Although there was much incredulity in regard to the Erie Canal, during all the period which we have been considering, yet the design met little or no opposition, so long as it was supposed that the necessary expenditures would be made by the Federal Government. But a severe scrutiny was encountered when it was avowed that the means for accomplishing so large a work must be derived from taxation, or from the use of the public credit. Erastus Root, in 1813, submitted a resolution by which the commissioners were to be called upon for a further report of their proceedings. The commissioners, in their report of 1814, reaffirmed their confidence in the feasibility of the enterprise, and adverted to the facilities which would be found for extending the communication to the valleys watered by the Susquehanna and its branches, whence they inferred that Pennsylvania would, at a proper time, coöperate in the enterprise. The commissioners also announced that grants of land would be made by the Holland Company of one hundred thousand six hundred thirty-two acres; by Le Roy Bayard and M'Evers of twenty-five hundred acres; by the heirs of the Pulteney estate, a large tract; and by Governor Hornby, thirty-five hundred acres. These cessions were ultimately realized, with a liberal donation from Gideon Granger.

Mr. Root introduced a bill into the Senate, which two days afterward passed that body, repealing so much of the act then in force as authorized the commissioners to borrow five million dollars. This repeal was a virtual abandonment of the policy of internal improvements. The divisions in the Assembly show a majority of eighteen in favor of the repeal; and in the Senate the majority was eight. In 1816, at the close of the war, Daniel D. Tompkins, Governor, in his annual speech, submitted, for the consideration of the Legislature, the expediency of prosecuting the canals. Citizens in various parts of the State, and especially in New York, Albany, and Troy, and in the towns and counties situated in the vicinity of the proposed routes, now earnestly applied for vigorous measures to accomplish the objects so long delayed. Among these petitions was a memorial by inhabitants of the city of New York, from the pen of De Witt Clinton.

The memorialists declared that since the object was connected with the essential interests of the country, and calculated in its commencement to reflect honor on the State, and in its completion to exalt it to an elevation of unparalleled prosperity, they were fully persuaded that centuries might pass away before a subject would be again presented so worthy of all the attention of the Legislature, and so deserving of all its patronage and support; that the improvement of intercourse between different parts of the same country had always been considered the first duty and the most noble employment of government; that canals united cheapness, celerity, certainty, and safety in the transportation of commodities; that they operated upon the general interests of society in the same way as machines for saving labor in manufactures; and, as to all the purposes of beneficial communication, they diminished the distances between places, and therefore encouraged the cultivation of the most remote parts of the country; that they created new sources of internal trade, and augmented the old channels, thus tending to enlarge old and erect new towns, increase individual and aggregate wealth, and extend foreign commerce. The memorialists attributed the prosperity of ancient Egypt and China to their inland navigation, and expressed the opinion that England and Holland, if deprived of their canals, would lose the most prolific sources of their prosperity and greatness. Inland navigation, they said, was to the same community what exterior navigation was to the great family of mankind; and that as the ocean connected the nations of the earth by the ties of commerce and the benefits of communication, so did lakes, rivers, and canals operate upon the inhabitants of the same country.

Applying these general arguments in favor of inland navigation, they showed that a great chain of mountains passed through the territory of the United States and divided it into Eastern and Western America; that the former, on account of the priority of its settlement, its vicinity to the ocean, and its favorable position for commerce, had many advantages, while the latter had a decided superiority in the fertility of its soil, the salubrity of its climate, and the extent of its territory; that to connect those great sections by inland navigation, to unite our Mediterranean seas with the ocean, was evidently an object of the first importance to the general prosperity; that the Hudson River offered superior advantages for effecting this connection, because it afforded a tide navigation through the Blue Ridge or eastern chain of mountains, and ascended above the eastern termination of the Catskills or great western chain, and that no mountains interposed between it and the great western lakes, while the tide in no other river or bay in the United States ascended any higher than Granite Ridge, or within thirty miles of Blue Ridge.

After showing the importance of the Hudson as a natural channel of trade, one hundred seventy miles in length, the petitioners showed that the canal would be virtually an extension of that channel three hundred miles through a fertile country, embracing a great population, and abounding with all the productions of industry; and they asked, if this work was so important when viewed in relation to this State alone, how unspeakably beneficial must it appear when the contemplation should be extended to the Great Lakes and the country that surrounded them—waters extending two thousand miles, and a country containing more territory than all Great Britain and Ireland, and at least as much as France. After demonstrating that New Orleans and Montreal were the only formidable rivals of New York for the great prize of the Western trade, and showing the advantages in that competition which New York would derive from the proposed Erie Canal, a glowing view of its prospective benefits was presented. Leaving to her rivals no inconsiderable portion of the Western trade, New York, said the memorialists, would engross more than sufficient to render her the greatest commercial city in the world. The whole line of the canal would exhibit boats loaded with the various productions of our soil, and with merchandise from all parts of the world; great manufacturing establishments would spring up; agriculture would establish its granaries and commerce its warehouses in all directions; villages, towns, and cities would line the banks of the canal and the shores of the Hudson from Erie to New York; the wilderness and the solitary place would become glad, and the desert would blossom as the rose.

The ground was broken for the construction of the Erie Canal on July 4, 1817, at Rome, with ceremonies marking the public estimation of that great event. De Witt Clinton, having just before been elected to the chief magistracy of the State, and being president of the Board of Canal Commissioners, enjoyed the high satisfaction of attending, with his associates, on the auspicious occasion.

In his annual speech to the Legislature in 1818, he congratulated the people on the commencement of the canals, rapidly reviewed the progress already made in their construction, remarked briefly on their advantages, and earnestly urged that the State was required to persevere, by every dictate of interest, by every sentiment of honor, by every injunction of patriotism, and by every consideration which ought to influence the councils and govern the conduct of a free, high-minded, enlightened, and magnanimous people. The Senate responded favorably to these sentiments, and the answer of the Assembly was in terms of spirited congratulation.

The commissioners made a report showing that they had engaged Isaac Briggs, an eminent mathematician, as an engineer on the middle section, and had let the work to be done in small portions by contract. At this session, laws were passed, authorizing the construction of the Chittenango Canal for navigation, and as a feeder to the Erie Canal, and an examination of the outlet of Buffalo Creek, with a view to form a harbor at the entrance of the Erie Canal into Lake Erie, and make improvements of the financial system adopted at the previous session. The act relating to the last-mentioned subject authorized the comptroller to borrow one million dollars for the general uses of the treasury, and to issue therefor stock redeemable on January 1, 1828. When this law was under consideration in the Assembly, Erastus Root moved that the power of the commissioners of the canal fund to borrow money for canal purposes should be suspended until the redemption of the stock debt to be created under the law. This was the last effort made in the Legislature to arrest the prosecution of the canals. The motion was lost, only twenty-one members voting therefor.

In 1819 Governor Clinton announced to the Legislature that the progress of the public works equalled the most sanguine expectations and that the Canal fund was flourishing. He recommended the prosecution of the entire Erie Canal. Enlarging upon the benefits of internal navigation, he remarked that he looked to a time, not far distant, when the State would be able to improve the navigation of the Susquehanna, the Allegheny, the Genesee, and the St. Lawrence; to assist in connecting the waters of the Great Lakes and the Mississippi; to form a junction between the Erie Canal and Lake Ontario through the Oswego River; and to promote the laudable intention of Pennsylvania to unite Seneca Lake with the Susquehanna, deducing arguments in favor of such enterprises, from the immediate com-

mercial advantages of extended navigation, as well as from its
tendency to improve the condition of society and strengthen the
bonds of the Union. Henry Yates Jr., in the Senate, and John
Van Ness Yates, in the Assembly, on behalf of the proper committees, submitted answers concurring in the opinions expressed
by the chief magistrate, and the same were adopted.

Joseph Ellicott having resigned the office of canal commissioner, Ephraim Hart was appointed in his place *ad interim*,
and subsequently Henry Seymour was called to fill the vacancy.

The canal commissioners, in their report, gave an interesting account of their proceedings, represented that the work on
the middle section, under the care of Benjamin Wright as principal engineer, had been conducted with great success, and
that Canvass White and Nathan S. Roberts, who had previously
been assistant engineers, were assigned, on account of their eminent skill, to higher duties. Mr. White was distinguished at this
time for his discovery of the manner of preparing a hydraulic
cement from a peculiar kind of limestone found in the vicinity
of the canal. He was the inventor, also, of the improvement in
the construction of upper gates of canal locks, which had been
said to be the only improvement in the mechanical construction
of canals made since the building of the Languedoc Canal.

The commissioners recommended that a navigable communication should immediately be opened from the Erie Canal to
the salt-works at Salina, and that the militia law should be so
modified as to excuse laborers on the canals from military duty,
and sustained the recommendation by the Governor of the simultaneous prosecution of all portions of the Erie Canal.

The joint committee on internal improvements consisted of
Jabez D. Hammond, Henry Seymour, and Walter Bowne, Senators, and Ezekiel Bacon, Jacob Rutsen, Van Rensselaer, John
Doty, Jedediah Miller, and Asahel Warner, of the Assembly.
Ezekiel Bacon submitted a report and introduced a bill embodying the recommendations of the canal commissioners. This
bill became a law, twenty-five members of the Assembly voting
against the section which empowered the canal commissioners
to commence the eastern and western portions of the Erie Canal
and the branch canal from the Erie Canal to Salina. A survey

was also authorized from the mouth of the Oswego River, up
the same, the Seneca River and the outlet of the Onondaga
River, with a view to improve the navigation of those streams.
This was the first legislative step toward the construction of the
Oswego Canal.

At this session a law was passed suspending the collection of
the local canal tax until further directions should be given by
the Legislature.   An act was also passed granting a loan to citizens of Buffalo, to be applied to the construction, under the direction of the canal commissioners, of a harbor at that place, and
providing for the assumption of the harbor if it should ultimately be deemed expedient.

On October 23, 1819, the portion of the Erie Canal between
Utica and Rome was opened to navigation, and on November
24th the Champlain Canal admitted the passage of boats.   Thus
in less than two years and five months one hundred twenty miles
of artificial navigation had been finished, and the physical as
well as the financial practicability of uniting the waters of the
western and northern lakes with the Altantic Ocean was established to the conviction of the most incredulous.

Governor Clinton announced these gratifying results to the
Legislature in 1820, and admonished that body that while efforts
directly hostile to internal improvements would in future be feeble, it became a duty to guard against insidious enmity; and
that in proportion as the Erie Canal advanced toward completion would be the ease of combining a greater mass of population against the further extension of the system.   Attempts, he
remarked, had already been made to arrest the progress of the
Erie Canal west of the Seneca River, and he anticipated their
renewal when it should reach the Genesee.   But the honor and
prosperity of the State demanded the completion of the whole
of the work, and it would be completed in five years if the representatives of the people were just to themselves and to posterity.

Referring to the local tax, he submitted whether it com-
ported with the magnanimity of Government to resort to partial
or local impositions to defray the expenses of a magnificent
work identified with the general prosperity.   The commissioners
informed the Legislature that they had employed David Thomas

to surwing the proposed harbor at Buffalo, and that plans for a similar improvement at Black Rock had been furnished

The committee on internal improvements in the Senate consisted of Jabez D. Hammond, Gideon Granger, and Stephen Barnum; and the committee on canals in the Assembly, of George Huntington, John T. Irving, David Austin, Elial T. Foote, and Thomas J. Oakley.

A law was passed suspending the collection of the tax on steamboat passengers, and imposing, by way of commutation, on the North River Steamboat Company an annual tax of five thousand dollars, for the benefit of the canal fund. This company then enjoyed, by grant from the Legislature, a monopoly of steam navigation upon all the waters within the State, as a reward to Robert Fulton, Robert R. Livingston, and their associates, as public benefactors. The grant was afterward adjudged by the Supreme Court of the United States to be void so far as it affected navigation in tide-waters, because it conflicted with the Constitution of the United States. The same law appropriated twenty-five thousand dollars for the improvement of the Oswego River; and by other acts, Grand Island in the Niagara River, and a portion of the reservation at the Onondaga salt springs, were directed to be sold for the benefit of the canal fund; and the Legislature prescribed a general system of police for the management and protection of the canals.

By an arrangement made by the commissioners, and sanctioned by the Legislature, three of the five commissioners were charged with active duties, to be compensated by salaries, while the other commissioners were relieved from such duties. The acting commissioners designated were Mr. Young, Mr. Seymour, and Mr. Holley. During the same year the title of the Western Inland Lock Navigation Company to its property and privileges was transferred to the State, and a compensation of one hundred fifty thousand eight hundred twenty-eight dollars was paid for the same.

In November, 1820, Governor Clinton congratulated the Legislature upon the progress of the public works. He urged the adoption of plenary measures to complete the Erie Canal within three years, enforcing the recommendation by the consideration that Ohio would thereby be encouraged to pursue her noble attempt to unite the waters of Lake Erie with the Ohio River. The canal commissioners showed in their report that the Erie Canal was navigable from Utica to the Seneca River, a distance of ninety-six miles, and that its tolls during four months had amounted to five thousand two hundred forty-four dollars.

An effort was made in the Assembly to abrogate the local tax, which failed, a result showing that distrust of the productiveness of the canals still lingered in the halls of the Legislature. This, however, was the last effort, and the law has been suffered to remain ever since unexecuted and unrepealed. William C. Bouck was, during the same session, appointed an acting canal commissioner.

Governor Clinton, in 1822, referred in his speech to the difficulties and embarrassments which had been encountered with regard to the most eligible routes for the canals, and the most proper designations for the termini of the Erie Canal, assuring the Legislature, however, that the Canal Board had not been led astray by local considerations or ephemeral expedients, and that they would be able to combine the accommodation of flourishing cities and villages with the promotion of the general convenience and welfare. He noticed that efforts on the part of Illinois to connect the river of that name with Lake Michigan, and those of Ohio to unite with Lake Erie the river which formed her southern boundary, commending those efforts to the munificent patronage of the National Government and the favorable countenance of New York. He recommended also the institution of a board of public improvements, to be composed of enlightened and public-spirited citizens, and invested with power to establish and facilitate all useful channels of communication and all eligible modes of improvement. The tolls on the portion of the Champlain Canal which had been completed amounted in the previous year to one thousand three hundred eighty-six dollars.

The Legislature at this session directed the canal commissioners to open a boat navigation between the village of Salina, Onondaga Lake, and the Seneca River. These improvements, when completed, together with those previously directed, created an artificial canal from the Erie Canal to Lake Ontario, and constituted a portion of what afterward became known as the Oswego Canal. Acts were also passed to encourage the construction of harbors at Buffalo Creek and Black Rock, and to adapt the Glens Falls feeder of the Champlain Canal to boat navigation.

On January 1, 1823, the Government went into operation under the new State constitution, Joseph C. Yates having been elected to the office of governor. The constitution declared that rates of toll not less than those set forth by the canal commissioners in their report of 1821 should be collected on the canals, and that the revenues then pledged to the canal fund should not be diminished nor diverted before the complete payment of the principal and interest of the entire canal debt, a pledge which placed the public credit on an impregnable basis.

It appeared at the commencement of the session of the Legislature in 1823 that the public debt amounted to five million four hundred twenty-three thousand five hundred dollars, of which the sum of four million two hundred forty-three thousand five hundred dollars was for moneys borrowed to construct the canals. The commissioners reported that boats had passed on the Erie Canal a distance of more than two hundred twenty miles, and that as early as July 1st ensuing that channel would be navigable from Schenectady to Rochester. The tolls collected in 1822 upon the Erie Canal were sixty thousand, and upon the Champlain Canal three thousand six hundred twenty-five dollars. The improvements of the outlet of Onondaga Lake had been completed, and the Glens Falls feeder was in course of rapid construction. Among the benefits already resulting from the Erie Canal, the commissioners showed that the price of wheat west of the Seneca River had advanced 50 per cent. To appreciate this result, it is necessary to understand that wheat is the chief staple of New York, and that far the largest portion of wheat-growing in this State lies west of the Seneca River. Attempts were again made in both branches to provide for collecting the local tax. The proposition was lost in the Senate by a vote of nineteen to ten, and in the Assembly by a division of sixty-five to thirty-one.

The Legislature expressed by resolution a favorable opinion of the inland navigation which New Jersey proposed to establish between the Delaware and Hudson rivers. A loan of one million five hundred thousand dollars was authorized for canal purposes, a survey of the Oswego River was directed to be made, and estimates of the expense of completing the canal from Salina to Lake Ontario. An association to construct such a canal was incorporated, and authority given to the commissioners to take the work when completed, leaving the use of its surplus waters to the corporators; and the eastern termination of the Erie Canal was fixed at Albany.

The canal commissioners reported in 1824 that the Champlain Canal was finished; that both canals had produced revenues during the previous year of one hundred fifty-three thousand dollars; and that the commissioners had decided that the Erie Canal ought to be united with the Niagara River at Black Rock and terminate at Buffalo.

Myron Holley now resigned the office of canal commissioner; and laws were passed appropriating one million dollars for canal purposes, and directing a survey for a canal from Lake Champlain to the St. Lawrence, with a view to complete the inland navigation between that river and the Hudson.

On April 25, 1824, John Bowman presented to the Senate a concurrent resolution that "De Witt Clinton, Esq., be and is hereby removed from the office of canal commissioner"; and it was carried on the same day through the Senate, by a vote of twenty-one to three, and through the Assembly by a vote of sixty-four to thirty-four.

As soon as partial navigation of the canals had commenced, the Government of the United States asserted a pretension to exact tonnage duties thereon. The Legislature of New York State, at its adjourned session, instructed its Senators and Representatives in Congress to use their utmost endeavors to prevent such unjust and impolitic exactions; and the claim of the Government of the United States, although not formally relinquished, has never since been urged.

On the reassembling of the Legislature in January, 1825, De Witt Clinton, who, in November of the preceding year, had been again called to the office of governor, congratulated the Legislature upon the prospect of the immediate completion of the Erie Canal, and the reasonable certainty that the canal debt might soon be satisfied, without a resort to taxation, without a

discontinuation of efforts for similar improvements, and without
staying the dispensing hand of Government in favor of education, literature, science, and productive industry.   Earnestly
renewing his recommendation that a board of internal improvement should be instituted, he remarked that the field of operations was immense, and the harvest of honor and profit unbounded, and that, if the resources of the State should be wisely
applied and forcibly directed, all proper demands for important
avenues of communication might be satisfied.

The primary design of our system of artificial navigation,
which was to open a communication between the Atlantic and
the Great Lakes, was already, he observed, nearly accomplished,
but would not be fully realized until Lake Ontario should be
connected with the Erie Canal and with Lake Champlain, and
the importance of these improvements would be appreciated
when it was understood that the lake coast, not only of this State,
but of the United States, was more extensive than their seacoast.   The next leading object, he remarked, should be to unite
the minor lakes and secondary rivers with the canals and to
effect such a connection between the bays on the seacoast as
would insure the safety of boat navigation against the tempests
of the ocean in time of peace, and against the depredations of an
enemy in time of war.

The public debt for canals in 1825 amounted to seven and a
half million dollars—all of which, it must be recorded to the
honor of the State and the country, had been borrowed of American capitalists—and the annual interest thereon, to three hundred
seventy-six thousand dollars.   The Governor estimated that the
tolls for the year would exceed three hundred ten thousand dollars; that the duties on salt would amount to one hundred thousand dollars, and that these, with the other income of the canal
fund, would produce a revenue exceeding, by three hundred thousand dollars, the interest on the canal debt.   He stated also that
ten thousand boats had passed the junction of the canals near
tide-water during the previous season.   Remarking that the cre-
ative power of internal improvement was manifested in the
flourishing villages which had sprung up or been extended; in
the increase of towns; and, above all, in the prosperity of the
city of New York.   And noticing the fact that three thousand

buildings had been erected in that city during the preceding year, Clinton predicted that in fifteen years its population would be doubled, and that in thirty years that metropolis would be the third city in the civilized world, and the second, if not the first, in commerce.

Adverting to the efforts which Ohio was making to connect Lake Erie—which, he remarked, might now be regarded as a prolongation of the Erie Canal—with the Ohio River, he declared that he should welcome the commencement and hail the consummation of that work as among the most auspicious events in our history; and he closed his review of the condition and prospects of the State with this exclamation: "How emphatically does is behoove us, in the contemplation and enjoyment of these abundant blessings, to remember that we derive them all from the great Fountain of Benevolence!"

The canal commissioners, alluding to the pressure of business on the eastern section of the canal and the probability of its rapid increase, announced to the Legislature that it would be necessary before long to exclude passenger-boats from this part of the line, unless double locks were made through the whole distance, and remarked that even then the crowd of boats in the spring and fall would produce great inconveniences and delay. Reasoning that in many places it would be almost impossible to construct double locks, and that in others it would be attended with great expense, they inferred that in a very few years it would be proper and perhaps indispensable to make a parallel canal along the valley of the Mohawk. They showed that, in 1820, the tolls of ninety-four miles of the Erie Canal were $5000; in 1821, on the same distance, $23,000; in 1822, on one hundred sixteen miles, $57,000; in 1823, on one hundred sixty miles, $105,000; and in 1824, on two hundred eighty miles, had reached the sum of $294,000. They submitted tables, in which they estimated the tolls on a basis of the increase of the population and the progress of agricultural improvement, and predicted that in 1836 two millions of people would be within the influence of the Erie Canal; that its tolls would in that year reach the sum of $1,000,000; and that, if the rates should not be reduced, they would amount in 1846 to $2,000,000, and in 1856 to $4,000,000.

At this session Samuel Dexter Jr. introduced a bill into the

Assembly for exploring a route to connect the waters of the
Black River with the Erie Canal, Jacob ... Van Der Hou
vel brought in a bill to construct a canal from Potsdam, in
St. Lawrence County, to the Oswegatchie, and to improve the
navigation of that river; and Thurlow Weed proposed a survey
with a view to connect the Allegheny River at Olean with the
Erie Canal at Rochester, by a navigable communication through
the valley of the Genesee River. Laws were passed at the same
session authorizing the construction of the Cayuga and Seneca
Canal, adopting the Oswego Canal as a State work, and providing for surveys for most of the other improvements recommended
by the Governor; and the Legislature, in view of the approaching completion of the main arteries of the system of inland navigation, directed that all the laws, reports, and documents relative to the canals, requisite for a complete official history of these
works, with necessary maps and profiles, should be carefully
collected and published. This duty was performed with much
accuracy by a legislative committee, with the assistance of John
Van Ness Yates, then Secretary of State, who had been one of
the most constant and efficient friends of the policy, of whose
history he thus became the guardian.

On October 26, 1825, the Erie Canal was in a navigable condition throughout its entire length, affording an uninterrupted
passage from Lake Erie to tide-water in the Hudson. Thus in
eight years artificial communications four hundred twenty-eight
miles in length had been opened between the more important
inland waters and the commercial emporium of the State. This
auspicious consummation was celebrated by a telegraphic discharge of cannon, commencing at Lake Erie, and continued
along the banks of the canal and of the Hudson, announcing to
the city of New York the entrance on the bosom of the canal of
the first barge that was to arrive at the commercial emporium
from the American Mediterraneans.

Borne in this barge, De Witt Clinton and his coadjutors enjoyed the spectacle of a free people rejoicing in the assurances
of prosperity increased and national harmony confirmed; and
were hailed, in their passage through towns and cities they
might almost be said to have called into existence, with the language of irrepressible gratitude and affection.

SIEGE OF MISSOLONGHI

A.D. 1825

GEORGE FINLAY

In 1822-1823 Missolonghi was successfully defended by the Greeks, under Marco Bozzaris, in their war of independence against Turkey. In 1825 the town was besieged by Turks and Egyptians, and although in the following year it fell, its defence was the most glorious event of the Greek revolution.

In the second year of the war (1822) the Greeks had won advantages that led them to proclaim their national independence. Then followed alternate victories and defeats, in which the deeds of Marco Bozzaris made his name famous in history and literature. His death in battle (1823) was a severe blow to the Greek cause. It is commemorated in a well-known poem by Fitz-Greene Halleck. From the time that the Provisional Government of Greece was set up (October, 1824), fighting was continuous in the mountain districts. The second siege of Missolonghi, by the Turks under Reshid Pacha and the Egyptians led by Ibrahim Pacha, is fully described and critically treated by Finlay, one of the most trustworthy and discriminating among the recent historians of Greece.

THE second siege of Missolonghi is the most glorious military operation of the Greek Revolution: it is also the most characteristic of the moral and political condition of the nation, for it exhibits the invincible energy of the Greek people in strongest contrast with the inefficiency of the military chiefs, and the inertness and ignorance of the members of the Government. Never were greater courage and constancy displayed by the population of a besieged town; rarely has less science been shown by combatants, at a time when military science formed the chief element of success in warfare.

Greek patriotism seemed to have concentrated itself within the strong walls of Missolonghi. Elsewhere hostilities languished. While the citizens of a small town, the fishermen of a shallow lagoon, and the peasants of a desolated district sustained the vigorous attack of a determined enemy, the fleets and armies of

Greece wasted their time and their strength in trifling and desultory operations. An undisciplined population maintained the entry of a trained garrison. Here, therefore, the valor of the individual demands a record in history. Yet, though private deeds of heroism were of daily occurrence, the historian shrinks from selecting the acts of heroism and the names of the warriors that deserve preëminence. All within the town seemed to be inspired by the warmest love for political liberty and national independence, and all proved that they were ready to guarantee the sincerity of their feeling with the sacrifice of their lives.

"Reshid, Pacha of Janina, or, as he was generally called, Kiutayhe, had distinguished himself at the Battle of Petta, and when he assumed the command of the Ottoman forces destined to invade Western Greece in the year 1825, much was expected by the Sultan (Mahmud II) from his well-known firmness and ability. On April 6th he seized the pass of Macronoros, which the Greek chieftains neglected to defend, and where the Greek Government had stationed only a few guards under the command of Noti Bozzaris, a veteran Suliote. No three hundred Greeks were now found to make an effort for the defence of this western Thermopylæ. The Turks advanced through Acarnania without encountering any opposition. The inhabitants fled before them, and many, with their flocks and herds, found shelter under the English flag in Calamo, where the poor were maintained by rations from the British Government; others retired to Missolonghi, and formed part of the garrison which defended that place. On April 27th Reshid established his headquarters in the plain, and two days afterward opened his first parallel against Missolonghi, at a distance of about six hundred yards from the walls. His force then consisted of only six thousand men and three guns.

Missolonghi was in a good state of defence. An earthen rampart two thousand three hundred yards in length extended from the waters of the lagoon across the promontory on which the town was built. This rampart was partly faced with masonry flanked by two bastions near the centre, strengthened toward its eastern extremity by a *lunette* and a *tenaille*, and protected where it joined the lagoon to the west by a battery on an islet called Marmora, about two hundred yards from the termination of the wall. In front of the rampart a muddy ditch, not easy to pass, separated the fortress from the adjoining plain. Forty-eight guns and four mortars were mounted in battery. The garrison consisted of four thousand soldiers and armed peasants, and one thousand citizens and boatmen. The place was well supplied with provisions and ammunition, but there were upward of twelve thousand persons to feed within the walls.

The army of Reshid never exceeded ten thousand troops, and a considerable part of it never entered the plain of Missolonghi, for he was obliged to employ about two thousand men in guarding a line of stations from Macronoros and Cravasara, on the Ambracian Gulf, to Cacescala on the Gulf of Patras, in order to keep open his communications with Arta, Prevesa, Lepanto, and Patras. But in addition to his troops, Reshid was accompanied by three thousand pioneers, muleteers, and camp-followers. It was not until the beginning of June that the besiegers obtained a supply of artillery from Patras, which increased their force to eight guns and four mortars. For several weeks, therefore, Reshid trusted more to the spade than to his artillery, and during this time he pushed forward his approaches with indefatigable industry. Early in June he had advanced to within thirty yards of the bastion Franklin, which covered the western side of the walls. But his ammunition was then so much reduced that he was compelled to fire stones from his mortars instead of shells. While the Turks were working at their approaches, the Greeks constructed traverses and erected new batteries.

Little progress had been made in the active operations of the siege, when a Greek squadron of seven sail arrived off Missolonghi on June 10th. It encouraged the besieged by landing considerable supplies of provisions and ammunition, and by announcing that Miaulis would soon make his appearance with a large fleet. The garrison, confident of success, began to make frequent and vigorous sorties. In one of these, Rutsos, a native of Missolonghi, was taken prisoner by the Turks, and was terrified into revealing to the enemy the position of the subterraneous aqueducts that supplied the town with water. The supply was immediately cut off, but fortunately the besieged found fresh water in abundance by digging new wells. The besiegers, who had pushed on their operations with great activity, at last made an attempt to carry the islot of Marmora by assault, which was repelled and entailed on them a severe loss.

The besieged now met with the first great trial of their firmness. They were eagerly awaiting the arrival of the fleet under Miaulis, which they fondly expected would compel Reshid to raise the siege. On July 10th several vessels were descried in the offing. Their joy reached the highest pitch, and they overwhelmed the advance-guard of the besiegers, which consisted of Albanians, with insulting boasts. Soon, however, fresh ships hove in sight, and it was evident that the fleet was too numerous and the ships too large to be Greek. The red flag became visible on the nearest brigs, and gradually the broad streaks of white on the hulls, and the numerous ports, showed plainly both to Greeks and Turks that this mighty force was the fleet of the Captain-Pacha. The besieged were greatly depressed, but their constancy was unshaken.

Reshid now assumed the offensive with great vigor. He introduced a number of flat-bottomed boats into the lagoon, gained possession of the islands of Aghiosostis and Procopanistos, which the Missolonghiots had neglected to fortify, and completely invested the place both by sea and land. On July 28th he made a determined attack on the bastion Bozzaris, and on August 2d he renewed the assault by a still more furious attempt to storm the bastion Franklin, in which a breach had been opened by his artillery; but both these attacks were gallantly repelled. Before the assault on the bastion Franklin, Reshid offered terms of capitulation to the garrison of Missolonghi. His offers were rejected, and, to revenge his defeat, he ordered Rutsos and some other prisoners to be beheaded before the walls. The cruisers of the Captain-Pacha informed him that the Greek fleet was approaching, before this was known to the besieged, and he made the assault on August 2d, with the hope of carrying the place before its arrival.

The Greek fleet, consisting of forty sail of the best ships that Greece still possessed, under the command of Miaulis, Sactures, Colandruzzos, and Apostoles, was descried from Missolonghi on August 3d. Next day the Ottoman fleet manœuvred to obtain an advantageous position. The Hydriot squadron in the end succceded in getting the weather-gage of the advanced ships of the Turks; yet the Greeks, in spite of this success, could not break the line of the main division, which consisted of twenty-two sail. Three fire-ships were launched in succession against the Captain-Pacha's flag-ship; but this mode of attack no longer threw the Turks into a panic terror, and they manœuvred so well that the blazing vessels drifted harmless to leeward without forcing them to break their line of battle. Chosref was, nevertheless, so intimidated by the determined manner in which the Greeks directed their attacks against his flag that he avoided a second engagement. He claimed the victory in this indecisive engagement merely because he had escaped defeat, and he made his orders to effect a prompt junction with the Egyptian fleet a pretext for sailing immediately for Alexandria. His cowardice left the flotilla of Reshid in the lagoon without support, and as the Greeks captured one of the transports laden with powder and shells for the army before Missolonghi, the besiegers were again inadequately supplied with ammunition for their mortars.

The command of the lagoons was of vital importance to the besieged. It was necessary to secure their communication with the fleet, and to prevent their being deprived of a supply of fish, which formed a considerable portion of their food. The Turks were not deprived of the advantages they had gained without a severe contest, but the skill of the Missolonghiot fishermen, who were acquainted with all the passages through the shallow water and deep mud, secured the victory, and, with the assistance of some Hydriot boats sent by Miaulis to their aid, the flotilla of Reshid was destroyed, and his Albanians were driven from the posts they had occupied in the islands. Five of the flat-bottomed boats were captured, and the Greeks recovered the command of the whole lagoon. The fleet then sailed in pursuit of the Captain-Pacha, leaving eight ships to keep open the communications between the besieged and the Ionian Islands, and prevent any supplies being sent by sea to the besieging army.

Reshid was now placed in a very difficult position. He received his supplies of provision with irregularity, both from Patras and Prevesa. His stores of ammunition were so scanty that he could not keep up a continuous fire from his guns, and was compelled to abandon the hope of carrying the place by an artillery attack. He had no money to pay his troops, and was unable to prevent great numbers of the Albanians from returning home, though he allowed all who remained double rations. On the other hand, the prospects of the besieged were very favorable. They felt confident that Reshid would be forced to raise the siege at the approach of winter, for they daily expected to hear that a Greek army had occupied the passes in his rear. It seemed therefore to be certain that if he persisted in maintaining his position, his army must perish by want and disease. The *armatoli* of Roumelia, who had quitted the Peloponnesus after their defeats at Navarin, were said to be marching into the mountains behind Lepanto, whose rugged surface is familiar to classic readers from the description which Thucydides has left us of the destruction of the Athenian army under Demosthenes.

Reshid weighed his own resources and estimated the activity of the Greek irregulars with sagacity. His guns could not render him much service, but he still believed that the spade would enable him to gain possession of Missolonghi before winter. To effect his purpose he adopted a singular but, under the circumstances in which he was placed, by no means an ill-devised method of covering the approach of a large body of men to the counterscarp of the ditch. He set his army to raise a mound by heaping up earth, and this primitive work was carried forward to the walls of the place in defiance of every effort which the besieged made to interrupt the new mode of attack. So strange a revival of the siege operations of the ancients excited the ridicule of the Greeks. They called the mound "the dike of union," in allusion to the mound which Alexander the Great constructed at the siege of Tyre. It was begun at about a hundred sixty yards from the salient angle of the bastion Franklin, and made an obtuse angle as it approached the place. Its base was from five to eight yards broad, and it was so high as to overlook the ramparts of the besieged.

By indefatigable perseverance, and after much severe fighting in the trenches, the Turks carried the mound to the ditch, filled up the ditch, and stormed the bastion Franklin. Even then they could not effect an entry into the place, for the Greeks cut off

this bastion from all communication with the rest of their defences, and soon erected batteries that completely commanded
it. They then became the assailants and after a desperate struggle drove the Turks from their recent conquest.

On August 31st all the ground they had lost was regained,
and preparations were begun for a great effort against the
mound. Several sorties were made in order to obtain exact
knowledge of the enemy's trenches. At last, on September 21st,
a great sortie was made by the whole garrison. The Turkish
camp was attacked in several places with such fury that Reshid
was unable to conjecture against what point the principal force
was directed. He was in danger of seeing his batteries stormed
and his guns spiked. After a bloody struggle the Greeks carried
the works that protected the head of the mound, and maintained
possession of their conquest until they had levelled that part of
it which overlooked their defences. While every spade in Missolonghi was employed in levelling the mound, bodies of troops
cleared the trenches and prevented the enemy from interrupt-
ing the work. As the Greeks had foreseen, rain soon rendered
it impossible for Reshid to repair the damage his works had sustained.

The garrison of Missolonghi received considerable reënforcements after the Captain-Pacha's departure. At the end of
September it still amounted to four thousand five hundred men
and was much more efficient than at the beginning of the siege.
Hitherto the fire of the Turkish artillery had been so desultory
and ill-directed that not more than one hundred persons had
been killed or wounded in the place. This trifling loss during a
six-months' siege induced the Greeks to form a very erroneous
idea of the efficiency of siege-artillery; while the facility with
which provisions and ammunition had been introduced inspired
them with a blind confidence in their naval superiority. The
only severe loss they had suffered had been in their sorties, and
in these they had hitherto been almost invariably the victors.

The Ottoman fleet, which returned to Patras on November
18th, saved Reshid's army from starvation, and furnished it with
some reënforcements and ample supplies of ammunition. The
Greek fleet ought to have engaged the Ottoman before it entered
the waters of Patras, but it did not reach the gulf until the Cap-

tain-Pacha had terminated the delicate operation of landing stores at Crioneri. A series of naval engagements then took place, in which the Turks baffled all the attempts of the Greeks to cut off their straggling ships and capture their transports. Both parties claimed the victory—the Captain-Pacha because he kept open the communications between Patras and Crioneri, and Miaulis because he succeeded in throwing supplies into Missolonghi and in keeping open its communications with the Ionian Islands. But the real victory remained with the Turks, whose fleet kept its station at Patras, while the Greeks retired from the waters of Missolonghi on December 4, 1825, and returned to Hydra.

Shortly before the departure of the Greek fleet, a new and more formidable enemy appeared before Missolonghi. The campaign in the Peloponnesus had proved that neither the courage of the *armatoli* nor the stratagems of the *clephts* were a match for the discipline and tactics of the Egyptians; and Ibrahim advanced to attack the brave garrison of Missolonghi, confident of success. He encountered no opposition in his march from Navarin to Patras. The pass of Clidi was left unguarded, and he captured large magazines of grain at Agulinitza, Pyrgos, and Gastuni, which ought either to have been previously transported to Missolonghi or now destroyed. These supplies proved of great use to Ibrahim's army during the siege.

The month of December was employed by Ibrahim in forming magazines at Crioneri, and bringing up ammunition to his camp before Missolonghi. Heavy rains rendered it impossible to work at the trenches. The whole plain, from the walls of the town to the bank of the Fidari, was either under water or formed a wide expanse of mud and marsh. The Egyptian soldiers labored indefatigably, and the order which prevailed in their camp astonished Reshid, who was said to have felt some irritation when he found that Ibrahim never asked him for any assistance or advice, but carried on his own operations with unceasing activity and perfect independence. A horrid act of cruelty perpetrated by Reshid was ascribed to an explosion of his suppressed rage. A priest, two women, and three boys, who were accused of having conveyed some intelligence to their relatives in the besieged town, were impaled by his order before the walls.

The Greeks now perceived that the progress of the besiegers, although not very rapid, would soon render the place untenable. The supplies of provisions received in January, added to what was then in the public magazines, ought to have furnished abundant rations to the whole population until the end of April; but these stores were wasted by the soldiery. Ibrahim and Reshid contrived to be well informed of everything that was said or done within the walls of Missolonghi, and they learned with pleasure that watchfulness and patience would soon force the Greeks to surrender the place or die of hunger.

The moment appeared favorable for offering a capitulation, but the besieged rejected all negotiation with disdain. Sir Frederick Adam, the Lord High Commissioner in the Ionian Islands, convinced that the loss of Vasiladi and Anatolicon rendered the fall of Missolonghi inevitable, endeavored to prevent further bloodshed. He visited Crioneri in a British ship-of-war and offered his mediation. But the two pachas were now sure of their prey, and as the Greeks refused to treat directly with them they refused all mediation, and Sir Frederick was obliged to retire without effecting anything—an example of the folly of too much zeal in other people's business.

As soon as he was gone, Ibrahim and Reshid, pretending that the Greeks had expressed a wish to learn what terms of capitulation could be obtained, sent a written summons to the garrison offering to allow all the Greek troops to quit Missolonghi on laying down their arms, and engaging to permit the inhabitants who desired to leave the town to depart with the garrison; at the same time they declared that all those who wished to remain should be allowed to retain possession of their property and should enjoy ample protection for themselves and their families. To this summons the Greeks replied that they had never expressed any wish to capitulate; that they were determined to defend Missolonghi to the last drop of their blood; that if the pachas wanted their arms they might come to take them; and that they remitted the issue of the combat to the will of God.

The only post in the lagoon of which the Greeks held possession was the small islet of Clissova, about a mile from Missolonghi, to the southeast. This post was defended by a hundred

fifty men under Cizzos Djavellas. The Greeks were advantageously posted, and protected by a rampart of earth from
the artillery of their assailants; while a low chapel, with an
arched roof of stone, served them as a magazine and citadel.
On April 6th the Albanians of Reshid attacked Clissova. The
shallow water prevented even the flat-bottomed boats of the
Turks from approaching close to its shore, so that the attacking
party was compelled to jump into the sea and wade forward
through the deep mud. While the gunboats fired showers of
grape the Greeks crouched in a ditch close to their earthen
rampart; but as soon as the Albanians jumped into the water,
they rose on their knees, and, resting the long guns on the para-
pet, poured such a well-directed volley on their enemies that the
foremost fell dead or wounded and the rest recoiled in fear. Several officers were standing up in the boats directing the landing:
they offered a conspicuous mark to the best shots among the
Greeks, and most of them fell mortally wounded. The Albanians retired in confusion.

Ibrahim then ordered his regular troops to renew the attack.
The result was similar; but the Egyptians were led back a second time to the attack, and again retreated under the deadly fire
of the Greeks. Seeing the advantage which the defenders of
Clissova derived from their position, Ibrahim ought to have
abandoned the assault and kept the islet closely blockaded until
he could bring up a few mortars. But he was eager to prove that
his regulars were superior to the Albanians of Reshid. He therefore ordered Hasan, the conqueror of Casos, Sphacteria, and
Vasiladi, to make a third attack. Hasan led his men bravely on,
but as he stood up in his boat giving orders concerning the formation of the storming parties he was struck by a musket-ball
and fell down mortally wounded. The steady fire of the Greeks
prevented the regulars from completing their formation. The
men turned and scrambled back into the boats in complete disorder. After this repulse the pachas drew off their troops. Five
hundred men were killed or wounded in this vain attempt to
storm a sand-bank defended by a hundred fifty good marks-
men.

The victory of Clissova was the last success of the Greeks
during the siege of Missolonghi. Provisions began to fail, and

rations ceased to be distributed to any but the men who performed service. Yet as relief by sea was hourly expected, the garrison remained firm.

Finally the magazines of Missolonghi did not contain rations for more than two days. The garrison had now to choose whether it would perish by starvation, capitulate, or cut its way through the besiegers. It resolved to face every danger rather than surrender. The inhabitants who were unable to bear arms, the women, and the children showed as much patience and courage in this dreadful situation as the veteran soldiers hardened in Turkish warfare. A spirit of heroism, rare in the Greek revolution — rare even in the history of mankind — pervaded every breast. After deliberate consultation in a numerous assembly, it was resolved to force a passage for the whole population through the besieging armies. Many would perish, some might escape; but those who fell and those who escaped would be alike free. A well-devised plan was adopted for evacuating the town, but its success was marred by several accidents.

About sunset on April 22, 1826, a discharge of musketry was heard by the besieged on the ridge of Zygos. This was a concerted signal to inform the chiefs in Missolonghi that a body of fifteen hundred armatoli, detached from the camp of Caraiscaci at Platanos, was ready to attack the rear of the Turks and aid the sorties of the besieged. The garrison was mustered in three divisions. Bridges were thrown across the ditch, and breaches were opened in the walls. There were still nine thousand persons in the town, of whom only three thousand were capable of bearing arms. Nearly two thousand men, women, and children were so feeble from age, disease, or starvation that they were unable to join the sortie.

Many of the relations of these helpless individuals voluntarily remained to share their fate. The noncombatants, who were to join the sortie, were drawn up in several bodies, according to the quarters in which they resided or the chiefs under whose escort they were to march. The Missolonghiots formed themselves into a separate band. They were less attenuated by fatigue than the rest; but being collected from every quarter of the town, their band was less orderly than the emigrants from the country, who had been disciplined by privation and accustomed to live and act together. Most of the women who took part in the sortie, dressed themselves in the *paramana* and carried arms, like the Albanians and armatoli; most of the children had also loaded pistols in their belts, which many had already learned to use.

At nine o'clock the bridges were placed in the ditch without noise, and a thousand soldiers crossed and ranged themselves along the covered way. Unfortunately a deserter had informed Ibrahim of the projected sortie, and both he and Reshid, though they gave little credit to the information that the whole population would attempt to escape, adopted every precaution to repulse a sortie of the garrison. When the noncombatants began to cross the bridges, the noise revealed to the Turks the positions in which the crowds were assembled, and on these points they opened a terrific fire. Crowds rushed forward to escape the shot. The shrieks of the wounded and the splash of those who were forced from the bridges were unnoticed; and in spite of the enemy's fire the greater part of the inhabitants crossed the ditch in tolerable order. The Missolonghiots still lingered behind, retarded by their interests and their feelings. It was no easy sacrifice to quit their homes and their relations. For a considerable time the garrison waited patiently for them under a heavy fire. At last the first body of the Missolonghiots crossed the ditch, and then the troops sprang forward with a loud shout and rushed sword in hand on the Turks.

Never was a charge made more valiantly. The eastern division of the garrison, under Noti Bozzaris, struggled forward to gain the road to Bochori; the central division, under Cizzos Djavellas, pushed straight through the enemy's lines toward the hills; and the western division, under Macry, strove to gain the road to the Clisura. All three intended when clear of the Turks to effect a junction on the slopes of Zygos, where the road ascends to the monastery of St. Simeon.

Almost at the moment when the garrison rushed on the Turks, that portion of the Missolonghiots which was then on the bridges raised a cry of "Back, back!" Great part of the Missolonghiots stopped, fell back, and returned into the town with the military escort which ought to have formed the rearguard of the sortie. The origin of this ill-timed cry, which weakened the force of the sortie and added to the victims in the place, has excited much unnecessary speculation. It evidently rose among those who were in danger of being forced into the ditch. Their cry was repeated so loudly that it created a panic.

The three leading divisions bore down all opposition. Neither the yataghan of Reshid's Albanians nor the bayonet of Ibrahim's Arabs could arrest their impetuous attack; and they forced their way through the labyrinth of trenches, dikes, and ditches with comparatively little loss. Only some women and children, who could not keep up with the column as it rushed forward over the broken ground, were left behind. Had it not been for the information given by the traitor, the greater part of the defenders of Missolonghi would have escaped. In consequence of that information Ibrahim and Reshid had taken the precaution to send bodies of cavalry to watch the roads leading to Bochori, St. Simeon, and Clisura. The horsemen fell in with the Greek columns when they were about a mile beyond the Turkish lines and were beginning to feel secure.

The division of Macry was completely broken by the first charge of the cavalry. The others were thrown into confusion. All suffered severely, yet small bands of the garrison still kept together, and, by keeping up a continuous fire, enabled numbers of women and children to rally under their protection. At last the scattered remnants of the three divisions began to recover some order on reaching the slopes of Zygos, where the irregularities of the ground forced the cavalry to slacken the pursuit.

The fugitives prepared to enjoy a short rest, and endeavored to assemble the stragglers who had eluded the swords of the horsemen. They were confident that the fire they had kept up against the cavalry would draw down the fifteen hundred men of Caraiscaci's corps to their assistance. While they were thus engaged in giving and expecting succor, a body of Albanians placed in ambuscade by Reshid to watch the road to the monastery of St. Simeon crept to their vicinity unperceived and poured a deadly volley into their ranks. Instead of friends to assist them, they had to encounter one thousand mountaineers, well posted, to bar their progress. The Greeks, surprised by these unseen enemies, could do nothing but get out of the range of the rifles of the Albanians. The Albanians followed and tracked them in order to secure their heads, for which the pachas had promised a high price. The loss of the Greeks was greater at the foot of the hills, where their own troops ought to have insured their safety, than it had been in forcing the enemy's lines and in resisting the charges of the cavalry. Most of the women and children who had dragged themselves thus far were so exhausted that they were taken prisoners.

About midnight small parties of the garrison, and a few women and children, succeeded in reaching the post occupied by the Greek troops; but instead of fifteen hundred men they found only fifty, with a very small supply of provisions to relieve their wants. Here they learned also, with dismay, that the camp at Platanos was a prey to the ordinary dissensions and abuses which disgraced the military classes of Greece at this period. The weary fugitives in order to escape starvation were soon compelled to continue their march to Platanos. Even there they obtained very little assistance from the chiefs of the arma-toli; and when they had rested about a week, they resumed their journey to Salona. Many perished from wounds, disease, and hunger on the road. About fifteen hundred reached Salona during the month of May, straggling thither generally in small bands, and often by very circuitous roads, which they followed in order to procure food. Of these about thirteen hundred were soldiers; there were several girls in the number of those who escaped, and a few boys under twelve years of age.

As soon as Ibrahim and Reshid found that the greater part of the garrison had evacuated Missolonghi, they ordered a general assault. Their troops occupied the whole line of the walls without encountering resistance. But it was not until morning dawned that the Turkish officers allowed their men to advance into the interior of the town, though several houses near the walls had been set on fire during the night. A whole day was spent by the conquerors in plundering Missolonghi. The Greek soldiers who were prevented from accompanying their comrades, either by wounds or sickness, intrenched themselves in the stone buildings best adapted for offering a desperate resistance. The party which occupied the principal powder-magazine, when closely attacked, set fire to the powder and perished in the explosion. A second powder-magazine was exploded by its defenders, who also perished with their assailants. A windmill, which served as a central depot of ammunition, was defended until April 24th, when its little garrison, having exhausted their provisions, set fire to the powder. All the soldiers preferred death to captivity.

The loss of the Greeks amounted to four thousand. Ibrahim boasted that the Turks had collected three thousand heads; and it is probable that at least one thousand perished from wounds and starvation beyond the limits which the besiegers examined. The nearest points where the fugitives could find security and rest were Petala, Salamis, and Salona. The conquerors took about three thousand prisoners, chiefly women and children. About two thousand escaped; for besides those who reached Salona, a few found refuge in the villages of Ætolia, and some of the inhabitants of Missolonghi and of the surrounding country evaded the Turkish pursuit by wading into the lagoon, and ultimately reached Petala and Salamis, where they received protection and rations from the British Government.

Many deeds of heroism might be recorded. One example deserves to be selected. The Morean primates have been justly stigmatized as a kind of Christian Turks; and, as a class, their conduct during the Greek revolution was marked by selfishness. Yet a Morean primate displayed a noble example of the purest patriotism at the fall of Missolonghi. Papadiamantopulos of Patras, a leading Hetairist,[1] was one of the members of the executive commission intrusted with the administration of Western Greece.

In the month of February he visited Zante to hasten the departure of supplies. His friends there urged him to remain. They said that as he was not a soldier he could assist in prolonging the defence of Missolonghi more effectually by remaining at Zante, to avail himself of every opportunity of sending over supplies, than by serving in the besieged town. But the noble old gentleman silenced every entreaty by the simple observation: "I invited my countrymen to take up arms against the Turks, and I swore to live and die with them. This is the

[1] The Hetairists were members of the Hetæria Philike, a secret political society founded in 1814 for the liberation of Greece. This organization was chiefly instrumental in bringing about the revolution.—ED.

hour to keep my promise." He returned to Missolonghi, and died the death of a hero in the final month.

John James Meyer, a young Swiss Philhellene, also deserves to have his name recorded. He came to Greece in 1821, married a maiden of Missolonghi, and at the commencement of the siege was elected a member of the military commission that conducted the defence. He was an enthusiastic democrat in his political opinions, and a man of indefatigable energy—acting as a soldier on the walls, as a surgeon in the hospital, as an honest man in the commissariat, and as a patriot in the military commission. A short time before it was resolved to force a passage through the Turkish lines, he wrote his last letter to a friend, which contains these words: "Our labors and a wound in the shoulder—a prelude to one which will be my passport to eternity—have prevented my writing lately. We suffer horribly from hunger and thirst; and disease adds to our calamities. In the name of our brave soldiers of Noti Bozzaris, Papadiamantopulos, and in my own, I declare that we have sworn to defend Missolonghi foot by foot, and to accept no capitulation. Our last hour approaches."

In the final sortie he reached the foot of the hills, carrying his child and accompanied by his wife. He was there slain, and his wife and child were made prisoners. Meyer entertained a firm conviction that constancy on the part of the Greeks would eventually force Christian nations to support their cause, and he deemed it to be his duty to exhibit an example of the constancy he inculcated. Greece owes a debt of gratitude to this disinterested stranger who served her before kings and ministers became her patrons.

The conduct of the defenders of Missolonghi will awaken the sympathies of freemen in every country as long as Grecian history endures. The siege rivals that of Platæa in the energy and constancy of the besieged; it wants only a historian like Thucydides to secure for it a like immortality of fame.

MASSACRE OF THE JANIZARIES

A.D. 1826

EDWARD UPHAM

By the destruction of the Janizaries, the Ottoman rulers—themselves oppressive despots—freed their empire from an internal despotism which for many years dominated their own. The history of the Janizaries in Turkey is much like that of the Mamelukes in Egypt. Both these military bodies were created and long recruited from the Christian slaves—" tribute children "—forced into the service of the sultans, and both were violently destroyed by the powers which had called them into existence, and which they had ruthlessly overridden.

The Janizaries were an infantry body, first organized as the sultan's guard in the fourteenth century. For three centuries they were levied as at first, and during that time they constituted the main standing army of Turkey. Afterward they were joined by Turks and other Mahometans, and became very numerous and powerful, and their history is marked by turbulence, conspiracies, and assassinations. Among their victims were sultans and viziers and other officials of the empire.

The Sultan Mahmud II, while engaged against the Greeks in their war of independence, also attempted internal reforms, with the object of Europeanizing Turkish manners and institutions. This endeavor gave offence to many of his subjects, and led to a collision with the Janizaries, whose revolt, provoked by the Sultan himself, ended in their dissolution, following the frightful scenes of massacre here described.

IT was reserved for the vigorous sceptre of Mahmud II, by one of the most sanguinary and terrific civil contests of modern history, to free the imperial throne of Othman from the intolerable yoke of the Janizary power.

To take a clear view of this important circumstance, we must advert to a name familiar in the first formation of this celebrated corps, as well as in many instances of their insubordination and rebellion under different sultans. Halet Effendi had been ambassador to the court of France, and was tinctured with the literature of Europe. The Sultan, pleased with his acquirements, appointed him to the situation of *nizamdge*, or keeper of the signet, and he became so useful to the Prince that for several years he was the mainspring of the Cabinet. The Janizaries, however, took great umbrage at this influence and employed the dervis Hadji Bektash to express their sentiments to the minister, confiding that his sacred caste would give an impunity to his interference. The Bektash dervises are a numerous and highly venerated community in Asia Minor, and the corps owed its institution and its sanctity to a dervis of this class in the reign of Amurath, whence one of these divines had always officiated in the *namaz* of prayer in the Orta mosque. Hadji Bektash ventured to speak freely to Halet Effendi, which gave great offence; and the Hadji disappeared, being probably privately strangled.

The Janizaries, indignant at this mysterious disappearance, held more frequent meetings, and the result was a demand for the dismissal of seven of the ministers the most obnoxious to the soldiery, which was presented to the Sultan on his way to the mosque. (A man stands in a conspicuous place in the street as the Sultan approaches, holding in both hands the paper which he sets over his head to mark that it is for the Sultan's eye; if the Sultan gives the sign an attendant takes the paper and puts it into a bag for inspection.) He did so, as the Sultan dismounted and as he performed his official duty of holding the Sultan's stirrup, when the Sultan declared his total ignorance of the subject. A great fermentation now arose in the public mind, and Mahmud paraded the streets of his capital to ascertain the public excitement; the consequence of this state of things was that the ministry was broken up, four of its members were exiled, and Halet Effendi was eventually decapitated.

Whether this sacrifice really grew out of any discoveries made to the disadvantage of the former favorite, or whether it became a necessary sacrifice to allay the discontent of the Janizaries, it is clear that though not the immediate, yet it was the remote cause of the extinction of that corps. Mahmud could bear the domination of his Janizaries no longer, and resolved to get rid of them altogether. It had long been the desire of the Government to introduce new systems of discipline; but every attempt had been fatal to the innovator: and yet the events of the Greek war, and the successes of the Egyptian forces, through their superior discipline, convinced every thinking man of its necessity.

The Sultan determined to make another attempt; and if the

Janizaries assented he designed to hold them in check with his disciplined troops, but if they resisted to extirpate them altogether. In conformity with his designs, the Janizaries were to furnish from each *orta* one hundred fifty men, who were to be instructed and drilled in European tactics by the Egyptian officers. As the Turks are so led away by terms, and a great offence had arisen from the term of *nizam-gedit*, a new institution, so the same thing was now called *nizam-gttei*, or the old regulation, and all were satisfied, it being declared to be merely a revival of an exercise used in Solyman's time.

They were so far advanced in the appointed evolutions that June 15, 1826, was appointed for a general review, at which the Sultan, the *ulema*, and ministers were to attend, and it was to take place in the great square of the Atmeidan. On the day preceding, the troops were brought together to exercise, that they might be expert in their movements on the grand day, and it was now for the first time that the Janizaries perceived that they were practising the very thing that they had all determined to resist. A *bairactar*, or standard-bearer, called out, "Why, this is very like Russian manœuvring!" A general discontent ensued; they instantly assailed the palace of the Janizary *aga*, who had scarcely time to escape, and they killed his *kiaia*, and even insulted his harem, and then spread themselves over the city to arouse their companions to a revolt. The Sultan was at this time at Beshiktash, a kiosk a few miles up the Bosporus; the Janizary aga, the grand vizier, and other ministers hastened thither from the Porte to inform him of what had happened. The ministers had scarcely left the palace of the Porte ere the mutineers arrived; the building was pillaged and stripped, and the archives were destroyed. The insurrection now assumed that desperate character which always announced, in the furious moments of the Janizaries, their settled resolve to proceed to extremities; their kettles sounded mournfully through the streets in the way to the Atmeidan, which immense square was soon filled with the insurgents, and above twenty thousand were thus assembled.

The crisis had arrived that had been both expected and feared by the Sultan, and he energetically resolved to call forth the resources which he had long secretly prepared. Immediate orders were transmitted to the Pacha-Aga of Yenikui, and to the Topgee Bashi, a commander of artillery, to hold themselves in readiness with their forces. A council was then called of all the principal members of the Divan; and Mahmud energetically stated the ill-conduct and mischief of the Janizaries, also the resolve he had formed to put an end to such a dangerous influence.

The Sultan added that rather than submit to such a system he would at once retire into Asia and leave Constantinople and European Turkey to its fate; and he proposed to display the *san-jak-she-riff*, as a measure of necessity, that all good Mussulmans might rally round it.

The proposition was unanimously approved of, and the various orders were rapidly issued. The standard was taken accordingly from the imperial treasury, and borne to the Sultan Achmet's mosque; the *ulemas* and the *softas* preceded, the Sultan and his court followed, all rehearsing the *Koran*. The zealous Mussulmans rushed from all quarters to gaze upon and rally under the sacred symbol. The standard, borne into the mosque, was placed in the pulpit, and the Sultan pronounced an anathema on all who refused to range themselves under it. The Pacha-Aga's troops now arrived from the Bosporus; the Topgee Bashi landed his artillery at the Yali kiosk, under the walls of the seraglio; the *galiendgoes*, or marines, and the *bostanji*, or household guard, were also in readiness; all seemed as perfectly matured as it was sagaciously planned.

Four officers of rank were now despatched by the Sultan to the Atmeidan to offer pardon to the Janizaries if they would immediately disperse; which offer was scornfully rejected and the four officers were wantonly put to death; for long experience had made them presume upon their most extravagant propositions being ultimately accepted. The Sultan demanded then of the *mufti* if he might kill his subjects in case of their rebellion? The mufti answered affirmatively; upon which the Sultan required a *fetsa*, and prepared to accomplish the long-projected design.

The Pacha-Aga had by this time collected about sixty thousand men on whom he could fully depend, and he received immediate orders to put the Janizaries down by force of arms, which he lost no time in executing. He entirely surrounded the

Atmeidan, where they were assembled in a dense crowd and were without the slightest intimation of the Sultan's intention. The first conviction of their horrid situation was from a general discharge of grape-shot, which did vast havoc upon their crowded masses; great numbers being killed, the survivors were obliged to retire to their *kislas*, or barracks, which were close by; here they shut themselves up, and, as the crisis had decided the Sultan to give no quarter, orders were given to set fire to the edifices and consume them together with all their unhappy inmates; and the dreadful command was faithfully performed.

The barracks were surrounded, like the Atmeidan, by cannon which thundered on the walls without intermission. No situation can be conceived more horrible than that of the Janizaries: the houses in flames over their heads, the buildings battered down and torn in pieces by grape-shot, and overwhelmed with ruins and burning fragments. As it was determined to exterminate them utterly, no quarter was given or received. The Janizaries, notwithstanding the great odds at which they were taken, defended themselves with extraordinary fierceness and slew a vast number of their assailants.

The work of death proceeded, and the infatuated victims were crushed, or destroyed by the devouring flames, and the smouldering ruins as they fell in. The burning fragments overwhelmed them all, until, the conflagration being at length extinguished by the lack of any proximate fuel to feed upon, the Atmeidan presented, on the ensuing morning, a hideous spectacle of burning ruins slaked in blood, and a mingled mass of dead bodies and smoking ashes.

For two days afterward the city gates continued closed, during which time, such was the relentless rigor of the Sultan, that the bostanghis searched every corner of the city for whatever Janizaries might have escaped the massacre of their comrades; these, when found, were led away to appointed spots, where executioners were stationed to decapitate their victims. Vast numbers were thus slaughtered in those human shambles, which were horrible to behold. The blaze of fires and the report of cannon ceased, and at length the public laborers were directed to cleanse the city, which had thus become one immense charnel-house. The number of Janizaries who perished could never be distinctly ascertained, but they evidently, in the capital alone, greatly exceeded twenty thousand, independently of the numbers which perished in the provinces

The gates of Constantinople were at length opened to Christians and all comers to pursue their customary avocations. The Sultan appeared in the uniform of a new corps, and went to the mosque, attended by the *seimen*, the *topgees*, the bostanji, instead of his usual guard of Janizaries, whose *nizams*, or badges, were everywhere torn down and trampled upon. On the next day, Mahmud, as the "Caliph of the Faithful," publicly anathematized the whole body of the Janizaries, inhibited the mention of their name or any allusion to them, and in their place solemnly conferred the appellation of "*Assakini-Muhamuditch*," or forces of Mahomet, on the new army forming to replace them; and.in the evening *fellahs*, or public criers, were everywhere sent about the city and suburbs, to proclaim that tranquillity was restored.

Thus, after four centuries and a half, the class of Janizaries perished, who had been the most powerful support of the empire in the first centuries of their institution, but who eventually became an inflexible barrier to all progressive improvement, and the fomenters of continued intestine troubles and commotions; being all-powerful to work evil, and incapacitated, by their ignorance, their enervated and licentious habits, to contribute in any degree to the well-being or advantage of the State.

It is certainly an anomaly in history, to behold a great empire thus shake off all its veteran force, its positive and existing strength, changing its long-recognized character and its entire system, and with so much of sternness massacring the bulk of its most efficient soldiery, at the very instant in which it is about to enter upon a contest not merely for power, but for its very existence, against a grasping, ambitious neighbor [Russia] of such superior strength. Had time been allowed to him, Mahmud had evidenced energies commensurate to the almost Herculean task of infusing life, vigor, and renovation into the inert mass of Turkish imbecility; but the alarms and the dangers of war had come on too instantly after the singular and astonishing event and the appalling catastrophes which we have just described.

The last mention made of the falling corps relates to a feeble and expiring effort in the month of August, 1828, when a number of the disbanded Janizaries, who had repaired to the capital under the pretext of enlisting in the new levies then making, were detected in a conspiracy which had been organized for calling on all their dispersed members throughout the Empire to rise in insurrection.

The Sultan gave orders for their immediate execution, and by his rigor stifled the plot.　Great alarm was, however, felt at the first moment; and it delayed for several days the march of the grand vizier with the reënforcements for the army in the camp at Shumla, opposed to the Russians.

THE BATTLE OF NAVARINO

A.D. 1827

HARRIET MARTINEAU

At Navarino Turkish sea power was destroyed. The Greeks, who for six years had been struggling to free themselves from the Ottoman yoke, were soon enabled to establish their independence. The Battle of Navarino was the turning-point of the Greek revolution, and is fairly numbered among the decisive battles of the world, although other events subsequently contributed to the liberation of Greece.

Navarino is a small seaport on the bay of the same name in the present Grecian nomarchy or district government of Messenia. It was captured in May, 1825, by Ibrahim Pacha, the Egyptian vassal of the Turks. Greek affairs were now in a precarious condition, which soon became more critical, and foreign aid was invoked.

In July, 1827, a treaty was made by England, Russia, and France whereby they agreed to mediate between Greece and Turkey. Mediation was refused by the Sultan, Mahmud II, who at once made thorough preparations for a new campaign. The allied powers were equally prepared to meet this move, and the ensuing operations are described by Miss Martineau. Her account also embraces preceding events, including operations in which two British officers, Admiral Cochrane and Sir Richard Church, respectively commanded the naval and land forces of the Greeks.

In 1828 and 1829 Russia alone, for her own purposes, warred successfully against Turkey, and in the Peace of Adrianople (September 14, 1829), that ended this conflict, the Sultan recognized the independence of Greece, and the resurrected state has ever since maintained its place in the family of nations.

B Y the end of 1826 the whole of Western Greece was recovered by the Turks; and the Greek Government had transferred itself to the islands. Men who find it at all times difficult to agree, are sure to fall out under the provocations of adversity, and the dissensions of the Greek leaders ran higher now than ever. It was this quarrelling which prevented the Greeks from taking advantage of some successes of their brave General Caraiscaci to attempt the relief of Athens, closely pressed by the Turks. The Turkish force was soon to be strengthened by troops already on their march; and now, before their arrival, was the time to at-

tempt to relieve Athens.   Some aid was sent, and some fighting
went on, on the whole with advantage to the Greeks; but nothing
decisive was done till Lord Cochrane arrived among them, rated
them soundly for their quarrels, and took the command of their
vessels, the Greek Admiral Miaulis being the first and most
willing to put himself under the command of the British officer.
In a little while Count Capo d'Istria, an official esteemed by the
Russian Government, was appointed President of Greece for
seven years.

The Turkish reënforcements had arrived, absolutely unopposed, before Athens, and this rendered necessary the strongest
effort that could be made for the deliverance of the place.   General Church brought up forces by land, and Lord Cochrane by
sea; and by May 1st the flower of the Greek troops, to the number of ten thousand, were assembled before the walls of Athens.
It was soon too clear to the British commanders that nothing was to
be done with forces so undisciplined and in every way unreliable.
The troops of Caraiscaci lost their leader, and incurred disaster
by fighting without orders, and then through a series of mistakes
and follies the issue became hopeless.

Between eight and ten o'clock in the morning of the 6th all
was ruined.   The killed and wounded of the Greeks amounted
to two thousand five hundred, and the rest were dispersed like
chaff before the wind.   Of those who escaped, the greater number took refuge in the mountains.   Lord Cochrane was compelled to throw himself into the sea and swim to his ship.   General Church strove hard to maintain his fortified camp at the
Phalerus, with three thousand men whom he had collected; but
when he found that some of the Greek officers were selling his
provisions to the enemy, he gave up and retired to Ægina, sorely
grieved, but not in despair.   Lord Cochrane kept the sea, generally with his single frigate, the Hellas, contributed to the cause
by the United States, and now and then with a few Greek vessels
when their commanders had nothing better to do than to obey
orders.   He was alone when he took his station off Navarino to
watch the fleet of the Egyptian Ibrahim; and he had better have
been alone when he went on to Alexandria to look after the fleet
which the Pacha was preparing there, for when the Egyptians
came out to offer battle the Greeks made all sail homeward.

The Turks now supposed they had everything in their own hands.   On the intervention of the French Admiral de Rigny they spared the lives of the garrison of the Acropolis, permitting them to march out with their arms and go whither they would. Then all seemed to be over.   The Greeks held no strong places but Corinth and Napoli, and had no army; while the Turks held all the strong places but Corinth and Napoli, and had two armies at liberty—that of the Egyptian leader in the West, and of the Turkish *seraskier* in the East—to put down any attempted rising within the bounds of Greece.   But at this moment of extreme humiliation for Greece aid was preparing, and hope was soon to arise out of despair.   While Canning was fighting his own battles in Parliament, he had his eye on what was passing in Greece; and the fall of Athens and the dispersion of the Greek forces only strengthened his resolution that the powers of Europe should hasten the interposition he had planned long before.

It was important to Russia that Turkey should be weakened in every possible way; and Russia was therefore on the side of the Greeks.   The sympathies of France and England were on the side of the Greeks, but they must also see that Greece should be freed in reality, and that Turkey should not be destroyed; so they were willing to enter into alliance with Russia to part the combatants, preserve both, impose terms on both, and see that the terms were observed.   The Duke of Wellington had gone to St. Petersburg to settle all this; and the ministers of the three courts laid before the Government of the Porte at Constantinople the requisition of the allies.   The great object was to separate the Turks and the Greeks—the faithful and the infidels—who could never meet without fighting; and it was proposed—or we may rather say ordained—by the allies, that all the Turks should leave Greece, receiving compensation—in some way to be devised—for the property they must forsake.   The Greeks were to pay a tribute to the Porte, and to be nominally its subjects, and the Turkish Government was to have some sort of veto on the appointment of officials, but substantially the choice of officers and the enjoyment of their own mode of living were to be left to the Greeks.

As might be expected, the victorious Turk was amazed at this interference between himself and his rebellious subjects; and if he would not listen to dictation before the fall of Athens, much less would he afterward. There was threat as well as dictation —threat of enforcing the prescribed conditions; but the Porte treated the threat as loftily as it rejected the interference.

The rejection was too natural and reasonable not to be received as final; and the three powers proceeded therefore to their acts of enforcement. Canning, ill and wearied after the close of the session, exerted himself to transact some public business. The chief item of this business was causing to be signed the treaty with France and Russia concerning the affairs of Greece, which was finished off in London and immediately despatched to Constantinople. In this treaty the alliance and its purposes were justified on the ground of " the necessity of putting an end to the sanguinary contests which, by delivering up the Greek provinces and the isles of the Archipelago to the disorders of anarchy, produce daily fresh impediments to the commerce of the European States and give occasion to piracies which not only expose the subjects of the contracting powers to considerable losses, but render necessary burdensome measures of suppression and protection." England and France, moreover, pleaded the appeals they had received from the Greeks. The treaty concluded with a declaration and pledge of disinterestedness—of desiring nothing which the whole world beside was not at liberty to obtain.

A month from the date of the arrival of the instructions to the ambassadors at Constantinople was the time allowed to the Porte for consideration. If the terms of the three powers were not by that time acceded to, they must proceed to the threatened enforcement, with every intention to preserve their own pacific relations with Turkey. The work of mediation was to be carried on by force in such a case under the plea that such a proceeding would be best for the interests of the contending powers, and necessary for the peace and comfort of the rest of the world. There were squadrons of all the three powers ready in the Levant—that of Russia being commanded by Admiral Heiden; that of France by Admiral de Rigny; and that of England by Sir Edward Codrington.

The formal note of the ambassadors at Constantinople was delivered in on August 16th, with a notification that an answer would be expected in fifteen days. On August 30th, no reply

having been volunteered, it was asked for, and given only verbally Again the Porte declined recognizing any interference be
tween itself and its rebellious subjects; and when the consequent
notice of enforcement was given, the Turkish Government became, as any other government would, in like circumstances,
bolder in its declaration of persistence in its own rights. Then
began a season of activity at Constantinople such as had seldom
been witnessed there; horses and provisions pouring in from the
country, and sent off, with ammunition, arms, and stores, to occupy the ports along the Bosporus and Dardanelles. There was
an incessant training of troops under the eye of the Sultan or his
vizier, and the capital seemed in a way to be turned into a camp.
There is something striking in the only words the Turkish minister would utter, in the final interview of September 14th. "God
and my right," said he, in the calmest manner; "such is the
motto of England. What better answer can we give when you
intend to attack us?"

Meantime the Egyptian fleet, strongly reënforced, had arrived
in the Morea, and the English commander had no right to interpose any obstacle, the time being the end of August, and the
answer of the Porte not being yet delivered. Sir Edward Codrington, however, hailed Ibrahim, informed him of what was
going on at Constantinople, and offered him a safe-conduct if he
wished to return to Egypt. But if he chose to enter the harbor
of Navarino, to join the Turkish fleet there, he must clearly understand that any of his vessels attempting to get out would be
driven back. Ibrahim chose to enter. There now lay the ninety-
two Egyptian vessels and the Turkish fleet crowded in the harbor;
and off its mouth lay the British squadron on the watch.

For some time Ibrahim occupied himself in preparing his
troops for action against the Greeks; but on September 19th he
determined to try an experiment. He sent out a division of the
Turkish fleet to see if the English would let them pass. Sir Edward Codrington warned them back, but the Turkish commander replied that he was under no other orders than those of
Ibrahim. The Egyptian Prince—being referred to by both parties
and afterward by the French Admiral, who had come up with his
squadron, and the danger of the case amply explained to him—
declared that he would recall the Turkish ships, and wait the re-

turn of couriers whom he would send to Constantinople and to
Alexandria; but that as soon as he received orders to sail, his
whole combined fleet would come out and brave all opposition.

A sort of armistice was agreed on, verbally, for twenty days,
during a long conference between the Egyptian, French, and English commanders, on September 25th. The two latter trusted to
Ibrahim's word that his ships would not leave the harbor for the
twenty days—ample facilities having been allowed by them for
the victualling of his troops; and they sailed for Zante to obtain
fresh provisions for their fleet. As soon as they were gone, only
five days after the conference, Ibrahim put out to sea, to sail to
Patras. On October 2d an armed brig brought notice to Sir
Edward Codrington of this violation of the treaty. The Admiral
immediately returned with a very small force, met successively
two divisions of the Turkish fleet, and turned them back to Navarino. In his wrath Ibrahim carried war inland, slaughtering
and burning, and driving the people to starvation, and even up-
rooting the trees wherever he went, that no resources might be
left to the wretched inhabitants.

As the spirit of the Treaty of London was thus broken through,
the three admirals concluded to compel an adherence to the terms
agreed upon at the conference, by entering the harbor and placing
themselves, ship by ship, in guard over the imprisoned fleets.
The strictest orders were given that not a musket should be fired
unless firing should begin on the other side. They were permitted to pass the batteries and take up their position; but a boat
was fired upon by the Turks, probably under the impression that
she was sent to board one of their vessels. A lieutenant and several of the crew were killed. There was a discharge of musketry
in return by an English and a French vessel; and then a cannon-
shot was received by the French Admiral's ship, which was answered by a broadside.

The action, probably intended by none of the parties, was
now fairly begun; and when it ended, there was nothing left of
the Turkish and Egyptian fleets but fragments of wrecks strewing
the waters. As the crews left their disabled vessels they set them
on fire; and among the dangers of the day to the allied squadrons, not the least was from these floating furnaces drifting about

among a crowd of ships. The battle, which took place on October 20th, lasted four hours. The Turkish and Egyptian forces
suffered cruelly. Of the Allies the English suffered the most, but
with them the loss was only seventy-five killed, and the wounded
were fewer than two hundred. The three British line-of-battle
ships had to be sent home after being patched up at Malta for the
voyage.

The anxiety of mind of the three admirals is said to have been
great—both on account of the calamity itself, and the doubt about
how their conduct of the affair would be viewed at home. One
reasonable apprehension was that there would be a slaughter of
the Christians at Constantinople. But things were now conducted there in a more cautious and deliberate manner than of
old. An embargo was laid on all the vessels in the harbor; but
the mob of the faithful were kept in check. There were curious
negotiations between the Government and the ambassadors,
while each party was in possession of the news and wanted to
learn how much the other knew. The Sultan himself wished to
declare war at once, but his counsellors desired to gain time; and
there were doubts, fluctuations, and bootless negotiations, in
which neither party would concede anything for several weeks.
The Turks would yield nothing about Greece, and the allies
would yield neither compensation nor apology for the affair of
Navarino.

On December 8th, however, it being clear that nothing could
be gained by negotiation, the ambassadors left Constantinople.
The Christian merchants might have embarked with them, but
they must have left their property behind; and some preferred
remaining. The Turkish authorities went to great lengths in
encouraging them to do so; but whether this was from pacific
inclinations, or from a sense of their value as hostages, could not
be certainly known; and the greater number did not relish trusting themselves to conjecture in such a case. The day before the
ambassadors left, an offer was made of a general amnesty to the
Greeks. But this was not what was required. As they sailed
out of the harbor, the Sultan must have felt that he was left deprived of his fleet, at war with Russia, England, and France.
But the coolness and ability shown by his Government in circumstances so extremely embarrassing as those of this autumn, were

evidence that there were minds about him very well able to see that if Russia desired to crush him, England and France would take care that she did not succeed.

As for the Greeks, their Government was thankful to accept the mediation of the allies, but so weak as to be unable to enforce any of their requisitions.   Piracy under the Greek flag reached such a pass in the Levant that Great Britain had to take the matter into her own hands.   In the month of November it was decreed, by an order in council, that the British ships in the Mediterranean should seize every vessel they saw under the Greek flag or armed and fitted out at a Greek port, except such as were under the immediate orders of the Greek Government.

Thus the British carried matters with a high hand in regard to both parties concerned in the unhappy Greek war.   It is a case on which so much is to be said on every side that it is impossible to help sympathizing with all parties in the transactions preceding and following the Battle of Navarino—with the Greeks, for reasons which the heart apprehends more rapidly than tongue or pen can state them; with the Porte, under the provocation of the interference of strangers between her and her rebellious subjects; with the Egyptians, in their duty of vassalage—however wrongly it might be performed; and with the allied powers in their sense of the intolerableness of a warfare so cruel and so hopeless going on amid the haunts of commerce, and to the disturbance of a world otherwise at peace; and with two of those three allies in their apprehension of Turkey being destroyed, and Greece probably once more enslaved by the power and arts of the third.

JACKSON ELECTED PRESIDENT OF THE UNITED STATES

A.D. 1828

JAMES PARTON

In the election of Andrew Jackson as seventh President of the United States the extreme elements and principles of the Democratic party of that period signally triumphed. The victory of Jackson and Calhoun, the Vice-President, over John Quincy Adams and Richard Rush, candidates of the National Republicans, introduced a new element into American national politics, which ever since has remained a cause of contention and the chief question of civil-service reform. It is known as the " Spoils System," and is " the practice or plan of distributing government patronage among the adherents of the political party in power, and displacing political opponents without regard to merit."

The origin of this practice in the United States is traced to New York and Pennsylvania, where as early as the beginning of the nineteenth century the honors and emoluments of public office were bestowed as rewards for partisan services. It is noteworthy that the application of this method on a national scale, which began early in Jackson's Administration, should soon have led to a popular naming of it from a phrase used by a New York statesman. This was Senator William L. Marcy,. who in a speech in the United States Senate, in 1831, declared that " to the victors belong the spoils."

General Jackson had become famous by his military services, and was greatly esteemed for his energy and courage and his rugged honesty, qualities which a certain narrowness of view, arbitrariness, and violence of temper never obscured. While amid the many strifes that disturbed his administration he did much to increase his popularity in some quarters, his inauguration of the Spoils System called forth widespread protest, which has never ceased to be repeated among those who would eliminate the practice from American politics.

THE most real issue in the Presidential contest of 1828 was one which was not stated at the time nor generally perceived. The question was whether "universal suffrage," so called, was to have any practical effect in the United States. Down to this period in the history of the Republic, the educated few had kept themselves uppermost. Cabinets, congresses, legislatures, governors, mayors, had usually been chosen from the same class of society as that from which the governing men of Europe are chosen.   Public life was supposed to require an apprenticeship, as much as any private profession.   In short, the ruling class in the United States, as in all other countries, was chiefly composed of men who had been graduated at colleges and had passed the greater part of their lives on carpets.

The truly helpful men and women of this Republic have oftenest sprung from the cabin, and learned to read by the light of pine-knots, and worked their way up to their rightful places as leaders of the people by the strength of their own arm, brain, and resolution.

The sceptre was about to be wrested from the hands of those who had not shown themselves worthy to hold it.   When they felt it going, however, they made a vigorous clutch, and lost it only after a desperate struggle.   In these Jacksonian contests, therefore, we find nearly all the talent, nearly all the learning, nearly all the ancient wealth, nearly all the business activity, nearly all the book-nourished intelligence, nearly all the silver-forked civilization of the country, united in opposition to General Jackson, who represented the country's untutored instincts.

The number of electoral votes in 1828 was two hundred sixty-one.   One hundred thirty-one was a majority.   General Jackson received one hundred seventy-eight; Adams eighty-three.   With the exception of one electoral district in Maine, Adams and Rush received the entire vote of New England.   Of the thirty-six electoral votes cast by the State of New York, Adams and Rush obtained sixteen; Jackson and Calhoun, twenty.   New Jersey voted entire for Adams and Rush; so did Delaware.   In Maryland, the same candidates obtained a bare majority—six votes to Jackson's five.   In Georgia, William H. Crawford had influence enough to withdraw seven votes out of nine from Calhoun, and throw them away upon William Smith, of South Carolina.   The entire vote of Georgia, however, was given to General Jackson, Crawford more than consenting thereto.

Every other State in the Union—Pennsylvania, Virginia, both Carolinas, Kentucky, Ohio, Tennessee, Indiana, Louisiana, Alabama, Mississippi, Missouri, Illinois—gave an undivided vote for Jackson and Calhoun.   For the Vice-Presidency Calhoun received one hundred seventy one votes, out of two hundred ninety-one.   There were no scattering or wasted votes except the seven cast for William Smith in Georgia.

In all Tennessee, Adams and Rush obtained fewer than three thousand votes.   In many towns every vote was cast for Jackson and Calhoun.   A distinguished member of the North Carolina Legislature told me that he happened to enter a Tennessee village in the evening of the last day of the Presidential election of 1828. He found the whole male population out hunting—the objects of the chase being two of their fellow-citizens.   He inquired by what crime these men had rendered themselves so obnoxious to their neighbors, and was informed that they had voted against General Jackson.   The village, it appeared, had set its heart upon sending up a unanimous vote for the General, and these two voters had frustrated its desire.   As the day wore on, the whiskey flowed more and more freely, and the result was a universal chase after the two voters, with a view to tarring and feathering them.   They fled to the woods, however, and were not taken.

Very many of the supporters of Adams felt, doubtless, as Ezekiel Webster felt, when he wrote to his brother Daniel, in February, 1829: "The people always supported Adams's cause from a cold sense of duty, and not from any liking of the man. We soon satisfy ourselves that we have discharged our duty to the cause of any man, when we do not entertain for him one personal kind feeling, and cannot, unless we disembowel ourselves, like a trussed turkey, of all that is human nature within us.   If there had been at the head of affairs a man of popular character, like Henry Clay, or any man whom we are not compelled by our natures, instincts, and fixed fate to dislike, the result would have been different."

So the whole country joined at last in the cry, "Hurrah for Jackson!"   Some few daring spirits at Hartford, we are told, burned the President-elect in effigy in the evening of the sacred January 8th; but the public indignation was such that the authorities of the city offered a reward of one hundred dollars for the "conviction of the persons engaged in it."   So says the sedate Niles, who also records, in his brief manner, without comment, that General Jackson did not call upon President Adams on his arrival in Washington. The reader knows why he did not. The precious *Register* of Mr. Niles rescues likewise from oblivion the fact that "General Merkle, of Franklin Market, New York," sent to General Jackson "a piece of the celebrated ox, Grand Canal, as a suitable tribute of General Merkle's high respect for the patriotism General Jackson has uniformly displayed in the public service of his country, and hopes at the same time it may arrive to grace his table on March 4th."

General Merkle had the pleasure of receiving an autograph acknowledgment from General Jackson: "Permit me, sir, to assure you of the gratification which I felt in being enabled to place on my table so fine a specimen of your market, and to offer you my sincere thanks for so acceptable a token of your regard for my character." "Hurrah for Jackson!" It was the universal cry. Adams would not have written to General Merkle, of Franklin Market, New York, perhaps. Was there a butcher in the Union who did not take the General's autograph as a personal compliment!

While General Jackson was receiving hundreds of visitors daily at his rooms in the Indian Queen Tavern, commonly styled the "Wigwam," the White House, we are informed, was nearly deserted. Judge Joseph Story mentions, in one of his letters to his wife, that the "birth-night ball" (February 22d) was thinly attended this year. "Adams has no more favors to bestow, and he is now passed by with indifference by all the fair-weather friends. They are all ready to hail the rising sun. Never have I felt so forcibly the emptiness of public honors and public favor." Eight years later there was a setting sun who was not "passed by with indifference" by friend or foe.

From the many rash and careless remarks of General Jackson some readers have inferred that the General was not, at all times, master of his tongue. Such an inference is incorrect. When it was his cue to be silent no man could keep his own counsel better. All Washington was busied, during these weeks, with conjectures as to the course of the President-elect, and, above all, as to his intentions with regard to appointments and removals. But all conjecturing was vain. Nothing was ascertained until he chose to reveal it. Daniel Webster wrote home just before the General's arrival: "General Jackson will be here about February

15th. Nobody knows what he will do when he does come. Many letters are sent to him; he answers none of them. His friends here pretend to be very knowing; but, be assured, not one of them has any confidential communication from him. Great efforts are making to put him up to a general sweep as to all offices, springing from great doubt whether he is disposed to go it."

A few days after General Jackson's arrival, Webster resumed his observations upon the scene around him. "Of course," said he, "the city is full of speculation and speculators. 'A great multitude,' too many to be fed without a miracle, are already in the city, hungry for office. Especially, I learn, that the typographical corps is assembled in great force—from New Hampshire, our friend Hill; from Boston, Greene; from Connecticut, Norton; from New York, Noah; from Kentucky, Kendall; and from everywhere else, somebody else. So many friends ready to advise, and whose advice is so disinterested, make somewhat of a numerous council about the President-elect; and, if report be true, it is a council which only 'makes that darker which was dark enough before.' For these reasons, or these with others, nothing is settled yet about the new Cabinet. I suppose Van Buren will be Secretary of State; but beyond that I do not think anything is yet determined." This was written on February 19th.

General Jackson, meanwhile, so closely concealed his intentions that, as late as March 2d, Webster still wrote home that nobody in Washington knew whether many or any changes in the subordinate offices of the Government would be made. "Probably," he wrote, "General Jackson will make some removals, but I think not a great many immediately. But we shall soon see." Yes, we shall soon see.

The day of the inauguration was one of the brightest and balmiest of the spring. An eye-witness shall describe to us the memorable scene:

"No one who was at Washington at the time of General Jackson's inauguration is likely to forget that period to the day of his death. To us, who had witnessed the quiet and orderly period of the Adams Administration, it seemed as if half the nation had rushed at once into the capital. It was like the inundation of the northern barbarians into Rome, save that the tumultuous tide came in from a different point of the compass.   The West and the South seemed to have precipitated themselves upon the North and overwhelmed it.   On that memorable occasion you might tell a 'Jackson man' almost as far as you could see him.   Their every motion seemed to cry out 'Victory!'   Strange faces filled every public place, and every face seemed to bear defiance on its brow.   It appeared to me that every Jackson editor in the country was on the spot.   They swarmed, especially in the lobbies of the House, an expectant host, a sort of Prætorian band, which, having borne in upon their shields their idolized leader, claimed the reward of the hard-fought contest.   His quarters were assailed, surrounded, hemmed in, so that it was an achievement to get into his presence.

" On the morning of the inauguration, the vicinity of the Capitol was like a great agitated sea; every avenue to the fateful spot was blocked up with people, insomuch that the legitimate procession which accompanied the President-elect could scarce make its way to the eastern portico, where the ceremony was to be performed.   To repress the crowd in front, a ship's cable was stretched across about two-thirds of the way up the long flight of steps by which the Capitol is approached on that side, but it seemed, at times, as if even this would scarce prove sufficient to restrain the eagerness of the multitude, every man of whom seemed bent on the glory of shaking the President's hand.   Never can I forget the spectacle which presented itself on every side, nor the electrifying moment when the eager, expectant eyes of that vast and motley multitude caught sight of the tall and imposing form of their adored leader, as he came forth between the columns of the portico; the color of the whole mass changed, as if by miracle; all hats were off at once, and the dark tint which usually pervades a mixed mass of men was turned, as by a magic wand, into the bright hue of ten thousand upturned and exultant human faces, radiant with sudden joy.   The peal of shouting that arose rent the air and seemed to shake the very ground.   But when the Chief Justice took his place and began the brief ceremony of administering the oath of office, it quickly sank into comparative silence; and as the new President proceeded to read his inaugural address, the stillness gradually increased; but all efforts to hear him, beyond a brief space immediately around, were utterly vain."

Webster, in his serio-comic manner, remarks: "I never saw such a crowd here before. Persons have come five hundred miles to see General Jackson, and they really seem to think that the country is rescued from some dreadful danger!"

The ceremony over, the President drove from the Capitol to the White House, followed soon by a great part of the crowd who had witnessed the inauguration. Judge Story, a strenuous Adams man, did not enjoy the scene which the apartments of the "palace," as he styles it, presented on this occasion. "After the ceremony was over," he wrote, "the President went to the palace to receive company, and there he was visited by immense crowds of all sorts of people, from the highest and most polished, down to the most vulgar and gross in the nation. I never saw such a mixture. The reign of 'King Mob' seemed triumphant. I was glad to escape from the scene as soon as possible."

Constitution-makers do all they can to support the weakness of human virtue when subjected to the temptations of power and place. But virtue cannot be dispensed with in this world. No system of "checks and balances" can be made so perfect but that much must be left, after all, to the honor of governing persons.

Among the powers intrusted to the honor of Presidents of the United States was the dread power of removing from office, without trial or notice, the civil employees of the Government. In the army and navy, no officer can be cashiered, no private dismissed, without trial—without being heard in his defence. In the civil service of the country, every man holds his place at the will of the head of government.

This fearful power over the fortunes of individuals and the happiness of families is held, necessarily, in our present imperfect civilization, by a large number of persons in private life; and it is one of the ten thousand proofs of the inherent loving-kindness of human nature that this power is generally exercised with a considerable regard for the feelings, the necessities, and the rights of the employed. The claim of old servants to indulgence and protection is almost universally recognized. The right, of a person about to be dismissed from an employment, to as long a notice of dismission beforehand as can be conveniently given, few persons are unfeeling enough to deny. The good policy of hold-

ing out to the faithful employee the prospect of a permanent retention of his place, and his promotion, by and by, to a better, no
one but a politician has been foolish enough to question.

It does not appear to have occurred to the gentlemen who
formed the Constitution under which we live, that there could
ever be a President of the United States who would abuse the
power of removal. His own responsibility for the conduct of
those whom he appointed was supposed to be sufficient to make
him careful to appoint the right men to the right places; and his
feelings, as a man and a gentleman, were deemed an adequate
protection to those right men in their right places.

It is delightful to observe with what a scrupulous conscien-
tiousness the early Presidents of this Republic disposed of the
places in their gift. Washington set a noble example. He demanded to be satisfied on three points with regard to an applicant
for office: Is he honest? Is he capable? Has he the confidence
of his fellow-citizens? Not till these questions were satisfactorily
answered did he deign to inquire respecting the political opinions
of a candidate. Private friendship between the President and an
applicant was absolutely an obstacle to his appointment, so fearful was the President of being swayed by private motives. "My
friend," he says, in one of his letters, "I receive with cordial welcome. He is welcome to my house, and welcome to my heart;
but with all his good qualities he is not a man of business. His
opponent, with all his politics so hostile to me, *is* a man of business. My private feelings have nothing to do in the case. I am
not George Washington, but President of the United States. As
George Washington, I would do this man any kindness in my
power—as President of the United States, I can do nothing."
There spoke the man who was a gentleman to the core of his
heart.

If General Washington would not appoint a friend because
he was a friend, nor a partisan because he was a partisan, still less
was he capable of removing an enemy because he was an enemy,
or an opponent because he was an opponent. During his administration of eight years, he removed nine persons from office;
namely, six unimportant collectors, one district surveyor, one
vice-consul, and one foreign minister. We all know that he recalled Charles C. Pinckney from Paris because that conservative

gentleman was offensive to the French Directory. The other dismissals were all "for cause." Politics had nothing to do with one of them.

The example of George Washington was followed by his successors. John Adams doubted, even, whether it was strictly proper for him to retain his son in a foreign employment to which President Washington had appointed him. He removed nine subordinate officers during his Presidency, but none for political opinion's sake. Jefferson, owing to peculiar circumstances well known to readers of history, removed thirty-nine persons; but he himself repeatedly and solemnly declared that not one of them was removed because he belonged to the party opposed to his own. The contrary imputation he regarded in the light of a calumny, and refuted it as such. In one respect Jefferson was even over-scrupulous. He would not appoint any man to office, however meritorious, who was a relative of his own. Madison made five removals; Monroe, nine; John Quincy Adams, two. Calhoun tells us that during the seven years that he held the office of Secretary of War only two of his civil subordinates were removed, both for improper conduct. In both cases, he adds, the charges were investigated in the presence of the accused, and "the officers were not dismissed until after full investigation, and the reason of dismission reduced to writing and communicated to them."[1] Colonel McKenney mentions, in his *Memoirs*, that when a vacancy occurred in one of the departments, the chief of that department would inquire among his friends for "a qualified" person to fill it.

Nor was this scrupulousness due to any lack of aspirants for governmental employment. John Quincy Adams says, in one of his letters, that he was tormented with ceaseless, with daily applications for office. In the last year of Monroe's Presidency, when the Fourth Auditorship of the Treasury fell vacant, there were, among the army of applicants for the place, five United States Senators and thirty members of the House of Representatives!

---

[1] Napoleon was a despot, it is said; yet he never dismissed anyone from public office without an inquiry and report of facts, and rarely ever without hearing the accused functionary, never when the questions involved were civil or administrative.—LOUIS NAPOLEON.

Up to the hour of the delivery of General Jackson's inaugural address, it was supposed that the new President would act upon the principles of his predecessors.   In his Monroe letters he had taken strong ground against partisan appointments, and when he resigned his seat in the Senate he had advocated two amendments to the Constitution designed to limit and purify the exercise of the appointing power.   One of these proposed amendments forbade the reëlection of a President, and the other the appointment of members of Congress to any office not judicial.

The sun had not gone down upon the day of his inauguration before it was known in all official circles in Washington that the "reform" alluded to in the inaugural address meant a removal from office of all who had conspicuously opposed, and an appointment to office of those who had conspicuously aided the election of the new President.   The work was promptly begun.   Figures are not important here, and the figures relating to this matter have been disputed.

Some have declared that during the first year of the Presidency of General Jackson two thousand persons in the civil employment of the Government were removed from office, and two thousand partisans of the President appointed in their stead. This statement has been denied.   It cannot be denied that in the first month of this Administration more removals were made than had occurred from the foundation of the Government to that time.   It cannot be denied that the principle was now acted upon that partisan services should be rewarded by public office, though it involved the removal from office of competent and faithful incumbents.

Colonel Benton will not be suspected of overstating the facts respecting the removals, but he admits that their number, during the year (1829), was six hundred ninety.   He expresses himself on this subject with less than his usual directness.   His estimate of six hundred ninety does not include the little army of clerks and others who were at the disposal of some of the six hundred ninety.   The estimate of two thousand includes all who lost their places in consequence of General Jackson's accession to power; and, though the exact number cannot be ascertained, I presume it was not less than two thousand.   Colonel Benton says that of the eight thousand postmasters, only four hundred ninety-one were removed; but he does not add, as he might have added, that the four hundred ninety-one vacated places comprised mainly all in the department that were worth having. Nor does he mention that the removal of the postmasters of half a dozen great cities was equivalent to the removal of many hundreds of clerks, bookkeepers, and carriers.

General Harrison, who had courteously censured General Jackson's course in the Seminole war, who had warmly defended his friend, Henry Clay, against the charge of bargain and corruption, was recalled from Colombia just four days after General Jackson had acquired the power to recall him. General Harrison had only resided in Colombia a few weeks when he received the news of his recall. A Kentuckian, who was particularly inimical to Clay, was sent out to take his place.

The appointment of a soldier so distinguished as General Harrison to represent the United States in the infant Republic of Colombia was regarded by the Colombians as a great honor done them, and an emphatic recognition of their disputed claim to a place among the nations. A purer patriot, a worthier gentleman, than General William Henry Harrison, has not adorned the public service of his country. His singular merits as a scholar, as a man of honor, as a soldier, and as a statesman, were only obscured by the calumny and eulogium incident to a Presidential campaign. My studies of the Indian affairs of the country have given me the highest idea of his valor, skill, and humanity.

Samuel Swartwout was among the expectants at Washington —an easy, good-natured man; most inexact and even reckless in the management of business; the last man in the whole world to be intrusted with millions. He had hopes of the collectorship of New York. On March 14th he wrote from Washington to his friend, Jesse Hoyt, to let him know how he was getting on, and to give Hoyt the benefit of his observations—Hoyt himself being a seeker. "I hold to your doctrine fully," wrote Swartwout, "that no d—d rascal who made use of his office or his profits for the purpose of keeping Adams in and General Jackson out of power is entitled to the least lenity or mercy, save that of hanging. So we both think alike on that head. Whether or not I shall get anything in the general scramble for plunder, remains to be proven; but I rather think I shall. What it will be is not yet so certain; perhaps keeper of the Bergen lighthouse.

"I rather think Massa Pomp stands a smart chance of going somewhere, perhaps to the place you have named, or to the devil. Your man, if you want a place, is Colonel Hamilton [Acting Secretary of State until the arrival of Van Buren]—he being now the second officer in the Government of the Union, and in all probability our next President. Make your suit to him, then, and you will get what you want."

The President, distracted with the number of applications for the New York collectorship, and extremely fond of Swartwout, gave him the place. Upon his return to New York his proverbial good-nature was put to a severe test; for the applicants for posts in the custom-house met him at every turn, crowded his office, invaded his house, and stuffed his letter-box. There was a general dismission of Adams men from the New York Custom-house, and the new appointments were made solely on the ground that the applicants had aided the election of General Jackson.

Henry Lee was appointed to a remote foreign consulship, a place which he deemed beneath his talents and an inadequate reward for his services. He would probably have obtained a better place but for the fear that the Senate would reject the nomination. The Senate did reject his nomination even to the consulship, and by such a decided majority that nothing could be done for him. Even Colonel Benton voted against him. Lee, I may add, died soon afterward in Paris, where he wrote part of a history of the Emperor Napoleon.

Terror, meanwhile, reigned in Washington. No man knew what the rule was upon which removals were made. No man knew what offences were reckoned causes of removal, nor whether he had or had not committed the unpardonable sin. The great body of officials awaited their fate in silent horror, glad, when the office hours expired, at having escaped another day. "The gloom of suspicion," says Stansbury, himself an office-holder, "pervaded the face of society. No man deemed it safe and prudent to trust his neighbor, and the interior of the department presented a fearful scene of guarded silence, secret intrigue, espionage, and tale-bearing. A casual remark, dropped in the street, would, within an hour, be repeated at headquarters; and many a man received unceremonious dismission who could not, for his life, conceive or conjecture why it is he had ~~~~~~~~~~.

At that period, it must be remembered, to be removed from office in the city of Washington was like being driven from the solitary spring in a wide expanse of desert. The public treasury was almost the sole source of emolument. Salaries were small, the expenses of living high, and few of the officials had made provision for engaging in private business or even for removing their families to another city. No one had anticipated the necessity of removal. Clerks, appointed by the early Presidents, had grown gray in the service of the Government, and were so habituated to the routine of their places that if removed they were beggared and helpless.

An old friend of General Jackson's was in Washington that summer. He wrote on July 4th to a friend: "I have seen the President, and have dined with him, but have had no free communication or conversation with him. The reign of this Administration—I wish another word could be used—is in very strong contrast with the mild and lenient sway of Madison, Monroe, and Adams. To me it feels harsh; it seems to have had an unhappy effect on the free thoughts and unrestrained speech which have heretofore prevailed. I question whether the ferreting out Treasury rats, and the correction of abuses, are sufficient to compensate for the reign of terror which appears to have begun. It would be well enough if it were confined to evil-doers, but it spreads abroad like a contagion: spies, informers, denunciations—the fecula of despotism. Where there are listeners there will be talebearers. A stranger is warned by his friend on his first arrival to be careful how he expresses himself in relation to anyone or anything which touches the Administration. I had hoped that this would be a national Administration; but it is not even an administration of a party. Our Republic henceforth will be governed by factions, and the struggle will be who shall get the offices and their emoluments—a struggle embittered by the most base and sordid passions of the human heart."

So numerous were the removals in the city of Washington that the business of the place seemed paralyzed. In July a Washington paper said:

"Thirty-three houses which were to have been built this year have, we learn, been stopped, in consequence of the unsettled and uncertain state of things now existing here; and the merchant cannot sell his goods or collect his debts, from the same cause. We have never known the city to be in a state like this before, though we have known it for many years. The individual distress, too, produced in many cases by the removal of the destitute officers, is harrowing and painful to all who possess the ordinary sympathies of our nature, without regard to party feeling. No man, not absolutely brutal, can be pleased to see his personal friend or neighbor suddenly stripped of the means of support, and cast upon the cold charity of the world without a shelter or a home. Frigid and insensible must be the heart of that man who could witness some of the scenes that have lately been exhibited here, without a tear of compassion or a throb of sympathy.

"But what is still more to be regretted is that this system, having been once introduced, must necessarily be kept up at the commencement of every Presidential term; and he who goes into office knowing its limited and uncertain tenure, feels no disposition to make permanent improvements or to form for himself a permanent residence. He therefore takes care to lay up what he can, during his brief official existence, to carry off to some more congenial spot where he means to spend his life, or reënter into business. All, therefore, that he might have expended in city improvements is withdrawn, and the revenue of the corporation, as well as the trade of the city, is so far lessened and decreased. It is obviously a most injurious policy as it respects the interests of our city. Many of the oldest and most respectable citizens of Washington, those who have adhered to its fortunes through all their vicissitudes, who have 'grown with its growth and strengthened with its strength,' have been cast off to make room for strangers who feel no interest in the prosperity of our infant metropolis, and who care not whether it advances or retrogrades."

BEGINNING OF RAILWAY LOCOMOTION

A.D. 1829

SAMUEL SMILES

Following closely upon the beginning of steam-navigation, the intro-duction of railways, with cars drawn by steam-locomotives, was the greatest triumph, up to that period, of mechanical invention. As early as 1759, according to James Watt, the application of the steam-engine to locomotion on land was suggested by the Scottish physicist John Robi-son. In 1784 Watt himself patented a locomotive-engine, but he never executed his plans. In 1804 or 1805 the first locomotive-engine was con-structed and used by Richard Trevithick and Andrew Vivian, English engineers.

Many experiments for improving the locomotive and adapting it for use upon a serviceable track were subsequently made before Stephenson succeeded in rendering railway locomotion clearly practicable.

George Stephenson was born near Newcastle-upon-Tyne, England, in 1781. The son of a workingman, educated himself in mechanics and en-gineering, and in 1812 became enginewright of a colliery at Killingworth. Here he constructed a " travelling engine," which in 1814 was successfully used on the Killingworth Railway. In 1825 the Stockton and Darling-ton Railway, built by Stephenson, was opened for traffic, and the cars drawn on this line by his locomotives were the first to be so moved for carrying both goods and passengers.

On the opening of the Liverpool and Manchester Railway, in 1830, Stephenson's achievement became fully established, and steam-locomo-tion was permanently installed for the service of mankind. The story of the official competitive trial of locomotives and the triumph of Stephen-son's Rocket is one of the most interesting among Smiles's many ac-counts of great achievements.

THE works of the Liverpool and Manchester Railway were approaching completion. But, strange to say, the directors had not yet decided as to the tractive power to be employed in working the line when opened for traffic. The differences of opinion among them were so great as apparently to be irrecon-cilable. It was necessary, however, that they should come to some decision without further loss of time, and many board meetings were accordingly held to discuss the subject. The old-fashioned and well-tried system of horse haulage was not without its advocates; but, looking at the large amount of traffic to be conveyed, and at the probable delay in the transit from station to station if this method were adopted, the directors, after a visit made by them to the Northumberland and Durham railways in 1828, came to the conclusion that the employment of horse-power was inadmissible.

Fixed engines had many advocates; the locomotive, very few: it stood as yet almost in a minority of one—George Stephenson. Grave doubts still existed as to the practicability of working a large traffic by means of travelling engines. The most celebrated engineers offered no opinion on the subject. They did not believe in the locomotive, and would scarcely take the trouble to examine it. The ridicule with which George Stephenson had been assailed by the barristers before the parliamentary committee had not been altogether distasteful to them. Perhaps they did not relish the idea of a man who had picked up his experience in Newcastle coalpits, appearing in the capacity of a leading engineer before Parliament, and attempting to establish a new system of internal communication in the country.

The directors could not disregard the adverse and conflicting views of the professional men whom they consulted. But Stephenson had so repeatedly and earnestly urged upon them the propriety of making a trial of the locomotive before coming to any decision against it, that they at length authorized him to proceed with the construction of one of his engines by way of experiment. In their report to the proprietors at their annual meeting on March 27, 1828, they say that they had, after due consideration, authorized the engineer "to prepare a locomotive-engine, which, from the nature of its construction and from the experiments already made, he is of opinion will be effective for the purposes of the company, without proving an annoyance to the public." The locomotive thus ordered was placed upon the line in 1829, and was found of great service in drawing the wagons full of marl from the two great cuttings.

In the mean time the discussion proceeded as to the kind of power to be permanently employed for the working of the railway.

The directors were inundated with schemes of all sorts for facilitating locomotion. The projectors of England, France, and America assailed in a lot loose upon them. There were plans for working the wagons along the line by water-power. Some proposed hydrogen, and others carbonic acid gas. Atmospheric pressure had its eager advocates. And various kinds of fixed and locomotive steam-power were suggested. Thomas Gray urged his plan of a greased road with cog-rails; and Messrs. Vignolles and Ericsson recommended the adoption of a central friction rail, against which two perpendicular rollers under the locomotive, pressing upon the sides of this rail, were to afford the means of ascending the inclined planes.

The directors felt themselves quite unable to choose from amid this multitude of projects. Their engineer expressed himself as decidedly as heretofore in favor of smooth rails and locomotive-engines, which, he was confident, would be found the most economical and by far the most convenient moving power that could be employed. The Stockton and Darlington Railway being now at work, another deputation went down personally to inspect the fixed and locomotive engines on that line, as well as at Hetton and Killingworth. They returned to Liverpool with much information; but their testimony as to the relative merits of the two kinds of engines was so contradictory that the directors were as far from a decision as ever.

They then resolved to call to their aid two professional engineers of high standing, who should visit the Darlington and Newcastle railways, carefully examine both modes of working—the fixed and the locomotive—and report to them fully on the subject. The gentlemen selected were Mr. Walker, of Limehouse, and Mr. Rastrick, of Stourbridge. After carefully examining the working of the Northern lines, they made their report to the directors in the spring of 1829. They concurred in the opinion that the cost of an establishment of fixed engines would be somewhat greater than that of locomotives to do the same work, but they thought the annual charge would be less if the former were adopted. They calculated that the cost of moving a ton of goods thirty miles by fixed engines would be 6.40 pence (twelve and one-fifth cents), and by locomotives 8.36 pence, assuming a profitable traffic to be obtained both ways.

At the same time it was admitted that there appeared more grounds for expecting improvements in the construction and working of locomotives than of stationary engines. "On the whole, however, and looking especially at the computed annual charge of working the road on the two systems on a large scale, Messrs. Walker and Rastrick were of opinion that fixed engines were preferable, and accordingly recommended their adoption to the directors." And in order to carry the system recommended by them into effect, they proposed to divide the railroad between Liverpool and Manchester into nineteen stages of about a mile and a half each, with twenty-one engines fixed at the different points to work the trains forward.

Such was the result, so far, of George Stephenson's labors. The two best practical engineers of the day concurred in reporting substantially in favor of the employment of fixed engines. Not a single professional man of eminence could be found to coincide with the engineer of the railway in his preference for locomotive over fixed engine power. He had scarcely a supporter, and the locomotive system seemed on the eve of being abandoned. Still he did not despair. With the profession against him and public opinion against him—for the most frightful stories went abroad respecting the dangers, the unsightliness, and the nuisance which the locomotive would create—Stephenson held to his purpose. Even in this, apparently the darkest, hour of the locomotive, he did not hesitate to declare that locomotive railroads would, before many years had passed, be the great highways of the world.

He urged his views upon the directors in all ways, in season, and, as some of them thought, out of season. He pointed out the greater convenience of locomotive power for the purposes of a public highway, likening it to a series of short unconnected chains, any one of which could be removed and another substituted without interruption to the traffic; whereas the fixed-engine system might be regarded in the light of a continuous chain extending between the two termini, the failure of any link of which would derange the whole. But the fixed-engine party were very strong at the board, and, led by Mr. Cropper, they urged the propriety of forthwith adopting the report of Messrs. Walker and Rastrick. Mr. Sandars and Mr. William Rathbone, on the other hand, desired that a fair trial should be given to the locomotive; and they with reason objected to the expenditure of the large capital necessary to construct the proposed engine-houses, with their fixed engines, ropes, and machinery, until they had tested the powers of the locomotive as recommended by their own engineer.

George Stephenson continued to urge upon them that the locomotive was still capable of great improvements, if proper inducements were held out to inventors and machinists to make them; and he pledged himself that, if time were given him, he would construct an engine that should satisfy their requirements, and prove itself capable of working heavy loads along the railway with speed, regularity, and safety. At length, influenced by his persistent earnestness not less than by his arguments, the directors, at the suggestion of Mr. Harrison, determined to offer a prize of five hundred pounds for the best locomotive-engine which on a certain day should be produced on the railway, and perform certain specified conditions in the most satisfactory manner. The conditions were these:

1. The engine must effectually consume its own smoke.

2. The engine, if of six tons' weight, must be able to draw after it, day by day, twenty tons' weight (including the tender and water-tank) at ten miles an hour, with a pressure of steam on the boiler not exceeding fifty pounds to the square inch.

3. The boiler must have two safety-valves, neither of which must be fastened down, and one of them be completely out of the control of the engineman.

4. The engine and boiler must be supported on springs, and rest on six wheels, the height of the whole not exceeding fifteen feet to the top of the chimney.

5. The engine, with water, must not weigh more than six tons; but an engine of less weight would be preferred on its drawing a proportionate load behind it; if of only four and a half tons, then it might be put on only four wheels. The company to be at liberty to test the boiler, etc., by a pressure of one hundred fifty pounds to the square inch.

6. A mercurial gauge must be affixed to the machine, showing the steam pressure above forty-five pounds per square inch.

7. The engine must be delivered, complete and ready for

trial, at the Liverpool end of the railway, not later than October 1, 1829.

8. The price of the engine must not exceed five hundred fifty pounds.

Many persons of influence declared the conditions published by the directors of the railway chimerical in the extreme. One gentleman of some eminence in Liverpool, Mr. P. Ewart, who afterward filled the office of government inspector of post-office steam-packets, declared that only a parcel of charlatans would ever have issued such a set of conditions; that it had been *proved* to be impossible to make a locomotive-engine go at ten miles an hour; but if it ever was done, he would undertake to eat a stewed engine-wheel for his breakfast!

The requirements of the directors as to speed were certainly not excessive. Perhaps they had in mind the animadversions of the *Quarterly Reviewer* on the absurdity of travelling at a greater velocity than ten miles an hour, and also the remarks published by Mr. Nicholas Wood, whom they selected to be one of the judges of the competition, in conjunction with Mr. Rastrick, of Stourbridge, and Mr. Kennedy, of Manchester.

It was now felt that the fate of railways in a great measure depended upon the issue of this appeal to the mechanical genius of England. When the advertisement of the prize for the best locomotive was published, scientific men began more particularly to direct their attention to the new power which was thus struggling into existence. In the mean time public opinion on the subject of railway working remained suspended, and the development of the undertaking was watched with intense interest.

During the progress of this important controversy with reference to the kind of power to be employed in working the railway, George Stephenson was in constant communication with his son Robert, who made frequent visits to Liverpool for the purpose of assisting his father in the preparation of his reports to the board on the subject. Mr. Swanwick remembers the vivid interest of the evening discussions which then took place between father and son as to the best mode of increasing the powers and perfecting the mechanism of the locomotive. He wondered at their quick perception and rapid judgment on each other's suggestions; at the mechanical difficulties which they anticipated and provided for in the practical arrangement of the machine; and he speaks of these evenings as most interesting displays of two actively ingenious and able minds stimulating each other to feats of mechanical invention, by which it was ordained that the locomotive-engine should become what it now is. These discussions became more frequent and still more interesting after the public prize had been offered for the best locomotive by the directors of the railway, and the working plans of the engine which they proposed to construct had to be settled.

One of the most important considerations in the new engine was the arrangement of the boiler and the extension of its heating surface to enable steam enough to be raised rapidly and continuously for the purpose of maintaining high rates of speed.

In Stephenson's first Killingworth engines he applied the ingenious method of stimulating combustion in the furnace by throwing the waste steam into the chimney after it had performed its office in the cylinders, thereby accelerating the ascent of the current of air, greatly increasing the draught and consequently the temperature of the fire. This plan was adopted by him as early as 1815, and it was so successful that he himself attributed to it the greater economy of the locomotive as compared with horse-power. Hence the continuance of its use upon the Killingworth Railway.

Though the adoption of the steam-blast greatly quickened combustion and contributed to the rapid production of high-pressure steam, the limited amount of heating-surface presented to the fire was still felt to be an obstacle to the complete success of the locomotive-engine. Mr. Stephenson endeavored to overcome this by lengthening the boilers and increasing the surface presented by the flue-tubes. The Lancashire Witch, which he built for the Bolton and Leigh Railway, and used in forming the Liverpool and Manchester Railway embankments, was constructed with two tubes, each of which contained a fire and passed longitudinally through the boiler. But this arrangement necessarily led to a considerable increase in the weight of those engines, which amounted to about twelve tons each; and as six tons were the limit allowed for engines admitted to the Liverpool competition, it was clear that the time was come when the Killingworth engine must undergo a further important modification.

For many years previous to this period, ingenious mechanics had been engaged in attempting to solve the problem of the best and most economical boiler for the production of high-pressure steam. The use of tubes in boilers for increasing the heating surface had long been known. As early as 1780, Matthew Boulton employed copper tubes longitudinally in the boiler of the Wheal Busy engine in Cornwall—the fire passing through the tubes—and it was found that the production of steam was thereby considerably increased.

The use of tubular boilers afterward became common in Cornwall. In 1803 Woolf, the Cornish engineer, patented a boiler with tubes, with the same object of increasing the heating-surface. The water was inside the tubes, and the fire of the boiler outside. Similar expedients were proposed by other inventors. In 1815 Trevithick invented his light high-pressure boiler for portable purposes, in which, to "expose a large surface to the fire," he constructed the boiler of a number of small perpendicular tubes "opening into a common reservoir at the top." In 1823 W. H. James contrived a boiler composed of a series of annular wrought-iron tubes, placed side by side and bolted together, so as to form by their union a long cylindrical boiler, in the centre of which, at the end, the fireplace was situated. The fire played round the tubes, which contained the water. In 1826 James Neville took out a patent for a boiler with vertical tubes surrounded by the water, through which the heated air of the furnace passed, explaining also in his specification that the tubes might be horizontal or inclined, according to circumstances. Mr. Goldsworthy Gurney, the persevering adapter of steam-carriages to travelling on common roads, applied the tubular principle in the boiler of his engine, in which the steam was generated within the tubes; while the boiler invented by Messrs. Summers and Ogle for their turnpike-road steam-carriage consisted of a series of tubes placed vertically over the furnace, through which the heated air passed before reaching the chimney.

About the same time George Stephenson was trying the effect of introducing small tubes in the boilers of his locomotives, with the object of increasing their evaporative power. Thus in 1829 he sent to France two engines constructed at the Newcastle works for the Lyons and St. Étienne Railway, in the boilers of which tubes were placed containing water. The heating-surface was thus considerably increased, but the expedient was not successful, for the tubes, becoming furred with deposit, shortly burned out and were removed. Then M. Seguin, the engineer of the railway, pursuing the same idea, is said to have adopted his plan of employing horizontal tubes through which the heated air passed in streamlets, and for which he took out a French patent.

In the mean time Henry Booth, secretary to the Liverpool and Manchester Railway, whose attention had been directed to the subject on the prize being offered for the best locomotive to work that line, proposed the same method which, unknown to him, Matthew Boulton had employed, but not patented, in 1780, and James Neville had patented, but not employed, in 1826; and it was carried into effect by Robert Stephenson in the construction of the Rocket, which won the prize at Rainhill in October, 1829. The following is Mr. Booth's account in a letter to the author:

"I was in almost daily communication with Mr. Stephenson at the time, and I was not aware that he had any intention of competing for the prize till I communicated to him my scheme of a multitubular boiler. This new plan of boiler comprised the introduction of numerous small tubes two or three inches in diameter and less than one-eighth of an inch thick, through which to carry the fire, instead of a single tube or flue eighteen inches in diameter and about half an inch thick, by which plan we not only obtain a very much larger heating-surface, but the heating-surface is much more effective, as there intervenes between the fire and the water only a thin sheet of copper or brass, not an eighth of an inch thick, instead of a plate of iron of four times the substance, as well as an inferior conductor of heat.

"When the conditions of trial were published I communicated my multitubular plan to Mr. Stephenson, and proposed to him that we should jointly construct an engine and compete for the prize. Mr. Stephenson approved the plan and agreed to my proposal. He settled the mode in which the fire-box and tubes were to be mutually arranged and connected, and the engine was constructed at the works of Messrs. Robert Stephenson and Company, Newcastle-on-Tyne.

"I am ignorant of M. Seguin's proceedings in France, but I claim to be the inventor in England, and feel warranted in stating, without reservation, that until I named my plan to Mr. Stephenson, with a view to compete for the prize at Rainhill, it had not been tried, and was not known in this country."

From the well-known high character of Mr. Booth we believe his statement to be made in perfect good faith, and that he was as much in ignorance of the plan patented by Neville as he was of that of Seguin. As we have seen, from the many plans of tubular boilers invented during the preceding thirty years, the idea was not by any means new; and we believe Mr. Booth to be entitled to the merit of inventing the method by which the multitubular principle was so effectually applied in the construction of the famous Rocket engine.

The principal circumstances connected with the construction of the Rocket, as described by Robert Stephenson to the author, may be briefly stated. The tubular principle was adopted in a more complete manner than had yet been attempted. Twenty-five copper tubes, each three inches in diameter, extended from one end of the boiler to the other, the heated air passing through them on its way to the chimney; the tubes being surrounded by the water of the boiler, it will be obvious that a large extension of the heating-surface was thus effectually secured. The principal difficulty was in fitting the copper tubes in the boiler-ends so as to prevent leakage. They were manufactured by a Newcastle coppersmith, and soldered to brass screws which were screwed into the boiler-ends, standing out in great knobs. When the tubes were thus fitted and the boiler was filled with water, hydraulic pressure was applied; but the water squirted out at every joint, and the factory floor was soon flooded.

Robert went home in despair; and in the first moment of grief he wrote to his father that the whole thing was a failure. By return of post came a letter from his father telling him that despair was not to be thought of—that he must try again; and he suggested a mode of overcoming the difficulty, which his son had already anticipated and proceeded to adopt. It was to bore clean holes in the boiler-ends, fit in the smooth copper tubes as tightly as possible, solder up, and then raise the steam. This plan succeeded perfectly, the expansion of the copper tubes completely filling up all interstices and producing a perfectly water-tight boiler fully capable of withstanding extreme external pressure

The mode of employing the steam-blast for the purpose of increasing the draught in the chimney was also the subject of numerous experiments. When the engine was first tried, it was thought that the blast in the chimney was not sufficiently strong for the purpose of keeping up the intensity of the fire in the furnace, so as to produce high-pressure steam with the required velocity. The expedient was therefore adopted of hammering the copper tubes at the point at which they entered the chimney, whereby the blast was considerably sharpened; and on a further trial it was found that the draught was increased to such an extent as to enable abundance of steam to be raised. The rationale of the blast may be simply explained by referring to the effect of contracting the pipe of a water-hose, by which the force of the jet of water is proportionately increased; widen the nozzle of the pipe, and the jet is in like manner diminished. So is it with the steam-blast in the chimney of the locomotive.

But doubts were expressed whether the greater draught obtained by the contraction of the blast-pipe was not counterbalanced in some degree by the negative pressure upon the piston. Hence a series of experiments was made with pipes of different diameters, and their efficiency was tested by the amount of vacuum that was produced in the smoke-box. The degree of rarefaction was determined by a glass tube fixed to the bottom of the smoke-box, and descending into a bucket of water, the tube being open at both ends. As the rarefaction took place, the water would of course rise in the tube, and the height to which it rose above the surface of the water in the bucket was made the measure of the amount of rarefaction. These experiments proved that a considerable increase of draught was obtained by the contraction of the orifice; accordingly, the two blast-pipes opening from the cylinders into either side of the Rocket's chimney, and turned up within it, were contracted slightly below the area of the steam-ports; and before the engine left the factory, the water rose in the glass tube three inches above the water in the bucket.

The other arrangements of the Rocket were briefly these:

The boiler was cylindrical, with flat ends, six feet in length and three feet four inches in diameter. The upper half of the boiler was used as a reservoir for the steam, the lower half being filled with water. Through the lower part the copper tubes extended, being open to the fire-box at one end and to the chimney at the other. The fire-box, or furnace, two feet wide and three feet high, was attached immediately behind the boiler, and was also surrounded with water. The cylinders of the engine were placed on each side of the boiler, in an oblique position, one end being nearly level with the top of the boiler at its after end, and the other pointing toward the centre of the foremost or driving pair of wheels, with which the connection was directly made from the piston-rod to a pin on the outside of the wheel. The engine, together with its load of water, weighed only four tons and a quarter; and it was supported on four wheels, not coupled. The tender was four-wheeled, and similar in shape to a wagon, the foremost part holding the fuel, and the hind part a water-cask.

When the Rocket was finished, it was placed upon the Killingworth Railway for the purpose of experiment. The new boiler arrangement was found perfectly successful. The steam was raised rapidly and continuously and in a quantity which then appeared marvellous. The same evening Robert despatched a letter to his father at Liverpool, informing him, to his great joy, that the Rocket was "all right," and would be in complete working trim by the day of trial. The engine was shortly afterward sent by wagon to Carlisle, and thence shipped for Liverpool.

The time so much longed for by George Stephenson had now arrived, when the merits of the passenger locomotive were about to be put to the test. He had fought the battle for it until now almost single-handed. Engrossed by his daily labors and anxieties, and harassed by difficulties and discouragements which would have crushed the spirit of a less resolute man, he had held firmly to his purpose through good and through evil report. The hostility which he experienced from some of the directors opposed to the adoption of the locomotive was the circumstance that caused him the greatest grief of all; for where he had looked for encouragement he found only carping and opposition. But his pluck never failed him; and now the Rocket was upon the ground to prove, to use his own words, "whether he was a man of his word or not."

Great interest was felt at Liverpool, as well as throughout the country, in the approaching competition. Engineers, scientific men, and mechanics arrived from all quarters to witness the novel display of mechanical ingenuity on which such great results depended. The public generally were no indifferent spectators either. The populations of Liverpool, Manchester, and the adjacent towns felt that the successful issue of the experiment would confer upon them individual benefits and local advantages almost incalculable, while populations at a distance waited for the result with almost equal interest.

On the day appointed for the great competition of locomotives at Rainhill the following engines were entered for the prize: (1) Messrs. Braithwaite and Ericsson's[1] Novelty. (2) Timothy Hackworth's Sanspareil. (3) Messrs. R. Stephenson and Company's Rocket. (4) Burstall's Perseverance. Another engine was entered by Mr. Brandreth, of Liverpool—the Cycloped—weighing three tons, worked by a horse in a frame, but it could not be admitted to the competition. These four were the only ones exhibited, out of a considerable number of engines constructed in different parts of the country in anticipation of this contest, many of which could not be satisfactorily completed by the day of trial.

The ground on which the engines were to be tried was a level piece of railroad, about two miles in length. Each was required to make twenty trips, or equal to a journey of seventy miles, in the course of the day, and the average rate of travelling was to be not under ten miles an hour. It was determined that, to avoid confusion, each engine should be tried separately and on different days. The day fixed for the competition was October 1, 1829, but, to allow sufficient time to get the locomotives into good working order, the directors extended it to the 6th. On the morning of the 6th the ground at Rainhill presented a lively appearance, and there was as much excitement as if the St. Leger were about to be run. Many thousand spectators looked on,

[1] John Ericsson (born in Sweden, 1803), who later came to the United States (1839) and, among other noted works, constructed the turreted ironclad Monitor (1862).—ED.

among whom were some of the first engineers and mechanicians of the day. A stand was provided for the ladies; the "beauty and fashion" of the neighborhood were present, and the side of the railroad was lined with carriages of all descriptions.

It was quite characteristic of the Stephensons that, although their engine did not stand first on the list for trial, it was the first that was ready, and it was accordingly ordered out by the judges for an experimental trip. Yet the Rocket was by no means the favorite with either the judges or the spectators. Nicholas Wood has since declared that the majority of the judges were strongly predisposed in favor of the Novelty (Ericsson's), and that "nine-tenths, if not ten-tenths, of the persons present were against the Rocket because of its appearance." Nearly every person favored some other engine, so that there was nothing for the Rocket but the practical test. The first trip made by it was quite successful. It ran about twelve miles, without interruption, in about fifty-three minutes.

The Novelty was next called out. It was a light engine, very compact in appearance, carrying the water and fuel upon the same wheels as the engine. The weight of the whole was only three tons and one hundredweight. A peculiarity of this engine was that the air was driven or forced through the fire by means of bellows. The day being now far advanced, and some dispute having arisen as to the method of assigning the proper load for the Novelty, no particular experiment was made further than that the engine traversed the line by way of exhibition, occasionally moving at the rate of twenty-four miles an hour. The Sanspareil, constructed by Timothy Hackworth, was next exhibited, but no particular experiment was made with it on this day. This engine differed but little in its construction from the locomotive last supplied by the Stephensons to the Stockton and Darlington Railway, of which Mr. Hackworth was the locomotive foreman.

The contest was postponed until the following day; but, before the judges arrived on the ground, the bellows for creating the blast in the Novelty gave way, and it was found incapable of going through its performance. A defect was also detected in the boiler of the Sanspareil, and some further time was allowed to get it repaired. The large number of spectators who had assembled to witness the contest were greatly disappointed at this postponement; but, to lessen it, Stephenson again brought out the Rocket, and, attaching to it a coach containing thirty persons, he ran them along the line at the rate of twenty-four to thirty miles an hour, much to their gratification and amazement. Before separating, the judges ordered the engine to be in readiness by eight o'clock on the following morning, to go through its definitive trial according to the prescribed conditions.

On the morning of October 8th the Rocket was again ready for the contest. The engine was taken to the extremity of the stage, the fire-box was filled with coke, the fire lighted, and the steam raised until it lifted the safety-valve loaded to a pressure of fifty pounds to the square inch. This proceeding occupied fifty-seven minutes. The engine then started on its journey, dragging after it about thirteen tons' weight in wagons, and made the first ten trips backward and forward along the two miles of road, running the thirty-five miles, including stoppages, in an hour and forty-eight minutes. The second ten trips were in like manner performed in two hours and three minutes. The maximum velocity attained during the trial trip was twenty-nine miles an hour, or about three times the speed that one of the judges of the competition had declared to be the limit of possibility.

The average speed at which the whole of the journeys were performed was fifteen miles an hour, or five miles beyond the rate specified in the conditions published by the company. The entire performance excited the greatest astonishment among the assembled spectators; the directors felt confident that their enterprise was now on the eve of success; and George Stephenson rejoiced to think that, in spite of all false prophets and fickle counsellors, the locomotive system was now safe. When the Rocket, having performed all the conditions of the contest, arrived at the grand-stand at the close of its day's successful run, Mr. Cropper, one of the directors favorable to the fixed engine system, lifted up his hands and exclaimed, "Now has George Stephenson at last delivered himself."

Neither the Novelty nor the Sanspareil was ready for trial until the 10th, on the morning of which day an advertisement appeared saying that the former engine was to be tried on that day, when it would perform more work than any engine on the ground. The weight of the carriages attached to it was only about seven tons. The engine passed the first post in good style; but, in returning, the pipe from the forcing-pump burst and put an end to the trial. The pipe was repaired, and the engine made several trips by itself, in which it was said to have gone at the rate of twenty-four to twenty-eight miles an hour.

The Sanspareil was not ready until the 13th; and when its boiler and tender were filled with water, it was found to weigh four hundredweight beyond the weight specified in the published conditions as the limit of four-wheeled engines; nevertheless, the judges allowed it to run on the same footing as the other engines, to enable them to ascertain whether its merits entitled it to favorable consideration. It travelled at the average speed of about fourteen miles an hour, with its load attached; but at the eighth trip the cold-water pump got wrong and the engine could proceed no farther.

It was determined to award the premium to the successful engine on the following day, the 14th, on which occasion there was an unusual assemblage of spectators. The owners of the Novelty pleaded for another trial, and it was conceded. But again it broke down. Then Mr. Hackworth requested the opportunity for making another trial of his Sanspareil. But the judges had now had enough of failures, and they declined, on the ground that not only was the engine above the stipulated weight, but that it was constructed on a plan which they could not recommend for adoption by the directors of the company. One of the principal practical objections to this locomotive was the enormous quantity of coke consumed or wasted by it—about six hundred ninety-two pounds an hour when travelling—caused by the sharpness of the steam-blast in the chimney, which blew a large proportion of the burning coke into the air.

The Perseverance of Mr. Burstall was found unable to move at more than six miles an hour, and it was withdrawn from the contest at an early period. The Rocket was thus the only engine that had performed, and more than performed, all the stipulated conditions, and it was declared to be entitled to the prize of five hundred pounds, which was awarded to the Messrs. Stephenson and Booth accordingly. And further to show that the engine had been working quite within its powers, George Stephenson ordered it to be brought upon the ground and detached from all encumbrances, when, in making two trips, it was found to travel at the astonishing rate of thirty-five miles an hour.

The Rocket had thus eclipsed the performances of all locomotive-engines that had yet been constructed, and outstripped even the sanguine expectations of its constructors. It satisfactorily answered the report of Messrs. Walker and Rastrick, and established the efficiency of the locomotive for working the Liverpool and Manchester Railway, and, indeed, all future railways.

The Rocket showed that a new power had been born into the world, full of activity and strength, with boundless capability of work. It was the simple but admirable contrivance of the steam-blast, and its combination with the multitubular boiler, that at once gave locomotion a vigorous life and secured the triumph of the railway system. As has been well observed, this wonderful ability to increase and multiply its powers of performance with the emergency that demands them has made this giant engine the noblest creation of human wit, the very lion among machines. The success of the Rainhill experiment, as judged by the public, may be inferred from the fact that the shares of the company immediately rose 10 per cent., and nothing further was heard of the proposed twenty-one fixed engines, engine-houses, ropes, etc. All this cumbersome apparatus was thenceforward effectually disposed of.

Very different now was the tone of those directors who had distinguished themselves by the persistency of their opposition to George Stephenson's plans. Coolness gave way to eulogy, and hostility to unbounded offers of friendship, after the manner of many men who run to the help of the strong. Deeply though the engineer had felt aggrieved by the conduct exhibited toward him during this eventful struggle by some from whom forbearance was to have been expected, he never entertained toward them in after-life any angry feelings; on the contrary, he forgave all. The directors afterward passed unanimous resolutions eulogizing "the great skill and unwearied energy" of their engineer.

When heavier and more powerful engines were brought upon the road, the old Rocket, regarded as a thing of no value, was

sold in 1837. It was purchased by Mr. Thompson, of Kirkhouse, the lessee of the Earl of Carlisle's coal and lime works,
near Carlisle. He worked the engine on the Midgeholme Railway five or six years, during which it hauled coal from the pits
to the town. There was wonderful vitality in the old engine, as
the following circumstance proves: When the great contest for
the representation of East Cumberland took place, and Sir James
Graham was superseded by Major Aglionby, the Rocket was
employed to convey the Alston express with the state of the poll
from Midgeholme to Kirkhouse. On that occasion the engine
was driven by Mr. Mark Thompson, and it ran the distance of
upward of four miles in four and a half minutes, thus reaching a
speed of nearly sixty miles an hour. But again it was superseded
by heavier engines; for it only weighed about four tons, whereas
the new engines were at least three times that weight. The
Rocket was consequently laid up in ordinary in the yard at
Kirkhouse, whence it was transferred to the Museum of Patents
at Kensington.

CATHOLIC EMANCIPATION

A.D. 1829

WILLIAM E. GLADSTONE   WILLIAM E. H. LECKY
DANIEL O'CONNELL

Scarcely less important in English history than the passage of the Reform Bill of 1832 was that of the Catholic Emancipation Act of 1829. This was an act repealing all laws that disqualified Roman Catholics from the enjoyment of civil rights and free disposal of property—the removal of their civil and political disabilities.

As early as 1793 a Catholic relief bill was passed by Parliament. It partially removed the disabilities under which Catholics had lain, but was far from being satisfactory to them, and did not prevent the Irish Catholics from taking part in the rising of 1798. The legislative union of Ireland with Great Britain (1800) left the demand of Catholics to be admitted to the common rights of citizens still ungranted. Pitt, as prime minister, had promised that Catholic emancipation should follow the union, but was prevented by King George III from redeeming the pledge.

The agitation for Catholic emancipation continued for some years without effectual combination for securing it. In Daniel O'Connell, sometimes called the " Liberator," born in County Kerry, in 1775, Ireland and the Catholic cause found a new and powerful advocate. While still a young man he appears to have formed the purpose of leading a fresh endeavor for the attainment of his country's liberties. By 1811 he had established his leadership of the movement for Catholic emancipation. The Relief Bill, as the Catholic Emancipation Act is also called, was introduced in the House of Commons, under sanction of Wellington the prime minister, by Sir Robert Peel, March 5, 1829. It passed both Houses of Parliament, and received the royal assent April 13th.

Meanwhile O'Connell had been elected to Parliament for Clare in 1828, but when he appeared, to take his seat, the following year, it was denied him on account of his refusal to subscribe to the Test Act, which, as well as the Corporation Act, required a virtual renunciation of Catholicism. In 1830, after the passage of the Catholic Emancipation Bill, removing the civil disabilities of Roman Catholics, O'Connell, who in 1829 was again returned for Clare, took his seat. The remainder of his life was devoted chiefly to agitation for repeal of the union between Ireland and Great Britain.

Besides the estimates of O'Connell and his work, to which the names

175

of Gladstone and Lecky give the weight of their authority, the reader, it is believed, will welcome, in O'Connell's letter to Sugrue, the "Liberator's" own note of jubilation for the victory won.

WILLIAM EWART GLADSTONE

O'CONNELL was, and was felt to be, not a name only, but a power. He had, in 1828–1829, encountered the victor of the Peninsula and of Waterloo on the battle-ground of the higher politics which lie truly *inter apices* and had defeated him, and obtained from his own lips the avowal of his defeat.

Moreover, O'Connell was a champion of whom it might emphatically be said, that alone he did it. True, he had a people behind him; but a people in the narrower, rather than in the wider, sense; the masses only, not the masses with the classes. The Irish aristocracy were not indeed then banded together, as they are now, in the cause that he thought the wrong one. Many of them supported Roman Catholic emancipation, but none of them comprehended that in the long reckoning of international affairs, that support would have to be carried onward and outward to all its consequences. He saw, at the epoch of the Clare election, what they did not see; that the time had come when, to save the nation, a victim must be dedicated even from among the nation's friends, like the great king's daughter at Aulis to preserve the host commanded by her own father.

O'Connell was the commander-in-chief, although as yet they hardly knew it; and even the most illustrious supporters of Roman Catholic emancipation, on whichever side the Channel, were but the rank and file behind him. His were the genius and the tact, the energy and the fire, that won the bloodless battle. By the force of his own personality he led Ireland to St. Stephen's[1] almost as much as Moses led the children of Israel to Mount Sinai; and he accomplished the promise of Pitt, which Pitt himself had labored, and labored not in vain, to frustrate.

There cannot be many in whose eyes O'Connell stands as clearly the greatest Irishman that ever lived. Neither Swift nor Grattan (each how great in their several capacities!) can be placed

---

[1] The British Houses of Parliament: a historic name figuratively applied especially to the House of Commons, sometimes also to the House of Lords. Both Houses are entered through St. Stephen's porch and St. Stephen's Hall.—ED.

in the scale against him. If there were to be a competition among the dead heroes of Irish history, I suppose that Burke and the Duke of Wellington would be the two most formidable competitors. But the great Duke is truly, in mathematical phrase, incommensurable with O'Connell. There are no known terms which will enable us fairly to pit the military faculty against the genius of civil affairs. It can hardly be doubted that if we take that genius alone into view, O'Connell is the greater man, and I will not so much as broach the question, in itself insoluble, whether and up to what point of superiority the exploits of the great Duke in the field establish an excess in his favor. With respect to Burke as against O'Connell, it seems safe to say that he was far greater in the world of thought, but also far inferior in the world of action.

There is another kind of comparison which this powerful figure obviously challenges, a comparison with the great demagogues or popular leaders of history. It is, however, a misnomer to call him a demagogue. If I may coin a word for the occasion, he was an "ethnagogue." He was not the leader either of *plebs* or *populus* against optimates: he was the leader of a nation; and this nation, weak, outnumbered, and despised, he led, not always unsuccessfully, in its controversy with another nation, the strongest perhaps and the proudest in Europe. If we pass down the line of history (but upward on the moral scale) from Cleon to Gracchus, to Rienzi, and even to Savonarola, none of these, I believe, displayed equal powers; but they all differed in this vital point, that they led one part of the community against another, while he led a nation, though a nation minus its dissentients, against conquerors, who were never expelled, but never domesticated.

For a parallel we cannot take Kossuth or Mazzini, who are small beside him; we must ascend more nearly to the level of the great Cavour, and there still remains this wide difference between them, that the work of Cavour was work in the Cabinet and Parliament alone, while O'Connell not only devised and regulated all interior counsels, but had also the actual handling, all along, of his own raw material—that is to say, of the people—and so handled them by direct personal agency that he brought them to a state of discipline unequalled in the history of the world.

His first, I believe, and not his last, memorable public utterance had been made in January, 1800, when he was twenty-four years old.   In writing to Lord Shrewsbury he says:

"For more than twenty years before emancipation the burden of the cause was thrown upon me.   I had to arrange the meetings, prepare the resolutions, furnish replies to the correspondence, examine the case of each person complaining of practical grievances, rouse the torpid, animate the lukewarm, control the violent and the inflammatory, avoid the shoals and breakers of the law, guard against multiplied treachery, and at all times to oppose, at every peril, the powerful and multitudinous enemies of the cause."

This was without doubt what may be called the opulent period of his life: but hear him as to even this period:

"For four years I bore the entire expenses of Catholic agitation without receiving the contributions of others to a greater amount than seventy-four pounds in the whole.   Who shall repay me for the years of my buoyant youth and cheerful manhood?   Who shall repay me for the lost opportunities of acquiring professional celebrity, or for the wealth which such distinction would insure?"

From, or shortly before, the epoch of the Clare election in 1828 dates the commencement of his absorption in public affairs.   He was now *totus in illis*.   He remained at his zenith until 1843, when the Peel Administration instituted the great prosecution against him.[1]   It can hardly be said that this prosecution was directly the cause of a decline in his power over the people.   But this much appears to be certain.   If his imprisonment in Richmond Bridewell did not break his spirit, it added heavily to that drain upon his nerve power which had for so many years been excessive and almost unparalleled.

WILLIAM EDWARD HARTPOLE LECKY

Few things are more striking to those who compare the present condition of Ireland with her past than the rapidity with which the power of the priests augmented during the nineteenth

---

[1] In 1844 O'Connell was convicted of conspiracy to raise sedition, and was sentenced to a year's imprisonment and a fine of two thousand pounds.   The verdict was set aside by the House of Lords, but O'Connell lay in prison for fourteen weeks.—ED.

century. Formerly they were much loved by their flocks but much despised by the Protestants, and they were contented with keeping alive the spiritual feeling of their people without taking any conspicuous part in politics. Once or twice, indeed, the bishops came forward to disclaim certain doctrines that were attributed to their Church and were advanced as an argument against emancipation. Once or twice they held meetings to further the movement by expressing their willingness to concede something to procure the boon.

The priests seem to have been at one time most reluctant to enter into the political arena, and the whole agitation was frequently in danger of perishing from very languor. There was a party supported by Keogh, the leader in 1793, who recommended what was called "a dignified silence"—in other words, a complete abstinence from petitioning and agitation. With this party O'Connell successfully grappled. His advice on every occasion was, "Agitate, agitate, agitate!" and Keogh was so irritated by the defeat that he retired from the society.

But the greatest of the early triumphs of O'Connell was on the veto question. It is evident that if the proposed compromise were made, the policy he had laid out for himself would be completely frustrated. A public spirit would not be formed among the Roman Catholics by a protracted struggle. Emancipation would be a boon that was conceded, not a triumph that was won, and the episcopacy would be in a measure dependent upon the Crown. In the course of the contest almost every element of power seemed against him. The bishops, both in 1799 and 1808, had declared themselves in favor of the veto. The English Roman Catholics led by Mr. Butler, the upper order of those of Ireland led by Lord Fingall, and the Protestant Liberals led by Grattan, warmly supported it. Sheil, who was thoroughly identified with the democratic party, and whose wonderful rhetorical powers gave him an extraordinary influence, wrote and spoke in favor of compromise; and, to crown all, Monsignor Quarantotti, who in a great measure managed affairs at Rome during the captivity of Pius VII, exhorted the bishops to accept it.

Over all these obstacles O'Connell triumphed. He succeeded in persuading or forcing the bishops into violent opposition to the scheme, and in throwing them on the support of the people. Doctor Milner wrote against the veto, and was accordingly censured by the English Roman Catholics; but O'Connell induced those of Ireland to support him. Grattan refused to place himself in the hands of the Catholic committee, and the petition was immediately taken out of his hands. Lord Fingall, Sir E. Bellew, and a few other leading Catholics would not yield, and were obliged to form a separate society, which soon sank into insignificance. Sheil was answered by O'Connell, and the answer was accepted by the people as conclusive; and, finally, the rescript of Quarantotti was disobeyed by the bishops and disavowed by the Pope. The results of the controversy were probably by no means beneficial to the country, but they at least served in an eminent degree the purposes of the agitator. The clergy were brought actively into politics. The lower orders were stirred to the very depths, and O'Connell was triumphant over all rivals.

In the course of this controversy it was frequently urged that O'Connell's policy retarded emancipation. This objection he met with characteristic frankness. He avowed himself repeatedly to be an agitator with an "ulterior object," and declared that that object was the repeal of the union. "Desiring, as I do, the repeal of the union," he said in one of his speeches, in 1813, "I rejoice to see how our enemies promote that great object. Yes, they promote its inevitable success by their very hostility to Ireland. They delay the liberties of the Catholics, but they compensate us most amply because they advance the restoration of Ireland. By leaving one cause of agitation, they have created, and they will embody and give shape and form to, a public mind and a public spirit."

In 1811, at a political dinner, he spoke to the toast of "Repeal," which had been given at his suggestion, and he repeatedly reverted to the subject. Nothing can be more untrue than to represent the repeal agitation as a mere afterthought designed to sustain his flagging popularity; nor can it be said that the project was first started by him. The deep indignation that the union had produced in Ireland was fermenting among all classes, and assuming the form, sometimes of a French party, sometimes of a social war, and sometimes of a constitutional agitation. The repeal agitation directed, but did not create, the national feeling. It merely gave it a distinct form, a steady action, and a constitutional character. In 1810 a very remarkable movement in this direction took place in Dublin. The grand jury passed a resolution declaring that "the union had produced an accumulation of distress; and that, instead of cementing, they feared that if not repealed it might endanger the connection between the sister-countries."

In the same year a meeting communicated on the subject with Grattan, who was member for the city. Grattan replied that a repeal agitation could only be successful if supported by the people; that if that support were given, he would be ready to advocate the movement; and that he considered such a course perfectly consonant with devoted attachment to the connection. Lord Cloncurry relates that he was a member of a deputation which on another occasion waited on Grattan, and that Grattan said to them, "Gentlemen, the best advice I can give my fellow-citizens upon every occasion is to keep knocking at the union."

It would be tedious to follow into minute detail the difficulties and the mistakes that obstructed the Catholic movement, and were finally overcome by the energy or the tact of O'Connell. For some time the gravest fears were entertained that the Pope would pronounce in favor of the veto. A strong party at Rome, headed by Cardinal Gonsalvi, was known to advocate it, and the deputy of the Irish bishops adopted so importunate a tone that he was peremptorily dismissed, and pronounced by His Holiness to be "intolerable." Innumerable dissensions dislocated the movement and demanded all the efforts of O'Connell to appease them.

When the Roman Catholic gentry had seceded, a multitude of those eccentric characters who are ever ready to embark in agitation from the mere spirit of adventure assumed a dangerous prominence, and it was found necessary to adopt a most despotic tone to repress them.

In 1815 O'Connell fought a duel with a gentleman named D'Esterre, which was attended by some very painful circumstances and gave rise to much subsequent discussion. It arose out of the epithet "beggarly" which O'Connell had applied to the corporation of Dublin.   D'Esterre was killed at the first shot.   In the same year Mr. Peel had challenged O'Connell, on account of some violent expressions he had employed.   O'Connell, however, was arrested at his wife's information, and bound over to keep the peace.

Several times the movement was menaced by Government proclamations and prosecutions.   Its great difficulty was to bring the public opinion of the whole body of the Roman Catholics actively and habitually into the question.   The skill and activity of O'Connell in arousing the people were beyond all praise, and the consciousness of the presence of a great leader began to spread through the whole mass of the dispirited and dependent Catholics.   All preceding movements since the revolution (except the passing excitement about Wood's halfpence) had been chiefly among the Protestants or among the higher order of the Catholics.   The mass of the people had taken no real interest in politics, had felt no real pain at their disabilities, and were politically the willing slaves of their landlords.

For the first time, under the influence of O'Connell, the great swell of a really democratic movement was felt.   The simplest way of concentrating the new enthusiasm would have been by a system of delegates, but this had been rendered illegal by the Convention Act.   On the other hand, the right of petitioning was one of the fundamental privileges of the constitution.   By availing himself of this right O'Connell contrived, with the dexterity of a practised lawyer, to violate continually the spirit of the Convention Act, while keeping within the letter of the law.   Proclamation after proclamation was launched against his society, but by continually changing its name and its form he generally succeeded in evading the prosecutions of the Government.

These early societies, however, all sink into insignificance compared with that great Catholic association which was formed in 1824.   The avowed objects of this society were to promote religious education, to ascertain the numerical strength of the different religions, and to answer the charges against the Roman Catholics embodied in the hostile petitions.   It also recommended petitions (unconnected with the society) from every parish, and aggregate meetings in every county.   The real object was to form a gigantic system of organization, ramifying over the entire country, and directed in every parish by the priests, for the purpose of petitioning and in every other way agitating in favor of emancipation The Catholic "Rent" was instituted at this time, and it formed at once a powerful instrument of cohesion and a faithful barometer of the popular feeling.   It is curious that at the first two meetings O'Connell was unable to obtain the attendance of ten members to form a quorum.   On the third day the same difficulty at first occurred, but O'Connell at length induced two Maynooth students, who were passing, to make up the requisite number, and the introduction of this clerical element set the machine in motion.

Very soon, however, the importance of the new society became manifest.   Almost the whole priesthood of Ireland were actively engaged in its service, and it threatened to overawe every other authority in the land.   In the elections of 1826 sacerdotal influence was profoundly felt; and the defeat of the Beresfords in the Catholic county of Waterford, in which, in spite of their violent anti-Catholicism, they had for generations been supreme, foreshadowed clearly the coming change.   The people were organized with unprecedented rapidity, and O'Connell and Sheil traversed the country in all directions to address them.   Though both were marvellously successful in swaying and in fascinating the people, it would be difficult to conceive a greater contrast than was presented by their styles.

If we compare the two speakers, I would say that before an uneducated audience O'Connell was wholly unrivalled, while before an educated audience Sheil was more fitted to please and O'Connell to convince.   Both were powerful reasoners, but the arguments of O'Connell stood in bold and clear relief, while the attention was somewhat diverted from those of Sheil by the ornaments and mannerism that accompanied them.   Both possessed great powers of ridicule, but in O'Connell it assumed the form of coarse but genuine humor, and in Sheil of refined and pungent wit.   By too great preparation Sheil's speeches displayed sometimes an excess of brilliancy.   By elaborate preparation O'Connell occasionally fell into bombast.   O'Connell was much the greater debater, Sheil was much the greater master

---

[1] A system of small subscriptions, as low as a penny a month, collected from the peasantry throughout Ireland.—ED.

of composition.   O'Connell possessed the more vigorous intellect and Sheil the more correct taste.

The success of the Catholic Association became every week more striking.   The Rent rose with an extraordinary rapidity. The meetings in every county grew more and more enthusiastic, the triumph of priestly influence more and more certain.   The Government made a feeble and abortive effort to arrest the storm by threatening both O'Connell and Sheil with prosecution for certain passages in their speeches.   The sentence cited from O'Connell was one in which he expressed a hope that "if Ireland were driven mad by persecution a new Bolivar might arise"; but the employment of this language was not clearly established, and the bill was thrown out.   The speech which was to have drawn a prosecution upon Sheil was a kind of dissertation upon "Wolfe Tone's *Memoirs*," of which Canning afterward said that it might have been delivered in Parliament without even eliciting a call to order.

The Attorney-General was Plunket, who by this act completed the destruction of his influence in Ireland.   Sheil asked him, as a single favor, to conduct the prosecution in person. Had he done so, Sheil intended to cite the passages from Plunket's speeches on the union, which at least equalled in violence any that the "Repealers" ever delivered.   The dissolution of the Government prevented the intended prosecution.

One very serious consequence of the resistance to the demand for emancipation was the strengthening of the sympathy between Ireland and France.   The French education of many of the Irish priests, and the prominent position of France among Roman Catholic nations, had naturally elicited and sustained it. The sagacity of O'Connell readily perceived what a powerful auxiliary foreign opinion would be to his cause; and by sending the resolutions of the association to Catholic Governments, by translations of the debates, and by a series of French letters written by Sheil the feeling was constantly fanned.   Many Irishmen have believed that the existence of this sympathy is an evil. I confess I can hardly think so.   Irishmen should never forget how, in the hour of their deepest distress, when their energies were paralyzed by a persecuting code, and their land was wasted by confiscation and war, France opened her ranks to receive them, and afforded them the opportunities of honor and distinction they were denied at home.

Gratitude to the French nation is a sentiment in which both Irish Catholics and Irish Protestants may cordially concur. The first will ever look back with pride to the achievements of the Irish Brigade, which threw a ray of light over the gloomiest period of their depression. The second should not wholly forget that to the enterprise of French refugees is due a large part of the manufactures which constitute a main element of their prosperity. Nor is it possible for any patriotic Irishman to contrast without emotion the tone which has been adopted toward his country by some of the most eminent writers of France with the studied depreciation of the Irish character by some of the most popular authors and by a large section of the press of England. The character of a nation is its most precious possession, and it is to such writers as Montalembert and Gustave de Beaumont that it is mainly due that Ireland has still many sympathizers on the Continent.

But in addition to these considerations there are others of much weight that may be alleged. One of the most important intellectual advantages of Catholicism is that the constant international communication it produces corrects insular modes of thought, and it has been of no small benefit to Irishmen that they have never been altogether without some tincture of French culture. In the worst period of the last century this was secured by the French education of the priests; and, in spite of geographical position and of penal laws, a certain current of Continental ideas has always been perceptible among the people. The spirit of French Catholicism long gave a larger and more liberal character to Irish Catholicism, and in French literature Irish writers have found the supreme models of a type of excellence which is peculiarly congruous to the national mind. There have sometimes been political dangers arising from the sympathy between the nations; but on the whole it has, I believe, produced far more good than evil.

The formation of the Wellington Ministry seemed effectually to crush the present hopes of the Catholics, for the stubborn resolution of its leader was as well known as his Tory opinions. Yet this Ministry was destined to terminate the contest by establishing the principle of religious equality. The first great concession was won by Lord John Russell, who, by obtaining the repeal of the Corporation and Test acts, secured the admission of Dissenters to the full privileges of the constitution. The Tory theory that, the State having an established religion, the members of that religion had a right to a position of political ascendency, was thus for the first time rejected, and with it fell the most popular argument against Catholic emancipation. O'Connell and the Catholics warmly supported the Dissenters in their struggle for emancipation, but the "No Popery" feeling among the latter was so strong that they never reciprocated the assistance. Even at a time when they were themselves suffering from disabling laws, they were in general hostile to Catholic emancipation.

About this time a new project of compromise was much discussed, both in Parliament and by the public, which shows clearly how greatly the prospects of the cause had improved. This project was that the emancipation should be accompanied by the payment of the clergy by the State, and by the disfranchisement of the forty-shilling freeholders. It seems to have been very generally felt that while emancipation could not be long delayed, some measure should be taken to prevent the Roman Catholic body from being virtually independent of the Crown. It was felt that a body which was connected by interests, by sympathies, and allegiance with a foreign court might become very dangerous in Parliament. To pay the Roman Catholic clergy would be to unite them by a strong tie to England, and to place them in a measure under the control of the Government. It would also, in all probability, set at rest the long-vexed question of the Established Church.

Pitt had contemplated the measure, and it found very many able advocates in England. O'Connell at first thought that the clergy should demand this arrangement; but, on their vehement opposition, he renounced the idea. In 1837 he had a warm controversy on the subject with Smith O'Brien, who advocated payment. Each was probably right according to his own point of view.

On the accession of the Wellington Ministry to power the Catholic Association passed a resolution to the effect that they would oppose with their whole energy any Irish member who

consented to accept office under it. When the Test and Corporation acts were repealed, Lord John Russell advised the
withdrawal of this resolution, and O'Connell, who at that time
usually acted as moderator, was inclined to comply. Fortunately, however, this opinion was overruled. An opportunity for
carrying the resolution into effect soon occurred. Mr. Fitzgerald, the member for Clare, accepted the offer of president of the
Board of Trade, and was consequently obliged to go to his constituents for reëlection. An attempt was made to induce a
Major Macnamara to oppose him, but it failed at the last moment, and then O'Connell adopted the bold resolution of standing himself.

The excitement at this announcement rose at once to fever
height. It extended over every part of Ireland and penetrated
every class of society. The whole mass of the Roman Catholics
prepared to support him, and the vast system of organization
which he had framed acted effectually in every direction. He
went down to the field of battle, accompanied by Sheil, by
the well-known controversialist Father Maguire, and by Steele
and O'Gorman Mahon, two very ardent "Repealers," who proposed and seconded him. Steele began operations by offering
to fight a duel with any landlord who was aggrieved at the interference with his tenants—a characteristic but judicious proceeding, which greatly simplified the contest. O'Connell, Sheil, and
Father Maguire flew over the country, haranguing the people.
The priests addressed the parishioners with impassioned zeal from
the altar; they called on them, as they valued their immortal
souls, as they would avoid the doom of the apostate and the
renegade, to stand firm to the banner of their faith. Robed in the
sacred vestments and bearing aloft the image of God, they passed
from rank to rank, stimulating the apathetic, encouraging the
faint-hearted, and imprecating curses on the recreant. They
breathed the martyr-spirit into their people, and persuaded them
that their cause was as sacred as that of the early Christians. They
opposed the spell of religion to the spell of feudalism—the traditions of the chapel to the traditions of the hall.

The landlords, on the other hand, were equally resolute.
They were indignant at a body of men who had no connection with
the county presuming to dictate to their tenants. They protested

vehemently against the introduction of spiritual influence into a political election and against the ingratitude manifested toward a tried and upright member. Fitzgerald had always been a supporter of the Catholic cause. He was an accomplished speaker, a man of unquestioned integrity and of most fascinating and polished manners. His father, who was at this time lying on his deathbed, had been one of those members of the Irish Parliament who had resisted all the offers and all the persuasions of the Ministry, and had recorded their votes against the union. The landlords were to a man in his favor. Sir Edward O'Brien, the father of Smith O'Brien, and the leading landlord, proposed him, and almost all the men of weight and reputation in the county surrounded him on the hustings. Nor did he prove unworthy of the contest. His speech was a model of good taste, of popular reasoning, and of touching appeal. He recounted his services and the services of his father; and, as he touched with delicate pathos on this latter subject, his voice faltered and his countenance betrayed so genuine an emotion that a kindred feeling passed through all his hearers, and he closed his speech amid almost unanimous applause. The effect was, however, soon counteracted by O'Connell, who exerted himself to the utmost on the occasion, and withheld no invective and no sarcasm that could subserve his cause. After two or three days' polling the victory was decided, and Fitzgerald withdrew from the contest.

Ireland was now on the very verge of revolution. The whole mass of the people had been organized like a regular army, and taught to act with the most perfect unanimity. Adopting a suggestion of Sheil, they were accustomed to assemble in every part of the country on the same day, and scarcely an adult Catholic abstained from the movement. It was computed in 1828 that in a single day two thousand meetings were held. In the same year Lord Anglesey had written to Sir Robert Peel, stating that the priests were working most effectually on the Catholics of the army, that it was reported that many of these were ill-disposed, and that it was important to remove the depots of recruits, and supply their place by English or Scotchmen. The contagion of the movement had thoroughly infected the whole population. If concession had not been made, almost every Catholic county would have followed the example of Clare, and the ministers, feeling further resistance to be hopeless, brought in the Emancipation Bill, confessedly because to withhold it would be to kindle a rebellion that would extend over the length and breadth of the land.

It was thus that this great victory was won by the genius of a single man, who had entered on the contest without any advantage of rank or wealth or influence, who had maintained it from no prouder eminence than the platform of the demagogue, and who terminated it without the effusion of a single drop of blood. All the eloquence of Grattan and of Plunket, all the influence of Pitt and of Canning, had proved ineffectual. Toryism had evoked the spirit of religious intolerance. The pulpits of England resounded with denunciations; the Evangelical movement had roused the fierce passions of Puritanism, yet every obstacle succumbed before the energy of this untitled lawyer.

The most eminent advocates of emancipation had almost all fallen away from and disavowed him. He had devised the organization that gave such weight to public opinion; he had created the enthusiasm that inspired it; he had applied to political affairs the priestly influence that consecrated it. With the exception of Sheil, no man of commanding talent shared his labors, and Sheil was conspicuous only as a rhetorician. He gained this victory not by stimulating the courage or increasing the number of the advocates of the measure in Parliament, but by creating another system of government in Ireland, which overawed all his opponents. He gained it at a time when his bitterest enemies held the reins of power, and when they were guided by the most successful statesman of his generation, and by one of the most stubborn wills that ever directed the affairs of the nation. If he had never arisen, emancipation would doubtless have been at length conceded, but it would have been conceded as a boon granted by a superior to an inferior class, and it would have been accompanied and qualified by the veto. It was the glory of O'Connell that his Church entered into the constitution triumphant and unshackled—an object of fear and not of contempt —a power that could visibly affect the policy of the empire.

The Relief Bill of 1829 marks a great social revolution in Ireland—the substitution of the priests for the landlords as the leaders of the people. For a long time a kind of feudal system had existed, under which the people were drawn in the closest manner to the landlords. In estimating the character of this latter class we must make very large allowance for the singularly unfavorable circumstances under which they had long been placed. The Irish Parliament was governed chiefly by corruption, and as the landlords controlled most of the votes, and as the county dignities to which they aspired were all in the gift of the Government, they were, beyond all other classes, exposed to temptation. They were also subject to much the same kind of demoralizing process as that which in slave countries invariably degrades the slave-owner.

The estate of the Protestant landowner had in very many cases been torn by violence from its former possessors. He held it by the tenure and in the spirit of a conqueror. His tenants were of a conquered race, of a despised religion, speaking another language, denuded of all political rights, sunk in abject ignorance and poverty, and with no leader under whom they could rally. Surrounded with helots depending absolutely on his will, it was not surprising that he contracted the vices of a despot.

Arthur Young concludes a vivid description of the relation between the classes by the assertion that "a landlord in Ireland can scarcely invent an order which a servant or laborer or cottier dares to refuse to execute"; and the total absence of independence on the part of the lower orders, and the general tolerance of brutal violence on the part of the higher orders, struck most Englishmen in Ireland. Besides this, the penal laws which gave the whole estate of the Catholic to any son who would consent to abjure his religion, seemed ingeniously contrived to secure a perpetual influx of unprincipled men into the landlord class; while the vast smuggling trade which necessarily followed the arbitrary and ruinous prohibition of the export of wool conspired with other causes to make the landlords, like all other Irishmen, hostile to the law. The glimpses which are given incidentally of their mode of life by Swift, Berkeley, Chesterfield, and Dobbs, and at a later period by Arthur Young, are in many respects exceedingly unfavorable.

The point of honor in Ireland has always been rather in favor of improvidence than of economy. In dress and living a scale of reckless expenditure was common, which impelled the landlords to rackrents and invasions of the common land, and these in their turn produced the agrarian troubles of the "Whiteboys" and "Hearts of Steel." Hard drinking was carried to a much greater extent than in England, and both Berkeley and Chesterfield have noticed the extraordinary consumption of French wines, even in families of very moderate means. The character of the whole landed interest is always profoundly influenced by that of its natural leaders, the aristocracy and the magistracy; but in Ireland peerages were systematically conferred as a means of corruption, and the appointments to the magistracy were so essentially political that even in the present century landlords have been refused the dignity because they were favorable to Catholic emancipation.

A spirit of reckless place-hunting and jobbing was very prevalent, and combined curiously with that extreme lawlessness which was the characteristic of every section of Irish society. Duelling was almost universal, and it was carried largely into politics, and even into the administration of justice; for a magistrate who gave a decision in favor of a tenant against his landlord was liable to be called out; by the same process landlords are said to have defended their own tenants against prosecution. No Irish jury, Arthur Young assures us, would in duelling cases find a verdict against the homicide. It was a common boast that there were whole districts in which the King's writ was inoperative. In the early part of the eighteenth century "hell-fire clubs," which were scenes of gross vice, existed in Dublin, and the crime of forcible abduction was, through nearly the whole of the eighteenth century, probably more common in Ireland than in any other European country, and it prevailed both among the gentry and among the peasants. It is worthy of notice that Arthur Young observed in the former, as much as in the latter, a strong disposition to screen criminals from justice.

These are the shades of the picture, and they are sufficiently dark. On the other hand, as the eighteenth century advanced, the character of the higher classes improved. Drinking and duelling, though still very general, had appreciably diminished. The demoralizing influence of the penal laws was mitigated. The gentry were gradually rooted to the soil, and a strong national feeling having arisen, they ceased to look upon themselves as aliens or conquerors. The Irish character is naturally intensely aristocratic; and when gross oppression was not perpetrated, the Irish landlords were, I imagine, on the whole very popular, and the rude, good-humored despotism which they wielded was cordially accepted. Their extravagance, their lavish hospitality, their reckless courage, their keen sporting tastes, won the hearts of their people, and the feudal sentiment that the landlord should command the votes of his tenants was universal and unquestioned.

The measure of 1793, conferring votes on the Catholics, though it is said to have weakened the zeal of some of the advocates of Parliamentary reform, left this feeling unchanged. Nor were the Irish gentry without qualities of a high order. The love of witty society; the passion for the drama and especially for private theatricals, which was very general in Ireland through the eighteenth century; and above all, the great school of Parliamentary eloquence in Dublin, indicated and fostered tastes very different from those of mere illiterate country squires. The noble efflorescence of political and oratorical genius among Irishmen in the last quarter of the century, the perfect calm with which great measures for the relief of the Catholics which would have been impossible in England were received in Ireland; above all, the manner in which the volunteer movement was organized, directed, and controlled, are decisive proofs that the upper classes possessed many high and commanding qualities, and enjoyed in a very large measure the confidence of their inferiors.

They were probably less uncultivated, and they were certainly much less bigoted, than the corresponding class in England, and as long as they consented to be frankly Irish, their people readily followed them. Occasional instances of deliberate tyranny and much sudden violence undoubtedly took place; but it should be remembered that during the whole of the eighteenth century the greater part of Ireland was let at very long leases, and that the margin between the profits of the tenant and the rent of the landlord was so great that the former almost invariably sublet his tenancy to an increased rent. The distress of the people was much more due to this system of middlemen, and to their own ignorance and improvidence, than to landlord tyranny; and the faults of the upper classes, in dealing with their tenants, were rather those of laxity and imprudence than of harshness. The absence of any legal provision for the poor produced great misery, and had a bad economical effect in removing one of the great inducements to the gentry to check pauperism; but, on the other hand, it fostered a very unusual spirit of private charity through the country. Absenteeism was much complained of; but this probably sprang more from the great tracts of confiscated land which had been given to great English proprietors, than from the systematic absence of the natives. The presence of a Parliament secured a brilliant society in Dublin; and in the country travellers represent the roads as rather better than in England, and the country seats as numerous and imposing. The absence of rival authority and of religious intolerance, and the character of the people, made the social system work better than might have been expected.

Good-nature is, perhaps, the most characteristic Irish virtue; and if it is not one of the highest, it is at least one of the most useful, qualities that a nation can possess. It will soften the burden of the most oppressive laws and of the most abject poverty, and the only evil before which it is powerless is sectarian zeal. O'Connell evoked that zeal, and the bond between landlord and tenant was broken. "I have polled all the gentry and all the fifty-pound freeholders," wrote Fitzgerald to Sir Robert Peel when giving an account of his defeat—"the gentry to a man." The attitude which the landlord class afterward assumed during the agitation for repeal completed the change, and they have never regained their old position.

It must be added that another important train of causes was operating in the same direction. The economical condition of Ireland had long been profoundly diseased. The effect of the confiscations, and of the penal laws, had been that almost all the land belonged to Protestants, while the tenants were chiefly Catholics. The effect of the restrictions on trade had been that manufacturing industry was almost unknown, and the whole impoverished population was thrown for subsistence upon the soil. At the same time the English land laws, which are chiefly intended to impede the free circulation and the division of land, were in force in the country in which, beyond all others, such circulation is desirable. One of the most important objects of a wise legislation is to soften the antagonism between landlord and tenant by interweaving their interests, by facilitating the creation of a small yeoman class who break the social disparity, and by providing outlets for the surplus agricultural population. In Ireland none of the mitigations existed; and the difference of religion, and the memory of ancient violence, aggravated to the utmost the hostility.

The tithes, levied for the most part on the poor Catholics for the support of the church of the landlords, were another element of dissension. All the materials of the most dangerous social war thus existed, though the personal popularity of the landlords, and the prostrate condition of the Catholics, for a time postponed the evil. The habits of disorder, and the secret organizations which had arisen in the middle of the eighteenth century, continued to smoulder among the people, and in the great distress that followed the sudden fall of prices which accompanied the peace, they broke out afresh. The land, as I have said, in the closing years of the eighteenth century was chiefly let at moderate rents on long leases. The tenant usually sublet his tenancy, and on the great rise of prices resulting from the war, the subtenant usually took a similar course, and the same process continued till there were often four or five persons between the landlord and the cultivator of the soil.

The peasants, accustomed to the lowest standard of comfort, and encouraged by their priests to marry early, multiplied recklessly. The land was divided into infinitesimal farms, and all classes seemed to assume that war prices would be perpetual. Many landlords, bound by their leases, were unable to interfere with the process of division, while others acquiesced in it through laxity of temper or dread of unpopularity; and others encouraged it, as the multiplication of forty-shilling freeholders increased the number of voters whom they could control. In such a condition of affairs, the fall in the value of agricultural produce after the peace proved a crushing calamity. Large sections of the people were on the verge of starvation, and among all agricultural laborers there was a distress and a feeling of oppression which alienated them from their landlords, and predisposed them to follow new leaders.

When introducing the Roman Catholics to Parliament, the ministers brought forward two or three measures with the object of diminishing their power, the only one of any real value being the disfranchisement of the forty-shilling freeholders. This measure greatly lessened the proportion of the Roman Catholic electors. It struck off a number of voters who were far too ignorant to form independent opinions, and it in some degree checked the fatal tendency to subdivision of lands. It would have been well if the ministers had stopped here, but with an infatuation that seems scarcely credible they proceeded in this most critical moment to adopt a policy which had the effect of irritating the Roman Catholics to the utmost, without in any degree diminishing their power, and of completely preventing the pacific effects that concession might naturally have had.

Their first act was to refuse to admit O'Connell into Parliament without reëlection, on the ground that the Emancipation Act had passed since his election. It was felt that this refusal was purely political, and designed to mark their reprobation of his career. It was, of course, utterly impotent, for O'Connell was at once reëlected; but it was accepted by the whole people as an insult and a defiance. O'Connell himself was extremely irritated, and to the end of his life his antipathy to Sir Robert Peel was of the bitterest and most personal character. He said of him that "his smile was like the silver plate on a coffin." There was, perhaps, no single measure that did so much to foster the feeling of discontent in Ireland as this paltry and irrational proceeding.

It was succeeded by another indication of the same spirit. By the Emancipation Act the higher positions in the bar were thrown open, as well as the Parliament. A distribution of silk gowns naturally followed; and, while several Roman Catholic barristers obtained this distinction, O'Connell, who occupied the very foremost position, was passed over. Among those who were promoted was Sheil, who had cooperated with him through the whole struggle. It now, too, become manifest that the Tories were determined to render the Emancipation Act as nugatory as was possible by never promoting a Roman Catholic to the bench. For some time under their rule the exclusion was absolute. The Relief Bill was also accompanied by a temporary act suppressing the Catholic Association, and enabling the Lord-Lieutenant, during the space of rather more than a year, to suppress arbitrarily, by proclamation, any association or assembly he might deem dangerous. A measure of this kind suspended every vestige of political liberty, and left the people as discontented as ever. O'Connell declared that justice to Ireland was not to be obtained from an English Parliament, and the tide of popular feeling set in with irresistible force toward repeal.

Of all possible measures, Catholic emancipation might, if judiciously carried, have been most efficacious in allaying agitation, and making Ireland permanently loyal. Had it been carried in 1795 as it undoubtedly would have been if Pitt had not recalled Lord Fitzwilliam—the country would have been spared the Rebellion of 1798, and all classes might have rallied cordially round the Irish Parliament. Had it been carried at or immediately after the union, as it would have been if Pitt had not again betrayed the cause—it might have assuaged the bitterness which that measure caused, and produced a cordial amalgamation of the two nations. It was delayed until sectarian feeling on both sides and in both countries had acquired an enduring intensity, and it was at last conceded in a manner that produced no gratitude, and was the strongest incentive to further agitation.

In estimating the political character of Sir Robert Peel, it must never be forgotten that on the most momentous question of his time he was for many years the obstinate opponent of a measure which is now almost universally admitted to have been not only just, but inevitable; that, his policy having driven Ireland to the verge of civil war, he yielded the boon he had refused simply to a menace of force, and that he accompanied the concession by a display of petty and impotent spite which deprived it of half its utility and of all its grace.

The exasperation of O'Connell at these measures was extreme. He denounced the Ministry of Wellington and Peel with reckless violence, endeavored in 1830 to embarrass it by a mischievous letter recommending a run upon gold, revived the Catholic Association under new names and forms, and energetically agitated for the repeal of the union. The proclamations of the Lord-Lieutenant, however, suppressed these associations, and when he attempted to hold public meetings he was compelled to yield to a prosecution; the upper classes strongly discouraged the new agitation, and the Ministry of Wellington soon tottered to its fall. In the beginning of 1831 he accordingly desisted from agitation, ostensibly in order to test the effect of emancipation upon the policy of the Imperial Parliament.

The Reform question was at this time rising to its height. O'Connell advocated the most extreme radical views, and in 1830 brought in a bill for universal suffrage, triennial Parliaments, and the ballot. He wrote a series of letters on the question. He brought the whole force of his influence to act upon it, and his followers contributed largely to the triumph of the measure of 1832—a fact which was remembered with great bitterness when the Reformed Parliament began its career by an extremely stringent Coercion Bill for Ireland.

DANIEL O'CONNELL

"THE FIRST DAY OF FREEDOM!

"APRIL 14, 1829.

"To James Sugrue:

"MY DEAR FRIEND—I cannot allow this day to pass without expressing my congratulations to the honest men of Burgh Quay on the subject of the Relief Bill.

"It is one of the greatest triumphs recorded in history—a bloodless revolution more extensive in its operation than any other political change that could take place. I say *political* to contrast it with *social* changes which might break to pieces the framework of society.

"This is a good beginning, and now, if I can get Catholics and Protestants to join, something solid and substantial may be done for all.

"It is clear that, without gross mismanagement, it will be impossible to allow misgovernment any longer in Ireland. It will not be my fault if there be not a 'Society for the Improvement of Ireland,' or something else of that description, to watch over the rising liberties of Ireland.

"I am busily making my arrangements respecting my own seat. As soon as they are complete you shall hear from me.

"I reckon with confidence on being in the House on the 28th instant, the day to which the adjournment is to take place. I think my right now perfectly clear and beyond any reasonable doubt.

"Wish all and every one of 'The Order of Liberators' joy in my name.   Let us not show any insolence of triumph, but I confess to you, if I were in Dublin, I should like to laugh at the corporators.

"I am writing a congratulatory address to the people.   It will appear, I hope, on Easter Monday in Dublin.

"Believe me, etc.,

"Daniel O'Connell."

ALGIERS TAKEN BY THE FRENCH

A.D. 1830

FRANCIS PULSZKY

By the capture of Algiers, capital of Algeria, on the northern coast of Africa, the French began a conquest that ended in making the conquered country a colonial possession of France. In common with other countries, France had often warred against the Algerine pirates, who with their fellow-corsairs of the Barbary States long preyed upon the commerce of nations.

Although in 1815 an expedition under Decatur gave the death-blow to Algerine piracy against the United States, other countries still suffered from its depredations. In 1816 Algiers was bombarded and destroyed by the British, who compelled the Dey to liberate all his Christian slaves and to promise for the future to treat prisoners of war according to European usage.

While the United States and England thus accomplished important objects, for themselves and other nations, against the Algerines, France not only had grievances of long standing, but also received fresh provocations, and the consequences that followed proved far more serious to the piratical State than those resulting from the action of the former countries. The capture of Algiers, related below, was one of the most striking events in the history of European dealings with the Barbary States.

IN 1818 a French brig was plundered in Bona, and the Government of Algiers refused to indemnify the owners. In 1823 the house of the French consular agent was violated by the Algerine authorities, under the pretext of searching for smuggled wares, and no satisfaction was given. Roman vessels, sailing under the protection of the French flag, had been taken by Algerine corsairs. At last a rough insult was alleged as the ultimate cause of war—the way in which the Dey had treated the French consul publicly before the Divan. Bakri, a rich Jew of Algiers, had supplied the French commissariat with grain at the time of the Napoleonic expedition to Egypt in 1798, and Bakri's accounts had not been settled. In 1816 a commission was named to sift the claims of the Algerian creditor.

The commission acknowledged the justice of the claim, which amounted to about fourteen million francs; but that sum was reduced by consent, in 1819, to seven millions, with the stipulation that the French creditors of Bakri were first to be satisfied; and, in fact, several of them, influential persons at court and in the chambers, got their money. But the principal creditor of Bakri was the Dey himself, who had sold to him a considerable quantity of wool, and who looked upon the debt of France as the guarantee of his debtor. The rumor was spread that many of the French claims which had been paid by the first instalment were fictitious, and Deval, the French consul in Algiers, was suspected of being in secret understanding and partnership with some of the French claimants. This opinion prevailed both in France and in Africa. The Dey, seeing that the value of Bakri's guarantee was day by day decreasing, wrote an autograph letter to the King of France. The letter remained without answer. The Dey, therefore, when in 1827 he publicly received the foreign consuls at the Bairam feast, asked Deval for the reason of that silence. The consul answered in words conveying the idea that the King of France could not lower himself so much as to write to a Dey of Algiers. At any rate, it is believed that Deval, either from his deficient knowledge of the Arabic or from hastiness of temper, used expressions offensive to the Dey. The Moor Hamdan-ben-Othman-Khodja, who was present at the scene, assures us that the reply of the consul was literally the following: "The King of France does not think a man like thee worthy of an answer." The Dey was maddened by such insulting language; and, with a flyflap which he just happened to hold in his hand, he slapped the face of the consul, bursting out into a disrespectful speech against the King of France. Deval made his report to his Government. It was M. Villèle who at that time stood at the head of the Ministry, and the opposition had often charged him with weakness and cowardice toward foreign powers. M. Villèle, therefore, seized the opportunity of displaying cheap energy and silencing the opposition. He declared that the King would take revenge for such an insult; and the blockade of the harbor of Algiers was decreed, but it remained without result. The Ministry of Polignac, wishing to turn the attention of the nation to foreign affairs, and believing that military glory might blind the French to the restrictions of the press which were intended by the Government, resolved to send the unmentionable expedition to Africa.

On May 25, 1830, a fleet, consisting of a hundred men-of-war, among them eleven line-of-battle ships and twenty-four frigates, and of three hundred fifty-seven vessels hired for transport, weighed anchor from the road of Toulon. It carried an army of thirty-four thousand one hundred eighty-four men, the officers included. The commander of the fleet was Vice-Admiral Duperré, who had the reputation of being the best and most experienced French naval officer. The army was led by Lieutenant-General Bourmont, Minister of War, whose precedents did not justify the nomination, and whose name could not inspire the soldiers either with confidence or with courage, neither of which, however, was deficient. Many of the officers had served in the wars of the Republic and of the Empire, and were accustomed to enemies more terrible than the undisciplined hordes of savage Africans. Besides, the army had always been honored by the French youth, and it won fresh favor when they saw that it had a nobler task than the dry uniformity of drilling and barrack life. Many volunteers, admirers of the deeds of Napoleon, entered the ranks, not a few of them young men of wealth and education. They introduced a good spirit into the army, and communicated their fresh enthusiasm even to the more rough or apathetic of the common soldiers.

On the morning of June 13th the fleet came in sight of the African coast, and landed on the sandy shores of Sidi-Ferruh, thus called from the tomb of a Marabout, twenty-five miles west of Algiers. The landing began on the 14th at dawn, and everybody expected a considerable resistance from the enemy; but only a few hundred mounted Arabs were seen in the distance, who seemed to spy the movements of the fleet. Scarcely was the first division, under the command of General Berthezène, on shore, when it marched in columns against the enemy, who had taken position upon a hill at about half an hour's distance from the sea, and had covered it by his batteries. They opened fire, but could not check the advance of the French. At that moment, General Bourmont, who hastened onward to lead the attack himself, had a narrow escape; two balls fell at his feet, and covered him with sand. As the French approached the batteries, the janizaries fled; all their artillery was taken by the victors.

General Bourmont had much too favorable an opinion of African tactics. He expected to have to encounter a cavalry similar to that of the Mamelukes in Egypt. He had even announced to the army, in an order of the day, dated from Palma, that the enemy were to send a mass of camels into the first line of battle, with a view to intimidate the French horse; but only a few of those animals were seen at a distance, carrying the baggage of the Turks. The dreaded African cavalry avoided every encounter; their method of warfare was a succession of skirmishes. The horsemen advanced suddenly, one by one, stopped their horses, discharged their long muskets, and rode away as suddenly as they had come, in order to charge their muskets again and to repeat the manœuvre. The Algerine army was commanded by the son-in-law of the Dey, Ibrahim, the *aga* of the militia, a man without capacity. It amounted to thirty thousand men, one-fourth of them being the auxiliaries brought by the beys of the provinces. The Algerine Turks amounted to about five thousand men; the remainder were Arabs of the Metidja, and Kabyles from the Jurjura mountain, mostly of the Flissa tribe, and led by their *kaid*, Ben-Zamun.

As soon as the army had taken position on the coast, it built a fortified camp, as the over-prudent Bourmont did not dare immediately to attack the city. Since there was abundance of green trees in the neighborhood, green huts and halls soon rose by the industry of the French soldiers. The camp looked like a city and was enlivened by merry movement. In the mean time the struggle continued uninterruptedly at the outposts; the natives had a superiority in skirmishing over the French, because their muskets were of a longer range; but they dreaded the artillery, especially the howitzers. As often as a shell exploded, the crowds of horsemen dispersed in all directions.

On the 18th some Arabs came stealthily to the French outposts, and disclosed to General Berthezène that he was to be attacked on the next day by all the forces of the Dey. One of them, a sheik of the Beni-Jad, told the General that the Arabs were tired of the war, and that his tribe was favorable to the

French; he himself promised to pass over to them with all his followers. This promise was not fulfilled, but the predicted attack really took place. The battle was stoutly contested, especially by the Turks, yet the natives were everywhere routed, and lost many men. The struggle lasted long, for General Bourmont lingered in giving the order to attack. At last he mounted his horse and gave the signal, and the first two divisions advanced rapidly over the broken ground, covered with bushes. The Algerines fled; their artillery, camp, and baggage were taken, and with it the splendid tent of the aga, sixty feet long. This battle (called that of Staueli, from the name of the plain on which it was fought) cost the Dey from three thousand to four thousand men in dead and wounded; but the French, too, lost six hundred men. All the natives say that had the French continued the pursuit of their routed enemy, they could have immediately taken the city, as the troops fled in such unruly disorder and consternation that nobody thought of a serious defence of the gates. But Bourmont remained faithful to his system of prudence and slow progress; he did not advance, and remained in Staueli up to June 24th.

Ibrahim Pacha, the commander of the Algerines, had lost his wits after the battle. He hid himself in his country-place, and did not dare to appear before his father-in-law, who sent the Moor Hamdan-ben-Othman-Khodja to him to cheer him up, in order to collect the remnants of the army. In the mean time the French entered into communication with one of the Arab tribes. The interpreter visited even one of their encampments and bought some oxen. The Arabs assured the French again that they felt weary of the war, and were ready to provide the French camp with victuals if protected against the revenge of the Turks, and principally if paid in cash. The French promised it; they were not yet aware of the character of this people, and put more trust in those overtures than they deserved. Bourmont exhorted the army to treat the Arabs kindly and honestly, as they were on the point of joining the French and fighting their oppressors the Turks. But a few days dispelled the delusion; on the 24th a new general attack was made on the French, both by Turks and by Arabs, who thought that the lingering of their enemies was a sign of weakness and cowardice.

They were once more defeated, and yet the undecided Bourmont did not allow his men to pursue the enemy to the city.

The French army was occupied in building a solid highway for the convoy and baggage-wagons. The generals and engineers were so little accustomed to Arab war that they went forward only with the greatest prudence and circumspection. A few years later the most wanton rashness succeeded to the over-anxious system of tarrying. While Bourmont required three weeks in summer to advance twenty-five miles on a field comparatively little broken, Marshal Clauzel undertook, in winter, 1836, an expedition to Constantine, across dangerous mountain-ridges and ravines, without having had the path reconnoitred. On the 28th a column of the enemy surprised a battalion of the Fourth Light-infantry Regiment, just in the act of cleaning their muskets, which they had unscrewed, and killed one hundred fifty of them, who were unable to make any resistance.

On the 29th the army advanced and occupied the heights and slopes of the Bujarea mountain, which commands the city and the forts of Algiers. The resistance of the enemy was not very serious, though they had now a more energetic commander than heretofore. The Dey, convinced by the failure of June 24th, of the incapacity of his son-in-law, had given the chief command to Mustapha-Bu-Mesrag, the Bey of Titteri, a courageous Turk. The trenches were at last opened on July 3d, and Admiral Duperré appeared on the same day in the roadstead of Algiers. On the 4th the French batteries began their fire at once against the "Emperor's Fort" and the Kasbah, the two principal defences of the city. The Turkish batteries returned the shots with great energy for four hours. When, however, the majority of their cannons were dismounted and the walls riddled by the balls, the fire slackened, and was silenced toward noon. The Emperor's Fort was evacuated, and its powder-magazine set on fire by order of the Dey. The explosion destroyed all the vaults and the inside walls. A few French companies immediately rushed forward and occupied the fort. They found three Turkish cannon still in good order; two French ones were carried into the fort, and with those five the fort Bab-a-Zun, on the shore, was fired upon and its batteries silenced. The fleet likewise attacked the fortifications on the sea side, but the fire made no impression on account of the distance.

Great consternation prevailed in the town after the fall of the Emperor's Fort. The inhabitants, who dreaded the capture of the city by storm, and the disorder and outrages usual on such occasions, rushed in crowds to the Kasbah, and with great noise demanded that the Dey should capitulate. Hasan now sent his chief clerk to General Bourmont with the promise to pay the costs of war and to give any satisfaction. As the French General declined that proposal, the chief clerk, a worthless traitor, as were nearly all the grandees of that pirate State, offered to kill his master, saying that it would be easier to treat advantageously with the new Dey. But the French General, who had orders to extinguish the domination of the deys, rejected those proposals as incompatible with the honor of France.

Hasan Dey hereupon sent the Moors Achmet-Buderbah and Hamdan-ben-Othman-Khodja as negotiators to General Bourmont. Both were clever and cunning; they had lived a long time in Europe and spoke French with great facility. After a negotiation of about two hours a capitulation was brought about according to which the Kasbah and all the forts and gates of the city were to be delivered to the French army. The Dey was permitted to remove from the country with his family and his private property whither he pleased. An escort was to provide for his safety. The same concession was granted to the Turkish militia. On the other side, General Bourmont further pledged his honor to respect the religion, the personal freedom, property, commerce, and industry of the inhabitants. Hasan Dey accepted this capitulation, which was equivalent to an abdication.

On July 6th the French entered Algiers as victors; and their white flag, which soon was to change its color, was reared on the Kasbah and on the Emperor's Fort. On the day after the capture of Algiers, General Bourmont, who soon afterward received the marshal's baton, sent a column to Cape Matifu to take possession of the stud and herds which were kept by the Dey on the Haush el Kantara (now Maison Carrée) and Rassata (Rassota), two important crown domains. But Ahmet, the Bey of Constantine, had, on his return to his province, anticipated the French: he had plundered those two establishments, and the French found nothing but bare walls.

The army remained quietly in the neighborhood of Algiers up to July 23d. The destruction of the luxuriant gardens and handsome villas by the French took place in that time. Nobody knew then whether Algiers would be retained, and nobody cared for its future. The officers, therefore, remained indifferent when the first palms and orange-trees were felled by the axes of the soldiers, to be used for camp-fires. Gangs of Frenchmen broke into the neat villas, deserted by their frightened inhabitants, and destroyed even the walls in the hope of finding hidden treasures. The traces of this vandalism are not yet all obliterated, especially on the Bujarea, where we often suddenly fall in with modern ruins in the midst of the finest gardens.

THE END OF ABSOLUTISM IN FRANCE

A.D. 1830

RICHARD LODGE   ALPHONSE LAMARTINE

In passing, at this period, from absolute to constitutional government, France took one of many preparatory steps—often followed by reaction —whereby she was gradually fitted for republicanism. It had been the aim of 'Charles X to restore the despotic system of the Bourbons and to rehabilitate the ecclesiastical authorities. But this policy was widely disapproved among his people, and for a time affairs were controlled by a liberal ministry. The ministry of Prince Polignac, which soon succeeded to power, represented the narrow views of the King. It was opposed by some of the most celebrated men of France—Lafayette, Guizot, Thiers, Benjamin Constant, and others—to whom constitutional government in that country owes a great debt.

The most important effects of this revolution were those that influenced the course of affairs in other countries. Discontent had been growing for years among the liberals of various European States. The repressive policy of Metternich controlled all the Continental rulers. But when France broke the spell of despotism, the example of revolution was followed in other countries, the liberal elements in all making common cause against the reactionary powers. First Belgium rose and won her independence. Then followed outbreaks, or milder demonstrations, in Poland, Italy, and Germany, while even England, in more peaceable ways, gave manifestations of the revolutionary spirit. The fruits of long agitation there at length appeared in the Reform Bill of 1832. The passage of this bill in Parliament was itself a peaceful revolution.

RICHARD LODGE

A MODERATE Ministry came into office (1828), in the Presidency of M. de Martignac. A law was introduced which imposed only slight restrictions upon the press, and a number of ordinances were issued against the Jesuits. But Martignac found that he had a very difficult position to occupy. Charles X regarded the ministers as forced upon him, and refused to give them his confidence. At the same time the majority of Deputies were hostile to them for not carrying liberal measures, which their relations to the King made impossible. Martignac wished to strengthen the monarchy and to give stability to the constitution by freeing the provinces from the excessive preponderance of the capital. Early in 1829 he brought forward a proposal to give to colleges in the communes and departments some control over the authority of the mayors and prefects. But this was not well received by the liberals, who had matters their own way in Paris, and who feared the preponderance of conservative and clerical influence in the country.

On July 30, 1829, the King dissolved the Chambers, and seized the opportunity to dismiss Martignac and his colleagues. He had convinced himself that concessions only encouraged more extreme demands, and he was determined not to yield. At the head of the new Ministry was Prince Jules de Polignac, the son of Marie Antoinette's favorite and the representative of the Emigrant nobles. The choice was an unfortunate one, as Polignac was incapable as well as unpopular, but it was dictated to some extent by foreign politics. It was just at this time that Russia and Turkey were negotiating at Adrianople, and Austria and England were anxious to prevent the former from obtaining excessive advantages from its victory. Martignac had been altogether on the side of Russia, and one of his chief supporters had been Pozzo di Borgo, the Russian envoy at Paris. Polignac was a personal friend of Wellington, the head of the Tory Ministry in England, and this contributed to his elevation. Still more unfortunate was the choice of the Minister of War, General Bourmont, who had deserted to the allies at the beginning of the Battle of Waterloo, an act which the French could neither forget nor forgive.

The appointment of the new Ministry was greeted with general indignation. Lafayette came forward as the leader of the agitation, and formed a secret society named "*Aide toi, et le Ciel t'aidera*" ["Help thyself, and Heaven will help thee"], which exercised considerable influence over the elections. When the Chambers met in March, 1830, the Liberals had an overwhelming majority among the Deputies. Their leaders were Royer-Collard and Guizot, the representatives of the constitutional theorists or *doctrinaires*, and the former was elected President. A number of royalist peers, influenced either by jealousy of Polignac or by Russian intrigues, deserted the Ministry, and an address expressing want of confidence was carried by large majorities. Charles

X dissolved the Chambers again, and determined to make a bold bid for popularity by an expedition against the Dey of Algiers, who had insulted the French consul. The French have always been eager for military glory, and it was hoped that the news of a brilliant success just at the time of the election would secure a majority for the Government. But the scheme was too obvious not to be seen through, and unforeseen accidents postponed the expected triumph until the elections were over (July 4th). A Chamber was returned which was still more hostile to the Government than its predecessor.

Matters had now reached a crisis, but Charles X was resolute to make no concessions. On July 25th a ministerial conference at St. Cloud drew up the celebrated "Ordinances," which were issued on the next day. The press was subjected to a strict censorship and the chief liberal papers were suppressed. The number of electors was diminished by raising the property qualification, and elections were to be no longer direct, but indirect. The recently chosen Chamber was dissolved before it had even met, and a new one was summoned for September 8th. These exceptional measures were justified by the fourteenth article of the Charter— "The King makes regulations and ordinances for the execution of the laws and the safety of the State."

The Ordinances were wholly unexpected in Paris, where the first feeling was one of stupefied astonishment. If the Government had been fully prepared for active measures, an easy triumph was assured. But there were only twelve thousand troops in the capital, and the command was in the hands of Marmont, who was unpopular among the soldiers as a traitor to Napoleon, and who personally disapproved of the Ordinances. The first opposition came from the journalists headed by Thiers and Mignet, who refused to recognize the suppression of their papers as a legal act. The liberal Deputies assembled at the house of Casimir Périer, but they distrusted the chances of a popular revolt, and contented themselves with a written protest against the dissolution of a Chamber which had never met.

Among the citizens there were bolder spirits. The manufactories were closed, the workmen crowded the streets, and a number of collisions with the troops occurred on July 28th. Marmont advised concessions, but Charles X, who had gone on a hunting-party as if nothing was happening, sent him orders to stand firm.

On the 29th came the decisive conflict. Lafayette, who was absent when the Ordinances were issued, hurried back to Paris and assumed the command of the National Guard. The troops were concentrated to defend the Tuileries, the Louvre, and the Palais Royal, and an obstinate conflict took place, in which much blood was shed. At last Marmont's indecision allowed the populace to gain possession of the Louvre, from which the long gallery admitted them to the Tuileries. So strong was the feeling against disgracing the revolt, that the treasures of the palace were left undisturbed, and a man who was detected in the act of plunder was promptly executed. By the evening Paris was in the hands of the mob.

When the news of these events reached St. Cloud the old King was at last compelled to recognize the necessity of concessions. Polignac was dismissed, and the Duke of Mortemart, a moderate man and acceptable to the Russian court, was appointed in his place. Mortemart lost no time in sending to Paris and announcing the revocation of the Ordinances. But it was too late. The Deputies had recovered their courage when the victory had been won for them, and had intrusted the Provisional Government to a municipal commission, of which Lafayette, Laffite, Casimir Périer and Gérard were members. They refused to recognize Mortemart, and declared that "the stream of blood which has flowed in Charles X's name has separated him from France forever." The respectable *bourgeoisie* wished to secure themselves against anarchy and to form a durable government. The establishment of a republic would inevitably excite the enmity of the great powers, would lead to another European war, and probably to a third restoration.

These considerations urged all moderate men to maintain a monarchical government in France. Fortunately they had not far to look for a suitable candidate for the throne. The Duke of Orléans had been the acknowledged patron of the liberal party ever since his return to France in 1815, and the favor shown to him by Charles X had failed to draw him any closer to the elder branch of his family. He was a Bourbon and therefore might be expected to satisfy the scruples of the monarchical States of

Europe. At the same time he would owe his power altogether to the popular choice, and could hardly venture upon unconstitutional government. Laffite and Thiers were his active supporters, and found no difficulty in gaining over the majority of the Deputies. Messengers were sent to Neuilly, where the Duke was then residing, to ask him to undertake the office of Lieutenant-General of the Kingdom until the Chambers could meet to secure the observance of the Charter.

Louis Philippe, whose *role* was to profess a becoming want of ambition, waited to consult Talleyrand, on whose diplomatic experience he relied to conciliate the European courts. On receiving his approval, he at once journeyed to Paris and accepted the proffered office. At the same time, to secure himself on both sides, he sent a letter through Mortemart to assure Charles X of his fidelity. The King placed such confidence in these treacherous professions that he confirmed the Duke's appointment and thus helped to drive his own supporters to the side of the usurper. The municipal commission, which was suspected of republican tendencies, was not informed of the action of the Deputies until all had been settled. Lafayette, however, was soon won over by Louis Philippe's professions, and the name of Orléans was so popular in Paris that opposition was out of the question.

Charles X was still confident that his crown was secure, but the anxiety of the Duchess of Berry for the safety of her son induced him to move from St. Cloud to the Trianon and thence to Rambouillet. There he was persuaded that his own unpopularity endangered the dynasty, and both he and the Dauphin abdicated in favor of the Duke of Bordeaux (August 1st). The Duke of Orléans, whose honesty was still relied upon, was asked to assume the regency for the infant King. But Louis Philippe now saw the crown within his grasp, and was determined to drive his rivals from the Kingdom. The cry was raised that Charles X meditated an attack upon Paris, and a mob of sixty thousand men marched upon Rambouillet. At last Charles realized the treachery of his relative and gave up all hope. His misfortunes were respected by the people as he journeyed to Cherbourg, whence he sailed to England, and for the second time took up his residence at Holyrood. On August 3d the French Chambers were opened, and on the 7th they had decided the future of France.

The throne was declared vacant through the abdication of Charles X and the Dauphin, and no allusion was made to the Duke of Bordeaux. By two hundred nineteen to thirty-three votes Louis Philippe was raised to the throne with the title of "King of the French."

ALPHONSE LAMARTINE

Fortune had irrevocably abandoned King Charles. The insurrection had left him no part of his kingdom but the castle and park of Rambouillet, and the little army encamped in the forest. One of two courses must be taken—civil war or abdication. Before leaving St. Cloud the King had humbled his heart before God, and abdicated, beforehand, a crown which he could never recover only through streams of his people's blood. He therefore continued on his defence at Rambouillet to retain an attitude of authority, but not to fight.

Being apprised of the universal spread of the revolt, of the desertion and disaffection of the troops of the line, of the failure of his son to maintain the posts of St. Cloud and Trianon, and the course of the Seine, moreover that even the regiments of his guard had begun to waver, he thought the moment was come to declare his resolution to his family and to his people. He no longer gathered about him his ministers and his generals, but held a council made up of his own family: his son, the Duchess of Angoulême, the Duchess of Berry, and his grandson—the darling of so many hearts—too young as yet to understand the affecting solemnity of this meeting in which they were, at once, to give him an empire and to take it away. The doors were closed upon all who were not of the blood of Louis XIV. No one knows the language, the entreaties, the objections, the sublime resignation, the tears, both bitter and dutiful, that accompanied this secret council wherein two voluntary abdications were made.

It would be rash and impious to seek to unveil the secrets of family devotion and the policy of the heart. All we are permitted to say—on the evidence of some words which escaped the son of Charles X the next day, and the one following, and which the ill-concealed regrets of the Duchess of Angoulême, in her exile, testified to—is that the Prince did not for a moment resist his father's orders, when it was thought that the innocence of a child might prove a means of reconcilement more generally acceptable to France; that the Duchess of Angoulême bewailed her fate In having been twice pushed off the steps of a throne which was to have made her amends for so many reverses; and that, while she sacrificed herself to her nephew, she felt all the sharpness of the trial; that the Duchess of Berry acknowledged with tears of joy the greatness of this sacrifice which, by crowning her son, bestowed upon her the unhoped-for guardianship of an empire. Obeyed as a father but impotent and outraged as a king, Charles X, on the breaking up of his council, wrote that letter to the Duke of Orléans which announced the spirit and resolution of this council.

"I am," said he, "too deeply disturbed by the calamities which afflict and threaten my people not to have sought for a measure to prevent them. I have therefore formed the resolution to abdicate the crown in favor of my grandson. The Dauphin, who participates in my sentiments, has likewise renounced his rights in his nephew's favor. It will therefore devolve upon you, as Lieutenant-General of the Kingdom, to proclaim the accession of Henry V to the crown. You will take moreover all the necessary measures which belong to your office to settle the form of government during the new King's minority. In this letter I confine myself to the declaration of these settlements; it is a measure to prevent a host of calamities.

"You will communicate my intentions to the diplomatic body, and let me know as soon as possible the proclamation by which my grandson will be declared king with the name of 'Henry V.'

"I commission Lieutenant-General Viscount de Latour-Foissac to deliver this letter to you. He has orders to settle with you the arrangements to be made in behalf of the persons who have accompanied me, as well as the arrangements concerning myself and the rest of my family. We will regulate hereafter the other measures which will be the consequence of this alteration in the successsion.

"I renew to you, my cousin, the assurance of the sentiments with which I am your affectionate cousin

"CHARLES."

It was strange that Charles X should have drawn up in the form of a letter the important document which changed the succession to the crown. Such an instance of carelessness was remarkable, especially in a monarch who was a scrupulous observer of the laws of etiquette; but the pledges of fidelity contained in the letter of the Duke of Orleans had removed from the mind of Charles X every doubt. The very manner in which the act of abdication was indited was a solemn proof of it. The Duke of Orleans, in this act, was spoken of as the natural protector of the childhood of Henry V, and he was left the chief arbiter of every measure which the sinister state of affairs might demand.

Meanwhile the Duke of Orleans felt alarmed on knowing that Charles X was so near the capital and in the midst of an army which might either fall back upon Paris or become the vanguard of a Vendean force. Under the pretence of protecting the royal family from the vengeance of the people he sent commissioners to watch over his safety. These were M. de Schonen, M. Odilon Barrot, and Marshal Maison. These commissioners had presented themselves at the outposts of the royal army and been driven off. On their return to Paris the Duke sent them back with injunctions still more decisive. "Let him go!" said he to them with reference to the King, "let him go directly; and in order to compel him he must be frightened!"

"But if the Duke of Bordeaux is put into our hands to be brought back to Paris," inquired one of the commissioners of the Duke, "what are we to do?"

"The Duke of Bordeaux!" returned the Prince, with genuine or affected loyalty, "why, he is your King!"

"Ah!" exclaimed the Duchess of Orleans, embracing her husband as if to reward these noble sentiments, "you are the most upright man in the kingdom!" Nothing was then determined upon, and his heart expressed one idea while policy was brooding over another.

General Jacqueminot, and some other officers who had served the Emperor, disseminated a report that Charles X was marching toward Paris. Lafayette, who commanded the National Guard of the kingdom, caused the drums to beat to raise the army of the revolution. In the space of four hours from ten to twelve thousand men—most of them mere youths, flushed with

Liberty leads the people to battle
over barricades in the streets of
Paris; 28th of July, 1830,

Painting by Eugène Delacroix.

the "Three Days'" conflict[1]—enlisted, and, in order to accelerate their pursuit of royalty, threw themselves into private carriages and the vehicles of traffic and hurried along the road in Rambouillet. General Jacquemilnot, Georges Lafayette, the dictator's son, in whom liberty was but filial piety and revolution a duty, marched at the head of these columns. General Pajol, a valiant soldier, who sought renown in every danger, took upon him the chief command of this multitude which rather resembled a riotous procession than an army. The politicians in the victorious party watched with secret gratification these young revolutionists, still restless, carrying their excitement out of the capital. These columns advanced intrepidly toward Rambouillet. Excelmans, who, as a soldier, had offered his sword to Marmont during the Three Days, now restored to the free exercise of his political principles, directed a vanguard. The two armies came up to each other as the day declined. They postponed the attack until the arrival of the commissioners, whom Charles X, this time, had consented to receive.

Messieurs de Schonen, Odilon Barrot, and Maison arrived at the castle about dusk. They found the King vexed and irritated by the obstruction he met with in his endeavors to transfer the crown to his grandson, and beginning to suspect that he was making but a useless sacrifice. "What do you require of me?" said he to them in the tone of a sovereign. "I have settled everything with the Duke of Orleans, my lieutenant-general."

Odilon Barrot, whom the moderation of his opinions and the propriety of his sentiments rendered a more suitable speaker to the Prince than his colleagues, soothed his anger, spoke to him with respectful kindness of the impending danger of a mortal strife, for which he would be answerable; of the account which kings must render to mankind for the lives of their subjects; of the fire which would be kindled throughout the land by the first shot commanded by the King; of the danger and the fallacy of hoping to cement with the blood of Frenchmen the future chances of his grandson to the throne. The King seemed to be touched, and evidently wanted but a pretext to yield with honor to a force of circumstances manifestly too strong to be resisted. He took aside Marshal Maison, whose military authority would at least

[1] The Revolution of July 27–29, 1830.—ED.

serve him as an excuse to Europe and to himself, and led him into the embrasure of a window. "My Lord Marshal," said he, appealing to his good faith, "tell me on your honor whether the army of Paris, which is marching against my troops, is really eighty thousand strong!"

"Sire," answered the Marshal, desirous to deceive and remove the King he had deserted in his misfortunes, "I dare not positively specify the number, but that army is numerous and may possibly reach that number."

"Enough," replied the King; "I believe you; and I will agree to all you propose, to spare the lives of my guards."

Marshal Maison owed his reputation to his own valor and military talents, under the Republic and the Empire; but he owed to Charles X his command of the army in Greece and his elevated rank. He showed himself on this occasion to be one of those soldiers in whom the noble career of arms is rather a glorious pursuit than a dutiful obedience.

The King and the royal family departed for Cherbourg, under the escort of their army as far as the castle of Maintenon, an almost royal residence belonging to the family of Noailles, and which bears the name of its founder. Here they were received by the Duke and Duchess of Noailles, a royalist family, whose devotion to the Crown by traditional descent was now enhanced by pious sympathy with royal misfortune. These faithful servants and all their family pressed with affection round the King and the princesses, as if to prevent them from feeling, at their hearth, that they had only halted on the way to exile. The King, agreeably to his promise to the commissioners, now disbanded his royal guard in a short proclamation, ordering the regiments to make their way to Paris and there to submit to the Lieutenant-General of the Kingdom; for such was the title which, on August 4th, Charles X still gave to the Duke of Orleans.

He retained as escort only the bodyguards and the gendarmerie, with six pieces of cannon. Marshal Marmont, who accompanied him, received again the chief command of these troops; an atonement which the King's goodness considered to be due to the Marshal's vexation after his son's violence. Marshal Maison, who was quartered with his colleagues at the castle of Maintenon, marked out on the map, rather as a proconsul of the people than as a marshal of France, the route of the King's progress and his resting-places on the way to Cherbourg, forgetting that it was he himself who had had the honor, in the name of the French Army, to go and meet Louis XVIII at Calais, when he landed, sixteen years before.

The next morning, after the King had breakfasted, the whole army drew up in battle order before the castle and along the road to give vent to its last shout of fidelity to the monarch, and to take its last look at the royal family. The Duchess of Noailles stood at the threshold, weeping and courteseying to her august guests. The King's face was sorrowful but resigned, expressive of a conscience overcome by fate, but confident in the uprightness of its purposes; the Duke of Angoulême, more mindful of his father's affliction than of the loss of a crown; the Duchess of Angoulême, whose noble stateliness grew with adversity, gave her hand to be kissed by the officers of the guard, who idolized her, and said to them through her sobs which she could not quite restrain, "My friends, may you be happy." The Duchess of Berry, dressed in male attire, and leading her son by the hand, could not believe that so high a fortune would be long eclipsed. Her thoughts seemed to dwell on the return rather than on the departure.

The people all along the road were still decorous and respectful. The shadow of this monarchy impressed them with awe more than the monarchy itself; there was as much nature as royalty in men's imaginations. They respected the King's fall the more that they no longer dreaded his return. They spared him almost everywhere, with instinctive decorum, the sight of the tricolored flag and cockade—palpable signs of his dethronement. In one or two of the manufacturing towns of Normandy there was an anticipation of taunts and insults on the part of the workmen. These fears proved to be vain. The marks of disfavor were confined to a few threats and groans aimed at Marmont[1] whose unsoldierly act in 1814 was everywhere remembered and condemned. On approaching Cherbourg he was under the necessity of removing the orders which he wore on his breast to hide his rank, his dignity, and his name from the rancor of the people.

[1] He surrendered his army to the Provisional Government in April, 1814.—ED.

The King read the *Moniteur* every morning to watch the progress of his own ruin with his own eyes. At Carentan he learned that the Duke of Orleans had consummated his usurpation. He uttered neither a reproach nor made a single unkind remark on that Prince's acts. Whether he still relied on the assurances which the Duke of Orleans had transmitted to him at St. Cloud and Rambouillet, or whether he thought that Prince accepted the crown only through the temporary force of circumstances, to return it afterward to his grandson, or whether he thought it more congenial to his soul to bear silently and without complaining the last and most cruel of all felonious acts—and that perpetrated by one of his own blood—it is hard to determine.

He stopped for two days at Valognes, in order to give time to the vessels prepared for his use to reach Cherbourg. He there collected around him the officers and six of the oldest guardsmen of each of the companies that escorted him—more like a father than a king. The tricolored flags had been taken down from the windows of the private houses as the *cortège* moved along, to spare the conquered monarch an unnecessary humiliation.

The King and his escort did not alight within the town, but entered a railed enclosure between the market-place and the strand at Cherbourg, and the iron gate was closed upon them. The people hurried there and clung to the rails in crowds to contemplate the strange spectacle of the ostracism of a king, the heir of sixty kings, without a country. The royal family, for the last time, alighted from their carriages on the edge of the beach washed by the waves; the Duchess of Angoulême, bathed in tears and staggering under the shock of her last exile, was deprived at once of a kingdom and a crown. M. de Larochejaquelein assisted her to pass over the last ground, leaning at least on a heroic arm. M. de Charette,[1] another Vendean officer—whose name might be considered an omen—escorted the Duchess of Berry. More of indignation than sorrow was visible in the countenance of that young widow on leaving a land which had drunk the blood of her husband, and which was now proscribing her innocent and helpless child. The Baron of Damas,

---

[1] Probably a son of François Athanase Charette, a noted leader of the Vendean insurgents, 1793–1795, who was taken prisoner at St. Cyr, March 25, 1796, and executed at Nantes three days later.—ED.

representatives, might have realized this desideratum in the fifteenth century; and, by establishing their dominion from the English Channel and the North Sea to the borders of the Rhine and the Moselle, might have secured a balance of power in Europe which would have saved it from the conflicts between Spain and her revolted colonies a century later. But the selfish ambition of Philip the Good—as history has nicknamed him—and the lust of conquest in Charles the Rash (or "Bold," as English writers generally mistranslate his *sobriquet*) blinded them to so vast a scheme of real greatness, and left Europe still in want of the basis of repose to be found in such an equilibrium. The facilities which not only favored, but seemed to demand, the realization of such a plan previous to the Reformation have been, no doubt, greatly weakened by its results. But nearly four centuries later, at the fall of Napoleon and the dismemberment of his Empire, another opportunity offered was lost.

The marriage of Mary, the daughter of Charles the Rash, with Maximilian, son of the Emperor of Germany, prepared the way for the political annihilation of the Low Countries, by their gradual descent into an appendage of the house of Austria. During the domination of Charles V, and the tyranny of Philip II, these countries, reduced to the rank of colonies, were but so many depots for the production of men and arms, as Peru and Mexico were for that of gold. At once the cause, the theatre, and the victim of the most bloody wars, they sank under the exactions of regal spoliation, at the very time that intellect and civilization were most flourishing.

Philip II, the odious type of tyranny, at once terrible and contemptible, gave a vigorous impulse to the spirit of nationality which so many causes had hitherto repressed. He attempted to establish the Inquisition in the Low Countries, less as a religious tribunal than as an instrument of government. The early resistance to this project was, like it, political. The struggle became religious at a much later period, and only in the North. William of Orange, the greatest of those princes of a house which has produced so many that were great, made the question of religious reform the watchword of national resistance in those provinces where the former had grown into a passion, through the fostering action of the latter, and thus he separated the cause of Holland from that of Belgium.   The successful though tardy issue of the struggle left Holland a free republic under the guidance of its stadtholders, and secured to Belgium its ancient but imperfect portion of nationality as an integral part of the great monarchy of which it still formed a fief.   The Spanish troops quitted its soil; its commercial privileges were guaranteed; and the sovereignty was conferred on Albert and Isabella in a modified form of Spanish power and feudal sway.   Their death, without posterity, threw Belgium back under the unmitigated mismanagement of Spain.   The benevolent reign of those archdukes—a title which they bore without distinction of sex—was a truce of happiness between the domestic sufferings of the sixteenth century and the desolating wars of Louis XIV.   But thenceforward Belgium, subjected to the paralyzing action of the court of Madrid, and thrown into the shade by the vigorous liberty of Holland, sank lower and lower in the scale of nations.

The Treaty of Westphalia, in 1648, regulated in many respects the situation of Europe, placing Holland in the foremost rank among the powers, concentrating religious toleration, and proclaiming a law of nations—imperfect, but still acknowledged as the law.   But it left the Belgian provinces in complete dependence on the throne of Spain, without fixing those questions of succession, which soon furnished Louis XIV with pretexts that legalized invasion and left the country a prize for chance adventurers in the bloody lottery of war.

From the Treaty of Westphalia until that of Vienna, in 1814, the Low Countries were little more than the arena to gladiatorial Europe.   The house of Austria, which acquired the sovereignty over them from Spain by the Treaty of Utrecht in 1713, never considered its new possessions in the light of an inheritance, and, in order to conciliate Holland, permitted her to establish a footing of supremacy in the country—which generated a notion of mastery that subsequently proved so fatal to her power—when Belgium was joined to her under the absurd and disproportioned title of " an increase of territory."   In 1715 Holland obtained the right of placing garrisons in several Belgian fortresses, having previously insured the commercial ruin of Antwerp, by the closing of the Schelde.

Ostend alone remained, to keep alive the spirit of enterprise

on which the ancient prosperity of Flanders was founded. A
company for the furtherance of the East India trade was established in 1722 (to be suspended in two years and never revived)
by the Emperor Charles VI, who felt himself too weak, or considered the object as too little understood, to resist the jealousy,
the intrigues, and the threats of the maritime powers. Thus the
country remained in a state of colonial vassalage, maintaining in
turbulent discontent the memory of former days whose only relics
were the municipal privileges, sufficiently powerful to foster a
narrow spirit of locality, but ineffectual toward procuring the
broad advantages of independence.

For seventy years the Low Countries seemed satisfied to forget the moral rights of nationality in the enjoyment of a physical
existence, which was called "prosperity." The misfortunes and
romantic energy of Maria Theresa and the entire sway she exercised over the provinces excited a feeling of religious loyalty
which overcame the general repugnance to the Austrian *régime*.
But no sooner did the death of the great Empress give her son and
successor, Joseph II, an opportunity of attempting his well-meant
but illegal and unreasonable reforms, than the old fire of liberty
burst forth from the embers in which it had been so long buried.
The insurrection of Brabant, in 1788, failed, from a total want of
large political views in the leaders, and from the absence of enlightened views of religion in the people whom they made their
tools. Its failure threw the country back under the feet of Austrian domination until republican France, victorious in 1795,
broke the chains of one slavery to rivet them more firmly for another. And when, vanquished in her turn, in 1814, she loosed
herself from her exhausted conquests, Belgium, among the rest,
was thrown loose on the political waters, like a waif, to be
picked up and appropriated by the first discoverers.

In the month of December, 1813, Holland had shaken off the
imperial yoke of Napoleon. By the Treaty of Paris of May 30th
following, she was promised an increase of territory. In 1815
she entered on the forced partnership with Belgium; and the
experience of the subsequent fifteen years of union proved that
the incompetent monarch, to whom was confided the task of
forming both nations into one, never acted but in the spirit of
the fatal flaw in the title which bound them together.

Reverting to four great facts of history with reference to the fate of Belgium, it must be borne in mind that it was *by force* she submitted to the dominion of the four powers to whom during the last two centuries she was joined: To Spain, by the Treaty of Westphalia, in 1648; to Austria, by that of Utrecht, 1713; to France, by that of Campo Formio, 1797; to Holland, by that of London, 1814; and that therefore she was not bound in allegiance to any of those powers by any ties sanctioned by the laws of reason or justice.

No sooner was the decree promulgated which established the existence of the Kingdom of the Netherlands than a course of misgovernment began, which it may be necessary shortly to capitulate.

The fundamental law, rejected by the majority of the Belgian notables, was forced upon the people. The nationality of Holland being considered as the basis of the Kingdom, every measure was regulated on it, without reference to the wishes, the wants, or the prejudices of Belgium. The Dutch language was considered as the national and official medium of communication. The great establishments of the Government were fixed in Holland. The reforms in the civil and criminal law were in accordance with Dutch, not Belgian views. The system of taxation was accordant with Dutch interests. Preference was given to the Dutch in the nominations to all civil and military posts. The laws and their administration were stamped with a marked anti-Catholic tendency. Finally, the whole nature of the Government was that of the old stadtholders' *régime*, disguised under monarchical denominations; a power said to be limited, but considering itself irresponsible.

The representative system, which was established in the new kingdom, became an instrument for the imposition of Dutch supremacy. The population of Belgium was, in round numbers, double that of Holland. The number of representatives was, however, equal; and repeated trials of strength in the Chamber of Deputies gave the following results:

All the laws that pressed heavily on the interests and liberties of Belgium were carried by a Dutch majority. Every such law, when rejected, was supported by a large number of Dutch members. All the proposed laws favorable to Belgian interests that were not carried failed through Dutch majorities. All such propositions as passed into laws were opposed by a formidable Dutch majority.

Such were the minutiæ of Belgian grievances; such the difficulties the Government had to surmount. But the grievances themselves were aggravated and increased a thousand-fold by the temptations offered to the Government to push them into oppression. Had a ruler of large and enlightened views, seconded by a ministry of practical talent, given his conscientious energy to the amelioration of mischievous legislation, the list of evils above enumerated would not have been enough to force a people into revolt, or to justify it in the eyes of the world at large. But, independently of the faults of William, and of Van Maanen and his other instruments of misgovernment, there was in the construction of the new State one positive evil, which human ingenuity could scarcely have overcome. That evil was the disproportion of population between the two divisions of the kingdom, considering, as they unfortunately did, their interests totally distinct. It was a manifest but an unavoidable injustice to Belgium to give her but the same number of Deputies as were allowed to Holland. Yet, had the representation of Belgium been proportioned to her population, she would assuredly have acquired that supremacy which she so loudly complained of when exercised by Holland; and the latter would have become, by the force of things, what Belgium had been pronounced to be by the folly of diplomacy, "an increase of territory."

The absolute establishment of the Kingdom of the Netherlands (so constituted) on a permanent footing of equalized nationality was perhaps impossible. But that such a kingdom might have been constructed, effectual for the intended purpose of the one which fell to pieces, there is no doubt. To raise up a barrier between France and Germany, a real balance of European power, was the design of the Congress of Vienna (in 1814), which had the materials for construction in its hands, but possessed no head sufficiently clear and disinterested to plan and execute the work. Had a great principle of forethought or a freedom from the desire of personal aggrandizement guided the counsels of the allies, the Rhenish provinces had been, without doubt, included with Holland and Belgium in the formation of that barrier kingdom, which, as it was constructed, was but a piece of frail and perishable patchwork. Had such an element. as those provinces been added to the imperfect combination, a self-righting action had been certainly superinduced, an internal umpire had existed when difficulties of self-government arose, and a balance of national interests and feelings would have been created that must have rendered the perpetual collision of petty passions and small jealousies impossible. The advantages of such a wholesale scheme to Europe at large may be hereafter discovered. Suffice it to say here that such a combination would have turned to the best account the dismemberment of Napoleon's enormous Empire, by giving one great and solid pledge to European peace, instead of frittering away so vast a guarantee into three unsettled, discontented fragments.

During fifteen years the Kingdom of the Netherlands struggled on through a frequently shifting atmosphere of political light and shade. Abandoned in a great measure by the rest of Europe to its own action, scarcely capable of appreciating its own situation, dazzled at times by certain false and forced indications of prosperity, oppressed at others by exaggerated fears of ill, agitated by antagonistic interests and passions, it presented the most violent contrasts, and was to foreign observers most difficult of comprehension.

King William had acquired a reputation for sagacity and liberality by some acts springing rather from constitutional than from moral causes. His plain manners and domestic habits were joined to an indifference to the pomps of royalty, and he wandered about the streets and wards, a daylight adventurer, without much dignity of bearing and none at all of purpose. The personal character of William had certainly a considerable influence on the secondary causes which led to the Belgian Revolution of 1830. He never forgot his Dutch origin and the stadtholderate principles of his ancestors. He always considered Holland as his country, and Belgium but as a part of his possessions. His constant efforts were directed to condense in himself the whole action of the Government, to mix himself up in every operation of finance and industry, to check and humiliate the nobility, and to ingratiate himself with the commercial and manufacturing classes by large loans of the public money.

By these means he succeeded in forming a body of personal partisans; while a certain result of this peculiar policy was to alienate the great mass of influential men, who smarted under his system of exclusion, and who would not consent to separate the great questions of national good from the selfish speculations of the monarch. It was in vain that the Treaty of London, of July 21, 1814, stipulated that the amalgamation between Holland and Belgium should be intimate and complete, while the royal artisan to whom the task was intrusted was incapable of performing it.

The three revolutions in Belgium had different results. That of the sixteenth century restored to Belgium its internal liberties without giving independence to the country. That of 1789, failing from the incapacity of its leaders, threw Belgium, exhausted and demoralized, underneath the feet of France. That of 1830 gave Belgium independence, neutrality, a dynasty of its choice, and an opportunity, never before possessed, for the development of its great and unsuspected resources, moral and physical.

The French Revolution, begun and finished in three days in July, 1830, was unquestionably the proximate cause of that of Belgium, two months later. But the latter was widely different in its outbursts and progress, although the provocations of both were similar. No violent *coup d'état* roused the people of Belgium to an abrupt resistance; nor did a contest of sixty or seventy hours in a single city suffice to establish their sovereignty on the ruins of the throne. The contest was not confined to the capital, but was spread all over the country during a period of some weeks. But it is not merely in these respects that the difference lies. The French people were suddenly forced into rebellion against an old hereditary dynasty, for the vindication of national rights. The Belgians were gradually worked up to revolt against a new-made sovereign, the type and instrument of foreign domination. France had to drive out a family; Belgium to conquer an army. The first fought a domestic battle for the recovery of its liberties. The latter combated an alien foe, for the deliverance of the soil. In one main point, and one only, those memorable events were strictly alike—in the total absence of preparation for the conflict, and of expectation that it was at hand.

Remonstrances, petitions, and declamation were the only means of redress attempted in Belgium, until the infatuated confidence of the authorities, acting in the spirit and under the order of the monarch, encouraged the people to proceed in preparations for the insurrection which their rulers seemed to court. Had King William shown the least foresight, had he listened in time to the popular complaints, dismissed his obnoxious minister, Van Maanen, abolished a few odious imposts, and removed the absurd restriction against the use of the French language in the public pleadings—all reasonable demands, and all conceded, but invariably too late—he might have been King of the Netherlands to the day of his death. Belgium was led on, coaxed as it may be said, from step to step; so that remonstrance, riot, revolt, and revolution followed in a gradual succession, that seemed arranged by the monarch, rather than intended by the people. Everything renders it likely that William calculated that his irritated subjects would proceed to excess, and that his foreign allies would then interfere, to uphold him by force, with increased prerogative over a prostrate people.

It is impossible, in the limits of this sketch, to detail the progress of the public discontent, or the various acts by which King William effectually alienated the affections of his subjects. The prosecution of Louis de Potter, for some seditious publications in a Brussels newspaper, was the last immediate measure of irritation previous to the outbreak in Paris. When this great event occurred, the people of all Belgium were quite prepared for an explosion, as soon as the signal should be given.

The Regency of Brussels (as the city government was called), as if for the purpose of giving this signal, commanded the representation, at the principal theatre, of the *Muette de Portici*, for the evening of August 25th; this opera having been considered, from its political bearing, so exciting and dangerous as to have been specially prohibited for several weeks previously. The civil authorities having thus admirably played their part, the people entered upon theirs; and the Dutch military commanders effectively joined, by their incapacity or cowardice, to bring about the *dénouement*.

On that memorable night, marking the opening of the Belgian Revolution, the rioters were almost unopposed. One movement of ordinary vigor on the part of the authorities would have stopped the tumult which the next day assumed so grave a character. The second day, August 26th, was decisive of the fate of the Kingdom of the Netherlands. But its dismemberment was solely due to the wavering and uncandid conduct of the King; for during four ensuing weeks sufficient opportunities occurred to remedy the successive evils so rapidly accumulated. On the morning of the 26th the affrighted Regency made some show of authority. They issued a proclamation promising certain measures of political redress; and they sanctioned the formation of a "burgher guard," to whom arms were freely issued, and for whom a chief was found in the person of Baron Vanderlinden d'Hoogvorst, an amiable, benevolent, incapable person, who consequently stood well with all classes, being neither feared nor envied by any.

The Revolution had now made its second step. Power had passed from the hands of the populace into those of the people. The Burgher Guard rapidly increased in numbers and soon began to exercise the authority now wholly vested in it. Baron d'Hoogvorst called a meeting of the notables of the city to take into consideration the perilous state of affairs. A deputation was ordered to proceed to The Hague with an address to the King; and a council was elected for the staff of the Burgher Guard, in whom the whole executive authority was vested. The deputation from the notables was received by the King. Professions of loyalty on the one side and of confidence on the other were bandied between them. A royal ordinance summoned the States-General to assemble on the 13th of the ensuing month. While the King was thus deceiving the deputation with fair words, military preparations were making, on a grand scale, to overawe Brussels if possible, and, at any rate, to force it into submission.

On August 29th the Prince of Orange, charged by the King with a temporizing mission, and his brother Prince Frederick, intrusted with the command of the troops, arrived at Antwerp, and on the following day their headquarters were established at Vilvorde, within five miles of Brussels. By this time the excitement within the capital had reached a very high pitch, influenced by the Jesuitical answers of the King to the various deputations which had been sent to him from Liège and other places, the concentration of an army close to the walls, the insulting tone of the Dutch journals, and the vague and suspicious wording of the proclamation issued by the Princes from Antwerp on the morning of the 30th.

Several interviews took place at Vilvorde during that and the following day between the Prince of Ligne and other representatives of the citizens of Brussels. After some animated discussions the Prince of Orange, yielding to the entreaties of the deputation, pledged his word that he would enter Brussels the following day attended solely by three or four officers of his staff, Prince Frederick engaging to remain at Vilvorde with the troops.

The following morning, September 1st, at daybreak, a proclamation of the Regency announced the news to the people, and a number of the Burgher Guard was required, at ten o'clock, to meet the Prince and escort him into the city. Before eleven, not less than eight thousand men were assembled on their parade-ground in the Grande Place, in their respective divisions and under the standard of Brabant. A finer body of volunteers, perhaps, was never collected in arms, even in the palmy days of Flemish freedom, when struggles, not dissimilar to the present, were so common between the burghers of the various cities and their feudal chiefs. Nor did the old and picturesque towers of the Town Hall, and the Gothic structures which surround it, ever witness a more stirring display than this rival exhibition of the many grand historical scenes which had been acted there.

But this day is more particularly memorable as forming an epoch of individual heroism almost without parallel, which proved that though the days of chivalry are gone their spirit still exists. To understand the extent to which that quality was displayed by the Prince of Orange on this occasion it must be borne in mind that, independently of the odium he shared in common with his father, as a Dutchman and a Nassau, he was also the brother-in-law of the Autocrat of Russia, and thus identified with the system of foreign influence, to shake off which those armed thousands stood in serried ranks; and that he was at that moment laboring under a load of personal calumny of the most base and brutal kind, propagated by the Belgian press. In defiance of all this, he now came forward from the ranks of his devoted army, to throw himself alone among a host of armed and inveterate enemies, in fulfilment of his promise, and under the sole guarantee of his innocence and courage.

Every arrangement of the day was made for the purpose of appalling as well as humiliating him. A treble line of bayonets bristled along the streets. Barricades were left standing to embarrass his path. A band of savage-looking men, bare-armed, and carrying knives, pikes, and hatchets, headed the column which received him beyond the gates; and strict orders were given, and frequently repeated as he came on, for the observance of a stern look and total silence throughout the whole array. The manner in which the gallant Prince conducted himself through this trying scene, the unfeeling reception given to him, and the perils he encountered on that day found a prominent place in the history of the times and form an episode of no small interest.

Repeated conferences, between the Prince and the members of a committee chosen by him from among the principal persons then in Brussels, consumed two days and nights. After much discussion as to the best means to use for conciliating the Government at The Hague and the people in Belgium, it was decided that the Prince should remove from Brussels with the whole of the regular garrison, leaving the entire control of the place in the hands of the citizens. At the moment of his departure with the troops there was a confident hope that the King, yielding to his representation of the true state of things, would have consented to a prompt and effectual legislative separation between Holland and Belgium; but not a notion was put forward, nor, as we believe, conceived, of the total independence of Belgium under any form of government whatever.

To the Prince's further honor it must be mentioned that during these two days he was repeatedly urged to place himself at the head of the movement, as his father's self-named viceroy, and thus identify himself with the cause of Belgium. This he at once declined as inconsistent with his duty both as a son and a subject. He saw the necessity for a separation; and, had his advice been followed, the monarchy had certainly been saved and the Nassaus had still ruled in Belgium. But such a measure was never contemplated by the King. He indeed pretended to take it into consideration; but, in flagrant violation of justice and humanity, he sent a powerful army to attack Brussels even while the States-General was debating the wisdom or impolicy of the measure of separation, which the expected success of that attack was intended to set completely at rest.

The mission of the Prince of Orange only raised against him a spirit of odious virulence in the Dutch people. More desirous even than the Belgians for the separation required by the latter, they could not tolerate him who admitted the justice of the claim, although he had risked his life and compromised his dignity for conciliation's sake. They would have been well pleased that a separation from Belgium should have been of their own prompting. But to *concede* it was gall and wormwood to their pride; and they consequently called loudly for the suppression of the revolt before the Legislature might entertain proposals of which the Prince was the bearer and the conscientious advocate.

In the mean time the chief towns of Belgium were successively following the example of the capital by loudly demanding a legislative separation between the Northern and Southern divisions of the Kingdom of the Netherlands. Some tumultuous proceedings took place; and, as was to be expected, the exasperation caused by the King's policy forced the people into strong measures for the furtherance of what had now become the general desire. Political clubs were formed; the language of the newspapers became more violent; and a "committee of safety" was decided on, a moderate title for the executive, which left everything open for the resumption of authority by a legally constituted government.

The Committee of Public Safety was specially charged with three main objects: First, with the care of preserving the rights of the dynasty. Second, with obtaining the separation by legal means. Third, with protecting the commercial and manufacturing interests of the country.

For a fortnight after the departure of the Prince of Orange this committee fulfilled the conditions of its nomination. The greatest difficulties consisted in finding employment for the poor, and in counteracting the violent conduct of the revolutionary clubs, by whom they were daily menaced and denounced. The committee consisted of eight persons. Four of them were noblemen, of no talent, whose names had been inserted merely to give the appearance of aristocratic sympathy with the four plebeians who were the active members. These latter were Messrs. Gendebien, Meéus, Rouppe, and Vandeweyer. The first was hasty and rash; the second and third were timid and temporizing; the fourth was cautious and cunning.

Elements of character such as these could form no combination fit to cope with the vigorous energy of such daring spirits as Charles Rogier, Feigneaux, Niellon, and Van Halen, the leading men of the clubs. The confidence of the people was soon given to those strenuous haters of Dutch connection in every shape; and the Committee of Public Safety, yielding to the uncontrollable influence that pressed on them, only wished to be driven from the post which they had not sufficient courage to maintain or resign.

It now became clear that the King had no intention of acceding to the proposed separation, which he talked of in his opening speech to the States-General at The Hague on September 13th, but which he carefully abstained from recommending, and toward the consideration of which, for several days following, they made no progress. It cannot be too forcibly impressed on those who would rightly understand the question, that, up to the very last moment of apparent security on the part of the King, the Belgian people were anxious to effect the separation on amicable and equitable terms. And it must also be observed that this proposed separation was not a mere revolutionary crotchet or a fanciful remedy for the existing evils. It might have been effected without any violation of the treaties of 1815, at that time forming the public law of Europe, and without the least attaint to the privileges of nations or individuals. It would have been a certain security against any wish on the part of Belgium for a reannexation to France, by founding a distinct nationality; and it would have conciliated all the great powers while it healed the discontent existing between the two divisions of the Kingdom of the Netherlands.

It must be admitted, to account for, but by no means to justify, the policy of the King and the Government, that they were in a state of most culpable ignorance of the real nature of public feeling in Belgium. The great bugbear which frightened them from their political propriety was the fear of republicanism in France, and of its spread in Belgium. This delusion was combated by a few disinterested observers; but their reasoning was not listened to when they pointed out the necessity for promptitude in the legislative proceedings, and an abstinence from all hostile measures.

Events now hurried on. Brussels was invested by an army of fourteen thousand men. The people, roused to desperation, and led on by Feigneaux and other clubmen, on the night of September 20th forced the doors of the Town Hall, seized on a depot of arms which was placed there for greater security, and drove out the incompetent committee, who, abandoning the care of the public safety, now only sought their own. They fled the country, and left the people to their fate—even Gendebien, the only one of the members from whom more resolution was expected; Baron D'Hoogvorst being the only one who remained, but in close concealment until the fearful events of the ensuing days had passed by.

The whole power now devolved, as if in the regular succession of revolutionary inheritance, to the people and their immediate chiefs. Yet it cannot be truly said that anarchy at any time reigned in Brussels. No act of spoliation or violence took place during the last three days, from September 20th to 23d, during which the very rabble formed the Government, and pike and bayonet were the law. All the degrading impulses of mob ferocity were suppressed; and every feeling was concentrated in the one absorbing object of a desperate defence. At length the agony of expectation was set at rest by the fiercer excitement of actual combat. On the morning of the 24th the attack on the city was made at three several points; and, to the great astonishment of Prince Frederick and his troops, they found at all a determined resistance instead of the easy triumph on which they had reckoned.

Among those who particularly distinguished themselves during the four days in which the people of Brussels fought so gallantly, and conquered, was Charles Rogier, who gave to the country the first impulse of armed resistance; who had been foremost in leading his detachment of the men of Liège to the attack on the Dutch at Diegham the day before the assault of Brussels took place; and who had, as soon as resistance was actually offered to that assault, boldly taken upon himself—in company with M. Jolly, a retired officer of engineers—the responsibility of a government, and the organization of the desultory and scattered elements, which ended in so complete a triumph. Van Halen, the commander-in-chief appointed by Rogier and Jolly, fought bravely; as did also Messrs. Niellon, Mellinet, Kessels, Vandermeere, Borremans, Grégoire, and Baron Felner (killed on the field of battle); besides a host of others equally brave and more or less celebrated.

The news of the heroic defence of Brussels was borne across the frontiers in every direction, and, while it created in Holland consternation and rage, it caused unbounded joy in France. Several of the runaway members of the Committee of Public Safety were assembled at Valenciennes, where they had been joined by Louis de Potter, one of the early causes and victims of government severity, who had hurried from Paris, and now waited with Vandeweyer and some others, not to mix in the *mêlée* and take chance with the country they had roused to resistance, but to "await the triumph and partake of the gale." The first of those who repassed the frontiers was Gendebien, a man of energy and nerve, notwithstanding his recent flight, led away by the bad example of his colleagues. The others followed; and the generous people of Brussels, drowning resentment and reproach in the shouts of victory, and feeling the urgent necessity of union, consented to the nomination of D'Hoogvorst, Gendebien, and Vandeweyer, as joint members of the Provisional Government, with Charles Rogier and Jolly, to whose intrepid firmness the preservation of order had been entirely owing. To maintain a show of aristocratic support the name of Count Felix de Merode was added, but he did not reappear from his hiding-place for some days after the expulsion of the Dutch.

Thousands upon thousands crowded into Brussels, as soon as the attacking army had fairly retreated, to view the different places of combat, to gaze on the shattered buildings, the torn-up and lacerated trees, the smoking ruins, the barricades and batteries, and above all to see the heroic defenders, some living and unhurt, the wounded stretched on their pallets in the hospitals and churches, and finally the glorious dead carried to their last common resting-place. It was altogether a combination exciting and affecting in no ordinary degree, and one never to be forgotten by those who witnessed it.

But the victors did not suffer themselves to be, in their turn, overcome by the delirium of triumph. They organized themselves under chosen leaders and pushed on to new combats and successes. They pursued the retreating army, hung on and harassed them, and had several severe though irregular actions with them, up to the walls of Antwerp, to which sanctuary Prince Frederick had conducted his discomfited troops.

The Provisional Government promptly proceeded to dispose of and secure the important interests confided to their care. And their first act in compliance with the popular will was to add De Potter's name to their number, and to recall him from a now nominal banishment to a sure ovation. But his worst enemy could not have done him a worse service. Happy had it been for him that he had remained an exile and a martyr. No stronger example was ever afforded of that fatality which places men on the highest pinnacle of their ambition, merely to dash them down to a surer destruction. De Potter now hastened across the frontier he had so lately shrunk from passing; and from the hour he touched the soil of Belgium he was borne forward to Brussels on the tide of popular enthusiasm; the members of the Provisional Government hailing his coming with pretended sympathy but with serious misgivings. They knew his vast ambition—they saw his unlimited influence. But they had yet to learn that he, who for the best years of his life had labored to bring about a crisis like that, was, at the moment of its realization, impotent to turn it to account.

Van Halen, a man of different stamp, was another most prominent person at that period. De Potter saw a dangerous rival in the gallant Spaniard, who had rendered such good service to his adopted country; and he had sufficient cunning to propagate suspicions against him in the public mind, which forced him to resign his command and leave to others to follow up his victory.

The effect produced throughout the Belgian provinces by

the events of Brussels was instantaneous and general. In a few days all the fortresses, with the exception of Antwerp, Maestricht, and Venlo, surrendered to the commanders named by the Provisional Government, which had by October 10th entirely supplanted the authority of the King.

The defence of Brussels had decided the States-General to consent to the legislative separation so long demanded by Belgium, but now forgotten, in the broad prospect of absolute independence which opened out before the nation's view. The King, seeing the state of the public mind, tried a new course of policy. He despatched the Prince of Orange once more to Belgium; and Antwerp was chosen as the stronghold whence he might with most effect send forth his emissaries or issue his addresses to the now formidable rebels in the hope of persuading them into submission. The Prince, sanguine and confiding, readily undertook to attempt this impracticable scheme. But there was no good faith in his father who sent him, nor any sincerity in the council of Belgians who were appointed to act with him; and no chance of coöperation on the part of the millions who identified him with all the violence and hypocrisy of his brother and his father. After some weeks of humiliating failure, deceived, abandoned, and exposed to all the bitterness of regret, he quitted Antwerp on the night of October 25th, in a steamboat for Rotterdam, lighted by the flames from the burning houses set on fire by the Dutch troops in their retreat from the pursuing Belgians. He now returned to Holland for the second time during six weeks, as pure as any public man who ever went through ordeals so severe and so unfortunate.

The Prince's departure from Antwerp immediately led to a state of total anarchy. On the 27th matters came to a fearful crisis. The populace, having risen in arms on the previous day, at length obtained possession of two of the gates of the town and opened them to the patriot forces. These, flushed with success, easily drove the scattered detachments of the royal troops into the citadel. A truce, hastily concluded, was quickly violated by some desultory acts of warfare between the vedettes on either side; upon which General Chassé, the Dutch commander, commenced a bombardment of the defenceless city, assisted by the artillery of the Dutch flotilla moored in the river Schelde before the quay, and bringing to bear a combination of nearly one hundred pieces of cannon.

This was unquestionably one of the most important events of the Revolution. Had the Belgian volunteers not been checked in their triumphant career, they would certainly have crossed the frontiers and have overrun Holland altogether. But although the Revolution was by this catastrophe paralyzed in its most important extremities, the vital principle of national independence was untouched. And it was perhaps favorable for its preservation that the inflated valor of the people, from which it apprehended its greatest risks, should have met this great, but not the most serious, check.

In the mean while the Prince of Orange had returned to The Hague, under circumstances the most mortifying, unthought of amid the rejoicing which the vindictive people indulged in in honor of their avenger Chassé; and the heir to the throne took possession, almost by stealth, of the homely residence, that presented so humiliating a contrast to the splendid palace which by no fault of his he had forever lost at Brussels. The stirring interest of the Belgian Revolution expired amid the embers of the conflagration of Antwerp. The social and political disruption was complete. Violence and the force of arms had done their work. To reorganize the materials of this moral chaos was the business of diplomacy; and under its tutelage the destinies of the country immediately passed.

Belgium having thrown off the yoke of Holland had now to decide between two alternatives: a republic, leading to a junction with France and a general war; or an independent monarchy, and negotiation. The latter of these was chosen; and from the moment her decision was known, she became identified with the interests of Europe, as she had been already admitted to its sympathies. The first great object of the Provisional Government was to put the country in harmony with the great powers, and then to proceed to the arrangement of several serious topics of domestic importance. Missions were despatched to Paris and London; but a great want of competent persons was evident from the first. The lucky accident of an acquaintance with the English language was allowed to stand in the stead of higher qualifications in the individuals chosen for the latter place. But the dearth of talent and the lack of station in the plebeian agitators, thrown to the surface by the late commotions, were for a long time serious obstacles to their success.

On November 10th the National Congress, which had been summoned some weeks previously, began its sittings; and its business commenced by an address from De Potter, who represented the Provisional Government.

On the 18th the Congress unanimously proclaimed the independence of Belgium. On the 22d it decreed, by a majority of one hundred seventy-four votes against thirteen, that the form of the government should be monarchical. Other important measures were passed within a few months of busy and turbulent discussion. The perpetual exclusion of the Nassaus, the adoption of the constitution, and the election of a sovereign were the other great questions on which the fate of the country hinged; and they were all debated, and decided in accordance with the convictions of Europe at large.

On November 4th the Conference of London, composed of representatives of the five great powers, commenced their long series of protocols, which began by pronouncing the existence of an armistice between Holland and Belgium, and assigning the same boundaries to the two States as existed before the union; that is to say, before the Treaty of Paris of May 30, 1814. By a protocol of December 20, 1830, the conference pronounced the dissolution of the Kingdom of the Netherlands. Several circumstances occurred in rapid succession and of almost miraculous coincidence, in favor of the new State still struggling on to independence. The first was the singular want of sense, spirit, and common powers of calculation, which hurled De Potter from his eminence to the lowest level, political and personal; until, within a few weeks from his triumphal entry into Brussels, he was driven from its gates, reviled and unpitied, an outcast too happy to escape with his life. The second was the unlooked-for forbearance of Louis Philippe (no matter from what source it sprang), making him repress the national longing of all France to seize on Belgium, as a recovered portion of its territory. The third was the breaking out of the Polish Revolution, November 29, 1830, turning the attention, and calling for the whole force, of the Russian despot to internal affairs, and paralyzing all his plans for offensive operations against France, and for a restoration in Belgium.

Fortuitous circumstances of minor moment might be adduced, all tending toward the same great end. Altogether, the good genius of Belgium triumphed over a thousand obstacles raised up by domestic faction, Dutch intrigue, and foreign jealousies; and the crowning measure, the election of Prince Leopold of Saxe-Coburg to be king, completed the series of events which marked Belgium as the only perfect political result of the Revolution of 1830, and led to her becoming a model for the monarchical States of Europe.

With this result before us, it is unnecessary to dwell on the minute details of seventy protocols, issued by the Conference of London, in reference to the Dutch and Belgic question. The multifarious state papers relative to this remarkable affair have been collected and printed. Their examination may be useful for the student of diplomatic anatomy; and they certainly form a monument of statesmanlike forbearance and forethought.

The question of the choice of a king offered a most curious spectacle to the world at large, and its progress abounded in important lessons to both monarchs and people. From the various persons named by the public voice or actually put upon the list as candidates in the first instance, the most remarkable were the Duke of Leuchtenberg, the eldest son of Eugene Beauharnais, and the Duke of Nemours, second son of Louis Philippe, King of the French. Of these rivals it may be stated that the choice of the first would have been anti-French, without being European; that of the latter exclusively French, but anti-European. Louis Philippe and the Conference of London declared against both; and while the election was nevertheless proceeding at Brussels, the Prince of Orange was proclaimed at Ghent, in an unsuccessful attempt for his succession, by Colonel Ernest Grégoire, one of the defenders of the Brussels barricades against the Dutch attack.

From that period the necessity became evident of finding some individual to fill the vacant throne, who would unite in himself the confidence of all the European powers without being a mark for the jealousy of any. To occupy the interregnum by a neutral measure of preparation, Surlet de Chokier, a respectable Belgian gentleman, was named regent February 24, 1831, The National Congress having adjourned on March 9th, reassembled on the 29th of the same month, separated once more on April 12th, and did not meet again till May 18th. During these intervals they completed the work of the Revolution in the spirit of European policy; and they consummated the most important of its acts—for a false step *then* had irretrievably ruined the country—by making a formal offer of the throne to Prince Leopold.

The conferences between the Prince and the commissioners deputed by the Congress to wait on him in London afforded many proofs of his good sense and good feeling. He came forward at their solicitation, backed by the entreaties of the principal powers of Europe; and he accepted the great, but most troublesome trust they reposed in him, from an exalted regard for the public good. The only conditions for which he stipulated were such as related to the well-being of the country he was chosen to rule over. He left London on July 16, 1831, and made his entry into Brussels on the 21st, when he was at once inaugurated, with all due solemnity, the National Congress being, by this act, dissolved.

Scarcely was Leopold seated on his uneasy throne when the King of Holland, true to his treacherous character, sent forward his son, the Prince of Orange—unfortunately, on this as on former occasions, too subservient to his father's will—to invade Belgium at the head of an army of fifty thousand men and seventy pieces of cannon, in defiance of the existing armistice, and while the Dutch plenipotentiaries at the Conference of London were giving written assurances of the King's ardent desire to conclude a definitive treaty of peace!

After a campaign of ten days, in which a scrambling action—called by courtesy the "*battle* of Louvain"—was fought, having put to complete rout the undisciplined volunteers of Belgium, the Prince of Orange retreated to Holland to reap the honors of his poor triumph. The appearance of the French army, which Leopold called to his assistance, was the cause of this retrograde movement. The rival commanders had good opportunities afforded them for proving once more their personal courage;

the Prince of Orange having a horse killed under him, and one of King Leopold's aides-de-camp being wounded by his side, in the thickest of the fight.

This battle of Louvain, like the bombardment of Antwerp by General Chassé, had a highly salutary effect on the character of the Belgian nation. Had it not been for these checks to their overweening pride, which may be fairly pardoned in consideration of their great successes, Leopold would have found it perhaps impossible to govern the country with the ease he did. The influence of his firm yet forbearing temperament has been immense on a people at once so susceptible and so reflective. The wisdom of his administration produced the happiest effects; shown forth in the return to tranquillity and order; in commercial, agricultural, and manufacturing enterprise; and in the establishment of a solid and to all appearances a lasting system of prosperity.

INSURRECTION IN RUSSIAN POLAND

A.D. 1831

ALFRED RAMBAUD

At the Congress of Vienna, in 1815, a new kingdom of Poland was created and placed under the government of Alexander I, Emperor of Russia. It was not to be incorporated with the Russian Empire, but to be governed separately, having its own constitution and administrative organization. The Czar appointed as commander-in-chief of the new kingdom his brother, the Grand Duke Constantine, who inaugurated a strict military rule, and by his errors and want of tact offended the Polish people, and at length provoked them to revolt.

Alexander, who during most of his reign was a sovereign of enlightened and liberal purposes, died in 1825, and was succeeded by his brother, Nicholas I, a man of quite opposite views. He supported Constantine in his misgovernment of Poland, and the insurrection against it was a manifestation of the old-time Polish passion for liberty, but also of the old incapacity of the people to unite effectively for its achievement. As on other matters of Russian history, Rambaud, the French Academician, here speaks with highest authority.

TOWARD 1830 Russia found herself in a singular state of uneasiness. The cholera had just made its appearance; fierce revolts had broken out at Sebastopol, Novgorod, and Staraia-Roussa. The Emperor seemed agitated by gloomy presentiments. He had been shocked by the news of the July revolution which had expelled his ally, Charles X, from France; the Belgian and Italian revolutions followed close on each other. The tricolored flag, the flag of 1799 and 1812, floating over the French consulate at Warsaw, hastened the explosion of the Polish Revolution.

The time was already far behind when Alexander, while opening the Diet of 1818, boasted of "those liberal institutions which had never ceased to be the object of his solicitude," and which allowed him to show to Russia herself "what he had for so long prepared for her." The time was far away when he congratulated the Polish Deputies on having rejected the proposed law of divorce, and proclaimed that, "freely elected, they must freely vote."

No doubt the prosperity of the kingdom was increasing. Commerce and industry had developed, the finances were in a satisfactory state, and from the remnant of the Napoleonic legions the Grand Duke Constantine had formed an excellent army of sixty thousand men. Unhappily it was very difficult for Alexander, who had become more and more autocratic in Russia, to accommodate himself in Poland to the liberty of a representative government. The Diet of 1820 had irritated him profoundly by its attack on the ministers and its rejection of certain projects of law. He looked on these ordinary incidents of parliamentary life as an attempt to undermine his authority. He lent an ear to the counsels of Karamzin and Araktcheyeff. He put forth an "additional act of the constitution" which suppressed the public sittings of the Diet. After the session of 1822 the convocation of the Estates was adjourned indefinitely. The liberty of the press was restrained, and the police became more vexatious. The soldiers complained of the severity and sometimes of the brutality of the Grand Duke Constantine, who was full of good intentions, who loved Poland, and had given proof of it by sacrificing the crown of Russia for a Polish lady, but who could never control his impetuous and eccentric character. The officers who had served under Dombrowski, Poniatowski, and Napoleon could scarecly reconcile themselves to the Muscovite discipline. Ancient jealousies and national hate were on the point of breaking out between the two peoples. Besides the Polish malcontents who grumbled at the violations of the Constitution in 1815, there was the party which dreamed of the Constitution of May 3, 1791, or of a republic, and which desired to reëstablish Poland in her ancient independence and within her ancient limits. The secret associations of the Templars and the Patriotic Society were formed. The trial of the Russian *Décembristes* had revealed an understanding between the conspirators of the two nations.

Constantine had made another mistake, that of persuading the Emperor Nicholas that the Polish army should not be employed against the Turks. He loved this army after his own fashion, and his saying has been quoted: "I detest war; it spoils an army." Victories gained in common over the ancient enemy of the two peoples might have created a bond of military fraternity between the Russian and Polish armies, given an opening to the warlike ardor of the Polish youth, and crowned with glory the union of the two crowns. Constantine's unpopularity increased in consequence of this error. Nothing, however, was as yet imperilled. When the Emperor Nicholas came to open the Diet of May, 1830, in person, his presence in Warsaw excited some hopes. In spite of the reserve which the deputies had imposed on themselves, they could not refrain from rejecting the unhappy scheme of the law of divorce, from lodging complaints against the ministers, and uttering a wish for the reunion with the Lithuanian provinces. This wish could not, of course, be granted by Nicholas without deeply wounding the patriotism and the rights of Russia. The "King of Poland" and his subjects separated with discontent on both sides; the secret societies were more active in their conspiracies, and the news from Paris found all the elements of a revolution already prepared.

On the evening of November 17th (29th) the youths belonging to the School of the Standard-bearers revolted at the command of the Sublieutenant Wysoki. They demanded cartridges: "Cartridges," cried Wysoki, "you will find them in the boxes of the Russians! Forward!" While one hundred thirty of them surprised the barracks of the Russian cavalry, a handful rushed to the palace of the Belvedere, where the Czarevitch resided. Constantine had just time to escape; the director of police and other officials fell beneath the blows of the conspirators. In a few moments all the Polish troops, the infantry, a battalion of sappers, the horse artillery, and a regiment of grenadiers, hastened to the arsenal, seized forty thousand muskets, and distributed arms among the insurgent people. Five Polish generals, accused of treason to the national cause, were put to death. The brave General Noviki, victim of a mistaken identity, suffered the same fate. The Grand Duke, seeing the insurrection spread, decided to evacuate the town and retire to the village of Wirzba; he even sent back to Warsaw the Polish regiment of mounted sharpshooters who had alone remained loyal.

Prince Lubek hastened to convoke the council of administration, to which was added a certain number of influential citizens. The majority of this council considered the struggle with Russia an act of madness, and entreated the people to "end all their agitations with the night, which had covered them with her mantle." This advice was not listened to: the crowd summoned other men to the head of affairs—the Princes Czartoryski and Ostrovski, Malakhowski, and the celebrated professor and historian Lelewel. The students were organized into a crack regiment; Lelewel opened a patriotic club and published a daily paper; the patriot Chlopicki, a brave officer who had served with distinction under Napoleon, was appointed generalissimo, but Chlopicki saw no hope for Poland save in a prompt reconciliation with the Emperor. He despatched envoys to St. Petersburg, to the Grand Duke's headquarters, and even to London and Paris, to obtain the mediation of the Western powers.

Two parties were concerned in this movement—the moderate party, who wished to mend the link that they had broken with the legal government by soliciting, at the most, a reform of the constitution and the annexation of the Lithuanian palatinates; and the party of the democrats, who insisted on the abdication of the Romanoffs, the restoration to the country of its independence, and the recovery by arms of the lost provinces. Nicholas repelled all efforts to treat which were not preceded by an immediate and unconditional submission. His proclamation deprived the insurgents of all hopes "of obtaining concessions as the price of their crimes." From that time the war party at Warsaw triumphed over the peace party. Chlopicki, disgusted with the conduct of the more advanced spirits, had resigned the post of generalissimo. He finally accepted the dictatorship, and gave himself up, without any hope of success, to organizing the defence, while continuing the negotiations. He and Lelewel were particularly uncongenial: the latter was of opinion that the Poles ought to take the offensive, throw themselves into Lithuania and Volhynia, arm the peasants, and raise a levy *en masse*, declaring that when an insurrection did not spread it was certain to fail. "Well, then," exclaimed Chlopicki impatiently, "make war with your reapers yourself," and he resigned his command a second time for a subordinate post.

The Diet now assembled and appointed Prince Radziwill, a weak man, without military talents, generalissimo. His election

was hailed by cries of "To Lithuania! to Lithuania!" In the
session of January 13th (25th), Count Ezerski, one of the two
magistrates sent by Constantine to St. Petersburg, gave an account
of their interview with the Emperor. The replies of Nicholas
did not give more ground for hope than his proclamation of December 17th. He refused to parley with rebel subjects. He at
once rejected the idea of despoiling Russia of the Lithuanian
provinces for the benefit of Poland. He considered it a sacred
duty to stifle the insurrection and punish the guilty, adding that
if the nation took up arms against him Poland would be crushed
by Polish guns. Then the Diet proclaimed the Romanoffs to
have forfeited the throne. It hoped by this step to engage the
sympathy of the Western courts, but in reality it rendered all
attempts at pacific mediation impossible, the Poles having abandoned the ground of the treaties of 1815, the only ones to which
European diplomacy could appeal. As to an armed intervention in the presence of the hostility of the German powers, neither England nor France could dream of such a thing. In vain
the population of Paris made energetic manifestations of its
sympathies, in vain the Chambers resounded with warlike addresses; all these demonstrations had no effect. Six days after
its declaration of freedom, the Polish Government instituted a
provisional government composed of five members: Adam Czartoryski, president; Barzikowski, Niemoiewski, Morazski, and
Joachim Lelewel, who represented democratic tendencies in this
Supreme Council.

The Czarevitch had completely evacuated the kingdom;
Modlin and all the other fortresses were in the hands of the
rebels. To protect Warsaw on the east, they had thrown up a
formidable work to cover the bridge; the Polish forces with the
new levies amounted to ninety thousand men, well provided
with artillery. In February, 1831, an army of one hundred
twenty thousand Russians, under the command of Diebitsch
Sabalkanski (the hero of the Balkans), entered Poland in a severe frost, driving back the Polish detachments into Warsaw.
The insurgent General Dverniki gained an advantage at the
skirmish of Stokzek. A two-days' battle at Grochow, glorious for
Poland (February 19th–20th), did not hinder the Russians from
approaching Warsaw, and the combats of Bialolenska and of the

wood of Praga (February 24th–25th) brought them nearly up to the Praga quarter. Radziwill then resigned his office, and was succeeded by Skrzynecki. The main body of the Russian army had abandoned the bank of the Vistula, with the exception of three small corps—that of Rosen at Dembe Wielke, that of Geismar at Wawre, and a third under Praga. The Polish general attacked them suddenly, and defeated Geismar at Wawre and Rosen at Dembe Wielke and Iganie, but did not dare to push his advantages further. An expedition directed against Volhynia by Dverniki failed completely; he was driven back into Galicia.

The Lithuanian expedition ended in a disaster under Wilna; the Poles had to cross the Prussian frontier, and only one division, that of Dembinski, reëntered Warsaw. In the interval, Skrzynecki having attacked the right wing of the Russians at Ostrolenka on the Narew, was after a severe fight forced back on the other side of the river (May 26th). Cholera raged in both armies, and carried off successively Diebitsch and the Grand Duke Constantine.

Political divisions now as always ruined Poland. After some violent scenes, Skrzynecki was replaced by Dembinski, and then by Malakhowski. Two days' revolt made the streets run with blood, and the people committed massacres in the prisons. The moderate party took flight, and Czartoryski fled in disguise. The Provisional Government resigned its power into the hands of the Diet, who invested General Krukoviecki with the office of dictator. He had some of the mutineers executed, but was not able to reëstablish order.

Paskewitch Erivanski, Diebitsch's successor, strengthened by the benevolent help of Prussia, which had thrown open to him her arsenals and magazines of Dantzig and Koenigsberg, had crossed the Vistula below Warsaw, and transported the theatre of war to the left bank. He intended to attack the capital, not from the side of Praga, as Suvaroff had done, but from the side of Vola and the Czyste quarter. Two semicircles of concentric intrenchments corresponded to these two quarters, but the Russians had no longer, as on the side of Praga, to overcome the obstacle of the Vistula. On September 6th the Russians attacked Vola, where General Sovinski, who had lost a leg at

the Moskva, and Wysocki, who began the revolution, were killed.
The same day Paskewitch began to cannonade Czyste and the
town. The next morning Krukoviecki asked to capitulate.
Paskewitch exacted the unconditional submission of the army
and the people, the immediate surrender of Warsaw, the reconstruction of the bridge of Praga, and the retreat of the troops on
Plock. The Diet having allowed the time fixed for a reply to
pass, Paskewitch began the attack. Krukoviecki had accepted
his terms, but he had been replaced in the interval by Niemoiewski. Czyste was already in flames, and the Russians were scal-
ing the ramparts, when the Poles capitulated. "Sire, Warsaw is
at your feet," wrote Paskewitch to the Emperor. "Order
reigns at Warsaw," such was the funeral oration pronounced by
official Europe over the insurrection. Twenty thousand soldiers laid down their arms at Plock, fifteen thousand of whom
Ramorino took into Galicia.

Not only Warsaw, but Poland herself, lay at the feet of Nicholas. Partial insurrections and new plots were later to revive
his resentment. At present he was happy at being able to make
an example and intimidate the European revolution. Seques-
trations, confiscations, imprisonments, and banishments to Sibe-
ria served as commentaries on the amnesty. The constitution
granted by Alexander was annulled; the public offices were
abolished and replaced by mere commissions emanating from
the public offices of Russia; the directors of these commissions
formed, under the management of the *Namiestnik*, the council of
government. No more diets; Poland was administered by the
officials of the Czar. No more Polish army; it was lost in the
imperial army. The national orders were only preserved as Russian orders, distributed among the most zealous servants of the
Government. The Russian systems of taxes, justice, and coin-
age were successively introduced into the kingdom. The ancient historical palatinates gave way to Russian provinces.

PASSAGE OF THE ENGLISH REFORM BILL

A.D. 1832

SIR THOMAS ERSKINE MAY

This measure, closely following upon Catholic emancipation, was one of the most memorable legislative reforms of modern times. It not only readjusted the basis of parliamentary representation and extended the suffrage, but by suppression of bribery and the abolition of "rotten boroughs" went far toward securing honest elections.

Before the Reform Bill went into effect the English people never had anything like direct control of their government. From the revolution of 1688, which put an end to the autocratic pretensions of the Crown, the Government was that of an aristocratic Parliament, in which none but privileged classes were represented. With the operation of the Reform Bill the Constitution and Government became in some measure democratic, and they have grown more so ever since.

Defects in the electoral system and corruption in connection with its workings had led to many earlier attempts at reform. Unequal representation was from the first a source of discontent with the composition of Parliament. Systematic bribery at elections appears to have become a practice during the reign of Charles II. This evil increased after the revolution, when the House of Commons obtained greater power. Bribery acts were passed, but did little to check the abuse. Seats in Parliament continued to be bought and sold.

In the eighteenth century many schemes of reform were proposed, notably, toward its close, by William Pitt, and at one period of his career by Charles James Fox, both of whom died in 1806; but, as will be seen in the following pages, in the early years of the nineteenth century little progress had been made in this direction.

No authority on this subject is to be placed above Sir Thomas Erskine May, the eminent English historian and jurist, whose various historical works, as well as his legal writings, are noted for their learning and impartiality.

IN 1809 the question of reform was revived in Parliament. Pitt and Fox, who had first fought together in support of the same principles, and afterward on opposite sides, were both no more; Mr. Grey and Mr. Erskine had been called to the House of Peers; and the cause was in other hands. Sir Francis Burdett was now its advocate, less able and influential than his predecessors, and an eccentric politician, but a thoroughbred English gentleman. His scheme was such as to repel the support of the few remaining reformers. He proposed that every county should be divided into electoral districts; that each district should return one member; and that the franchise should be vested in the taxed male population. So wild a project found no more than fifteen supporters.

On June 13, 1810, Earl Grey, in moving an address on the state of the nation, renewed his public connection with the cause of reform, avowed his adherence to the sentiments he had always expressed, and promised his future support to any temperate and judicious plan for the correction of abuses in the representation. He was followed by Lord Erskine, in the same honorable avowal.

In 1818 Sir Francis Burdett, now chairman of the Hampden Club of London, proposed resolutions in favor of universal male suffrage, equal electoral districts, vote by ballot, and annual Parliaments. His motion was seconded by Lord Cochrane, but found not another supporter in the House of Commons. At this time there were numerous public meetings in favor of universal suffrage; and reform associations, not only of men, but of women, were engaged in advancing the same cause. And as many of these were advocating female suffrage, Sir Francis Burdett, to avoid misconstruction, referred to male suffrage only.

In 1819 Sir Francis Burdett again brought forward a motion on the subject. He proposed that the House should, early in the next session, take into consideration the state of the representation. In the debate Lord John Russell, who had recently been admitted to Parliament, expressed his opinion in favor of disfranchising such boroughs as were notoriously corrupt. The motion was superseded by reading the orders of the day.

At the beginning of the following session Lord John Russell, whose name has ever since been honorably associated with the cause of reform, proposed his first motion on the subject. In the preceding session he had brought under the notice of the House scandalous proceedings at Grampound. He now took broader ground, and embraced the general evils of the electoral system. The time was not favorable to moderate counsels.

On one side were the intemperate advocates of universal suffrage; on the other the stubborn opponents of all change in the representation. But such was the moderation of Lord John's scheme of reform that it might have claimed the support of the wiser men of all parties. He showed, in a most promising speech, that in former times decayed boroughs had been discharged from sending Members, and populous places summoned by writ to return them; he described the wonderful increase of the great manufacturing towns which were unrepresented; and the corruption of the smaller boroughs which sold their franchise. He concluded by moving resolutions: 1. That boroughs in which notorious bribery and corruption should be proved to prevail should cease to return Members; the electors not proved guilty being allowed to vote for the county. 2. That the right thus taken from corrupt boroughs should be given to great towns with a population of not less than fifteen thousand, or to some of the largest counties. 3. That further means should be taken to detect corruption; and lastly, that the borough of Grampound should cease to send Members.

As the motion was met by the Government in a conciliatory manner, and as Lord Castlereagh was ready to concur in the disfranchisement of Grampound, Lord John Russell consented to withdraw his resolutions and gave notice of a bill for disfranchising Grampound. The progress of this bill was interrupted by the death of the King; but it was renewed in the following session, and reached the House of Lords, where, after evidence being taken at the bar, it dropped by reason of the prorogation. Again it was passed by the Commons, in 1821. That House had given the two vacant seats to the great town of Leeds; but the Lords still avoided the recognition of such a principle, by assigning two additional Members to the county of York, in which form the bill was at length agreed to.

In 1821 two motions were made relating to Parliamentary reform, the one by Mr. Lambton, and the other by Lord John Russell. On April 17th the former explained his scheme. In lieu of the borough representation he proposed to divide counties into districts containing twenty-five thousand inhabitants, each returning a Member; to extend the franchise for such districts to all householders paying taxes; to facilitate polling by means of numerous polling-booths and by enabling overseers to receive votes; and to charge the necessary expenses of every election upon the poor rates. To the county constituencies he proposed to add copyholders, and leaseholders for terms of years. After a debate of two days his motion was negatived by a majority of twelve. On May 9th Lord John Russell moved resolutions with a view to the discovery of bribery, the disfranchisement of corrupt boroughs, and the transfer of the right of returning Members to places which had increased in wealth and population. His resolutions were superseded by the previous question, which was carried by a majority of thirty-one.

In 1822 Lord John Russell, having, as he said, "served an apprenticeship in the cause of reform," again pressed the matter upon the notice of the House. The cry for universal suffrage had now subsided, tranquillity prevailed throughout the country, and no circumstance could be urged as unfavorable to its fair consideration. After showing the great increase of the wealth and intelligence of the country, he proposed the addition of sixty Members to the counties and forty to the great towns; and, not to increase the total number of the House of Commons, he suggested that one hundred of the smallest boroughs should each lose one of their two Members. His motion, reduced to a modest resolution, "that the present state of representation required serious consideration," was rejected by a majority of one hundred five.

In 1823 Lord John renewed his motion in the same terms. He was now supported by numerous petitions, and among the number by one from seventeen thousand freeholders of the county of York, but, after a short debate, was defeated by a majority of one hundred eleven.

Again, in 1826, Lord John proposed the same resolution to the House, and pointed out forcibly that the increasing wealth and intelligence of the people were daily aggravating the inequality of the representation. Nomination boroughs continued to return a large proportion of the Members of the House of Commons, while places of enormous population and commercial prosperity were without representatives. After an interesting debate his resolution was negatived by a majority of one hundred twenty-four.

In 1829 a proposal for reform proceeded from an unexpected quarter and was based upon principles entirely novel. The measure of Catholic emancipation had recently been carried; and many of its opponents, of the Tory party, disgusted with their own leaders, by whom it had been forwarded, were suddenly converted to the cause of parliamentary reform. Representing their opinions, Lord Blandford on June 2d submitted a motion on the subject. He apprehended that the Roman Catholics would now enter the borough-market and purchase seats for their representatives in such numbers as to endanger our Protestant Constitution. His resolutions condemning close and corrupt boroughs found only forty supporters and were rejected by a majority of seventy-four. At the beginning of the next session Lord Blandford repeated these views in moving an amendment to the address, representing the necessity of improving the representation. Being seconded by Mr. O'Connell, his anomalous position as a reformer was manifest.

Soon afterward he moved for leave to bring in a bill to restore the constitutional influence of the Commons in the Parliament of England, which contained an elaborate machinery of reform, including the restoration of wages to Members. His motion served no other purpose than that of reviving discussions upon the general question of reform.

But in the mean time questions of less general application had been discussed, which eventually produced the most important results. The disclosures that followed the general election of 1826, and the conduct of the Government, gave a considerable impulse to the cause of reform. The corporations of Northampton and Leicester were alleged to have applied large sums, from the corporate funds, for the support of ministerial candidates. In the Northampton case Sir Robert Peel went so far as to maintain the right of a corporation to apply its funds to election purposes; but the House could not be brought to concur in such a principle; and a committee of inquiry was appointed. In the Leicester case all inquiry was successfully resisted.

Next came two cases of gross and notorious bribery—Penryn and East Retford. They might have been easily disposed of; but, treated without judgment by the ministers, they precipitated a contest, which ended in the triumph of reform.

Penryn had long been notorious for its corruption, which had been already twice exposed; yet the ministers resolved to deal tenderly with it. Instead of disfranchising so corrupt a borough, they proposed to embrace the adjacent hundreds in the privilege of returning Members. But true to the principles he had already carried out in the case of Grampound, Lord John Russell succeeded in introducing an amendment in the bill by which the borough was to be entirely disfranchised.

In the case of East Retford a bill was brought in to disfranchise that borough and to enable the town of Birmingham to return two representatives; and it was intended by the reformers to transfer the franchise from Penryn to Manchester. The session closed without the accomplishment of either of these objects. The Penryn Disfranchisement Bill, having passed the Commons, had dropped in the Lords; and the East Retford bill had not yet passed the Commons.

In the next session two bills were introduced: one by Lord John Russell, for transferring the franchise from Penryn to Manchester; and another by Mr. Tennyson, for disfranchising East Retford and giving representatives to Birmingham. The Government proposed a compromise. If both boroughs were disfranchised, they offered, in one case to give two Members to a populous town, and in the other to the adjoining hundreds. When the Penryn bill had already reached the House of Lords, where its reception was extremely doubtful, the East Retford bill came on for discussion in the Commons. The Government now opposed the transferrence of the franchise to Birmingham. Mr. Huskisson, however, voted for it; and his proffered resignation being accepted by the Duke of Wellington, led to the withdrawal of Lord Palmerston, Lord Dudley, Mr. Lamb, and Mr. Grant, the most liberal Members of the Government, the friends and colleagues of the late Mr. Canning. The Cabinet was now entirely Tory, and less disposed than ever to make concession to the reformers. The Penryn bill was soon afterward thrown out by the Lords on the second reading; and the East Retford bill, having been amended so as to retain the franchise in the hundreds, was abandoned in the Commons.

It was the opinion of many attentive observers of these times that the concession of demands so reasonable would have arrested, or postponed for many years, the progress of reform. They were resisted; and further agitation was encouraged. In 1830 Lord John Russell, no longer hoping to deal with Penryn and East Retford, proposed at once to enfranchise Leeds, Birmingham, and Manchester, and to provide that the three next places proved guilty of corruption should be altogether disfranchised. His motion was opposed, mainly on the ground that if the franchise were given to these towns, the claims of other large towns could not afterward be resisted. Where, then, was such concession to stop? It is remarkable that on this occasion Mr. Huskisson said of Lord Sandon, who had moved an amendment, that he "was young, and would yet live to see the day when the representative franchise must be granted to the great manufacturing districts. He thought such a time fast approaching; and that one day or other His Majesty's ministers would come down to that House to propose such a measure as necessary for the salvation of the country." Within a year this prediction had been verified; though the unfortunate statesman did not live to see its fulfilment. The motion was negatived by a majority of forty-eight; and thus another moderate proposal, free from the objections which had been urged against disfranchisement, and not affecting any existing rights, was sacrificed to a narrow and obstinate dread of innovation.

In this same session other proposals were made of a widely different character. Mr. O'Connell moved resolutions in favor of universal suffrage, triennial Parliaments, and vote by ballot. Lord John Russell moved to substitute other resolutions providing for the enfranchisement of large towns and giving additional Members to populous counties; while any increase of the numbers of the House of Commons was avoided by disfranchising some of the smaller boroughs, and restraining others from sending more than one Member. Sir Robert Peel, in the course of the debate, said: "They had to consider whether there was not, on the whole, a general representation of the people in that House, and whether the popular voice was not sufficiently heard. For himself he thought that it was." This opinion was but the prelude to a more memorable declaration, by the Duke of Wellington. Both the motion and the amendment failed; but discussions so frequent served to awaken public sympathy in the cause, which great events were soon to arouse into enthusiasm.

At the end of this session Parliament was dissolved in consequence of the death of George IV. The Government was weak, parties had been completely disorganized by the passing of the Roman Catholic Relief Act; much discontent prevailed in the country; and the question of parliamentary reform, which had been so often discussed in the late session, became a popular topic at the elections. Meanwhile a startling event abroad added to the usual excitement of a general election. Scarcely had the writs been issued when Charles X of France, having attempted a *coup-d'état*, lost his crown, and was an exile on his way to England. As he had fallen in violating the liberty of the press and subverting the representative Constitution of France, this sudden revolution gained the sympathy of the English people and gave an impulse to liberal opinions. The excitement was further increased by the revolution in Belgium, which immediately followed. The new Parliament, elected under such circumstances, met in October. Being without the restraint of a strong government, acknowledged leaders, and accustomed party connections, it was open to fresh political impressions; and the first night of the session determined their direction.

A few words from the Duke of Wellington raised a storm, which swept away his government and destroyed his party. In the debate on the address Earl Grey adverted to reform, and expressed a hope that it would not be deferred, like Catholic emancipation, until Government would be "compelled to yield to expediency what they refused to concede upon principle." This elicited from the Duke an ill-timed profession of faith in our representation. "He was fully convinced that the country possessed, at the present moment, a legislature which answered all the good purposes of legislation, and this to a greater degree than any legislature ever had answered, in any country whatever. He would go further, and say that the legislature and system of representation possessed the full and entire confidence of the country, deservedly possessed that confidence, and the discussions in the legislature had a very great influence over the opinions of the country. He would go still further, and say that if at the present moment he had imposed upon him the duty of forming a legislature for any country, and particularly for a country like this, in possession of great property of various descriptions, he did not mean to assert that he could form such a legislature as they possessed now, for the nature of man was incapable of reaching such excellence at once; but his great endeavor would be to form some description of legislature which would produce the same results. Under these circumstances he was not prepared to bring forward any measure of the description alluded to by the noble lord. He was not only not prepared to bring forward any measure of this nature, but he would at once declare that, as far as he was concerned, as long as he held any station in the government of the country, he should always feel it his duty to resist such measures when proposed by others."

At another time such sentiments as these might have passed unheeded, like other general panegyrics upon the British Constitution, with which the public taste had long been familiar. Yet, so general a defence of our representative system had never, perhaps, been hazarded by any statesman. Ministers had usually been cautious in advancing the theoretical merits of the system, even when its abuses had been less frequently exposed and public opinion less awakened. They had spoken of the dangers of innovation; they had asserted that the system, if imperfect in theory, had yet "worked well"; they had said that the people were satisfied and desired no change; they had appealed to revolutions abroad and disaffection at home, as reasons for not entertaining any proposal for change; but it was reserved for the Duke of Wellington, at a time of excitement like the present, to insult the understanding of the people by declaring that the system was perfect in itself and deservedly possessed their confidence.

On the same night Mr. Brougham gave notice of a motion on the subject of parliamentary reform. Within a fortnight the Duke's administration resigned, after an adverse division in the Commons, on the appointment of a committee to examine the accounts of the civil list. Though this defeat was the immediate cause of their resignation, the expected motion of Mr. Brougham was not without its influence in determining them to withdraw from further embarrassments.

Earl Grey was the new minister, and Mr. Brougham his Lord Chancellor. The first announcement of the Premier was that the Government would "take into immediate consideration the state of the representation, with a view to the correction of those defects which have been occasioned in it by the operation of time, and with a view to the reëstablishment of that confidence upon the part of the people which he was afraid Parliament did not at present enjoy to the full extent that is essential for the welfare and safety of the country and the preservation of the Government."

The Government were now pledged to a measure of parliamentary reform, and during the Christmas recess were occupied in preparing it. Meanwhile the cause was eagerly supported by the people. Public meetings were held, political unions established, and numerous petitions signed in favor of reform. So great were the difficulties with which the Government had to contend that they needed all the encouragement that the people could give. They had to encounter the reluctance of the King; the interests of the proprietors of boroughs, which Mr. Pitt, unable to overcome, had sought to purchase; the opposition of two-thirds of the House of Lords and perhaps of a majority of the House of Commons, and, above all, the strong Tory spirit of the country. Tory principles had been strengthened by a rule of sixty years. Not confined to the governing classes, but pervading society, they were now confirmed by the fears of impending danger. On the other hand, the too ardent reformers, while they alarmed the opponents of reform, embarrassed the Government and injured the cause by their extravagance.

On February 3d, when Parliament reassembled, Lord Grey announced that the Government had succeeded in framing "a measure which would be effective, without exceeding the bounds of a just and well-advised moderation," and which "had received the unanimous consent of the whole Government."

On March 1st this measure was brought forward in the House of Commons by Lord John Russell, to whom, though not in the Cabinet, this honorable duty had been justly confided. In the House of Commons he had already made the question his own; and now he was the exponent of the policy of the Government. The measure was briefly this: To disfranchise sixty of the smallest boroughs; to withdraw one Member from forty-seven other boroughs; to add eight Members for the metropolis; thirty-four for large towns; fifty-five for counties in England; and to give five additional Members to Scotland, three to Ireland, and one to Wales. By his new distribution of the franchise the House of Commons would be reduced in number from six hundred fifty-eight to five hundred ninety-six, or by sixty-two Members.

For the old rights of election in boroughs a ten-pound household franchise was substituted; and the corporations were deprived of their exclusive privileges. It was computed that half a million of persons would be enfranchised. Improved arrangements were also proposed for the registration of votes and the mode of polling at elections.

This bold measure alarmed the opponents of reform, and failed to satisfy the radical reformers; but on the whole, it was well received by the reform party and by the country. One of the most stirring periods in our history was approaching: but its events must be rapidly passed over. After a debate of seven nights, the bill was brought in without a division. Its opponents were collecting their forces, while the excitement of the people in favor of the measure was continually increasing. On March 22d the second reading of the bill was carried by a majority of one only, in a House of six hundred eight, probably the greatest number which up to that time had ever been assembled at a division. On April 19th, on going into committee, ministers found themselves in a minority of eight on a resolution proposed by General Gascoyne, that the number of Members returned for England ought not to be diminished. On the 21st, ministers announced that it was not their intention to proceed with the bill. On that same night they were again defeated on a question of adjournment, by a majority of twenty-two.

This last vote was decisive. The very next day Parliament was prorogued by the King in person, "with a view to its immediate dissolution." It was one of the most critical days in the history of our country. At a time of grave political agitation, the people were directly appealed to by the King's Government to support a measure by which their feelings and passions had been aroused, and which was known to be obnoxious to both Houses of Parliament and to the governing classes.

The people were now to decide the question; and they decided it. A triumphant body of reformers was returned, pledged to carry the Reform Bill; and on July 6th the second reading of the renewed measure was agreed to, by a majority of one hundred thirty-six. The most tedious and irritating discussions ensued in committee, night after night; and the bill was not disposed of until September 21st, when it was passed by a majority of one hundred nine.

That the Peers were still adverse to the bill was certain; but whether, at such a crisis, they would venture to oppose the national will was doubtful. On October 7th, after a debate of five nights, one of the most memorable by which that House has ever been distinguished, and itself a great event in history, the bill was rejected on the second reading by a majority of forty-one.

The battle was to be fought again. Ministers were too far pledged to the people to think of resigning; and on the motion of Lord Ebrington they were immediately supported by a vote of confidence from the House of Commons.

On October 20th Parliament was prorogued; and, after a short interval of excitement, turbulence, and danger, it met again on December 6th. A third reform bill was immediately brought in, changed in many respects, and much improved by reason of the recent census and other statistical investigations. Among other changes the total number of Members was no longer proposed to be reduced. The bill was read a second time on Sunday morning, December 18th, by a majority of one hundred sixty-two. On March 23d it was passed by the House of Commons, and once more was before the House of Lords.

Here the peril of again rejecting it could not be concealed; the courage of some was shaken, the patriotism of others aroused; and after a debate of four nights the second reading was affirmed by the narrow majority of nine. But danger still awaited it. The Peers who would no longer venture to reject such a bill, were preparing to change its essential character by amendments. Meanwhile the agitation of the people was becoming dangerous. Compulsion and physical force were spoken of; and political unions and monster meetings assumed an attitude of intimidation. A crisis was approaching, fatal, perhaps, to the peace of the country; violence, if not revolution, seemed impending.

The disfranchisement of boroughs formed the basis of the measure; and the first vote of the Peers, in committee on the bill, postponed the consideration of the disfranchising clauses, by a

majority of thirty-five. Notwithstanding the assurances of opposition Peers that they would concede a large measure of reform, it was now evident that amendments would be made to
which ministers were bound in honor to the people and the Commons not to assent. The time had come when either the Lords
must be coerced or the ministers must resign. This alternative
was submitted to the King. He refused to create Peers: the
ministers resigned, and their resignation was accepted. Again
the Commons came to the rescue of the bill and the Reform Ministry. On the motion of Lord Ebrington, an address was immediately voted by them renewing their expressions of unaltered
confidence in the late ministers, and imploring His Majesty "to
call to his councils such persons only as will carry into effect, unimpaired in all its essential provisions, that bill for reforming the
representation of the people which has recently passed this House."

The King meanwhile insisted upon one condition, that any
new ministry, however constituted, should pledge themselves to
an extensive measure of reform. But, even if the Commons and
the people had been willing to give up their own measure, and
accept another at the hands of their opponents, no such ministry
could be formed. The public excitement was greater than ever;
and the Government and the people were in imminent danger of
a bloody collision, when Earl Grey was recalled to the councils of
his sovereign. The bill was now secure. The Peers averted
the threatened addition to their numbers, by abstaining from
further opposition; and the bill, the Great Charter of 1832, at
length received the royal assent. The main evil had been the
number of nomination (or rotten) boroughs enjoying the franchise. Fifty-six of these, having fewer than two thousand inhabitants and returning one hundred eleven Members, were swept
away. Thirty boroughs, having fewer than four thousand inhabitants, lost each a Member. Weymouth and Melcombe Re-
gis lost two.

This disfranchisement extended to one hundred forty-three
Members. The next evil had been, large populations unrepresented; and this was now redressed. Twenty-two large towns,
including metropolitan districts, received the privilege of returning two Members; and twenty more, of returning one. The
large county populations were also regarded in the distribution

of seats, the number of county Members being increased from ninety-four to one hundred fifty-nine. The larger counties were divided, and the number of Members adjusted with reference to the importance of the constituencies.

Another evil was the restricted and unequal franchise. This, too, was corrected. All narrow rights of election were set aside in boroughs; and a ten-pound household franchise was established. The freemen of corporate towns were the only class of electors whose rights were reserved; but residence within the borough was attached as a condition to their right of voting. Those freemen, however, who had been created since March, 1831, were excepted from the electoral privilege. Crowds had received their freedom in order to vote against the reform candidates at the general election: they had served their purpose and were now disfranchised. Birth or servitude was to be the sole claim to the freedom of any city which should confer a vote.

The county constituency was enlarged by the addition of copyholders and leaseholders, for terms of years, and of tenants-at-will paying a rent of fifty pounds a year. The latter class had been added in the Commons on the motion of the Marquess of Chandos, in opposition to the Government. The object of this addition was to strengthen the interests of the landlords, which it undoubtedly effected; but as it extended the franchise to a considerable class of persons, it was at least consistent with the liberal design of the Reform Act.

Another evil of the representative system had been the excessive expenses at elections. This, too, was sought to be mitigated by the registration of electors, the division of counties and boroughs into convenient polling-districts, and the reduction of the days of polling.

It was a measure at once bold, comprehensive, moderate, and constitutional. Popular, but not democratic—it extended liberty without hazarding revolution. Two years before, Parliament had refused to enfranchise a single unrepresented town; and now this wide redistribution of the franchise had been accomplished! That it was theoretically complete, and left nothing for future statesmen to effect, its authors never affirmed; but it was a masterly settlement of a perilous question. No law since the Bill of Rights is to be compared with it in importance.

The defects of the Scotch representation, being even more flagrant and indefensible than those of England, were not likely to be omitted from Lord Grey's general scheme of reform. On March 9, 1831, a bill was brought in to amend the representation of Scotland; but the discussions on the English bill, and the sudden dissolution of Parliament, interrupted its further progress. The same lot awaited it in the short session of 1831; but in 1832 its success was assured in the general triumph of the cause. The entire representation was remodelled. Forty-five Members had been assigned to Scotland at the Union: this number was now increased to fifty-three, of whom thirty were allotted to counties and twenty-three to cities and burghs. The county franchise was extended to all owners of property of ten pounds a year and to certain classes of leaseholders; and the burgh franchise to all ten-pound householders.

The representation of Ireland had many of the defects of the English system. Several rotten and nomination boroughs, however, had already been disfranchised on the union with England; and disfranchisement, therefore, did not form any part of the Irish Reform Act. But the right of election was taken away from the corporations, and vested in ten-pound householders; and large additions were made to the county constituency. The number of Members in Ireland, which the Act of Union had settled at one hundred, was now increased to one hundred five.

This measure was the least successful of the three great reform acts of 1832. Complaints were immediately made of the restricted franchise which it had created; and the number of electors registered proved much less than had been anticipated. After repeated discussions a measure was passed in 1850 by which the borough franchise was extended to householders rated at eight pounds; and additions were made to the county franchise.

The representation of the country had now been reconstructed on a wider basis. Large classes had been admitted to the franchise; and the House of Commons represented more freely the interests and political sentiments of the people. The reformed Parliament, accordingly, has been more liberal and progressive in its policy than the Parliament of old; more vigorous and active; and more secure in the confidence of the people.

NULLIFICATION IN SOUTH CAROLINA

A.D. 1832

JAMES PARTON AND JOHN C. CALHOUN

President Jackson had almost reached the end of his first term when a crisis second in gravity only to that of the Civil War threatened the peace and integrity of the American Union. The passage of the Ordinance of Nullification by a State convention of South Carolina, in November, 1832, accompanied with the threat of secession, filled the whole country with apprehension and alarm. By his energetic measures in dealing with this critical state of affairs, Jackson confirmed his reputation for courage and decision, and, what was far more important, averted for the time the danger of civil conflict between the States.

The doctrine of nullification, or the constitutional right of a State of the American Union to refuse obedience to an act of Congress, was introduced as early as 1798, when the "Virginia Resolutions," prepared by James Madison, declared that the Alien and Sedition acts were "palpable and alarming infractions of the Constitution," and that when the Federal Government assumed powers not delegated by the States "a nullification of the act was the rightful remedy." It was but the extended reaffirmation of this doctrine when in 1832 South Carolina, objecting to the collection of duties in Charleston harbor, made the declaration, virtually, "that any State had a right to nullify such of the laws of the United States as might not be acceptable to her."

The nullifiers of 1798 protested against what they regarded as Federal usurpation. Those of 1832 were divided in their interpretation of the Virginia Resolutions, extremists holding that they implied the right of any State to secede at will. It is commonly held to-day that this was the real meaning of the nullifiers of 1832. The soul of the South Carolina nullification was John C. Calhoun. "Calhoun began it; Calhoun continued it; Calhoun stopped it," says one historian. But such political acts have causes that are more than personal. The South Carolina Ordinance of Nullification grew out of questions connected with the tariff, which had long been a source of disagreement and perplexity among the American people. The War of 1812 had been expensive, and in order to pay the interest on the debt and reduce the principal, the Government had greatly to increase its revenues. The growing manufacturing interests of the North asked and received protection. The early protectionists were led by Calhoun and Clay, Calhoun being especially zealous. From this period the tariff became one of the most difficult and persistent subjects of American statesmanship. Calhoun's attitude underwent a complete change, and matters reached a climax in South Carolina.

Parton, who, in a wide range of authorship, devoted particular attention to this passage in American history, gives us a comprehensive and lucid presentation of the whole subject, with the historical background essential to its full understanding; and his important citations from Calhoun add the authority of that eminent name to the following narrative.

THE protectionists triumphed in 1816. In the tariff bill of 1820 the principle was carried further, and still further in those of 1824 and 1828. Under the protective system manufactures flourished and the public debt was greatly diminished. It attracted skilful workmen to the country, as John C. Calhoun had said it would, and contributed to swell the tide of ordinary emigration.

But about the year 1824 it began to be thought that the advantages of the system were enjoyed chiefly by the Northern States, and the South hastened to the conclusion that the protective system was the cause of its lagging behind. There was, accordingly, a considerable Southern opposition to the tariff of 1824, and a general Southern opposition to that of 1828. In the latter year, however, the South elected to the Presidency General Jackson, whose votes and whose writings had committed him to the principle of protection. Southern politicians felt that the General, as a Southern man, was more likely to further their views than Messrs. Adams and Clay, both of whom were peculiarly devoted to protection.

As the first years of General Jackson's Administration wore away without affording to the South the "relief" which they had hoped from it, the discontent of the Southern people increased. Circumstances gave them a new and most telling argument. In 1831 the public debt had been so far diminished as to render it certain that in three years the last dollar of it would be paid. The Government had been collecting about twice as much revenue as its annual expenditures required. In three years, therefore, there would be an annual surplus of twelve or thirteen millions of dollars. The South demanded, with almost a united voice, that the duties should be reduced so as to make the revenue equal to the expenditure, and that, in making this reduction, the principle of protection should be, in effect, abandoned. Protection should thenceforth be "incidental" merely.

The session of 1831–1832 was the one during which Southern gentlemen hoped to effect this great change in the policy of the country. The President's message announced that, in view of the speedy extinction of the public debt, it was high time that Congress should prepare for the threatened surplus.

Clay, after an absence from the halls of Congress of six years, returned to the Senate in December, 1831—an illustrious figure, the leader of the opposition, its candidate for the Presidency, his old renown enhanced by his long exile from the scene of his well-remembered triumphs. The galleries filled when he was expected to speak. He was in the prime of his prime. He never spoke so well as then, nor as often, nor so long, nor with so much applause. But he either could not or dared not undertake the choking of the surplus. He proposed merely "that the duties upon articles imported from foreign countries, and not coming into competition with similar articles made or produced within the United States, be forthwith abolished, except the duties upon wines and silks, and that those be reduced." After a debate of months' duration, a bill in accordance with this proposition passed both Houses, and was signed by the President. It preserved the protective principle intact; it reduced the income of the Government about three million dollars; and it inflamed the discontent of the South to such a degree, that one State, under the influence of a man of force became capable of—nullification.

The President signed the bill, as he told his friends, because he deemed it an approach to the measure required. His influence, during the session, had been secretly exerted in favor of compromise. Major Lewis, at the request of the President, had been much in the lobbies and committee-rooms of the Capitol, urging members of both sections to make concessions. The President thought that the just course lay between the two extremes of abandoning the protective principle and reducing the duties in total disregard of it.

"You must yield something on the tariff question," said Major Lewis to the late Governor Marcy, of New York, "or Van Buren will be sacrificed." Said Governor Marcy in reply: "I am Van Buren's friend, but the protective system is more important to New York than Van Buren."

To return to Calhoun. He had been elected Vice-President, but soon disagreed with Jackson's measures. His hostile correspondence with the President was published by him in the spring of 1831. The President retorted by getting rid of the three members of the Cabinet who favored the succession of Calhoun to the Presidency. Three months afterward, in the Pendleton *Messenger* of South Carolina, Calhoun continued the strife by publishing his first treatise upon nullification. As there was no obvious reason for such a publication at that moment the Vice-President began his essay by giving a reason for it.

"It is one of the peculiarities," said he, "of the station I occupy that while it necessarily connects its incumbent with the politics of the day, it affords him no opportunity officially to express his sentiments, except accidentally on an equal division of the body over which he presides. He is thus exposed, as I have often experienced, to have his opinions erroneously and variously represented. In ordinary cases the correct course I conceive to be to remain silent, leaving to time and circumstances the correction of misrepresentations; but there are occasions so vitally important that a regard both to duty and character would seem to forbid such a course; and such I conceive to be the present. The frequent allusions to my sentiments will not permit me to doubt that such also is the public conception, and that it claims the right to know, in relation to the question referred to, the opinions of those who hold important official stations; while on my part desiring to receive neither unmerited praise nor blame, I feel, I trust, the solicitude which every honest and independent man ought, that my sentiments should be truly known, whether they be such as may be calculated to recommend them to public favor or not. Entertaining these impressions, I have concluded that it is my duty to make known my sentiments; and I have adopted the mode which, on reflection, seemed to be the most simple and best calculated to effect the object in view."

The essay is divided into two parts. First, the Vice-President endeavors to show that nullification is the natural, proper, and peaceful remedy for an intolerable grievance inflicted by Congress upon a State or upon a section; secondly, that the Tariff Law of 1828, unless rectified during the next session of Con-

gress, will be such a grievance. He went all lengths against the
protective principle. It was unconstitutional, unequal in its
operation, oppressive to the South, an evil "inveterate and dangerous." The reduction of duties to the revenue standard could
be delayed no longer "without the most distracting and dangerous consequences." "The honest and obvious course is to prevent the accumulation of the surplus in the treasury by a timely
and judicious reduction of the imposts, and thereby to leave the
money in the pockets of those who made it, and from whom it
cannot be honestly nor constitutionally taken unless required by
the fair and legitimate wants of the Government.

"If, neglecting a disposition so obvious and just, the Government should attempt to keep up the present high duties when
the money was no longer wanted, or to dispose of this immense
surplus by enlarging the old or devising new schemes of appropriations; or, finding that to be impossible, it should adopt the
most dangerous, unconstitutional, and absurd project ever devised by any Government, of dividing the surplus among the
States—a project which, if carried into execution, could not fail
to create an antagonistic interest between the States and General
Government on all questions of appropriations, which would
certainly end in reducing the latter to a mere office of collection
and distribution—either of these modes would be considered by
the section suffering under the present high duties as a fixed determination to perpetuate forever what it considers the present
unequal, unconstitutional, and oppressive burden; and from
that moment it would cease to look to the General Government
for relief."

Nullification is distinctly announced in this passage. It
seems to be again announced, as a thing inevitable, in the con-
cluding words of the essay: "In thus placing my opinions before
the public I have not been actuated by the expectation of changing the public sentiment. Such a motive, on a question so long
agitated and so beset with feelings of prejudice and interest,
would argue on my part an insufferable vanity and a profound ignorance of the human heart. To avoid as far as possible the imputation of either, I have confined my statements
on the many and important points on which I have been compelled to touch, to a simple declaration of my opinion, without

advancing any other reasons to sustain them than what appeared to me to be indispensable to the full understanding of my views.

"With every caution on my part I dare not hope, in taking the step I have, to escape the imputation of improper motives; though I have without reserve freely expressed my opinions, not regarding whether they might or might not be popular. I have no reason to believe that they are such as will conciliate public favor, but the opposite; which I greatly regret, as I have ever placed a high estimate on the good opinion of my fellow-citizens. But, be this as it may, I shall at least be sustained by feelings of conscious rectitude. I have formed my opinions after the most careful and deliberate examination, with all the aids which my reason and experience could furnish; I have expressed them honestly and fearlessly, regardless of their effects personally; which, however interesting to me individually, are of too little importance to be taken into the estimate where the liberty and happiness of our country are so vitally involved."

In this performance Calhoun did not refer to his forgotten championship of the protective policy in 1816. The busy burrowers of the press, however, occasionally brought to the surface a stray memento of that championship, which the press of South Carolina denounced as slanderous. A Mr. Reynolds, of South Carolina, was moved, by his disgust at such reminders, to write to Calhoun, asking him for information respecting "the origin of a system so abhorrent to the South." Calhoun, replying to the inquiry, said that "he had always considered the tariff of 1816 as in reality a measure of revenue—as distinct from one of protection"; that it reduced duties instead of increasing them; that the protection of manufactures was regarded as a mere incidental feature of the bill; that he had regarded its protective character as temporary, to last only until the debt should be paid; that in fact he had not paid very particular attention to the details of the bill at the time, as he was not a member of the committee that had drawn it; that "his time and attention were much absorbed with the question of the currency," as he was chairman of the committee on that subject; that the Tariff Bill of 1816 was innocence itself compared with the monstrous and unconstitutional tariff of 1828, and had no principle in common with it.

These assertions may not all be destitute of truth, but the impression created by them is most erroneous. The reader has but to turn to the debates of 1816 to discover that the whole discussion of the tariff bill turned entirely on its protective character, and that Calhoun was the special defender of its protective provisions. The strict constructionist or State Rights party was headed then in the House by John Randolph, who, on many occasions during the long debate, rose to refute Calhoun's protective reasoning. Calhoun was then a member of the other wing of the Republican party. He was a bank man, an internal improvement man, a protectionist, a consolidationist—in short, a Republican of the Hamiltonian school, rather than the Jeffersonian. He was strenuous in asserting, among other things, that protection would benefit the planter as much as it benefited the manufacturer. In fact, there is no protective argument that cannot be found in the speeches of Calhoun upon the tariff of 1816. Indeed, it was Calhoun's course on this question in 1816 which gave him that popularity in Pennsylvania which induced his friends in that State to start him for the Presidency in 1824. His principal tariff speech had been printed upon a sheet, framed, hung up in bar rooms and parlors along with the Farewell Address of General Washington. A Member of Congress from Pennsylvania reminded Calhoun of this fact during the session of 1833.

Nicholas P. Trist, then of the State Department, in a series of articles in the Richmond *Inquirer*, fell upon Calhoun's Reynolds letter, and tore it to shreds. He found that (to use his own language) it contained more errors than it contained words. He copied from the old newspapers column after column of the debates of 1816, in which Calhoun figured as the most active and even enthusiastic of the protectionists. He showed that his name was associated with that of Henry Clay in the defence of the principle, and that both were frequently replied to at the same time by members of the other division of the party. These articles of Trist created what is now termed a "sensation." The President was greatly pleased with them, and had not the least difficulty in accepting Trist's conclusion, "that Calhoun was totally destitute of all regard for truth."

Calhoun's article in the Pendleton *Messenger* was dated July

26, 1831. Congress met in December following, and debated the tariff all the winter and spring. Late in the month of June, by a majority of thirty-two to sixteen in the Senate, by a majority of one hundred twenty-nine to sixty-five in the House, Clay's bill, reaffirming the protective principle and abolishing duties on articles not needing protection, was passed. A month afterward Congress adjourned; the Vice-President went home to South Carolina; and that State soon prepared to execute the threats contained in the Vice-President's Pendleton manifesto.

The Legislature of the State, early in the autumn, passed an act calling a convention of the citizens of South Carolina, for the purpose of taking into consideration the late action of Congress, and of suggesting the course to be pursued by South Carolina in relation to it. At Columbia, on November 19th, the convention met. It consisted of about one hundred forty members, the *elite* of the State. The Hamiltons, the Haynes, the Pinckneys, the Butlers, and, indeed, nearly all the great families of a State of great families were represented in it. It was a body of men as respectable in character and ability as has ever been convened in South Carolina. Courtesy and resolution marked its proceedings, and the work undertaken by it was done with commendable thoroughness. A committee of twenty-one was appointed to draw up an address to the people of the State, or rather a programme of the proceedings best calculated to promote the end designed. The chief result of the labors of this committee was the celebrated Ordinance of Nullification, signed by the entire convention, which consisted of five distinct decrees, to the execution of which the members pledged themselves. It was ordained:

1. That the tariff law of 1828, and the amendment to the same of 1832, were "null, void, and no law, nor binding upon this State, its officers or citizens."

2. No duties enjoined by that law or its amendment shall be paid, or permitted to be paid, in the State of South Carolina, after February 1, 1833.

3. In no case involving the validity of the expected nullifying act of the Legislature, shall an appeal to the Supreme Court of the United States be permitted. No copy of proceedings shall

be allowed to be taken for that purpose. Any attempt to appeal to the Supreme Court "may be dealt with as for a contempt of the court" from which the appeal is taken.

4. Every office-holder in the State, whether of the civil or the military service, and every person hereafter assuming an office, and every juror, shall take an oath to obey this ordinance, and all acts of the Legislature in accordance therewith or suggested thereby.

5. If the Government of the United States shall attempt to enforce the tariff laws, now existing, by means of its army or navy, by closing the ports of the State, or preventing the egress or ingress of vessels, or shall in any way harass or obstruct the foreign commerce of the State, then South Carolina will no longer consider herself a member of the Federal Union: "the people of this State will thenceforth hold themselves absolved from all further obligation to maintain or preserve their political connection with the people of the other States, and will forthwith proceed to organize a separate Government, and do all other acts and things which sovereign and independent States may of right do."

The convention issued an address to the people of the other States of the Union, justifying its proceedings, and then adjourned. The people of South Carolina accepted the ordinance with remarkable unanimity. There was a Union party in the State, respectable in numbers and character, but the Nullifiers commanded an immense, an almost silencing majority. Robert Y. Hayne, a member of the convention, was elected Governor of the State, and the Legislature that assembled early in December was chiefly composed of Nullifiers. The message of the new Governor approved the acts of the convention in the strongest language possible. "I recognize," said the Governor, "no allegiance as paramount to that which the citizens of South Carolina owe to the State of their birth or their adoption. I here publicly declare, and wish it to be distinctly understood, that I shall hold myself bound, by the highest of all obligations, to carry into full effect, not only the ordinance of the convention, but every act of the Legislature, and every judgment of our own courts, the enforcement of which may devolve on the executive. I claim no right to revise their acts. It will be my duty to execute them; and that duty I mean, to the utmost of my power, faithfully to perform."

He said more: "If the sacred soil of Carolina should be polluted by the footsteps of an invader, or be stained with the blood of her citizens, shed in her defence, I trust in Almighty God that no son of hers, native or adopted, who has been nourished at her bosom, or been 'cherished by her bounty, will be found raising a parricidal arm against our common mother. And even should she stand alone, in this great struggle for constitutional liberty, encompassed by her enemies, I trust that there will not be found, in the wide limits of the State, one recreant son who will not fly to the rescue, and be ready to lay down his life in her defence. South Carolina cannot be drawn down from the proud eminence on which she has now placed herself, except by the hands of her own children. Give her but a fair field, and she asks no more. Should she succeed, hers will be glory enough to have led the way in the noble work of reform. And if, after making these efforts due to her own honor, and the greatness of the cause, she is destined utterly to fail, the bitter fruits of that failure, not to herself alone, but to the entire South, nay, to the whole Union, will attest her virtue."

The Legislature instantly responded to the message by passing the acts requisite for carrying the ordinance into practical effect. The Governor was authorized to accept the services of volunteers, who were to hold themselves in readiness to march at a moment's warning. The State resounded with the noise of warlike preparation. Blue cockades, with a palmetto button in the centre, appeared upon thousands of hats, bonnets, and bosoms. Medals were struck ere long, bearing this inscription: "John C. Calhoun, First President of the Southern Confederacy." The Legislature proceeded soon to fill the vacancy created in the Senate of the United States by the election of Hayne to the governorship. John C. Calhoun, Vice-President of the United States, was selected, and he accepted the seat. He resigned the Vice-Presidency and began his journey to Washington in December, leaving his State in the wildest ferment.

Two months of the autumn of this year General Jackson spent in visiting his beloved Hermitage. But he had had an eye upon South Carolina. Soon after his return to Washington in October came news that the convention of the South Carolina Nullifiers was appointed to meet on November 19th. On the 6th of that month the President sent secret orders to the collector of the port of Charleston of an energetic character:

"Upon the supposition that the measures of the convention or the acts of the Legislature may consist, in part at least, in declaring the laws of the United States imposing duties unconstitutional, and null and void, and in forbidding their execution and the collection of the duties within the State of South Carolina, you will, immediately after it shall be formally announced, resort to all the means provided by the laws, and particularly by the Act of March 2, 1799, to counteract the measures which may be adopted to give effect to that declaration.

"For this purpose you will consider yourself authorized to employ the revenue cutters which may be within your district, and provide as many boats and employ as many inspectors as may be necessary for the execution of the law and for the purposes of the act already referred to. You will, moreover, cause a sufficient number of officers of cutters and inspectors to be placed on board and in charge of every vessel arriving from a foreign port or place with goods, wares, or merchandise, as soon as practicable after her first coming within your district, and direct them to anchor her in some safe place within the harbor, where she may be secure from any act of violence and from any unauthorized attempt to discharge her cargo before a compliance with the laws; and they will remain on board of her at such place until the reports and entries required by law shall be made, both of vessel and cargo, and the duties paid, or secured to be paid to your satisfaction, and until the regular permit shall be granted for landing the cargo; and it will be your duty, against any forcible attempt, to retain and defend the custody of the said vessel, by the aid of the officers of the customs, inspectors, and officers of the cutters, until the requisitions of the law shall be fully complied with; and in case of any attempt to remove her or her cargo from the custody of the officers of the customs, by the form of legal process from State tribunals, you will not yield the custody to such attempt, but will consult the law officer of the district, and employ such means as, under the particular circumstances, you may legally do, to resist such process and prevent the removal of the vessel and cargo.

"Should the entry of such vessel and cargo not be completed and the duties paid, or secured to be paid by bond or bonds with sureties to your satisfaction, within the time limited by law, you will at the expiration of that time take possession of the cargo, and land and store the same at Castle Pinckney or some other safe place, and in due time, if the duties are not paid, sell the same, according to the direction of the fifty-sixth section of the Act of March 2, 1799: and you are authorized to provide such stores as may be necessary for that purpose."

A few days after the despatch of these orders General Scott was quietly ordered to Charleston, for the purpose, as the President confidentially informed the collector, "of superintending the safety of the ports of the United States in that vicinity." Other changes were made in the disposition of naval and military forces, designed to enable the President to act with swift efficiency if there should be occasion to act.

Calhoun was in his place in the Senate-chamber when Congress convened. He had arrived two weeks before, after a journey which one of his biographers compares to that of Luther to the Diet of Worms. He met averted faces and estranged friends everywhere on his route, we are told; and only now and then some daring man found courage to whisper in his ear: "If you are sincere, and are sure of your cause, go on, in God's name, and fear nothing." Washington was curious to know, we are further assured, what the arch-Nullifier would do when the oath to support the Constitution of the United States was proposed to him. "The floor of the Senate-chamber and the galleries were thronged with spectators. They saw him take the oath with a solemnity and dignity appropriate to the occasion, and then calmly seat himself on the right of the Chair, among his old political friends, nearly all of whom were now arrayed against him."

After the President's message had been read, Calhoun rose to vindicate himself and his State, which he did with that singular blending of subtlety and force which characterized his later efforts. He declared himself still devoted to the Union, and said that if the Government were restored to the principles of

1798 he would be the last man in the country to question its authority.

February 1st, the dreaded day which was to be the first of a fratricidal war, went by, and yet no hostile and no nullifying act had been done in South Carolina. How was this? Did those warlike words mean nothing? Was South Carolina repentant? The President was resolved, and avowed his resolve, that the hour which brought the news of one act of violence on the part of the Nullifiers should find Calhoun a prisoner of state upon a charge of high treason—and not Calhoun only, but every Member of Congress from South Carolina who had taken part in the proceedings which had caused the conflict between South Carolina and the General Government.

Whether this intention of the President had any effect upon the course of events, we cannot know. It came to pass, however, that, a few days before February 1st, a meeting of the leading Nullifiers was held in Charleston, who passed resolutions to this effect: that, inasmuch as measures were then pending in Congress which contemplated the reduction of duties demanded by South Carolina, the nullification of the existing revenue laws should be postponed until after the adjournment of Congress; when the convention would reassemble, and take into consideration whatever revenue measures may have been passed by Congress. The session of 1833 being the "short" session, ending necessarily on March 4th, the Union was respited thirty-two days by the Charleston meeting.

The President, in his annual message, recommended Congress to subject the tariff to a new revision, and to reduce the duties so that the revenue of the Government, after the payment of the public debt, should not exceed its expenditures. He also recommended that, in regulating the reduction, the interests of the manufacturers should be duly considered. We discover, therefore, that while the President was resolved to crush nullification by force if it opposed by force the collection of the revenue, he was also disposed to concede to nullification all that its more moderate advocates demanded. Accordingly, McLane, the Secretary of the Treasury, with the assistance of Gulian C. Verplanck, of New York, and other Administration members, prepared a new tariff bill, which provided for the reduction of duties to the revenue standard, and which was deemed by its authors as favorable to the manufacturing interest as the circumstances permitted.

This bill, reported by Verplanck on December 28th, and known as the Verplanck Bill, was calculated to reduce the revenue thirteen million dollars, and to afford to the manufacturers about as much protection as the tariff of 1816 had given them. It put back the "American System," so to speak, seventeen years. It destroyed nearly all that Clay and the protectionists had effected in 1820, 1824, 1828, and 1832. Is it astonishing that the manufacturers were panic-stricken? Need we wonder that, during the tariff discussions of 1833, two Congresses sat in Washington, one in the Capitol, composed of the Representatives of the people, and another outside of the Capitol, consisting of representatives of the manufacturing interest? Was it not to be expected that Clay, seeing the edifice which he had constructed with so much toil and talent about to tumble into ruins, would be willing to consent to any measure which could even postpone the catastrophe?

The Verplanck Bill made slow progress. The outside pressure against it was such that there seemed no prospect of its passing. The session was within twenty days of its inevitable termination. The bill had been debated and amended, and amended and debated, and yet no apparent progress had been made toward that conciliation of conflicting interests without which no tariff bill whatever can pass. The dread of civil war, which overshadowed the Capitol, seemed to lose its power as a legislative stimulant, and there was a respectable party in Congress, led by Webster, who thought that all tariff legislation was undignified and improper while South Carolina maintained her threatening attitude. The Constitution, Webster maintained, was on trial. The time had come to test its reserve of self-supporting power. No compromise, no concession, said he, until the nullifying State returns to her allegiance.

No question of so much importance as this can be discussed in Congress without a constant, secret reference to its effect upon the next Presidential election. "It is mortifying, inexpressibly disgusting," wrote Clay to Judge Brooke, in the midst of the debate upon his own compromise bill of this session, "to find that

considerations affecting an election now four years distant influence the fate of great questions of immediate interest more
than all the reasons and arguments which intimately appertain
to those questions.   If, for example, the tariff now before the House
should be lost, its defeat will be owing to two causes: First, the
apprehension of Van Buren's friends that, if it passes, Calhoun
will rise again as the successful vindicator of Southern rights.
Second, its passage might prevent the President from exercising
certain vengeful passions which he wishes to gratify in South
Carolina.   And if it passes, its passage may be attributed to the
desire of those same friends of Van Buren to secure Southern
votes."

On February 12th Clay introduced his celebrated Compromise Bill for the regulation of the tariff. It differed from the
measure devised by the Administration and engineered by Verplanck chiefly in this: Verplanck proposed a sudden, and Clay
a gradual, reduction of duties.   The Verplanck Bill tended mainly
to the conciliation of the Nullifiers; the Clay compromise, to the
preservation of the manufacturers.   Clay's bill provided that on
the last day of the year 1833 all *ad-valorem* duties of more than
20 per cent. should be reduced one-tenth; on the last day of the
year 1835 there should be a second and a similar reduction;
another, to the same amount, at the close of 1837; and so on,
reducing the duties every two years, until on June 31, 1842, all
duties should be reduced to or below the maximum of 20 per cent.
The object of Clay was to save all that he could save of the protective policy, and to postpone further action upon the tariff to
a more auspicious day.

The most remarkable narrative left by Colonel Benton for
the entertainment of posterity is that which he gives, in his
Thirty Years' View, of the strange coalition between Clay and
Calhoun for the passage of the Compromise Bill. Clay, he tells
us, had introduced the measure into the Senate, but the manufacturers could not be reconciled to some of its provisions; and
without their consent nothing could be done. At this stage of
the affair Senator John M. Clayton, of Delaware, a protectionist, gave Clay a piece of advice, which he followed. "These
South Carolinians," said Clayton to Clay, "are acting very
badly, but they are fine fellows, and it is a pity to let Jackson

hang them." He urged Clay to make a "new move" with his bill, get it referred to a select committee, and so modify it as to render it acceptable to a majority.

The bill was referred to a select committee, accordingly, and that select committee was appointed, of course, by Judge White, the President of the Senate. Respecting the appointment of this important committee Judge White has left on record a little tale which shows, among other things, how keenly the President watched the proceedings of Congress, and how resolved he was to deprive the Opposition of all the glory of pacificating the country.

"Before the members of the committee were named," writes Judge White, "I received a note from the President requesting me to go to his house, as he wished to see me. I returned for answer that while the Senate was in session it was out of my power to go, but that as soon as it adjourned I would call on him. I felt the high responsibility which rested on me in appointing the committee: the fate of the bill, in a good degree, depended on it; and if the bill failed, we would probably be involved in a most painful conflict. I endeavored to make the best selection I could, by taking some tariff men, some antitariff men, one Nullifier, and Clay himself—hoping that if a majority of a committee, in which all interests and views were represented, could agree on anything, it was likely it would pass.

"Taking these principles for my guide, I wrote down the names of seven members, Clayton, of Delaware, being one; and immediately before we adjourned handed the names to the secretary, with directions to put them on the Journal, and in the course of the evening waited on the President. Soon after we met, he mentioned that he had wished to see me on the subject of appointing a committee on Clay's bill, to ask that Clayton might not be put on it; as he was hostile to the Administration and unfriendly to McLane, he feared he would use his endeavor to have a preference given to Clay's bill over that of the Secretary of the Treasury, or words to that effect. I observed, in answer, that it would always give me great pleasure to conform to the wishes of my political friends, whenever I could do so with propriety; but that the Treasury Bill had been so altered and mangled, and that, as I understood, in a good degree by the votes of

his own party, that it had but few friends; that we seemed to be
on the ove of a civil war, and that, for the sake of averting such
a calamity, I would further all in my power any measure, from
from whom it might, which would give peace to the country;
and that any bill having that for its object was esteemed by me
a measure above party, and any man who was the author of it
was welcome to all the credit he could gain by it.   But, at all
events, it was too late to talk on the subject, as I had handed the
names of the committee to the secretary before we adjourned;
and that as I had a very high opinion of Mr. Clayton's talents
and liberal feelings, I had put him on the committee, without
knowing he was personally unkind to the Secretary of the Treasury.   He then asked me if I could not see the secretary of the
Senate that evening, and substitute some other name for Clayton,
before the Journal was made up.   I told him I could not—in my
judgment it would be wrong; and then the interview terminated."

Clayton was retained on the committee, therefore, and it was
directly owing to his tact and firmness, according to Colonel
Benton, that the bill was passed.   He began by making it a *sine
qua non* that the Compromise Bill, with all the amendments
agreed upon, should be voted for by Calhoun and the other Nullifiers, so as to commit them to the principles involved in the
bill, and to give the manufacturers an assurance of the perpetuity
of the compact.   He was equally explicit in demanding that Clay,
also, should record his vote upon the bill and its amendments.
The closing struggle between policy and principle let our eye-
witness, Colonel Benton, describe:

"Clayton being inexorable in his claims, Clay and Calhoun
agreed to the amendments, and all voted for them, one by one, as
Clay offered them, until it came to the last—that revolting measure of the home valuation.   As soon as it was proposed, Calhoun
and his friends met it with violent opposition, declaring it to be
unconstitutional, and an insurmountable obstacle to their votes
for the bill if put into it.   It was then late in the day, and the
last day but one of the session, and Clayton found himself in the
predicament which required the execution of his threat to table
the bill.   He executed it, and moved to lay it on the table, with
the declaration that it was to lie there.   Clay went to him and

besought him to withdraw the motion; but in vain — he remained inflexible; and the bill then appeared to be dead. In this extremity, the Calhoun wing retired to the colonnade behind the Vice-President's chair, and held a brief consultation among themselves; and presently Bibb, of Kentucky, came out and went to Clayton and asked him to withdraw his motion to give him time to consider the amendment. Seeing this sign of yielding, Clayton withdrew his motion — to be renewed if the amendment was not voted for.

"A friend of the parties immediately moved an adjournment, which was carried; and that night's reflections brought them to the conclusion that the amendment must be passed, but still with the belief that, there being enough to pass it without him, Calhoun should be spared the humiliation of appearing on the record in its favor. This was told to Clayton, who declared it to be impossible; that Calhoun's vote was indispensable, as nothing would be considered secured by the passage of the bill unless his vote appeared for every amendment separately, and for the whole bill collectively. When the Senate met, and the bill was taken up, it was still unknown what he would do; but his friends fell in, one after the other, yielding their objections upon different grounds, and giving their assent to this most flagrant instance (and that a new one) of that protective legislation against which they were then raising troops in South Carolina! and limiting a day, and that a short one, on which she was to be, *ipso facto*, a seceder from the Union.

"Calhoun remained to the last, and only rose when the vote was ready to be taken, and prefaced a few remarks with the very notable declaration that he had then to 'determine' which way he would vote. He then declared in favor of the amendment, but upon conditions which he desired the reporters to note, and which, being futile in themselves, only showed the desperation of his condition, and the state of impossibility to which he was reduced. Several Senators let him know immediately the futility of his conditions; and without saying more, he voted on ayes and noes for the amendment, and afterward for the whole bill."

The Compromise Bill, which passed in the Senate by a vote of twenty-nine to sixteen, was sprung upon the House of Representatives, and carried in that body by a *coup-de-main*. The Verplanck Bill, Colonel Benton indignantly informs us, was afloat in the House, "upon the wordy sea of stormy debate," as late as February 25th. "All of a sudden," he continues, "it was arrested, knocked over, run under, and merged and lost in a new one, which expunged the old one and took its place. It was late in the afternoon when Letcher, of Kentucky, the fast friend of Clay, rose in his place, and moved to strike out the whole Verplanck Bill—every word except the enacting clause—and insert, in lieu of it, a bill offered in the Senate by Clay, since called the 'Compromise.' This was offered in the House without notice, without signal, without premonitory symptom, and just as the members were preparing to adjourn. Some, taken by surprise, looked about in amazement; but the majority showed consciousness, and, what was more, readiness for action.

"The bill, which made its first appearance in the House when members were gathering up their overcoats for a walk home to their dinners, was passed before those coats had got on their backs; and the dinner which was waiting had but little time to cool before the astonished members, their work done, were at the table to eat it. A bill without precedent in the annals of our legislation, and pretending to the sanctity of a compromise, and to settle great questions forever, went through to its consummation in the fragment of an evening session, without the compliance with any form which experience and parliamentary law have devised for the safety of legislation." The bill passed in the House by a vote of one hundred nineteen to eighty-five.

That the President disapproved of this hasty, and, as the event proved, unstable compromise is well known. The very energy with which Colonel Benton denounces it shows how hateful it was to the Administration. President Jackson, however, signed the bill concocted by his enemies. It would have been more like him to have vetoed it and I do not know why he did not veto it. The time may come when the people of the United States will wish he had vetoed it, and thus brought to an issue, and settled finally, a question which, at some future day, may assume more awkward dimensions, and the country have no Jackson to meet it.[1]

[1] This was written a year or two before the Civil War.—ED.

Calhoun left Washington, and journeyed homeward post haste, after Congress adjourned. "Travelling night and day, by the most rapid public conveyances, he succeeded in reaching Columbia in time to meet the convention before they had taken any additional steps. Some of the more fiery and ardent members were disposed to complain of the Compromise Act, as being only a half-way, temporizing measure; but when his explanations were made, all felt satisfied, and the convention cordially approved of his course. The Nullification Ordinance was repealed (March, 1833), and the two parties in the State abandoned their organizations, and agreed to forget all their past differences." So the storm blew over.

CARLIST REVOLT IN SPAIN

A.D. 1833

CHARLES A. FYFFE

This uprising was more than the attempt of the pretender Don Carlos to seat himself upon the Spanish throne. It was one of many struggles in Europe that received the support of the same influences that, through the Holy Alliance, had sought to repress the growth of constitutional liberty. The revolt also marks the rise of a Spanish party, the Carlists, who have continued, with fresh risings from time to time, to serve the cause of Don Carlos and several subsequent claimants under his assumed title.

The Carlist revolt followed soon upon the Revolution of 1820, which three years later was suppressed with the help of French arms. King Ferdinand VII then abrogated the liberal Constitution of 1812, which the revolutionists had restored, and for the rest of his reign he ruled absolutely.

FROM the time of the restoration of absolute government in Spain in 1823, King Ferdinand, from his abject weakness and ignorance, had not given complete satisfaction to the people. He had been thrice married; he was childless, his state of health miserable, and his life likely to be short. The succession to the throne of Spain had, moreover, since 1713, been governed by the Salic Law, so that even in the event of Ferdinand leaving female issue Don Carlos would nevertheless inherit the crown. These confident hopes were rudely disturbed by the marriage of the King with his cousin, Maria Christina of Naples, followed by an edict, known as the Pragmatic Sanction, repealing the Salic Law which had been introduced with the first Bourbon, and restoring the ancient Castilian custom under which women were capable of succeeding to the crown. A daughter, Isabella, was shortly afterward born to the new Queen.

On the legality of the Pragmatic Sanction the opinions of publicists differed; it was judged, however, by Europe at large not from the point of view of antiquarian theory, but with direct reference to its immediate effect. The three Eastern courts emphatically condemned it, as an interference with established monarchical right, and as a blow to the cause of European absolutism through the alliance which it would almost certainly produce between the supplanters of Don Carlos and the Liberals of the Spanish Peninsula. To the clerical and reactionary party at Madrid, it amounted to nothing less than a sentence of destruction, and the utmost pressure was brought to bear upon the weak and dying King with the object of inducing him to undo the alleged wrong which he had done to his brother.

In a moment of prostration Ferdinand revoked the Pragmatic Sanction; but subsequently, regaining some degree of strength, he reënacted it, and appointed Christina regent during the continuance of his illness. Don Carlos, protesting against the violation of his rights, had betaken himself to Portugal, where he made common cause with Miguel.[1] His adherents had no intention of submitting to the change of succession. Their resentment was scarcely restrained during Ferdinand's lifetime, and when, in September, 1833, his long-expected death took place, and the child Isabella was declared queen under the regency of her mother, open rebellion broke out, and Carlos was proclaimed king in several of the Northern Provinces.

For the moment the forces of the Regency seemed to be far superior to those of the insurgents, and Don Carlos failed to take advantage of the first outburst of enthusiasm and to place himself at the head of his followers. He remained in Portugal, while Christina, as had been expected, drew nearer to the Spanish Liberals, and ultimately called to power a Liberal minister, Martinez de la Rosa, under whom a constitution was given to Spain by a royal statute (April 10, 1834). At the same time negotiations were opened with Portugal and with the Western powers, in the hope of forming an alliance which should drive both Miguel and Carlos from the Peninsula.

On April 22, 1834, a quadruple treaty was signed at London, in which the Spanish Government undertook to send an army into Portugal against Miguel, the Court of Lisbon pledging itself in return to use all the means in its power to expel Don Carlos from Portuguese territory. England engaged to cooperate by

[1] Dom Miguel, third son of John VI of Portugal, was head of the Absolutist party in that country, whose throne he usurped in 1828.—ED.

means of its fleet. The assistance of France, if it should be deemed necessary for the attainment of the objects of the treaty, was to be rendered in such manner as should be settled by common consent. In pursuance of the policy of the treaty, and even before the formal engagement was signed, a Spanish division under General Rodil crossed the frontier and marched against Miguel. The forces of the usurper were defeated. The appearance of the English fleet and the publication of the Treaty of Quadruple Alliance rendered further resistance hopeless, and on May 22d Miguel made his submission, and, in return for a large pension, renounced all rights to the crown, and undertook to quit the Peninsula forever. Don Carlos, refusing similar conditions, went on board an English ship and was conducted to London.

With respect to Portugal, the Quadruple Alliance had completely attained its object; and in so far as the Carlist cause was strengthened by the continuance of civil war in the neighboring country, this source of strength was no doubt withdrawn from it. But in its effect upon Don Carlos himself the action of the Quadruple Alliance was worse than useless. While fulfilling the letter of the treaty, which stipulated for the expulsion of the two pretenders from the Peninsula, the English Admiral had removed Carlos from Portugal, where he was comparatively harmless, and had taken no effective guarantee that he should not reappear in Spain itself and enforce his claim by arms. Carlos had not been made a prisoner of war; he had made no promises and incurred no obligations; nor could the British Government, after his arrival in that country, keep him in perpetual restraint. Quitting England after a short residence, he travelled in disguise through France, crossed the Pyrenees, and appeared on July 10, 1834, at the headquarters of the Carlist insurgents in Navarre.

In the country immediately below the western Pyrenees, the so-called Basque Provinces, lay the chief strength of the Carlist rebellion. These Provinces, which were among the most thriving and industrious parts of Spain, might seem by their very superiority an unlikely home for a movement which was directed against everything favorable to liberty, tolerance, and progress in the Spanish Kingdom. But the identification of the Basques with the Carlist cause was due in fact to local, not to general, causes; and in fighting to impose a bigoted despot upon the Spanish people, they were in truth fighting to protect themselves from a closer incorporation with Spain. Down to the year 1812 the Basque Provinces had preserved more than half of the essentials of independence.

Owing to their position on the French frontier, the Spanish monarchy, while destroying all local independence in the interior of Spain, had uniformly treated the Basques with the same indulgence which the Government of Great Britain has shown to the Channel Islands, and which the French monarchy, though in a less degree, showed to the frontier Province of Alsace in the seventeenth and eighteenth centuries. The customs-frontier of the North of Spain was drawn to the south of these districts. The inhabitants imported what they pleased from France without paying any duties; while the heavy import-dues levied at the border of the neighboring Spanish Provinces gave them the opportunity of carrying on an easy and lucrative system of smuggling. The local administration remained to a great extent in the hands of the people themselves; each village preserved its active corporate life; and the effect of this survival of a vigorous local freedom was seen in the remarkable contrast described by travellers between the aspect of the Basque districts and that of Spain at large. The *Fueros* (or local rights, as the Basques considered them) were in reality, when viewed as part of the order of the Spanish State, a series of exceptional privileges; and it was inevitable that the framers of the Constitution of 1812, in their attempt to create a modern administrative and political system doing justice to the whole of the nation, should sweep away the distinctions which had hitherto marked off one group of Provinces from the rest of the community.

The continuance of war until the return of Ferdinand, and the overthrow of the constitution, prevented the plans of the Cortes from being at that time carried into effect; but the Revolution of 1820 brought them into actual operation, and the Basques found themselves, as a result of the victory of Liberal principles, compelled to pay duties on their imports, robbed of the profits of their smuggling, and supplanted in the management of their local affairs by an army of officials from Madrid. They had gained by the constitution little that they had not possessed before, and their losses were immediate, tangible, and substantial. The result was that, although the larger towns, like Bilbao, remained true to modern ideas, the country districts took up arms on behalf of the absolute monarchy, assisted the French in the restoration of despotism in 1823, and remained the permanent enemies of the constitutional cause. On the death of Ferdinand they declared at once for Don Carlos, and rose in rebellion against the Government of Queen Christina, by which they considered the privileges of the Basque Provinces and the interests of Catholic orthodoxy to be alike threatened.

There was little in the character of Don Carlos to stimulate the loyalty even of his most benighted partisans. Of military and political capacity he was totally destitute, and his continued absence in Portugal when the conflict had actually begun proved him to be wanting in the natural impulses of a brave man. It was, however, his fortune to be served by a soldier of extraordinary energy and skill; and the first reverses of the Carlists were speedily repaired, and a system of warfare organized which made an end of the hopes of easy conquest with which the Government of Christina had met the insurrection. Fighting in a worthless cause, and commanding resources scarcely superior to those of a brigand chief, the Carlist leader, Zumalacarregui, inflicted defeat after defeat upon the generals who were sent to destroy him. The mountainous character of the country and the universal hostility of the inhabitants made the exertions of a regular soldiery useless against the alternate flights and surprises of men who knew every mountain track and who gained information of the enemy's movements from every cottager.

Terror was added by Zumalacarregui to all his other methods for demoralizing his adversary. In the exercise of reprisals he repeatedly murdered all his prisoners in cold blood, and gave to the war so savage a character that foreign governments at last felt compelled to urge upon the belligerents some regard for the usages of the civilized world. The appearance of Don Carlos himself in the summer of 1834 raised still higher the confidence already inspired by the victories of his general. It was in vain that the old constitutionalist soldier, Mina, who had won so great a name in these Provinces in 1823, returned after long exile to the scene of his exploits. Enfeebled and suffering, he was no longer able to place himself at the head of his troops, and he soon sought to be relieved from a hopeless task. His successor, the War Minister, Valdes, took the field announcing his determination to act upon a new system, and to operate with his troops in mass instead of pursuing the enemy's bands with detachments. The result of this change of tactics was a defeat more ruinous and complete than had befallen any of Valdes's predecessors. He with difficulty withdrew the remainder of his army from the insurgent Provinces; and the Carlist leader, master of the open country up to the borders of Castile, prepared to cross the Ebro and to march upon Madrid.

The ministers of Queen Christina, who till this time had professed themselves confident in their power to deal with the insurrection, could now no longer conceal the real state of affairs. Valdes himself declared that the rebellion could not be subdued without foreign aid; and after prolonged discussion in the Cabinet it was determined to appeal to France for armed assistance. The flight of Don Carlos from England had already caused an additional article to be added to the Treaty of the Quadruple Alliance, in which France undertook so to watch the frontier of the Pyrenees that no reënforcements or munition of war should reach the Carlists from that side, while England promised to supply the troops of Queen Christina with arms and stores, and, if necessary, to render assistance with a naval force (August 18, 1834).

The foreign supplies sent to the Carlists had thus been cut off both by land and sea; but more active assistance seemed indispensable if Madrid was to be saved from falling into the enemy's hands. The request was made to Louis Philippe's Government to occupy the Basque Provinces with a corps of twelve thousand men. Reasons of weight might be addressed to the French court in favor of direct intervention. The victory of Don Carlos would place upon the throne of Spain a representative of all those reactionary influences throughout Europe which were in secret or in open hostility to the house of Orléans, and definitely mark the failure of that policy which had led France to combine with England in expelling Dom Miguel from Portugal.

On the other hand, the experience gained from earlier military enterprises in Spain might well deter even bolder politicians than those about Louis Philippe from venturing upon a task whose ultimate issues no man could confidently forecast. Napoleon had wrecked his empire in the struggle beyond the Pyrenees not less than in the march to Moscow: and the expedition of 1823, though few from military difficulties had exposed France to the humiliating responsibility for every brutal act of a despotism which, in the very moment of its restoration, had scorned the advice of its restorers. The constitutional Government which invoked French assistance might, moreover, at any moment give place to a democratic faction which already harassed it within the Cortes, and which, in its alliance with the populace in many of the great cities, threatened to throw Spain into anarchy, or to restore the ill-omened Constitution of 1812.

But above all, the attitude of the three Eastern powers bade the ruler of France hesitate before committing himself to a military occupation of Spanish territory. Their sympathies were with Don Carlos, and the active participation of France in the quarrel might possibly call their opposing forces into the field and provoke a general war. In view of the evident dangers arising out of the proposed intervention, the French Government, taking its stand on that clause of the Quadruple Treaty which provided that the assistance of France should be rendered in such manner as might be agreed upon by all the parties to the treaty, addressed itself to Great Britain, inquiring whether this country would undertake a joint responsibility in the enterprise and share with France the consequences to which it might give birth. Lord Palmerston in reply declined to give the assurance required. He stated that no objection would be raised by the British Government to the entry of French troops into Spain, but that such intervention must be regarded as the work of France alone, and be undertaken by France at its own peril.

This answer sufficed for Louis Philippe and his ministers. The Spanish Government was informed that the grant of military assistance was impossible, and that the entire public opinion of France would condemn so dangerous an undertaking. As a proof of goodwill, permission was given to Queen Christina to enroll volunteers both in England and France. Arms were supplied; and some thousands of needy or adventurous men ultimately made their way from England as well as from France, to earn under Colonel De Lacy Evans and other leaders a scanty harvest of profit or renown.

The first result of the rejection of the Spanish demand for the direct intervention of France was the downfall of the minister (Valdes) by whom this demand had been made.   His successor, Toreno, though a well-known patriot, proved unable to stem the tide of revolution that was breaking over the country.   City after city set up its own Junta, and acted as if the central Government had ceased to exist.   Again the appeal for help was made to Louis Philippe, and now not so much to avert the victory of Don Carlos as to save Spain from anarchy and from the Constitution of 1812.   Before an answer could arrive, Toreno in his turn had passed away.

Mendizabal, a banker who had been intrusted with financial business at London, and who had entered into friendly relations with Lord Palmerston, was called to office, as a politician acceptable to the democratic party, and the advocate of a close connection with England rather than with France.   In spite of the confident professions of this minister, and in spite of some assistance actually rendered by the English fleet, no real progress was made in subduing the Carlists or in restoring administrative and financial order.   The death of Zumalacarregui, who was forced by Don Carlos to turn northward and besiege Bilbao instead of marching upon Madrid immediately after his victories, had checked the progress of the rebellion at a critical moment; but the Government, distracted and bankrupt, could not use the opportunity which thus offered itself, and the war soon blazed out anew, not only in the Basque Provinces but throughout the North of Spain.   For year after year the monotonous struggle continued, while Cortes succeeded Cortes and faction supplanted faction until there remained scarcely an officer who had not lost his reputation or a politician who was not useless and discredited.

The Queen Regent, who from the necessities of her situation had for a while been the representative of the popular cause, gradually identified herself with the interests opposed to democratic change; and although her name was still treated with some respect and her policy was habitually attributed to the misleading advice of courtiers, her real position was well understood at Madrid, and her own resistance was known to be the principal obstacle to the restoration of the Constitution of 1812.   It was therefore determined to overcome this resistance by force; and on

August 13, 1836, a regiment of the garrison of Madrid, won over by the *Exaltados*, marched upon the palace of La Granja, invaded the Queen's apartments, and compelled her to sign an edict restoring the Constitution of 1812 until the Cortes should establish that or some other.

Scenes of riot and murder followed in the capital. Men of moderate opinions, alarmed at the approach of anarchy, prepared to unite with Don Carlos. King Louis Philippe, who had just consented to strengthen the French legion by the addition of some thousands of trained soldiers, now broke entirely from the Spanish connection, and dimissed his ministers who refused to acquiesce in this change of policy. Meanwhile the Eastern powers and all rational partisans of absolutism besought Don Carlos to give those assurances which would satisfy the wavering mass among his opponents, and place him on the throne without the sacrifice of any right that was worth preserving. It seemed as if the opportunity was too clear to be misunderstood; but the obstinacy and narrowness of Don Carlos were proof against every call of fortune. Refusing to enter into any sort of engagement, he rendered it impossible for men to submit to him who were not willing to accept absolutism pure and simple.

On the other hand, a majority of the Cortes, whose eyes were now opened to the dangers around them, accepted such modifications of the Constitution of 1812 that political stability again appeared possible (June, 1837). The danger of a general transferrence of all moderate elements in the State to the side of Don Carlos was averted; and, although the Carlist armies took up the offensive, menaced the capital, and made incursions into every part of Spain, the darkest period of the war was now over; and when Don Carlos fell back in confusion to the Ebro, the suppression of the rebellion became a certainty.

General Espartero forced back the adversary step by step, and carried fire and sword into the Basque Provinces, employing a system of devastation for exhausting the endurance of the people. Reduced to the last extremity, the Carlist leaders turned their arms against one another.

Finally, on September 14, 1839, after the surrender of almost all his troops to Espartero, Don Carlos crossed the French frontier, and the conflict was at an end.

ABOLITION OF THE SLAVE-TRADE

A.D. 1833

JOHN KELLS INGRAM

By the passage of the Act of 1833 abolishing slavery throughout the British colonies, the English people, through their Parliament, set the world an example, not only of humanity, but also of wise statesmanship obeying the voice of political progress. Like the United States, Great Britain had abolished the slave-trade early in the nineteenth century, and the abolition of slavery itself was, as Fox declared, the natural consequence. During the late years of the seventeenth century, and throughout the greater part of the eighteenth, negro slaves were held in England. In 1764 there were more than twenty thousand in London alone, and there they were openly bought and sold. From its introduction in Virginia in 1619, slavery spread throughout the English colonies in North America.

In the British West Indies traffic in negro slaves early attained greater proportions than on the American Continent. From the days of John Hawkins (1562) dates the beginning of English enterprise in the New World, and his slave-trading voyages, in which he carried human cargoes to the Spanish colonists in the West Indies, were followed by a great increase in the traffic among those islands. During the first quarter of the eighteenth century the English slave-trade there reached its height, and tens of thousands of slaves were imported each year, not only into the Spanish colonies, but into the British as well, no fewer than seventy thousand being taken to Jamaica alone between 1752 and 1762.

Ingram's story of the revolt of English feeling against the slave system, both at home and in the colonies, and of the gradual growth and final triumph of the abolition movement, which at last freed Great Britain from this curse, is as interesting in its narration as it is instructively specific in details.

IT may be truly said that from the latter part of the seventeenth century, when the nature of the slave-trade began to be understood by the public, all that was best in England was adverse to it. Among those who denounced it—besides some whose names are now little known but are recorded in the pages of Clarkson —were Baxter, Sir Richard Steele, Southerne (in *Oroonoko*), Pope, Thomson, Shenstone, Dyer, Savage, and, above all, Cowper (in

Charity and *The Task*), Thomas Day (author of *Sandford and Merton*), Bishop Warburton, Hutcheson, Beattie, John Wesley, Whitefield, Adam Smith, Millar, Robertson, Dr. Joseph Johnson, Mrs. Barbauld, Paley, Gregory, Gilbert Wakefield, Bishop Porteus, and Dean Tucker.

The question of the legal existence of slavery in Great Britain and Ireland was raised in consequence of an opinion given in 1729 by York and Talbot, Attorney- and Solicitor-General at the time, to the effect that a slave by coming into these countries from the West Indies did not become free, and might be compelled by his master to return to the plantations.   Chief Justice Holt had expressed a contrary opinion; and the matter was brought to a final issue by Mr. Granville Sharpe in the case of the negro Somerset.   It was decided by Lord Mansfield, in the name of the whole bench, on June 22, 1772, that as soon as a slave set his foot on the soil of the British Isles he became free.   In 1776 it was moved in the House of Commons by David Hartley, son of the author of *Observations on Man*, that "the slave-trade was contrary to the laws of God and the rights of men"; but this motion—the first which was made on the subject—failed: public opinion on the question was far from being yet fully ripe.

The first persons in England who took united practical action against the trade were the Quakers, inspired by the humane sentiments which had been expressed so early as 1671 by their founder, George Fox.   In 1727 they declared it to be "not a commendable or allowed" practice; in 1761 they excluded from their society all who should be found concerned in it, and issued appeals to their members and the public against the system.   In 1783 there was formed among them an association "for the relief and liberation of the negro slaves in the West Indies, and for the discouragement of the slave-trade on the coast of Africa."   This was the first society established in England for the purpose.

The Quakers in America had taken action on the subject still earlier than those in England.   The Pennsylvania Quakers advised their members against the trade in 1696; in 1754 they issued to their brethren a strong dissuasive against encouraging it in any manner; in 1774 all persons concerned in the traffic, and in 1776 all slaveholders who would not emancipate their slaves, were excluded from membership.   The Quakers in the other

American provinces followed the lead of their brethren in Pennsylvania. The persons among the American Quakers who labored most earnestly and indefatigably on behalf of the Africans were John Woolman (1720–1773) and Anthony Benezet (1713–1784), the latter a son of a French Huguenot driven from France by the Revocation of the Edict of Nantes. The former confined his efforts chiefly to America and indeed to his coreligionists there; the latter sought, and not without a large measure of success, to found a universal propaganda in favor of abolition. A Pennsylvanian society was formed in 1774 by James Pemberton and Doctor Benjamin Rush, and in 1787 (after the war) was reconstructed on an enlarged basis under the presidency of Benjamin Franklin. Other similar associations were founded about the same time in different parts of the United States.

The next important movement took place in England. Doctor Packard, Vice-Chancellor of the University of Cambridge, who entertained strong convictions against the slave-trade, proposed in 1785, as subject for a Latin prize dissertation, the question, "*An liceat invitos in servitutem dare.*" Thomas Clarkson resolved to compete for the prize. Reading Anthony Benezet's *Historical Account of Guinea*, and other works in the course of his study of the subject, he became so powerfully impressed with a sense of the vile and atrocious nature of the traffic that he ere long determined to devote his life to the work of its abolition—a resolution which he nobly kept. His essay, which obtained the first prize, was translated into English in an expanded form by its author, and published in 1786 with the title *Essay on the Slavery and Commerce of the Human Species*. In the process of its publication he was brought into contact with several persons already deeply interested in the question; among these were Granville Sharp, William Dillwyn (an American by birth, who had known Benezet), and the Reverend James Ramsay, who had lived nineteen years in St. Christopher, and had published an *Essay on Treatment and Conversion of the African Slaves in the British Sugar Colonies.*

The distribution of Clarkson's book led to his forming connections with many persons of influence, and especially with William Wilberforce, who, having already occupied himself with the subject, went fully into the evidence bearing on it which

Clarkson laid before him, and, as the result of his inquiries, undertook the Parliamentary conduct of the movement which was now
decisively inaugurated.   A committee was formed on May 22,
1787, for the abolition of the slave-trade, under the presidency of
Granville Sharp, which after twenty years of labor succeeded,
with the help of eminent men, in effecting the object of its foundation, thus removing a great blot on the character of the British
nation and mitigating one of the greatest evils that ever afflicted
humanity.   It is unquestionable that the principal motive power
which originated and sustained their efforts was a Christian principle and feeling.   The most earnest and unremitting exertions
were made by the persons so associated in investigating facts and
collecting evidence, in forming branch committees and procuring petitions, in the instruction of the public and in the information and support of those who pleaded the cause in Parliament.
To the original members were afterward added several persons, among whom were Josiah Wedgwood, Bennet Langton
(Doctor Johnson's friend), and, later, Zachary Macaulay, Henry
Brougham, and James Stephen.

In consequence of the numerous petitions presented to Parliament, a committee of the Privy Council was appointed by the
Crown in 1788 to inquire concerning the slave-trade; and Mr.
Pitt moved that the House of Commons should early in the next
session take the subject into consideration.   Wilberforce's first
motion for a committee of the whole House upon the question was
made on March 19, 1789, and this committee proceeded to business on May 12th of the same year.   After an admirable speech,
Wilberforce laid on the table twelve resolutions which were intended as the basis of a future motion for the abolition of the
trade.   The discussion of these was postponed to the next session, and in 1790–1791 evidence was taken upon them.   At
length, on April 18th of the latter year, a motion was made for
the introduction of a bill to prevent the further importation of
slaves into the British colonies in the West Indies.   Opinion had
been prejudiced by the insurrection in Santo Domingo and Mar-
tinique, and in the British island of Dominica; and the motion
was defeated by one hundred sixty-three votes against eighty-
eight.

Legislative sanction was, however, given to the establishment of the Sierra Leone Company for the colonization of a district on the west coast of Africa and the discouragement of the slave-trade there.   It was hoped at the time that that place would become the centre from which the civilization of Africa would proceed; but this expectation was not fulfilled.   On April 2, 1792, Wilberforce again moved that the trade ought to be abolished; an amendment in favor of gradual abolition was carried, and it was finally resolved that the trade should cease on January 1, 1796. When a similar motion was brought forward in the Lords the consideration of it was postponed to the following year, in order to give time for the examination of witnesses by a committee of the House.   A bill in the Commons in the following year to abolish that part of the trade by which British merchants supplied foreign settlements with slaves was lost on the third reading; it was renewed in the Commons in 1794 and carried there, but defeated in the Lords.

Then followed several years during which efforts were made by the abolitionists in Parliament with little success.   But in 1806, Lord Grenville and Fox having come into power, a bill was passed in both Houses to put an end to the British slave-trade for foreign supply, and to forbid the importation of slaves into the colonies won by the British arms in the course of the war.   On June 10th of the same year Fox brought forward a resolution "that effectual measures should be taken for the abolition of the African slave-trade in such a manner and at such a period as should be deemed advisable," which was carried by a large majority.   A similar resolution was successful in the House of Lords.   A bill was then passed through both Houses forbidding the employment of any new vessel in the trade.   Finally, in 1807, a bill was presented by Lord Grenville in the House of Lords providing for the abolition of the trade; was passed by a large majority; was then sent to the Commons (where it was moved by Lord Howick); was there amended and passed, and received the royal assent on March 25th.   The bill enacted that no vessel should clear out for slaves from any port within the British dominions after May 1, 1807, and that no slave should be landed in the colonies after March 1, 1808.

In 1807 the "African Institution" was formed, with the primary objects of keeping a vigilant watch on the slave-traders and procuring, if possible, the abolition of the slave-trade by the other European nations. It was also to be made an instrument for promoting the instruction of the negro races and diffusing information respecting the agricultural and commercial capabilities of the African Continent.

The Act of 1807 was habitually violated, as the traders knew that if one voyage in three was successful they were abundantly remunerated for their losses, so that the enormous profits of the traffic afforded an insurance against the consequences of capture. This state of things, it was plain, must continue as long as the trade was only a contraband commerce involving merely pecuniary penalties. Accordingly, in 1811, Brougham carried through Parliament a bill declaring the traffic to be a felony punishable with transportation. Some years later another act was passed making it a capital offence, but this was afterward repealed. The Law of 1811 proved effectual and brought the slave-trade to an end so far as the British dominions were concerned. Mauritius, indeed, continued it for a time. That island, which had been ceded by France in 1810, three years after the abolition, had special facilities for escaping observation in consequence of the proximity of the African coast; but it was soon obliged to conform.

England had not been the first European power to abolish the slave-trade; that honor belongs to Denmark: a royal order was issued on May 16, 1792, that the traffic should cease in the Danish possessions from the end of 1802. The United States had in 1794 forbidden any participation by American citizens in the slave-trade to foreign countries; they now prohibited the importation of slaves from Africa into their own dominion. This act was passed on March 2, 1807; it did not, however, come into force until January 1, 1808. At the Congress of Vienna (opened November 1, 1814) the principle was acknowledged that the slave-trade should be abolished as soon as possible; but the determination of the limit of time was reserved for separate negotiation between the powers. It had been provided in a treaty between France and Great Britain, May 30, 1814, that no foreigner should in future introduce slaves into the French colonies, and that the trade should be absolutely interdicted to the French themselves after June 1, 1819. This postponement of abolition was dictated by the wish to introduce a fresh stock of slaves into Haiti if that island should be recovered. Bonaparte, as we have seen, abolished the French slave-trade during his brief restoration, and this abolition was confirmed at the second Peace of Paris, November 20, 1815, but it was not effectually carried out by the French Legislature until March, 1818.

In January, 1815, Portuguese subjects were prohibited from prosecuting the trade north of the equator, and the term after which the traffic should be everywhere unlawful was fixed to end January 21, 1823, but was afterward extended to February, 1830; England paid three hundred thousand pounds as a compensation to the Portuguese. A royal decree was issued on December 10, 1836, forbidding the export of slaves from any Portuguese possession. But this decree was often violated. It was agreed that the Spanish slave-trade should come to an end in 1820, England paying to Spain an indemnification of four hundred thousand pounds. The Dutch trade was closed in 1814; the Swedish had been abolished in 1813. By the Peace of Ghent, December, 1814, the United States and England mutually bound themselves to do all in their power to extinguish the traffic. It was prohibited in several of the South American States immediately on their acquiring independence, as in La Plata, Venezuela, and Chile. In 1831 and 1833 Great Britain entered into an arrangement with France for a mutual right of search within certain seas, to which most of the other powers acceded; and, by the Ashburton Treaty (1842) with the United States, provision was made for the joint maintenance of squadrons on the west coast of Africa. By all these measures the slave-trade, so far as it had been carried on under the flags of Western nations, or for the supply of their colonies, ceased to have a legal existence.

Meantime another and more radical reform had been in preparation and was already in progress, namely, the abolition of slavery itself in the foreign possessions of the several States of Europe. When the English slave-trade had been closed, it was found that the evils of the traffic, as still continued by several other nations, were greatly aggravated. In consequence of the activity of the British cruisers the traders made great efforts to carry as many slaves as possible in every voyage, and practised atrocities to get rid of the slaves when capture was imminent. It was besides the interest of the cruisers, who shared the price of the captured slave-ship, rather to allow the slaves to be taken on board than to prevent their being shipped at all. Therein meant a number of negroes as before, it was said, was exported from Africa, and two-thirds of these perished on the high seas.

It was found also that the abolition of the British slave-trade did not lead to an improved treatment of the negroes in the West Indies. The agents who cultivated those islands had different interests from their employers, who were commonly absentees; and even the latter too often in their haste to be rich, or under the pressure of distressed circumstances, forgot the lessons of humanity in the thirst for immediate gain. The slaves were overworked now that fresh supplies were stopped, and their numbers rapidly decreased. In 1807 there were in the West Indies eight hundred thousand; in 1830 they were reduced to seven hundred thousand. It became more and more evident that the root of the evil could be reached only by abolishing slavery altogether. At the same time, by the discussions which had for years gone on throughout English society on the subject of the slave-trade, men's consciences had been awakened to question the lawfulness of the whole system of things out of which that trade had taken its rise.

An appeal was made by Wilberforce in 1821 to Thomas Fowell Buxton to undertake the conduct of this new question in Parliament. An antislavery society was established in 1823, the principal members of which, besides Wilberforce and Buxton, were Zachary Macaulay, Doctor Lushington, and Lord Suffield. Buxton moved on May 5th of the same year that the House should take into consideration the state of slavery in the British colonies. The object he and his associates had then in view was gradual abolition by establishing something like a system of serfdom for existing slaves, and passing at the same time a measure emancipating all their children born after a certain day. Canning carried against Buxton and his friends a motion to the effect that the desired ameliorations in the treatment of the slaves should be recommended by the Home Government to the colonial legislatures, and enforced only in case of their resistance.

A well-conceived series of measures of reform was accordingly proposed to the colonial authorities. Thereupon a general outcry was raised by the planters at the acquiescence of the Government in the principles of the antislavery party. A vain attempt being made in Demerara to conceal from the knowledge of the slaves the arrival of the order in council, they became impressed with the idea that they had been set free, and accordingly refused to work, and, compulsion being resorted to, offered resistance. Martial law was proclaimed; the disturbances were repressed with great severity; and the treatment of the missionary Smith awakened strong feeling in England against the planters.

The question, however, made little progress in Parliament for some years, though Buxton, William Smith, Lushington, Brougham, Mackintosh, Butterworth, and Denman, with the aid of Zachary Macaulay, James Stephen, and others, continued the struggle, only suspending it during a period allowed to the local legislatures for carrying into effect the measures expected from them. In 1828 the free people of color in the colonies were placed on a footing of legal equality with their fellow-citizens. In 1830 the public began to be aroused to a serious prosecution of the main issue. It was becoming plain that the planters would take no steps tending to the future liberation of the slaves, and the leaders of the movement determined to urge the entire abolition of slavery at the earliest practicable period. The Government continued to hesitate, and to press for mitigations of the existing system. At length, in 1833, the Ministry of Earl Grey took the question in hand and carried the abolition with little difficulty, the measure passing the House of Commons on August 7, 1833, and receiving the royal assent on the 28th of the same month. A sum of twenty million pounds sterling was voted as compensation to the planters. A system of apprenticeship for seven years was established as a transitional preparation for liberty. The slaves were bound to work for their masters during this period for three-fourths of the day, and were to be liable to corporal punishment if they did not give the due amount of labor. The master was in return to supply them with food and clothing. All children under six years of age were to be at once free, and provision was to be made for their religious and moral instruction. Many thought the postponement of emancipation unwise. Immediate liberation was carried out in Antigua, and the Christmas of 1833 was the first for twenty years during which martial law was not proclaimed in order to preserve the peace.

THE TEXAN REVOLUTION

A.D. 1836

SAM HOUSTON   CHARLES EDWARDS LESTER

If only as marking a transition from one political connection to another, the revolt of Texas against Mexico was an event of no slight historical significance. It led, in 1836, to the establishment of the Republic of Texas, which maintained an independent existence until its annexation to the United States in 1845. From the time of its exploration by La Salle (1684) the Texas region was occupied by settlers from different countries, especially, at first, by Spaniards, who in the eighteenth century established missions there. Rival missions were planted by the French. The strife of contesting claimants was increased in the early years of the nineteenth century, when adventurers from many quarters entered the territory. From 1820 to 1830, while it was part of a Mexican State, Texas was settled by numerous American colonists, and this colonization from the United States had much to do with the movement for Texan independence, in obtaining which many Americans took part. The first conflicts, in 1835, were between Americans and Mexicans.

The most prominent among the American actors in the uprising was General Sam Houston. He was born in Virginia in 1793, served in the War of 1812, and afterward in Congress, and in 1827–1829 was Governor of Tennessee. He then spent three years among the Cherokee Indians, and later went to Texas, where he attained political and military prominence, and upon the outbreak of the revolution the Provisional Government elected him commander-in-chief of the Texan forces.

Of the following accounts, that of Houston himself narrates the early steps of the struggle ; while Lester, its historian, gives a spirited description of the Battle of San Jacinto, which proved decisive for the success of the movement.

SAM HOUSTON

IN December, 1835, when the troubles began in Texas, in the inception of its revolution, Houston was appointed major-general of the forces by the consultation then in session at San Felipe. He remained in that command. Delegates, one from each municipality, or what would correspond to counties here, were to constitute the government, with a governor, lieutenant-governor, and council. They had the power of the country. An army was requisite, and means were necessary to sustain the revolution. This was the first organization of anything like a government, which absorbed the power that had previously existed in committees of vigilance and safety in different sections of the country. When the General was appointed, his first act was to organize a force to repel an invading army which he was satisfied would advance upon Texas.

A rendezvous had been established, at which the drilling and organization of the troops were to take place, and officers were sent to their respective posts for the purpose of recruiting men. Colonel Fannin was appointed at Matagorda, to superintend that district, second in command to the General-in-Chief; and he remained there until the gallant band from Alabama and Georgia visited that country. They were volunteers under Colonels Ward, Shackleford, Duvall, and other illustrious names. When they arrived, Colonel Fannin, disregarding the orders of the Commander-in-Chief, became, by countenance of the Council, a candidate for commander of the volunteers. Some four or five hundred of them had arrived, all equipped and disciplined; men of intelligence, men of character, men of chivalry and of honor. A more gallant band never graced the American soil in defence of liberty. He was selected; and the project of the Council was to invade Matamoras, under the auspices of Fannin. San Antonio had been taken in 1835. Troops were to remain there. It was a post more than seventy miles from any colonies or settlements by the Americans. It was a Spanish town or city, with many thousand population, and very few Americans. The Alamo was nothing more than a church, and derived its cognomen from the fact of its being surrounded by poplars or cottonwood trees. The Alamo had been known as a fortress since the Mexican revolution in 1812. The troops remained at Bexar until about the last of December.

The Council, without the knowledge of the Governor, and without the concurrence of the Commander-in-Chief of the army, had secretly sent orders authorizing Grant and others to invade Matamoras, some three hundred miles, I think, through an uninhabited country, and thereby to leave the Alamo in a defenceless position. They marched off, and left only one hundred fifty effective men, taking some two hundred with them. Fannin was to unite with them from the mouth of the Brazos, at Copano, and there the two forces were to unite under the auspices of Colonel Fannin, and were to proceed to Matamoras and take possession of it. The enemy, in the mean time, were known to be advancing upon Texas; and they were thus detaching an inefficient force, which, if it had been concentrated, would have been able to resist all the powers of Mexico combined. The Commander-in-Chief was ordered by the Governor to repair immediately to Goliad, and if the expedition surreptitiously ordered by the Council should proceed to Matamoras, to take charge of it. Under his conduct it was supposed that something might be achieved, or, at least, disaster prevented.

The Council, on January 7th, passed an edict creating Fannin and Johnson military agents, and investing them with all the power of the country, to impress property, receive troops, command them, appoint subordinates throughout the country, and effectually supersede the Commander-in-Chief in his authority. He was ordered to repair to Capano, and did so. While at Goliad he sent an order to Colonel Neill, who was in command of the Alamo, to blow up that place and fall back to Gonzales, making that a defensive position, which was supposed to be the farthest boundary the enemy would ever reach.

This was on January 17th. That order was secretly superseded by the Council; and Colonel W. B. Travis, having relieved Colonel Neill, did not blow up the Alamo and retreat with such articles as were necessary for the defence of the country; but remained in possession from January 17th until the last of February, when the Alamo was invested by the force of Santa Anna. Surrounded there, and cut off from all succor, the consequence was they were destroyed; they fell victims to the ruthless Santa Anna, by the contrivance of the Council, and in violation of the plans of the Major-General for the defence of the country.[1]

[1] The massacre of the Alamo is one of the most memorable tragedies in American military history. Of the men—about one hundred fifty in number—under Colonel Travis in the fort, only one is known to have remained alive, and he escaped before the butchery began. The defenders had made a desperate resistance during the terrible siege, but not even desperation could enable valor to prevail against the fury of an overwhelming force. Among those killed in this slaughter were David Crock-

What was the fate of Johnson, of Ward, and of Morris? They had advanced beyond Capano previous to forming a junction with Fannin, and they were cut off. Fannin subsequently arrived, and attempted to advance, but fell back to Goliad. When the Alamo fell, he was at Goliad. King's command had been left at Refugio, for the purpose of defending some families, instead of removing them. They were invested there; and Ward, with a battalion of gallant volunteers, was sent to relieve King; but he was annihilated. Fannin was in Goliad. Ward, in attempting to come back, had become lost or bewildered. The Alamo had fallen.

On March 4th the Commander-in-Chief was reëlected by the convention, after having laid down his authority. He hesitated for hours before he would accept the situation. He had anticipated every disaster that befell the country, from the detached condition of the troops, under the orders of the Council, and the inevitable destruction that awaited them, and to this effect had so reported to the Governor on February 4th.

When he assumed the command, what was his situation? Had he aid and succor? He had conciliated the Indians by treaty while he was superseded by the unlawful edicts of the Council. He had conciliated thirteen bands of Indians, and they remained amicable throughout the struggle of the revolution. Had they not been conciliated, but turned loose upon our people, the women and children would have perished in their flight arising from panic. After treaty with the Indians, he attended the conventions, and acted in the deliberations of that body, signing the declaration of independence, and was there elected. When he set out for the army, the only hope of Texas remained then at Gonzales.

Men with martial spirit, with well-nerved arms and gallant hearts, had hastily rallied there as the last hope of Texas. The Alamo was known to be in siege. Fannin was known to be em-

ett, the famous pioneer, hunter, and politician, and Colonel James Bowie, an American soldier, notorious as a duellist, and as the inventor of the bowie-knife. The feature of extreme atrocity consisted in the murder, by order of Santa Anna, of six men—among them Crockett—who surrendered after the death of their comrades. This outrage rankled in the memory of the men who continued the fight for Texan independence, and, as will be seen below, inspired their vengeful battle-cry.—ED.

barrassed; Ward, also, and Morris and Johnson, destroyed.
All seemed to bespeak calamity of the most direful character. It
was under those circumstances that the General started; and
what was his escort? A general in chief, you would suppose,
was at least surrounded by a staff of gallant men. It would be
imagined that some prestige ought to be given to him. He was
to produce a nation; he was to defend a people; he was to command the resources of the country; and he must give character
to the army. He had two aides-de-camp, one captain, and a
youth. This was his escort in marching to the headquarters of
the "army," as it was called. The Provisional Government had
become extinct; self-combustion had taken place, and it was utterly consumed.

The General proceeded on his way and met many fugitives.
The day on which he left Washington, March 6th, the Alamo had
fallen. He anticipated it; and marching to Gonzales as soon as
practicable, though his health was infirm, he arrived there on
March 11th. He found at Gonzales three hundred seventy-four
men, half fed, half clad, and half armed, and without organization. That was the nucleus on which he had to form an army
and defend the country. No sooner did he arrive than he sent a
despatch to Colonel Fannin, fifty-eight miles, which would reach
him in thirty hours, to fall back. He was satisfied that the
Alamo had fallen. Colonel Fannin was ordered to fall back from
Goliad twenty-five miles to Victoria, on the Guadalupe, thus
placing him within striking distance of Gonzales, for he had only
to march twenty-five miles to Victoria to be on the east side of the
Colorado, with the only succor hoped for by the General. He
received an answer from Colonel Fannin, stating that he had received his order; had held a council of war; and that he had
determined to defend the place, and called it Fort Defiance, and
had taken the responsibility to disobey the order.

Under these circumstances the confirmation of the fall of the
Alamo reached the General. He ordered every wagon but one
to be employed in transporting the women and children from the
town of Gonzales, and had only four oxen and a single wagon, as
he believed, to transport all the baggage and munitions of war
belonging to Texas at that point. That was all he had left. He
had provided for the women and children; and every female and

child left but one, whose husband had just perished in the Alamo; and, disconsolate, she would not consent to leave there until the rear-guard was leaving the place, but invoked the murderous Mexicans to fall upon and destroy her and her children.

Though the news of the fall of the Alamo arrived at eight or nine o'clock at night, that night, by eleven o'clock, the Commander-in-Chief had everything in readiness to march, though panic raged, and frenzy seized upon many; and though it took all his personal influence to resist the panic and bring them to composure, with all the encouragement he could use, he succeeded.

Fannin, after disobeying orders, attempted, on the 19th, to retreat, and had only twenty-five miles to reach Victoria. His opinions of chivalry and honor were such that he would not avail himself of the night to do it in, although he had been admonished by the smoke of the enemies' encampment for eight days previous to attempt a retreat. He then attempted to retreat in open day. The Mexican cavalry surrounded him. He halted in a prairie, without water; commenced a fortification, and there was surrounded by the enemy, who, from the hill-tops, shot down upon him. Though the most gallant spirits were there with him, he remained in the situation all that night and the next day, when a flag of truce was presented; he entered into a capitulation, and was taken to Goliad, on a promise to be returned to the United States with all associated with him. I believe some few did escape, most of whom came afterward and joined the army.

The General fell back from the Colorado. The artillery had not yet arrived. He had every reason to believe that the check given to General Sesma, opposite to his camp on the west side of the Colorado, would induce him to send for reënforcements, and that Fannin having been massacred, a concentration of the enemy would necessarily take place, and that an overwhelming force would soon be upon him. He knew that one battle must be decisive of the fate of Texas. If he fought a battle and many of his men were wounded, he could not transport them, and he would be compelled to sacrifice the army to the wounded. He determined to fall back, and did so, and on falling back received an accession of three companies that had been ordered from the mouth of the Brazos.

He marched and took position on the Brazos, with as much ⟨illegible⟩ ⟨illegible⟩ ⟨illegible⟩ he found a spirit of dissatisfaction in the troops. The Government had removed east. It had left Washington and gone to Harrisburg, and the apprehension of the settlers had been awakened and increased, rather than decreased. The spirits of the men were bowed down. Hope seemed to have departed, and with the little band alone remained anything like a consciousness of strength.

At San Felipe objection was made to marching up the Brazos. It was said that settlements were down below, and persons interested were there. Oxen could not be found for the march, in the morning, of a certain company. The General directed that they should follow as soon as oxen were collected. He marched up the Brazos, and, crossing Mill Creek, encamped there. An express was sent to him asking his permission for that company to go down the Brazos to Fort Bend, and to remain there. Knowing that it arose from a spirit of sedition, he granted that permission, and they marched down. On the Brazos the efficient force under his command amounted to five hundred twenty men. He remained there from the last of March until April 13th. On his arrival at the Brazos he found that the rains had been excessive. He had no opportunity of operating against the enemy. They marched to San Felipe, within eighteen miles of him, and would have been liable to surprise at any time, had it not been for the high waters of the Brazos, which prevented him from marching upon them by surprise. Thus he was pent up. The portion of the Brazos in which he was became an island. The water had not been so high for years.

On arriving at the Brazos, he found that the Yellowstone, a very respectable steamboat, had gone up the river for the purpose of transporting cotton. She was seized by order of the General, to enable him, if necessary, to pass the Brazos at any moment, and was detained with a guard on board. She remained there for a number of days. The General had taken every precaution possible to prevent the enemy from passing the Brazos below. He had ordered every craft to be destroyed on the river. He knew that the enemy could not have constructed rafts and crossed; but, by a ruse they obtained the only boat that was in that part of the country, where a command was stationed. They came and spoke English. The boat was sent over, and the Mexicans surprised the boatmen and took possession of it. Those on the east side of the river retreated; and thus Santa Anna obtained an opportunity of transporting his artillery and army across the Brazos.

The General anticipated that something of the kind must have taken place, because his intelligence from San Felipe was that all was quiet there. The enemy had kept up a cannonade on the position across the river, where over one hundred men were stationed. The encampment on the Brazos was the point at which the first piece of artillery was ever received by the army. They were without munitions; old horseshoes and all pieces of iron that could be procured had to be cut up; various things were to be provided; there were no cartridges and but few balls. Two small six-pounders, presented by the magnanimity of the people of Cincinnati, and subsequently called the "Twin Sisters," were the first pieces of artillery that were used in Texas. From there the march commenced at Donoho's, three miles from Groce's. It had required several days to cross the Brazos with the horses and wagons.

The march to Harrisburg was effected through the greatest possible difficulties. The prairies were quagmired. The contents of the wagons had to be carried across the bogs, and the horses attached to empty wagons had to be assisted. No less than eight impediments in one day had to be overcome in that way. Notwithstanding that, the remarkable success of the march brought the army in a little time to Harrisburg, opposite which it halted. "Deaf" Smith (known as such—his proper name was Erasmus Smith), with other spies, had gone over by rafts, and, after crossing, arrested two couriers and brought them into camp. Upon them was found a buckskin wallet containing despatches of General Filosola to General Santa Anna, as well as from Mexico, and thereby we were satisfied that Santa Anna had marched to San Jacinto with the *elite* of his army, and we resolved to push on. Orders were given by the General immediately to prepare rations for three days, and to be at an early hour in readiness to cross the bayou. The next morning the Commander-in-Chief addressed a note in pencil to Colonel Henry Raguet, of Nacogdoches, in these words:

"CAMP AT HARRISBURG, April 19, 1836.

"SIR: This morning we are in preparation to meet Santa Anna. It is the only chance of saving Texas. From time to time I have looked for reënforcements in vain. The convention adjourning to Harrisburg struck panic throughout the country. Texas could have started at least four thousand men. We will only have about seven hundred to march with, besides the camp-guard. We go to conquer. It is wisdom, growing out of necessity, to meet the enemy now; every consideration enforces it. No previous occasion would justify it. The troops are in fine spirits, and now is the time for action.

"We shall use our best efforts to fight the enemy to such advantage as will insure victory, though odds are greatly against us. I leave the result in the hands of a wise God, and rely upon his providence. My country will do justice to those who serve her. The rights for which we fight will be secured, and Texas free."

A crossing was effected by the evening, and the line of march was taken up. The force amounted to a little over seven hundred men. The camp-guard remained opposite Harrisburg. The cavalry had to swim across the bayou, which is of considerable width and depth. General Rusk remained with the army on the west side. The Commander-in-Chief stepped into the first boat of the pioneers, swam his horse with the boat, and took position on the opposite side, where the enemy were, and continued there until the army crossed. The march was then taken up. A few minutes or perhaps an hour or so of daylight only remained. The troops continued to march until the men became so exhausted and fatigued that they were falling against each other in the ranks, or some falling down.

The General ordered a halt after marching a short distance from the road to secure a place in a chapparal. The army rested for perhaps two hours, when, at the tap of the drum given by the General, they were again on their feet, and took up the line of march for San Jacinto and Buffalo Bayou. It was necessary for Santa Anna to cross the San Jacinto to unite with the Mexicans in Nacogdoches County, and excite the Indians to war. Santa Anna had provided a boat through the instrumentality of Texans who had joined him, and was in readiness to cross. He had marched down to New Washington, some seven or eight miles below the San Jacinto, and was returning to take up his march eastward.

After sunrise some time, the army having halted to slaughter beeves and refresh, the signal was given that our scouts had encountered those of the enemy; eating was suspended, everything packed, and we were on the march. We marched down to the ferry of San Jacinto and there halted. There was no word of the enemy. About half a mile or a mile up the bayou, where the timber commenced, we fell back and formed an encampment in the timber, so as to give security from the brow of the hill, as well as the timber that covered it, at the same time running up the boat which he had provided, and securing it in the rear of our encampment.

That was the position taken. The artillery was planted in front, for it had never been fired, and the enemy were really not apprised that we had a piece. The troops were secured so as to expose none but the few artillerists to view. There were but eighteen of them, and nine were assigned to each piece. The enemy, within about three hundred yards, I think, took position with their artillery and infantry, and opened fire from a twelve-pounder. It continued until evening. It did no execution, however, with the exception of one shot. Colonel Neill, of the artillery, was wounded, though not mortally. That was the only injury we sustained. At length Santa Anna ordered his infantry to advance. They were advancing, when our artillery were ordered to fire upon them; but they being so much depressed, it passed over their heads and did no injury; but they returned in such haste and confusion to their encampment that it inspirited our troops and caused the welkin to ring.

Upon our left, a company of infantry was, by Santa Anna, posted in an "island" of timber, within one hundred fifty yards of our encampment. An officer desired the General to let him charge, which was readily conceded. He wished to, and did, make the charge on horseback, though not in accordance with the General's opinion. It proved unsuccessful. The enemy, after receiving some injury from the discharge of our artillery, fell back to the heights of San Jacinto, and commenced fortifying.

In the evening, the General ordered a reconnoitring party, under Colonel Sherman, to reconnoitre; but they were ordered not to go within the fire of the enemy's guns or to provoke an attack; but if he could, by his appearance, decoy them into the direction of a certain island of timber, they would be received there by the artillery and infantry that had been ordered to be in readiness to march to that point. No sooner was he out of sight, than a firing commenced, with a view, as Sherman himself declared, to bring on a general action, in violation of the General's orders. Confusion was the result of it. Two men were wounded in our line. A confused retreat took place; and the consequence was that two gallant men were wounded, and one subsequently died of his wounds. This was done in direct violation of the General's orders; for it was not his intention to bring on a general action that day. The guards that night were doubled. The next day, about nine o'clock, troops were discovered advancing along the prairie ridge in the direction of the Mexican encampment, which produced some excitement. The General, not wishing the impression to be received that they were reënforcements, suggested that it was a ruse of the Mexicans, that they were the same troops that were seen yesterday; that they were marching around the swell in the prairie for the purpose of display, because they were apprehensive of an attack from the Texans. He sent out two spies secretly—Deaf Smith and Karnes—upon their track, with directions to report to him privately. They did so, and reported that the reënforcement which the enemy had thus received amounted to five hundred forty men.

Things remained without any change until about twelve o'clock, when the General was asked to call a council of war. No council of war had ever been solicited before: it seemed strange to him. What indications had appeared he did not know. The council was called, however, consisting of six field officers and the Secretary of War. The proposition was put to the council, "Shall we attack the enemy in position, or receive their attack in ours?" The two junior officers—for such is the way of taking the sense of courts in the army—were in favor of attacking the enemy in position. The four seniors, and the Secretary of War, who spoke, said that "to attack veteran troops with raw militia is a thing unheard of; to charge upon the enemy, without bayonets, in an open prairie, had never been known; our situation is strong; in it we can whip all Mexico." Understanding this as the sense of the council, the General dismissed them. They went to their respective places.

CHARLES EDWARDS LESTER

The night that preceded the bloody slaughter of San Jacinto rolled anxiously away, and brightly broke forth the morning of the last day of Texan servitude. Before the first gray streaks shot up in the east, three taps of a drum were heard in the camp, and seven hundred soldiers sprang to their feet as one man. The camp was busy with the soldiers' hum of preparation for battle, but in the midst of it all Houston slept on calmly and profoundly. The soldiers had eaten the last meal they were to eat till they had won their independence. They were under arms, ready for the struggle.

At last the glorious sun came up over the prairie, without a single cloud. It shone full and clear in the face of the hero, and it waked him to battle. He sprang to his feet and exclaimed, "The sun of Austerlitz has risen again!" His face was calm, and, for the first time in many weeks, every shade of trouble had left his brow. He ordered his commissary-general, Colonel John Forbes, to provide two good axes, and then sent for "Deaf" Smith. He took this faithful and intrepid man aside, and ordered him to conceal the axes in a safe place near by where he could lay his hands on them at a moment's warning, and not to pass the lines of the sentinels that day without his special orders, nor to be out of his call.

Morning wore away, and about nine o'clock a large body of men were seen moving over a swell of the prairie in the direction of Santa Anna's camp. They were believed to be a powerful force which had come to join the Mexicans, and the spectacle produced no little excitement in the Texan lines. Houston saw it at a glance, and quelled the apprehension by coolly remarking that "they were the same men they had seen the day before.

They had marched round the swell in the prairie and returned in sight of the Texan camp to alarm their foe with the appearance of an immense reënforcement, for it was very evident Santa Anna did not wish to fight. But it was all a *ruse de guerre* that could be easily seen through—a mere Mexican trick."

All this did very well, and yet Houston, of course, had quite a different notion on the subject. He sent Deaf Smith and a comrade with confidential orders as spies on their rearward march. They soon returned, and reported publicly that "the General was right—it was all a humbug." A few minutes after, Deaf Smith whispered quite another story in the private ear of the commander. The enemy they saw was a reënforcement of five hundred forty men, under General Cos, who had heard Santa Anna's cannon the day before on the Brazos, and come on by forced marches to join his standard. But the secret was kept until it did no harm to reveal it. A proposition was made to the General to construct a floating bridge over Buffalo Bayou, "which might be used in the event of danger." Houston ordered his adjutant and inspector-generals and an aide to ascertain if the necessary materials could be obtained. They reported that by tearing down a house in the neighborhood they could. "We will postpone it awhile, at all events," was Houston's reply.

In the mean time he had ordered Deaf Smith to report to him with a companion well mounted. He retired with them to the spot where the axes had been deposited in the morning. Taking one in either hand and examining them carefully, he handed them to the two trusty fellows, saying: "Now, my friends, take these axes, mount, and make the best of your way to Vince's Bridge; cut it down and burn it, and come back like eagles or you will be too late for the day." This was the bridge over which both armies had crossed in their march to the battle-ground of San Jacinto, and it cut off all chance of escape for the vanquished. "This," said Deaf Smith, in his droll way, "looks a good deal like fight, General."

The reader will not fail to notice the difference between Houston's calculations of the results of that day and those of some of his officers. They bethought themselves of building a new bridge—he of cutting down and burning up the *only* bridge in the neighborhood. The fact was Houston was determined his army should come off victorious that day or leave their bodies on the field.

The day was now wearing away; it was three o'clock in the afternoon, and yet the enemy kept concealed behind his breast-works and manifested no disposition to come to an engagement. Events had taken just such a current as Houston expected and desired, and he began to prepare for battle.

In describing his plan of attack we borrow the language of his official report after the battle was over: "The First Regiment, commanded by Colonel Burleson, was assigned the centre. The Second Regiment, under the command of Colonel Sherman, formed the left wing of the army. The artillery, under the special command of Colonel George W. Hockley, inspector-general, was placed on the right of the First Regiment, and four companies of infantry, under the command of Lieutenant-Colonel Henry Millard, sustained the artillery upon the right. Our cavalry, sixty-one in number, commanded by Colonel Mirabeau B. Lamar, placed on our extreme right, completed our line. Our cavalry was first despatched to the front of the enemy's left, for the purpose of attracting their notice, while an extensive 'island' of timber afforded us an opportunity of concentrating our forces and displaying from that point, agreeably to the previous design of the troops. Every evolution was performed with alacrity, the whole advancing rapidly in line and through an open prairie without any protection whatever for our men. The artillery advanced and took station within two hundred yards of the enemy's breast-work."

The two armies were now drawn up in complete order. There were seven hundred Texans on the field, and Santa Anna's troops numbered over eighteen hundred. Houston had informed Thomas J. Rusk of the plan of the battle, and he approved of it as perfect. The Secretary, it is true, had never been a soldier—he understood little of military evolutions or the discipline of an army—but Houston knew he carried a lion heart in his bosom, and he assigned him the command of the left wing. The General, of course, led the centre.

Everything was now ready, and every man at his post waiting for the charge. The two six-pounders had commenced a well-directed fire of grape and canister, and they shattered bones and baggage where they struck—the moment had at last come. Houston ordered the charge and sounded out the war-cry, "*Remember the Alamo!*" These magic words struck the ear of every soldier in the ranks instant and "The Alamo! The Alamo!" went up from the army in one wild yell which sent terror through the Mexican host. At that moment a rider came up on a horse covered with foam and mire, swinging an axe over his head, and dashed along the Texan lines, crying out, as he had been instructed to do, "I have cut down Vince's bridge—now fight for your lives and remember the Alamo!" Then the solid phalanx which had been held back for a moment at the announcement, launched forward upon the breastwork like an avalanche of fire. Houston spurred his horse on at the head of the centre column right into the face of the foe.

The Mexican army was drawn up in perfect order ready to receive the attack, and when the Texans were within about sixty paces, and before they had fired a rifle, a general flash was seen along the Mexican lines and a storm of bullets went rushing over the Texan army. They fired too high; several balls struck Houston's horse in the breast, and one ball shattered the General's ankle. The noble animal staggered for a moment, but Houston spurred him on. If the first discharge of the Mexicans had been well directed, it would have thinned the Texan ranks. But they pressed on, reserving their fire until each man could choose some particular soldier for his target; and before the Mexicans could reload, a murderous discharge of rifle-balls was poured into their ranks.

The Texan soldiers rushed on. They were without bayonets, but they converted their rifles into war-clubs and levelled them upon the heads of Santa Anna's men. Along the breastwork there was little more firing of muskets or rifles—it was a desperate struggle hand to hand. The Texans, when they had broken off their rifles at the breech by smashing the skulls of their enemies, flung them down and drew their pistols. They fired them once, and having no time to reload, hurled them against the heads of their foes, and then, drawing forth their bowie-knives, literally cut their way through the dense masses of the enemy.

It would be a mistake to suppose that the Mexicans played the coward that day. They were slain by hundreds in the ranks

where they stood when the battle began, but the fierce and vengeful onslaught of the Texans could not be resisted.   They fought
as none but freeman can fight when they are striking for their
homes, their families, and to revenge their dead kindred.   The
Mexican officers and men stood firm for a time, but the Texans
stamped on them as fast as they fell, and trampled down the prostrate and the dying with the dead, and, clambering over the
groaning bleeding mass plunged their knives into the breasts of
those in the rear.   When the Mexicans saw that the onset of their
foe could not be resisted they either attempted to fly and were
stabbed in the back, or fell on their knees to plead for mercy, crying, "Me no Alamo!   Me no Alamo!   Me no Alamo!"   These
unfortunate slaves of the Mexican tyrant had witnessed that
brutal massacre of brave men, and now they could think of no
other claim for mercy but the plea they were not there, for they
knew the day of vengeance for the Alamo had come at last.

But before the centre breastwork had been carried, the right
and left wing of the enemy had been put to the rout or the slaughter.   The Mexicans, however, not only stood their ground at first,
but made several bold charges upon the Texan lines.   A division
of their infantry of more than five hundred men made a gallant
charge, in handsome order, upon the battalion of Texan infantry.
Seeing them hard pressed by a force of three to one, the Commander-in-Chief dashed between them and the enemy's column,
exclaiming, "Come on, my brave fellows, your General leads
you!"   The battalion halted and wheeled into perfect order, like
a veteran corps, and Houston gave the order to fire.   If the guns
of the Texans had all been moved by machinery they could not
have been fired more instantaneously.   There was a single explosion; the battalion rushed through the smoke, and those who
had not been mowed down by the bullets were felled by smashing
blows from the rifle-butts, and the prostrate column was trampled
into the mire.   Of the five hundred, only thirty-two lived, to surrender as prisoners of war.

In the mean time, although Houston's wound was bleeding
profusely, and his dying horse could scarcely stagger his way over
the slain, yet the Commander-in-Chief saw every movement of
his army, and followed the tide of battle as it rolled over the field.
Wherever his eye fell he saw the Mexicans staggering back under

the resistless shock of his heroic soldiers.   Regiments and battalions, cavalry and infantry, horses and men were hurled together, and every officer and every man seemed to be bent upon
ꞏ ꞏꞏꞏ ꞏꞏ ꞏꞏꞏꞏꞏꞏꞏ ꞏꞏꞏ ꞏꞏꞏꞏꞏꞏꞏ.

The Mexican army had now been driven from their position,
and were flying before their pursuers.   Houston saw that the battle was won, and he rode over the field and gave his orders to stop
the slaughter of the wounded and of those who surrendered.
But it would have been easier to stop the inrolling tide of the sea.
He had given "The Alamo" for their war-cry, and the magic
word could not be recalled.   The ghosts of brave men, massacred
at Goliad and the Alamo, flitted through the smoke of battle, and
the uplifted hand could not be stayed.   "While the battle was in
progress," says General Rusk, "the celebrated Deaf Smith, although on horseback, was fighting with the infantry.   When they
got near the enemy Smith galloped on ahead, and dashed directly
up to the Mexican line.   Just as he reached it his horse stumbled
and fell, throwing him on his head among the enemy.   Having
dropped his sword in the fall, he drew one of his pistols from his
belt and presented it at the head of a Mexican who was attempting to bayonet him, but it missed fire.   Smith then hurled the
pistol itself at the head of the Mexican, and, as he staggered back,
he seized his gun and began his work of destruction.   A young
man named Robbins dropped his gun in the confusion of the
battle, and happening to run directly in contact with a Mexican
soldier who had also lost his musket, the Mexican seized Robbins, and both being stout men, they fell to the ground.   Robbins
drew his bowie-knife and ended the contest by cutting the Mexican's throat.   On starting out from our camp to begin the attack
I saw an old man, named Curtis, carrying two guns.   I asked
him what reason he had for carrying more than one gun.   He
answered: 'D—n the Mexicans; they killed my son and son-
in-law in the Alamo, and I intend to kill two of them for it, or be
killed myself.'   I saw the old man again during the fight, and he
told me he had killed his two men; and 'if he could find Santa
Anna himself he would cut out a razor-strop from his back.'"

Such was the day of vengeance.   It was not strange that no
invading army, however brave, could long withstand so dreadful
an onset.   "When the Mexicans were first driven from the point

of woods where we encountered them," continues General Rusk, "their officers tried to rally them, but the men cried, 'It's no use, it's no use; there are a thousand Americans in the woods!' When Santa Anna saw Almonte's division running past him he called a drummer and ordered him to beat his drum. The drummer held up his hands and told him he was shot. He called to a trumpeter near him to sound his horn. The trumpeter replied that he also was shot. Just at that instant a ball from one of our cannon struck a man who was standing near Santa Anna, taking off one side of his head. Santa Anna then exclaimed, 'D—n these Americans; I believe they will shoot us all!' He immediately mounted his horse, and commenced his flight."

The flight had now become universal. The Texans had left dead and dying on the ground where the battle began (more Mexicans than their own entire number), and far over the prairie they were chasing the flying and following up the slaughter. Many were overtaken and killed as they were making their escape through the high grass. The Mexican cavalry was well mounted, and after the defeat they spurred their horses and turned their heads toward Vince's bridge. They were hotly pursued by the victors, and when the latter came up the most appalling spectacle perhaps of the entire day was witnessed.

When the fugitive horsemen saw that the bridge was gone, some of them, in their desperation, spurred their horses down the steep bank; others dismounted and plunged into the stream; some were entangled in their trappings, and were dragged down with their struggling steeds, others sank at once to the bottom; while those whose horses reached the opposite bank fell backward into the river. In the mean time, while they were struggling with the flood, their pursuers, who had come up, were pouring down upon them a deadly fire which cut off all escape. Horses and men, by hundreds, rolled down together; the water was red with their blood and filled with their struggling bodies. The deep, turbid stream was literally choked with the dead.

A similar spectacle was witnessed on the southern verge of the island of trees, near the Mexican encampment, in the rear of the battle-ground. There was little chance of escape in this quarter, for a deep morass had to be passed, and yet a great number of the fugitives, in their desperation, had rushed to this spot as a forlorn hope. They had plunged into the water and mud with horses and mules, and, in attempting to cross, had been completely submerged; those who seemed likely to escape soon fell victims to the unerring aim of a practised rifleman until the morass was literally bridged over with carcasses of dead mules, horses, and men.

A company of about two hundred fifty cooler and braver men, under Almonte, had rallied in the island of trees, prepared to resist or surrender rather than fly. Houston rallied as large a body of men as could be assembled and was preparing to lead them to the charge, when his gallant horse, that had so nobly borne his rider through the thickest of the battle, with seven bullets in his body, at last staggered and fell dead. Houston, in dismounting, struck upon his wounded leg and fell to the earth. It was now discovered, for the first time, that he was wounded. Alarm immediately spread over the field. Houston called for General Rusk, and gave him the command. He was then helped upon another horse, and General Rusk advanced with his newly formed company upon the last remnant of the Mexican army. Its commander, however, came promptly forward and surrendered his sword. Houston then cast a glance over the field and said, "I think now, gentlemen, we are likely to have no more trouble to-day, and I believe I will return to the camp."

The party then rode slowly off from the field of victory and the resting-place of the dead, and returned to the oak at whose foot the hero of San Jacinto had slept till the "sun of Austerlitz" had awakened him that morning. All resistance to the arms of Texas ceased. The pursuers returned to the camp, where a command was left to guard the spoils taken from the enemy. As the Commander-in-Chief was riding across the field the victorious soldiers came up in crowds, and slapping him rudely on his wounded leg, exclaimed "Now, aren't we brave fellows, General?"

"Yes, boys, you have covered yourselves with glory, and I decree to you the spoils of victory; I will reward valor. I claim only to share the *honors* of our triumph with you!"

While he was giving his orders, after he reached the Texas encampment and before he had dismounted, General Rusk came in and presented his prisoner, Almonte. It was the first time they had ever met.   This seemed to give a finishing stroke to the victory, and Houston, who was completely exhausted from fatigue and loss of blood, fainted and fell from his horse.   Colonel Hockley caught him in his arms and laid him at the foot of the oak.

Thus ended the bloody day of San Jacinto—a battle that has scarcely a parallel in the annals of war.   The immediate fruits of victory were not small, as the spoils were of great value to men who had nothing in the morning but the arms they carried; scanty, coarse clothing, and the determination to be free.   About nine hundred stands of English muskets (besides a vast number that were lost in the morass and bayou), three hundred sabres, two hundred pistols, three hundred valuable mules, and a hundred fine horses; a large amount of provisions, clothing, tents, and paraphernalia for officers and men; and twelve thousand dollars in silver, constituted the spoil taken from the enemy.

On that well-fought field Texan independence was won.   A brave but outraged people, in imitation of their fathers of the century before, had intrusted their cause to the adjudication of battle, and had gained the victory.   It was not a struggle for the aggrandizement of some military chieftain, nor was it a strife for empire.   The soldiers who marched under the "Lone Star" into that engagement were free, brave, self-relying men.   Some of them, indeed, had come from a neighboring Republic, as Lafayette crossed the sea to join in the struggle for freedom, but most of them were men who cultivated the soil they fought on, and had paid for it with their money or their labor.   Hundreds of them had abandoned their homes to achieve everlasting freedom for their children.   They were fighting for all that makes life worth living or gives value to its possession.

THE CANADIAN REBELLION

A.D. 1837

GEORGE BRYCE

After the War of 1812, while Canada was making satisfactory material progress, its political condition was deplorable. In both Provinces of Upper and Lower Canada public feeling was aroused over the irresponsible character of the Executive Council, and found vent in many stormy scenes in the Legislature and in angry outbursts in the press. In Lower Canada, the English minority were indignant at the misappropriation of public funds and the high-handed acts of the Governor and the Executive. In the Upper Province there was a plentiful crop of grievances. Among these were the scandalous system on which the public lands were granted, and the partiality shown in the issue of land-patents and other favors in the gift of the Crown. A vigorously enforced Alien Act, directed against immigrants from the United States supposed to be tainted with republicanism, added to the ferment of the time.

The chief authors of these abuses were the members of the Executive and Legislative Councils, who, by their close alliances for mutual advantage, came to be known by the rather sinister designation of the "Family Compact." Strongly attached to the latter, in their disposal of offices of emolument and other Crown patronage, was a somewhat unscrupulous and dishonest following.

Other causes were also at work which produced disaffection in both Provinces and finally led to rebellion. Of these causes, one was the political game of the dominant ruling party to thwart the Assembly in its efforts to remove the abuses that had crept in with irresponsible government, and to obtain control of the revenues. A radical change in the constitution was sought to be made to remedy matters, including a demand that the Executive Council should in some measure become responsible to the people, and that the Legislative Council should be made an elective rather than a Crown-nominated body. As these demands and suggestions were not complied with, the next step, as will be seen from the appended article, was rebellion.

THE conflict for free government in Lower Canada was intensified by the fact that while the Assembly was chiefly French-Canadian, in the Legislative and Executive Councils there was a British majority. The Earl of Dalhousie, who had been for some years Governor of Nova Scotia, arrived in Lower Canada in 1820. Belonging to the class of high disciplinarians, though he had shown himself a friend of education and social progress in Nova Scotia, he was yet, as has been said, a soldier rather than a statesman. The Lieutenant-Governor of Lower Canada, Mr. Burton, was popular, but the French-Canadians were never reconciled to the stern commander. Lord Dalhousie was much hampered by the vacillating policy of the British Ministry, and as he was a man with whom there was no finesse or intrigue, his position was often unenviable.

The Lower Canadian Assembly, year after year, passed resolutions declaring their grievances, the people sent "monster petitions"; the French-Canadian press, and an English newspaper published in Montreal, the *Vindicator*, constantly excited the populace to discontent. The idol of the French-Canadians at this time was Speaker Papineau, of whom we shall hear more anon.

In the excited state of public feeling, Papineau had given expression to opinions about the Governor which, as proceeding from the Speaker of the Assembly, especially from one who had served as speaker in six Parliaments, were considered disrespectful to the Crown. On the summoning of the new House, in 1827, though it was known that Lord Dalhousie disapproved of him, Papineau was, by a large majority, chosen Speaker of the Assembly. The Governor refused to recognize the agitator. The House persisted in its course, when the old soldier prorogued the Assembly. Lord Dalhousie also deprived a number of the militia officers of their commissions for insolence. In 1827 petitions, largely signed, were presented to the King, asking for legislative control of Lower Canadian affairs.

New fuel was added to the flame by a statement of Sir John Colborne to the Upper Canadian Legislature, in his last message, to the effect that the Lower Canadian agitation had filled his mind with deep "regret, anxiety, and apprehension," and had done injury to the country. The Lower Canadian Assembly repudiated these statements, and in 1836 Speaker Papineau addressed to Mr. Bidwell, Speaker of the Upper Canadian Assembly, a lengthy letter, defending their agitation, and adding certain remarks which were regarded by some as seditious. It was unfortunate that Sir John Colborne, a natural despot, should have been at this juncture appointed to Lower Canada to command the forces.

The agitation among the French-Canadians began to assume a serious aspect. Loud appeals were made for an equality of rights with their British fellow-subjects. The Assembly, which was chiefly French-Canadian, threw off all reserve, and by all classes sentiments hostile to Britain were freely uttered from the platform and upon the streets. The cry was that the Legislative Council should be elective, and that the Assembly ought to control the provincial exchequer. The control of the revenue had been, in 1832, given over to the Assembly by the British Government to quiet the clamor. Now it was determined by the Assembly to compel further concessions by refusing to pay the judges and other executive officers.

A British commission was appointed in 1835 to inquire into the state of Lower Canada; and the possibility that a report favorable to French-Canadian desires might be made, led the British people of Montreal, Quebec, and the English settlements in Lower Canada to organize themselves into "Constitutional Associations." The main questions of liberty were now obscured. The leaders of the French-Canadians appealed to their following to support the cause of their downtrodden race.

On constitutional questions, such as the Executive Council being responsible to the Assembly, many of the English people of Lower Canada agreed with the French-Canadians, but it seemed as if the French leaders were making the matter one of British connection and British influence rather than of executive reform. In consequence, the appeals of the Constitutional Associations were much more moderate and statesmanlike than the wild denunciations of the authors of the "ninety-two resolutions." And yet the success of the British party, in their contention, meant welding the fetters of an oligarchy upon the people. It was a perplexing case for British statesmen.

On the report of the "Commission" coming before the Imperial Parliament, Lord John Russell, in 1837, moved four resolutions, reciting that the Lower Canadian Assembly had granted no supplies since 1832; that upward of one hundred forty-two thousand pounds was due to the judges and civil servants; that the request to have the Legislative Council made elective be not granted; but that that branch of the Legislature be changed, that it might secure a greater degree of public confidence.

The so-called "patriots" were infuriated when the news of this action reached Canada. The *Vindicator* declared: "Henceforth there must be no peace in the Province—no quarter for the plunderers. Agitate! Agitate! Agitate! Destroy the revenue; denounce the oppressors. Everything is lawful when the fundamental liberties are in danger. The guards die—they never surrender!" These were certainly extravagant expressions. They were the outburst of feeling after five years of agitation.

The leader of the movement was Speaker Papineau. In 1817 he was elected Speaker of the Assembly, and with one short interval he continued so until the rebellion. Papineau was a brilliant orator, an energetic and useful member of Assembly, a political student, though somewhat vain and aggressive, and on the whole lacking in balance of mind.

At this juncture of the Russell resolutions Papineau was prepared to go wildly into anything—even independence, or annexation to the United States. Associated with the rebellious Speaker in the agitation was a man of very different qualities— this was Doctor Wolfred Nelson. He was a man of high scholastic attainments, of calm and ready judgment, was highly respected, and had a boundless influence over the people in the southern counties of Lower Canada. Believing that the struggle in Lower Canada was one for liberty, and that the oligarchy in the Lower Province was as tyrannical and self-seeking as the Family Compact in Upper Canada, Nelson had allied himself with Papineau and the French-Canadians.

At a great indignation meeting of twelve hundred persons, held on May 7, 1837, on the Richelieu River, near St. Denis, at which Doctor Nelson presided, strong resolutions were adopted against the course taken by Lord John Russell. The example of the Irish patriot, Daniel O'Connell, was held up for admiration, and it was agreed that all should rally around one man as their chief—and that man, Papineau.

Encomiums were passed on Papineau's force of mind, eloquence, hatred of oppression, and love of country; and it was determined, with much enthusiasm, to give up the use of imported articles, in order that the revenue might be crippled. With much zeal the assemblage decided to raise a fund, to be known as the "Papineau Tribute," for the support of their idol. Similar meetings to that at St. Denis were being held throughout the country, when Lord Gosford, the Governor-General, becoming alarmed, issued a proclamation forbidding such gatherings, and summoning those loyal to the country to support his action. This but increased the agitation. "Anti-coercion meetings," as they were now called, were widely held. The young French-Canadians organized themselves into societies, known as the "Sons of Liberty," while the loyal inhabitants, by meeting and petition, threw back the rebellious challenges.

A most important meeting of the agitators took place at St. Charles, on the Richelieu, on October 23d, including delegates from the "six confederated counties." There were present at the meeting, it is estimated, five thousand persons. Doctor Nelson presided, and his outspoken declaration, the extravagant resolutions adopted, and the excited speeches delivered left no longer any doubt as to the intentions of the agitators. A handsome column, surmounted with a "cap of liberty," was erected at this time in honor of Papineau at St. Charles.

The threatening clouds of sedition now grew so heavy that the Roman Catholic Bishop, Monsignor Lartigue, a relative of Papineau, issued an earnest pastoral, imploring the people to avoid the horrors of a civil war. The agitators continually grew bolder, and began to drill at different points throughout the country. In the mean time several additional French-Canadians were placed upon the Legislative and Executive Councils, but the concession had come too late to abate the excitement.

The Sons of Liberty and the Constitutionalists met in conflict in the streets of Montreal in November of this year, and the odds were slightly in favor of the former. Proclamations forbidding the drilling of the patriots were issued. Sir John Colborne had now made his headquarters in Montreal, and in October all the British troops in Upper Canada had been brought to his aid, while the Loyalists of Glengarry had tendered their services to the General. Soon the blow fell. News came that bands of insurgents were collecting at St. Charles and St. Denis, and an expedition under Colonels Wetherall and Gore was sent against the rebels.

At St. Denis, on November 23d, Doctor Nelson had fortified a stone distillery, three stories high, belonging to himself; had cut down the bridges, and awaited the attack of the approaching troops, of whose movements he had learned from despatches taken on Lieutenant Weir, a captured officer. The attack on the improvised fort was made, but without success, Doctor Nelson showing himself a skilful tactician. After several hours'· fruitless effort, the troops retired. By their success the insurgents were encouraged.

At St. Charles was the more important centre of revolt. A General Brown was the rebel leader. The insurgents had at this point fifteen hundred men, two twenty-four pounders, and a well-provisioned fort. The attack was made upon the rebel position by Colonel Wetherall, and after a severe struggle resulted in the taking of the fort, the defenders losing one hundred fifty killed and three hundred wounded. Brown escaped to Vermont.

The arrival at St. Denis of the news from St. Charles caused Nelson's followers to vanish like the mist, and the brave St. Denis leader, seeing all lost, fled toward the American boundary, but was captured in the county of Shefford. Papineau, who was at St. Denis, is said to have escaped to the United States while the fight at the fortified distillery was still going on. It is of interest to know that among Nelson's followers at St. Denis was young George Étienne Cartier, afterward a prominent statesman of Canada.

A most tragic occurrence took place at St. Denis. A dashing young officer, Lieutenant Weir, carrying despatches for Colonel Wetherall, had lost his way and fallen into the hands of the rebels at St. Denis. For safe keeping he had been placed under the charge of three French-Canadian guards. His keepers were removing their prisoner to a distance from the scene of conflict when the mettlesome young officer attempted to escape. Thinking themselves justified by Weir's insubordination, the guards fell upon their prisoner, shot him with their pistols, and cut him to pieces with sabres. This cruel deed was enacted without the knowledge of the leader, Doctor Nelson, who deeply regretted the outrage. In revenge for the barbarities practised on Lieutenant Weir, the infuriated loyal soldiery burned Doctor Nelson's extensive buildings at St. Denis.

The insurgents made unsuccessful demonstrations at St. Eustache and St. Benoit, in the district northwest of Montreal, as well as along the international boundary line. Though an attack, led by Robert, the brother of Doctor Wolfred Nelson, was made at Odelltown from across the boundary line in the following year—which was easily suppressed by Sir John Colborne—yet the danger to Canada was over when St. Charles had been taken. Though troops were during the winter of 1837–1838 sent through the wilderness from New Brunswick to Quebec, their services were but little required. Thus ended the appeal to arms—a mad attempt at the best!

Great expectations were indulged by the opposition in Upper Canada, when in place of the discredited Governor Colborne it was learned that a more liberal-minded Lieutenant-Governor was on his way to York [Toronto]. Their supposed "crowning mercy" was Sir Francis Bond Head, a retired army officer, and late poor-law guardian. The new appointee had a taste for book-making, and had written certain very readable books of travel. His previous experience, however, did not in any way justify his appointment as ruler of a province on the verge of rebellion. The reasons for his selection have always been a mystery, and the shortest explanation of it is that it was a Downing Street blunder.

Sir Francis boasted of having no political views, and of having had no political experience. He was a man whose shallow nature, flippant letters and despatches, and speedy subserviency to the Family Compact rendered him in the end an object of detestation in Canada. Denunciation too severe can scarcely be visited upon a man who deliberately proceeds to aggravate and irritate a disturbed community. The new Governor was surprised, as he himself tells us, to see in large letters on the walls of Toronto on his arrival, "Sir Francis Head, a tried reformer," and before four months had elapsed those who had made the placards were possessed with still greater surprise and vexation when they looked back at what they had done.

Governor Head, shortly after his arrival, was called on to fill three vacancies in the Executive Council, one-half of the offices being already held by adherents of the Family Compact. The Governor, passing over Mr. Bidwell, for whom he from the first took a strong dislike, called to the Council Messrs. Baldwin, Rolph, and Dunn. Soon finding that Chief-Justice Robinson and Doctor Strachan, who were not in the Executive Council at all, were the virtual advisers of the Governor, the new councillors resented the interference and resigned in three weeks' time. The new Governor was no more independent than Sir John Colborne had been, and was less dignified.

Sir Francis concluded, soon after his arrival, that the oppositionists were not a party of gentlemen, and was in a short time engaged in discrediting them before the country, utterly forgetful of his position. The Assembly sought to protect itself, and adopted a formal deliverance, charging the Governor with "deviations from truth and candor."

A general election was soon to follow, and the opposition found to their cost that the Provincial electorate had much changed since the year 1830. Since that date the population of Upper Canada had nearly doubled. The new inhabitants were largely from the British Isles, and were strongly monarchic in their views. While a section of the opposition desired a constitution which would be "an exact transcript" of that of Great Britain, it was well known that some of them favored an approximation to republican forms. Bidwell and perhaps Mackenzie were among the latter.

Governor Head threw himself heartily into the struggle in the election of 1836, and, no doubt honestly believing there was a section of the late Assembly disloyal to Britain, stirred up the new British electors, who had not a single principle in common with the Family Compact, to look upon Bidwell, Mackenzie, and their followers as untrue to British connection, pointing as he did to the disloyal letter from Papineau, which had been read by Speaker Bidwell in the Upper Canada Assembly.

But the Governor, though but "winning his spurs" as a political manipulator, showed evidence of talent in not trusting to appeals to sentiment alone. He used the stronger inducements of self-interest. It was given out that settlers who voted with the Government would receive the patents for their lands, for which in some cases they had waited long, and these patents were openly distributed on the days of polling. The Family Compact organized the "British Constitutional Society" in Toronto, the more effectually to fasten the charge of disloyalty on their opponents. "Hurrah for Sir Francis Head and British Connection!" was their rallying-cry. The influence of that redoubtable politician Egerton Ryerson was likewise thrown in the same direction.

The election was a political Waterloo for the Governor's opponents. Bidwell, Perry, Lount, and even Mackenzie were all defeated. The Family Compact had changed a minority of eleven in the late Assembly into a majority of twenty-five in the new, and now they were able to contend that constitutional harmony between Governor, Executive and Legislative Councils, and the Legislative Assembly had been completely restored.

Mackenzie was exasperated, revived his *Colonial Advocate*, under the name of the *Constitution*, and was now more fierce in his attacks than he had ever been before. Those in power, confident of their majority, heard his denunciations without attempting to repress their vilifier. Soon the Governor's influence began to wane. Even the Parliament elected through his interference to some extent asserted its liberties as against his arbitrary control, and the whole population saw the error that had been committed in returning a Legislature subject to the Family Compact.

Now was the time for wisdom and self-control on the part of the leaders of the opposition. Sad indeed was it for the country that the unwise and unpatriotic counsel of Mackenzie was that which asserted itself most strongly. No doubt the malign influence of the Lower Canadian party of sedition, led by Papineau, with whom Mackenzie and others were in constant communication, was felt in Upper Canadian affairs. The French-Canadians spoke with the utmost freedom of a resort to arms should their demands be refused.

About the end of July, 1837, an organization, known as the "Committee of Vigilance," was formed in Upper Canada, and William Lyon Mackenzie was chosen as "agent and corresponding secretary." This society did not professedly aim at rebellion; the great majority certainly did not suspect outward violence; a few ardent spirits may from the first have intended sedition. Mackenzie was most active: he stirred up the Province from end to end by incendiary addresses, and professed to have obtained thousands of names of those willing to make a hostile demonstration against the Governor, and to form a provisional government.

Bidwell would have nothing to do with violent measures; Rolph played a double part. He was in secret with Mackenzie planning mischief, and was the man selected by the plotters to be the head of the new government proposed, but he succeeded in imposing on the Governor as to his loyalty.

The Governor had but invited a rising by allowing the British troops to go to Sir John Colborne's aid in Montreal. Everything favored the fulfilment of Mackenzie's schemes. The rising in Lower Canada brought on the crisis in Upper Canada, or more correctly the two movements had been concerted in order to help each other. On November 24th, less than twenty-four hours before the St. Charles defeat, Mackenzie left Rolph's house in Toronto to rouse his followers. Next day a revolutionary appeal was printed, headed "Proclamation by William Lyon Mackenzie, chairman *pro tem.* of the Provisional Government of the State of Upper Canada," and containing such incendiary sentiments as "Rise, Canadians! Rise as one man, and the glorious object of our wishes is accomplished." The document said that the "patriots" had established a provisional government on Navy Island, in the Niagara River. The well-known names of Mackenzie, Gorham, Lount, and Duncombe were attached to the manifesto, and it was declared that two or three other names were, for powerful reasons, withheld from view.

Samuel Lount was appointed a commander, and a well-known resort, "Montgomery's Tavern," on Yonge Street, a few miles north of Toronto, was made the rebel rendezvous. The outbreak was planned for December 7, 1837. Mackenzie, who knew the country well and had been hither and thither for several days, returned to Montgomery's to find that the time of the rising had been antedated by Doctor Rolph to December 4th.

At that time the first detachment of insurgents arrived under Lount, eighty or ninety strong.

Blood was soon shed. One, Captain Powell, a Loyalist, had been taken prisoner by the rebels, but escaped from their hands by shooting his guard—a man named Anderson. A most sad event was the death of Colonel Moodie, a Family Compact favorite. He had rashly attempted, on horseback, to force the rebel line on Yonge Street. He was fired upon, and fell from his horse mortally wounded.

The insurgents numbered at length eight hundred or nine hundred. Had they marched at once on Toronto, it must have fallen into their hands, for though a place of twelve thousand people, the apathy was so great that none of its citizens took up arms to defend it, but were content to rely for defence upon the men of Gore District from the west. The Governor sought to gain time by negotiating with the rebels. He asked the assistance of Bidwell, who refused the commission.

At last, by the hand of Baldwin and Rolph, a flag of truce was sent, and a reply brought to the Governor with certain demands of the insurgents. The Governor refused to grant the requests made. It was in carrying back Governor Head's unfavorable answer that Doctor Rolph showed his duplicity. Though acting as the Governor's messenger, he took aside certain of the rebel leaders and secretly encouraged them to attack Toronto.

An advance was made to within a mile of the city, when a collision took place, and the rebels retired to Montgomery's. Mackenzie succeeded in a sally on the western mail in capturing certain important letters. The delay in attacking Toronto made Rolph's position very precarious, and so he hastened from Toronto, professedly to the western district, but really to seek shelter in the United States.

The time for action was allowed to slip by the aforetime courageous regulators. Colonel Allan McNab arrived in Toronto from Hamilton, with his militia, and without delay attacked the rebels remaining at Montgomery's. After a short but severe skirmish, the militia were victors; the motley gathering of discontented farmers fled; and Mackenzie, on whose head a reward of one thousand pounds had been set, after a toilsome and adventurous journey escaped to the United States by way of the Niagara frontier.

The Provisional Government was now organized on Navy Island, in the Niagara River. The patriot flag, with twin stars and the motto "Liberty and Equality," was hoisted, and planted in the face of Colonel McNab, who held the Canadian shore. A daring action was performed on December 29th by Captain Drew, R.N., one of McNab's command. The insurgents had made use of a vessel, the Caroline, in carrying supplies from the American shore to Navy Island. The vessel lay moored for the night under the very guns of Fort Schlosser, indeed the shadows of the fort enveloped the Caroline. With seven boats, carrying some sixty men in all, who were armed with pistols, cutlasses, and pikes, the captain boarded the ill-fated vessel, captured her, but not being able, on account of the current, to bring her to the Canadian side, sent her flaming over the Niagara Falls. The vessel proved to be an American bottom, and so Britain was compelled to disavow the seizure, but nothing could blot out the bravery of the deed.

The ardent leader, Doctor Duncombe, succeeded in gathering some three hundred men on Burford Plains, intending to pass by way of Brantford and seize Hamilton, and thus advance the rebel cause. Colonel McNab, however, with five hundred men, hastened west, and reached the village of Scotland, but the insurgent band melted away on his approach. For some time afterward, an irritation continued along the Niagara frontier, a number of characterless scoundrels seeking to keep up strife for the sake of plunder. The archrebel Mackenzie was at length seized by the law authorities of the State of New York, and tried at Albany, "for setting on foot a military enterprise against Upper Canada." He was found guilty, and sentenced to one and a half years' imprisonment, but was released in response to numerous petitions after some ten months had expired.

The utter want of tact, and even of fair dealing, shown by Sir Francis Bond Head, resulted in his recall. He was succeeded by Sir George Arthur, who had in Hobart Town been accustomed to rule the convict settlements. He was harshness itself. Lount and Matthews, two of the rebel leaders, were well regarded by all classes of the people notwithstading their false movement in the rebellion. Large petitions in their favor were presented to the Governor, and Lount's wife made before Sir George a most heartrending appeal for her husband, but all was of no avail, and they were hanged on the gallows April 11, 1838. On June 28th an amnesty was granted to all suspected persons, who had not been actively engaged in the rebellion. It was not until 1843 that Rolph, Duncombe, Morrison, Gibson, Gorham, and Montgomery were pardoned, though the general amnesty was not granted until 1849. Thus in reality terminated this wretched affair, dishonoring to the enemies of liberty who forced it on, and reflecting only disgrace on those who conceived and so badly executed it.

THE INVENTION OF PHOTOGRAPHY

A.D. 1838

WILLIAM JEROME HARRISON[1]

Among modern inventions, that of photography is one of the most valuable for varied usefulness, while few are more wonderful on the score of ingenuity. The steps of its later development have been universally observed, and its new processes and applications popularly described as fast as they appeared. But not less important, and scarcely less interesting, is the story of its beginnings and early advance through the labors of patient experimenters.

Photography—that is, the process of forming and fixing images of objects by the chemical action of light—was not at all understood before the nineteenth century. The effect of light upon various substances had been much earlier observed, as in the fading of dyed materials, and the blackening of paper, etc., when moistened with silver solutions. But not till the close of the eighteenth century does anyone appear to have thought of applying the discovery of the changes of color produced by the action of light upon silver compounds to any practical purpose.

The earliest experiments leading to photographic results occurred in connection with the camera-obscura, a chamber or box in which the image of an exterior object is projected upon a plane surface. From experiments with the camera-obscura, which was invented by Baptista Porta, an Italian philosopher, in the sixteenth century, the photographic camera was developed. It is a camera-obscura in miniature—a box having a lens at one end and a ground-glass screen at the other, but now highly perfected and equipped.

The discovery of photography, properly so called, has been claimed for at least two men, who are said to have made it in the latter part of the eighteenth century—Professor Charles, a French physicist, and Matthew Boulton, an English inventor and engineer, the partner of James Watt. In the case of Charles, the claim is regarded as merely traditional, and the best authorities consider it " too vague and improbable to be taken into serious account." Boulton and Watt sold pictures that have been described as photographic, but are now known to have been executed by a mechanical process with which photography had nothing to do.

[1] From W. J. Harrison's *History of Photography* (New York: Anthony & Scovill Company), by permission.

338

Early in the nineteenth century the first definite progress in true photography was made and duly recorded. From this period to the full accomplishment of the results attained by Nièpce and his more distinguished associate, Daguerre, the history of the art is clearly set forth in Harrison's account.

WITH the dawn of the nineteenth century all things were propitious for the rapid advancement of matters scientific. Great progress had by this time been made both in chemistry and in optics; while the art of experimenting—the knowledge of how to question nature—had become familiar to many men of talent and education. Thomas Wedgwood, fourth son of the great potter, earnestly studied the action of light upon certain compounds of silver. He was encouraged and assisted by Humphry Davy, then just rising into fame as a chemist, and after Wedgwood's death Davy wrote an account of their work, which appeared in the *Journal of the Royal Institution* for 1802.

Wedgwood's best results were obtained by coating paper or white leather with a weak solution of silver nitrate. The more or less opaque object which it was desired to copy was then placed on the prepared surface, and the whole exposed to sunlight. In a few minutes the unprotected portions of the paper were darkened, and when the opaque object was removed its form remained in white upon a black ground. Paintings on glass could be copied in this way, the light passing through the transparent and semitransparent portions, and blackening the sensitive paper placed underneath. Wedgwood noticed that "red rays, or the common sunbeams passed through red glass, have very little action upon paper prepared in this manner; yellow and green are more efficacious, but blue and violet light produce the most decided and powerful effects."

These facts had been previously published by Scheele and by Senebier, but Wedgwood does not appear to have known of their work. The scantiness of scientific literature at that time and the difficulty of communication between different countries were, indeed, great hinderances to progress. The workers in any one country were usually ignorant of what had been done elsewhere; so that the same track was pursued again and again, and the same discoveries made several times over. Davy made some important additions to Wedgwood's work. He found that the chloride was much more sensitive to light than the nitrate of silver. Both Wedgwood and Davy attempted to secure the pictures formed within a camera, upon paper coated with these salts of silver, but without success. Davy, however, using the more concentrated light of the solar microscope, readily obtained images of small objects on paper prepared with silver chloride.

But there was another and more fatal objection to this method of "picturing by light," which not even Davy, with all his chemical knowledge, was able to surmount. When the copies obtained were exposed to daylight, the same agency which had produced the picture proceeded to destroy it. The action of sunlight upon the white or lightly shaded portions constituting the picture speedily blackened the entire surface of the paper or leather, causing the whole to become of one uniform tint, in which nothing could be distinguished. To prevent this it was clearly necessary to remove the unacted-on silver salt after the image had been formed, and before the paper was exposed, as a whole, to daylight. Long-continued washing in water was tried, but proved ineffectual; nor was a coating of transparent varnish found of any service. Davy does not seem to have pursued the process with much energy, and the whole thing dropped into obscurity. Still he clearly recognized its capabilities, for he writes: "Nothing but a method of preventing the unshaded parts of the delineations from being colored by exposure to the day is wanting to render this process as useful as it is elegant." In this copying process, devised by Wedgwood and improved by Davy, we see the germ of the ordinary method by which our negative photographs on glass are made to yield a positive proof or impression upon sensitized paper.

The first man to obtain a permanent photograph was Joseph Nicéphore Nièpce, who was born at Châlons-sur-Saône, March 7, 1765. He was well educated and designed for the Church, but the outbreak of the French Revolution upset all plans, and in 1794 Nièpce fought in the ranks of the Republican army which invaded Italy. Ill health soon compelled his retirement from active service, and marrying, he settled down at Châlons; his brother Claude, to whom he was devotedly attached, residing with him.

Even during childhood, the fondness of the brothers Nièpce

for scientific pursuits had been very noticeable, and they now applied themselves to the task of invention, bringing out a machine called the pyrelophore, which propelled vessels by the aid of hot air, and a velocipede, the ancestor of our modern bicycle. Endeavoring to bring these inventions before the public, Claude went to Paris in 1811, and afterward crossed over to England, where he settled down at Kew.

It was, apparently, about the year 1813 that Nicéphore Nièpce began the experiments which resulted in his discovery of what may be called the bitumen process in photography. From his correspondence with his brother Claude, we learn something of this method; and when, in 1827, Nicéphore visited his brother at Kew, he brought with him many specimens of his work. These pictures, the first permanent photographs ever produced, Nièpce desired to bring before the notice of the Royal Society, but, as he declined to publish the process by which they were produced (being desirous to perfect it before making it public), the rules of the society compelled them to refuse Nièpce's communication. Having examined several of the specimens presented by this early French experimenter to his English friends, we can testify to the successful manner in which he had copied engravings.

Making but a short stay in England, Nièpce returned to France, where, in 1829, he entered into a partnership with another investigator named Daguerre. But Nièpce was not destined to complete his work, or even to publish his results; he died in 1833, at the age of sixty-eight. Although it is impossible to assign the title of "Inventor of Photography" to any one man, yet Nièpce has probably the best claim to it. A statue of Nièpce has been erected at Châlons.

Lithography, invented by a German, Senefelder, in 1798, was successfully practised in France in 1812. Expert draughtsmen were required to execute the necessary drawings upon the prepared surfaces of the smooth blocks of limestone employed. Now Nièpce thought that it might be possible, by the action of light, to cause designs, engravings, etc., to copy themselves upon the lithographic stone. The basis of all his work was the discovery that bitumen, or "Jew's pitch," as it was then commonly called, is rendered insoluble by the action of light. Nièpce dissolved bitumen in oil of lavender, and spread a thin layer of it upon the stone. Next he varnished the drawing on paper, of which he desired to secure an impression—the varnish rendering the paper fairly transparent—and laid it upon the bitumenized stone.

After exposing the whole to sunlight for an hour or so, the paper was removed and oil of lavender poured upon the bitumen, by which those portions of it that had been protected from light by the opaque lines of the drawing were dissolved away, and the surface of the stone beneath was in those parts exposed. Thus the outlines of the original subject were reproduced with perfect truth. Lastly, by treating the stone with an acid, the exposed portions could be "bitten" or eroded more deeply, and it was then ready for printing from. Finding much difficulty in securing stone of a sufficiently fine and close grain, Nièpce substituted metal, employing plates of polished tin, etc., on which to spread the bitumen. Although the results he obtained were far from perfect, yet they were very promising, and heliography, as Nièpce named this method, has since proved very useful.

Having obtained pictures by what we may call contact-printing, Nièpce's next endeavor was to apply his process to securing the beautiful views produced by the aid of a camera. For this purpose he tried the chlorides of silver and of iron, and gum guaiacum, whose sensibility to light had been investigated by Wollaston in 1804. Nothing, however, answered so well in his hands as the surface of bitumen or asphalt, with which he had already been successful in heliography. When exposed to the action of the light forming the picture within the camera, the bitumen became insoluble in proportion to the intensity of the light by which the various parts of the image were produced, an effect which we now know to be due to the oxidation and consequent hardening of this resinous substance.

When the resinized plate was removed from the camera, no picture at all was visible on its surface. But by steeping the exposed plate in a mixture of oil of lavender and petroleum, the still soluble portions of the bitumen were removed. The shadows of the landscape were then represented by bare portions of the metal plate, while the insoluble resin which remained indicated the brightest parts, or "high-lights," of the orginal. Obviously such a picture would look more natural if the portions of polished metal exposed could be darkened, and for this purpose we know that Nièpce employed various chemicals, and among others iodine.

It is unfortunate that Nicéphore Nièpce never published a single line descriptive of his methods, so that it is only from his correspondence—and more especially his letters to his brother Claude—that we can glean our information. The difficulties of an experimenter in an obscure French town, at that time, were indeed great. Nièpce tells us that his first camera was fashioned out of a cigar-box, while his lenses were "the lenses of the solar microscope which belonged to our grandfather Barrault."

In a letter written to his brother in 1816 Nièpce describes how he secured what was probably the first picture ever taken in a camera. "My object-glass being broken, and being no longer able to use my camera, I made an artificial eye with Isidore's ring-box, a little thing from sixteen to eighteen lines square. I placed this little apparatus in my workroom, facing the open window looking upon the pigeon-house. I made the experiment in the way you are acquainted with, and I saw on the white paper the whole of the pigeon-house seen from the window. One could distinguish the effects of the solar rays in the picture from the pigeon-house up to the window-sash. The possibility of painting by this means appears almost clear to me. I do not hide from myself that there are great difficulties, especially as regards fixing the colors, but with work and patience one can accomplish much."

"Work" and "patience"! Truly Nièpce himself combined these in no common degree. From the reference to white paper used in this early experiment, it would seem probable that silver chloride was employed. We know that Nièpce used the substance, and that he gave it up, because, like Wedgwood and Davy, he was unable to fix or render permanent the pictures secured by its aid.

In December, 1829, Nièpce drew up the following important statement:

"The discovery which I have made, and to which I give the name of 'heliography,' consists in producing spontaneously, by the action of light, with gradations of tints from black to white, the images received by the camera-obscura. Light acts chemically upon bodies. It is absorbed; it combines with them, and communicates to them new properties. Thus it augments the natural consistency of some of these bodies; it solidifies them, even, and renders them more or less insoluble, according to the duration or intensity of its action. The substance which has succeeded best with me is asphaltum dissolved in oil of lavender. A tablet of plated silver is to be highly polished, on which a thin coating of the varnish is to be applied with a light roll of soft skin. The plate when dry may be immediately submitted to the action of light in the focus of the camera. But even after having been thus exposed a length of time sufficient for receiving the impressions of external objects, nothing is apparent to show that these impressions exist. The forms of the future picture remain still invisible. The next operation then is to disengage the shrouded imagery, and this is accomplished by a solvent consisting of one part by volume of essential oil of lavender and ten of oil of white petroleum.

"Into this liquid the exposed tablet is plunged, and the operator, observing it by reflected light, begins to perceive the images of the objects, to which it had been exposed, gradually unfolding their forms. The plate is then lifted out, allowed to drain, and well washed with water."

"It were however to be desired that, by blackening the metal plate, we could obtain all the gradations of tone from black to white. The substance which I now employ for this purpose is iodine, which possesses the property of evaporating at the ordinary temperature."

We cannot but admire the graphic description of the phenomena of development here given by Nièpce, and, without doubt, it formed the foundation of all the discoveries in photography that followed. It will be noticed that Nièpce's method of development was a physical one only, for it consisted in simply washing away by a suitable solvent the unacted-on and therefore still soluble parts of the bitumen.

The chief objection to the beautiful and ingenious process discovered by Nicéphore Nièpce was the great length of time for which the bitumenized plate needed to be exposed in the camera. For an ordinary landscape an exposure of six to eight hours was required. During this time the shadows of objects changed from one side to the other so that the resulting pictures were comparatively flat and spiritless, being devoid of the charming effects resulting from the contrast of light and shade. Another trouble arose from the fact that in the half-tones of the picture the bitumen was only hardened at the surface, the layer beneath remaining soft and soluble. When the developing liquid was applied this lower layer was apt to be dissolved, and in the final washing it sometimes carried away with it the hardened upper portion, so producing bare patches or defects.

Most black varnishes are made from asphalt, and we can easily imitate Nièpce's process by coating a glass or metal plate with a thin layer of such varnish and exposing it under a negative to bright sunshine. By subsequent washing with petroleum the picture is readily developed.

Nicéphore Nièpce was a man of a quiet and retiring disposition, a student who was so immersed in his work and so desirous of perfecting it that he hesitated—while as yet he felt it to be incomplete—to publish even the smallest details with regard to it.

But the man with whom Nièpce entered into partnership, Louis Jacques Mandé Daguerre, was of a very opposite temperament—bold and energetic, desirous of fame and its accompanying rewards, accustomed to success and to the applause of the public.

Daguerre was born at Cormeilles, a village near Paris, in 1789. Neglected by his parents, his native talents asserted themselves, and while still young he became known as a scene painter of great power and originality; while the mechanical effects which he introduced to add to the realism of his stage views were the admiration of all Paris.

In 1822 Daguerre opened a diorama in Paris, for which he executed paintings on a colossal scale for such scenery as the "Village of Goldau," the "Valley of Sarnem," etc. By painting on both sides of the canvas, and showing the picture first by reflected and then by transmitted light, very remarkable changes and effects could be produced.

In the sketches from nature which Daguerre made as a preliminary aid to the execution of these immense pictures, he frequently employed the camera-obscura; and it was the remarkable beauty and perfection of the images produced by this instrument that determined the artist to attempt the discovery of some means by which they could be permanently retained.

Without any scientific education or training this task would have seemed to most persons a hopeless one; but perhaps Daguerre's very ignorance of the difficulties to be encountered was one cause of his perseverance. The date of his first attempts appears to have been about 1824, and during the next two or three years we hear of his paying frequent visits to the shop of Chevalier, a well-known optician, of whom Daguerre purchased the camera, lenses, and other articles necessary to his new pursuit.

In 1826 Daguerre was informed—probably by Chevalier—that a gentleman at Châlons had already made considerable progress toward the end which he was himself desiring to attain. Letters addressed to Nièpce received, however, but curt responses, and it was not till 1827, when Nièpce passed through Paris on his way to England, that he entered into cordial relations with Daguerre. The partnership between these two workers, which was established in 1829, was continued after the death of the elder Nièpce, Isidore Nièpce taking the place of his father.

Year after year passed away and left our scene painter still toiling after his ideal — ever endeavoring to fix the fleeting images formed by the lens of his camera. His ordinary work is neglected, but he passes nine-tenths of his time in his laboratory.

It was at this period that Madame Daguerre sought advice as to the sanity of her husband, and was not perhaps much comforted by the assurance of the men of science whom she consulted that the object of her husband's researches was "not absolutely impossible." Five years after the death of Nièpce his partner was able to announce that he had overcome all difficulties, and that henceforth Nature would depict her own likeness with a pencil of light.

In 1838 Daguerre attempted to form a company which should acquire and work the new process; but the Parisian public were utterly incredulous, and the shares were not taken up. In this extremity Daguerre showed his specimens, and in confidence explained his method to the eminent French astronomer and physicist Arago. Arago's admiration and delight with this new and wonderful process by which objects were made to draw their own pictures were unbounded.   As a man of science and of world-wide reputation, his endorsement of the value of Daguerre's discovery at once established its worth, and on his recommendation the French Government awarded to Daguerre a life pension of six thousand frances, and to Isidore Nièpce one of four thousand frances per annum, on the condition that the invention should be published without patenting it; this money being paid by France for "the glory of endowing the world of science and of art with one of the most surprising discoveries that honor their native land."   Notwithstanding this official statement, a patent was taken out by Daguerre in one country, England, in 1839.

Daguerre is said to have placed a written account of his process in the hands of Arago in January, 1839, and at the same time to have publicly exhibited specimens of the results which he had up to that time obtained; but no details were revealed, nor was the paper published until the meeting of the Academy in August of that year.   The new process was named "daguerreotype," and the excitable inhabitants of the French metropolis went into ecstasies over it.   Nevertheless, the daguerreotype process was, at the time of its publication, very imperfect, and it was destined to undergo important modifications and improvements during the next three or four years.

The news of Daguerre's wonderful discovery soon spread to other countries, and the inventor obtained a rich reward by the sale of apparatus and by the instruction of hundreds who flocked to Paris to learn the details of the new art.   A keen observer—Sir John Robinson—wrote as follows in 1839 to a friend in the United States:

"Circumstances led to my being included in a small party of English gentlemen who were lately invited to visit the studio of M. Daguerre to see the results of his discovery.   I satisfied myself that the pictures produced by his process have no resemblance of anything, as far as I know, that has yet been produced in this country.   Excepting the absence of color, they are perfect images as seen by reflection from a highly polished surface.   The subjects which I saw were views of streets, boulevards, and buildings; vacillating objects made indistinct pictures.   There can be no doubt that when the daguerreotype process is known to the

public it will be immediately applied to numberless useful processes, and even the fine arts will gain; for the eye, accustomed to
the accuracy of the Daguerre pictures, will no longer be satisfied with bad drawing, however splendidly it may be colored."
Every word of this prediction has since been fulfilled.

Daguerre died in 1851, aged sixty-two. In 1883 a bust of
this ardent worker was unveiled at Cormeilles; funds for its execution having been contributed by photographers of all civilized
nations. Viewing his whole career, Daguerre must be considered as a fortunate man. Not only did he reap much honor and
material benefit from his discovery, but he lived to see photography rise to an important place among the arts and sciences.

The materials employed by Daguerre in his early experiments—between 1824 and 1829—appear to have been the same
as those used by Wedgwood and Davy—the chloride and nitrate
of silver spread upon paper—and he did not advance upon, if indeed he equalled, the results obtained by the two English chem-
ists. After entering into partnership with Nièpce, and learning
the details of his bitumen process, Daguerre followed for a time
in the same track; but further study enabled him to work out
improvements and modifications which led him ultimately to a
greater success. We know that Nièpce sometimes used metal
plates coated with silver; moreover, he employed iodine to darken
these plates after the picture had been developed. Using these
two materials, plates of silver and vapor of iodine, Daguerre
found that the iodide of silver, formed by exposing silver to the
vapor of iodine, was sensitive to light. When such "iodized
silver plates" were exposed within the camera, faint images of
bright objects were impressed upon them in the course of two or
three hours.

At this stage a happy "accident" occurred, which revealed
to Daguerre a method by which not only was the time of exposure
necessary to secure a good picture greatly reduced, but the dis-
tinctness and beauty of the image were much enhanced.

It appears that one day Daguerre removed from his camera
a plate, which either from the shortness of the exposure or the
dulness of the light, showed no sign of an image. He placed
this blank plate in a store-cupboard, intending to clean the surface and use it again. But what must have been our photog-

rapher's surprise when, on taking out this plate the next morning, he found upon its surface a distinct and perfect picture.

Another prepared plate was quickly exposed for an equally short time within the camera, and again a sojourn of twenty-four hours within the magic cupboard sufficed to bring out a picture. The next step was to ascertain to which of the numerous chemicals kept within the cupboard this marvellous effect was due. By a process of elimination it was at last traced to a dish full of mercury.

Delighted by this fortunate discovery Daguerre at once proceeded to place his exposed plates over a dish of warm mercury, when the vapor proceeding from the liquid metal was found to settle upon the iodized silver in exact proportion to the intensity of the light by which each part of the plate had been affected. This was, in fact, a process of "development," an invisible or "latent" image being strengthened and thereby made visible. Some such method of "developing" the originally feeble impressions produced upon sensitive plates by a short exposure to light has been found necessary in every photographic process.

Another advance made by the French artist was the discovery of a fixing agent. This was neither more nor less than a strong solution of common salt, in which the plates were soaked after development, and which dissolved and washed away the iodide of silver that had not been acted on by light. But when, almost immediately after the publication of the daguerreotype process in 1839, Sir John Herschel drew attention to the superior qualities of hyposulphite of soda as a solvent of the silver salt, Daguerre immediately adopted it for clearing and fixing his exposed plates. We may mention that this substance, so valuable to every photographer, was discovered by Chaussier, in 1799, and its power of dissolving the haloid salts of silver had been described by Herschel as early as 1819.

The first daguerreotypes were so delicate that the merest touch of the finger was sufficient to mar their beauty, and when exposed to the air they rapidly tarnished and deteriorated. This defect was remedied by M. Fizeau, who gilded the image by means of a mixture of chloride of gold and hyposulphite of soda. This solution was poured over the silver plate, which was then heated until the liquid evaporated, leaving a thin coating of gold upon the picture, which was thereby rendered more distinct as well as more permanent.

Another great improvement was introduced by Mr. Goddard, a London science lecturer, in 1840. He exposed the iodized silver plate to the action of bromin vapors, thereby forming a bromide of silver upon the plate in addition to iodide of silver. In 1841 M. Claudet used chlorin vapors in a like manner. Plates prepared by either of these methods were found to be far more sensitive to light than those which had been simply iodized. In fact, the time required to produce a picture in the camera was thereby reduced to from one to five minutes, or, with a very good light, to less than one minute.

As the three elements referred to above were only discovered, chlorin in 1774, iodine in 1811, and bromin in 1826, we see that photography was hardly possible before the nineteenth century. After the improvements of Goddard and Claudet, which were quickly adopted by Daguerre, the production of portraits by the daguerreotype process became comparatively easy.

In the very first attempts at portraiture, which appear to have been made in America by Draper and Morse, in 1839, the sitter's face was covered with white powder, the eyes were closed, and the exposure, lasting for perhaps half an hour, was made in bright sunshine. To lessen the glare of light, which painfully affected the sitter, Draper caused the sunlight to pass through a large glass tank containing a clear blue liquid—ammonia sulphate of copper—before falling upon the sitter, thus filtering out most of the heat rays, which could well be spared, as they possess little or no actinic value. In 1840 Beard and Claudet opened photographic studios in London; Davidson followed suit in Edinburgh, and Shaw in Birmingham, and soon daguerreotypy became a trade. For landscapes, etc., the daguerreotype process was but seldom employed, though we read of a fine instantaneous picture of New York harbor being secured by its aid.

The expense of the plates, which were usually of copper plated with silver, was a serious objection to the daguerreotype process. As late as 1854 we find the price of daguerreotypes in England was two and a half guineas each for the quarter-plate size (4¼ by 3¼ inches); and for half-plate size, four guineas.

The cleansing and polishing of the silver surface on which the picture was to be produced were a most troublesome task, necessitating great care and a vast amount of labor in the production of the "black polish" which was necessary. It must also be remembered that there was practically no way of multiplying a daguerreotype—a fact due to the opacity of the silver plate. It is true that Grove devised a method of etching daguerreotypes with acid, so that they could be used in a printing-press, but, practically, this method was a failure.

The daguerreotype held sway for about ten years only, from 1839 to 1851. It was more popular in America than in England; indeed, in the latter country, specimens of the art are now quite rare. With all its faults it was an immense advance on anything previously known, and entitles Daguerre to rank with the leading inventors of the nineteenth century.

THE OPIUM WAR

A.D. 1840

DEMETRIUS CHARLES BOULGER

This conflict was the immediate result of the attempt of the Chinese Government to prevent the importation of opium. At the end of the war Great Britain had won her object of opening China to general English trade and to the opium trade in particular. By the Treaty of Nanking (1842) Hong-Kong was ceded to the conquering power, and later that island became a British Crown colony and naval station. By the same treaty Canton, Amoy, Shanghai, Fuchow, and Ningpo were opened to British commerce. China also paid an indemnity equal to twenty-one million dollars.

The proximate causes of the war arose several years earlier. Up to 1833 the English East India Company held a monopoly of the Chinese trade. In that year the monopoly was withdrawn by the British Government in its own interest. This meant that England had determined upon the opening of Chinese trade. The opposition of the Chinese officials led Great Britain to the conclusion that China must take her place, through compulsion if necessary, in the family of nations, as the only solution of the question of foreign intercourse with the Oriental power. England prepared to carry out her policy by appointing Lord Napier chief superintendent of trade with China. On his arrival there, in 1834, he attempted to open diplomatic intercourse, but his overtures met with a refusal. Reaching Canton, he found that the authorities would not recognize him, and that his presence placed a new barrier in the way of the trade he had been sent to promote. Such a storm was raised that he left Canton and went to Macao, where he soon died.

The Chinese now believed that they had defeated the English purpose implied in the transfer of authority from the East India Company to the Crown; but when in 1837 Captain Elliot, the new superintendent of trade, arrived at Canton, the former irritation was renewed, and hostilities soon began to appear inevitable. In January, 1839, the Emperor Taoukwang ordered Lin Tsihseu, Viceroy of Houkwang, to Canton, as a special commissioner to report on the situation and suggest a remedy for the opium evil, which had become serious through the increasing trade in that commodity. At this time the anti-opium party controlled the Imperial Council. Commissioner Lin was instructed to take extreme measures for doing away with the buying and selling of opium. But already Elliot had come into collision with the mandarins, and the arrival of Lin in Canton was the beginning of still more serious complications. After much controversy, and great concessions by Elliot, the Chinese prepared for summary measures. Lin destroyed ten million dollars' worth of opium. For this and other high-handed acts he was rewarded with the viceroyalty of the Two Kiang. The seat of his government was at Nanking.

Collisions between Chinese and foreigners soon became frequent, and hostilities may be said to have begun November 3, 1839, when two British men-of-war, having already had encounters with the Bogue forts at the entrance to Canton River, fought twenty-nine Chinese junks off Chuenpec. The Chinese were worsted, but this only increased their determination to keep Europeans out of China. Soon an expedition was on its way from England to Chinese waters, and the military operations following its arrival marked a more definite beginning of the war. Boulger, who here describes the contest, is the author of the most complete history of China that thus far has appeared.

THE British expedition arrived at the mouth of the Canton River in the month of June, 1840. It consisted of four thousand troops on board twenty-five transports, with a convoy of fifteen men-of-war. If it was thought that this considerable force would attain its objects without fighting and merely by making a demonstration, the expectation was rudely disappointed. The reply of Commissioner Lin was to place a reward on the persons of all Englishmen, and to offer twenty thousand dollars for the destruction of an English man-of-war. The English fleet replied to this hostile step by instituting a close blockade at the mouth of the river, which was not an ineffectual retort. Sir Gordon Bremer, the commander of the first part of the expedition, came promptly to the decision that it would be well to extend the sphere of his operations, and he accordingly sailed northward with a portion of his force to occupy the island of Chusan, which had witnessed some of the earliest operations of the East India Company two centuries before.

The capture of Chusan presented no difficulties to a well-equipped force, yet the fidelity of its garrison and inhabitants calls for notice as a striking instance of patriotism. The officials at Tinghai, the capital of Chusan, refused to surrender, as their duty to their Emperor would not admit of their giving up one of his possessions. It was their duty to fight, and although they admitted resistance to be useless, they refused to yield, save to force. The English commander reluctantly ordered a bombardment, and after a few hours the Chinese defences were demolished, and Tinghai was occupied. Chusan remained with the English as a base of operations during the greater part of the war, but its insalubrity rather dissipated the reputation it had acquired as an advantageous and well-placed station for operations on the coast of China.

Almost at the same time as the attack on Chusan, hostilities were resumed against the Chinese on the Canton River, in consequence of the carrying off of a British subject, Mr. Vincent Stanton, from Macao. The barrier forts were attacked by two English men-of-war and two smaller vessels. After a heavy bombardment, a force of marines and blue-jackets was landed and the Chinese positions carried. The forts and barracks were destroyed, and Mr. Stanton released. Then it was said that "China must either bend or break," for the hour of English forbearance had passed away, and unless China could vindicate her policy by force of arms there was no longer any doubt that she would have to give way.

While these preliminary military events were occurring, the diplomatic side of the question was also in evidence. Lord Palmerston had written a letter stating in categorical language what he expected at the hands of the Chinese Government, and he had directed that it should be delivered into nobody else's hands but the responsible ministers of the Emperor Taoukwang. The primary task of the English expedition was to give this despatch to some high Chinese official who seemed competent to convey it to Peking. This task proved one of unexpected difficulty, for the mandarins, basing their refusal on the strict letter of their duty, which forbade them to hold any intercourse with foreigners, returned the document and declared that they could not receive it. This happened at Amoy and again at Ningpo, and the occupation of Chusan did not bring the English any nearer to realizing their mission.

Baffled in these attempts, the fleet sailed north for the mouth of the Peiho, when at last Lord Palmerston's letter was accepted by Keshen, the Viceroy of the Province, and duly forwarded by him to Peking. The arrival of the English fleet awoke the Chinese court for the time being from its indifference, and Taoukwang not merely ordered that the fleet should be provided with all the supplies it needed, but appointed Keshen high commissioner for the conclusion of an amicable arrangement. The difficulty thus seemed in a fair way toward settlement, but as a matter of fact it was only at its commencement, for the wiles of Chinese diplomacy are infinite and were then only partially understood. Keshen was remarkable for his astuteness and for the yielding exterior which covered a purpose of iron, and in the English political officer, the Captain Elliot of Canton, he did not find an opponent worthy of his steel. Although experience had shown how great were the delays of negotiations at Canton, and how inaccessible were the local officials, Captain Elliot allowed himself to be persuaded that the best place to carry on negotiations was at that city, and after a brief delay the fleet was withdrawn from the Peiho, and all the advantages of the alarm created by its presence at Peking were surrendered.

Relieved by the departure of the foreign ships, Taoukwang sent orders for the despatch of forces from the inland Provinces, so that he might be able to resume the struggle with the English under more favorable conditions, and at the same time he hastened to relieve his overcharged feelings by punishing the man whom he regarded as responsible for his misfortunes and humiliation. The full weight of the imperial wrath fell on Commissioner Lin, who from the position of the foremost official in China fell at a stroke of the vermilion pencil to a public criminal arraigned before the Board of Punishments to receive his deserts. He was stripped of all his offices, and ordered to proceed to Peking, where, however, his life was spared.

Keshen arrived at Canton on November 29, 1840, but his despatch to the Emperor explaining the position he found there shows that his view of the situation did not differ materially from that of Lin: "Night and day I have considered and examined the state of our relations with the English. At first, moved by the benevolence of His Majesty and the severity of the laws, they surrendered the opium. Commissioner Lin commanded them to give bonds that they would never more deal in opium—a most excellent plan for securing future good conduct. This the English refused to give, and then they trifled with the laws, and so obstinate were their dispositions that they could not be made to submit. Hence it becomes necessary to soothe and admonish them with sound instruction, so as to cause them to change their mien and purify their hearts, after which it will not be too late to renew their commerce. It behooves me to instruct and persuade them so that their good consciences may be restored, and they reduced to submission."

The language of this document showed that the highest Chinese officers still believed that the English would accept trade facilities as a favor, that they would be treated *de haut en bas*, and that China possessed the power to make good her lofty pretensions. China had learned nothing from her military mishaps at Canton, Amoy, and Chusan, and from the appearance of an English fleet in the Gulf of Petchili. Keshen had gained a breathing-space by procrastination in the north, and he resorted to the same tactics at Canton. Days expanded into weeks, and at last orders were issued for an advance up the Canton River, as it had become evident that the Chinese were not only bent on an obstructive policy, but were making energetic efforts to assemble a large army. On January 7, 1841, orders were consequently issued for an immediate attack on the Bogue forts, which had been placed in a state of defence, and which were heavily manned.

Fortunately for the English, the Chinese possessed a very rudimentary knowledge of the art of war, and showed no capacity to take advantage of the strength of their position and forts, or even of their excellent guns. The troops were landed on the coast in the early morning to operate on the flank and rear of the forts at Chuenpee. The advance squadron, under Captain (afterward Sir Thomas) Herbert, was to engage the same forts in front, while the remainder of the fleet proceeded to attack the stockades on the adjoining island of Taikok. The land force of fifteen hundred men and three guns had not proceeded far along the coast before it came across a strongly intrenched camp in addition to the Chuenpee forts, with several thousand troops and many guns in position. After a sharp cannonade the forts were carried at a rush, and a formidable army was driven ignominiously out of its intrenchments with hardly any loss to the assailants. The forts at Taikok were destroyed by the fire of the ships, and their guns spiked and garrisons routed by storming parties. In all, the Chinese lost five hundred killed, besides an incalculable number of wounded, and many junks. The Chinese showed courage as well as incompetence, and the

English officers described their defence as "obstinate and honorable."

The capture of the Bogue forts produced immediate and important consequences. Keshen at once begged a cessation of hostilities, and offered terms which conceded everything the English had demanded. These were the payment of a large indemnity, the cession of Hong-Kong, and the right to hold official communication with the Central Government. In accordance with these preliminary articles, Hong-Kong was proclaimed, on January 29, 1841, a British possession, and the troops evacuated Chusan to garrison the new station. It was not considered at the time that the acquisition was of much importance, and no one would have predicted for it the brilliant and prosperous position it has since attained. But the promises given by Keshen were merely to gain time and to extricate him from a very embarrassing situation. The morrow of what seemed a signal reverse was marked by the issue of an imperial notice breathing a more defiant tone than ever.

Taoukwang declared in this edict that he was resolved "to destroy and wash the foreigners away without remorse," and he denounced the English by name as "staying themselves upon their pride of power and fierce strength." He therefore called upon his officers to proceed with courage and energy, so that "the rebellious foreigners might give up their ringleaders, to be sent encaged to Peking, to receive the utmost retribution of the laws." So long as the sovereign held such opinions as these it was evident that no arrangement could endure. The Chinese did not admit the principle of equality in their dealings with the English, and this was the main point in contention, far more than the alleged evils of the opium traffic. So long as Taoukwang and his ministers held the opinions which they did not hesitate to express, a friendly intercourse was impossible. There was no practical alternative between withdrawing from the country altogether and leaving the Chinese in undisturbed seclusion, or forcing their Government to recognize a common humanity and an equality in national privileges.

It is not surprising that under these circumstances the suspension of hostilities proved of brief duration. The conflict was hastened by the removal of Keshen from his post, in consequence of his having reported that he considered the Chinese forces un-equal to the task of opposing the English.   His candor in recog-nizing facts did him credit, while it cost him his position; and his successor, Eleang, was compelled to take an opposite view, and to attempt something to justify it.   Eleang refused to ratify the convention signed by Keshen, and on February 25th the English commander ordered an attack on the inner line of forts which guarded the approaches to Canton.   After a brief engagement the really formidable lines of Anunghoy, with two hundred guns in position, were carried at a nominal loss.   The many other posi-tions of the Chinese, up to Whampoa, were occupied in succes-sion; and on March 1st the English squadron drew up off How-qua's Folly, in Whampoa Reach, at the very gateway of Canton. On the following day the dashing Sir Hugh Gough arrived to take the supreme direction of the English forces.

After these further reverses the Chinese again begged a sus-pension of hostilities, and an armistice for a few days was granted. The local authorities were on the horns of a dilemma.   They saw the futility of a struggle with the English, and the Cantonese had to bear all the suffering for the obstinacy of the Peking Gov-ernment;   but, on the other hand, no one dared to propose con-cession to Táoukwang, who, confident of his power and ignorant of the extent of his misfortunes, breathed nothing but defiance. After a few days' delay, it became clear that the Cantonese had neither the will nor the power to conclude a definite arrangement, and consequently their city was attacked with as much forbear-ance as possible.   The fort called "Dutch Folly" was captured, and the outer line of defences was taken possession of, but no attempt was made to occupy the city itself.   Sir Hugh Gough stated, in a public notice, that the city was spared because the Queen [Victoria] had desired that all peaceful people should be tenderly considered.

The first English successes had entailed the disgrace of Lin, the second were not less fatal to Keshen.   Keshen was arraigned before the Board at Peking, his valuable property escheated to the Crown, and he himself was sentenced to decapitation, which was commuted to banishment to Tibet, where he succeeded in amassing a fresh fortune.   The success of the English was pro-claimed by the merchants reoccupying their factories on March

18, 1841, exactly two years after Lin's first fiery edict against opium. It was a strange feature in this struggle that the instant they did so the Chinese merchants resumed trade with undiminished ardor and cordiality. The officials even showed an inclination to follow their example, when they learned that Taoukwang refused to listen to any conclusive peace, and that his policy was still one of expelling the foreigners. To carry out his views the Emperor sent a new commission of three members to Canton, and it was their studious avoidance of all communication with the English authorities that again aroused suspicion as to the Chinese not being sincere in their assent to the convention which had saved Canton from an English occupation.

Taoukwang was ignorant of the success of his enemy, and his commissioners, sent to achieve what Lin and Keshen had failed to do, were fully resolved not to recognize the position which the English had obtained by force of arms, or to admit that it was likely to prove enduring. This confidence was increased by the continuous arrival of fresh troops, until at last there were fifty thousand men in the neighborhood of Canton, and all seemed ready to tempt the fortune of war again and to make another effort to expel the hated foreigner. The measure of Taoukwang's animosity may be taken by his threatening to punish with death anyone who suggested peace with the barbarians.

While the merchants were actively engaged in their commercial operations, and the English officers in conducting negotiations with a functionary who had no authority, and who was only put forward to amuse them, the Chinese were busily employed in completing their warlike preparations, which at the same time they kept as secret as possible, in the hope of taking the English by surprise. But it was impossible for such extensive preparations to be made without their creating some stir, and the standing aloof of the commissioners was in itself ground of suspicion. Suspicion became certainty when, on Captain Elliot paying a visit to the prefect in the city, he was received in a disrespectful manner by the mandarins and insulted in the streets by the crowd. He at once acquainted Sir Hugh Gough, who was at Hong-Kong, with the occurrence, and issued a notice, on May 21, 1841, advising all foreigners to leave Canton that day. This notice was not a day too soon, for during the night the Chinese made a desperate attempt to carry out their scheme. The batteries which they had secretly erected at various points in the city and along the river-banks began to bombard the factories and the ships at the same time that fire-rafts were sent against the latter in the hope of causing a conflagration.

Fortunately the Chinese were completely baffled, with heavy loss to themselves and none to the English; and during the following day the English assumed the offensive, and with such effect that all the Chinese batteries were destroyed, together with forty war-junks. The only exploit on which the Chinese could compliment themselves was that they had sacked and gutted the English factory. This incident made it clearer than ever that the Chinese Government would only be amenable to force, and that it was absolutely necessary to inflict some weighty punishment on the Chinese leaders at Canton, who had made so bad a return for the moderation shown them, and had evidently no intention of complying with the arrangement to which they had been a party.

Sir Hugh Gough arrived at Canton with all his forces on May 24th, and on the following morning the attack commenced with the advance of the fleet up the Macao Passage, and with the landing of bodies of troops at different points which appeared well suited for turning the Chinese position and attacking the gates of Canton. The Chinese did not molest the troops in landing, which was fortunate, as the operation proved exceedingly difficult and occupied more than a whole day. The Chinese had taken up a strong position on the hills lying north of the city, and they showed considerable judgment in their selection and no small skill in strengthening their ground by a line of forts. The Chinese were said to be full of confidence in their ability to reverse the previous fortune of the war, and they fought with considerable confidence, while the turbulent Cantonese populace waited impatiently on the walls to take advantage of the first symptoms of defeat among the English troops. The English army, divided into two columns of nearly two thousand men each, with a strong artillery force of seven guns, four howitzers, five mortars, and fifty-two rockets, advanced on the Chinese intrenchments across paddy-fields, rendered more difficult of passage by numerous burial-grounds. The obstacles were considerable and the progress was slow, but the Chinese did not attempt any opposition.

Then the battle began with the bombardment of the Chinese lines, and after an hour a general advance was ordered.

But the Chinese thought better of their intention, or their movement was misunderstood, for when the English streamed up the hill to attack them they stood to their guns and presented a brave front. Three of their forts were carried with little or no loss, but at the fourth they offered a stubborn, if ill-directed, resistance. Even then the engagement was not over, for the Chinese rallied in an intrenched camp one mile in the rear of the forts, and, rendered confident by their numbers, they resolved to make a fresh stand, and hurled defiance at the foreigners. The English troops never halted in their advance, and, led by the Eighteenth or Royal Irish, they carried the intrenchment at a rush and put the whole Chinese army to flight. The English lost seventy killed and wounded; the Chinese losses were never accurately known. It was arranged that Canton was to be stormed on the following day, but a terrific hurricane and deluge of rain prevented all military movements on May 26th.

Once more Chinese diplomacy came to the relief of Chinese arms. To save Canton the mandarins were quite prepared to make every concession, if they only attached a temporary significance to their language, and they employed the whole of that lucky wet day in getting round Captain Elliot, who once more allowed himself to place faith in the promises of the Chinese. The result of this was seen on the 27th, when, just as Sir Hugh Gough was giving orders for the assault, he received a message from Captain Elliot stating that the Chinese had come to terms and that all hostilities were to be suspended. The terms the Chinese had agreed to in a few hours were that the commissioners and all the troops should retire sixty miles from Canton, and that six million dollars should be paid "for the use of the English Crown."

Five of the six million dollars had been handed over to Captain Elliot, and amicable relations had been established with the city authorities, when the Imperial commissioners, either alarmed at the penalties their failure entailed, or encouraged to believe in the renewed chances of success from the impotence into which the English troops might have sunk, made a sudden attempt to surprise Sir Hugh Gough's camp and to retrieve a succession of disasters at a single stroke. The project was not without a chance of success, but it required prompt action and no hesitation in coming to close quarters—the two qualifications in which the Chinese were most deficient. So it was on this occasion. Ten or fifteen thousand Chinese braves suddenly appeared on the hills about two miles north of the English camp; but instead of seizing the opportunity created by the surprise at their sudden appearance and at the breach of armistice, and delivering home their attack, they merely waved their banners and uttered threats of defiance. They stood their ground for some time in face of the rifle and artillery fire opened upon them, and then they kept up a running fight for three miles as they were pursued by the English.

They did not suffer any serious loss, and when the English troops retired in consequence of a heavy storm they became in turn the pursuers and inflicted a few casualties. The advantages they obtained were due to the terrific weather more than to their courage, but one party of Madras sepoys lost its way, and was surrounded by so overwhelming a number of Chinese that it would have been annihilated but that its absence was fortunately discovered and a rescuing party of marines, armed with the new percussion-gun, which was to a great degree secure against the weather, went out to its assistance. They found the sepoys, under their two English officers, drawn up in a square firing as best they could and presenting a bold front to the foe— "many of the sepoys, after extracting the wet cartridge very deliberately, tore their pocket handkerchiefs or lining from their turbans and, baling water with their hands into the barrel of their pieces, washed and dried them, thus enabling them to fire an occasional volley." Out of sixty sepoys one was killed and fourteen were wounded. After this Sir Hugh Gough threatened to bombard Canton if there were any more attacks on his camp, and they at once ceased, and when the whole of the indemnity was paid the English troops were withdrawn, leaving Canton as it was, for a second time "a record of British magnanimity and forbearance."

After this, trade reverted to its former footing, and by the Canton Convention, signed by the Imperial commissioners in July, 1841, the English obtained all the privileges they could hope for from the local authorities. But it was essentially a truce, not a treaty, and the great point of direct intercourse with the Central

Government was no nearer settlement than ever. At this moment Sir Henry Pottinger arrived as plenipotentiary from England, and he at once set himself to obtaining a formal recognition from the Peking Executive of his position and the admission of his right to address him on diplomatic business. With the view of pressing this matter on the attention of Taoukwang, who personally had not deviated from his original attitude of emphatic hostility, Sir Henry Pottinger sailed northward with the fleet and a large portion of the land forces about the end of August.

The important seaport of Amoy was attacked and taken after what was called "a short but animated resistance." This town is situated on an island, the largest of a group lying at the entrance to the estuary of Lungkiang, and it has long been famous as a convenient port and flourishing place of trade. The Chinese had raised a rampart of one thousand one hundred yards in length, and this they had armed with ninety guns, while a battery of forty-two guns protected its flank. Kulangsu was also fortified, and the Chinese had placed in all five hundred guns in position. They believed in the impregnability of Amoy, and it was allowed that no inconsiderable skill as well as great expense had been devoted to the strengthening of the place. When the English fleet arrived off the port the Chinese sent a flag of truce to demand what it wanted, and they were informed the surrender of the town.

The necessity for this measure would be hard to justify, especially as the British were nominally at peace with China, for the people of Amoy had inflicted no injury on their trade, and their chastisement would not bring them any nearer to Peking. Nor was the occupation of Amoy necessary on military grounds. It was strong only for itself, and its capture had no important consequences. As the Chinese determined to resist the English, the fleet engaged the batteries, and the Chinese, standing to their guns "right manfully," only abandoned their position when they found their rear threatened by a landing party. Then, after a faint resistance, the Chinese sought safety in flight; but some of their officers, preferring death to dishonor, committed suicide, one of them being seen to walk calmly into the sea and drown himself in face of both armies. The capture of Amoy followed.

As the authorities at Amoy refused to hold any intercourse

with the English, the achievement remained barren of any useful consequence, and after leaving a small garrison on Kulangsu and three warships in the roadstead, the English expedition continued its northern course. After being scattered by a storm in the perilous Formosa Channel, the fleet reunited off Ningpo, whence it proceeded to attack Chusan for a second time. The Chinese defended Ting-hai, the capital, with great resolution. At this place General Keo, the chief naval and military commander, was killed, and all his officers, sticking to him to the last, also fell with him. Their conduct in fact was noble; nothing could have surpassed it. On the reoccupation of Chusan, which it was decided to retain until a formal treaty had been concluded with the Emperor, Sir Henry Pottinger issued a proclamation to the effect that years might elapse before that place would be restored to the Emperor's authority, and many persons wished that it should be permanently annexed as the best base for commercial operations in China. A garrison of four hundred men was left at Ting-hai, and then the expedition proceeded to attack Ching-hai on the mainland, where the Chinese had made every preparation to offer a strenuous resistance. The Chinese suffered the most signal defeat and the greatest loss they had yet incurred during the war. The victory at Ching-hai was followed by the unopposed occupation of the important city of Ningpo, where the inhabitants shut themselves up and wrote on their doors "Submissive People."

Ningpo was put to ransom, and the authorities informed that unless they paid the sum within a certain time their city would be handed over to pillage and destruction. As the Peking Government had made no sign of giving in, it was felt that no occasion ought to be lost of overawing the Chinese, and compelling them to admit that any further prolongation of the struggle would be hopeless. The arrival of further troops and warships from Europe enabled the English commanders to adopt a more determined and uncompromising attitude, and the capture of Ningpo would have been followed up at once but for the disastrous events in Afghanistan, which distracted attention from the Chinese question and delayed its settlement. It was hoped, however, that the continued occupation of Amoy, Chusan, and Ningpo would cause sufficient pressure on the Peking Government to induce it to yield all that was demanded.

These anticipations were not fulfilled, for neither the swift-recurring visitation of disaster nor the waning resources of the Imperial Government in both men and treasure could shake the fixed hostility of T'aoukwang or induce him to abate his proud pretensions. Minister after minister passed into disgrace and exile. Misfortune shared the same fate as incompetence, and the more the embarrassments of the State increased the heavier fell the hand of the ruler and the verdict of the Board of Punishments upon beaten generals and unsuccessful statesmen. The period of inaction which followed the occupation of Ningpo no doubt encouraged the Emperor to think that the foreigners were exhausted or that they had reached the end of their successes, and he ordered increased efforts to be made to bring up troops and to strengthen the approaches to Peking. The first proof of his returning spirit was shown in March, 1842, when the Chinese attempted to seize Ningpo by a *coup de main*.

Suddenly, and without warning, a force of between ten and twelve thousand men appeared at daybreak outside the south-west gates of Ningpo, and many of them succeeded in making their way over the walls and gaining the centre of the town; but, instead of proving the path to victory, this advance resulted in the complete overthrow of the Chinese. Attacked by artillery and foot in the market-place they were almost annihilated, and the great Chinese attack on Ningpo resulted in a fiasco. Similar but less vigorous attacks were made about the same time on Ching-hai and Chusan, but they were both repulsed with heavy loss to the Chinese. In consequence of these attacks and the improved position in Afghanistan it was decided to again assume the offensive, and to break up the hostile army at Hangchow, of which the body that attacked Ningpo was the advanced guard. Sir Hugh Gough commanded the operations in person, and he had the co-operation of a naval force under Sir William Parker.

The first action took place outside Tszeki, a small place ten miles from Ningpo, where the Chinese fancied they occupied an exceedingly strong position. But careful inspection showed it to be radically faulty. Their lines covered part of the Segaou Hills, but their left was commanded by some higher hills on the right of the English position, and the Chinese left again commanded their own right. It was evident, therefore, that the capture of the left wing of the Chinese encampment would entail the surrender or evacuation of the rest. The difficulties of the ground caused a greater delay in the advance than had been expected, and the assault had to be delivered along the whole line, as it was becoming obvious that the Chinese were growing more confident, and more to be feared from the delay in attacking them.

The assault was made with the impetuosity good troops always show in attacking inferior ones, no matter how great the disparity of numbers; and here the Chinese were driven out of their position—although they stood their ground in a creditable manner—and chased over the hills down to the rice-fields below. The Chinese loss was over a thousand killed, including many of the Imperial Guard, of whom five hundred were present, and whom Sir Hugh Gough described as "remarkably fine men," while the English had six killed and thirty-seven wounded. For the moment it was intended to follow up this victory by an attack on the city of Hangchow, the famous Kincsay of mediæval travellers; but the arrival of fresh instructions gave a complete turn to the whole war.

Little permanent good had been effected by these successful operations on the coast, and Taoukwang was still as resolute as ever in his hostility; nor is there any reason to suppose that the capture of Hangchow or any other of the coast towns would have caused a material change in the situation. The credit of initiating the policy which brought the Chinese Government to its knees belongs exclusively to Lord Ellenborough, then Governor-General of India. He detected the futility of operations along the coast, and he suggested that the great waterway of the Yang-tse-Kiang, perfectly navigable for warships up to the immediate neighborhood of Nanking, provided the means of coercing the Chinese and effecting the objects of the English Government.

The English expedition, strongly reënforced from India, then abandoned Ningpo and Ching-hai, and, proceeding north, began the final operations of the war with an attack on Chapu, where the Chinese had made extensive measures of defence. Chapu was the port appointed for trade with Japan, and the Chinese had collected there a very considerable force from the levies of Chekiang, which ex-Commissioner Lin had been largely instrumental in raising. Sir Hugh Gough attacked Chapu with two thousand

men, and the main body of the Chinese was routed without much
difficulty, but three hundred desperate men shut themselves up
in a walled enclosure and made an obstinate resistance.   They
held out until three fourths of them were slain, when the survivors, seventy-five wounded men, accepted the quarter offered
them from the first.   The English lost ten killed and fifty-five
wounded, and the Chinese more than a thousand.

After this the expedition proceeded northward for the Great
River, and it was found necessary to attack Woosung, the port of
Shanghai, *en route*.   This place was also strongly fortified with
as many as one hundred seventy-five guns in position, but the
chief difficulty in attacking it lay in that of approach, as the channel had first to be sounded, and then the sailing-ships towed into
position by the steamers.   Twelve vessels were in this manner
placed broadside to the batteries on land, a position which obviously they could not have maintained against a force of anything
like equal strength; but they succeeded in silencing the Chinese
batteries with comparatively little loss, and then the English army
was landed without opposition.   Shanghai is situated sixteen
miles up the Woosung River, and while part of the force proceeded
up the river another marched overland.   Both columns arrived
together, and the disheartened Chinese evacuated Shanghai after
firing one or two random shots.   No attempt was made to retain
Shanghai, and the expedition reëmbarked, and proceeded to attack Chankiang or Chinkiangfoo, a town on the southern bank of
the Yang-tse-Kiang, and at the northern entrance of the southern
branch of the Great Canal.

This town has always been a place of great celebrity, both
strategically and commercially, for not merely does it hold a very
strong position with regard to the Canal, but it forms with the
Golden and Silver Islands, the principal barrier in the path of
those attempting to reach Nanking.   At this point Sir Hugh
Gough was reënforced by the Ninety-eighth Regiment, under
Colonel Colin Campbell.   The difficulties of navigation and the
size of the fleet, which now reached seventy vessels, caused a delay in the operations, and it was not until the latter end of July,
or more than a month after the occupation of Shanghai, that the
English reached Chinkiangfoo, where, strangely enough, there
seemed to be no military preparations whatever.   A careful re-

connoissance revealed the presence of three strong encampments at some distance from the town, and the first operation was to carry them, and to prevent their garrisons joining such forces as might still remain in the city. This attack was intrusted to Lord Saltoun's brigade, which was composed of two Scotch regiments and portions of two native regiments, with only three guns. The opposition was almost insignificant, and the three camps were carried with comparatively little loss and their garrisons scattered in all directions.

At the same time the remainder of the force assaulted the city, which was surrounded by a high wall and a deep moat. Some delay was caused by these obstacles, but at last the western gate was blown in by Captain Pears, of the Engineers, and at the same moment the walls were escaladed at two different points, and the English troops, streaming in on three sides, fairly surrounded a considerable portion of the garrison, who retired into a detached work, where they perished to the last man either by rifle fire or in the flames of the houses which were ignited partly by themselves and partly by the fire of the soldiers. The resistance did not stop here, for the Tartar or inner city was resolutely defended by the Manchus, and owing to the intense heat the Europeans would have been glad of a rest; but, as the Manchus kept up a galling fire, Sir Hugh Gough felt bound to order an immediate assault before the enemy grew too daring. The fight was renewed, and the Tartars were driven back at all points; but the English troops were so exhausted that they could not press home this advantage. The interval thus gained was employed by the Manchus, not in making good their escape, but in securing their military honor by first massacring their women and children, and then committing suicide. It must be remembered that these were not Chinese, but Manchu Tartars of the dominant race.

The losses of the English army at this battle—forty killed and one hundred thirty wounded—were heavy, and they were increased by several deaths caused by the heat and exhaustion of the day. The Chinese, or rather the Tartars, never fought better, and it appears from a document discovered afterward that if Hailing's recommendations had been followed, and if he had been properly supported, the capture of Chinkiangfoo would have been even more difficult and costly than it proved.

Some delay at Chinkiangfoo was rendered necessary by the exhaustion of the troops and by the number of sick and wounded; but a week after the capture of that place in the manner described the arrangements for the further advance on Nanking were com pleted. A small garrison was left in an encampment on a height commanding the entrance to the canal; but there was little reason to apprehend any fresh attack, as the lesson of Chinkiang-foo had been a terrible one. That city lay beneath the English camp like a vast charnel-house, its half burned buildings filled with the self-immolated Tartars who had preferred honor to life; and so thickly strewn were these and so intense the heat that the days passed away without the ability to give them burial, until at last it became absolutely impossible to render the last kind office to a gallant foe. Despite the greatest precautions of the English authorities, Chinkiangfoo became the source of pestilence, and an outbreak of cholera caused more loss in the English camp than befell the main force intrusted with the capture of Nanking.

Contrary winds delayed the progress of the English fleet, and it was not until August 5th, more than a fortnight after the Battle at Chinkiangfoo, that it appeared off Nanking, the second city in reputation and historical importance of the empire, with one million inhabitants and a garrison of fifteen thousand men, of whom two-thirds were Manchus. The walls were twenty miles in length, and hindered, more than they promoted, an efficient defence; and the difficulties of the surrounding country, covered with the débris of the buildings which constituted the larger cities of Nanking at an earlier period of history, helped the assailing party more than they did the defenders. Sir Hugh Gough drew up an admirable plan for capturing this vast and not defenceless city with his force of five thousand men, and there is no reason to doubt that he would have been completely successful, but by this the backbone of the Chinese Government had been broken, and even the proud and obstinate Taoukwang was compelled to admit that it was imperative to come to terms with the English and to make some concessions in order to get rid of them.

The minister Elepoo, who once enjoyed the closest intimacy with Taoukwang, and who was the leader of the peace party, which desired the cessation of an unequal struggle, had begun informal negotiations several months before they proved successful at Nanking. He omitted no opportunity of learning the views of the English officers, and what was the minimum of concession on which a stable peace could be based. He had endeavored also to give something of a generous character to the struggle, and he had more than once proved himself a courteous as well as a gallant foe. After the capture of Chapu and Woosung he sent back several officers and men who had at different times been taken prisoners by the Chinese, and he expressed at the same time the desire that the war should end. Sir Henry Pottinger's reply to this letter was to inquire if he was empowered by the Emperor to negotiate. If he had received this authority the English plenipotentiary would be very happy to discuss any matter with him, but, if not, the war must proceed.

At that moment Elepoo had not the requisite authority to negotiate, and the war went on until the victorious English troops were beneath the walls of Nanking. At the same time as these *pourparlers* were held with Elepoo at Woosung, Sir Henry Pottinger issued a proclamation to the Chinese stating what the British Government required to be done. In this document the equality of all nations as members of the same human family was pointed out, and the right to hold friendly intercourse insisted on as a matter of duty and common obligation. Sir Henry said that "England, coming from the utmost West, has held intercourse with China in this utmost East for more than two centuries past, and during this time the English have suffered ill-treatment from the Chinese officials, who, regarding themselves as powerful and us as weak, have thus dared to commit injustice." Then followed a list of many of the high-handed acts of Commissioner Lin and his successors.

The Chinese, plainly speaking, had sought to maintain their exclusiveness and to live outside the comity of nations, and they had not the power to attain their wish. Therefore they were compelled to listen to and to accept the terms of the English plenipotentiary, which were as follows: The Emperor was first of all to appoint a high officer with full powers to negotiate and conclude arrangements on his own responsibility, when hostilities would be suspended. The three principal points on which these negotiations were to be based were compensation for losses and expenses, a friendly and becoming intercourse on terms of equal-

ity between officers of the two countries, and the cession of insular
territory for commerce and for the residence of merchants, and as
a security and guarantee against the future renewal of offensive
acts. The first step toward the acceptance of these terms was
taken when an imperial commission was formed of three members, Keying, Elepoo, and Niu Kien, Viceroy of the Two Kiang;
and to the last named, as Governor of the Provinces most affected,
fell the task of writing the first diplomatic communication of a
satisfactory character from the Chinese Government to the English plenipotentiary.

This letter was important for more reasons than its being of a
conciliatory nature. It held out to a certain extent a hand of
friendship, and it also sought to assign an origin to the conflict,
and Niu Kien could find nothing more handy or convenient than
opium, which thus came to give its name to the whole war. With
regard to the Chinese reverses, Niu Kien, while admitting them,
explained that "as the central nation had enjoyed peace for a
long time the Chinese were not prepared for attacking and
fighting, which had led to this accumulation of insult and disgrace." In a later communication Niu Kien admitted that "the
English at Canton had been exposed to insults and extortions
for a series of years, and that steps should be taken to insure in
future that the people of your honorable nation might carry on
their commerce to advantage, and not receive injury thereby."
These documents showed that the Chinese were at last willing to
abandon the old and impossible principle of superiority over other
nations, for which they had so long contended; and with the
withdrawal of this pretension negotiations for the conclusion of a
stable peace became at once possible and of hopeful augury.

UNION OF UPPER AND LOWER CANADA

A.D. 1841

JOHN CHARLES DENT[1]

While the Canadas, in 1838, were in the throes of rebellion, the British Government commissioned the Earl of Durham, an able statesman of the Liberal party at the time in power in England, to go to Canada and report on the state of affairs in the colony, and to fill the then vacant office of Governor-General. During his brief rule, Lord Durham sought to allay political commotion and soften the asperities of party strife, and with laudable intent stretched his authority on the side of clemency in dealing with the rebels. His able state paper, on his return to England, was made by the English Ministry the basis of certain political changes in the constitution of the colony, which were of lasting benefit to Canada. These changes were acted upon, in spite of the opposition of the " Family Compact" in Upper Canada and of the governing party in the Lower Province, both of whom dreaded the termination of their despotic rule.

LORD DURHAM'S report was seed sown in good ground. From the time when it became public property it formed a prominent topic of discussion among British statesmen, and added not a little to his reputation, as well as to that of his secretary, Mr. Charles Buller. Most people approved of it; a few found fault with some of its clauses; but there was no difference of opinion as to the great ability and industry which had gone to its production as a whole. In Upper Canada, the Reform party, which had long been struggling against the Family Compact under great disadvantages, and which had strenuously contended for many of the principles recognized by the report, received it with enthusiasm. The Legislative Assembly of that Province passed a resolution in favor of union. The Conservatives, however, were very well satisfied with the existing order of things, and were, almost to a man, opposed to any change.

The Honorable (afterward Sir) John Beverley Robinson, Chief Justice of Upper Canada, who had long been the chief

---

[1] From J. C. Dent's *The Last Forty Years* (of Canadian history) (Toronto, Canada: Virtue and Company), by permission.

guide, philosopher, and friend of the dominant faction in the Province, went to England at this time, and during his stay there, toward the close of the year 1839, published what was intended as a counterblast to Lord Durham's report, under the title of "Canada and the Canada Bill." It strove to show that the division of the Provinces in 1791 had worked satisfactorily, and that the carrying out of Lord Durham's recommendations would by no means remove existing evils or promote the welfare of the country. Mr. Robinson had sixteen years before been an advocate of such a union as he now opposed, but had subsequently seen reason for changing his views. His little book was well written, and presented the case from his side with clearness, but it was like arguing against the doctrine of gravitation.

In Lower Canada public opinion was much divided. A large majority of the British population approved of the project of union, but there was a considerable minority on the other side. The French-Canadians were almost unanimous in their disapproval of the scheme. It thus seemed probable that there would be no slight difficulty in obtaining general assent to the carrying out of Lord Durham's recommendations. But, the will being present, a way was soon found. During the session of 1839 a bill for reuniting the Canadas was introduced into the Imperial Parliament by Lord John Russell. When it came to be dealt with by a committee of the House of Commons it was found that some additional information was needed. It was also thought desirable to obtain the formal concurrence of the Canadians, as expressed through their respective Legislatures. To effect these objects it was necessary to send out some clear-headed man, possessed of a large share of tact, and with a due sense of how much was involved in his enterprise.

The gentleman fixed upon to undertake this important mission was Charles Poulett Thomson, better known to Canadians by his subsequent title of Lord Sydenham. Mr. Thomson, though still a young man to be intrusted with a matter of such importance, had had large experience as a politician and diplomatist. He was particularly well informed respecting mercantile affairs, having been bred to commercial pursuits, and was an ardent disciple of free-trade doctrines. Though neither a thorough nor a profound statesman, he was at least a very clever politician, and it is doubtful whether any man could have been found throughout England better fitted, alike by nature and by training, to carry out Lord Durham's policy in Canada than was Charles Poulett Thomson. He at this time sat in the House of Commons for the important constituency of Manchester, and held the office of president of the board of trade in the Ministry of the day. Having been appointed Governor-General of Canada, and having enjoyed the great advantage of frequent personal interviews with Lord Durham on the subject of his mission, he set out for Quebec in September, 1839. He reached his destination on October 17th following, and two days afterward issued a proclamation announcing that he had assumed the reins of government.

The task before him was one of no ordinary difficulty. It has been seen that the people and the Legislatures were by no means unanimous in approving the proposed measures, and yet it was necessary that he should obtain their consent. Owing to the suspension of the Lower Canadian Constitution, there was, strictly speaking, no Legislature in that Province to be consulted. The body that did duty for a Legislature was the Special Council, and this was summoned to meet at Montreal on November 11th.

No change whatever was made in its composition. It consisted of eighteen members, nearly all of whom belonged to the British party. It had been nominated (after Lord Durham's departure from Canada) by Sir John Colborne, acting in behalf of the Crown, and the body as a whole did not by any means represent the views generally entertained among the inhabitants of the Lower Province. It was Lord Sydenham's mission, however, to carry out his instructions, and to obtain a formal consent from the existing body which stood in the place of a Legislature. Had a fairly representative body been in existence, it would never have given its consent to a union which for a time blotted out the political influence of the French-Canadian population. But no potent opposition was to be dreaded from such a body as the Special Council. The Provincial Constitution was suspended, and the factious spirits were either effectually silenced or in exile. After several days' discussion the Council adopted the union resolutions by a majority of twelve to three. The Governor-General was thus enabled to report to the Secretary of State in England that the assent of the Lower Province had been obtained. He then made his way without loss of time to Toronto, to obtain the concurrence of the Legislature of the Upper Province.

In the Upper Canadian Legislature His Excellency had no Special Council to deal with, but a regularly constituted legislative body, with a due sense of its own importance and an unequivocal disposition to stand upon its rights. With the Assembly no trouble was to be anticipated, as it had already passed resolutions in favor of union, and was desirous of seeing responsible government conceded without delay. In the Legislative Council very different sentiments prevailed. Its members had everything to lose and nothing to gain by the proposed change. A large majority of them belonged to the Family Compact. Their power and patronage would go, and the principles to which they had always opposed themselves would triumph, in the event of a union of the Provinces and the concession of executive responsibility. They dreaded a coalition between the Liberals of the two Provinces. Their position, however, was such that they could not with any show of consistency refuse their assent to the resolutions proposed by His Excellency.

Those resolutions were known to embody the Imperial will, and the members of the Family Compact were nothing if not loyal. For years past, and more especially since the suppression of the recent rebellion (of 1837), their loyalty had become positively, albeit honestly, effusive. They had proclaimed it through the public prints, at the corners of the streets, and—literally— from the housetops. Some of them had talked a great deal of hysterical nonsense, and had propounded theories better suited to the early years of the Restoration than to the times in which they lived. How then could they venture to oppose the Imperial mandate, as proclaimed to them by the Governor-General in person? His Excellency was an adept in the science of finesse, and used all his arts to win them over. He appealed in the strongest terms to their lifelong fealty. He materially strengthened his position by the publication in the *Upper Canada Gazette* of a despatch from the Colonial Minister.

"You will understand, and will cause it to be generally

known," said the despatch, "that hereafter the tenure of colonial offices, held during Her Majesty's pleasure, will not be regarded as equivalent to a tenure during good behavior; but that not only such officers will be called upon to retire from the public service as often as any sufficient motives of public policy may suggest the expediency of that measure, but a change in the person of the Governor will be considered as a sufficient reason for any alterations which his successor may deem it expedient to make in the list of public functionaries—subject, of course, to the future confirmation of the sovereign. These remarks do not extend to judicial officers, nor are they meant to apply to places which are altogether ministerial, and which do not devolve upon the holders of them duties in the right discharge of which the character and policy of the British Government are directly involved. They are intended to apply rather to the heads of departments than to persons serving as clerks or in similar capacities under them; neither do they extend to officers in the service of the Lords Commissioners of the Treasury. The functionaries who will be chiefly, though not exclusively, affected by them are the Colonial Secretary; the Treasurer, or Receiver-General; the Surveyor-General; the Attorney- and Solicitor-General; the Sheriff, or Provost-Marshal; and other officers who, under different designations from these, are intrusted with the same or similar duties. To this list must also be added the members of the Council, especially in those colonies in which the Legislative and Executive Councils are distinct bodies."

The meaning of this was obvious enough. It meant that for the future the persons indicated would have to merit and enjoy a share of public confidence or else resign their places. It also meant that the Home Government had set its mind on passing a union bill, and that no caprice or obstruction on their part would be allowed to stand in the way of such a consummation. It was evident that they might as well bow to the inevitable with a good grace, as, in the event of their refusal, means would be found to get rid of them and supply their places with more manageable material. They yielded.

Resolutions expressive of assent to the union were passed, on condition that there should be an equal representation of each Province in the united Legislature; that a sufficient permanent civil list should be voted to secure the independence of the judges; and that the public debt of Upper Canada should be a charge upon the joint revenue of the United Province. In the Assembly certain conditions were pressed upon the consideration of His Excellency which the latter saw fit to oppose, as being unjust to the French-Canadian population in the Lower Province. The Governor's views finally prevailed. On the last day of the year he was able to announce to a correspondent that he had satisfactorily accomplished the objects of his mission, and that nothing further remained but for Parliament to pass the Union Bill, a draught of which, he added, would soon be forwarded from Canada.

The draught of the Union Bill, founded upon the resolutions of the Legislature of Upper Canada and the Special Council of the Lower Province, was chiefly prepared by the Honorable James Stuart, Chief Justice of the Court of Queen's Bench for Lower Canada, who for his great services to Lord Durham and Mr. Thomson was subsequently elevated to the rank of a baronet of the United Kingdom. The successive clauses of the bill were separately and carefully discussed between the Governor and the Chief Justice before transmission to England. It provided for the union of the two Provinces under the name of the Province of Canada. It further provided that there should be one Legislative Council and one Assembly, with an equal representation from each of the former Provinces; the Legislative Council to consist of not fewer than twenty life members, appointed by the Crown, and the Assembly to consist of eighty-four members (forty-two from each of the former Provinces), elected by the people.

The property qualification for candidates for seats in the Assembly was fixed at five hundred pounds sterling in lands or tenements. The Governor was authorized to fix the time and place of holding Parliaments, and to prorogue or dissolve the latter at his pleasure. The Speaker of the Legislative Council was to be appointed by the Governor, and the Speaker of the Assembly to be elected by its members. A permanent civil list of seventy-five thousand pounds annually was provided for, instead of all territorial and other revenues then at the Crown's disposal; and the judges were made independent of the votes of the Assembly. All writs, proclamations, reports, journals, and public documents were to be in the English language only; and it was provided that the public debt of the two Provinces should be assumed by the united Province.

Such, in so far as it is now necessary to specify them, were the principal provisions of the Union Bill transmitted to England by Mr. Thomson. The Imperial Parliament was then in session, and the Colonial Secretary, Lord John Russell, lost no time in presenting the measure. It underwent some slight modifications in the course of its passage through the Commons. Certain clauses relating to local municipal institutions were struck out, and left to be dealt with by the Provincial Legislatures, but the bill, as a whole, commended itself to the wisdom of the House of Commons, and was passed with but little opposition. Some of the Irish members, led by O'Connell, raised their voices against it, on the ground that it sanctioned a disproportionate representation of the French and British races; that the former had not assented to the measure, and that in consequence of the suspension of the Lower Canadian Constitution, they had no means of expressing their assent. It was further argued that it was unjust to saddle Lower Canada with a share of liability in respect of the debt of the Upper Province. Opposition from this quarter, however, was regarded by the Ministry very much as a matter of course, and was of no special significance.

In the House of Lords the objections to the measure were urged with more vigor than commonly characterizes the debates there, and among those who spoke most strongly against it were Lords Gosford and Seaton, both of whom had been Governors of Canada, and might be supposed to bring special knowledge to bear upon the subject. The act passed, however, and was to come into operation by virtue of a royal proclamation, to be issued within fifteen calendar months. The issuing of the proclamation was deferred until February 5, 1841, when it appeared under the authority of the Provincial Secretary, the Honorable Dominick Daly. By its terms the Act of Union was to take effect from the 10th of the month; and at that date the union of the Provinces was accordingly complete.[1]

[1] The day upon which the union of the Provinces took effect was the anniversary of two events of some importance in Canadian history; viz.,

The French population of Lower Canada generally, and even some of the British, were much averse to the project of union on the terms proposed, and an impartial critic must confess that their discontent was not wholly groundless. In the first place, the population of the Lower Province was considerably in excess of that of Upper Canada; whereas the latter, by the terms of union, were granted an equal Parliamentary representation with the former. The financial condition of the two Provinces was still more unequal than the population. In Lower Canada the public debt was insignificant, and, if there was less public enterprise than in the Upper Province, there was no financial embarrassment. The revenue was small, but it was ample for the public requirements. In Upper Canada, on the other hand, for some years past an amount of enterprise had been displayed which was altogether out of proportion to the age and financial condition of the Province. The construction of the great canals and other important public works had involved what for those times must be pronounced to have been an enormous expenditure, and for this there had so far been little or no return. A good deal of the expenditure had been unnecessary — the result of mismanagement and inexperience — and would never produce any return. The public debt was large. Further outlay was imperative, and the exchequer was empty. Some important public enterprises had been temporarily abandoned for want of funds. The Province seemed to be on the verge of bankruptcy.

By the imposition of the public debt on the united Province, therefore, Upper Canada was clearly a gainer. But, it was argued, this was only fair, inasmuch as Lower Canada would participate in the advantages derivable from the public works which had given rise to the debt. Lower Canada, moreover, had long reaped an undue advantage in respect of the revenue from imports collected at Montreal and Quebec. That revenue was chiefly paid by the Upper Province, where a majority of the consumers resided; yet Lower Canada had for years received the lion's share of it, and surrendered even the smallest proportion with reluctance. The argument as to the representation

of the signing of the Treaty of 1763, and of the royal assent being accorded to the suspension of the Lower Canadian Constitution in 1838.

of the two Provinces being equal, and therefore disproportionate to the population, was met by the plea that the disproportion would soon disappear, inasmuch as the population of Upper Canada had been largely recruited by immigration; that it was rapidly increasing, and would continue to increase; whereas immigration to the Lower Province was insignificant in comparison, and the increase of population proportionately slow.

The Lower Canadians were not disposed to regard this argument as conclusive. They argued, with some show of reason, that it would be time enough to equalize the representation when the prediction as to equality of population should be realized. The practical proscription of the French language in all public proceedings, moreover, was keenly felt by the French-Canadians, and they never ceased to clamor for the repeal of the clause effecting it — a repeal which was finally accomplished after the accession to power of the second Lafontaine-Baldwin Ministry in 1848. The French-Canadians, indeed, looked upon the Union Act as the result of a predetermination to destroy their nationality and their religion. It was evident that if the British representatives from Lower Canada should act in unison with their conationalists from the Upper Province, the combination would be all-powerful in the Legislature.

The discontent in the Lower Province over the terms of union made itself felt in various quarters before the passing of the act. In the districts of Quebec and Three Rivers a petition was set on foot under the auspices of the clergy, and erelong forty thousand signatures were appended to it. Some of the signatories were influential members of the British party. It expressed strong hostility to the proposed union, and prayed that the Constitution of 1791 might be maintained. It was sent over to England and laid before the Imperial Parliament, and doubtless influenced the Government there to the extent of inducing them not to legislate without due deliberation. A large meeting was also held at Montreal, where, on motion of Mr. Lafontaine, an address to the Imperial Parliament protesting against the proposed union was adopted; but, owing to a want of concord among its promoters, it was not forwarded to England.

Dissatisfaction, however, was now of no further avail. The

Union of the Provinces was an accomplished fact, and it only remained for the representatives of both to accept the situation and make the best of it. The Governor-General, for his arduous and indefatigable services, was in August, 1840, raised to the peerage with the title Baron Sydenham of Sydenham in Kent and of Toronto in Canada. His exertions had not been without their effect on his physical frame, which was even more weakly than Lord Durham's had been; but he was keenly ambitious, and not disposed to sit down and brood over his maladies. He was authorized by the thirtieth clause of the Union Act to fix the capital of the United Province at such place as he might be advised. He chose to fix it at Kingston, in the Upper Province. This was another step which was keenly felt by the inhabitants of Lower Canada, who had hoped that the capital would be either Montreal or Quebec, both of which, as compared with Kingston, were large towns. The pressure from Upper Canada on this point, however, was overwhelming, and the Governor-General exercised a wise discretion in placing the seat of government in the centre of a district where the unwavering loyalty of the people was a guarantee for free and undisturbed legislation.

The appointment of the Executive Council was a matter which could no longer be delayed, and which required some deliberation on the part of the Governor-General. On February 13th—three days after the Union proclamation took effect—His Excellency, having made his selection, called to his Council eight gentlemen who already occupied the highest offices of state. They consisted of Messrs. Sullivan, Dunn, Daly, Harrison, Ogden, Draper, Baldwin, and Day. A month later—on March 17th—Mr. H. H. Killaly was added to the list. The principle of executive responsibility having been conceded, it was necessary that the members of the Council holding seats in the Assembly should be reëlected. This was duly accomplished at the general elections for members to serve in the first House of Assembly. These elections began on March 8, 1841, and were concluded early in the following month.

In the Lower Province they were marked by a violence and acrimony unprecedented at any election which had ever taken place in the colony. The British party and the national party had never been arrayed against each other with such bitterness. The latter smarted under a sense of defeat, while the former did not in all cases attempt to disguise their consciousness of triumph. There was a desire for revenge on the one side, and an ill-concealed complacency or contempt on the other. These sentiments, for some weeks before the elections, found frequent expression through the Provincial press, and a large proportion of the lower orders of electors was roused to a condition bordering on ferocity. In some constituencies another "reign of terror" prevailed during the progress of the election, and the ruffianism seems to have been pretty equally apportioned between the representatives of the different nationalities.

Mr. Lafontaine, whose name has already been mentioned, offered himself to the electors of Terrebonne. He was opposed by Doctor Michael McCulloch, of the British party, who was successful in securing his election. The violence displayed on both sides was disgraceful to the causes which they respectively represented, but there seems to be no reasonable doubt that had the franchise been perfectly free and untrammelled, Mr. Lafontaine's election would have been assured. He himself afterward admitted, however, that a large number of his supporters had set out from their homes armed with cudgels, and that those who had not been so provided at starting had made a détour into a wood on the road in order to supply their deficiencies. Upon nearing the polling-place they found Doctor McCulloch's supporters (many of whom were canal laborers and navvies who were not entitled to exercise the franchise at all) armed and ready for them; and as the latter had contrived to secure an advantageous position for a hand-to-hand fight, the French-Canadians adopted the better part of valor and withdrew from the field without recording their votes.

At the election for the county of Montreal the opposing forces came into actual collision, and one man, a member of the British party, was slain on the spot. With regard to the possession of the poll itself, Rob Roy's "good old rule" was the order of the day—those took who had the power, and those kept who could. The French-Canadians kept possession the first day, and it was in the struggle of a British elector to record his vote that he met his doom as above narrated. Next day the British mustered in such force that their opponents abandoned the struggle, and the French candidate retired. The Lower Canadian elections, therefore, did not in all cases represent the voice of the people. The French-Canadians were vehement in their denunciations of the Governor-General, who was allied, in their minds, with the British party, and was responsible for all the excesses of the latter. To say that he was not so responsible would, it is to be hoped, be a work of supererogation, but it must be owned that his determination to carry out the object of his mission to Canada was great, and that he was not over-scrupulous as to the means employed to secure that end. His conduct with regard to the electoral limits of Quebec and Montreal lent some color to the not unreasonable supposition that his sympathies were entirely with the British party, and that he did not intend to allow any impediment to stand in the way of the accomplishment of his wishes.

By the Union Bill, as originally draughted by him and Chief Justice Stuart, only one member was assigned to each of those cities. When the measure was laid before the Commons, Sir Robert Peel suggested that a larger representation was due to the commercial interest, and a clause was accordingly inserted assigning two members to each of the two principal cities of Lower Canada. The act, as finally passed, authorized the Governor to define the boundaries of the various cities and towns mentioned in the act. Lord Sydenham's attention was drawn to the fact that if the electoral limits of Montreal and Quebec were made to coincide with their municipal limits, the increased representation contemplated by the Union Act would not take effect, as the numerical superiority of electors in the suburbs would enable them to return both members. The number of French-Canadian representatives—and by consequence the number of opponents of the Union—would thus be increased. Lord Sydenham's first object was to make the Union a success, and to have a majority of members returned to Parliament who should be favorable to the Government policy. He accordingly exercised the power granted him by the act, and by a proclamation issued from Government House, Montreal, on March 4, 1841, defined the boundaries of Quebec and Montreal in such a manner as to exclude the suburbs, which for electoral purposes were amalgamated with the counties in which they were situated. He by this means practically disfranchised a large number of the inhabitants, and secured the return of members pledged to support his favorite project—an achievement for which the French-Canadians have never forgiven him.

It is believed that at least ten of the members who sat in the first Parliament were returned either by violence or by corruption. The violence, though chiefly manifested in Lower Canada, was by no means wholly confined to that Province. There were "gentle and joyous" passages of arms in all parts of the country. One life was lost in Toronto, and another in the county of Durham. Intelligence of broken heads and arms was received from various quarters. It was even feared lest the published accounts of the innumerable election riots would disseminate such an impression of the lawless state of affairs as to check immigration to Canada. Happily the fear proved not to be well grounded.

During the second week in April the returns were tolerably well known, and the Governor made up his accounts. Twenty-four out of the eighty-four members were pledged supporters of his policy. Only twenty French members—French in spirit as well as in nationality—appeared on the list. Of the remainder, twenty were classed as moderate and five as ultra Reformers. Only seven members of the Compact had found seats. All things considered, the two opposing parties of Conservatives and Reformers were divided almost equally.

CHRONOLOGY OF UNIVERSAL HISTORY

EMBRACING THE PERIOD COVERED IN THIS VOLUME

A.D. 1816–1844

JOHN RUDD, LL.D.

CHRONOLOGY OF UNIVERSAL HISTORY

EMBRACING THE PERIOD COVERED IN THIS VOLUME

A.D. 1816–1844

JOHN RUDD, LL.D.

Events treated at length are here indicated in large type; the numerals following give volume and page.

Separate chronologies of the various nations, and of the careers of famous persons, will be found in the INDEX VOLUME, with references showing where the several events are fully treated.

A.D.

1816. Indiana admitted into the Union. A second Bank of the United States chartered by Congress. James Monroe elected President. Outbreak of the First Seminole War.

"EUROPEAN REACTION UNDER METTERNICH: THE HOLY ALLIANCE." See xvi, 1.

A new tariff in Russia prohibits almost all British manufactures; Moscow rebuilt.

Independence of the Plata Provinces declared by the Congress of Tucuman.

Agitation in England for Parliamentary reform; Henry Hunt a popular leader. Invention of the miners' safety-lamp by Humphry Davy. Bombardment of Algiers by Lord Exmouth.

1817. Admission of Mississippi into the Union. Inauguration of James Monroe.

Formation of the United Evangelical Church in Prussia.

Bolivar assumes the chief power in Venezuela and establishes a supreme council.

Distress in England leads to continued rioting; march of the Blanketeers from Manchester. The Mahratta War begins; their power broken. Issue of "sovereigns," a new gold coin.

The Burschenschaft formed in Germany.

1818. Jackson's campaign against the Seminoles; he occupies Pensacola. Illinois admitted into the Union.

Establishment of Chilean independence follows the Battle of Maypu.

Celebration in England of the tercentenary of the Reformation. A convicted murderer escapes punishment by availing himself of an ancient statute allowing him to demand the "wager of battle." Subjugation of the Pindarees; the English also acquire the territories of Mulhar Row Holkar.

1819. Alabama admitted into the Union. Treaty for the cession of Florida by Spain to the United States. First voyage across the Atlantic by a steamship, the Savannah, from New York to Liverpool.

Riot and deaths in England, arising from widespread distress.

Kotzebue assassinated at Mannheim. Adoption of the Carlsbad resolutions against freedom of the press and the universities.

Complete independence of Venezuela and New Granada, under Bolivar's lead.

1820. "PASSAGE OF THE MISSOURI COMPROMISE;" see xvi, 14. Maine admitted to the Union. James Monroe reëlected to the Presidency.

Assassination in France of the Duke of Berry, second son of the future Charles X; Decazes dismissed; Richelieu again becomes premier.

"SPANISH DEMAND FOR A CONSTITUTION." See xvi, 41.

Death of George III; accession of his son, George IV. Trial of Queen Caroline; her name omitted in the liturgy. Cato Street conspiracy for the murder of the ministers.

Successful rising of the Carbonari in Naples. Sicilian insurrection.

Insurrection in Haiti; Cristophe, the ruler, puts an end to his life.

1821. Missouri admitted into the Union. "FLORIDA ACQUIRED BY THE UNITED STATES;" see xvi, 57.

Successful revolution of Iturbide in Mexico; independence secured.

San Martin and the Chileans liberate Peru.

King John VI returns to Portugal from Brazil.

"THE GREEK WAR FOR INDEPENDENCE." See xvi, 65.

Congress of the Great Powers at Laybach, to maintain absolutism.

Saint-Simon, in France, introduces his *Système industriel*.

1822. Liberia colony established by the American Colonization Society.

Triumph of the Constitutionalists over the Royalists in Spain; at Verona a congress of the Great Powers resolves to suppress the Constitutionalists.

At Epidaurus the National Assembly proclaims Greek independence.

Iturbide proclaimed Emperor of Mexico; Santa Anna and others proclaim a republic.

Separation of Brazil from Portugal; Dom Pedro I first constitutional Emperor.

Canning becomes Foreign Secretary of the British Government.

1823. James Monroe, in his annual message, enunciates the doctrine bearing his name. See "THE MONROE DOCTRINE," xvi, 80.

A French army enters Spain to restore the authority of Ferdinand VII; it storms the Trocadero; crushing of the Constitutionalists.

Death of Marco Bozzaris, the Greek revolutionary hero.

The abdication of Iturbide; the republic of Mexico founded.

Wilberforce forms the British Antislavery Society.

Denham and Clapperton, English explorers, reach Lake Tchad.

1824. Presidential election in United States; no choice results in the Electoral College; John Quincy Adams elected by House of Representatives. Lafayette visits the United States.

Mexico constituted a federal republic. Iturbide, who had visited England, returns and is shot.

Bolivar becomes dictator of Peru. Battle of Ayacucho; Sucre overwhelms the Spaniards; Spanish power in South America at an end.

Death of Byron. See "THE GREEK WAR FOR INDEPENDENCE," xvi, 65. Miaulis defeats the efforts of Ibrahim Pacha to restore the Turkish authority in Greece.

First war between England and Burma; Rangoon taken by the English. Formation of the Catholic Association in Ireland. Founding of the National Gallery.

1825. "OPENING OF THE ERIE CANAL." See xvi, 94.

Brazilian independence recognized by Portugal. France recognizes the independence of Haiti. Bolivar resigns his dictatorship in Peru. The republic of Bolivia formed.

A grant of one thousand millions of francs awarded by France to the *Émigrés*.

"SIEGE OF MISSOLONGHI." See xvi, 112.

Opening of the Stockton and Darlington Railway, England; the first use of steam locomotion for the conveyance of passengers and goods. Abolishment in England of state lotteries.

1826. Antimasonic excitement in New York due to the abduction of William Morgan.

Evacuation of Callao, their last port in Peru, by the Spaniards.

"MASSACRE OF THE JANIZARIES." See xvi, 128.

Close of the First Burmese War; acquisition by England of Arcan, Assam, and other territories. The University of London founded. Commercial distrust and distress throughout Britain; Sir Walter Scott and his publishers involved in the general wreck.

1827. Slavery abolished in the State of New York.

Charles X of France dissolves the Chamber of Deputies and the National Guard.

Treaty of London between Great Britain, France, and Russia to settle Greek affairs. Destruction of the Turkish by the allied fleet. See "BATTLE OF NAVARINO," xvi, 135.

Sir William Edward Parry on his arctic expedition reaches latitude 82° 45'. First printing for the blind, in England.

1828. Election to the Presidency of the United States of Andrew Jackson. See "JACKSON ELECTED PRESIDENT OF THE UNITED

STATES," xvi, 143. Construction of the Baltimore and Ohio Railroad begun.

A successful insurrection is headed by Guerrero against the government in Mexico. Recognition of Uruguay as an independent republic.

Russo-Turkish War; Paskevitch takes Kars; Varna falls to the Russians.

Formation of Wellington's ministry in England. Political disabilities of dissenters removed by act of Parliament.

1829. Jackson inaugurated President of the United States; the " spoils system " introduced into American politics.

Fruitless effort by the Spaniards to recover Mexico. Revolt against Guerrero. Venezuela separates from Colombia. Rosas attains supreme power in Argentina.

Peace of Adrianople between Turkey and Russia; the former cedes much territory to the Russians; the independence of Greece recognized.

Passage by Parliament of the Catholic Emancipation Act; O'Connell takes his seat. See " CATHOLIC EMANCIPATION," xvi, 175.

" BEGINNING OF RAILWAY LOCOMOTION." See xvi, 157.

1830. Church of the Latter-day Saints of Jesus Christ (Mormons) founded by Joseph Smith, at Manchester, New York. Debate in Congress between Webster and Hayne on the sale of the public lands: Foote's Resolution.

"ALGIERS TAKEN BY THE FRENCH;" see xvi, 199. Revolution in Paris; overthrow of the Bourbons. See " END OF ABSOLUTISM IN FRANCE," xvi, 207.

Assumption by Bustamante of the executive power in Mexico. Ecuador founded from part of Colombia. Death of Bolivar, after resigning the Presidency of Colombia.

" THE REVOLUTION IN BELGIUM." See xvi, 220.

Death in England of George IV; his brother, William IV, succeeds. Incendiary fires and antimachinery riots prevail.

1831. Insurrection of slaves under Nat Turner in Virginia. William Lloyd Garrison and Benjamin Lundy agitate for abolition.

Deposition of Dom Pedro I in Brazil; Dom Pedro II succeeds.

Louis Philippe makes Casimir Périer Prime Minister of France. The hereditary peerage abolished. Insurrectionary riots of silk-workers in Lyons and Southern France.

Leopold of Saxe-Coburg elected King of the Belgians.

" INSURRECTION IN RUSSIAN POLAND." See xvi, 245.

Austria crushes out revolutions in the Papal States.

Central Europe ravaged by the cholera.

Defeat of the first ministerial bill for Parliamentary reform; dissolution of Parliament and appeal to the people. Assumption of the name Conservatives by the advanced Tories. National schools founded in Ireland by the Government. The position of the magnetic pole (Boothia Felix) determined by James Clarke Ross. Riots mark the rejection of the Reform Bill; Nottingham castle burned and destroyed.

BUILDERS OF THE CANADIAN COMMONWEALTH

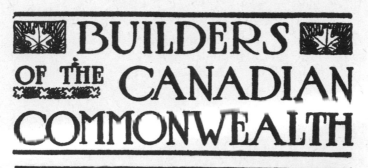

BUILDERS OF THE CANADIAN COMMONWEALTH

BY GEORGE H. LOCKE

With an Introduction by A. H. U. Colquhoun

Essay Index Reprint Series

BOOKS FOR LIBRARIES PRESS, INC.

FREEPORT, NEW YORK

First Published 1923
Reprinted 1967

920.071
L796
68562

January, 1970

LIBRARY OF CONGRESS CATALOG CARD NUMBER:
67-28755

PRINTED IN THE UNITED STATES OF AMERICA

CONTENTS

v

CONTENTS

Contents

INTRODUCTION

IN any collection of the speeches of Canadian public
men the political element would predominate.
This does not mean that the men themselves lacked
the literary equipment or that they were without
views upon literature, art, or the criticism of life.
The contrary is the case. The general culture of
those from whose addresses extracts are given in this
volume was not inferior. But the speeches that have
been preserved are naturally those dealing with the
great episodes in our constitutional development.
Such subjects inspired the deepest emotions and the
most striking thoughts. If one were able to find
the utterances of the same speakers on other themes
a wider presentation of their intellectual qualities and
tastes could be made. But the purpose is, primarily,
to relate present problems of national life back to
some of the men who helped to mould history and to
include some of those still living who have, incidentally or chiefly, laboured to the same end. Having
this object in view Dr. Locke has performed a difficult
task with impartial judgment, while the industry required to do it—as one who has worked a little in
the same vineyard can testify—must have received
its impetus from nothing less than an abiding love
of Canada. The Canadian has, in some degree, the

cosmopolitan mind. Notable speeches by British or foreign statesmen dwell as vividly in his memory as some delivered by his own countrymen, and the former are usually more accessible.

To read the following pages is to gain some idea of the mental powers, the earnest sincerity and the eloquence of those Canadian·leaders whose voices we shall hear no more. To hear and to read are two vastly different things. As the great French critic declared, there is as much eloquence in the tone of the voice, in the eyes, and in the air of a speaker as in his choice of words. Something of this is supplied by the brief appreciation that the editor has prefixed to each speech, written with a sympathy and a kindliness that are as valuable as the insight and knowledge displayed. But even so, the reader must supply for himself, by the exercise of his imagination, the quality that made these speeches tell—the flashing eye, the thrilling tone, the gesture (and some were prodigal of gesture). The events that inspired the speech must also be understood. The reader should not expect to find this volume a royal road to complete knowledge of the subject, but will feel himself compelled, if he is a Canadian of the right kind, to make excursions farther afield into history, into the fascinating by-paths of biography and into the principles of political progress that make Canada—in its own place and within its limits,—so interesting and profitable an area for research because the solution of our problems, and the ways by which we came to solve them, may constitute Canada's most useful legacy to posterity.

Introduction

The Canadian statesmen of former periods filled a
great space in the popular mind. They gave, for
the most part, the whole of their lives to public
affairs. Either in Parliament, or outside of it, they
represented causes. Their speeches were usually
addressed to the people at large. There are persons
still living who remember well some of these orators
at the zenith of their influence and power—Joseph
Howe, Sir John Macdonald, George Brown, Principal
Grant, Edward Blake, Sir Antoine Dorion. It
seems but yesterday since Cartwright, Mowat, Ross,
and Laurier left the scene of so many triumphs.
Who can forget who has heard the sonorous accents
of Blake, as he stood, an impressive and dignified figure on the platform swaying an audience as Antony is
pictured as moving the Roman crowds after the
death of Cæsar? Who was willing to miss a single
word of Cartwright's scornful indictment of the foe,
as he poured forth in perfectly-constructed sentences
and from a richly-dowered vocabulary, his denunciations of men and measures alike unworthy, in his
view, of respect and confidence? The charm of Sir
John Macdonald's speeches lay not in oratorical declamation, but in the easy and simple grasp of the
dullest questions which he exhibited, enlivened by a
droll humour that made an old story seem new because its application was so apt and appropriate.
At such a function as a St. Andrew's Society dinner,
where politics were rigidly debarred, Macdonald the
man was, perhaps, seen at his best, for his affectionate
raillery at those of his own racial origin, and the
stories at his own expense which he enjoyed as much

as his audience, give a more certain clue to his power over the masses of his fellow-countrymen than the more weighty deliverances on the Washington Treaty or the Letellier constitutional dispute, in which no trace of humour was permitted to creep in, but which were the true index of his intellectual capacity. In reading these speeches, we should, therefore, keep before us, if we can, the personality behind each of them, because the career, the manner, and the point of view are inseparable from the particular utterance.

A word may be said, in conclusion, as to the admirable purpose which a work like the present fulfills. Even in large libraries all the sources from which the material must have been drawn cannot be consulted. The editions of Canadian books are not large and are thus soon exhausted. While Canadian biography figures creditably in the national literature few biographies include the speeches which must be sought elsewhere. With the exception of the modern edition of Howe, to whose editor a debt of gratitude is due, biographers have, naturally enough, been unable to include the speeches. There are the parliamentary debates, but these, too, are not readily obtainable. Strange as it may sound, Dr. Locke has gathered together much information and enlightenment not actually accessible to the average Canadian, and for whom in most cases it is a locked door of knowledge. It may confidently be hoped that a work that should stimulate a healthy interest in the national history will be found to produce, in time, far-reaching effects in study and in comprehension of the past.

A. H. U. Colquhoun

PREFACE

IN the definitely educational aspect of our work in the Public Library we have felt the need of a history of our country as revealed in the speeches of her public men where they are discussing the contemporary problems of national life with which they were confronted. History in the process of making with all the ardour of advocacy or the fervour of denunciation has a personal interest which is almost impossible to arouse by a calm logical treatment in the light of after years. The individual becomes less and less and the facts more and more, which may be suitable for historians but well-nigh useless in training for citizenship and developing intelligent patriotism in the youth of our land. The struggle for responsible government, for representation by population or for the confederation of the provinces was carried on by men, and it is worth while to know who they were and what they actually said "in the fell clutch of circumstance."

GEORGE H. LOCKE

The Public Library
Toronto

LOUIS JOSEPH PAPINEAU

LOUIS JOSEPH PAPINEAU

1786-1871

THE name of Papineau is one to conjure with in French Canada. The personality, genius and patriotism of this outstanding Canadian have stamped themselves ineffaceably on the hearts of his romantic countrymen. Canadians of English descent, more responsive to the prose than to the poetry of life, may be inclined to remember the least attractive side of Papineau's history, but the most ardent lover of British institutions cannot fail to appreciate the single-minded devotion of this well-meaning, though mistaken, patriot to the land of his birth.

Louis Papineau was born in Quebec, in 1786, at a period of great political turmoil. His father, Joseph Papineau, was himself a politician of no mean repute, and it was natural that, at an early age the brilliant young Louis should turn his attention to the welfare of his countrymen in their struggle for political self-expression. While attending the Quebec Seminary, his intellectual brilliance and his marvellous oratorical powers pointed to a great future, and his passionate enthusiasm, coupled with fearlessness, determination and a love of freedom, seemed to supply all the requisites for a Superman.

But one great thing was lacking in his composition, the absence of which made a tragedy of the great

1

orator's life: he was entirely without self-restraint, and, entering the political arena at a time when patience and moderation were sorely needed, the outcome was inevitable.

In 1812 Papineau entered the Lower Canadian Assembly, and from the beginning enlisted his sympathies and his magnificent gifts in the struggle of the Assembly against the corruptions and injustices which were rife in the Legislative and Executive Councils, dominated by a narrow, place-seeking English oligarchy. In 1815 he was elected Speaker of the House, and from this date until the fateful days of 1837 he held first place in the hearts of his countrymen, swaying his imaginative disciples, both in and out of the Assembly, with his burning eloquence and his magnetic personality.

In 1822 he was sent as a delegate to London with a petition from his people against a proposed union with Upper Canada, which threatened to undermine the French nationality in Canada. The mission was successful, and his great charm and dignity impressed London society very favourably. He returned to Canada to renew his fight against the tyranny of the English faction in Parliament, and was the leader in the battle over the finances which animated Lower Canadian politics for fifteen years.

By 1827 the situation was critical indeed, and Governor Dalhousie, fearing Papineau's mighty influence, refused to sanction his re-election to the speakership. This action resulted in a petition to London by Papineau's idolizers, asking for the Governor-General's recall. The petition was granted, but matters were not improved. A change of policy, not of governors, was what was needed, and when Papineau became convinced of the stolid indifference of the British Government to the wrongs of French Canada, he became embittered, and from 1830 onward he was as violent an agitator against British institutions as he had earlier been an admirer of them.

His radical utterances in the Assembly soon lost him the support of his more moderate countrymen, and jealousy helped to increase the volume of vindictive sarcasm and rage which he poured forth daily in the Assembly—stubbornly refusing all compromises which the British Government offered him, and, by his rashness, rendering inevitable the foolish uprising which has gone down into history as the "Rebellion of 1837 in Lower Canada."

During the rebellion, Papineau escaped to the United States, and though in 1842 his former disciple, LaFontaine, secured a pardon for him, he deemed it inadvisable to return to Canada just then, and spent three years in France, where he devoted himself to historical research, and where, unfortunately, his impressionable mind was influenced by ultra-Radicals, such as Louis Blanc. When he returned to Canada in 1847 he again entered politics, and constituted himself a bitter minority against the moderate Liberals who had agreed to the Union of the Provinces. For some years he continued to raise his voice against British institutions, and in favor of a French-Canadian democracy, fashioned on American lines; but, although his great eloquence and commanding personality were still influential with the younger section of his people, his efforts were, on the whole, futile, and he retired to private life in 1854.

In 1867 he was lured out of his domestic retreat for a moment to give a lecture at the Canadian Institute, where he gave a lucid summary of British rule in Canada, and reaffirmed his distrust of English institutions—but after this final challenge he went back to the felicity of home life, where he remained until his death in 1871.

Such were the high spots in the life of this misguided patriot, whose gravest faults sprang from the intensity of his patriotism. In spite of his excesses, the stimulus he gave to Canadian political development was considerable, and though to-day unbiassed Canadians deplore his mistakes, they must feel the tenderest admiration for a man who, out of the fulness of his heart, uttered, in his last public speech, words which should kindle the pulses of all loyal Canadians:

"I love my country—I have loved her wisely!— I have loved her madly! 'My country first!' I learned to lisp at my father's knee."

Louis Joseph Papineau

THE REPRESENTATIVE SYSTEM
LOUIS JOSEPH PAPINEAU

From a speech on the hustings at the opening of the election for the west ward of Montreal, August 11, 1827.

YOU are assembled to exercise an important right, that of choosing freely, with the sole view to your own interests, men whom you think most capable of upholding them; to exercise a right which for several centuries (until quite recent times, in fact) was enjoyed exclusively by British subjects:—the privilege of choosing Representatives to act as legislators. The men of your choice, cannot, it is true, be called legislators in a strict and absolute sense, because they share this power with other authorities, who, in this country especially, could never become the objects of your choice; but, as those authorities, in their turn, cannot alter the laws nor create new ones without the assent of your Representatives, these latter may, in a restricted sense, be called your legislators.

Nothing has received greater emphasis in our public and constitutional law than the maxim that governments are constituted only with a view to the common weal, and not principally for the advantage of the public functionaries. The truth of this maxim has been conceded even by despotic governments, which raise themselves above the laws; but in our present situation in this province it is only an illusion, a dead letter, a cheat, and is productive of no real advantage. Our government professes to be immeasurably superior to a despotism, but of what use are the frequent relations with the people of which the administrators of our government boast, if instead of ascertaining

5

the wishes of the people with the intention of fulfilling them, they use the Representative system merely as a blind, and having learned the tenor of public opinion ignore it, and govern in their own selfish interests?

In our government these frequent relations with the mass of the people take place periodically by means of elections, daily by means of petitions, annually through the mediation of the Representatives, who are an integral part of the government, and at the same time, an organ and a voice for the people. Their decisions ought to be adopted, except in singular cases where it is evident that they are counter to the wishes of the majority of their constituents. The nearer the other authorities,—the Legislative and Executive Councils—come to the views and the desires of the representative body in our constitutional government, so much the more exactly do they move in conformity with the laws of their nature and so much the more accurately do they correspond to the end, and approach the scope, of their institution. On the other hand, in proportion as they are indifferent or opposed to the wishes of a representative body true to its constituents, the more do they swerve from the purposes of their institution. In their abnormal course they threaten the political world with afflictions and disorders more real than those which our fathers feared in the physical world on the appearance of planets with whose devious courses they were unacquainted. History demonstrates that in England kings have been adjudged good or bad according to the degree of concord which prevailed between them

6

and the people's Representatives. If discord reigned the fault was attributed to tyrannical or incapable Princes, who desired to raise themselves above the laws.

If the House of Commons in England could receive the laws from its Kings, if it could be reprimanded by them with arrogance, it would never have become the admiration and study of other nations, and the model which they endeavoured to copy. The Representative system is becoming the desire of all civilized nations, because it promises to them a powerful lever to extirpate abuses; because it affords a popular efficacious action which penetrates into all the parts of administration, and influences, in a salutary manner, all its agents, from the Sovereign to the lowest officer, reminding them of their mission, which is to secure the peace and prosperity of nations. It seems as if republicanism and absolute monarchy will exist for them, at no distant period, only in the pages of past history, that the human race will be divided into two great classes: freemen, who will have representatives, and slaves who will have none, or whose representatives, instead of being counsellors of an executive power which ought to receive their advice with deference, will be vicegerents of a degraded people, who would allow their representatives to be insulted with impunity by men who (supposedly) are paid only on condition that they shall consult and procure the public welfare.

*   *   *   *   *   *

You see at present in Lower Canada, Legislative and Executive Councillors treating the electors with an exaggerated and hitherto-unpractised courtesy, venting an extreme rudeness of old standing against the Representatives, very busy, running about, agitating, strutting, stirring and torturing both themselves and yourselves, in order to decide your choice according to their wishes. Those gentlemen are familiar with only the smallest portion of the English constitution, and that portion the least applicable to the state of this country. They adopt that part which relates to the splendour and privileges of Royalty and Aristocracy, though our Sovereign and his nobles are little inclined to settle amongst us; but ignore the enactments upholding the privileges of the nation, although there is a people settled on these lands which sees a great deal less of real distance grounded on reason between the administrators and themselves, than exists in England between the administrators of the government and the people. Well, in England, the House of Commons having declared that the interference of the Lords in election is contrary to principle, the people are so tenacious of their rights, and so careful of their Representatives, that they would resent the intrusion of a lord who took an active and open part in the election. Here, in Lower Canada, the example set by our great personages has been followed by a retinue of great and little, high and low officers whom they draw after them and keep in chains.

This proposition I advance, and no man who has studied the situation will deny it, namely, that in no other part of the British Empire is it so essential as in this province, to find great independence and energy in the Representative body, because in that body alone can be found a counterpoise to the excesses of power concentrated in a small number of persons having for the most part no link of permanent interests with the country. When the same persons unite the legislative, executive, and judiciary powers in themselves, the abuses which they shall have committed in one of these capacities they are endowed with sufficient means to uphold in the other; and from abuses to abuses the laws would soon be powerless, unless there was an unceasing and fearless watch over them on the part of your Representatives.

WILLIAM LYON MACKENZIE

WILLIAM LYON MACKENZIE

1795-1861

THE moderate Canadian in full enjoyment of the privileges of self-government is inclined to minimize the debt which he owes to the great Canadian rebel, William Lyon Mackenzie, and to magnify his indiscretions. But a careful examination of all the circumstances connected with his career, will reveal the magnitude of his service to Canadian constitutional development, and will soften the memory of his faults.

Gifted with a keen intellect, an indomitable will, high personal courage, and an extraordinary reserve of energy, Mackenzie was destined to play an important part in the life of a young colony, which stood in urgent need of strong men, and from his arrival in Canada in 1820, until his death forty-one years later, his history is interwoven with the development of the province.

When Mackenzie left Scotland to make his fortune in Canada, the "Family Compact" of Upper Canada was at its zenith. The corruption and favouritism which held sway under this narrow oligarchy paralyzed the efforts of would-be reformers, and to Mackenzie, with his constitutional hatred of tyranny

13

and injustice, this was intolerable. He had come to Canada for purely business reasons, but indignation at the behaviour of the Compact, and sympathy for the struggling party of Reform drew him into the crux of the situation and kept him there for the remainder of his life.

In 1824 he established *The Colonial Advocate* to espouse the cause of self-government, and to protest against the attitude of the existing government. For ten years he continued its publication in the teeth of violent opposition and at a financial loss, uniting the scattered ranks of Reformers, and crystallizing the principles of Reform.

At first his statements were moderate in the extreme, for in spite of his defect of temper he honestly strove to preserve a calm and judicial attitude in his criticism. But the repeated acts of violence, and the bitter rejoinders of his adversaries, drove him to an intemperance of speech which widened the breach between the opposing parties and made reconciliation impossible.

In 1828 he entered the Legislative Assembly, determined to break the back of the Family Compact. In the Assembly he continued the spirited criticism of the Government which he was conducting simultaneously in his journal, and infuriated his political foes by this double attack. During his short parliamentary career he was expelled three times from the Assembly on various pretexts of libel, though his electorate was almost unanimous in his favour.

In 1832 Mackenzie went to England as the bearer of petitions by the Reformers of Upper Canada, seeking redress of the most glaring evils practised by the Executive. During his stay in England he drew up several detailed reports of the colony which were valuable in throwing light upon Canadian affairs, of which the Imperial Government had a very superficial knowledge. He interested several influential English statesmen in the sufferings of the Colony, and obtained a number of concessions from the Colonial Secretary.

When he returned to Canada in 1833 it was with renewed hope for the future, but, unfortunately, a new Colonial Secretary had been appointed, who cancelled all the concessions granted by his predecessor. Yet Mackenzie did not despair, and in 1835 he made another attempt to enlist British sympathy for Upper Canada, by sending to the Imperial Government a detailed report of the chief grievances and recommendations as to means of their removal.

As a result of this report, Sir Francis Bond Head was sent out to Upper Canada, with instructions to adopt conciliatory measures. Instead he decided upon a policy of repression, controlled the elections to secure a Tory majority, and having adopted this high-handed method, lacked both the strength and the intelligence to carry it through. His conduct drove Mackenzie to desperation. Balked of a seat in the Assembly, his party completely blocked in their efforts to reform the administration, he became convinced of Great Britain's apathy to the wrongs of her colony, and determined to resort to arms.

During the course of the rebellion which he had so largely instigated, he was obliged to seek safety in flight, for a price was on his head, and with great difficulty he made his escape to the United States. Here he renewed his agitation for the independence of Canada, and his efforts met with some response. He was arrested, however, on a charge of violating the American Neutrality Act, was tried, found guilty, and spent a term of eighteen months in prison. On his release he struggled against ill-health and poverty to support his family, and realized the unalloyed bitterness of an exile's lot. In 1849 he was pardoned by the Imperial Government, and returned to Canada where he spent the remainder of his life.

He again entered political life to find that the principle for which he had suffered so keenly—Responsible Government—was firmly established, and the credit given to Baldwin and LaFontaine. The experiences of his life had cast his mind in such a radical mould that he lost sympathy with all but the extreme wing of the Reform party which had once idolized him, and he remained a tireless critic of the Government to the end. He died in 1861, worn out by poverty and the hardships of his career.

It is difficult to estimate the exact share of credit due to William Lyon Mackenzie in the constitutional development of Canada, for after the rebellion Baldwin and LaFontaine took up the thread of Reform, and with a moderation of which he was incapable, wove it gradually into the fabric of Responsible Government. But had it not been for Mackenzie's courageous opposition to the principles represented by the Family Compact, and the powerful impetus that he gave to the cause of Reform, the task of

enjoy with the evils of which you complain, and readily admit that your lot even as contrasted with that of your most favoured neighbours is not that of misfortune or which justifies discontent. But, although no human institutions are without imperfections, the blessings enjoyed by the inhabitants of this fine country should not be adduced as a reason why they should remain satisfied with real grievances which can and ought to be removed.

I earnestly entreat you, Brother Reformers, to rouse yourselves, using every exertion until the elections are completed in order to secure throughout the province true and faithful representatives, men who would unite with the present enlightened government of Great Britain in spreading far and wide the elements of useful knowledge, men who would combine and direct the physical energy of the people to purposes of general and individual usefulness, men who would hold no fellowship with those misguided legislators who in the late Legislative Council and Assembly insulted their Sovereign and reproved his Ministers for harkening to your petitions and desiring favourably to entertain your just complaints.

To the resident land-owners of Upper Canada, the lords of the soil, the men who seek for themselves and their children enduring tranquillity, free institutions, just laws well administered, I would say that unless they unite in securing the election of men of other principles than have hitherto formed the majorities in the Upper Canadian Parliament, they will assuredly sacrifice their children's best interests. Unless a Legislature elected by the freeholders have the control of the public lands and the whole revenue raised from the people, with the power to enact laws of general utility and to repeal statutes found inconvenient, this fine country cannot flourish as it otherwise would. To obtain that control and that power the Executive Council must be removable at the will of the House of Assembly, and the Governor bound to consult them as his constitutional advisers agreeable to British usage; and the authority hitherto exercised in Downing Street of granting large sums of money belonging to the people of Upper Canada without their consent, to purposes they would not sanction, withdrawn. There is good reason to believe that if you elect an intelligent and patriotic House of Assembly all or nearly all of these points will be conceded and it is well known that the British Government is as much opposed to the establishment or continuation of the temporal supremacy of any one class of religious teachers in Canada as the most steady reformer among you.

Under the protection of Great Britain, this Province may arrive at a very great height of prosperity. It is an advantage to have our imports and exports clogged with as few duties as possible at Quebec, and to be under the wing of an old, a rich and powerful nation, able and willing to protect and encourage our trade and agriculture. We cannot be independent. Three hundred thousand settlers, thinly scattered over a vast extent of territory and far distant from the sea, could not possibly set up for themselves, and even if they could it would be an expensive and hazardous experiment. Who would protect their foreign trade? Who would guard their immense frontiers? How could they secure a free navigation of the St. Lawrence? But England will throw no obstacle in the way of the settled population if they will but use the power they have to select an honest and capable domestic legislature with whom her present enlightened government can act in concert for the general good.

The chief cause or origin of the grievances which retard the progress of this colony is the power given to successive Secretaries for the Colonies to exercise an undue influence in our domestic affairs. Until now these Secretaries have been free from the control of public opinion in England, and even at this day, when a reformed parliament can check their errors, they may at four thousand miles distance commit many fatal mistakes in directing by deputy the energies of a country few of them ever saw or ever expect to behold.

It is they who appoint our Executive and Legislative Council—it is they who grant places, pensions, sinecures, lands and reserves—it is they who give monopolies to land companies—it is they who direct the expenditure of our land revenue—it is they who select our military governors—it is they who tell us we must pay a chaplain of the House of Assembly a salary to the day of his death for praying, even although we do not employ any person in that capacity —it is they who threw the war losses debt on our shoulders by refusing to apply the land revenue to its liquidation—it is they who, after declaring the principles of the Upper Canada Commercial Bank charters unfit for the colony, sanctioned institutions which they admitted were built on foundations inconsistent with the permanent interests and future welfare of the people.

When I was in England the leading men there freely admitted that a Colonial Minister could not wisely direct our internal concerns—that he would have to be guided by the governor who acts as his agent here and that as the people here cannot control that governor he in his turn would have to yield to the wishes of his advisers. This system Mr. Hume justly terms a baneful domination, and although he detested the arbitrary acts of Mr. Stanley he now comes forward to acknowledge his conviction that if the freeholders of Upper Canada are ready to do their duty at the ensuing elections they will find Mr. Stanley's successor both able and willing to do his.

Up, Brother Reformers! organize committees; appoint canvassers; call meetings; put forth your strength in a good cause, and manifest at the hustings that to you the peace and prosperity of Upper Canada are dear. Be diligent, untiring, faithful and watchful—bring up your brethren who are unable to walk to the polls—cheer the hearts of the downcast—confirm the wavering—and let the frowns of honest men abash every mercenary hireling. Vote for no man whose conduct in private and public life is not above suspicion, and inquire with due diligence before you give your suffrages. Do all this in the strength of that God who has implanted feelings of love and pity and compassion in your breasts towards your brethren—who has the destiny of empires in His hands—and who will in His good time deliver this beautiful land from the thraldom of wicked and ambitious men, if its inhabitants truly and sincerely porform their duties, actuated by principles and with a single eye to the welfare of their country.

ROBERT BALDWIN

ROBERT BALDWIN

1804-1858

CANADA'S debt to Robert Baldwin is immense. Canadians to-day may well pay homage to the memory of this great patriot, who, without compromising his reputation for honesty, humanity and moderation, fought and won one of the most memorable campaigns in history—the fight for Responsible Government—nobly dedicating his life to this great cause, and dying, old and exhausted, in the prime of life.

Robert Baldwin was born in 1804, at "Muddy York." The son of an ambitious Irishman, who combined in his person the triple offices of doctor, lawyer and schoolmaster, he was himself destined, though devoid of intellectual brilliance, to climb to a high place in the young colony, through sheer industry and perseverance.

After a creditable career in Grammar and Law Schools, he was called to the Bar in 1825 and practised law successfully until the political distresses of his country drew him into the parliamentary ranks to make his great stand for Government by the People.

Baldwin's political career covered a period of twenty years—a period most significant in the development of Canadian history. As early as 1836 he had become the recognized leader of Reform in Upper Canada, and he was offered a seat in the Executive by the Governor-General, Sir Francis Head, a position which he declined when he divined the governor-general's motive, which was to pacify the Reform party without yielding to their demand for the responsibility of the Executive to the majority of the people.

In 1841 he was again appointed to the Executive Council, and again resigned because he refused to compromise himself or his party on the question of Ministerial Responsibility, but from his position as a member of the Legislature he brought his influence to bear on the question, and, together with LaFontaine, his colleague from Lower Canada, forced the Government to define its attitude toward Responsible Government, and, subsequently, to resign.

In 1842, Sir Charles Bagot, the new Governor-General, having diagnosed the political situation correctly, acceded to the demands of the Reformers, and invited Baldwin and LaFontaine to form a ministry, on the principle of Responsible Government, and though its career was brief, this first Baldwin-LaFontaine administration deserves lasting recognition as the first real cabinet in Canadian history fashioned on the British system of popular control of the Executive.

In 1843, Sir Charles Metcalfe, Bagot's successor, came to Canada, resolved to nip the career of Responsible Government in the bud, and from the outset a series of battles royal ensued between the determined governor, and his equally determined ministers. In a few months the position of Baldwin and his colleague became intolerable, and they resigned, as a protest against the unconstitutional actions of the Governor-General.

Then began a struggle of prodigious importance into which both sides poured all the fervour and energy which they possessed. Baldwin was the leader in Upper Canada of the agitation against Metcalfe, and spared no effort in the cause of Reform. He delivered many striking speeches throughout the province, bravely holding up his head amid the sneers and accusations of his enemies, and fighting with a gentleman's weapons the battle against prejudice and reaction.

The arrival of Lord Elgin in 1847 terminated the long battle of the Reformers against the Government, and with his advent the victory of Responsible Government was assured. Baldwin and LaFontaine were invited to form a second ministry, and this administration, which was known as the " Great Ministry," signalized the ultimate triumph of the principle for which Baldwin had given his life.

The new ministry entered on a crusade against the reigning evils—economic, educational, judicial and political, and to Robert Baldwin is due great credit for the initiation and careful preparation of many prominent measures, chief among which was the Municipal Act of 1849, which carried the principle of self-government to the smallest unit of the state.

Having achieved the boon of self-government, the extreme wing of the Reform party was not content, but sought more radical changes. Baldwin, an enthusiastic admirer of British institutions, lost sympathy with the extreme wing of his party and, in 1851, resigned from the head of the ministry, proving himself, by this action, a disinterested and consistent disciple of Ministerial Responsibility to the last. He had accomplished the end for which he had striven, and seven years later he died, worn out by his unselfish devotion to his country.

Robert Baldwin has been termed "the man of one idea" and to the tenacity with which he clung to this idea is due in great measure the political freedom of Canada to-day. Without outstanding gifts of oratory, intellect or social charm, his unassuming and kindly manner, deep sincerity and strength of conviction carried him to a high place in the regard of his countrymen, and won for him the well-deserved title of "a political saviour."

Robert Baldwin

RESPONSIBLE GOVERNMENT

ROBERT BALDWIN

Delivered at the first meeting of the Reform Association of Canada, in Toronto, on March 25th, 1844.

I FEEL particularly gratified at the honour which has been conferred upon me in calling upon me to preside at the First General Meeting of the Reform Association of Canada, because it affords the most unquestionable evidence that in your opinion I have proved myself the firm and uncompromising friend of that great and vital principle of British Constitutional Liberty which it is the great object of the Association to support ; and because it shows that, while exerting yourselves to insure your country the practical application of that great principle to the administration of all our local affairs, you have repudiated the ungenerous cause of casting by the men who had stood firm to that principle through evil report and good report, in the darkest hour of our country's history ; when the doing so was denounced in the highest quarters as incipient treason, as well as when emerging from the cloud of calumny, in which interest and ignorance and despotism had for a time succeeded in enveloping it, this great and truly British principle shone forth in all the splendour of its native truth and excellence, under the expressed sanction of one of the brightest ornaments of the proud aristoccracy of the Mother Country, and the specially-appointed High Commissioner and Representative of the Sovereign herself. I refer to Lord Durham.

It affords me also the opportunity of giving expression, in the most unequivocal manner, to my entire approval of the Association; and no exertion, on my part, I can assure you, shall be wanted to forward its object, and make the organization you have recommended as effectual as possible ; and I most earnestly recommend to all who value the principles of the British Constitution, and to whom the preservation of the connection with the Mother Country is dear, to lend your aid by joining such an organization. For, depend upon it, the day will come when one of the proudest boasts of our posterity will be, that they can trace their descent to one who had his name inscribed on this great Roll of the contenders for Colonial rights.

Our objects are open and avowed. We seek no concealment, for we have nothing to conceal. We demand the practical application of the principles of the Constitution of our beloved Mother Country to the administration of our local affairs. Not one hair's breadth farther do we go, or desire to go; not with one hair's breadth short of that will we be ever satisfied. The nature and extent of the demand has never been better expressed than by the great Statesman to whom I have already alluded. Lord Durham, in his report to Her Majesty, has nobly vindicated the Reformers of the Province from the foul imputation which had been cast upon them, and I will trespass upon the meeting for a few moments, while I read a few extracts from that great Text Book of Colonial Rights: "The views," says his Lordship, "of the great body of the Reformers appear to have

been limited, according to their favourite expressions,
to the making of the Colonial Constitution 'an exact
transcript' of that of Great Britain, and they only
desire that the Crown should in Upper Canada, as at
home, entrust the administration of affairs to men
possessing the confidence of the Assembly."

And, after pointing out the nature of the evil, to
the existence of which he attributes the unsatisfactory
condition of the Province, he proceeds:—"It is not
by weakening but by strengthening the influence of
the people on its Government, by confining within
much narrower bounds than those hitherto allotted
to it and not by extending the interference of the
Imperial authorities in the details of Colonial affairs,
that I believe that harmony is to be restored where
dissension has so long prevailed, and a regularity and
vigour hitherto unknown introduced into the administration of these Provinces. It needs no change
in the principles of Government—no invention of a
new Constitution theory—to supply the remedy
which would, in my opinion, completely remove the
existing political disorders. It needs but to follow
out consistently the principles of the British Constitution, and introduce into the Government of those
great Colonies those wise provisions, by which alone
the working of the Representative system can, in
any country, be rendered harmonious and efficient.
We are not now to consider the policy of establishing
Representative Government in the Colonies. That
has been irrevocably done and the experiment of
depriving the people of their present constitutional
powers is not then to be thought of. To conduct

their Government harmoniously, in accordance with its established principles, is now the business of its rulers, and I know not how it is possible to procure that harmony in any other way than by administering the Government on those principles which have been found perfectly efficacious in Great Britain. I would not impair a single prerogative of the Crown; on the contrary, I believe that the interests of the people of the Colonies require the protection of the prerogatives which have not hitherto been exercised. But the Crown must, on the other hand, submit to the necessary consequences of Representative institutions, and if it has to carry on the Government in unison with a representative body, it must consent to carry it on by means of those in whom that representative body has confidence."

Then, after referring to the idle attempt of some to deny the applicability of this principle to a Colony, he proceeds:—"I admit that the system which I propose would, in fact, place the internal Government of the Colonies in the hands of the Colonists themselves, and that we should thus leave to them the execution of the laws, of which we have long entrusted the making, solely to them. I know not in what respect it can be desirable that we should interfere with their internal legislation in matters which do not affect their relations with the Mother Country. Nor can I conceive that any people, or any considerable portion of the people, will view with dissatisfaction a change which would amount simply to this:— that the Crown would, henceforth, consult the wishes of the people in the choice of its servants."

Robert Baldwin

For my part I have taken my stand upon the rock of the British Constitution, and I feel assured that whatever the difficulties are with which we may have to contend, and from whatever quarter they may come, ultimate success is sure to crown our efforts—but we want not only the Constitution, but as regards the administration of our local affairs, the whole Constitution and nothing but the Constitution. By the Constitution the Ministers of the Crown are responsible to Parliament for appointments to office, as well as for every other act of the Government—and was not one of the modes suggested by Lord Durham for carrying out his proposed change in the practical administration of Provincial affairs, though not the only nor the best one, "that the official acts of the Governor" should be "countersigned by some public functionary"? Does he not expressly deprecate as most injurious to the relations subsisting between the Colony and the Parent State the maintenance of a contest in order that a Governor or Secretary of State may be able to confer Colonial appointments on one rather than on another set of men in the Colonies? And, do not Lord Sydenham's Resolutions of 1841 most distinctly point out the express object of the constitutional necessities for the management of our local affairs, being conducted by and with the assistance, counsel and information of a provincial administration, under the head of the Government, to be for the purpose of affording a guarantee "that the well-understood wishes and interests of the people should, on all occasions, be faithfully represented and advocated"?

How can such wishes and interests be represented or advocated if those who are so to represent and advocate them are not to be consulted? And yet in the face of all this, with the very same breath that it is admitted that "appointments and proposals to make appointments" had been made without consulting his Ministers, the head of the Government is advised to declare that he had hitherto pursued the system of Responsible Government without deviation, and to profess his concurrence in the Resolutions of 1841. And a hope appears to be entertained that by a constant repetition of the assertion in the shape of answers to addresses, the people of Canada have so little of intelligence and so crude a notion of their rights that they will at least be persuaded to believe it.

I doubt not that the head of the Government has practised Responsible Government as the Governor-General has been pleased to interpret it—and of course being in his estimation a "yet undefined question" we cannot wonder if in preparing a definition for his own particular convenience he left a large margin for the benefit of that constitution which favoured the exercise of a practically irresponsible and despotic power. But I feel convinced that the people of this country are not such a set of children as to be satisfied with a mere bauble because it is called "Responsible Government." You have been contending for a substance not for a shadow. And the question for the country to decide, is whether we are in effect to go back to the old system under the new name, or whether we are to have Responsible Government in reality, as practically acted upon in the Mother

Country. "A rose," it was said, "by any other name would smell as sweet," and I will venture to say that the poppy would be equally disagreeable to the sense and equally deleterious in its effect, though dignified with the name of the Queen of flowers. If we are to have the old system let us have it under its new name, "the Irresponsible System," "the Compact System," or any other adapted to its hideous deformities; but let us not be imposed upon by a mere name. We were adjured with reference to this new-fangled Responsible Government in a style and manner borrowed with no small degree of care from that of the eccentric Baronet who once represented the Sovereign in this part of her Majesty's Dominion (Sir F. B. Head), "to keep it," "cling to it" and "not to throw it away." You all, no doubt, remember the story of little Red Riding Hood, and the poor child's astonishment and alarm as she began to trace the features of the wolf instead of those of her venerable grandmother. Let the people of Canada beware lest when they begin to trace the real outlines of this newfangled Responsible Government, and are calling out in the simplicity of their hearts, "Oh! Grandmother what great big eyes you have! Oh! Grandmother what a great big nose you've got!" it may not, as in the case of poor little Red Riding Hood, be too late, and the reply to the exclamation "Oh! Grandmother what a great big mouth you have!" be, "That's to gobble you up the better, my child!"

LOUIS LAFONTAINE

LOUIS LAFONTAINE
1807-1864

LOUIS LAFONTAINE will not soon be forgotten in French Canada. The romantic glamour which surrounds the memory of Papineau dims the milder lustre of his less picturesque countryman, but in the page of actual achievement, LaFontaine far outshines his eloquent rival. He possessed that sense of proportion which Papineau lacked and which, at all times necessary for high statesmanship, was indispensable in the critical period to which both men belonged.

At the beginning of his public career LaFontaine pledged himself to the cause of French nationalism in Canada, and throughout his life he was a jealous guardian of the privileges of his race. His patient endeavours to place Lower Canada on a basis of equality with Upper Canada, in language, laws and representation met with a success which was denied the agitations of more impetuous leaders.

He was a man of impressive personality, with keen mentality, an indomitable will, and a love of moderation which fitted him admirably for the position of leader of the Reform party in Lower Canada. His countrymen supported him with loyal enthusiasm, and relied on his ability to save them from the jaws of political extinction.

At first LaFontaine was a bitter opponent of Union, but when he saw that his efforts to avert it were hopeless, he resigned himself to the inevitable, and espoused the cause of Responsible Government as the one salvation of his race. With commendable wisdom he united with Robert Baldwin, the Reform leader of Upper Canada, and despite the radical differences of race and religion, the two Reformers worked harmoniously over a period of twenty years, demonstrating by their concerted action that a political union of two races was not impossible, and initiating the policy which remained the backbone of the Canadian political system until Confederation.

During the anxious years between the passing of the Union Act, and the final adoption of Responsible Government, the successive Governor-Generals sought to conciliate LaFontaine, who held Lower Canada in the hollow of his hand, by offers of various political sinecures, but he remained true to his trust and refused to sacrifice the interests of his race to private gain. He had one mission to perform,—the preservation of French nationality through the medium of Responsible Government—and he would accept no compromise which might impede or delay the realization of his aim.

In the two "LaFontaine-Baldwin" ministries he played an important part, effecting many badly-needed reforms in Lower Canada, and in 1849 introducing the Rebellion Losses Bill which established on a firm base the loyalty of French Canadians to the British Government.

When the triumph of Responsible Government was

assured, LaFontaine retired from political life, confident that his task was accomplished. French-Canadianism was a recognized factor in Canadian life, the privileges of his race were identical with those of British Canadians, and the successful workings of Responsible Government offered a security for the future.

Subsequently, as a jurist in Lower Canada, La-Fontaine won a reputation which rivalled his success as a politician, but it is for his great contribution to Canadian political development that his name will be longest remembered. He died in 1864 deeply lamented by a large following of both nationalities.

The study of history reveals the significance of personality in the shaping of great events. Had a statesman with LaFontaine's wisdom, tact and moderation not appeared at the crucial moment in Canadian politics, the union of the Canadas would doubtless have ended in disaster, and the history of Canada been radically changed. He succeeded in proving, for the guidance of future statesmen, that the union of two distinct nationalities was compatible with peace and harmony, and obliterated the dismal picture which Lord Durham had painted "of two races warring within the bosom of a single state."

FRENCH CANADA AND RESPONSIBLE GOVERNMENT

Louis LaFontaine

Delivered at Montreal, October, 1851, at a banquet given in his honour upon his withdrawal from public life.

TWENTY-ONE years ago, when I first entered upon political life, we were under a very different government. I refer to the method of its administration. We had a government in which the parliament had no influence,—the government of all British colonies. Under this government the people had no power, save only the power of refusing subsidies. This was the sole resource of the House of Assembly, and we can readily conceive with what danger such a resource was fraught. It was but natural that this system should give occasion to many abuses.

We commenced, therefore, our struggle to extirpate these abuses, to establish that form of government that it was our right to have and which we have to-day,—true responsible English government. Let it be borne in mind that under our former system of government all our struggles were vain and produced only that racial hate and animosity which is happily passing from us to-day, and which, I venture to hope, this banquet may tend still further to dissipate.

I hope that I give offence to none if, in speaking of the union of the provinces, I say that history will record the fact that the union was a project which, in the mind of its author, aimed at the annihilation of the French-Canadians. It was in this light that I regarded it. But after having subsequently ex-

amined with care this rod of chastisement that had
been prepared against my compatriots, I besought
some of the most influential among them to let me
make use of this very instrument to save those whom
it was designed to ruin, to place my fellow-countrymen in a better position than any they had ever
occupied. I saw that this measure contained in itself
the means of giving to the people the control which
they ought to have over the government, of establishing a real government in Canada. It was under
these circumstances that I entered parliament. The
rest you know. From this moment we began to
understand responsible government, the favourite
watchword of to-day,—it was then that it was understood that the governor must have as his executive
advisers men who possessed the confidence of the
public, and it was thus that I came to take part in
the administration.

For fifteen months things went fairly well. Then
came the struggle between the Ministry, of which I
formed part, and Governor Metcalfe. The result of
this struggle has been that you now have in this
country not merely the form of Responsible Government, but the spirit—indeed, the thing itself; the true
counterpart of the British Constitution. Power to-
day is in the hands of the people, who exercise a
salutary action on the Government; and a vote of
want of confidence in the Ministry passed by the
majority of the House of Assembly, will constrain the
Representative of the Crown to call other and more
popular men to his Councils.

Let us take a glance at the present Administration

—at what it has done. We see to-day united under it the different parts of the country; canals which cannot fail to be of immense advantage to the country's future. Has one measure which commanded the approval of the people been rejected by the Imperial Government or its representative in this Province, since 1848? No,—and this fact should convince you that there need be no more fears entertained for the fate of measures truly necessary and beneficial as in times past. The danger to-day is the facility with which we may legislate; and if we continue to disregard the possibility of the abuse which may arise from this power, your code will shortly become a labyrinth from which it will be difficult, when once you have entered it, to extricate yourself. But, if this be an abuse, it tends to prove my proposition that the popular will reigns, and that all measures proceeding from the people are well received . . .

I have said that the union was intended to annihilate the French-Canadians. But the result has been very different. The author of the union was mistaken. He wished to degrade one race among our citizens, but the facts have shown that both races among us stand upon the same footing. The very race that has been trodden under foot now finds itself, in some sort by this union, in a position of command to-day. Such is the position in which I leave the people of my race.

THOMAS CHANDLER HALIBURTON

THOMAS CHANDLER HALIBURTON
1796-1865

THE author of Sam Slick stands in the forefront of Canadian literary history. Unique in Canadian literature, "The sayings and doings of the Clockmaker" reveal a spontaneous humour and a profound philosophy of life. If Haliburton was not as Artemus Ward has said "The founder of the American school of humour," there is no doubt that he was "one of the shrewdest of humourists," and his writings both humorous and historical had a distinct influence on later American authors.

This brilliant writer, lawyer and politician was born in Windsor, Nova Scotia, in 1796. Educated at the Windsor Grammar School and Kings College, he became a member of the House of Assembly for Annapolis in the year 1826. His debates were naturally characterized by a tendency toward humour, but at times he was a forceful and effective speaker. It is said that on one occasion a youthful reporter, afterwards Nova Scotia's greatest orator, paused pen in hand, to listen to his eloquence. Thus the record of a memorable speech was lost.

In 1829 he was appointed Chief Justice of the Inferior Court of Common Pleas for the Middle Division of Nova Scotia, the youngest judge in that court. A justice of the Supreme Court in 1841, he came

49

closely in touch with all classes, and his experience gave him a keen insight into human nature. His writings are replete with allusions to the foibles and weaknesses of his countrymen. In 1856 he left his native province for England, where he lived for the remainder of his life.

He was always a strong advocate of imperialism and when in 1859 he became a member of the House of Commons for Launceston he thanked his electors "on behalf of four million of British subjects on the other side of the water, who, up to the present time, had not had one individual in the House of Commons through whom they might be heard."

Though a prophet in his own country he could not foresee that while he was urging imperial unity in the House of Commons, fifteen miles from his home in the village of Grand Pré was a boy who was to be the first colonial premier summoned to an Imperial Conference. Nor, when he defended the rights of the timber merchants of New Brunswick against an act which threatened seriously to injure their interests, could he foresee that a native of that very province would in 1922 become prime minister of England.

Author of the first history of Nova Scotia, creator of the inimitable Sam Slick, Judge Haliburton died at Isleworth on the Thames in 1865.

Thomas Chandler Haliburton

IMPERIAL FEDERATION

From an address at Glasgow, 1857.

MY object is to draw together in more intimate bonds of connection the two countries, to remove distrust, to assimilate interests, to combine the raw material of the New, with the manufacturing skill of the Old World, to enlarge the boundaries, to widen the foundations, to strengthen the constitution, and to add to the grandeur of the Empire. My object is to unite indissolubly the two parties of the Empire, so that there may be but one interest, one country with one constitution, one parliament, one language, one literature, one and the same monarch and one and the same great and glorious old flag, "that for a thousand years has braved the battle and the breeze." This is my object, and I trust it will be yours also, now, while it yet can be effected, ere separate interests, and the angry passions they engender, draw us asunder too widely and too rudely ever to admit of reunion.

The retention or loss of your colonies is, in my opinion, a question of infinitely more importance than all others put together. We have heard of justice to Ireland till we have caught the Irish accent, and more recently, with more reason, of justice to Scotland; but if you think I am going to raise the cry of "justice to the colonies," you are mistaken. We are able to do ourselves justice, and most assuredly will do so, when occasion requires. I come not here to threaten you, I know you too well for that, and I come not to supplicate you, for I am too much of a Scotchman, and too proud for that also. But I come to warn you, in sorrow, and not in anger, seriously, but amicably, that if there be not a change in the colonial policy of this Empire, the distant extremities will inevitably fall off from the body-politic, from their own unwieldy bulk and ponderosity.

Previous to the American Revolution, Dr. Benjamin Franklin visited this country, and warned the government that, unless its policy was more judicious and more conciliatory, it would lose the old colonies. His advice was unheeded and his prophecy was fulfilled. I do not pretend to compare myself with him; I have neither his talents nor his knowledge. But I know as much of the feeling of my countrymen as he did, and without any disparagement to him, I am infinitely more attached to this country than he ever was. For all my predilections are monarchical, and not republican. In like manner I now warn you that there are other subjects more important than the bombardment of Canton, the fall of Herat, or the establishment of the Danubian boundary. And first and foremost among them is the retention of British America. Don't mistake me, I am no agitator; I don't like agitation, even for a good object. I am not a man with a hobby to ride on perpetually—for such a person is a great bore; nor a man with a grievance, a character that is very troublesome; but a loyal colonist, very fond of his own country, enthusiastically attached to this, and an advocate for an intimate and indissoluble union of both. You may here say, as has often been said: "You have a responsible government; you manage your own affairs, what do you complain of?"

I shall answer this question, and I am happy to do so, here among practical, reflecting, thinking men, among men who will understand me when I do speak, and who, I am certain, will agree with me when they hear me. First, I say, we don't complain; and, secondly, we not only don't govern our own affairs, but have no voice in their management, and are not even consulted about them. I say we don't complain, and for two short reasons; first, we have nobody to complain to; and, secondly, if we had, we have no means of making ourselves heard. We have been told with much superciliousness by a noble Lord, who had the happy knack of embroiling himself with every colony in turn, that, "when we are ripe for independence, and desire it, no objection will be made to it." We are obliged to him for his permission, but assure him his consent is not required. He cannot accelerate it, or his insolence would long since have accomplished it; he cannot retard it, for no one values his opinion. Neither do we govern our own affairs; we manage our local matters, and there our power ends, as I shall show you. But if we don't complain, I shall tell you what we say. We say that our Eastern and Western provinces, together with our other foreign possessions, contain a population of one hundred millions of colonists, and that they are all unrepresented; that they are all so distinct and disjointed that England, in her hour of need, as lately in the Crimea, could draw no assistance in men or money from them, though they were able and willing to have contributed both; and that where this is the case, there is something wrong in the organization of the empire. We say that, in North America there are five colonies, covering a space larger than all Europe, unconnected among themselves, and unconnected with England, with five separate jurisdictions, five separate tariffs, five different currencies, and five different codes of laws; with no common bond of union, and no common interest; with no power to prevent the aggression of strangers, or of one on the other; no voice in the regulation of their trade, their intercourse with each other, with foreign powers, or with England. We say that our rights are bartered away without our concurrence, and without our knowledge; that recently a treaty, relative to the fisheries of Nova Scotia, was entered into with the United States, with no other notice to us than to choose delegates to attend and advise (the delegates were chosen, but were never asked to meet the Commissioner, and the treaty was signed without them), that the people were compelled to submit and adopt it, by a threat from the Americans that they would punish their refusal by discriminating duties. This was done in such haste that the fishery limits were left unsettled, and greater confusion and trouble has ensued than previously existed.

When Lord Ashburton ceded more than four millions of the best timber lands of New Brunswick, together with nearly 150 miles of the St. John, and a right of passage through the remainder of the River to the Ocean (also the best mail route to Canada), we think it not unreasonable that the people of the

Province should have had a voice in the arrangement
of the treaty, or the right, and the power to call
him to account in Parliament. We ask, if Canada
had had a representative in the House of Commons,
or delegates in the Colonial Office, whether Newfoundland would have been permitted to grant, as
it has done, a monopoly to an American company
for a European line of telegraph to her exclusion, so
that she must now derive her English news from New
York; or if Great Britain thinks proper to give a
permission of registration to Americans for their
vessels, without an equivalent, whether it is equally
right to grant a similar privilege to them in the
Colonies, without their consent, or in like manner to
grant them a coasting trade, without reciprocity in
their ports, whereby our commerce is crippled in a
way only intelligible to merchants. For instance,
an American steamer can leave Boston, with freight
and passengers for St. John, New Brunswick, touching
at all the intermediate ports of the States, but a
colonial vessel must proceed direct to her port of
destination, nor can she take freight from any port
or place on the Atlantic, to California or any port in
the Pacific, because that they interpret to be a coasting voyage. I stop not to enquire if this is right or
wrong, but it seems to be no more than decent, when
the rights of others are legislated away in this manner, that their concurrence should at least be asked.
It may be as well here to state what our neighbours
the Americans say, who never lose an opportunity of
sowing the seeds of disaffection among our people:—
"Why do you," they say, "continue in the degraded

position of a dependency to England, when you might become free and independent by joining us? Instead of having your territory ceded to others, your fisheries bartered away, and your rights denied or withheld, you would be protected and incorporated with us; you would return above a hundred members for Congress (you are not entitled to one in Parliament); you and your children would be eligible to the highest offices in our great nation (you are excluded from all in Great Britain); your real estate would be increased in value, and your commerce immensely enlarged, and you would at once take your place among the nations of the Earth; but there is no accounting for taste, bondage may have its charms, though we do not understand them," and so on. On all this I have but one observation to make, and it is this: an allegiance like ours, that neither neglect nor indifference can extinguish, nor reward nor ridicule seduce, would, in the estimation of any other Government under Heaven but that of England, be considered above all praise and beyond all price. In your turn, you may well say: "Do you put forward your bonfires, your illuminations and rejoicings at our success at Sebastopol (if success it was), and your legislative grants in aid of the compassionate fund, as a suitable contribution to the expenses of war?"

It is a reasonable and a rational question to ask, and there is an answer to it. An offer was made to raise two regiments in Canada, and conduct them to the Crimea, to be commanded by colonial officers, but to be, like others, under the command of the General-in-Chief, whoever he might be. The offer was returned from London unanswered—*it had been addressed to the wrong office.*

But I have done—I have stated to you a situation of affairs that cannot last. There are four remedies: First, Annexation to the States. Secondly, A Federal Union of the Colonies, a Colonial Board of Control, instead of the Downing Street Bureau, and what the Americans call Territorial Representation, that is Delegates in Parliament, to advocate colonial rights, and vote on them, and them only. Thirdly, Incorporation with Great Britain, and a fair share of full representation. Fourthly, Independence. Time forbids me to enter upon these topics: I submit them for your calm and deliberate consideration. The period has arrived when you and your colonists must take counsel together. All my wishes and my hopes point to a union between you, and my last words are *"esto perpetua."*

OLIVER MOWAT

OLIVER MOWAT

1820-1903

FIFTY years of disinterested public service have entitled Oliver Mowat to a prominent place on Canada's scroll of Fame. Whether as alderman, judge, cabinet minister, senator, premier or lieutenant-governor, his energies were devoted to the development of his country, and throughout his long career his reputation remained untarnished.

He was descended from the ancient family of Mowats of Caithness, Scotland, and was born in Kingston, Upper Canada, where his parents had settled in their youth. He was educated in private schools, carefully grounded in classics, and at the age of sixteen years entered the law office of John A. Macdonald, who was destined to become his political opponent.

In the crisis of 1837 young Mowat enlisted in the First Battalion of Frontenac Militia, and for a time it appeared as if the son were to inherit the political beliefs of his father, who was a Conservative by temperament and conviction. But politics attracted him little at this juncture, for he was absorbed in his legal studies, and as late as 1844 he refused to vote because of his avowed ignorance of the political situation in Canada.

In 1840 he came to Toronto to complete his legal education, and in the following year he was admitted to the Bar. His success was assured from the first, for besides his enthusiasm for his work he possessed accuracy of judgment, a clear, logical mind, and a strong, independent spirit. By 1854 he was one of the leaders in his profession, and his love of honesty and fair play increased the prestige which his ability had won for him.

As his legal success increased his interest in politics deepened, and he devoted his leisure to the study of the situation in Canada, weighing the merits of both parties with impartial judgment. Eventually he decided that the ideals of the Reform party were more conducive to the development of Canada, and, consequently, he attached himself to George Brown and his followers. In 1857, after a year of municipal service as a preface to public life, he entered the Legislature, upholding, as did his more explosive leader, the principles of "representation by population" and "free non-sectarian education." He became a power among the Liberals, and at the Reform Convention held in 1859 to seek a panacea for the ills which beset the government, he made a memorable speech in favour of Federal union, as opposed to Legislative union. This meeting was the tiny mustard seed out of which the mighty tree of Confederation evolved.

In 1863 he joined the Cabinet as Postmaster-General, and, again after the deadlock occurred, resumed his portfolio in the Brown-Macdonald Cabinet which was formed in 1865 to support Confederation. He was one of the so-called Fathers of Confederation, and although absent from the Charlottetown Conference, was an important figure at the Quebec Convention, where he stood up manfully for provincial autonomy and opposed John A. Macdonald's demand for centralization.

Just before the dawn of Confederation he retired from politics to accept the Vice Chancellorship of Upper Canada, a position for which he was well fitted with his fairness and soundness of judgment, and which he held until 1872, when he left it to assume the Premiership of Ontario.

During his long term of office as Premier, Ontario made remarkable progress. His industry was unremitting, and he fathered many valuable reforms which set the pace for the other provinces. Roads were built, public buildings erected, education and immigration were encouraged, and hosts of other valuable measures were introduced. But it was for his stoic defence of provincial rights, when Sir John Macdonald made repeated attempts to encroach on provincial autonomy, that he deserves lasting credit. In eight famous cases the Privy Council decided in Mowat's favour, and an enduring recognition of provincial rights was secured.

In 1896 the Liberal Party came into power at Ottawa, and Mowat resigned the premiership on Laurier's appeal for support. He entered the Liberal Cabinet as Minister of Justice, but after a year of hard work, decided that his new duties were too strenuous for his impaired vitality, and accepted instead the Lieutenant-Governorship of Ontario, in which office he died in 1903.

Sir Oliver Mowat was a strong Imperialist and

vigorously opposed the Annexation movement which had found favour in some quarters. He was not a bigoted party man for he weighed every political measure with impartial judgment. It was only natural that a man of his moral fibre should prefer the blunt honesty of George Brown and Alexander Mackenzie to the humorous blandishments of Sir John A. Macdonald, but apart from the individual characters of the Liberal leaders, he approved of the policy which the Reform party had adopted, and having made his decision, he stuck to it loyally. He was not an eloquent orator, and he often lacked the saving sense of humour which characterized Sir John, but his genuine ability, integrity, and sympathy won him the respect of Conservative and Liberal alike. At his death the mourning was universal and no one denied the aptness of the quotation which his subordinate and successor, George W. Ross, employed, to describe his public life:

"Not making his high place the lawless perch
  Of winged ambition, but through all that tract of
      years,
Wearing the white flower of a blameless life."

THE FAILURE OF LEGISLATIVE UNION

OLIVER MOWAT

*Delivered at the Reform Association, Toronto,
November 9, 1859.*

IT requires little to convince this assembly or the
people of this country that we can no longer delay
the making of some change in the constitution. The
feeling in favour of representation according to population has for some time been general, and there has
been an impression, as strong as any that ever was
formed, that if the Union is to continue in its present
form, that is the only principle that can be regarded
as just or equal. It is not because I have less zeal
for that principle than I have hitherto had, that I
now come forward to advocate a change in—or, I
should say rather, an addition to—the platform we
have assumed in the struggle now making in favour
of good government. The question has been put—
and it was right that it should be put—as to the
necessity which exists for making any such alteration.
We have fought long for representation according to
population, but we have discovered that it will take
a much longer time than many of us have supposed
to secure the recognition of that principle. It is
certain that there is the most resolute determination
on the part of Lower Canada to resist this demand;
and if we ask for dissolution pure and simple it will
take a long time to remove the obstacles thus presented. The only alternative is an appeal to the
Home Government; and we ought not to call upon
them unnecessarily. We may be driven to it, but

it should be the last resort. We must first try to settle our difficulties among ourselves. Again, it is doubtful whether the Home Government would interfere to give us representation according to population till after a long continued application; and in the meantime what are we not enduring? If we were only well governed by Lower Canada; if she gave us good laws, such as we desire, we might bear with the power she has of preventing us from making such laws for ourselves—we might afford to wait. But she does not do so. The Lower Canadians impose upon us laws which we do not want. The legislation of the last two years has been legislation directed against Upper Canada, and in favour of Lower Canada.

It is plain that if we desire the interests of this country, if we wish to secure ourselves against bankruptcy, we must look out for some other measure than representation according to population in order to obtain relief.

Is there, then, a shorter method to obtain those rights of which for some time past we have been deprived? That is the question to be decided. Before the period of Responsible Government there was a state of things in this country which no free people would endure. I do not sympathize with those who tried to alter it by force, but I do feel that when an eminent English statesman said our Government was one for which, had he lived under it, he would not fight, the state of things must have been very deplorable indeed. But let us ask ourselves if our present condition is not worse than that of which

Lord Sydenham made the observation I have quoted,
—when the country was ruled by the Family Compact; when the legislation desired by the majority of
the people and of their representatives was checked
by a party with whom the people did not sympathize, and when the Executive Government was
in the hands of that party. I ask if the state of
things which now prevails is not still worse? It is
true that we were not then ruled by the majority,
but by the minority; but, after all, it was an English
influence which prevailed. Our affairs were controlled by those who should not have managed them;
but at least they were controlled by men living among
ourselves, brought up as we were, understanding our
language, reading our newspapers and to whose
minds we had access through these and through our
speeches. But those who rule us now are of another
language, another race, another country; knowing
nothing of Upper Canada, with other views, other
sympathies and other interests. Is there any comparison between the condition of things then and
now? If, in the minds of English statesmen—with
whom, however, I do not agree—there was enough to
induce them to say that men were justified in resisting
then, what are we to say of our condition now?

Our remedy, however, is a constitutional one; but
we do right to remember and reflect upon the evils
that we suffer in order that we may not be heedless
of the remedy. As freemen we cannot help loving
liberty, and what we have to do is to see whether by
constitutional means we may not obtain the reform
of our grievances, and that by a course shorter than

the one which we have hitherto been following.
Without going into all these evils and remedies, I
will say a word or two here of the two remedies between
which I believe Upper Canada is now hesitating,
namely: a separation from Lower Canada at all haz-
ards, or a separation which would continue the connection for some purposes with freedom from its controlling influence in regard to others. As to a
dissolution of the Union pure and simple there are
immense difficulties. There are the geographical relations of the two provinces, the tariff, the navigation
of the St. Lawrence, and the debt, all to be arranged.
If the relations between the two provinces before the
Union created bad feeling, the antagonism of that
day would be greatly magnified now, when we possess
public works not then in existence, and when the
population, wealth and trade of Upper Canada are so
enormously augmented. Is it likely that all these
things can be arranged in any reasonable time?
There are doubtless many in Lower Canada who, notwithstanding their favourable position, are in favour
of a repeal of the Union; but they simply desire a return to the former state of things. There is no like-
lihood of the majority in that part of the country
consenting to the necessary arrangements within a
time shorter than would be requisite even to obtain
representation by population; and, of course, without
violence, there is only one other method than persuasion, and that is by means of an appeal to the Imperial Government. But every one who has studied
the feeling of the British people, or the dealings of
the British Government with this country, must be

satisfied that that Government will not like the Union to be repealed. Its repeal will certainly take a long time. I am not satisfied that it can be accomplished at all.

But supposing the dissolution of the Union to be that desirable thing at which we should aim, is not the shortest way to accomplish even that, the obtaining in the first instance of this federation, which will be more easily carried? The statesmen of England are not opposed to federation in the Maritime Provinces, and they will therefore not be against it here. There is also strong reason to think that Lower Canada is prepared to favour the scheme; for though the Lower Canadians have the power now, they feel that the unjust exercise of it may come home to them; that the more they abuse their power now, the more we may be disposed to retaliate when we shall have the power in our hands. Federation will vest the local government of each part of the two provinces within itself, so that we may get by it all the advantages of dissolution without its difficulties. As to the subject of expense, there can be no doubt that in Upper Canada, at least, the federal system will be much cheaper than the present one; and, on the whole, looking at the two systems together, and even regarding them from the point of view taken by those who are in favour of dissolution, I can see no objection whatever to the federation now proposed.

JOHN A. MACDONALD

JOHN A. MACDONALD

1815-1891

AT no period in Canadian history has personality been such a potent force as in the movement for Confederation. Strong men of widely divergent temperaments upheld the cause of union in the various provinces, but without the welding power exerted by Sir John A. Macdonald Confederation would have been impossible. With his genial common sense, tact and immense personal magnetism, he united the varying elements in the struggle and converted into reality the dream of visionaries throughout British North America.

John A. Macdonald came from Glasgow in 1820, with his parents, and received his education at Kingston where the family settled. He studied law, was called to the Bar in 1836, and practised successfully until he was drawn into politics in 1844. He entered the legislature as Conservative member for Kingston, and represented this constituency for over forty years.

At the beginning of his political career he was conservative in the extreme, and sympathized with the "Family Compact" in Upper Canada, even taking up arms against the rebels in 1837. Throughout his life he was slow to adopt new policies, but when convinced of the wisdom of a proposed measure, was resolute in its execution. Nor was he a narrow partisan, for he recognized genius in the ranks of his opponents, and united with men of opposite politics to secure the achievement of his aims.

In 1847 Macdonald entered the Cabinet under Draper, and by 1854 became, with Cartier, the dominating force in the Ministry. Their influence was effectual in securing the abolishment of Seigniorial Tenure in Lower Canada, and the secularization of Clergy Reserves in Upper Canada. Macdonald consistently upheld the French and Roman Catholic interests, and came into open conflict with George Brown, who was the special champion of Upper Canadian and Protestant rights. In 1857 Macdonald became Premier, but despite his political genius, he was unable to avert the approaching deadlock, due to the opposing forces in the Legislature, and the crisis came in June, 1864.

George Brown suggested a scheme of federation as a solution of the difficulty, and Macdonald seized upon the plan with enthusiasm, agreeing to unite with his rival to ensure its success. A coalition government was formed which devoted itself to the task of confederation, and Macdonald became the leader of the movement.

He was a prominent speaker at the Charlottetown Conference, dominated the Quebec Conference, and introduced the measure in the Canadian Assembly, where it was passed, after a struggle, with a large majority. Throughout the dark days when the Maritime Provinces opposed the measure, his faith and good humour were unfailing, and in 1867, when the British North America Act was framed at a conference in London, Macdonald was recognized as the controlling power among the Fathers of the Confederation.

He was chosen as first Premier of the Dominion. and ably performed the task of reconciling the provinces to their new position. A less magnetic statesman would have found the task impossible, but Sir John's power to transform enemies to friends seldom failed him, and by 1872 the new Dominion was secure. He sought to cement the union by the construction of the Canadian Pacific Railway, but, always a Machiavelli in his politics, allowed his zeal to override his scruples, and was ousted from power by the resulting "Pacific Scandal" of 1873.

His buoyant nature could not be long suppressed, however, and, five years later, he was returned to office, his popularity as strong as ever, on the impetus of the National Policy. During his second administration the construction of the Canadian Pacific Railway was completed, and various legislative measures were passed which contributed to the development of the country. He remained in harness to the end, carrying his last election in 1891 by his personality alone and dying a few weeks later mourned by the nation which his magic had called into existence.

Imperialism was one of the strongest tenets of Sir John A. Macdonald's political creed, and throughout his life his imperialistic principles suffered no change. But his love for the Empire did not lessen his affection for the young nation which he had fostered into life.

Instead, it gave a broader significance to his nationalism. Indeed, the secret of his success as a statesman lay in the breadth of his views, and the great encompassing love of humanity and life which characterized this lovable, humorous, scheming, wholly-human veteran of Canadian politics.

THE ADVANTAGES OF CONFEDERATION

JOHN A. MACDONALD

*From his address introducing the Act of
Confederation, 1865*

THE colonies are now in a transition state. Gradually a different colonial system is being developed—and it will become, year by year, less a case of dependence on our part, and of overruling protection on the part of the Mother Country, and more a case of a healthy and cordial alliance. Instead of looking upon us as a merely dependent colony, England will have in us a friendly nation—a subordinate but still a powerful people—to stand by her in North America in peace or in war. The people of Australia will be such another subordinate nation. And England will have this advantage, if her colonies progress under the new colonial system, as I believe they will, that, though at war with all the rest of the world, she will be able to look to the subordinate nations in alliance with her, and owning allegiance to the same Sovereign, who will assist in enabling her again to meet the whole world in arms, as she has done before. And if, in the great Napoleonic war, with every port in Europe closed against her commerce, she was yet able to hold her own, how much more will that be the case when she has a colonial empire rapidly increasing in power, in wealth, in influence, and in position? It is true that we stand in danger, as we have stood in danger again and again in Canada, of being plunged into war, and of suffering all its dreadful consequences, as the result of causes over which we have no control, by reason of their connection. This, however, did not intimidate us. At the very mention of the prospect of a war some time ago, how were the feelings of the people aroused from one extremity of British America to the other, and preparations made for meeting its worst consequences!

Although the people of this country are fully aware of the horrors of war—should a war arise, unfortunately, between the United States and England, and we all pray it never may—they are still ready to encounter all perils of that kind, for the sake of the connection with England. There is not one adverse voice, not one adverse opinion on that point. We all feel the advantages we derive from our connection with England. So long as that alliance is maintained, we enjoy, under her protection, the privileges of constitutional liberty according to the British system. We shall enjoy here that which is the great test of constitutional freedom—we shall have the rights of the minority respected. In all countries the rights of the majority take care of themselves, but it is only in countries like England, enjoying constitutional liberty, and safe from the tyranny of a single despot or of an unbridled democracy, that the rights of the minorities are regarded. So long, too, as we form a portion of the British Empire, we shall have the example of her free institutions, of the high standard of the character of her statesmen and public men, of the purity of her legislation, and the upright administration of her laws. In this younger country one great advantage of our connection with Great Britain will be, that, under her auspices, inspired by her example, a portion of her empire, our public men will be actuated by principles similar to those which actuate the statesmen at home. These, although not material, physical benefits, of which you can make an arithmetical calculation, are of such overwhelming advantage to our future interests and standing as a nation, that to obtain them is well worthy of any sacrifices we may be called upon to make, and the people of this country are ready to make them.

We should feel, also, sincerely grateful to beneficent Providence that we have had the opportunity vouchsafed us of calmly considering this great constitutional change, this peaceful revolution, that we have not been hurried into it, like the United States, by the exigencies of war, that we have not had a violent revolutionary period forced on us, as in other nations, by hostile action from without, or by domestic dissensions within. Here we are in peace and prosperity, under the fostering government of Great Britain—a dependent people, with a government having only a limited and delegated authority, and yet allowed, without restriction, and without jealousy on the part of the Mother Country, to legislate for ourselves, and peacefully and deliberately to consider and determine the future of Canada and of British North America.

GEORGE BROWN

GEORGE BROWN

1818-1880

THE keynote of George Brown's character was sounded by an Edinburgh schoolmaster in the remark: "He is not only endowed with high enthusiasm, but possesses the faculty of creating enthusiasm in others." The deep imprint which he made subsequently on Canadian history is attributable to the zest with which he flung himself into the political affairs of his adopted country, and the kindred spark he roused in the breasts of his followers.

George Brown was born near Edinburgh in 1818, the son of a Lowland father and a Celtic mother. From his parents he imbibed a strong love of freedom and justice which found expression in his later struggles against negro slavery, clerical domination, and political tyranny.

In 1838 business reverses led the Browns to New York, where, a few years later, they established a magazine called the *British Chronicle*, for Scottish readers in the United States and Canada. In 1843 George Brown came to Canada to promote the Canadian circulation of the journal, and became keenly interested in the political situation of Upper Canada. As a result of this visit the Browns moved to Toronto and established the *Banner* in the interests of Presbyterianism and Self-Government.

By 1844 the *Banner*, avowedly non-partisan, was drawn into the political embroglio, and was reincarnated under the name of *The Globe*, a Liberal journal devoted to the cause of Responsible Government, and a staunch ally of Baldwin and LaFontaine. It grew rapidly in size and importance and throughout George Brown's life exerted a powerful influence on Canadian public opinion.

In 1851 George Brown made his début in the Legislative Assembly, as an advocate of the separation of Church and State, non-sectarian education, Reciprocity with the United States and a reform of parliamentary representation. Throughout his career he was a consistent adherer to his first principles, and spared neither time nor talents in seeking to convert them into laws.

His influence in the Assembly was marked from the outset. His honesty, courage and vigour won the confidence of his party, and by 1856 he was the recognized leader of the Liberals in Upper Canada. Later he became the very mouthpiece of Upper Canadian sentiment. He was energetic in behalf of the secularization of Clergy Reserves, and in the fight for religious equality. So strong was his opposition to clerical domination that he incurred the violent antipathy of the Roman Catholic body, and was regarded as the especial champion of Protestantism. He alienated the Conservatives of Lower Canada still further by his agitation for a reform of the representation, for to them the famous slogan "Representation by Population" meant the decline of French Canadian power in the Assembly.

Meanwhile, the political situation of United Canada grew more and more unstable. The interests of the two provinces were distinctly opposed, and deadlock threatened the administration. The leaders of the various factions vainly sought a solution of the coming crisis. Brown urged Representation by Population as the one way of escape, but Lower Canada, led by Cartier, refused his solution. His persistent efforts to secure justice for his province embarrassed the successive ministers beyond endurance, and hastened the political deadlock which made Confederation inevitable.

In the actual scheme of Confederation, George Brown played an important part. As early as 1859 he had advocated a federal union of the Canadas to overcome the obstacles raised by the less flexible legislative union, but the ministry rejected his proposal. On June 14, 1864, as chairman of a committee appointed to consider the difficulties connected with the government, he recommended a federative system applied either to the Canadas alone or to all the British North American provinces. On the same day the ministry resigned and the long-threatened deadlock arrived. Brown was asked to join a proposed Coalition ministry pledged to evolve a workable form of government for Canada, and in spite of the strong distaste which a man of his decided temperament must have felt in uniting with Sir John A. Macdonald, his lifelong enemy, and Sir George Cartier, his political rival of Lower Canada, he consented for his country's sake. Immediately the Coalition Government set on foot Brown's federative scheme, and he himself accelerated the movement with his customary impetuosity.

He was an impressive figure at the conferences held at Charlottetown and Quebec, and delivered many powerful speeches throughout the Provinces which carried conviction in their train. In the Assembly as well, he battered down arguments of the anti-unionists of whom his lifelong friend and co-worker, Antoine Dorion, was the leader. Finally, he represented Upper Canada at the Imperial conference held in London to frame the Confederation Act, and was foremost in the rejoicing over the success of the movement.

In 1867 he retired from the Assembly, and a few years later was appointed to the Senate, but except for his visit to Washington in 1873 in an unsuccessful attempt to renew the Reciprocity Treaty with the United States, his name figured no more in great political measures. In March, 1880, he was shot at the *Globe* office by a former employee, and he died a few weeks later, mourned by the entire province.

To-day George Brown is remembered chiefly as a Father of Confederation, and the founder of *The Globe*, but, great as these activities undoubtedly were, they claimed only a part of his unflagging vitality. He was actively concerned in every question relating to Canadian development, and supported with his many talents the cause of freedom in every branch of public life. Prison reform, temperance, the abolition of slavery in America, the development of the North West, education, farming—these and other reforms received a measure of his boundless enthusiasm. His fiery disposition and ingrained obstinacy often antagonized his fellow-workers, but the rugged honesty and large-souled generosity of the great Scotsman easily atoned for his faults, and made the name of George Brown prominent among the list of Canadian patriots.

THE UNION OF THE BRITISH NORTH AMERICAN COLONIES

GEORGE BROWN

From the debate in the Legislature, February 8, 1865

THE scene presented by this chamber at this moment, I venture to affirm, has few parallels in history. One hundred years have passed away since these provinces became by conquest part of the British Empire. I speak in no boastful spirit—I desire not for a moment to excite a painful thought—what was then the fortune of war of the brave French nation, might have been ours on that well-fought field. I recall those olden times merely to mark the fact that here sit to-day the descendants of the victors and the vanquished in the fight of 1759, with all the differences of language, religion, civil law and social habit, nearly as distinctly marked as they were a century ago. Here we sit to-day seeking amicably to find a remedy for constitutional evils and injustice complained of—by the vanquished? No, but complained of by the conquerors! Here sit the representatives of the British population claiming justice—only justice; and here sit the representatives of the French population, discussing in the French tongue whether we shall have it. One hundred years have passed away since the conquest of Quebec, but here sit the children of the victor and the vanquished, all avowing hearty attachment to the British Crown —all earnestly deliberating how we shall best extend the blessings of British institutions—how a great people may be established on this continent in close and hearty connection with Great Britain. Where, in the page of history, shall we find a parallel to this? Will it not stand as an imperishable monument to the generosity of British rule?

And it is not in Canada alone that this scene is being witnessed. Four other colonies are at this moment occupied as we are—declaring their hearty love for the parent state, and deliberating with us how they may best discharge the great duty entrusted to their hands, and give their aid in developing the teeming resources of these vast possessions. And well may the work we have unitedly proposed rouse the ambition and energy of every true man in British America. Look at the map of the continent of America, and mark that island (Newfoundland) commanding the mouth of the noble river that almost cuts our continent in twain. Well, that island is equal in extent to the kingdom of Portugal. Cross the straits to the mainland, and you touch the hospitable shores of Nova Scotia, a country quite as large as the kingdom of Greece. Then mark the sister province of New Brunswick—equal in extent to Denmark and Switzerland combined. Pass up the River St. Lawrence to Lower Canada—a country as large as France. Pass on to Upper Canada, twenty thousand square miles larger than Great Britain and Ireland put together. Cross over the continent to the shores of the Pacific, and you are in British Columbia, the land of golden promise—equal in extent to the Austrian Empire. I speak not now of the vast Indian territories that lie between—greater in extent than the whole soil of Russia—and that will ere long,

I trust, be opened up to civilization under the auspices of the British American confederation. Well, the bold scheme in your hands is nothing less than to gather all these countries into one—to organize them all under one government, with the protection of the British flag, and in heartiest sympathy and affection with our fellow-subjects in the land that gave us birth. Our scheme is to establish a government that will seek to turn the tide of European emigration into this northern half of the American continent—that will strive to develop its great natural resources—and that will endeavour to maintain liberty, and justice, and Christianity throughout the land.

The honourable member for North Hastings asks when all this can be done. The great end of this confederation may not be realized in the lifetime of many who now hear me. We imagine not that such a structure can be built in a month or in a year. What we propose now is but to lay the foundations of the structure—to set in motion the governmental machinery that will one day, we trust, extend from the Atlantic to the Pacific. And we take special credit to ourselves that the system we have devised, while admirably adapted to our present situation, is capable of gradual and efficient expansion in future years to meet all the great purposes contemplated by our scheme. But if the honourable gentleman will only call to mind that when the United States seceded from the mother country, and for many years afterwards, their population was not nearly equal to ours at this moment—that their internal improvements did not then approach to what we have already attained, and that their trade and commerce was not then a third of what ours has already reached—I think that he will see that the fulfilment of our hopes may not be so very remote as at first sight might be imagined. And he will be strengthened in that conviction if he remembers that what we propose to do is to be done with the cordial sympathy and assistance of that great power of which it is our happiness to form a part.

Such are the objects of attainment to which the British American Conference pledged itself in October. And said I not rightly that such a scheme is well fitted to fire the ambition and rouse the energies of every member of this House? Does it not lift us above the petty politics of the past, and present to us high purposes and great interests that may well call forth all the intellectual ability and all the energy and enterprise to be found among us? I readily admit all the gravity of the question, and that it ought to be considered cautiously and thoroughly before adoption. Far be it from me to deprecate the closest criticism, or to doubt for a moment the sincerity or patriotism of those who feel it their duty to oppose the measure. But in considering a question on which hangs the future destiny of half a continent, ought not the spirit of mere fault-finding to be hushed?—ought not the voice of partisanship to be banished from our debates?—ought we not sit down and discuss the arguments presented in the earnest and candid spirit of men bound by the same interests, seeking a common end, and loving the same country? Some honourable gentlemen seem to imagine that the members of government have a deeper interest in this scheme than others—but what possible interest can any of us have except that which we share with every citizen of the land? What risk does any one run from this measure in which all of us do not fully participate? What possible inducement could we have to urge this scheme, except our earnest and heartfelt conviction that it will inure to the solid and lasting advantage of our country?

THOMAS D'ARCY McGEE

THOMAS D'ARCY McGEE
1805-1868

THOMAS D'ARCY McGEE was born in 1805 in
Carlingford—one of the most picturesque spots in
Ireland. Gifted with a glowing imagination and an
ardent nature—both intensified, no doubt, by his
romantic surroundings—McGee possessed also the
proverbial Celtic fluency of speech. This happy
combination made him temperamentally fitted to
arouse others emotionally when he appealed to them
later in literature and in the legislature.

Emigrating to America he joined the Boston
Pilot, and soon rose to the co-editorship of it. His
articles were so clever that they attracted Daniel
O'Connell's attention to their author, and led to an
invitation to McGee to return to Ireland to give his
services to the Dublin *Freeman*. The offer was accepted but it was not long before the youth found the
limits put upon his ardour too circumscribed; so he
left the *Freeman* and united with Duffy and the host
of other brilliant young writers who thought to hasten
right conditions for their country by a more expedi-
tious means than O'Connell's slow but sure legislative
measures. It was first of all a literary movement
that these young Irelanders intended, and so they
aimed to publish a library of patriotic books, of which
McGee contributed two—"The Life of Art Mc-

Murrough" and "Irish Writers of the Seventeenth Century." But before long, their indignation burst into flame when English law was perverted, for the purpose of imprisoning O'Connell in 1844. Then followed conditions so bad that the famine of 1848 fanned the flame to gigantic proportions, culminating in the Confederation scheme and finally in an uprising.

It was a foolish rebellion—evident from the first—and McGee felt this, but as secretary of the Confederation he was commissioned to play a certain perilous part, which he did satisfactorily. Of course the uprising was discovered, quelled, and the leaders exiled,—McGee escaping to the United States, where he again took up work on the *American Nation*. This he made an organ of anti-English feeling.

In 1857 he took the advice of some Canadian friends who assured him of the urgent need of an Irish leader in Montreal. Here he edited a paper which he called *The New Era*—prophetically named in view of the developments of 1867. In spite of his earlier political follies, but not without strenuous opposition in some quarters, in view of his rebel reputation, McGee was returned as one of the three representatives for Montreal in the Legislative House in 1858.

McGee's attitude towards England underwent a gradual change due to Canada's happy colonial connection with the Mother Country. In his *New Era* he suggested a union of the provinces which his statesmanlike mind saw would spell security for Canada, especially in view of possible effects of the American Civil War upon the country. In his travels throughout what is now the Dominion of Canada he had seen the great possibilities for the united provinces, with a prospective railway to join them together, and so when in Parliament, Cartier, Macdonald, and the others were voicing the same opinion, in their advocacy of a federation, McGee went about the country making brilliant speeches on its advantages—speeches which, even now, charm the reader by their impassioned beauty and sincerity.

His generosity was almost limitless. It has been said that he delivered more than a thousand lectures during twenty years for charitable purposes; and that it is due to his exertions that night schools were established in New York.

Owing to McGee's denunciations of the Fenians who were stirring up strife in the New Dominion, one of them assassinated him in 1868 on his return home one night from the House of Parliament. His last speech—made that very evening—had embodied in it sentiments testifying to his nobility of soul; and his last letter, which had not yet reached its destination, was wending its way to Lord Mayo in Ireland, pleading for fuller rights for Ireland. That this letter led to the reforms which followed, we have Gladstone's own public statement.

The loss to Canada's literature by the untimely death of McGee cannot be measured, as with the prospect of release from political life he had hoped to give much time to writing, the character of which can be judged by the more than ordinary ability displayed in his histories, his speeches and his poetry, though these were written in the press of a busy life.

THE PRINCIPLE OF CONFEDERATION
Thomas D'Arcy McGee
Delivered before the Legislative Assembly, February 9, 1865.

I TRUST the House will permit me to say a few words as to the principle of Confederation, considered in itself. In the application of this principle to former constitutions, there certainly always was one fatal defect, the weakness of the central authority. Of all the Federal constitutions I have ever heard or read of, this was the fatal malady: they were short-lived, they died of consumption. But I am not prepared to say that because the Tuscan League elected its chief magistrates but for two months and lasted a century, that therefore the Federal principle failed. On the contrary, there is something in the frequent, fond recurrence of mankind to this principle, among the freest people, in their best times and in their worst dangers, which leads me to believe that it has a very deep hold in human nature itself—an excellent basis for a government to have. But, indeed, Sir, the main question is the due distribution of powers in a Federal Union—a question I dare not touch to-night. The principle itself seems to me to be capable of being so adapted as to promote internal peace and external security, and to call into action a genuine, enduring, and heroic patriotism. It is a principle capable of inspiring a noble ambition and a most salutary emulation. You have sent your young men to guard your frontier. You want a principle to guard your young men, and thus truly defend your frontier. For what do good men who make the best

soldiers fight? For a line of Scripture or chalk-line—
for a text or for a pretext? What is a better boundary
between nations than a parallel of latitude, or even a
natural obstacle?—what really keeps nations intact
and apart?—a principle. When I can hear our young
men say as proudly, "our Federation," or "our
Country," or, "our Kingdom," as the young men of
other countries do, speaking of their own, then I
shall have less apprehension for the result of whatever
trials the future may have in store for us.

It has been said that the Federal Constitution of
the United States has failed. I, Sir, have never said
it. It may be a failure for us, paradoxical as this
may seem, and yet not a failure for them. They have
had eighty years' use of it, and having discovered its
defects, may apply a remedy and go on with it eighty
years longer. But we also were lookers-on, who saw
its defects as the machine worked, and who have prepared contrivances by which it can be improved and
kept in more perfect order when applied to ourselves.
And one of the foremost statesmen in England, distinguished alike in politics and literature, has declared that we have combined the best part of the
British and the American systems of government; an
opinion deliberately formed at a distance, without
prejudice, and expressed without interested motives
of any description. We have, in relation to the head
of the government, in relation to the judiciary, in
relation to the second chamber of the Legislature, in
relation to the financial responsibility of the General
Government, and in relation to the public officials
whose tenure of office is during good behaviour in-

stead of at the caprice of a party—in all these respects we have adopted the British system; in other respects we have learned something from the American system, and I trust and believe we have made a very tolerable combination of both.

The principle of Federation is a generous one. It is a principle that gives men local duties to discharge, and invests them at the same time with general supervision, that excites a healthy sense of responsibility and comprehension. It is a principle that has produced a wise and true spirit of statesmanship in all countries in which it has ever been applied. It is a principle eminently favourable to liberty, because local affairs are left to be dealt with by local bodies, and cannot be interfered with by those who have no local interest in them, while matters of a general character are left exclusively to a General Government. It is a principle inseparable from every government that ever gave extended and important services to a country, because all governments have been more or less confederations in their character. Spain was a Federation, for although it had a king reigning over the whole country, it had its local governments for the administration of local affairs. The British Isles are a quasi Confederation, and the old French dukedoms were confederated in the States-General. It is a principle that runs through all the history of civilization in one form or another, and exists alike in monarchies and democracies; and having adopted it as the principle of our future government, there were only the details to arrange and agree upon. Those details are before you. It is not in our power to alter any of them even if the House desires it. If the House desires it can reject the treaty, but we cannot, nor can the other Provinces which took part in its negotiation, consent that it shall be altered in the slightest particular.

We stand at present in this position: we are bound in honour, we are bound in good faith, to four Provinces occupied by our fellow colonists, to carry out the measure of Union agreed upon here in the last week of October. We are bound to carry it to the foot of the Throne, and ask there from Her Majesty, that She will be graciously pleased to direct legislation to be had on this subject. We go to the Imperial Government, the common arbiter of us all, in our true Federal metropolis—we go there to ask for our fundamental Charter. We hope, by having that Charter, which can only be amended by the authority that made it, that we will lay the basis of permanency for our future government. What I should like to see is—that fair representatives of the Canadian and Acadian aristocracy should be sent to the foot of the Throne with that scheme, to obtain for it the royal sanction—a scheme not suggested by others, or imposed upon us, but one the work of ourselves, the creation of our own intellect and of our own free, unbiassed, and untrammelled will. I should like to see our best men go there, and endeavour to have this measure carried through the Imperial Parliament—going into Her Majesty's presence, and by their manner, if not actually by their speech, saying—"During Your Majesty's reign we have had Responsible Government conceded

101

to us: we have administered it for nearly a quarter of a century, during which we have under it doubled our population, and more than quadrupled our trade. The small colonies which your ancestors could hardly see on the map, have grown into great communities. A great danger has arisen in our near neighbourhood. Over our homes a cloud hangs, dark and heavy. We do not know when it may burst. With our own strength we are not able to combat against the storm; but what we can do, we will do cheerfully and loyally. We want time to grow; we want more people to fill our country, more industrious families of men to develop our resources; we want to increase our prosperity; we want more extended trade and commerce; we want more land tilled—more men established through our wastes and wildernesses. We of the British North-American Provinces want to be joined together, that, if danger comes, we can support each other in the day of trial. We come to Your Majesty, who has given us liberty, to give us unity, that we may preserve and perpetuate our freedom; and whatsoever charter, in the wisdom of Your Majesty and of Your Parliament, you give us, we shall loyally obey and observe as long as it is the pleasure of Your Majesty and Your Successors to maintain the connection between Great Britain and these Colonies."

CHARLES TUPPER

CHARLES TUPPER

1821-1915

CONSPICUOUS in the annals of Canadian history is the name of Charles Tupper who for a half century employed his great talents and prodigious energy in the service of his country. He lived to see the nation which he had helped into existence justify its claim to nationhood on the battle ground of Europe, and in the development of its national consciousness himself played a major part.

Charles Tupper came of Puritan stock, and inherited the dauntless courage of his ancestors. He was born in Amherst, Nova Scotia, in 1821, and received his elementary education in the local schools. But ambition prompted him to enter the medical profession, and, despite great obstacles, he obtained his medical education at Edinburgh, returning to assume the arduous duties of a country physician for twelve years.

In 1855 Tupper entered politics, defeating the popular idol, Joseph Howe, in the Cumberland riding. His rise was phenomenal, for at the outset he was offered the leadership of the Conservative party by the aged leader, J. W. Johnstone, and though he refused the nominal headship, he performed the actual work. In Opposition he poured an unremitting stream of criticism on the heads of the

Government, and in 1863, when his party triumphed at the polls, he became Premier of Nova Scotia.

Almost at once he set on foot a scheme to unite the Maritime Provinces, for he had long been an advocate of union. His proposal for a conference to facilitate the movement for federation resulted in the Charlottetown Conference, which was followed by the decisive one at Quebec. At both of these conventions he was a prominent figure, and an impetuous disciple of Confederation.

To him was entrusted Nova Scotia's share in the common struggle, and his task was singularly difficult. Nova Scotia, led by Joseph Howe, was almost unanimous in its opposition to union. But Tupper, like Lloyd George, gloried in a fight, and with his usual bulldog courage threw himself into the thick of the battle, braving the wrath of his countrymen,—confident of the outcome.

He dodged an impending election, kept the minds of the legislators occupied with other issues, and secretly made his plans. In 1866 he secured a vote for a conference with the Imperial authorities on a scheme of union more favourable to Nova Scotia than the Quebec Resolutions. The following year Confederation came into being, and the indignation of Nova Scotia was revealed very clearly at the first Dominion election. Tupper was the only union candidate returned for Nova Scotia, and the old battle was renewed with unrelenting fury in the new Assembly. In the midst of it Howe slipped off to England to seek the repeal of the Confederation Act, and Tupper, following, faced him there. He convinced him of the hopelessness of his mission, and urged his rival to join him in an attempt to convert Nova Scotia to union. At a great personal sacrifice Howe finally consented, and together they achieved the ultimate acceptance of the Confederation idea.

Tupper then applied his colossal energy to the task of national development. In 1870 he formulated the National Policy which was later adopted by the Conservative Party. He was invited to join the Dominion Cabinet, and became the moral support of Sir John A. Macdonald, defending him vigorously in the "Pacific Scandal" crisis, and persuading him to retain the leadership of his party, when the overwhelming criticisms, resulting from the Scandal, had sapped his self-confidence. During the second Macdonald administration, Tupper, in the capacity of Minister of Railways, initiated the policy pursued in the construction of the Canadian Pacific Railway, and by his unswerving faith in the wisdom of the undertaking helped to keep up the courage of the Government.

In 1884 Tupper disappeared from Canadian politics for a time, to accept the position of Canadian High Commissioner in England, but he responded to the urgent appeal of his party to accept the Premiership in 1896. He occupied the Premier's chair for a few weeks, at the end of which his party met with their long-threatened defeat, and he was driven into Opposition. He retained the leadership of the Conservatives until 1900, when he withdrew from public life, and spent the remainder of his days in England. He died in 1915, regretted by a large circle of friends in England, and by the entire Canadian nation.

Sir Charles Tupper was a distinct contrast to his rival, Joseph Howe. His self-confident manner, pugnacity and deadly earnestness contrasted unfavourably with the subtle humour, delicacy and charm of his poetic countryman. But "the Cumberland war horse" caught and held the vision of a greater nationality when his more magnetic rival was groping in the dusk of provincialism, and to him is due, in great measure, the ultimate triumph of Confederation.

THE NECESSITY FOR UNION—A PLEA FOR NATIONALITY

Charles Tupper

From a Speech on the Union of the Colonies, 1865

INSTEAD of looking to the Union of British North America as tending to weaken the bond of connection that binds us to the parent state, no one who reads the resolutions of the conference, but must see that there was placed in the forefront the principle that that bond should be strengthened, and that we should be connected with the parent state by a more indissoluble tie than ever before existed. I need not tell the House that these results have been submitted to the attention of the Imperial Government, and that the statesmen of England have looked upon them not as likely to separate these dependencies, but as the best means of uniting them more indissolubly to the crown.

I need not state that the same bond which exists between Canada and England—between Nova Scotia, New Brunswick and England, was determined upon when the scheme was contemplated that the Queen should place a Viceroy or Governor-General over these dependencies thus united, and the surest guarantee was given that the great object was to preserve the bonds that connect us with the parent state. And that view has been accepted not only by the government but by the people and press of England, and by statesmen in every quarter of the globe.

I have glanced at the more leading features connected with the constitution, and it will be perhaps desirable that I show what necessity there existed, and what ground there was for having this union. I have already called the attention of the House to the singular fact that rife as party feeling has been in this country—that strong as have been the divisions and lines of demarcation between existing parties—from the time the great question of union was first submitted to the notice of the legislature and people of this country, there has been an amount of unanimity of sentiment among all classes of public men of all parties, such as has never been exhibited on any other question. It is not singular that such should be the case when we look at our present position. Who is there who does not feel that the first principle of manhood imprinted in the breast of man is that the country with which he is connected should occupy a position of influence of which he need not be ashamed? Who is there with a spark of manliness in his bosom who does not feel that he has a right to be proud of his country in proportion to the position it occupies in the scale of nations? I need not tell the House that surrounded as we are by many blessings—owing fealty as we do to the first empire in the world—enjoying the protection of one of the greatest powers on the globe—having free institutions in all their entirety—possessing as we do peace and plenty—that we enjoy advantages for which we ought to be profoundly grateful; but I can discover no other cause why there has been so great a co-operation among all classes of intelligent people of our country in respect to a union of these colonies than the desire that possessing these advantages we should at the same time advance to a more national position and render our institutions more secure. Who does not feel mortified when he takes up the report of the discussion that recently took place in the Commons, and finds that although the subject under debate was the security of British America, yet the only one of the provinces that appeared to be known to British statesmen—that was deemed worthy of their notice—was Canada?

We have had evidence of the most positive and tangible character, both in Nova Scotia and New Brunswick, how insignificant is our position in the estimation of the parent state. What was the complaint when the Reciprocity Treaty was submitted to the House, that came from both sides? That the Imperial Parliament, in negotiating that treaty, had not thought it necessary to ask the opinion of Nova Scotian statesmen, although the great fisheries that surrounded this country were to be surrendered. Mr. Johnstone was invited by the Lieutenant-Governor, although in opposition at that time, to go in conjunction with Mr. Young to attend the meeting of delegates, for the purpose of considering the question. He found, however, that he was required to give his assent to what had been done already. Therefore, in the arrangement of a treaty so intimately affecting our interests, the views of not a single public man in Nova Scotia were considered worthy of attention, and I presume it was the same with New Brunswick.

Where was New Brunswick when a large slice was cut off from her territory, when the whole of

British North America was disfigured by the Ashburton Treaty? The opinion of a single statesman in New Brunswick was not asked.

The fact is, if we are known at all across the Atlantic, notwithstanding the immense resources of these Maritime Provinces, it is because we happen to be contiguous to Canada. Everything connected with our interests tells us of the insignificance of our position. Therefore it is not a matter of surprise, in view of these facts, and of the position we occupy, that the intelligent men of these Provinces have long since come to the conclusion that, if these comparatively small countries are to have any future whatever in connection with the crown of England, it must be found in a consolidation of all British North America. I regret that this harmony does not exist down to the present moment, but I am dealing with the position the question opened at the time these negotiations were going on.

GEORGES ETIENNE CARTIER

GEORGES ETIENNE CARTIER
1814-1873

GEORGES ETIENNE CARTIER, a descendant of the same family as the famous navigator, was destined to make the name twice famous in the annals of Canadian history. He was one of the ablest of French Canadian statesmen, supported by the British of his province as well as the French, and the chief influence in bringing Lower Canada into the Confederation in 1867.

Cartier was born in the village of St. Antoine, Quebec, on September 6, 1814. After the usual preliminary education, he began to practise law in Montreal in 1835, and by his tireless energy and industry quickly won prominence in his profession. He early became interested in politics and was naturally drawn into the rebellion of 1837. As a result he was obliged to live in seclusion for a time, and almost ten years elapsed before he again took any active part in public life.

He first entered parliament in 1848 and for the rest of his life was largely engaged in affairs of government. In 1858 he became joint-premier with Sir John A. Macdonald. Under their administration the first serious efforts were made toward a federal union and though they were defeated in the 1862 election, Cartier continued to speak and write unceasingly and convincingly in favour of Confederation. Finally he succeeded against the strongest opposition in carrying the scheme through his own province. He took an active part in the conferences that drew up the British North America Act of 1867 and the following year was awarded a baronetcy for his services.

In the first Confederation Cabinet Cartier was Minister of Militia. Though he still remained Quebec's foremost leader, his political influence began to decline and in the elections of 1872 his own country failed to support him. A Manitoban constituency then returned him to parliament but he never recovered from the mortification of the defeat. He died the following year.

Though he lacked many of the qualities that characterized the finest of his contemporaries, he was unexcelled in energy, knowledge of parliamentary strategy, and ability in contest, and he was most faithful in devoting his powers to the political and material advancement of his native province.

Georges Etienne Cartier

THE UNION OF THE PROVINCES
GEORGES ETIENNE CARTIER
From a speech delivered in 1865 in the Legislative Assembly

I DO not intend to enter into the details of the confederation project. I simply desire now to expose
the principal reasons which should induce members
to approve of the resolutions proposed by the Government. Confederation is, so to speak, a necessity for
us at this time. It is impossible to close our eyes to
what is happening on the other side of the line. We
see that there a government established not more
than eighty years ago has not been able to keep united
the family of states which shares that vast country.
We cannot hide from ourselves that the result of this
terrible struggle, the progress of which we all follow
with such anxiety, must affect our political existence.
We do not know what the result will be—whether this
great war will end by the establishment of two confederations or by the re-establishment of that which
has already existed.

It is for us to act so that five colonies inhabited by
people whose interests and sympathies are the same
shall form a great nation. The way is for all to unite
under a general government. The question reduces
itself to this—we must either have a confederation
of British North America or be absorbed by the
American Union. Some are of the opinion that it is
not necessary to form such a confederation to prevent
our absorption by the neighbouring republic, but they
are mistaken. We know that England is determined
to aid us, to support us in any possible struggle against

our neighbours. The English provinces, separated as they are at present, cannot alone defend themselves. We have duties to fulfil towards England; if we desire to obtain her support for our defence, we must help ourselves, which we cannot very well do without a confederation. When we are united the enemy will know that if he attacks any province, either Prince Edward Island or Canada, he will have to deal with the combined forces of the Empire. Canada, remaining separate from the others, would be in a dangerous position if war was declared. When we have organized a system of defence, suitable for our mutual protection, England will not fail us in case of need, either in soldiers or in money. In territory, population and riches, Canada excels any of the other provinces, but it lacks an element essential to its national greatness—the maritime element. The trade of Canada is now so considerable that it is absolutely necessary to have means of communication with England at all seasons of the year. Twenty years ago the summer season was sufficient for the movement of our commerce, but now it is insufficient, and for our communication with the outside world during the winter we are at the mercy of our neighbours, through whose territory we are obliged to pass. In the situation in which we are at present a war with the United States will deprive us of our winter port.

The question to ask ourselves is this: Shall we live apart, will we be content to preserve a mere provincial existence when united we may become a great nation? No union of small communities ever was able to hope to reach national greatness with such facility as we are. In past centuries warriors have struggled for long years to give to their country a strip of territory. In our own days Napoleon III, after an enormous expense of treasure and blood in the war with Italy, acquired Savoy and Nice, which added about a million people to France. If any one were to calculate the value of these acquisitions compared with what they cost, he would be struck with the disproportion and convinced that the territory acquired had perhaps been secured too dearly.

In British North America we are five different groups inhabiting five separate provinces. We have the same commercial interests and the same desire to live under the British Crown. Why should New Brunswick, Nova Scotia and Newfoundland retain their several customs tariffs against our trade, and why should we maintain similar duties to their disadvantage? In ancient times the manner in which nations developed was not the same as it is to-day. Then a weak settlement developed into a village, the village into a town or a city, which in turn became the nucleus of a nation. This is not the case in modern times. Nations now are formed by the joining together of various people having similar interests and sympathies. Such is our position at the present time. Objection is made to our project, because of the words "a new nationality." But if we unite we shall form a political nationality independent of the national origin and religion of individuals. Some have regretted that we have a distinction of races, and have expressed the hope that, in time, this diversity will disappear. The idea of a fusion of all races is Utopian; it is an impossibility. Distinctions of this character will always exist; diversity is the order of the physical, moral and political world. As to the objection that we cannot form a great nation because Lower Canada is French and Catholic, Upper Canada English and Protestant, and the Maritime Provinces mixed, it is futile. Take for example the United Kingdom, inhabited as it is by three great races. Has the diversity of races been an obstacle to the progress and the welfare of Great Britain? Have not the three races, united by their combined qualities, their energy and their courage, contributed to the glory of the Empire, to its laws so wise, to its success on land, on sea and in commerce? In our confederation there will be Catholics and Protestants, English, French, Irish and Scotch, and each by its efforts and success will add to the prosperity of the Dominion, to the glory of the new confederation. We are of different races, not to quarrel, but to work together for the common welfare. We cannot by law make the differences of race disappear, but I am convinced that the Anglo-Canadians and the French-Canadians will appreciate the advantages of their position. Set side by side, like a great family, their contact will produce a happy spirit of emulation. The diversity of races will in fact, believe me, contribute to the common prosperity. The whole difficulty will be in the manner of rendering justice to minorities. In Upper Canada the Roman Catholics will be in the minority, in Lower Canada it will be the Protestants who will be in the minority, whilst in the Maritime Provinces the two communions will equalize each other. Is it possible then to suppose that the general government or the provincial governments can become guilty of arbitrary acts? What would be the result, even supposing that one of the provincial governments should attempt it? Measures of such a character would undoubtedly be repudiated by the mass of the people. There is no reason then to fear that it will ever be sought to deprive a minority of its rights. Under the federal system, which leaves to the central government the control of questions of general interest, to which differences of races are foreign, the rights of race and of religion cannot be invaded. We shall have a general parliament to deal with questions of defence, tariff, excise, public works and all matters affecting individual interest. I will therefore ask those defenders of nationality who have accused me of bartering fifty-eight counties of Lower Canada with my colleague who sits near me (George Brown), how can injustice be done to the French-Canadians by the general government?

RICHARD JOHN CARTWRIGHT

RICHARD JOHN CARTWRIGHT

1835-1912

FOR practically a half century Sir Richard Cartwright dwelt in the forefront of politics. He saw the birth of a nation, saw it grow yearly in national consciousness—and died too early to behold its triumphant debût at the first Assembly of the League of Nations, held at Geneva in 1920.

Richard Cartwright was born in Kingston, in 1835. He came of loyal British stock, his grandfather, the Hon. Richard Cartwright, having been a United Empire Loyalist who later became very prominent in political and business circles in Canada.

He obtained his early education at Kingston, but received his university training at Trinity College, Dublin. After graduation he returned to Canada, and studied law, but, obeying the impulse to enter politics which had obsessed him from childhood, he was initiated into the secrets of political life in 1863, and devoted his energies to public service for the remainder of his life.

Cartwright was a firm believer in Confederation, and at the beginning of his career was a staunch supporter of Sir John A. Macdonald. Later he opposed his Chief on the question of banking reforms, and in 1872 his antipathy to the proposed Canadian

Pacific Railway Bill was so violent that he transferred his allegiance to the Liberal party.

In the general election of 1872, his popularity was demonstrated by his election as a Liberal member to Parliament for the same constituency for which he had formerly stood as a Conservative. After the downfall of Macdonald, subsequent to the "Pacific Scandal" disclosures, Cartwright became Minister of Finance in the Mackenzie Cabinet and during his five years of office was responsible for several important measures which tended to stabilize financial conditions in Canada.

The Mackenzie Government was defeated in 1878, and Sir John A. Macdonald came back to the helm on the wave of the National Policy. Sir Richard, in opposition, was merciless in his criticisms of the new protection scheme throughout the sixteen years of the Conservative regime, for he was a thoroughgoing free trader. Upon the election of Laurier to the Premiership in 1896, Cartwright was appointed Minister of Trade and Commerce, and secured several necessary reforms in trade relations, though his attempt to introduce unrestricted reciprocity with the United States was unsuccessful. In 1902 he was made a member of the Imperial Privy Council, and from 1904 until his death in 1912 was one of the Liberal leaders in the Senate.

Cartwright's pronounced ability and long years of experience entitled him to rank as a foremost authority on tariff and financial problems. As a public speaker and debater he was surpassed by few of his contemporaries. His annual oratorical duel, first with Sir Charles Tupper, and later with Sir George Foster, was hailed with delight by parliamentary audiences, bored with the dull routine of ordinary procedure, and his speech in seconding the vote of thanks to the volunteers in the North West Rebellion of 1885, is regarded as a masterpiece of Canadian political oratory.

A COALITION GOVERNMENT IN THE FACE OF AN EMERGENCY

Richard Cartwright

From a speech delivered March 9, 1865, in the debates on Confederation

SO far from regarding the union of parties which has taken place as a political misfortune in itself, or as tending to deprive the people of any safeguard, I say that it was of the greatest importance to our people that they should be relieved, if only for a brief period, from the desperate party struggles in which they have been engaged—that a lull of some kind should be afforded, that they should have some opportunity of considering the grave dangers which encompass them, some chance of escaping from the state of practical anarchy into which they had been drifting. It is to their credit, Mr. Speaker, and to the credit of those who control the press of this country, that ever since this project has been fairly before us a very marked improvement has taken place in the whole tone and temper of public discussion. Of the press, in particular, I must say that the moment they were relieved of the necessity of supporting party manœuvres—the moment a subject of sufficient importance was submitted for consideration, they seem to have risen at once to the level of the subject and to have abandoned all those unhappy and rancorous personalities which, in times past, were too apt to disfigure their pages.

Sir, I believe the people of Canada have learned a lesson which they will not easily forget. I believe that henceforward it will not be found so easy to array citizen against citizen, race against race, as it has been heretofore. I believe that our people have discovered that men who rise to be the heads of great parties are not of necessity villains and scoundrels—that both sides may have great political principles to maintain—that the words Reformer and Revolutionist, Conservative and Corruptionist, are not absolutely convertible terms, and that men who have given up the best of their lives, and sacrificed, too often, the best part of their fortunes in the service of their country, have had some better and higher reasons than mere love of jobbery and intrigue for doing so. To me, Sir, this appears a matter of great moment. It is only too notorious how much of the misery and misfortune which has befallen the United States is to be traced to the systematic degradation of their public men. It is well for us that the matter is still in our own power. It is well for us that we have still the choice whether we will have statesmen or stump orators to rule over us—whether this House shall maintain its honourable position as the representatives of a free people, or whether it shall sink into a mere mob of delegates, the nominees of caucuses and of wire-pullers. It is still in our power to decide whether we shall secure a fair share of the best talent we possess to carry on the affairs of the country, or whether we will ostracize from our councils every man of superior ability, education or intelligence—with what practical results we need not look far abroad to see; and, I think, Sir, it is fast becoming apparent that in this, as in other matters, the people of Canada are well disposed to adhere to the traditions of their British ancestry.

There is one objection, Mr. Speaker, which has been advanced perpetually throughout this debate by some honourable gentlemen who, while unable or unwilling to show any valid reason against Confederation in itself, profess themselves bitterly scandalized at the political combination by which it is likely to be brought about. Now, Sir, I admit at once that there is a prejudice, a just and wholesome prejudice, against all coalitions in the abstract. I admit that that prejudice is especially strong in the minds of Englishmen, and that, in point of fact, a coalition is always an extreme measure, only to be had resort to in cases of extreme emergency. A coalition, Mr. Speaker, may be a very base act, but it may also be a very noble one. It may be a mere conspiracy, for purposes of revenge or plunder, on the part of men hating and detesting each other to the uttermost— or it may be an honourable sacrifice of private personal enmity before the pressure of overwhelming public necessities, to escape from great danger or to carry a great object.

Sir, I shall not insult the intelligence of the House by inquiring whether this present existing Coalition has proposed to itself an object of sufficient importance to warrant its formation. Even those who censure the details of this scheme most strongly are fain to do homage to the grandeur of the project, and are compelled to admit that a union which should raise this country from the position of a mere province to that of a distinct nation, is a project well worthy of the utmost efforts of our statesmen. To determine the remaining question whether the position of our affairs was so critical as to require the utmost energy of all our leaders, and to justify any union which gave a reasonable hope of extricating ourselves from our difficulties, I must again revert to the condition in which we found ourselves during the last few years, and I ask every honourable member to answer for himself whether it was one which it gives him any pleasure to look back upon?

Was it pleasant for us, Mr. Speaker, a young country without one penny of debt which has not been incurred for purposes of public utility—was it pleasant for us, I ask, to find our revenue yearly outrunning our expenditure in the ratio of 20, 30 or even 40 per cent. per annum? Was it pleasant for us to know that some of our once busiest and most prosperous cities were being depopulated under the pressure of exorbitant taxation? Was it pleasant for us, inhabiting a country able to sustain ten times its present population, to find capital and immigrants alike fleeing from our shores, even if they had to take refuge in a land desolated by civil war? Was it pleasant for us, Sir, the only colony of England which has ever vindicated its attachment to the Empire in fair fight, to know that our apathy and negligence in taking steps for our own defence was fast making us the byword to both friend and foe? And lastly, Mr. Speaker, I ask was it pleasant for us, needing and knowing that we needed a strong government above all things, one which should maintain a firm and steady policy, and possess the good will and support of at least a large majority of our people—I say, Sir, was it pleasant for us at such a crisis to find ourselves the victims of a mere political see-saw—to be sure only of this one fact, that whatever course of policy was adopted, the circumstance that it emanated from one party would cause it to be viewed with jealousy and suspicion by the whole remaining moiety of the nation?

I would not have it thought, Mr. Speaker, that in saying this I am blind to the difficulties with which our statesmen have had to struggle. So far from this I believe that it has been quite too much the fashion to underrate them in times past. We have spoken of them as if it were the easiest task in the world to blend together, in less than one generation, two distinct peoples—peoples differing from one another in race, in language, in laws, customs and religion—in one word, in almost every point in which it is possible for men of European origin, and professing one common Christianity, to differ from each other. Sir, this could never have been an easy task. It is one which has again and again baffled the ablest statesmen of the most powerful monarchies of Europe; and I will not undertake to say whether it is ever capable of complete accomplishment. Be that as it may, I know that in every empire which has ever existed, from the English to the Roman, which has held different races under its sway, it has always been found necessary to make large allowances for distinctive national traits—has, in fact, been found necessary to introduce in some measure, the Federal element, though it is equally true that in every state which deserved the name of an empire, the supreme authority of the central power in all that concerns the general welfare has been acknowledged unreservedly.

And, Sir, it is just because this seems to have been effectual in all essential points in the scheme now before us—because, while reserving to the general government the power of the purse and the sword, it accords the amplest defensive powers to the various local bodies—because, even where there may be some conflict of jurisdiction on minor matters, every reasonable precaution seems to have been taken against leaving behind us any reversionary legacies of sovereign state rights to stir up strife and discord among our children. For all these reasons, I say, I am disposed to give my hearty support to the scheme as a whole, without criticizing too narrowly the innumerable details which it must inevitably present to attack.

ANTOINE AIMÉ DORION

ANTOINE AIMÉ DORION
1818-1891

THE character of Antoine Dorion lends a touch of poetry to the story of Confederation. Judged by political standards of success his public life was a pathetic failure, for during a political career of twenty years he held but seldom the reins of office, and it was his misfortune to oppose a movement which was destined to become the greatest force in the history of Canadian development. But no one who reads of the sweetness and magnetism of Dorion's personality can pronounce his career a failure. Not only does it adorn the somewhat sordid annals of politics with a rare beauty and charm, but in the inspiration which it gave to later politicians, notably Sir Wilfrid Laurier, who worshipped at the shrine of Dorion, its fruitfulness is proven beyond fear of denial.

Dorion came of a noted family of French Canadian public men, his father, grandfather and brother having each in turn been members of the Assembly. He was born at St. Anne de la Perade, Champlain County, in 1818, was educated at Nicolet College, and in 1842 was called to the Bar. His rise to distinction was rapid, for the charm of his personality augmented the prestige which his natural ability won for him, and he was soon recognized as a potential leader of Quebec.

In 1850 the Parti Rouge was founded by Papineau and other brilliant Radicals, animated with the fervour and rash idealism of youth. Dorion became an active member of the party, and in 1854, on the retirement of Papineau, was chosen leader of the Rouges. In the same year he entered the Assembly, together with nineteen others of his party, and for a time the influence of the Parti Rouge was dominant in Quebec. Dorion allied himself with George Brown, the leader of the Clear Grits in Upper Canada, and a warm friendship sprang up between the two leaders, which the combined differences of temperament, race and religion could not destroy.

In 1858 Brown invited Dorion to join him in an administration pledged to seek a solution for the ills of government which were crippling the development of the country. Dorion accepted, but Sir Edmund Head, who distrusted the Liberals, refused a dissolution of the House, and the Brown-Dorion government lasted but two days. Brown was an eager disciple of Representation by Population, and Dorion agreed to a modification of the measure, with checks attached which would safeguard the rights of the Lower Canadians. As an alternative he proposed a loose federation of the two provinces. But in the succeeding administrations neither of the suggestions was adopted, and though Dorion held office for a short time under two different administrations his efforts were futile to shelve the approaching crisis, and the famous deadlock took place in 1864.

When the actual scheme of Confederation was evolved, Dorion distrusted the measure and set his face against it like flint. He was wholly conscientious in his opposition, for though he approved of the principle of Confederation he believed that the scheme was premature, and deplored the terms of the union. He refused to join a Coalition government which espoused the movement, and for the first time in the history of their friendship became alienated from George Brown. Both in and out of the Assembly he criticized the measure and exerted a great deal of influence over his young compatriots in Quebec, but the movement was triumphant in spite of his earnest opposition.

After Confederation Dorion became a vigilant critic of the new government, and was relentless in his attitude to the Pacific Scandal. When the Mackenzie government came into power Dorion was appointed Minister of Justice, but poverty and ill health forced him to abandon politics, and in 1874 he accepted the position of Chief Justice of Quebec, which he held until his death in May, 1891.

Antoine Dorion was a gentleman of the old school, —courteous, polished and dignified. Yet with all his aristocracy of bearing he was thoroughly democratic in his principles. In his youth he was radical to the extreme, but age modified his views and he became ultimately the founder of the Liberal party of Quebec which under Laurier rose to a position of distinction throughout the country. But Dorion's heart was in his profession, and he never craved the spoils of office nor the adulation of the crowd. His love for his country was far-reaching, and in his quiet and self-effacing way he served her nobly.

His lack of vision at the crisis in Canadian history was the tragic point in his career, but there is a heroism in his honest opposition to Confederation more poignant than the reckless courage of George Brown and John A. Macdonald who both rode triumphant over obstacles at which he faltered. His attitude toward union may have lessened his fame as a politician, but nothing can sully his reputation as a magnanimous and single-minded patriot of Canada.

Antoine Aimé Dorion

THE WEAKNESS OF THE CONFEDERATION SCHEME

ANTOINE DORION

From a speech in the Legislative Assembly, February 16, 1865

THIS scheme is submitted to us on two grounds; first, the necessity for meeting the constitutional difficulties which have arisen between Upper and Lower Canada, owing to the growing demands on the part of Upper Canada for representation by population; and, secondly, the necessity of providing more efficient means for the defence of the country than now exist. These are the only two grounds we have heard stated for the propositions now submitted to us; and I shall apply myself to explain my views on these two subjects, and also upon the scheme generally. When upon the first question I trust I shall be permitted to go a little into the history of the agitation for representation by population, for I owe it to myself, to my constituents and the country. My name has been used in various ways. It has sometimes been said that I was entirely favourable to representation by population—at other times that I was entirely favourable to the Confederation of the provinces, and I shall now endeavour, once more, to state as clearly as possible what my real views have been, and still are.

The first time representation by population was mooted in this House, on behalf of Upper Canada, was, I believe, in the Session of 1852, when the Conservative party took it up, and the Hon. Sir Allan Macnab moved resolutions in favour of the principle. We then found the Conservatives arrayed in support of this constitutional change. It had been mooted before on behalf of Lower Canada, but the Upper Canadians had all opposed it. In 1854 the Macnab-Morin coalition took place and we heard no more of representation by population from that quarter—that is, as mooted by the Conservative party, who from that time forth uniformly opposed it on every occasion. It was, however, taken up by the present Hon. President of the Council, the member for South Oxford, and with the energy and vigour that he brings to bear on every question that he takes in hand, he caused such an agitation in its behalf as almost threatened a revolution. As the agitation in the country increased, so did the vote for it in this House increase, and on several occasions I expressed my views upon the subject. I never shirked the question—I never hesitated to say that something ought to be done to meet the just claims of Upper Canada, and that representation based on population was in the abstract a just and correct principle. I held, at the same time, that there were reasons why Lower Canada could not grant it; and I entreated Lower Canadian representatives to show themselves disposed to meet the views of Upper Canada by making, at any rate, a counter proposal; and in 1856, when Parliament was sitting in Toronto, I, for the first time, suggested that one means of getting over the difficulty would be to substitute for the present Legislative union a Confederation of the two Canadas, by means of which all local questions could be consigned to the deliberations of local

legislatures, with a central government having control of commercial and other questions of common or
general interest. I stated that considering the
different religious faith, the different language, the
different laws that prevailed in the two sections of
the country, this was the best way to meet the
difficulty; to leave to a general government questions
of trade, banking, public works of a general character,
etc., and to commit to the decision of local legislatures
all matters of a local bearing. At the same time I
stated that, if these views should not prevail, I would
certainly go for representation by population, and
such checks and guarantees as would secure the interests of each section of the country, and to preserve
to Lower Canada its cherished institutions.

Well, Sir, I have not a word of all this to take back.
I still hold to the same views. I still think that a
Federal union of Canada might hereafter extend so
as to embrace other territories either east or west;
that such a system is well adapted to admit of territorial expansion without any disturbance of the
federal economy, but I cannot understand how this
plain sentence should be considered by the President
of the Council as any indication that I have ever
been in favour of Confederation with the other
British Provinces. There is nothing I have ever
said or written that can be construed to mean that
I was ever in favour of such a proposition. On the
contrary, whenever the question came up I set my
face against it. I asserted that such a union could
only bring trouble and embarrassment, that there
was no social, no commercial connection between the

provinces whose union was proposed,—nothing to justify their union at the present juncture. Of course I do not say that I shall be opposed to their Confederation for all time to come. Population may extend over the wilderness that now lies between the Maritime Provinces and ourselves, and commercial intercourse may increase sufficiently to render Confederation desirable. But I say here, as I said in 1856, and in 1861 also, that I am opposed to this Confederation now.

Sir, I may be asked what difference our bringing in the Maritime Provinces can make. This I shall endeavour to explain. When they went into the Conference, the honourable gentlemen opposite submitted to have the votes taken by provinces. Well, they have brought us in, as was natural under the circumstances, the most conservative measure ever laid before a Parliament. The members of the Upper House are no longer to be elected, but nominated. Were we not expressly told that it was the Lower Provinces who would not hear of our having an elective Legislative Council? If instead of going into the Conference with the people of the Lower Provinces, our Government had done what they pledged themselves to do, that is, to prepare a Constitution themselves, they would never have dared to bring in such a proposition as this which is now imposed upon us by the Lower Colonies,—to have a Legislative Council, with a fixed number of members, nominated by four Conservative governments.

If the two Canadas were alone interested, the majority would have its own way—would look into

the Constitution closely—would scan its every
doubtful provision, and such a proposal as this about
the Legislative Council would have no chance of
being carried, for it is not long since the House, by
an overwhelming majority, voted for the substitution of an elected for a nominated Upper Chamber.
In fact, the nominated Chamber had fallen so low
in public estimation—I do not say it was the fault
of the men who were in it, but the fact is nevertheless, as I state it—that it commanded no influence.
There was even a difficulty of getting a quorum of it
together. So a change became absolutely necessary,
and up to the present moment the new system worked
well; the elected members are equal in every respect
to the nominated ones, and it is just when we see an
interest beginning to be felt in the proceedings of the
Upper House that its Constitution is to be changed,
to return back again to the one so recently condemned. Back again, did I say? No, sir, a Constitution is to be substituted, much worse than the
old one, and such as is nowhere else to be found.
Why, even the British House of Lords, conservative
as it is, is not altogether beyond the influence of the
popular sentiment of the country. Their number
may be increased on the recommendation of the
responsible advisers of the Crown, if required to
secure united action or to prevent a conflict between
the two Houses. From the position its members
occupy, it is a sort of compromise between the popular element and the influence or control of the
Crown.

But the new House for the Confederation is to be

a perfectly independent body—these gentlemen are to be named for life—and there is to be no power to increase their number. How long will the system work without producing a collision between the two branches of the Legislature? Suppose the Lower House turns out to be chiefly Liberal, how long will it submit to the Upper House, named by Conservative administrations which have taken advantage of their temporary numerical strength to bring about such a change as is now proposed? Remember, Sir, that after all, the power, the influence of the popular branch of the Legislature is paramount. We have seen constitutions like that of England adopted in many countries, and where there existed a nobility, such as in France in 1830, the second chamber was selected from this nobility. In Belgium, where the Constitution is almost a fac-simile of that of England, but where there are no aristocracy, they adopted the elective principle for the Upper House, and nowhere in the world is there a fixed number for it, unless it is also elective.

It must be fresh in the memory of a great many members of this House how long the House of Lords resisted the popular demand for reform, and what great difficulties were threatened. At last in 1832 the agitation had become so great that the Government determined to nominate a sufficient number of peers to secure the passage of the Reform Bill. The members of the House had to choose between allowing the measure to become law, or to see their influence destroyed by the addition of an indefinite number of members. They preferred the first alternative, and thereby quieted an excitement, which, if not checked in time, might have created a revolution in England The influence of the Crown was then exerted in accordance with the views of the people; but here we are to have no such power existing to check the action of the Upper Chamber, and no change can be made in its composition except as death might remove its members. I venture to prophesy, Sir, that before a very short time has elapsed a deadlock may arise, and such an excitement be created as has never yet been seen in this country.

JOSEPH HOWE

JOSEPH HOWE

1804-1873

FROM the little province of Nova Scotia many of Canada's greatest sons have sprung, but none of these later constellations can dim the lustre which surrounds the name of Joseph Howe. Apart from his vast political service to his province—for to him is due the lion's share in the establishment of Responsible Government in Nova Scotia—his personal charm, magnetic eloquence and mighty intellect alone, accord him first place in the hearts of his countrymen.

He was born in Halifax in 1804, of United Empire stock, and after a childhood characterized by fun and mischief, with glintings of the poetic nature which afterwards found expression in charming verse, he became printer's devil to the Halifax *Gazette* at the age of thirteen. During his boyhood he devoured the classics, and with such a background his natural gift for writing rapidly expanded, so that at the age of twenty-four he felt qualified to assume the editorship of the *Novascotian*.

By 1830 the political situation in Nova Scotia was precarious, and Howe instituted a vigorous campaign against the autocracy of the government, through the pages of his journal. He was indicted for libel in 1835 for attacking the City Magistrates, and spoke in his own defence, having studied law books for a week. Contrary to the expectations of a sympathetic populace, he was acquitted, and from that day forward he became the idol of his countrymen, and the champion of their rights.

In 1836 Howe was elected to the Legislature. The "Family Compact" of Nova Scotia was flourishing, and Howe never ceased to strike at it, both in the House and in his newspaper. His peerless eloquence and nimble wit made him the terror of his opponents, and his strong hold on the people outside fortified his position in the Assembly. A reform agitation was in progress, simultaneously, in the Canadas, and Howe sympathized warmly with their effort, but his ingrained loyalty to Great Britain led him to decline their invitation to join them in the appeal to arms. He refused "to bully the British Government," and the wisdom of his course was proven when in 1847 the hostile faction surrendered and Nova Scotia was granted Responsible Government, a year earlier than the Canadas.

He had early conceived a desire for the federation of the British provinces, and to further his scheme, secured the offer of an Imperial guarantee to build an intercolonial railway. He negotiated with the Canadas for their share in the great project, and his ardent imagination flamed with the latent possibilities of the plan, when, unfortunately, Lord Grey limited the guarantee, wet-blanketed the scheme, and wounded Howe's sensibilities to the core.

From this date Howe's attitude to federation underwent a severe change, and when Charles Tupper proposed and secured a conference at Charlottetown (at which Howe was not present) to consider the advantages of Confederation, he opposed it with his whole strength. The people of Nova Scotia, themselves, heartily resisted the plan, and Howe became their spokesman. He maintained that the rights and the individuality of Nova Scotia would be swamped in the interests of the larger provinces, and threw himself bitterly into the anti-union cause.

But, thanks to Tupper, Confederation carried in Nova Scotia, after a three-year struggle, and though Howe went to England to seek its repeal, his efforts were unavailing. Sir John Macdonald convinced him of the futility of his task, and persuaded him to reconcile his countrymen to Confederation, and to accept a seat in the Cabinet of the new Dominion. He accepted reluctantly and, broken-hearted, sought to quell the agitation against union. Together with Tupper he accomplished his task, though at the expense of his popularity in the province.

In April, 1873, he was appointed Lieutenant Governor of Nova Scotia, but he lived only a few weeks after the appointment, worn out as he was with worry and disappointment. He was buried in Halifax, near the home of his boyhood, and at his death, recollections of his kindness, geniality and charm swarmed back into the memory of his former admirers and reinstated him in his position as a popular idol and the pride of Nova Scotia—a position which he will hold for time immemorial.

COMMERCIAL RELATIONS BETWEEN CANADA AND THE UNITED STATES

Hon. Joseph Howe

From an address in Detroit, in July, 1865

I NEVER prayed for the gift of eloquence till now. Although I have passed through a long public life, I never was called upon to discuss a question so important in the presence of a body of representative men so large. I see before me merchants who think in millions and whose daily transactions would sweep the harvest of a Greek island or a Russian principality. I see before me the men who whiten the ocean and the great lakes with the sails of commerce—who own the railroads, canals and telegraphs which spread life and civilization through this great country, making the waste plains fertile and the wilderness to blossom as the rose. I see before me the men whose capital and financial skill bulwark and sustain the Government in every crisis of public affairs. On either hand I see the gentlemen who control and animate the press, whose laborious vigils mould public sentiment—whose honourable ambitions I can estimate from my early connection with the profession. On these benches, Sir, or I mistake the intelligence to be read in their faces, sit those who will yet be governors and ministers of State. I may well feel awed in the presence of such an audience as this; but the great question which brings us together is worthy of the audience and challenges their grave consideration.

What is that question? Sir, we are here to deter-

mine how best we can draw together in the bonds of
peace, friendship and commercial prosperity the
great branches of the British family.   In the presence
of this great theme all petty interests should stand
rebuked—we are not dealing with the concerns of a
city, a province, or a state, but with the future of
our race in all time to come.   Some reference has
been made to "elevators" in your discussions.   What
we want is an elevator to lift our souls to the height
of this great argument.   Why should not these three
great branches of the family flourish, under different
systems of government, it may be, but forming one
grand whole, proud of a common origin and of their
advanced civilization?   We are taught to reverence
the mystery of the Trinity, and our salvation depends
on our belief.   The clover lifts its trefoil leaves to the
evening dew, yet they draw their nourishment from a
single stem.   Thus distinct, and yet united, let us
live and flourish.

Why should we not?   For nearly two thousand
years we were one family.   Our fathers fought side
by side at Hastings, and heard the curfew toll.
They fought in the same ranks for the sepulchre of
our Saviour—in the earlier and later civil wars.
We can wear our white and red roses without a blush,
and glory in the principles those conflicts established.
Our common ancestors won the Great Charter and
the Bill of Rights—established free Parliaments, the
Habeas Corpus and trial by jury.   Our jurisprudence
comes down from Coke and Mansfield to Marshall
and Story, rich in knowledge and experience which
no man can divide.   From Chaucer to Shakespeare

our literature is a common inheritance. Tennyson
and Longfellow write in one language which is en-
riched by the genius developed on either side of the
Atlantic. In the great navigators, from Cotterel to
Hudson, and in all their "moving accidents by flood
and field," we have a common interest. On this side
of the sea we have been largely reinforced by the
Germans and French, but there is strength in both
elements. The Germans gave to us the sovereigns
who established our freedom, and they give to you
industry, intelligence and thrift; and the French, who
have distinguished themselves in arts and arms for
centuries, now strengthen the Provinces which the
fortune of war decided they could not control.

But it may be said we have been divided by two
wars. What then? The noble St. Lawrence is
split in two places—by Goat Island and by Anticosti
—but it comes to us from the same springs in the
same mountain sides; its waters sweep together past
the pictured rocks of Lake Superior, and encircle in
their loving embrace the shores of Huron and
Michigan. They are divided at Niagara Falls as
we were at the revolutionary war, but they come
together again on the peaceful bosom of Ontario.
Again they are divided on their passage to the sea;
but who thinks of divisions when they lift the keels
of commerce, or, when drawn up to heaven they form
the rainbow or the cloud? It is true that in eighty-
five years we have had two wars—but what then?
Since the last we have had fifty years of peace, and
there have been more people killed in a single campaign in the late civil war, than there were in the

two national wars between this country and Great Britain. You hope to draw together the two conflicting elements and make them one people. And in that task I wish you Godspeed! And in the same way I feel that we ought to rule out everything disagreeable in the recollection of our old wars, and unite together as one people for all time to come. I see around the door the flags of the two countries. United as they are there, I would ever have them draped together, fold within fold—and let

> "Their varying tints unite,
> And form in Heaven's light
> One arch of peace."

SIR JOHN A. MACDONALD

THE RELATIONSHIP OF CANADA TO GREAT BRITAIN

SIR JOHN A. MACDONALD

From a Speech made in the House of Commons, May 8, 1872

IT has been said by the honourable gentleman on my left (Mr. Howe), in his speech to the Young Men's Christian Association, that England had sacrificed the interests of Canada. If England has sacrificed the interests of Canada, what sacrifice has she not made in the cause of peace. Has she not, for the sake of peace between those two great nations, rendered herself liable, leaving out all indirect claims, to pay millions out of her own treasury? Has she not made all this sacrifice, which only Englishmen and English statesmen can know, for the sake of peace— and for whose sake has she made it? Has she not made it principally for the sake of Canada? Let Canada be severed from England—let England not be responsible to us, and for us, and what could the United States do to England? Let England withdraw herself into her shell, and what can the United States do? England has got the supremacy of the sea, she is impregnable in every point but one, and that point is Canada; and if England does call upon us to make a financial sacrifice, does find it for the good of the Empire that we, England's first colony, should sacrifice something, I say that we would be unworthy of our proud position if we were not prepared to do so. I hope to live to see the day, and if I do not that my son may be spared to see Canada the right arm of England, to see Canada a powerful auxiliary to the Empire, not, as now, a cause of anxiety and a source of danger. And I think that if we are worthy to hold that position as the right arm of England, we should not object to a sacrifice of this kind when so great an object is attained, and the object is a great and lasting one.

It is said that amities between nations cannot be perpetual. But I say that this Treaty which has gone through so many difficulties and dangers, if it is carried into effect, removes almost all possibility of war. If ever there was an irritating cause of war, it was from the occurrences arising out of the escape of those vessels, and when we see the United States people and government forget this irritation, forget those occurrences, and submit such a question to arbitration, to the arbitration of a disinterested tribunal, they have established a principle which can never be forgotten in this world. No future question is ever likely to arise that will cause such irritation as the escape of the *Alabama* did, and if they could be got to agree to leave such a matter to the peaceful arbitrament of a friendly power, what future cause of quarrel can in the imagination of man occur that will not bear the same pacific solution that is sought for in this? I believe that this Treaty is an epoch in the history of civilization, that it will set an example to the wide world that must be followed; and with the growth of the great Anglo-

Saxon family, and with the development of that mighty nation to the south of us, I believe that the principle of arbitration will be advocated and adopted as the sole principle of settlement of differences between the English-speaking peoples and that it will have a moral influence in the world. And, although it may be opposed to the antecedents of other nations, that great moral principle which has now been established among the Anglo-Saxon family will spread itself over all the civilized world. It is not too much to say that it is a great advance in the history of mankind, and I should be sorry if it were recorded that it was stopped for a moment by a selfish consideration of the interests of Canada.

EDWARD BLAKE

EDWARD BLAKE

1833-1912

EDWARD BLAKE was the son of William Hume Blake, a noted lawyer and politician of Upper Canada, and descendant of the Blakes of Galway, famous in history and romance. He was born in Middlesex county in 1833, but when he was a few months old the family moved to Toronto. He entered Upper Canada College at the age of eleven years, but, though he possessed an intellect far above the average, he showed no inclination to study. In 1848, however, his father took him on a tour abroad, and the vivid impressions which he received of revolutionary Europe gave him a burning zeal for knowledge. From that date he studied assiduously, and obtained first place in the final examinations. In 1854 he graduated from the University of Toronto with high honours in Classics, and begahe stun tdy of law. He was called to the bar in 1857, and during his career won a brilliant reputation in his profession not only in Canada, but in England and the outlying posts of the Empire as well.

His political life began in 1867, when he was elected both to the Provincial and the Federal Parliament. In 1869 he accepted the leadership of the Liberal party in Ontario, and in 1871, on the resignation of the Sandfield Macdonald ministry, became Premier of Ontario. Unfortunately his health became impaired at this juncture, and he was obliged to resign the Premiership in 1872.

He was returned to the Dominion Parliament in 1872, and was urged to accept the leadership of the Liberal party in the Federal House, but declined. He accepted a place in the Mackenzie Cabinet in 1873, and became Minister of Justice in 1875. Again ill health forced his resignation although during his term of office he was chiefly instrumental in perfecting the constitution of the Supreme Court at its establishment by the Mackenzie administration.

After the downfall of the Mackenzie Government in 1878, Blake accepted the leadership of the Liberal Party, and although he was never a popular leader, his magnificent intellectual gifts and his moral integrity commanded the respect of his party. He was a champion of Canadian autonomy, and was one of the leaders of the "Canada First" party. During his regime as leader of the Opposition he kept a vigilant watch on the actions of the Government, particularly with regard to the North West Rebellion and the construction of the Canadian Pacific Railway. In 1887 he retired from political life in Canada to the deep regret of his followers, and was succeeded by Wilfrid Laurier as Liberal leader.

In 1892 he accepted an invitation to represent an Irish constituency in the British House of Commons, and was elected with a large majority, for South Longford. He became an earnest supporter of Home Rule and the rights of the Irish, and made many striking speeches on their behalf. He was elected a member of the Executive Committee of the Irish Parliamentary party in 1894 and was included in the Royal Commission appointed to investigate the financial situation between Great Britain and Ireland.

In 1896 he was one of the members of the Imperial Parliament selected to investigate the causes of the Transvaal Raid in Africa, and served also as an arbitrator between the Government of New Zealand and the New Zealand Midland Railway. He continued his activities in the Imperial Parliament until 1907, when increased ill-health forced him to retire from political life. He returned to Toronto, where he died in 1912.

Edward Blake's genuine interest in education was evinced throughout his career. In 1873 he was appointed Chancellor of the University of Toronto, and his liberality, when in this position, is well known.

As a citizen his name ranks among the greatest that Canada has produced—as a politician, his title is dubious. While possessing one of the mightiest intellects ever recorded in the annals of the Dominion Parliament, his over-strong individuality and his lack of personal magnetism deprived him of the warm-hearted devotion which was bestowed on Sir John Macdonald and Sir Wilfrid Laurier. But, for his uprightness, his benevolence and his unusual oratorical and intellectual ability—he lives in the memory of his countrymen, as one of the most noble and distinguished of Canadian public men.

CANADA'S RELATION TO THE EMPIRE
EDWARD BLAKE

Delivered at Aurora, 1874.

LET me turn to another question which has been adverted to on several occasions, as one looming in the not very distant future. I refer to the relations of Canada to the Empire. Upon this topic I took, three or four years ago, an opportunity of speaking, and ventured to suggest that an effort should be made to reorganize the Empire upon a Federal basis. I repeat what I then said, that the time may be at hand when the people of Canada shall be called upon to discuss the question. Matters cannot drift much longer as they have drifted hitherto. The Treaty of Washington produced a very profound impression throughout this country. It produced a feeling that at no distant period the people of Canada would desire that they should have some greater share of control than they now have in the management of foreign affairs; that our Government should not present the anomaly which it now presents—a Government the freest, perhaps the most democratic in the world with reference to local and domestic matters, in which you rule yourselves as fully as any people in the world, while in your foreign affairs, your relations with other countries, whether peaceful or warlike, commercial or financial, or otherwise, you may have no more voice than the people of Japan. This, however, is a state of things of which you have no right to complain, because so long as you do not choose to undertake the responsibilities and burdens which

attach to some share of control in these affairs, you
cannot fully claim the rights and privileges of free-
born Britons in such matters.

But how long is this talk in the newspapers and
elsewhere, this talk which I find in very high places,
of the desirability, aye, of the necessity of fostering
a national spirit among the people of Canada, to be
mere talk? It is impossible to foster a national
spirit unless you have national interests to attend to,
or among people who do not choose to undertake the
responsibilities and to devote themselves to the
duties to which national attributes belong. We have
been invited by Mr. Gladstone and other English
statesmen, notably by Mr. Gladstone, in the House
of Commons, very shortly before his Government
fell, to come forward. Mr. Gladstone, speaking
as Prime Minister of England, expressed the hope he
cherished, that the Colonies would some day come
forward and express their readiness and desire to
accept their full share in the privileges and responsibilities of Britons. It is for us to determine—not
now, not this year, not perhaps during this Parliamentary term, but yet, at no distant day—what our
line shall be. For my part I believe that while it is
not unnatural, not unreasonable, pending that process of development which has been going on in our
new and sparsely settled country, that we should
have been quite willing—we so few in numbers, so
busied in our local concerns, so engaged in subduing
the earth and settling up the country—to leave the
cares and privileges to which I have referred in the
hands of the parent State; the time will come when

that national spirit which has been spoken of will be truly felt among us, when we shall realize that we are four millions of Britons who are not free, when we shall be ready to take up that freedom, and to ask what the late Prime Minister of England assured us we should not be denied—our share of national rights.

To-morrow, by the policy of England, in which you have no voice or control, this country might be plunged into the horrors of a war. It is but the other day that, without your knowledge or consent, the navigation of the St. Lawrence was ceded forever to the United States. That is a state of things of which you may have no right to complain, as long as you can choose to say: "We prefer to avoid the cares, the expenses and charges, and we are unequal in point of ability to discharge the duties which appertain to us as free-born Britons;" but while you say this, you may not yet assume the lofty air, or speak in the high-pitched tones which belong to a people wholly free.

The future of Canada, I believe, depends very largely upon the cultivation of a national spirit. We are engaged in a very difficult task—the task of welding together seven Provinces which have been accustomed to regard themselves as isolated from each other, which are full of petty jealousies, their provincial questions, their local interests. How are we to accomplish our work? How are we to effect a real union between these Provinces? Can we do it by giving a sop now to one, now to another, after the manner of the late Government? By giving

British Columbia the extravagant terms which have been referred to; by giving New Brunswick $150,000 a year for an export duty which cannot be made out as worth more than $65,000 a year? Do you hope to create or to preserve harmony and good feeling upon such a false and sordid and mercenary basis as that? Not so! That day I hope is done for ever, and we must find some other and truer ground for Union than that by which the late Government sought to buy love and purchase peace. We must find some common ground on which to unite, some common aspiration to be shared, and I think it can be found alone in the cultivation of that national spirit to which I have referred.

I observe that those who say a word on this subject are generally struck at by the cry that they are practically advocating annexation. I believe that the feeling in the neighbouring Republic has materially changed on this subject, and that the notions which were widely spread there some years ago, and the desire to possess, as one Republic, under one Government, the whole of this continent, from north to south, have died away. A better and a wiser spirit, I believe, now prevails—largely due, perhaps, to the struggles which are unhappily occurring in that country. The attempt to reorganize the South has been going on for some years, and owing, I think, to a very great error in judgment as to the way in which it should be effected, it has been largely a failure. There is great difficulty, and there are frequent disorders in the South. Then there are the conflicts of interest between the Eastern and Western

States, very great conflicts and heartburnings. Then there are the alarming difficulties and complications arising from the inordinate political power which has been grasped by great corporations. And I think that the best and wisest minds in the United States have settled down to the conviction that the management of the United States with its present territory is just as difficult a task as their best men can accomplish, and that it would not be wise to add to their existing complications and difficulties by any such unwieldy accession or unmanageable increase as this great domain, the larger half of the whole continent, would be. I think that among those circles in the United States which are to be looked to as influencing the future, there is a great modification of view on this point, and there would be, even were we disposed, as I hope we shall never be disposed, to offer to join them, a great reluctance to take us.

But I believe we have a future of our own here. My opinion coincides with those to which I have been referring in the United States. I believe that that country is even larger than it ought to be in order to be well governed, and that an extension of its territory would be very unfortunate in the interests of civilization. "Cribbed, cabined and confined" as we ourselves are to the South by the unfortunate acts of English diplomatists in the past, giving up to the United States territory which, if we had it to-day, would make our future absolutely assured, but still retaining as we do the great North-West, I believe we can show that there is room and verge enough in North America for the maintenance of two distinct governments, and that there is nothing to be said in favour but on the contrary everything to be said against, the notion of annexation. These are the material reasons, independent altogether of the very strong and justly adverse feeling arising from our affection for and our association with England, and the well settled conviction which, I believe, exists among the people of this country that a constitutional monarchy is preferable to a republican government. The monarchical government of England is a truer application of real Republican principles than that of the United States, and I have no hesitation in saying that the government of Canada is far in advance, in the application of real republican principles, of the Government of either England or the United States.

But, with the very great advantages which we enjoy over that portion of our fellow-subjects living in England, by reason of our having come into a new country, having settled it for ourselves, and adapted our institutions to modern notions by reason of our not being cumbered by the constitution of a legislative chamber on the hereditary principle, by reason of our not being cumbered with an aristocracy, or with the unfortunate principle of primogeniture and the aggregation of the land in very few hands, by reason of our not being cumbered with the difficulties which must always exist where a community is composed of classes differing from one another in worldly circumstances so widely as the classes in England differ, where you can go into one street of the City of London and find the extreme of wealth, and a mile or two away the very extreme of poverty; living, as we do, in a country where these difficulties do not exist, where we early freed ourselves from the incubus of a State Church, where we early provided for the educational needs of our people, under these happy circumstances, with these great privileges, there are corresponding responsibilities.

WILFRID LAURIER

WILFRID LAURIER
1841-1919

THE elevation of a French Canadian to the Premiership of Canada was a subtle testimony to the success of Confederation. The honours heaped upon this French Canadian premier at the Diamond Jubilee of 1897 were a striking demonstration of the tremendous stride which Canada had made politically during the first sixty years of Victoria's sovereignty. And no more fitting representative of Canada's best, or one more worthy to receive the highest honours of a nation, could have been selected than Sir Wilfrid Laurier, the brilliant, broad-minded and courtly statesman of French Canadian birth.

Wilfrid Laurier was born at St. Lin, Quebec, in 1841, and received his primary education at the Parish School, but was sent at an early age to the Protestant school at New Glasgow to acquire a knowledge of English. Later he took the Classical course at L'Assomption College; still later he undertook the study of law at Laval University, and in 1864 was admitted to the Bar.

At a very early age he obtained a profound influence over his fellow students, and many prophecies were made concerning his future. His marked intellectual ascendency, strength of character, and personal charm were in evidence when he was but a child. As he grew to manhood his natural gifts developed, and the rich background he had formed from constant reading of the best in both English and French literature gave him a breadth of view and a mental balance which fitted him admirably for the part he was destined to play in Canadian political life.

In 1871 he entered the Quebec Legislature as Liberal member for Arthabaska, and was quickly recognized as the future leader of the Quebec Liberals. His eloquence, philosophic outlook, and lofty intellect won the admiration and confidence of a large following throughout his province, and in 1874 he was elected to the Dominion Legislature.

A bitter conflict had been brewing in Quebec between the Catholic clergy and the Liberals, and Laurier took his stand boldly against clerical control of politics and education. He was himself a Catholic, but had been an enthusiastic member of L'Institut Canadien, a club devoted to intellectual freedom, and his wide reading combined with his youthful experience in the Protestant community of New Glasgow gave him a love of religious toleration, which characterized his whole political career. In 1877, during the height of the quarrel between church and state, he delivered a powerful speech on Political Liberalism which sharply defined the position of his party toward the Catholic clergy—and won him the concentrated hostility of the ecclesiastical body, as well as the far-reaching admiration of broad-minded Catholics and Protestants alike.

In the same year he entered the Mackenzie Administration as Minister of Inland Revenue, but the

ministry was forced to resign in the following year
and he had no opportunity to display his ability as an
administrator. His reputation was steadily increasing however, and when in 1887 Edward Blake,
Mackenzie's successor, resigned, Laurier was chosen
as Liberal leader of the House of Commons. The
few speeches which he had delivered had given him a
prestige which few members in the House enjoyed,
and in spite of his French origin, and the racial
troubles which divided the country, he received the
full confidence of his party throughout the country.

In 1896 the Conservative Government resigned
on the Manitoba Separate School question, and
Laurier became premier of Canada. He remained
at the helm for a period of fourteen years, and attempted to put into practice the beliefs which he had
held since boyhood. He steadily upheld the principle of federalism, and of civil and religious freedom, and was moderate and rationalistic in his
views. His attitude to Imperialism was especially
noteworthy, for though his enthusiasm for the
Empire was stimulated by the pageantry and glory of
the Diamond Jubilee in England, he strove faithfully
to maintain Canada's autonomy within the Empire,
and resisted the strong movement for Imperial
Federation which swept over England in the early
part of the century.

In 1911 he was defeated on the proposed bill for
Reciprocity with the United States, but retained the
leadership of the Liberal party. During the war he
lost his grip on his party by his attitude toward con-
scription. He favoured Canada's participation in

the war, but, out-and-out advocate of freedom that he was, opposed enforced enlistment. As a result he was placed in an uncomfortable position, for pro-conscriptionist Liberals deserted him, and the Nationalists under Bourassa slipped out of his grasp. His declining years were spent under trying circumstances, as, struggling against ill health and war conditions, he strove pathetically to regain his former place in the affections of his people. He succeeded shortly before his death in 1919, and when he at last laid down the sceptre, all Canada, and many in Europe as well, mourned the loss of the statesman, courtier and scholar who had made such a profound impression on the public life of his day.

Sir Wilfrid Laurier's fascinating personality has left an indelible stamp on the memory of his countrymen, but admiration for his personal charms should not cloud the significance of his political achievements. His master diplomacy preserved Canadian autonomy at a critical period and paved the way for Canada's new conception of nationhood. But above all he deserves lasting gratitude in that he, a Frenchman and a Catholic, swept aside the barrier of ecclesiastical control of politics, and placed the welfare of the Dominion of Canada before sect, creed, or race.

Wilfrid Laurier

POLITICAL LIBERALISM

WILFRID LAURIER

Speech delivered before the Club Canadien, Quebec, June, 1877.

NOW, it should not be overlooked that our form of government is a representative monarchy. This is the instrument which throws into relief and brings into action the two principles, Liberal and Conservative. We Liberals are often accused of being Republicans. I do not note this reproach for the purpose of taking it up, for it is not worth taking up. I merely state that the form matters little; whether it be monarchical or republican, the moment the people exercise the right to vote, the moment they have a responsible government, they have the full measure of liberty. Still, liberty would soon be no more than an empty name, if it left without control those who have the direction of power. A man, whose astonishing sagacity has formulated the axioms of governmental science with undeviating accuracy, Junius, has said: "Eternal vigilance is the price of liberty." Yes, if a people want to remain free, they must, like Argus, have a hundred eyes and be always on the alert. If they slumber, or relax, each moment of indolence loses them a particle of their rights. Eternal vigilance is the price which they have to pay for the priceless boon of liberty. Now, the form of a representative monarchy lends itself marvellously—much more, perhaps, than the republican form—to the exercise of this necessary vigilance. On the one hand, you have those who govern and, on the other, those who watch. On the one hand you have those who are in power and have an interest in remaining there, and, on the other, those who have an interest in getting there. What is the bond of cohesion to unite each individual of the different groups? What is the principle, the sentiment, to range these divers elements of the population either among those who govern or those who watch? It is the Liberal principle or the Conservative principle. You will see together those who are attracted by the charm of novelty and you will see together those who are attracted by the charm of habit. You will see together those who are attached to all that is ancient and you will see together those who are always disposed to reform.

Now, I ask, between these two ideas which constitute the basis of parties, can there be a moral difference? Is the one radically good and the other radically bad? Is it not evident that both are what are termed in moral philosophy "indifferents," that is to say that both are susceptible of being appreciated, pondered and chosen? Would it not be as unfair as it would be absurd to condemn or approve either the one or the other as absolutely bad or good?

Both are susceptible of much good, as they are also of much evil. The Conservative, who defends his country's old institutions, may do much good, as he also may do much evil, if he be obstinate in maintaining abuses which have become intolerable. The Liberal, who contends against these abuses, and who, after long efforts, succeeds in extirpating them, may be a public benefactor, just as the Liberal who lays a rash hand on hallowed institutions may be a ocourge not only for his country, but for humanity at large.

The constitution of the country rests on the freely expressed wish of each elector. It intends that each elector shall cast his vote freely and willingly as he deems best. If the greatest number of the electors of a country are actually of an opinion and that, owing to the influence exercised upon them by one or more men or owing to words they have heard or writings they have read, their opinion changes, there is nothing in the circumstance but what is perfectly legitimate. Although the opinion they express is different from the one they would have expressed without such intervention, still it is the one they desire to express conscientiously, and the constitution meets with its entire application. If, however, notwithstanding all reasoning, the opinion of the electors remains the same, but that, by intimidation or fraud they are forced to vote differently, the opinion which they express is not their opinion, and the constitution is violated. As I have already said, the constitution intends that each one's opinion shall be freely expressed as he understands it at the moment of expression, and the collective reunion of the individual opinions, freely expressed, forms the government of the country.

The law watches with so jealous an eye the free expression of the elector's opinion as it really is, that, if in a constituency the opinion expressed by a single one of the electors is not his real opinion, but an opinion forced upon him by fear, fraud or corruption, the election must be annulled.

It is therefore perfectly legitimate to alter the elector's opinion by argument and all other means of persuasion, but never by intimidation. As a matter of fact, persuasion changes the elector's conviction; intimidation does not. When, by persuasion, you have changed the elector's conviction, the opinion he expresses is his own opinion, but when, by terror, you force him to vote, the opinion he expresses is your opinion; remove the cause of his fear and he will then express another opinion, which is his own.

Now, it will be understood, if the opinion expressed by the majority of the electors is not their real opinion, but an opinion snatched from them by fraud, by threats or by corruption, the constitution is violated and you have not the government of the majority, but the government of a minority. Well, if such a state of things continues and is repeated,— if, after each election, the will expressed is not the real will of the country,—once more you do violence to the constitution, responsible government is no longer anything but an empty name, and, sooner or later, here as elsewhere, the pressure will culminate in explosion, violence and ruin.

GEORGE M. GRANT

GEORGE MUNRO GRANT

1835-1902

GEORGE MUNRO GRANT was a native Canadian. He was born at Albion Mines, Nova Scotia, December 22, 1835, of Scottish parentage. The simple life of his early years on the farm gave him two of his outstanding characteristics—practical ability and a deep love of nature. He was a very vivacious lad and enjoyed his share of boyhood pranks.

His school days were spent at Pictou Academy and West River Seminary where he showed promise of a brilliant career. At the age of eighteen he went to Glasgow University. Here he entered into every activity of college life, winning laurels in scholastic, debating, and athletic circles.

In 1860 he was ordained to the Ministry of the Presbyterian Church in Canada. After short pastorates in River John and Prince Edward Island he was called to St. Matthew's Church, Halifax, of which he was the eminently successful minister for fourteen years.

A momentous era was dawning in Canada. The proposal of a confederation of the provinces was before the people. In Nova Scotia there was strong opposition to the scheme, but it had a powerful champion in Grant. He did much to foster and strengthen faith in the new Dominion. In 1872 he accompanied Sanford Fleming, engineer-in-chief of the Canadian Pacific Railway on a surveying tour through the then unknown West. On his return he published an account of his travels in the book "From Ocean to Ocean" which revealed to Canadians the glories of their Northern and Western territories.

But it was in a wider sphere that Dr. Grant found his true life work. In 1877 he accepted the principalship of Queen's University, Kingston, and as the beloved Principal Grant of Queen's he touched thousands of young lives, inspiring them towards a pursuit of knowledge, the upbuilding of a free, self-reliant personality, and high ideals of Canadian citizenship. Early and late he toiled for Queen's; his boundless energy and enthusiasm built up a great institution of learning.

Not only as a college president was Dr. Grant of note. As a public man he watched the trend of events in Canadian national life and spoke out sanely and fearlessly on questions of the day.

Principal Grant never spared himself. As preacher, writer, lecturer, and student of affairs he had many interests and responsibilities which greatly taxed his strength. His sudden death came as a great shock to the whole country, for he had been carrying out his duties at the University a few days before the end. He passed away May 10, 1902, and was laid to rest in beautiful Cataraqui Cemetery, Kingston. Canada mourned the loss of one of her truest and greatest sons.

George M. Grant

CANADA FIRST

PRINCIPAL GEORGE MUNRO GRANT

From an address to the Canadian Club of New York City, 1887.

I MAY be asked: How can Canada have at the same time the position of a nation and a colony? I may answer that no country any more than an individual attains to complete self-realization at once; but, until it does so it is allowed a place among the nations only by courtesy. As I have already hinted, the War of Independence was made much more difficult than it otherwise would have been, from the fact that each of the thirteen colonies thought itself supreme and the Union secondary. Even that war for bare life did not teach the lesson that a real Union was necessary to constitute a great State. It took some years of deadlocks before the present constitution was adopted. We know how weak the bond that held the States together was felt to be—for a long time even after that. We see it in the action of State Legislatures in 1812-15, justifying Great Britain and Canada, threatening secession and refusing quotas of troops; from subsequent attempts at nullification North and South; from political compromises and conflicts at various times; and, at last, from the great war of Secession, when thousands of men like Lee and Jackson, who cared nothing for slavery, fought for it rather than fight against their own native State. It took nearly a century for the great Republic to realize itself, to understand that its life was a sacred thing, and that whosoever or whatsoever stood in the way or interfered with its legitimate development must be swept out of the way. It accomplished the necessary task—consequently its present proud position. It stands out before the world a power so mighty that we can hardly conceive of a force, internal or external, great enough to threaten it.

Well, Canada stands now about where the United States stood a century ago. The circumstances are different, for though history repeats itself, it does not do so slavishly. We have had a different historical development. We have more radical racial diversities. We have a less genial climate and larger breadths of land of which nothing can be made. But we are near where the Republic stood a century ago. Canada is in its infancy and must expect infantile troubles. It must go through the hard experience of measles, teething, calf-fears and calf-love; must be expected to spend its pocket-money foolishly, suffer from explosions of temper, get slights that are hard to bear and abrasions of the skin that will make it think life not worth living. But, it is a big, healthy child, comes of a good stock, has an enormously large farm, which is somewhat in need of fencing and cultivation, and I think it may be depended on to pull through. It is growing up under stern conditions, and, as a Scotch-Canadian, taught in his youth to revere Solomon and to believe therefore in the efficacy of the rod and the yoke for children, I am inclined to think that it is none the worse for that. The climate is most trying to tramps. Geography and treaties have united to make its material unification difficult. Much of its property is not worth stealing; but all the more will it hold on with grim tenacity to all that is worth anything.

But, no matter what may be said in its disparagement, it is a wide and goodly land, with manifold beauties of its own, with boundless resources that are only beginning to be developed, and with room and verge for Empire. Each Province has attractions for its children. One would need to live in it to understand how strong these attractions are. Only when you live among the country people do they reveal themselves. Strangers or tourists are not likely to have the faintest conception of their deepest feelings. Thus a man who lives in his study, or in a select coterie, or always in a city, may—no matter how great his ability—utterly misconceive the spirit of a province or nation and the vigour of its life. It has been my lot to live for a time in almost every one of our provinces, and to cross the whole Dominion, again and again, from ocean to ocean, by steamer or canoe, by rail and buckboard, on horseback and on foot, and I have found, in the remotest settlements, a remarkable acquaintance with public questions and much soundness of judgment and feeling in regard to them; a high average purity of individual and family life, and a steady growth of national sentiment. I have sat with the blackened toilers in the coal mines of Pictou and Cape Breton, the darkness made visible by the little lamps hanging from their sooty foreheads; have worshipped with pious Highlanders in log huts in fertile glens and on the hillsides, where the forest gives place slowly to the plough, and preached to assembled thousands, seated on grassy hillocks and prostrate trees; have fished and sailed with the hardy mariners, who find "every harbour, from Sable to Canseau, a home;" have ridden under the willows of Evangeline's country, and gazed from North and South Mountain on a sea of apple-blossoms; have talked with gold miners, fishermen, farmers, merchants, students, and have learned to respect my fellow countrymen and to sympathize with their provincial life, and to see that it was not antagonistic, but intended to be the handmaid to a true national life.

Go there, not altogether in the spirit of "Baddeck, and that sort of thing." Pass from Annapolis Royal into the Bay of Fundy, and then canoe up the rivers, shaded by the great trees of New Brunswick. Live a while with the habitants of Quebec, admire their industry, frugality and courtesy; hear their carols and songs, that blend the forgotten music of Normandy and Brittany with the music of Canadian woods; music and song, as well as language and religion, rooting in them devotion to "Our Language, our Laws, our Institutions." Live in historic Quebec, and experience the hospitality of Montreal. Pass through the Province of Ontario, itself possessing the resources of a kingdom. Sail on lakes great enough to be called seas, along rugged Laurentian coasts, or take the new Northwest passage by land, that the Canadian Pacific has opened up from the Upper Ottawa, through a thousand miles once declared impracticable for railways, and now yielding treasures of wood and copper and silver, till you come to that great prairie ocean, that sea of green and gold in this month of May, whose billows extend for nigh another thousand miles to the Rocky Mountains, out of which great Provinces like Minnesota and Dakota will be carved in the immediate future. And when you have reached the Pacific, and look back over all the panorama that unrolls itself before your mental vision, you will not doubt that the country is destined to have a future. You will thank God that you belong to a generation to whom the duty has been assigned of laying its foundations; and knowing that the solidity of any construction is in proportion to the faith, the virtue and the self-sacrifice that has been wrought into the foundation, you will pray that you for one may not be found wanting.

JOHN A. MACDONALD

CANADA'S RELATIONSHIP TO GREAT BRITAIN AND THE UNITED STATES

SIR JOHN A. MACDONALD

From the last address to the people of Canada and in connection with the Unrestricted Reciprocity Campaign of 1891

FOR a century and a half this country has grown and flourished under the protecting aegis of the British Crown. The gallant race who first bore to our shores the blessings of civilization passed by an easy transition from French to British rule, and now form one of the most law-abiding portions of the community. These pioneers were speedily reinforced by the advent of a loyal band of British subjects, who gave up everything that most men prize, and were content to begin life anew in the wilderness rather than forego allegiance to their Sovereign. To the descendants of these men, and of the multitude of Englishmen, Irishmen, and Scotchmen who emigrated to Canada, that they might build up new homes without ceasing to be British subjects, to you Canadians I appeal, and I ask you what have you to gain by surrendering that which your fathers held most dear? Under the broad folds of the Union Jack, we enjoy the most ample liberty to govern ourselves as we please, and at the same time we participate in the advantages which flow from association with the mightiest Empire the world has ever seen. Not only are we free to manage our domestic concerns, but, practically, we possess the privilege of making our own treaties with foreign countries, and, in our relations with the outside world, we enjoy the prestige inspired by a consciousness of the fact that behind us towers the majesty of England.

The question which you will shortly be called upon to determine resolves itself into this: shall we endanger our possession of the great heritage bequeathed to us by our fathers, and submit ourselves to direct taxation for the privilege of having our tariff fixed at Washington, with a prospect of ultimately becoming a portion of the American Union? I commend these issues to your determination, and to the judgment of the whole people of Canada, with an unclouded confidence that you will proclaim to the world your resolve to show yourselves not unworthy of the proud distinction that you enjoy, of being numbered among the most dutiful and loyal subjects of our beloved Queen.

As for myself, my course is clear. A British subject I was born—a British subject I will die. With my utmost effort, with my latest breath, will I oppose the "veiled treason" which attempts by sordid means and mercenary proffers to lure our people from their allegiance. During my long public service of nearly half a century, I have been true to my country and its best interests, and I appeal with equal confidence to the men who have trusted me in the past, and to the young hope of the country, with whom rest its destinies for the future, to give me their united and strenuous aid in this my last effort for the unity of the Empire and the preservation of our commercial and political freedom.

SIR WILFRID LAURIER

DEATH OF SIR JOHN A. MACDONALD

SIR WILFRID LAURIER

From a Speech in the House of Commons, June 8, 1891

SIR JOHN MACDONALD now belongs to the ages, and it can be said with certainty that the career which has just been closed is one of the most remarkable careers of this century. It would be premature at this time to attempt to fix or anticipate what will be the final judgment of history upon him; but there were in his career and in his life, features so prominent and so conspicuous that already they shine with a glow which time cannot alter, which even now appear before the eye such as they will appear to the end in history. I think it can be asserted that for the supreme art of governing men, Sir John Macdonald was gifted as few men in any land or in any age were gifted; gifted with the most high of all qualities which would have made him famous wherever exercised and which would have shone all the more conspicuously the larger the theatre. The fact that he could congregate together elements the most heterogeneous and blend them into one compact party, and to the end of his life keep them steadily under his hand, is perhaps altogether unprecedented. The fact that during all those years he retained unimpaired not only the confidence, but the devotion—the ardent devotion and affection of his party—is evidence that beside those higher qualities of statesmanship to which we were the daily witnesses, he was also endowed with those inner, subtle, undefinable graces of soul which win and keep the hearts of men.

As to his statesmanship, it is written in the history of Canada. It may be said without any exaggeration whatever, that the life of Sir John Macdonald, from the date he entered Parliament, is the history of Canada, for he was connected and associated with all the events, all the facts which brought Canada from the position Canada then occupied—the position of two small provinces, having nothing in common but a common allegiance, united by a bond of paper, and united by nothing else—to the present state of development which Canada has reached. Although my political views compel me to say that, in my judgment, his actions were not always the best that could have been taken in the interest of Canada, although my conscience compels me to say that of late he has imputed to his opponents motives as to which I must say in my heart he has misconceived, yet I am only too glad here to sink these differences, and to remember only the great services he has performed for our country—to remember that his actions always displayed great originality of views, unbounded fertility of resources, a high level of intellectual conceptions, and, above all, a far-reaching vision beyond the event of the day, and still higher, permeating the whole, a broad patriotism, a devotion to Canada's welfare, Canada's advancement and Canada's glory.

Death of Sir John A. Macdonald

The life of a statesman is always an arduous one, and very often it is an ungrateful one. More often than otherwise his actions do not mature until he is in his grave. Not so, however, in the case of Sir John Macdonald. His career has been a singularly fortunate one. His reverses were few and of short duration. He was fond of power, and, in my judgment, if I may say so, that may be the turning point of the judgment of history. He was fond of power, and he never made any secret of it. Many times we have heard him avow it on the floor of this Parliament, and his ambition in this respect was gratified as, perhaps, no other man's ambition ever was. In my judgment, even the career of William Pitt can hardly compare with that of Sir John Macdonald in this respect; for although William Pitt, moving in a higher sphere, had to deal with problems greater than our problems, yet I doubt if in the intricate management of a party William Pitt had to contend with difficulties equal to those that Sir John Macdonald had to contend with. In his death, too, he seems to have been singularly happy. Twenty years ago I was told by one who at that time was a close personal and political friend of Sir John Macdonald, that in the intimacy of his domestic circle he was fond of repeating that his end would be as the end of Lord Chatham, that he would be carried away from the floor of Parliament to die. How true that vision into the future was we now know, for we saw him to the last, with enfeebled health and declining strength, struggling on the floor of Parliament until the hand of fate pinned him to his bed to die. And thus to die with his armour on was probably his ambition. Sir, death is the law—the supreme law. Although we see it every day in every form, although session after session we have seen it in this Parliament striking right and left without any discrimination as to age or station, yet the ever-recurring spectacle does not in any way remove the bitterness of the sting. Death always carries with it an incredible sense of pain; but the one thing sad in death is that which is involved in the word separation—separation from all we love in life. This is what makes death so poignant when it strikes a man of intellect in middle age. But when death is the natural termination of a full life, in which he who disappears has given the full measure of his capacity, has performed everything required of him, and more, the sadness of death is not for him who goes, but for those who loved him and remain. In this sense I am sure the Canadian people will extend unbounded sympathy to the friends of Sir John Macdonald—to his sorrowing children, and, above all, to the brave and noble woman, his companion in life and his chief helpmate.

Thus, Mr. Speaker, one after another, we see those who have been instrumental in bringing Canada to its present stage of development removed from amongst us. To-day we deplore the loss of him who, we all unite in saying, was the foremost Canadian of his time, and who filled the largest place in Canadian history. Only last week was buried in the city of Montreal, another son of Canada, one who at one time had been a tower of strength to the Liberal party, one who will ever be remembered as one of the noblest, purest and greatest characters that Canada has ever produced, Sir Antoine Aimé Dorion. Sir Antoine Aimé Dorion had not been in favour of Confederation. Not that he was opposed to the principle; but he believed that the Union of these provinces, at that day, was premature. When, however, Confederation had become a fact, he gave the best of his mind and heart to make it a success. It may indeed happen, Sir, that when the Canadian people see the ranks thus gradually reduced and thinned of those upon whom they have been in the habit of relying for guidance, that a feeling of apprehension will creep into the heart lest, perhaps, the institutions of Canada may be imperilled. Before the grave of him who, above all, was the father of Confederation, let not grief be barren grief; but let grief be coupled with the resolution, the determination, that the work in which Liberals and Conservatives, in which Brown and Macdonald united, shall not perish, but that though United Canada may be deprived of the services of her greatest men, still Canada shall and will live.

GEORGE W. ROSS

GEORGE W. ROSS

1841-1914

SIR GEORGE ROSS is held in grateful remembrance by the people of Ontario for his generous contribution to the development of the province. But he was not a merely provincial figure, and Canada, too, owes him thanks for his faithful political service in the Dominion Parliament, extending over a period of eighteen years.

George Ross began life in a humble way on a farm in Middlesex county, in 1841, was educated at the local public school, and at Toronto Normal School, and entered upon his public career at the age of fifteen years as a country school teacher. His natural gift for public speaking and debating, and his capacity for leadership were quickly recognized and he was persuaded to enter politics. With a political goal in view he became in turn journalist, Public School and Model School Inspector, and by 1872 his prestige was sufficient to effect his election to the Dominion Legislature as Liberal Member for Middlesex County. Once inside the parliamentary walls, his rise was steady, though by no means spectacular.

In 1883 he joined the Mowat Administration in Ontario as Minister of Education, and his work in this capacity was of lasting benefit to the education system of the province, several badly-needed reforms having been achieved. His efforts were rewarded with the Premiership in 1899, which he retained until 1905, when the Liberal party went down to defeat after an uninterrupted reign of thirty-three years.

During his term of administration Ontario's economic development was facilitated greatly by the construction of the Temiskaming and Northern Ontario Railway, which opened up the vast treasures of Northern Ontario to the world. Ross was energetic in behalf of the scheme, and hoped to extend the railway eventually to Hudson Bay. Throughout his premiership he continued his educational reforms, and was active in advancing Temperance reform.

In 1907 he was appointed to the Senate and became one of the Liberal leaders, but he was not slavishly attached to his party and retained his individual viewpoint to the end. Thus, though a life-long Liberal, he opposed the Reciprocity Bill of 1911, because it conflicted with his Imperialistic principles. He died in 1914, active to the last in the service of his country.

Sir George Ross was a staunch Imperialist and an enthusiastic student of the Empire in its various phases. He was an author and publicist of repute, and has left behind him a number of books and treatises on education, history and politics. He was, besides, a master of oratory, and delivered many public speeches, commendable alike for their logic and eloquence. His cheerful and kindly disposition, lofty idealism and broad-minded enthusiasm added to the esteem to which his long years of public service have entitled him.

George W. Ross

THE EVOLUTION OF CANADIAN SENTIMENT

Hon. George W. Ross

From a speech at the Empire Club, 1905

IT is not hard to believe, I think you will accept the proposition readily, that there was a time when there was no such thing as Canadian loyalty. I suppose that is true in the evolution of a family. There is no such thing as the full development of the spirit of home in man until he feels he has a home for himself. When our fathers came here they came to a land in which they had their fortunes to make if there was a chance for them; which land was entirely destitute of a history and in order to give themselves any identity or individuality at all they had to attach themselves to the land from which they came. It is only, Sir, within the last few years we knew we were Canadians. I am sorry to say in Great Britain they hardly know we are Canadians yet. They generally speak of us as Americans, as if there was not in the term "Canadian" a sweetness and a power which cannot issue, and which we must not allow to issue from the rather mal-appropriated term "American" which some people in this country use for themselves. I said our first sentiments of connection with Canada were entirely that of British connection, and all our first efforts to preserve our identity were efforts not to preserve the identity or the existence of Canada, but were to preserve that British connection which we transferred, or our fathers transferred, to this country by their settlement here.

The War of 1812 was not a war engaged in by Canadians for Canada, it was a war to maintain British connection. The object of the Americans was to annex us. We fought to maintain British connection. There may have been perhaps a scintilla of Canadian love and loyalty; there may have been in the minds of some of us the idea that we were fighting for the land in which we live and for the property which we possess and for our homes, but these ideas were in the form in which a man fights for any goods he may have in his possession when waylaid by the highwayman. But the prevailing idea and the main consideration which led to the fight of 1812, so far as we were concerned, was to preserve Canada to Great Britain and not to preserve it to Canadians. When we came to the rebellion of 1837 many years afterwards, that trouble was suppressed through the idea that the promoters of the Rebellion had in their minds the diversion of Canada to the United States. We fought then in 1837 without any prevailing or predominating idea that we were fighting for Canada or fighting for Canadian privileges; we were fighting to remain under the British flag.

Really as I read history, Canadians did not feel even then that we had a Canada to fight for. And what is true of our efforts, and very proper and praiseworthy efforts they were, to maintain British connection is also true of much of our trade arrangements of the time. For instance, if you read the life of Lord Elgin, you will find that the Treaty of Reciprocity was made not from a Canadian stand-

point as much as from the British standpoint. By
the abolition of the Corn Laws and the abrogation of
the Preferential Tariff which existed then between
Canada and Great Britain in the matter of lumber
and wheat and flour, our trade with Great Britain
was practically destroyed and the instructions to
Lord Elgin were, in order to overcome the discontent
which prevailed in Canada at the loss of business, to
make an effort to establish better trade relations with
the United States in order that the Canadians might
be content and continue their allegiance to the
British Crown. So that the whole history of Canada
up to Confederation, and that itself, as I shall show
in a moment, was a history in which the standpoint
of the Canadian was that of British connection, a
worthy standpoint to be sure, but yet a standpoint
which had not in it those elements of loyalty which
were subsequently injected into the Canadian mind.

And, coming to the Confederation itself, if you read
the discussion in the House of Lords when the Bill
was introduced by the Colonial Secretary you will
there find one of the objects of Confederation was to
unite the Canadian Provinces so that they might
present a united front to the Americans should the
Americans be too aggressive. The preamble of that
Act shows that pretty clearly because it refers to the
establishment in Canada of a Government after the
model of the Government of the United Kingdom of
Great Britain and Ireland. So that even in that very
recent stage in our history the Canadian standpoint
was one of British connection rather than of, shall I

say, an integral, ingrained, devoted loyalty to Canada itself.

The next stage was a different one that practically grew out of the Confederation of 1867, largely moved, too, by a party organization at that time known as the Canada First party, which had some excellent qualities and which for some time endeavoured to direct Canadian sentiment; in some respects I think wrongfully, in other respects rightfully, towards the intrinsic merits of Canada itself and directing us also to the duty of loving Canada because it was great enough to be loved, because it was good enough to be loved and because it had in its constitution those elements of freedom and liberty which made for greatness; that it was our duty not to fear about greatness but to look boldly upon the future and to meet it with a loyal heart, remembering the words of Tennyson:

"We sailed wherever ship could sail;
We founded many a mighty state.
Pray Heaven our greatness may not fail
Through craven fear of being great."

And we got that sentiment, and that sentiment grew in the Canadian mind. I do not want to call it Canada First sentiment except for the convenience of the term; for I would like to sever it from some elements that constituted the Canada First party. Let us look at the evolution from the time of the Confederation of 1867. I believe we builded better than we knew then. I believe the Fathers of Confederation, like the Fathers of the American Republic, even like the great Bismarck who founded the German Confederation, did not conceive of the future which we now see, much less of the future which our children shall see, as the .foundation of that Confederation was laid in 1867. The first thing we did was to look around and with true Scotch frugality and British prudence endeavoured to see if we were having a clear title to the half of this Continent and we immediately negotiated with Great Britain or with the Hudson's Bay Company for the possession of Rupert's Land, thus getting our hands upon practically a great empire, that which may be the greatest part of Canada yet, reaching from the boundary of Ontario on the west to the foot of the Rocky Mountains and north as far as ship can sail and farther still.

That showed that before we were practically twelve months old we had caught the inspiration of true Canadianism and we were seeking to clear the decks, as it were, for greater prosperity and progress, and we got that great territory and it was well we got it then, for had we delayed the purchase thereof it would have cost us much more. Then, having got the territory, what did we do? We began as four Provinces and immediately this little family of four members multiplied and increased and we, as by a repetition of history, became possessed with the same spirit which animated the founders of the American Republic. They began with thirteen States and in a few years there were fifteen, and seventeen and so on. As Madison said to Jefferson when they were trying to get the Constitution of the United

States adopted by the other States: "We must not allow State rights to interfere nor must we look upon this Federation of ours from the standpoint of individual States, but we must think continentally." And the Americans thought continentally and they got Florida from Spain, and Louisiana from France, and they took Texas for themselves. They would have done more if we had let them. Think of their getting from France the vast territory which they did! They thought continentally.

The ink was scarcely dry upon our Constitution when we began to think constitutionally. We began to think federally; we carved out Manitoba in 1869, we federated with British Columbia in 1871, with Prince Edward Island in 1873. We are making two more Provinces just now. Amid a great deal of confusion and a great deal of debate and discussion this new baby is born under certain disquieting circumstances but we shall have two Provinces more. These twins will add to our Provinces and make them nine, and the true Canadian will not rest until Newfoundland is within the boundaries of the Constitution. That was the spirit that was born in 1867 and that is the spirit still. We must have elbow room. Britain has about one-quarter of the whole habitable portion of the globe to-day, and John Bull sometimes feels himself a little squeezed in approaching certain portions of his territory. We must have elbow room, not for ourselves simply, but for the generations yet to come. We have got it and therefore we have territory enough to call forth the highest demands upon our loyalty.

STEPHEN LEACOCK

STEPHEN LEACOCK

1869-

THERE are three Stephen Leacocks wrapped up in the one personality; the university professor of academic mind and writer of "Elements of Political Science;" the political speaker and popular lecturer; and the humourist and writer of the "Sunshine Sketches of a Little Town," "Literary Lapses." "Behind the Beyond," and other "Nonsense Novels."

Stephen Butler Leacock was born in England on December 30, 1869, at Swanmoor, Hants, but came to Canada as a boy. He was educated at Upper Canada College, Toronto, and at the University of Toronto. After graduation he engaged in school-teaching and for several years taught languages at Upper Canada College. In his preface to the "Sunshine Sketches" he tells us that in 1899 he "gave up school-teaching in disgust, borrowed enough money to live upon for a few months and went to the University of Chicago to study economics and political science." He was soon appointed to a Fellowship in political economy and in 1903 he took the degree of Doctor of Philosophy. Since then he has belonged to the staff of McGill University, Montreal, first as lecturer in political science, then as associate professor in political science and history, and finally as head of the department of Economics and Political Science.

C.—14

Having solved the problem of a livelihood—"the emolument is so high as to place me distinctly above the policemen, postmen, street-car conductors and other salaried officials of the neighbourhood"—he was able to devote his leisure to writing and to spreading the Gospel of Humour.

The world seems as a rule to accept Stevenson's theory that a man's recreations make up his real life, and it is as a humorous writer that Professor Leacock is most widely known. He himself has said that he would rather have written "Alice in Wonderland" than the whole Encyclopædia Britannica. Occasionally his humour lacks spontaneity, but his masterpieces effervesce with fun and wit. On the whole his writings entitle him to the first place among Canadian humourists, and he is hailed with joy as a bringer of laughter from coast to coast.

Stephen Leacock

EDUCATION AND EMPIRE UNITY
Professor Stephen Leacock.

From an address made before the Empire Club, Toronto, 1907.

WE must realize, and the people of England must realize, the inevitable greatness of Canada. This is not a vainglorious boast. This is not a rhodomontade. It is a simple fact. Here we stand, six million people, heirs to the greatest legacy in the history of mankind, owners of half a continent, trustees, under God Almighty, for the fertile solitudes of the West. A little people, few in number, say you? Ah, truly such a little people! Few as the people of the Greeks that blocked the mountain gates of Europe to the march of Asia, few as the men of Rome that built a power to dominate the world, nay, scarce more numerous than they in England whose beacons flamed along the cliffs a warning to the heavy galleons of Spain. Aye, such a little people, but growing, growing, growing, with a march that shall make us ten millions to-morrow, twenty millions in our children's time and a hundred millions yet ere the century runs out.

What say you to Fort Garry, a stockaded fort in your father's day, with its hundred thousand of to-day and its half a million souls of to-morrow? What think you, little River Thames, of our great Ottawa that flings its foam eight hundred miles? What does it mean when science has moved us a little further yet, and the wheel of the world's work turns with electric force? What sort of asset do you think then our melting snow and the roaring river-flood of our

223

Canadian spring shall be to us? What say you, little puffing steam-fed industry of England, to the industry of coming Canada? Think you, you can heave your coal hard enough, sweating and grunting with your shovel, to keep pace with the snow-fed cataracts of the north? Or look, were it but for double conviction, at the sheer extent and size of us. Throw aside, if you will, the vast districts of the frozen north; confiscate, if you like, Ungava, still snow-covered and unknown, and let us talk of the Canada that we know, south of the sixteenth parallel, south of your Shetland Islands, south of the Russian Petersburg and reaching southward thence to where the peach groves of Niagara bloom in the latitude of Northern Spain. And of all this take only our two new provinces, twin giants of the future, Alberta and Saskatchewan. Three decades ago this was a great lone land, the frozen west, with its herds of bison and its Indian tepees, known to you only in the pictured desolation of its unending snow; now crossed and inter-crossed with railways, settled 400 miles from the American frontier, and sending north and south the packets of its daily papers from its two provincial capitals. And of this country, fertile as the corn plains of Hungary, and the crowded flats of Belgium, do you know the size? It is this. Put together the whole German Empire, the republic of France and your England and Scotland, and you shall find place for them in our two new provinces. Or take together across the boundary from us, the States of Maine, New Hampshire, Vermont, Massachusetts, Rhode Island and Connecticut—all the New England States

—and with them all the Middle States of the North—
New York, New Jersey, Pennsylvania, Delaware,
Ohio, Indiana, Michigan, Illinois and Wisconsin
till you have marked a space upon the map from the
Atlantic to the Mississippi and from Ohio to the Lakes
—all these you shall put into our two new provinces
and still find space for England and for Scotland in
their boundaries.

The signs of the times are written large as to what
the destiny of Canada shall not be. Not as it is—
not on this colonial footing—can it indefinitely last.
There are those who tell us that it is best to leave well
enough alone, to wait for the slow growth, the evolution of things. For herein lies the darling thought
of the wisdom of the nineteenth century, in the same
evolution, this ready-made explanation of all things;
hauled over the researches of the botanist to meet
the lack of thought of the philosopher. Whatever
is, is; whatever will be, will be—so runs its silly creed.
Therefore let everything be, that is; and all that shall
be, shall be. This is but the wisdom of the fool wise
after the fact. For the solution of our vexed colonial
problem this profits nothing. We cannot sit passive
to watch our growth. Good or bad, straight or
crooked, we must make our fate.

Nor is it even possible or desirable that we in
Canada can form an independent country. The little
cry that here and there goes up among us is but the
symptom of an aspiring discontent, that will not let
our people longer be colonials. 'Tis but a cry forced
out by what a wise man has called "the growing
pains of a nation's progress." Independent, we could

not survive a decade. Those of us who know our country realize that beneath its surface smoulder still the embers of racial feud and of religious bitterness. Twice in our generation has the sudden alarm of conflict broken upon the quiet of our prosperity with the sound of a fire-bell in the night. Not thus our path. Let us compose the feud and still the strife of races, not in the artificial partnership of Independent Canada, but in the joint greatness of a common destiny.

Nor does our future lie in union with those that dwell to the southward. The day of annexation to the United States is past. Our future lies elsewhere. Be it said without concealment and without bitterness. They have chosen their lot; we have chosen ours. Let us go our separate ways in peace. Let them keep their perennial Independence Day, with its fulminating fireworks and its Yankee Doodle. We keep our Magna Charta and our rough-and-ready Rule Britannia, shouting as lustily as they! The propaganda of annexation is dead.

JAMES A. MACDONALD

JAMES A. MACDONALD

1862-1923

REV. DR. JAMES ALEXANDER MACDON-
ALD, preacher, lecturer and journalist, was born
in Middlesex County, Ontario, in 1862. His forceful,
independent spirit can be traced in his forefathers
through the pioneer in Ontario and Nova Scotia
back to the Macdonalds and Grants, warriors in
the Highlands of Scotland.

J. A. Macdonald attended collegiate institute in
Toronto and Hamilton, studied at Toronto and
Edinburgh Universities, and was trained for the
ministry at Knox College, Toronto. From 1881 to
1896 he was pastor of a Presbyterian church in St.
Thomas. There he established his reputation as a
powerful preacher and a magnetic lecturer.

But he soon turned to work in which he could send
his message over a larger field. Evidences of his gift
for journalism had appeared while he was still a
student, for he had edited the *Knox College
Monthly*. In 1896 he returned to Toronto as editor of the *Westminster*, a religious monthly magazine, in which his articles on topics of the day were
widely read. His interests were diverse, for during
this period he acted also as Principal of the Presbyterian Ladies' College. In 1902 he became
editor-in-chief of the *Daily Globe*, Toronto, and won

a very high place among Canadian journalists. In 1909 he was a delegate to the Imperial Press Conference in London, England, and was given an honorary degree by the University of Glasgow. A similar honour was conferred on him later by the University of Birmingham.

While upholding the principles of the Liberal party, Dr. Macdonald showed an unusual fairness and independence of thought, that gave weight to his opinions on any phase of politics in Canada. His interest in national and international affairs, his advocacy of democratic ideals, his work toward arbitration and world peace, combined to give his writings a widespread appeal. In 1911 he was appointed a director of the World's Peace Foundation for promoting the settlement of international disputes by judicial arbitration. After an illness extending over a number of years he passed away in Toronto, in May, 1923.

James A. Macdonald

INTERNATIONAL RELATIONS

Rev. J. A. Macdonald

From an address before the Canadian Club, Toronto, 1911

IF Canada would, indeed, play a great part
among the nations, her standing must be maintained as free among the free nations comprising the
British Empire, without abatement of any powers
of self-government and with due regard for the obligations of Empire. None of the rights of responsible
government won half a century ago can be surrendered to any theory of imperialism. And those rights,
which give dignity and worth to all other privileges,
must be made to match the new obligations which
the relations of world-wide empire impose. Canada
must make and administer her own laws, police her
own shores, and do her share in keeping the peace
on the high seas. But all this she must do in alliance
with the rest of the Empire, and in the free exercise
of her own responsible judgment. National autonomy is of the very essence of national freedom, and
freedom is the source and secret of enduring loyalty.
This is the glorious British way. By it Canada has
grown in loyalty as she grew in power. And by it
South Africa, that a decade ago was seething with
rebellion, is now justifying once more to the world
the all-conquering power of Britain's confidence in
that liberty by which she makes free all the nations
under the flag. Let us not doubt it. We may have
no precedent for a world empire of free nations.

Let us make one. Britain had to blaze the way for responsible government. Canada blazed the way for overseas confederation. Let Britain and Canada and the other British dominions give the world a new type of empire in which the measure of individual freedom is the measure of imperial loyalty.

But Canada's relations are not with Britain alone, but with America as well. A partner in the English-speaking fraternity, a factor in Anglo-American arbitration proposals, an ally for the security of America, Canada's position on this continent is a pledge of peace, not for America alone, but for the world. Believe me, the problem of Canada's future and the part and place of this young nation in the development of American life, while uncertain enough to command our severest thought, is hopeful enough to inspire our highest effort.

Time was, and not many years ago, when many thoughtful Canadians saw no future for this country except in political union with the United States. Some who were then not averse to such an issue are now the stoutest protesters against even ordinary trade relations. Time was, too, when thoughtful men in the United States looked forward to the annexation of Canada as an inevitable and not far-off event. The situation has completely changed. Annexation is no longer an open question. I do not know one informed and respectable leader of opinion in the United States who advocates it or wishes it. In a chance, but not unfruitful, conference which I had with President Taft in March of last year, when the ground was covered from the maximum and minimum tariff clause to the proposed Anglo-American arbitration treaty, the Chief Executive of the Republic assured me in terms and with an emphasis not to be mistaken, that the political union of these two nations is, from the American point of view, not only not desired, but not desirable. Since the incident at Manila Bay; since the United States was pushed out into world-politics; since the Orient loomed large on the horizon, there has come to their men of thought and leadership a new experience and a new insight. They appreciate now as they never did before the significance of the Union Jack on the north half of this continent. "The Pacific is a safer situation," said President Taft, "because two flags, not one, represent the power of English-speaking civilization." The past half-dozen years of diplomatic history illustrates this new attitude. To-day not one commanding voice, either in Canada or in the United States, would be given for annexation. That is the great new fact which shines on the horizon of Canada's international relations.

But through all these problems there runs the question: How is the ideal of the nation of eight millions to be kept unlowered and unspoiled against the day when Canada shall have eighty millions? In answering that question each man of us has his opportunity for service. Parliament and the politicians have their tasks, but the real chance is for the man out of office. Official obligations smother and hamper. In the freedom of simple citizenship the man who has a message will get his audience. The dignities of office are insignificant compared with the chance to awaken and direct the opinion of the people. Let who will be Premier or President; it is the man who moulds the people's thoughts that rules the democracies of America.

GEORGE E. FOSTER

GEORGE E. FOSTER

1847-

SIR GEORGE FOSTER is a well-known figure in Canadian political life. For forty years he has been an active member of the Dominion Parliament and he has had the unparalleled record of serving under every Conservative Prime Minister of Canada. His powerful intellect, strong moral convictions, and his wonderful gifts of oratory have made him a mighty influence among the Conservative ranks, and though by nature unfitted to lead a party, he has often been "the power behind the throne."

He was born in New Brunswick in 1847, was educated in the local schools, and in the University of New Brunswick, and began his public career as a school teacher. In this profession he was decidedly successful, but in 1879 he resigned the professorship of classics in New Brunswick University to enter the business world, from which he retired in 1906.

His political career commenced in 1882, and from the outset he made his presence felt in the House. He was tireless in exposing negligence and corruption, and was a scourge to political offenders. His marvellous capacity for combining reason with passion, and of humanizing statistics, gave him a position of great prestige, on the parliamentary floor as well as on the public platform.

C.—15

He joined Sir John A. Macdonald's Cabinet in 1885 as Minister of Marine and Fisheries, became Minister of Finance in 1889, and Minister of Trade and Commerce from 1911 until the fall of the Unionist Government in 1921. In all three of these portfolios he laboured with characteristic zeal, especially during the Great War, when he instituted a campaign in favour of economy and greater production.

He is a fervent Imperialist, and in 1903 gave a series of powerful addresses in Great Britain supporting Chamberlain's agitation for Imperial Trade Preference. He was called to the Imperial Privy Council in 1916, and was appointed one of the four representatives of Great Britain to the Economics Conference of the Allies, at Paris, in the same year. He was also actively interested in the League of Nations, and was elected Vice-President of the Canadian branch of the League of Nations in 1920. In 1921 he was elevated to the Senate, where he still takes a strong interest in national affairs.

Throughout his life he has followed the dictates of conscience, and his efforts at moral reform have been ceaseless. For years he has been identified with the Temperance movement, and he has given a number of eloquent addresses in its behalf. His passionate earnestness and moral intensity, while robbing him of the personal charm and humorous appeal which characterized his great Conservative Chief, Sir John A. Macdonald, have given him a convincing personality and an outstanding place among Canadian statesmen.

George E. Foster

THE CALL OF CANADA

Sir George E. Foster

From an address before the Royal Colonial Institute, June, 1913

WHEN a man from Nova Scotia goes to British Columbia he is not called an emigrant. He has simply moved. What reason is there in the world, when a man goes from Scotland to Australia or to Canada, that he should not be put in the same class as the man who has simply moved and not emigrated? The head and centre of the Empire is poorer by 138,000 people, provided they have not moved to another portion of the Empire. Therein lies the whole question. There should be but one Empire. The citizen of one portion of it should be a citizen in every other portion of it; the man who goes from one to another has simply transferred his home, and not transferred his national characteristics. If these great, mighty outlying dominions continue to grow, as they will grow, and their populations increase, fifty years will put the heart of the Empire and the outlying portions of the Empire in a very different position the one to the other. Are we not going to think about these things? Shall it always be *laissez faire?*

Yonder are indications of fire, behind it the wind is driving the flames towards your home; here you are, in your own home, asking yourself how many rooms you shall have within your dwelling, what compartments they shall be divided into, and what furniture shall be placed in each. You are warned of the danger. "But," you say, "let us settle this business first. Let us see how we are going to locate our own compartments and furnish our own rooms. Do not be excited over the fire," you say. "God is good, anyway—the wind may change." You can take that and translate it into a thought of Empire. From this day forward, "accursed be *laissez faire.*" Call it laziness—incapacity if you like; call it cowardice if that be the best name; but in the name of Heaven, men who have done what the outside dominions have done, men who have done what the men of this great heart of Empire have done—shall we not come together and sit around one common table, put our wits to work, and join our hearts and brains, our wisdom and our experience, from every part of this Empire, and organize?

What would Canada have been to-day had she not organized? What would this Empire have been without organization? Within twenty-five years it has outgrown the old organization. Shall we lie down, or sit still, and confess that we are not able to make the new and necessary organization which shall keep this Empire one, which will make those outside dominions synonymous with the growth of Empire as a whole? Shall we not take counsel together, plan together, work together, and so build up for the future an Empire which in the past has done so much for civilization, and which has so much left to do? Does any man here believe that the British Empire has fulfilled its mission—the mission to its own generations unborn, if you go no further—its mission to the world, for which it has great things in trust? This work can only be carried on by the fullest co-operation, and by calling ultimately to the seats of council the best experience that the whole Empire grows beneath its wide skies and upon its broad fields.

SIR WILFRID LAURIER

WHEN GREAT BRITAIN IS AT WAR WE ARE AT WAR

SIR WILFRID LAURIER

From an address in the House of Commons, Ottawa
August 19, 1914

THE gravity of the occasion which has called us together makes it incumbent upon us even to disregard the formalities and conventionalities which in ordinary times the rules of the House, written and unwritten, enjoin as a wise safeguard against precipitate action, but which, on such an occasion as this, might impede us in dealing with the momentous question before us. This session has been called for the purpose of giving the authority of Parliament and the sanction of the law to such measures as have already been taken by the Government, and any further measures that may be needed, to insure the defence of Canada and to give what aid may be in our power to the mother country in the stupendous struggle which now confronts her. Speaking for those who sit around me, speaking for the wide constituencies which we represent in this House, I hasten to say that to all these measures we are prepared to give immediate assent. If in what has been done or in what remains to be done there may be anything which in our judgment should not be done or should be differently done, we raise no question, we take no exception, we offer no criticism, and we shall offer no criticism so long as there is danger at the front. It is our duty, more pressing upon us than all other duties, at once, on this first day of this extraordinary session of the Canadian Parliament, to let Great Britain know, and to let the friends and foes of Great Britain know, that there is in Canada but one mind and one heart, and that all Canadians stand behind the mother country, conscious and proud that she has engaged in this war, not from any selfish motive, for any purpose of aggrandizement, but to maintain untarnished the honour of her name, to fulfil her obligations to her allies, to maintain her treaty obligations and to save civilization from the unbridled lust of conquest and domination.

We are British subjects, and to-day we are face to face with the consequences which are involved in that proud fact. Long we have enjoyed the benefits of our British citizenship; to-day it is our duty to accept its responsibilities and its sacrifices. We have long said that when Great Britain is at war, we are at war; to-day we realize that Great Britain is at war and that Canada is at war also. Our territory is liable to attack and to invasion. So far as invasion is concerned, I do not see that there is any cause for apprehension, for it seems to me obvious that neither Austria nor Germany, our foes in this war, can command any able force to make an attack so far from their base. But no one pretends that our maritime cities on the Pacific and the Atlantic, are free from the possibility of insult by an audacious corsair, who, descending suddenly upon our shores, might subject them to an insolent raid and decamp with his booty before punishment could reach him. This is not an unfounded dread of danger; this is no mere illusion; it is a real and indeed a proximate danger, since it is a matter of notoriety that both on the Pacific and on the Atlantic there are German cruisers whose mission it is to inflict all the injury they can upon our commerce, and even to raid our cities should they find our harbours unguarded. We are aware that the Government has already taken measures, and very appropriately, to guard against this danger. We know that one of our battleships on the Pacific has been seeking the enemy, and if she has not yet engaged him, it is because the enemy has eluded her pursuit.

We have had another and more striking evidence that when Great Britain is at war we are at war, in this—that our commerce has been interrupted, and perhaps the expression would not be too strong if I were to say that it has been to some extent dislocated. From the day war was declared—nay, from the day the possibility of war was first mooted—our shipping to Great Britain and to Europe has been interrupted. Ships were lying at the docks fully loaded and ready to put to sea, but unable to do so because of the fact that when England is at war Canadian property on the high seas is liable to capture. Our ships therefore had to remain in port so long as precautions had not been taken to clear the way and to ensure their safe passage across the ocean. What measures have been taken in regard to that we have not yet been told, but I have no doubt that we shall have that information in due time.

The correspondence brought down yesterday, however, has informed us that the Canadian Government has already taken steps to send a contingent of twenty thousand men or thereabouts to take their place in the firing line. Upon this occasion I owe it to the House and to myself to speak with absolute frankness and candour. This is a subject which has often been an occasion of debate in this House. I have always said, and I repeat it on this occasion, that there is but one mind and one heart in Canada. At other times we may have had different views as to the methods by which we are to serve our country and our empire. More than once have I declared that if England were ever in danger—nay, not only in danger, but if she were ever engaged in such a contest as would put her strength to the test—then it would be the duty of Canada to assist the motherland to the utmost of Canada's ability. England to-day is not engaged in an ordinary contest. The war in which she is engaged will in all probability—nay, in absolute certainty—stagger the world with its magnitude and its horror. But that war is for as noble a cause as ever impelled a nation to risk her all upon the arbitrament of the sword. That question is no longer at issue; the judgment of the world has already pronounced upon it. I speak not only of those nations which are engaged in this war, but of the neutral nations. The testimony of the ablest men of these nations, without dissenting voice, is that to-day the allied nations are fighting for freedom against oppression, for democracy against autocracy, for civilization against reversion to that state of barbarism in which the supreme law is the law of might.

SIR GEORGE E. FOSTER

CANADA AND THE WAR

Sir George E. Foster

*From a speech at the close of the Special War Session of the
Parliament of Canada, 1914*

I DO not feel that I am capable of saying what I
would like to say. I feel at the present time a
great deal more than I have the power to express.   I
feel the solemnity of this hour.   We are meeting as a
band of Canadians of different races and nationalities
and languages; but never in the history of Canada
have we met feeling that we were one in the same
sense as at this hour of our history.   That generosity
which sometimes lies more or less concealed in partisan and racial disputes has burst all those ignoble
bonds, and a feeling of pure patriotism, love of
country and devotion to what the flag symbolizes,
has come to the front disfigured by no mean or petty
purpose.

The last four days of this session of Parliament have
vindicated Canadian public life and parliamentary
life for all time to come.   They have shown that it is
possible for us to forget all mean and petty things
when our country and its highest liberties are at
stake. We have these rooms to-day, and we may
meet again in some months; but what will have
happened in that intervening time? The issues of
war are never certain until they are settled.   It does
not always happen that the right triumphs in the one
battle or the one campaign.   In this war nearly
twenty millions of armed men will probably be face
to face or within range of each other before the
finality of the contest is determined.   What will

happen? Will the right and true prevail this time, or must there be more sacrifice and many years before they ultimately prevail?

The one solemn thing for us to remember to-day is that there is more to war than the first march out of the troops, the first blare of the trumpet and the first flaunting of the flag. What there is more to war has been demonstrated in Belgium in these last thirteen or fourteen days, when their homes have gone up in flames, when their wives and their children have been given over to hardship and death, and when their own bodies, as strong and valiant as ours, have been shattered by the grim weapons of war. We have not had that experience. But it may yet be ours, and my word to this House and to this country to-day is to put on the full armour of courage and confidence, not to be daunted by a temporary reverse or by a series of reverses, but to feel sure that justice will burn forth bright and strong in proportion to our readiness to make the necessary sacrifice, and as the fires of this sacrifice burn away what is selfish and base in our country, our people and ourselves.

Some of our companions and colleagues march out to-day and will go forward to the front. Let us remember with our best wishes and follow with our deepest prayers those of our comrades who are about to take the sword in defence of liberty and the right.

I cannot say more, and I should have been sorry to have said less. The time of trial is upon this country and the Empire. It will do us good in the end. God and the right will finally triumph.

RODOLPHE LEMIEUX

RODOLPHE LEMIEUX

1866-

PROMINENT among the orators of Canada stands Rodolphe Lemieux, the noted statesman and lawyer, with the blood of Normandy in his veins. His fluency in English and French is equally remarkable, yet notwithstanding his magnificent command of language he is never carried beyond the pale of reason and of practical common sense.

He was born in Montreal in 1866, and received his earlier education at Nicolet College. After a youthful venture in journalism, he studied law at Laval University, and was called to the Bar in 1891. He has achieved a brilliant record in his profession, and is recognized as one of the leaders of the Quebec Bar. In 1896 he became a member of the law faculty of Laval University, where until 1906 he lectured on the History of Canadian Law.

His parliamentary career dates from 1896, and he has served his country in the House of Commons for twenty-six years. In 1906 he entered the Laurier Cabinet as Postmaster General, but retired with the fall of the Laurier Government in 1911. He was offered a portfolio in the King Cabinet but declined it, and was elected Speaker of the House of Commons in March, 1922, a position for which he is pre-eminently fitted by virtue of his tact and his strong mental balance.

He is a born diplomatist, and has been sent as an ambassador to foreign countries on various missions. In 1907 he went to Japan in connection with the limitation of Japanese immigrants to Canada. In 1909 he represented Canada at the commemoration of the founding of the Postal Union held at Berne, Switzerland, and the following year was Canada's representative at the opening of the South African Union Parliament.

His knowledge of Canadian constitutional development is profound, and he is also a keen admirer of British institutions. He is a man of wide culture, has a thorough background of English literature and wields a very facile pen.

In 1903 he favoured the independence of Canada by peaceful means when the Chamberlain agitation for Imperial federation was at its height, but has since become a convinced Imperialist. During the war his loyalty to Great Britain was unmistakably demonstrated, for he was Quebec's most energetic recruiting sergeant, and was eloquent in maintaining the necessity for Canada's participation in the war, and in breaking down the objections of the Quebec Nationalists.

Lemieux's political creed is broad and uplifting. He is interested in social legislation, and was the father of the Lemieux Act of 1907, which provided a peaceful method for settling labour disputes. With his moral integrity, his intellectual brilliancy, and his sound common sense, he is a decided asset to Canadian politics.

Rodolphe Lemieux

THE QUEBEC ACT

Hon. Rodolphe Lemieux

From his address to the Canadian Club, Toronto, 1914

UNDER the benign influence of the Crown, our traditions have been preserved, our customs and our laws have been maintained. Religious liberty we fully enjoy. The French language is officially recognized. It is freely used in the courts of the land and in Parliament.

Indeed, if we did not cling to the memories of the past, we should be unworthy of the great nation which gave us life. If we did not proclaim our loyalty, we should be ungrateful to the great nation which gave us liberty. French by descent and affection, we are British by allegiance and conviction.

The Quebec Act is considered as the Magna Charta of the French Catholic subjects of Great Britain in North America. And by all Canadians, in my humble judgment, it should be looked upon as one of the foundation stones of that greatest of human fabrics—the modern British Empire.

The Act was brought before the House of Lords by the Earl of Dartmouth on May 2nd, 1774, and passed without any opposition on May 17th. From May 26th until June 13th it was discussed in the House of Commons. The principle of the Act fixed no territory limits for the Province. It comprised not only the country affected by the proclamation of 1763, but also all the eastern territory which had previously been annexed to Newfoundland. In the west and southwest the province was extended to the Ohio and the Mississippi, and, in fact, enclosed all the lands beyond the Alleghanies coveted and claimed by the old English colonies now hemmed in between the Atlantic and the Appalachian Range.

It was now expressly enacted that the Roman Catholic inhabitants of Canada should thenceforth "enjoy the free exercise" of their religion "subject to the King's supremacy declared and established" by law, and on condition of taking an oath of allegiance set forth in the Act. The Roman Catholic clergy was allowed "to hold, receive and enjoy their accustomed dues and rights, with respect to such persons only as shall confess the said religion"—that is, one twenty-sixth part of the produce of the land, Protestants being specially exempted. The French-Canadians were allowed to enjoy all their property, together with all customs and usages incident thereto, "in as large, ample and beneficial manner" as if the proclamation or other acts of the Crown "had not been made;" but the religious orders and communities were accepted in accordance with the terms of the capitulation of Montreal. In "all matters of controversy relative to property and civil rights," resort was to be had to the old civil law of French Canada "as the rule for the decision of the same;" but the criminal law of England was extended to the province on the indisputable ground that its "certainty and lenity" were already "sensibly felt by the inhabitants from an experience of more than nine years." The government of the province was entrusted to a Governor and a Legislative Council appointed by the Crown "inasmuch as it was inexpedient to call the

assembly." The council was to be composed of not
more than twenty-three residents of the province.
At the same time the British Parliament made
special enactments for the imposition of certain customs duties "towards defraying the charges of the
administration of justice and the support of the
civil government of the province." All deficiencies in
the revenues derived from these and other sources
had to be supplied by the Imperial treasury.

In French Canada the Act was received without
any popular demonstration, but the men to whom
the great body of people always looked for advice and
guidance, the priests, curés and seigneurs naturally
regarded these concessions to their nationality as giving most unquestionable evidence of the consideration and liberal spirit in which the British Government was determined to rule the Province. They
had had ever since the conquest satisfactory proof
that their religion was secure from all interference,
and now the British Parliament itself came forward
with legal guarantees not only for the free exercise of
that religion, with all its incidents and tithes, but
also for the permanent establishment of the civil law,
to which they attached so much importance.

The fact that no provision was made for a popular
assembly could not possibly offend the people to
whom local self-government in any form was entirely
unknown. It was not a measure primarily intended
to check the growth of popular institutions, but
solely framed to meet the actual conditions of a people
unaccustomed to the working of representative institutions. It was a preliminary step in the develop-

ment of self-government. Such as it was, the Quebec Act was the first real bond of friendship between Canada and Great Britain.

The strength of British statesmanship throughout the history of Canada, and the history of the Empire —the strength of British diplomacy lay in its wisdom. I may say: Its wisdom is its strength; its strength is its wisdom. Reviewing the constitutional growth of Canada, there are three outstanding stages of development, each marking a large, a very large, measure of liberty. First, England gave us a representative government—it educated the French Canadians to the notion of popular government; second, it gave us responsible government; third, it gave us federal government. And at each stage, I am proud to say, Great Britain made secure for the French Canadians, the minority, its religion, its laws and customs, and its language. The traditional policy of Great Britain, for the student of history, is that England trusts her own people. She made the French Canadians loyal in 1774, because she trusted the French Canadians.

May I say, might I suggest to this audience in Toronto, that in these days of monopoly and trusts and mergers, there must not be any such monopoly as a monopoly of loyalty? Loyalty is not in the trade; it is not even patented; it is in the heart of every man. We may differ as to the methods of how best to serve the British Empire, but our aims are all the same. We may disagree on details, but we are all agreed on essentials. And I don't see the object of advertising, say, one half of this country as disloyal.

We are all loyal. The great bond of union of all is, nor the Grit party nor the Tory party. The great bond of union for every Canadian, after all, is His Majesty the King and the Crown. And the great instrument of freedom, which belongs to me as well as it belongs to you, is the British Constitution, an unwritten instrument, which is as dear to me as it is to you. We may speak different languages, profess different creeds, but the French Canadian in Quebec, the Scotch in the Highlands, the Manxman, the Irishman, the Welshman, is as loyal, as patriotic, as the Englishman from Lancashire—or even from Toronto.

Then, if you ask me why I am a British subject, and why I wish to remain one? I reply, that I honour the flag that honours its obligations; that I prize most those institutions that secure me most strongly in my rights and liberties; and am proud to be a sharer in that great work of advancing peace and progress throughout the world, for which the British Empire stands; gratitude for what has been done for them in the past, contentment in the liberties which they to-day enjoy; pride in the greatness of England and her dominions scattered throughout the whole of the globe; this, and much more, warms the hearts of the French Canadians to the Motherland, and makes of them loyal subjects second to none under the British Crown. By the vastness of the Empire their imagination is stirred; by the self-government it insures, their confidence is secured.

Talk not of annexation of French Canada—because all that there is of charm in monarchy is retained in our constitution, and all that there is of democracy in a republic is retained.

ROBERT A. FALCONER

ROBERT A. FALCONER

1867-

TOLERATION, moderation, efficiency — Sir Robert Falconer stands for these three ideals in the University of Toronto. His calm, unimpassioned temperament assists him in his rather difficult task of preserving an equilibrium in the University, during an era marked by strong intellectual, as well as social, unrest. But despite his judicial air, he does not stand complacently outside the struggles of his age; his interest in national and international problems is sincere, and he has always aimed at a close co-operation between the world of ideas as represented by educational centres, and the world of facts as represented by the working-men in all countries.

Robert Falconer was born in Charlottetown, P.E.I., in 1867, but at an early age moved with his parents to Trinidad, B.W.I. where he received the groundwork of his education. He was chosen Gilchrist Scholar for London University, and in 1888 graduated with high honours in Classics. Later he received his M.A. degree in Classics at Edinburgh University, still later his B.D. degree, and in 1902 his degree of Doctor of Literature. He studied at famous German Universities as well, and on his return to Canada has received various honorary degrees from Canadian Universities.

In 1892 he was appointed lecturer in New Testament Exegesis at the Presbyterian College in Halifax, and his reputation increased steadily until, in 1904, he became Principal of the College. Meanwhile he declined various offers from American Universities to join their staff, but, after some hesitation, accepted the invitation to the Presidency of the University of Toronto in 1907. He was then but forty years of age, and was reluctant to accept a position entailing so great a responsibility, especially when his predecessors had been venerable men with long years of experience to temper their judgment. But during the fifteen years of his Presidency he has shouldered his tremendous executive responsibility with the coolness and method of a railway magnate, and the studied impartiality of a Chief Justice.

Sir Robert Falconer has been actively interested in the social conditions of his day. He has given his whole-hearted support to the University Extension idea, and heartily approves of any plan which will bring education to the masses. His generous services to Canada and education in the Khaki University during the war will long be remembered. He is, besides, a public speaker of note, and has written several books on history, theology and education. His writings and speeches are not characterized by strong originality or imaginative fire, for he is primarily an administrator, and is not temperamentally fitted to inflame the hearts of men. But in all of his works the strength of his intellect, and the accuracy of his judgments are clearly revealed.

Robert A. Falconer

THE MEANING OF THE WEST

SIR ROBERT FALCONER

From a Speech on "The Quality of Canadian Life," 1917

THE creation of Western Canada is the most splendid achievement of our life since 1867. Manitoba became a province in 1870, British Columbia in the following year, and Saskatchewan and Alberta fulfilled in 1905 the dream of the Fathers of Confederation. Had it not been for the mysterious potency of the West, awaiting the day when it should be incorporated in the Union, it is doubtful whether any Dominion would have been called into being. The hope of that great lone land has been realized beyond expectation, though that was too small a measure of its capacity because its resources had been of set purpose disparaged. It was the Eastern Canadian who in a true sense discovered it, for Hudson's Bay or North-West Company traders kept its wealth guarded, and when the intruder from the East disturbed those silent spaces, the traders, as well as the half-breeds and the Indians, felt aggrieved. Fears and jealousies were the source of much trouble and, as a matter of history, the rising of 1885 is of importance because it finally relieved the prairies of the unrest which was bound to smoulder until once and for all it was decided that not the Indian or the half-breed, but the Canadian white-man was to be master. Other sources of discontent between different races and religions are not yet completely removed, but the West has boldly faced its problems, and it seems to be on the way to solve them with justice and with as much compromise as is compatible with the determination that the English language and Canadian institutions are to prevail.

In the prairie provinces the history of the east repeats itself. There are the familiar stages of widening liberty; self-government was granted, with hesitation, to those who went in first, by the timid friends whom they had left behind and who were slow to believe that they were capable of exercising it. Of all the immigration in the earlier years that from Eastern Canada was the most abundant and forceful. Whole counties of Ontario seem to have been emptied into that new land. By heredity the people knew how to live in stern conditions and to face the unknown with courage. It is a fact of primary importance that the English-speaking Canadian first put the west in order, laid it out, stamped it with his own institutions and then invited in others; nor is it surprising that the vigorous spirit of himself and his children is still in control, even though of late a large and very effective body of Americans has entered from the Western States. They have not disputed his supremacy, and he may be proud of his accomplishments. These are a fine proof of his quality. He required imagination, courage, patience, the virtues on which the west is reared, and, had he not shown them, and had the American farmer gone in first, the future of this Dominion would have been different from that to which we look forward.

The stimulation of the climate may lead the Westerner to overmuch action and to make large drafts upon his future with confidence, but what he

has done is so wonderful that he has reason in venturing upon wide horizons. The Winnipeg of 1917, solid,
with a reserve of power, the home of well-educated
and comfortable people, so surpasses the loosely
developed Winnipeg of twenty years ago that one may
well hesitate to set bounds to its future. No city
of the west is likely to rival it, but Regina, Saskatoon,
Moosejaw, Calgary, Edmonton, all speak of Canadian pluck and energy. West of the mountains lies
another section of the Dominion. British Columbia
has a history of its own, but in Vancouver far east
and far west meet, for not a little of the energy of
that city of wonderful outlook comes from those who
have left the Maritime provinces or Ontario to make
their home on the Pacific slope. In the conduct of
the Canadian west nothing is finer than the treatment
of the Indian. The men sent out by the Dominion
Government were not border adventurers, but high-
minded and educated gentlemen who carried rigid
scrupulousness into their dealings with the natives
and made honourable treaties which have been
honourably observed.

Our west never went through a riotous youth; it
has few memories to be forgotten. From the first,
life has been held sacred and respect has been paid
to the law as rigidly as in the east, some of the
credit being undoubtedly due to the Royal North-
West mounted police force which the Dominion called
into existence and has kept in high efficiency.

By its well ordered society and its political,
educational and religious institutions, the west is
shown to possess firmly fixed principles which have

simply been transferred to their new home by the first settlers from Eastern Canada. But every thinking Canadian asks himself the question, how long will this similarity between the west and the east continue? Though we are convinced that Canadian unity will be maintained, it is already evident that the west will soon possess a marked individuality and that the older influences will become fainter. Already the western man is impatient of his eastern brother and the incoming of the American will probably increase the criticism. It is therefore prudent to strengthen by every means in our power the bond between east and west, which is in danger of being stretched too thin at the Great Lakes if the two sections of the Dominion should pull apart in interest. Now is the time of our opportunity, for the war has quickened our mutual sympathies and given us a new chance to coalesce.

So far I have spoken of the influence of the east upon the west, but already the west has begun to influence the policy of the east. Things have been done there which of ourselves we might have pronounced premature, if not impossible. In prohibition and woman suffrage they have led the way, and it is not improbable that they will be fertile in political, social and religious experiment and will compel the reluctant east to follow in their steps. Nor need we be alarmed at the prospect. They are still, in the majority, our kith and kin, they are as clear-headed as we and morally as sound, and one fact which we have learned of late is that policies which were deemed impossible may be quite practicable when men of resolute purpose determine to put them into action. If imitation is the sincerest flattery, the west may be not altogether insensible to the compliment we pay them when we follow their example.

LOMER GOUIN

LOMER GOUIN

1861-

SIR LOMER GOUIN holds a unique place among French Canadian statesmen. Though devoid of the romantic charm and poetic eloquence which characterize the Gallic temperament, he has won the implicit confidence of his people, and is known as the Father of Quebec. No Anglo-Canadian is more sober, practical or cautious in disposition and speech, and no bank president has a more technical mind, or a more comprehensive grasp of details, than this unusual French-Canadian who for fifteen years administered the government of his province with such outstanding success.

He was born at Grondines, Quebec, in 1861, the son of a physician who gave his child every educational advantage. After taking the classical course, he studied law at Laval University, and was admitted to the Bar in 1884. He was eminently successful in his profession, and for fourteen years was Attorney-General of Quebec.

With his fine intellectual attainments and his statesman-like qualities it was natural that politics should attract him. He entered the Provincial Legislature in 1897, joined the Parent Ministry three years later, and when, in 1905, his chief was forced to resign, Gouin became Premier in his stead.

During the fifteen years of his administration, Quebec forged ahead in almost every branch of her public life. He devoted himself with tireless energy to her uniform advancement—along financial, agricultural, industrial and educational lines. His detailed knowledge of the resources of his province is marvellous. Its highways, waterways, industries, and thousands of its inhabitants are personally known to him. Yet despite his pride in and knowledge of Quebec, he is never betrayed into extravagant demonstrations of affection for it. He is a firm believer in Federation, for Quebec's sake, as well as for the welfare of Canada as a whole. He is also a staunch Imperialist, and his attitude toward Great Britain has not been without influence among his countrymen, who respect his great talents and value his vast service to their province.

During his career he has received many high honours. At the Quebec Tercentenary he was knighted by the Prince of Wales, now King George V, and in 1920 he was made Commandeur de la Legion d'Honneur by the French Government. He holds besides several honorary degrees from Canadian universities, and is President of the University of Montreal.

He accepted the portfolio of Minister of Justice in the Federal Cabinet under Mackenzie King, and in the wider field of Dominion politics critics who taunted him with provincialism had an opportunity of watching his interests expand into a broader nationalism.

QUEBEC AND CONFEDERATION

SIR LOMER GOUIN

Delivered in the Legislative Assembly of Quebec,
January 23, 1918

I DESIRE to define my position on this question very clearly. Mr. Speaker, I believe in the Canadian Confederation. The Federal system of government seems to me to be the only possible one for Canada in view of the differences in race and creed and also in view of the variety and multiplicity of the local needs of our immense territory.

To be even more precise I would say that if I had been a party to the negotiations of 1864 I would certainly have tried, had I had the authority, to obtain for the French Canadian minority in the sister provinces the same protection that was secured for the English minority in the Province of Quebec. I would not have asked this as a concession, but as a measure of justice. And even if it had not been granted, I would have voted in favour of the resolutions of 1864.

When the project was debated in 1865 I would have renewed my demand for that measure of prudence and of justice and if I had not succeeded I would still have declared myself in favour of the system which was adopted on the 13th of March, 1865. And even at the present hour, Mr. Speaker, despite the conflicts that have taken place in the administration of our country since 1867, despite the distress caused to those from Quebec who constitute a minority in the other provinces, if I had to choose between Confederation and the Act of 1791 or the Act of 1840-41, I would be for Confederation.

For fifty years now, Mr. Speaker, we have lived under this system. We have had difficulties, it is true; we have had conflicts, more or less violent, but have we any right to say that the system has failed? *I believe just the contrary.*

When I regard the results achieved, when I mark the development that has taken place, when I take into account our progress, I am ready to say with Sir Wilfrid Laurier that "the hopes of the Fathers of Confederation have been surpassed."

Dorion, one of the finest and noblest figures of his time, dreaded the federal system because he feared that the Province of Quebec would be swamped in a great Canadian whole. The opponents of Confederation declared, as Dorion did, that Confederation was nothing more nor less than a step to legislative union. Can it be maintained to-day that those fears, that those misgivings were well founded? For fifty years now our Province has formed part of the Confederation and legislative union has not been brought about. We have legislated and we continue to freely legislate in the municipal and educational spheres and never have we been interfered with in the administration of our civil laws.

Our Province, as we have seen, thanks to Confederation, thanks to our union with the sister provinces, has progressed to a marvellous degree and certainly nobody can deny that it is due to Confederation that Montreal has in point of importance become the fourth city of North America. And if we regard the French groups settled in the other provinces, can it be said that Confederation has been unfavourable to them? Would their position, would their lot be improved if Quebec broke the federal pact? There are in Canada to-day, outside the Province of Quebec, at least 500,000 French Canadians, or more than half of the total number in the two Canadas in 1867. Would it be to the interest of our own people of whom I have spoken for the Province of Quebec to retire from the Confederation?

What would be the result, Mr. Speaker, if we were to separate from Confederation? I do not wish it to be thought for a moment that the honourable Member for Lotbiniere wished to raise that question. But as we are upon that ground it is better that each should express his thoughts. What position would we be in, shut off as we would be without any access to the sea during the winter months? How could we defend our immense frontier? What part of the national debt would we have to assume? What would be the customs tariffs of the Provinces with which we now trade freely? And finally, what would be the position of French Canadians outside of Quebec?

Lord Acton, the great English historian, has said that the liberty of a country is measured by the liberty of its minority. That is to say that if a minority is not well treated it is not it alone which suffers, as all those of the majority who have a right spirit, a just and generous heart, suffer with the minority and to the same extent as it does. We must not, Mr. Speaker, forget the good qualities of others, we must remember that it is due to the combined qualities of all groups and of all races in the Dominion that our country has become great.

His Excellency the Governor-General of Canada, the Duke of Devonshire, on the occasion of the celebration of the fiftieth anniversary of Confederation last year truly said:

"Confederation will stand for all time as the monument of the work accomplished by the devotion, the unselfishness and the far-sighted vision of those men whom we are all proud to call the Fathers of the Confederation. To those men and their work we owe a debt which we can never repay, and it is for us, in our generation, to see that the glorious heritage to which we have succeeded shall be handed to those who come after us, unimpaired and, as far as lies in our power, with added glory and lustre."

Let us preserve, yes, Mr. Speaker, let us preserve intact our field of action and guard against even dreaming of diminishing the great task it is our mission to continue. Let us in the accomplishment of that task be inspired by the courage, by the faith, by the ideals of our ancestors, the discoverers of this country, and by the splendid visions of the Fathers of Confederation; and thanks to our work, to our efforts and to our sacrifices, the twentieth century will count our country amongst the great nations of the earth.

When I regard our immense territory, when I admire our old Provinces with all their rich historical souvenirs, and the new born of yesterday from the prairies and the virgin forests with their teeming power. I am proud of the name of Canadian, proud of my country—Canada. I am thankful that Providence allowed me to be born in this new and fruitful land which is sheltered from the bloody carnage that is now devastating Europe, a land of liberty, a land of equality, which knows no castes and which recognizes no superiority save that of talent, of effort, and of rectitude, a land where fruitful peace will bring union and concord and promote more progress and prosperity than in any other corner of the world.

It is in order to preserve to our country her greatness, to guard in the hearts of our children their hopes and to transmit to them unimpaired the heritage received from our fathers, that we should fight fearlessly under the passing storm, that we should work ceaselessly and without faltering for the development and maintenance of the Canadian Confederation.

WILLIAM LYON MACKENZIE KING

WILLIAM LYON MACKENZIE KING

1874-

UNTIL his elevation to the Premiership of Canada William Lyon Mackenzie King, grandson of the famous Canadian rebel and patriot, has been better known in the economic world than in the field of politics. His fame in economics is continent-wide. His combined interest in sociology and politics fits him admirably for the premiership at the reconstruction stage in Canadian history, and his thorough knowledge of industrial and social conditions is an excellent background for broad statesmanship at any period.

Mackenzie King, born in Kitchener in 1874, received his early education in the local schools, and entered the Political Science course at the University of Toronto. His keen interest in sociology led him to pursue the subject after graduation, and having received his M.A. in Toronto, he undertook postgraduate work in Political Economy at the University of Chicago as well, and later at Harvard, where he received the degree of Ph.D. He won a Harvard fellowship, and studied economics at first hand in Great Britain, France, Germany, Switzerland and Italy.

Thus equipped, Mackenzie King made his debut in public life. In 1900 he became first Deputy Minister of Labour, under Sir William Mulock, and retained this position for eight years. He served on several Royal Commissions on industrial and immigration problems, and acted as government conciliator in important industrial disputes. He possessed a genius for conciliating groups, due, doubtless, to the fervency of his belief that industry and humanity are not essentially antagonistic and irreconcilable elements. In 1909 he was appointed Minister of Labour, which portfolio he held until the downfall of the Laurier Government in 1911.

Because of his intelligent interest in labour disputes he was invited in 1914 to join the staff of the Rockefeller Foundation to make a practical study of industrial problems. In this capacity he rendered valuable service during the war in the adjustment of relations between workers and employers in great war industries of America. The result of his investigations found expression in his book "Industry and Humanity," which is a study of the principles underlying industrial reconstruction, and is an appreciable addition to the sum total of economic literature.

In 1919 he returned to Canadian public life to accept the leadership of the Liberal party in Canada, and in 1921 on the defeat of the Unionist Government became Prime Minister of the Dominion. His endeavour has been to carry on the traditions of his late revered chief, Sir Wilfrid Laurier, and to incorporate in Canadian Liberalism the new sociological viewpoint which is not only the result of his personal studies and experience, but is the unmistakable trend of world politics in the new era heralded by the Great War.

William Lyon Mackenzie King

LIBERALISM AND RECONSTRUCTION
Wm. L. Mackenzie King

Being an Address delivered at National convention,

August, 1919

IT has been my desire to pay some small tribute
to the memory of our great and truly-revered
leader, Sir Wilfrid Laurier. I shall not attempt to
pay any tribute to his name or memory in words of
praise. What words of mine or of any man or woman
in this room could equal the praise that has come
from all countries and all continents? No, I will
give the praise which history will ever give, his own
words and his own life: "Whatever we may do, we
cannot deprive the people of the supreme command
which they must have over their Legislatures and the
members whom they elect. If there is one thing
that is to save nations from revolution, it is that the
governments of the different countries are truly
representative of the people as a whole. All history
has been a struggle to bring about that free and full
representation."

And so, I say, looking back at the memory of our
great Chief, and our great Leader, we Liberals of
Canada have reason to be proud that in him we have
one whose name will rank with those of Pym, Pitt,
Bright, Gladstone, Lincoln,—men who have given
their lives and existence in order that the right of
the people to control Parliament, and the right of
Parliament to control the Executive, might be preserved in the name of freedom. . . .

I shall, I am sure, be carrying out your wish if I

287

seek to the utmost of my ability in these great responsibilities to carry on the principles which he sought to make prevail throughout this vast Dominion and which I think can all be expressed in the maxim of an illustrious English statesman, Pym, who said that the form of government is best which doth actuate and dispose every part and member of the state to the common good. . . .

The Liberal party will continue to stand as its illustrious leaders stood in the past, for unity, good will, and the open mind. It has no prejudice of race, creed or class. It is for equal rights and justice to all. It believes that problems of industry and nationality, like all questions of race and religion, can only be solved by the application of these principles. We want no cleavage along racial or religious lines. In imperial relations we are opposed to centralization. We are advocates of British unity based upon human relations, rather than upon governmental machinery, unity based upon self-government and the quality of the British community of nations. We are for friendly relations with the United States, and we are in sympathy with the movement to substitute friendly co-operation for conflict and jealousy in international relations with all countries. . . .

If there is in Canada to-day one portion of its citizenry which more than any other is entitled to consideration, it is the men who risked their lives in battle and those who shared with them the dangers and privations of war, especially the families of those whose sons made the supreme sacrifice in the call of

With the liberal forces at work in Canada to-day among the farmers in the rural communities, among labourers in the cities and towns, among the returned soldiers, and among that great body of Canadian citizenry, men and women alike, who, apart from class affiliations or associations, are thinking and praying and striving for the dawn of that better day which the sacrifices and war were to usher in, there is nothing to withstay ultimate and speedy victory in the triumph of liberal ideals and policies, except a failure on the part of those who are opposed to a common enemy to co-operate in a spirit that has regard primarily for the good of all.

ARTHUR S. MEIGHEN

ARTHUR S. MEIGHEN

ARTHUR MEIGHEN was born on June 16th, 1874, on an Ontario farm. His grandfather, an Irishman, came to Canada in the early forties, taught school, and then settled on the farm where his son, Joseph, and his grandson, Arthur, were born. At school, Arthur showed remarkable ability as a scholar, but was of a deeply serious nature and took no part in sports. In 1896 he graduated in mathematics from the University of Toronto, and went to Winnipeg where he studied law and taught school. In 1903 he was called to the Bar and built up a successful practice at Portage-la-Prairie.

Mr. Meighen was elected to the House of Commons in 1909 and made his first speeches as a Conservative when the fortunes of his party were at a low ebb. His power of presenting facts clearly and logically, his faculty for sizing up a situation, and his love of hard work, caused his promotion to be rapid. He was appointed Solicitor-General in 1913, Secretary of State and Minister of Mines in 1917, and Minister of the Interior in October of the same year. He was responsible for the War Times Election Act, and drafted the bill for compulsory military service.

When, in 1920, Sir Robert Borden retired from the Premiership, Mr. Meighen was chosen in his stead. But he was not given a fair opportunity to demonstrate his capacity for high statesmanship, because, in the election of December, 1921, his party was defeated, and he found himself in opposition. As leader of the critics of the present government, he watches the new party at the helm with characteristic vigilance, and, with staunch loyalty, upholds the interests of the Conservative Party.

Throughout his years of political service, Mr. Meighen has won a reputation for honesty, courage and a love of thoroughness which necessitates constant and patient toil. He has a finely-balanced legal mind, and is recognized as one of the most logical debaters in the Dominion Parliament. Normally, he is not a great orator, but on rare occasions he has risen to heights of eloquence which rival the performances of the masters.

Arthur S. Meighen

THE GLORIOUS DEAD

HON. ARTHUR MEIGHEN

*From an address at Thelus Military Cemetery, Vimy Ridge,
July 3, 1921*

THE Great War is past; the war that tried through
and through every quality and mystery of the
human mind and the might of human spirit; the
war that closed, we hope for ever, the long, ghastly
story of the arbitrament of men's differences by force;
the last clash and crash of earth's millions is over now.
There can be heard only sporadic conflicts, the moan
of prostrate nations, the cries of the bereaved and
desolate, the struggling of exhausted peoples to rise
and stand and move onward. We live among the
ruins and the echoes of Armageddon. Its shadow is
receding slowly backward into history.

At this time the proper occupation of the living is,
first, to honour our heroic dead; next, to repair the
havoc, human and material, that surrounds us; and,
lastly, to learn aright and apply with courage the
lessons of the war.

Here in the heart of Europe we meet to unveil a
memorial to our country's dead. In earth which has
resounded to the drums and tramplings of many conquests, they rest in the quiet of God's acre with the
brave of all the world. At death they sheathed in
their hearts the sword of devotion, and now from
oft-stricken fields they hold aloft its cross of sacrifice,
mutely beckoning those who would share their immortality. No words can add to their fame, nor so
long as gratitude holds a place in men's hearts can

our forgetfulness be suffered to detract from their renown. For as the war dwarfed by its magnitude all contests of the past, so the wonder of human resource, the splendour of human heroism, reached a height never witnessed before.

Ours we thought prosaic days, when the great causes of earlier times had lost their inspiration, leaving for attainment those things which demand only the petty passing inconveniences of the hour. And yet the nobility of manhood had but to hear again the summons of duty and honour to make response which shook the world. Danger to the treasury of common things—for common things when challenged are the most sacred of all,—danger to these things ever stirred our fathers to action, and it has not lost its appeal to their sons.

France lives and France is free, and Canada is nobler for her sacrifice to help free France to live. In many hundreds of plots throughout these hills and valleys, all the way from Flanders to Picardy, lie fifty thousand of our dead. Their resting places have been dedicated to their memory forever by the kindly grateful heart of France, and will be tended and cared for by us in the measure of the love we bear them. Above them are being planted the maples of Canada, in the thought that her sons will rest the better in the shade of trees they knew so well in life. Across the leagues of the Atlantic the heartstrings of our Canadian nation will reach through all time to these graves in France; we shall never let pass away the spirit bequeathed to us by those who fell; "Their name liveth for evermore."

ROBERT LAIRD BORDEN

ROBERT LAIRD BORDEN

1854-

THE little village of Grand Pré in the centre of one
of Canada's most historic districts seemed a fitting
birthplace for a future premier of Canada; and from
the fact that his ancestors, staunch men of Britain,
were United Empire Loyalists, one could almost
predict his policy in the affairs of his country.

Robert Laird Borden was born on July 26, 1854,
and spent his boyhood and early manhood in the
historic country of Evangeline. He attended Acadia
Villa Academy, a private school near his home, then
after a year or two as a teacher he began the study
of law in Kentville under Sir R. L. Weatherbe and
Mr. Justice Graham. In his profession he proved
eminently successful and was admitted to the Bar in
1876. He practised first at Kentville in partnership
with the present Judge Chipman, and later at
Halifax, where his legal ability, coupled with unremitting industry, made him one of the leaders of
the Bar in his province.

Borden's political career began in 1898, when he
was elected to the Canadian House of Commons, as
a Conservative member for Halifax County. But
he did not crave public life; his heart was in his profession, and for the first term he took little part in
parliamentary affairs. His early speeches in Parlia-

ment were concerned with legal matters. In 1901, however, a crisis occurred in his life when, upon the resignation of Sir Charles Tupper, Borden was asked to assume the leadership of the Conservative Party. It was a difficult situation for a young man with little experience. To step into the shoes of parliamentary veterans like Sir John A. Macdonald and Sir Charles Tupper, at such an awkward stage in the fortunes of the Conservative Party, might terrify a much older man. Moreover, his opponent, Sir Wilfrid Laurier, was then at the zenith of his popularity. But Borden reluctantly accepted the task, and without the natural advantages of outstanding brilliancy, eloquence or charm which his rival possessed, piloted his party slowly, but surely, into safe waters.

His political beliefs were very conservative, and he opposed especially any policy which he felt would weaken the tie between Canada and the mother country. His opposition to the Reciprocity Bill, proposed by the Government in 1911, to facilitate trade relations between Canada and the United States, was the natural outcome of his political convictions. The question was decided in a general election that year, the Government was defeated, and Borden became Premier of Canada in October, 1911.

The nine years of Borden's premiership were years of arduous and faithful service to his country. He soon revealed unexpected qualities of leadership and while he lacked the brilliancy of Sir Wilfrid Laurier, his personal integrity and strong British qualities inspired confidence in him as a man able to guide the destinies of Canada.

Robert Laird Borden

During the war years 1914 1918 Canada took her place as an equal among the great nations of the world, and the name of Borden will always be associated with the annals of his country during the period of her most heroic history. His efforts on behalf of the war were most untiring both at home and in Great Britain where he took part in the Imperial war conferences in 1917 and in 1918. When the end of the conflict finally came he went to Paris in 1919 as Canada's representative at the Peace Conference.

In the following year, 1920, ill-health compelled Borden to retire from the premiership. General regret was felt, but after a well-earned holiday he was able to act as Canada's representative at the Conference for the disarmament of nations at Washington in 1921.

Many honours have been showered upon Robert Borden since his entrance into public life. Honorary degrees have been conferred upon him by both British and Canadian universities, and in 1914 he was knighted by the King. His best reward, however, is the respect and esteem of the people of Canada.

C.—2.

FROM CONFEDERATION TO THE WORLD WAR

Sir Robert Borden

From a Speech delivered in 1921

THE Canadian people accomplished Confederation by means of a statute enacted at their instance by the Parliament of the United Kingdom. Necessary amendments have been effected by subsequent Acts passed by that Parliament upon joint resolution of the Senate and Commons of Canada, and no such amendment has been refused. Thus the legal powers of the Parliament of the United Kingdom have been utilized as a convenient means of effecting constitutional amendments. Doubtless the Canadian Parliament would hesitate to pass any such resolution if its effect could properly be regarded as a violation of the original compact between the Provinces. In any such case it would be proper, and, indeed, necessary, to obtain the consent of every Province affected by the proposed amendment.

With the material growth and constitutional development of the overseas nations the Parliament of the United Kingdom has ceased to be an Imperial Parliament in any real sense so far as the Dominions are concerned. Its legal power is subject to the limitations of constitutional right. Theoretically it has power to impose direct taxation or compulsory military service upon the people of any Dominion; constitutionally and practically it possesses no such right or authority. The exercise of any power contrary to established or developing conventions would have legal sanction, but would not be respected, and in the end could not be enforced. In practice the position is becoming tolerably clear; in theory there remains a singular anomaly. Apprehensions may be quieted if we remember that under our system of government many such anomalies may be observed. The King's veto is legally existent but constitutionally dead. Effective administration of public affairs would be impossible if any instrument of government should continually exercise its legal powers to the legal limit.

In the half-century which elapsed between Confederation and the World War, constitutional development was notable both in character and extent. At the beginning the Governor General in his quality of Imperial officer exercised no inconsiderable influence over certain public affairs; at the close his functions in that character had practically ceased. Appointed with the consent of the Canadian Government, he had become in effect a nominated President, invested with practically the same powers and duties in this country as those appertaining to the King in the British Isles. New and convenient methods of consultation had been established through periodical conferences, in which at first the Dominions were regarded as subordinate dependencies attached to a department of the British Government, but in which they eventually took their places as sister nations upon equal terms with the United Kingdom. The Dominions were originally included in commercial treaties without much regard for their wishes or interests. Eventually no such treaty bound them except by the expressed consent of their Governments. At first Canada was told somewhat brusquely that no Canadian commissioner could take part in the negotiation of a treaty affecting his country; in the end Canada freely negotiated her own commercial treaties by her own commissioners, without control, or interference except of a formal character. Canadians acting as British agents represented the interests of Canada and the whole Empire in the Behring Seas and Alaskan Boundary arbitrations. Naturalization granted in Canada became effective in the United Kingdom. Notwithstanding unfortunate and formidable forces of reaction, the right of the Dominion to full control of its copyright laws was acknowledged. It was gradually realized that legal power is over-ridden by constitutional right. The power to disallow Canadian statutes fell into desuetude. Canada's right to a voice in foreign policy involving her interests as a great Dominion of the Empire, began to be recognized. Her complete control over her policy in respect of military and naval defence was acknowledged. By these sure steps, Canada was steadily mounting to the stately portal of nationhood.

Thus stood the relations of Canada to the Empire in the fateful month of August, 1914. There had arisen a truer comprehension of the ties uniting the overseas nations and the motherland. At last it began to be realized that upon complete liberty and full autonomy a unity and strength capable of resisting the severest shock could be established. When the day of trial came, the response of the Dominions vindicated forever the principle that they had consistently upheld.

NEWTON W. ROWELL

NEWTON W. ROWELL

1867-

HON. N. W. ROWELL has climbed to a high place in his country's regard through sheer ability and indefatigable toil, and in his case ambition has gone hand in hand with conscience.

He was born on a farm in Middlesex County in 1867, and attended the local public school, after which he entered a dry goods warehouse in London. But he had other plans for his future, and spent his evenings in preparation for a wider sphere in life. Unaided, he obtained his matriculation, and began the study of law, graduating with high honours. In 1891 he was called to the Bar, and he has since achieved a wide reputation in the legal profession.

In 1911 Mr. Rowell was asked to assume the leadership of the Liberal Party in the Ontario Legislature though he was without previous parliamentary experience. During the six years that he held this position, he devoted himself to the improvement of social conditions in his province. His name is associated with the Temperance movement in particular, for in 1914 he appealed to the electors on the issue of "Abolish the Bar," and though defeated, it was the impetus that he gave to the Government which resulted in the adoption of the Ontario Temperance Act in 1916.

In 1917 he resigned the leadership of the Provincial Opposition, to join the Federal Unionist Government in formation. He was reluctant to break with his former chief, Sir Wilfrid Laurier, but patriotic zeal overcame his personal scruples, and he threw himself wholeheartedly into the task of "winning the war."

As a colleague of Sir Robert Borden, he became a member of the Imperial War Cabinet, Sir Robert and he acting as Canada's representatives in the Imperial War Cabinet, 1918. During Sir Robert's prolonged absence in Europe, Mr. Rowell was Acting Secretary of State in External Affairs, and in this capacity displayed the keenness of his intellect and the strength of his patriotism. For years he had been an enthusiastic advocate of international co-operation, and henceforth used his great intellectual and oratorical gifts in effecting a better understanding between Canada and the Empire. He still found time for social legislation, however, and in 1919 organized and administered a Department of Health, and obtained a more stringent control of the Drug Traffic.

In London and Paris, Sir Robert Borden was fighting to have Canada represented at the Peace Conference and in the League of Nations, and to have the new status of the Dominions recognized by the other nations of the world. The struggle was intensified by the fact that the Imperial Government feared a departure from the traditional methods of diplomacy at such a crisis. At home in Canada, Mr. Rowell supported Sir Robert with his entire strength, and voiced the sentiments of the country as a whole. When the Imperial Government became convinced of the fairness of Canada's contention, which was supported by the other Dominions, they gave Sir Robert's proposal whole-hearted support at the Peace Conference. The united efforts of Sir Robert and Mr. Rowell—with the Imperial Government for backing—succeeded in establishing the precedent. Henceforth Canada was to be recognized as a distinct nation—one of the groups of nations forming the British Commonwealth.

Mr. Rowell was chosen to represent Canada at the first assembly of the League of Nations held at Geneva in 1920. His diplomatic talents were readily recognized and he succeeded in raising the status of his country in the esteem of the other delegates. In his address he pleaded for a World League rather than a European one, and presented the North American view with clarity and vigour.

He retired from the Unionist Cabinet at the time of Sir Robert Borden's resignation and later withdrew from active public life. But with his great vitality and his magnificent dowry of public spirit, it is safe to prophesy that his service to Canada has not yet ended.

The complete significance of Mr. Rowell's service to Canada may not be realized for some time to come, for, owing to post-war conditions, she has yet to reap the full benefit accruing from her new position among the nations of the world. But he has already won the lasting gratitude of his countrymen for his share in obtaining for Canada a voice in international affairs.

Builders of the Canadian Commonwealth

CANADA'S PLACE IN THE EMPIRE

Hon. N. W. Rowell

From one of his addresses in connection with the Burwash Memorial Lectureship at the University of Toronto, 1922

WHAT contribution has Canada made to the unity, the strength, and the stability of the Empire in the past?

Her first and perhaps greatest contribution was the successful working out of the problem of responsible self-government. Every one recognizes at this time how impossible it would have been to preserve the unity of the British Empire if the policy of attempting to govern the Overseas Colonies from Downing Street had been persisted in; and yet, when the agitation for Responsible Government in Canada was at its height, the view of responsible statesmen in the Motherland was that the granting of Responsible Government was entirely incompatible with the maintenance of Imperial connexion.

Lord Stanley, the Colonial Secretary in the Conservative Government of Great Britain in the year 1844, in what was known in Canada as the "Great Debate," stated that to place the Governor in a state of dependence upon his Council and Parliament was "a course which by no gradual steps but certainly and at once would place the whole authority in the hands of the dominant party for the time, and convert Canada into a republic, independent of the Crown of this country. It was inconsistent with monarchical government that the Governor who was responsible should be stripped of all authority and all power, and should be reduced to that degree of political power which was vested in the constitutional sovereign of the country. Not only would such a course be inconsistent with monarchical government, but also with the colonial dependence."

Lord Stanley concluded his address as follows:

"I believe when they seriously consider the results of the alternative I have put they will follow, not the advice of the unprincipled demagogues—bad, rash and interested counsellors—but take as their guide the liberal, sound and honest views of the Governor-General."

Baldwin and LaFontaine were the political leaders in Canada who were fighting the battle of Responsible Government, and Joseph Howe was fighting a similar battle in Nova Scotia. Lord Durham's report on political conditions in Canada, made in 1839, which is one of the most notable State documents in British Colonial history, had approved the principle for which Baldwin, LaFontaine and Howe were contending, but the British Government of the day did not agree with Lord Durham.

Lord Elgin was appointed Governor-General of Canada in 1847. He at once recognized the justice of the claim for Responsible Government and with the full approval of the British Ministry, which had in the meantime changed, he accepted and applied the principle. A new government was formed in 1848 by Baldwin and LaFontaine, who possessed the confidence of Parliament and of the country, and the great battle for Responsible Government was won.

Contrast the statement of Lord Stanley in 1844 with the statement made seventy years later by another British statesman, Sir Herbert Samuel, who, speaking before the British Association for the Advancement of Science, said: "Two great discoveries in the sphere of government have been made by the British people, discoveries which have moulded the shape of the modern world. The first was the principle of representation, which alone enabled order to be reconciled with liberty, and the other was Colonial self-government, which alone had enabled autonomy to be reconciled with unity."

Colonial self-government, one of the two great discoveries in the sphere of government made by the British people, was contended for and secured by the people of Canada, not because they desired separation from the Motherland, but because they believed self-government essential to the satisfactory management of their own affairs, and that with peace and contentment within Canada the ties that bound her to the Motherland would be strengthened rather than weakened. Events have justified their view, and this great principle of colonial self-government, thus established first in Canada, was subsequently successfully applied to all the Colonies of the Empire settled with European stock. It was the general recognition and adoption of this principle which has made possible the continued unity and strength of the Empire.

The second contribution of Canada was Canadian Confederation. Canada was the first country to apply the principles of Parliamentary Government

to a Federation. By the union first of the four
Provinces and later of the whole of Canada under one
central Federal Government, Canada not only laid
the foundations of a strong, prosperous and united
British nation on this half of the North American
Continent, but by her successful experiment she made
possible a similar union of the Australian Colonies and
later still a union of the South African Colonies.
To-day the scattered Colonies of Canada, Australia
and South Africa are three great self-governing
Dominions within the British Empire.

At the time Confederation was proposed by Canada
to the statesmen of Great Britain it was not looked
upon by them as a step that would strengthen the
Empire, but as one that would lead naturally and
inevitably toward the separation of Canada from the
Mother Country and the organization of an independent State. It was the desire of the late Sir John
Macdonald that the new Confederation should be
called the Kingdom of Canada, but the name was not
favoured by the British Government as it was thought
it might offend the sensibilities of the people of the
United States. The official trend of thought about
the time of Confederation is well illustrated by the
following extract from a letter of Lord Lyons, British
Ambassador to Paris, to Lord Clarendon, British
Foreign Secretary. Lord Clarendon had written
asking his advice on some question concerning Canada, as he had been British Ambassador to Washington for many years. After discussing the political
conditions in Canada, Lord Lyons expressed the
opinion that the great problem for Great Britain

in American politics was to find some fair and honourable way of dissolving all connexion between England and her North American Colonies. He concludes: "In fact, it seems to be in the nature of things that the United States' prestige should grow and ours should wane in North America and I wish we were well and creditably out of the scrape. . ." Lord Clarendon on his side was equally emphatic. "I agree," he wrote, "in every word you say about our position in North America and wish they would propose to be independent and to annex themselves. We can't throw them off and it is very desirable that we should part as friends."

It is clear that Canada was not the spoiled child of an over-indulgent mother.

Here again the statesmen of the Mother Country were mistaken in their view, and history has shown that, with the larger powers and the greater freedom of action which have come to the people of Canada through the Canadian Confederation, the ties that have bound Canada to the Motherland have been strengthened rather than weakened; and this also applied to the other self-governing Dominions.

The statesmen of Canada were the first to recognize that the strength and unity of the Empire could only be maintained by the recognition of the full equality of status of the Dominions with the Mother Country in the British family of nations.

This request for an equal status was supported by the representatives of the other Dominions, and when frankly presented to the statesmen of Great Britain was accepted by them as a necessary and logical constitutional development. This change in status has not been a sudden development, but a gradual growth, and the visible evidences of the change have been shown in the further recognition from time to time accorded to the Dominions in the Imperial family, rather than by specific acts which have changed the status.

The British Government has fully recognized in principle the equality of status of the Dominions with the Mother Country, and to-day the true definition of our constitutional relationship is that the members of the Britannic Commonwealth are a group or League of free, self-governing nations and India, united under a common Sovereign, bound together by ties of sympathy, of interest, and of common ideals, and preserving the strength and the unity of the whole through consultation and co-operation in all matters of common concern.

Do we appreciate all our citizenship means to us? We are full Canadian citizens, but we are much more than Canadian citizens—we are citizens of the whole Empire. A Canadian may travel in Europe, Asia, Africa, and Australasia, and still be a citizen—not a foreigner. We are the possessors of a great inheritance. Our task is to improve it, to endeavour to realize its ideals, and to transmit those ideals to those who come after us.